# EMERALD ILLUSIONS

## The Irish In Early American Cinema

GARY D. RHODES
Queen's University, Belfast

IRISH ACADEMIC PRESS
LONDON • PORTLAND, OR

*First published in 2012 by Irish Academic Press*

2 Brookside
Dundrum Road,
Dublin 14, Ireland

920 NE 58th Avenue, Suite 300
Portland, Oregon,
97213-3786 USA

www.iap.ie

British Library Cataloguing in Publication Data
An entry can be found on request

ISBN 978 0 7165 3143 2

Library of Congress Cataloging-in-Publication Data
An entry can be found on request

Typeset by FiSH Books, Enfield, Middx.
Printed by Short Run Press Ltd, Exeter, Devon.

# Contents

For Marina

# Acknowledgements

This book has only been possible due to the kindness and generosity of a large number of institutions and people. As a result, I would like to extend gratitude to the various archives, libraries and museums whose holdings have assisted this project. These include: the British Film Institute in London; the California Museum of Photography at the University of California/Riverside; the Chicago Public Library; the Free Library of Philadelphia; the George Eastman House in Rochester, New York; the Johnson-Shaw Stereoscopic Museum in Meadville, Pennsylvania; the Library of Congress in Washington, DC; the Lincoln Center for the Performing Arts in New York City; the Margaret Herrick Library of the Academy of Motion Picture Arts and Sciences in Beverly Hills, California; the Museum of Modern Art in New York City; the National Media Museum in Bradford; the New York Public Library; the University of California/Los Angeles; the University of Iowa at Iowa City; the University of Oklahoma in Norman, Oklahoma; the University of Southern California in Los Angeles and the University of Texas at Austin.

A number of scholars, archivists and collectors have also made available a range of documents, films, slides and other materials for my research. Others have kindly read drafts of this book and provided much-needed feedback. I would like to extend my thanks to each of them. They include: Paula Blair, Genoa Caldwell, Jared Case, Phillip Fortune, Rebecca Grant, Luke McKernan, Steve Massa, Roger Miller, Patrick Montgomery, Charles Musser, Oliver Nelson, Henry Nicolella, Betty Robbins, Mark Ryan, Kevin Rockett, Charles Silver, Zoran Sinobad, David Stenn, Brian Taves, Glenn White and Galen Wilkes.

In particular, I would like to acknowledge the crucial assistance provided by Margaret Bergh and the Marnan Collection, Bill Chase, Michael Lee and Martin McLoone, as well as to my good friend and colleague Desmond O'Rawe. Without the assistance and encouragement of these people, this book would not have been possible.

On a personal level, I would also like to thank my parents, Don and Phyllis Rhodes, as well as my wife, Marina, to whom this book is dedicated.

Gary D. Rhodes
Belfast, Northern Ireland, 2011

# Introduction

In 1908, the American Mutoscope & Biograph Company of New York City reigned as one of the most important American producers of moving pictures. Among their many releases that year was *Caught by Wireless*, directed by Wallace McCutcheon, who had previously directed such important films as *Kit Carson* (1903), *The Moonshiner* (1904), *Dream of a Rarebit Fiend* (1906) and *The Black Hand* (1906). The lead role in *Caught by Wireless* was performed by actor D.W. Griffith. Within a few months of his performance in the film, Griffith embarked on a directorial career at Biograph that would forever change American cinema. Accompanying him on that journey would be cinematographer G.W. 'Billy' Bitzer, the man who photographed *Caught by Wireless*.

The film features actor Edward Dillon as a villainous rent collector in Ireland who threatens Paddy (D.W. Griffith) and his family. After thrashing the rent collector, Paddy leaves for America, the land of opportunity. He becomes a successful policeman in New York City, and his salary soon pays for his family's passage to America, thus allowing for a happy reunion. On the same ocean liner with his family is the rent collector, who has fled Ireland after stealing money from his employer. Thanks to the 'efficacy of the marconigram', Scotland Yard has wired the New York police force of the rent collector's pending arrival. The villain is arrested after setting foot on American soil.[1]

Of the many Irish-themed films produced in America during the early cinema period, *Caught by Wireless* is certainly one of the most important, not least because of the involvement of Griffith, Bitzer and McCutcheon. It was the first film to depict an Irishman's emigration to the United States, a tale that had been a staple of the nineteenth-century American theatre and popular music. It was also a film structured to highlight the technological advances of the telegraph, which became, unlike its 'Irish' plotline, the key feature of its publicity. *Caught by Wireless* was thus an important moving picture for many reasons.

1

At least 75 per cent of all American silent films are lost, if not more.[2] Fortunately, however, *Caught by Wireless* survives and is readily available for viewing. As of spring 2011, a video company in America named Grapevine Video sells a DVD copy of it.[3] That is in addition to the coverage *Caught by Wireless* received on its original release in film industry trade publications. The most in-depth discussion of the film appeared in a 1908 issue of *Moving Picture World*, the trade publication most often used by modern film historians researching early American cinema.[4] In short, *Caught by Wireless* is not at all hard to find, even if one is not looking specifically for it.

However, until my research, studies of Irish Film has remained completely unaware of its existence. It has not been discussed or even mentioned in existing literature, and it has not been listed in catalogues of 'Irish Cinema'. For those working in the subject area – like so many other hitherto unknown Irish-themed films – it simply does not exist, and yet for scholars working in the area of early American cinema it very much does exist. As a result, *Caught by Wireless* represents a specific example of the larger, urgent need for rigorous historiographic practice in the area of 'Irish Cinema'.

# Why This Book?

In recent years, scholars and critics of 'Irish Cinema' have been excavating the archives of early American cinema for artefacts and evidence that might plausibly connect the history and traditions of that cinema with their own inquiries into the popular culture and artistic achievements of the Irish-American diaspora. I believe that this enterprise is fraught with conceptual and empirical problems, and that the notion of 'Irish-American Cinema', at least insofar as it has been conceived and is now being deployed by scholars and critics of 'Irish Cinema', says more about the needs of Irish Film Studies at the end of the twentieth and beginning of the twenty-first century than it does about an actual historical period of US cinema that might relate to a some discrete category of Irish-American film. While many Irish-themed moving pictures were produced and/or distributed in America from the 1890s to the year 1915 (which has commonly been accepted as the end of the 'early cinema' period), the assumption that they constituted a codified 'Irish-American Cinema' – or that they should now be considered part of 'Irish Cinema' – will be interrogated in this book.

The invention of 'Irish-American Cinema' has depended in no small measure on pragmatic classification by scholars of Irish film. Selecting a film or a group of films to discuss is accepted practice in film studies, for

Advertisement published in the
28 March 1908 issue of the *New York Clipper*.

obvious reasons. The sheer number of American films, for example, means that it is necessary to concentrate only on one film, or perhaps a group of films, for a research project, whether that project might be considered 'historical', 'critical' or 'theoretical' in its approach. To analyse a group of films on the basis of the fact that each was directed by the same person, or that each featured the same actor, or that each was released in the same period of time, or that each belongs to the same genre: certainly these are among the many reasons that exist for pragmatic classification.

However, classifying films because they are perceived to be 'Irish-American' poses important concerns. Early fictional films like *Caught by Wireless* might have sequences that take place in Ireland or that feature Irish/Irish-American characters living in America, but that is not the key category in which these films operated at the time. *Caught by Wireless* was a Biograph moving picture that bears important narrative and aesthetic commonalities to other, non-Irish-themed Biograph films of the period, as well as to the broader American cinema, particularly in its use of melodrama. The basic plotline of *Caught by Wireless* features a man who achieves the 'American Dream', hardly a narrative unique to Irish-themed films. It also features a villain, an antagonist who terrorizes the hero and his family before receiving his comeuppance. Such a plot template informed hundreds of American melodramas that had nothing to do with Ireland or 'Irish' stories. In other words, what I am suggesting is that segregating films because they are perceived to be 'Irish-American' tends to sever them problematically from the American cinema that produced them.

Reconnecting what I will refer to as 'Irish-themed' films to the American cinema also means reconnecting them to the pre-cinema influences on early American films. The decades preceding the first Irish-themed films offered an array of sources on which they would be dependent. These included live entertainment, such as theatre and variety programmes and sketches of the type that were staged at opera houses and vaudeville. Such influences also included lantern slides projected at various public events. These slides created a visual culture in the years before cinema that would inform both the topics and the cinematographic approach employed by Irish-themed moving pictures. At the same time, lantern slides and live theatre of the 1890s and early twentieth century bore the influence of moving pictures, as by that time all of these entertainment forms coexisted.

My goal is not merely to reconnect these Irish-themed films with the American cinema, but to reconnect the Irish-themed films produced in America with one another, by which I specifically mean examining both fiction and non-fiction Irish-themed American films. Early non-fiction films about Ireland have represented a curious problem for scholars of Irish Cinema, who have generally eschewed them in favour of writing about fictional 'Irish-American' films, thus creating what I would perceive to be an even more peculiar form of pragmatic classification. These non-fiction films about Ireland featured images, as well as educational goals, similar to non-fiction films produced before 1915 on other countries of the world and on specific sites within the United States. The stylistic and – certainly by the early years of the twentieth century – narrative similarities of non-fiction 'travelogues', as they were often called, featured entertainment goals not at all dissimilar to fictional films. Moreover, such non-fiction films were generally screened as part of larger programmes that included both fiction and non-fiction moving pictures. The history of non-fiction films in early American cinema is tethered to the history of fiction films, a fact that has been largely absent from existing literature on what has been called Irish Cinema.

The imperative of this book is thus to introduce a measure of revisionism into a developing research field that encompasses the historical and formal relationship between Irish-themed films and early American cinema. Such revisionism is the result of my undertaking an archive-based study that draws on empirically grounded primary sources. By constructing a history of Irish-themed films in early American cinema, it is my intention to redress the neglect of pre-cinema contexts and the relationship between those discourses and the formation of genres and the circulation of ethnic images and stereotypes within the broader context of early American cinema. Using such a film historical approach, it is hoped that this topic can be aligned more closely with the research traditions and methods of Film Studies.

## Survey of Existing Literature

In March 1998, the Irish President Mary Robinson famously talked about a 'global Irish family', by which she referred to people of Irish ancestry living outside of Ireland.[5] By the time Robinson spoke those words, scholars had already been working for years on the subject of Irish migration to countries such as the United States. Kerby A. Miller's *Emigrants and Exiles: Ireland and the Irish Exodus to North America* (1985) remains the landmark example of such scholarship.[6] Miller has continued to address similar issues in such texts as *Ireland and Irish America: Culture, Class, and Transatlantic Migration* (2008).[7] Other studies have offered insight into specific aspects of the Irish-American experience, including such published essays as 'St Patrick's Day Celebrations and the Formation of Irish-American Identity, 1845–1875' and 'Gaelic Sport and the Irish Diaspora in Boston, 1879–90'.[8] Not unexpectedly, the interest in Irish migration helped spawn Irish Diaspora Studies. Writing about Irish Diaspora Studies in 2003, Patrick O'Sullivan noted: 'No one academic discipline is going to tell us everything we want to know about the Irish Diaspora. The study of migration, emigration, immigration, population movements, flight, scattering, networks, transnational communities, diaspora – this study demands an interdisciplinary approach.'[9] However, while endorsing an interdisciplinary approach, O'Sullivan importantly requests that his 'readers' reflect upon 'the complexities, confusions, and the plain nonsense' that it can create.[10]

Irish Diaspora Studies has certainly afforded an important opportunity for many of those scholars interested in what has often been called 'Irish Cinema'. In some cases, the connection between the two areas has been implicit; in other cases, it has been actively promoted. For example, the blurb inside the dust jacket of Kevin Rockett's *The Irish Filmography* (1996) promised that the book would add a 'new dimension to the study of the Irish diaspora'.[11] Forging a relationship with Irish Diaspora Studies

Publicity photo of Sidney Olcott.

offered numerous benefits to scholars of Irish Cinema, not least of which were possible affiliations with various institutions in America and the potential for grants and international research network funding.

A connection to Irish Diaspora Studies also suited the kinds of narratives that some scholars of Irish Cinema desired to write. It is important to note that the major scholars working in this area have not generally been film historians or film theorists, but have instead been cultural theorists. For example, in her 'Introduction' to the anthology *Screening Irish-America* (2009), Ruth Barton speaks of the use of cultural theory – as well as 'gender studies, religious studies, [and] spatial and political theories' – to inform discussions of what she refers to as 'Irish-American Cinema'.[12] Nowhere does she mention current (or, for that matter, old) debates in film theory or film historiography. Rather than participate in those areas of Film Studies, scholars such as Ruth Barton, Luke Gibbons and others have often focussed on the politics of cultural representations.

Another result from the connection between 'Irish Cinema' and Irish Diaspora Studies has been the ability to broaden the canon of films that are 'Irish'. After all, the history of indigenous Irish film-making was quite sparse until the 1980s. It has been, as Martin McLoone has rightly suggested, 'the emergence of a contemporary cinema'.[13] However, by subsuming Irish-themed American films into Irish Cinema, a practice ostensibly justified at least in part by the diaspora, scholars in this area have been able to construct a more extensive (and, arguably, more grand) history of Irish Cinema than would otherwise exist. The process has resulted in a larger filmography, and, as a result, more films on which to expound. Nowhere does this appear more apparent to me than on the cover of Ruth Barton's book, *Irish National Cinema* (2004), which features not an image of an indigenous Irish production, as the term 'national cinema' would suggest, but rather a publicity still for a Hollywood movie.[14]

At least one scholar has recently identified problems in existing literature on Irish Cinema. In his book *The Myth of an Irish Cinema* (2008), Michael Gillespie suggests that the subject area is mired in problematic notions of 'national cinema'.[15] He adds:

> Just as *Irish cinema* [emphasis in original] stands as a term too often accepted without question, many film scholars still generate criticism based on the conception of Irish identity as a monolithic temperament, even when Irishness as a stable category finds itself under assault... To complicate circumstances, the institutions that have traditionally defined 'Irishness' are changing or becoming obsolete. This condition of flux does not mean that viewers should cease to take Irishness into consideration when interpreting specific films, but it does demand a refinement of one's point of view.[16]

Gillespie thus calls into question 'Irish Cinema', but importantly adds that he does not 'deny the value of looking at Irish-themed motion pictures from the points of view of communal identities'.[17]

The trajectory of scholarship on Irish Cinema did not necessarily need to unfold as it has. Anthony Slide's *The Cinema and Ireland* (McFarland, 1988) was at the vanguard of scholarship in this area, being published at roughly the same time as Kevin Rockett, Luke Gibbons and John Hill's seminal book *Cinema and Ireland* (1987). Slide's book addresses both indigenous film-making in Ireland and the Irish-themed American film, but consciously and quite carefully separates those discussions. Thus, at the onset of scholarship in this area, Slide's work proposed the possibility of examining Irish film and Irish-themed American films without conflating the two. However, his approach was generally eschewed by subsequent scholars in favour of that employed by Kevin Rockett in *Cinema and Ireland*, who readily placed early American films into the category of Irish Cinema.

Rockett's approach, which also manifested in his book *The Irish Filmography*, has proved influential on literature in this area, far more so than Slide's, and has thus resulted in what I view as a problematic expansion of Irish Cinema. More recently, scholars like Ruth Barton, in *Screening Irish-America*, have offered another, related invention, the category of 'Irish-American Cinema'. Here a distinction is sometimes made between Irish-themed films produced in Ireland and Irish-themed films produced in America; however, those films produced in America are 'Irish-American', thus constituting a diasporic cinema that I do not believe exists, certainly not in its current formulation. However, many scholars working in this area have readily accepted the viability of these categories. It is my belief that Rockett and Barton have employed three narratives to categorize Irish-themed American films, and that all three categories are problematic.

The first narrative – which helped place Irish-themed films from early American cinema into the category of 'Irish Cinema' – is founded on those fictional American films with plots set in Ireland, particularly those that were shot on location in Ireland. For example, in *Cinema and Ireland*, Rockett crafts a chapter called 'Silent Films' that begins with the dawn of film exhibition in Ireland and ends with a discussion of indigenous Irish film production, such as those films produced by the Film Company of Ireland. Both issues make much sense in a discussion about silent Irish films. In the middle of that chapter, however, he discusses Sidney Olcott and Walter MacNamara, both of whom shot American films with Irish story-lines on location in Ireland. Approximately seventeen years later, in her book *Irish National Cinema*, Ruth Barton adopts the same narrative structure and intellectual strategy in a chapter entitled 'A Silent Revolution'.[18]

Both Rockett and Barton thus subtly place the Olcott and MacNamara films into the category of Irish Cinema by virtue of the fact that they were shot in Ireland. However, in the aforementioned books, they do not address, for example, the large array of American films set in Ireland that were shot in the United States. Their discussions also avoid addressing the complexities of films featuring Irish characters that were either set in America or that had ill-defined settings. It is true that Rockett later included many of these kinds of films in *The Irish Filmography*, but in that case, rather than playing a role in a narrative argument, the films are subsumed unproblematically into the category of Irish Cinema/Irish Film by process of being catalogued in an encyclopaedia bearing the title that it does.

The second narrative – which also helped place Irish-themed films from early American cinema into the category of Irish Cinema – involves ethnic origins. Writing about the Kalem Company in *Cinema and Ireland*, Kevin Rockett notes that director Sidney Olcott was 'born in Toronto, Canada, of Irish parents'.[19] Rockett also refers to the O'Kalem films as 'the films Olcott made in Ireland for his American employers', as if to distance the diasporic director from his American producers.[20] He then claims that it was Olcott who 'chose Ireland' for location shooting, the suggestion being that the director with Irish heritage wanted to shoot a film in Ireland. However, at least one primary source indicates that it was Frank Marion – one of the three men who started the Kalem Company – who 'chose' Ireland as a location, not Olcott.[21] Moreover, Kalem's 1910 location shoot in Ireland was part of a trip that also included location shooting in Germany. That is all in addition to the fact that the bulk of Olcott's film career was spent directing non-Irish-themed films on American soil. Rockett then proposes a similar argument involving Walter MacNamara, director of *Ireland a Nation*, noting that he was 'an Irishman who had been living in the US for a few years'.[22] MacNamara was Irish-born, but the bulk of his American film career involved non-Irish-themed films.

In *Irish National Cinema*, Barton echoes Rockett, noting that Sidney Olcott was a 'colourful character whose parents had emigrated to Toronto from Cork'.[23] She also draws attention to the fact that Walter MacNamara was born in Ireland.[24] Five years later, writing in her 'Introduction' to *Screening Irish-America*, Barton continues to discuss ethnic heritage, citing such film-makers as Herbert Brenon, William Desmond Taylor and Raoul Walsh, as well as actors of 'Irish descent' like Mary Pickford. In this case, she uses ethnicity in an attempt to support claims of an Irish-American Cinema rather than an Irish Cinema or – in the words of her previous book – an 'Irish National Cinema'. However, her 'Introduction' in *Screening Irish-America* omits discussion of the vast array of writers, directors, producers, actors and others involved in a large number of Irish-themed films in early American cinema that were not Irish-American; she also does not mention the large array of Irish-Americans working in early cinema on films that were not Irish-themed.

The third narrative Rockett and Barton propose also involves ethnic origins, not of film-makers in this case, but instead of the audiences who attended 'Irish' or, as the case might be, 'Irish-American Cinema'. For example, in *Cinema and Ireland*, Rockett claims that Kalem's Irish-themed films were 'orientated towards an (Irish) American audience', but he provides absolutely no supporting evidence for that monumental claim.[25] Subsequently, Rockett, Barton and others removed the parenthetical, speaking more directly about an 'Irish-American audience'. Such an Irish-American audience was necessary to complete the invention of an 'Irish-American Cinema'. In other words, these films, so the story goes, were not only made by Irish-Americans, but also viewed by them as well. Films produced by the Irish (-Americans) for the Irish (-Americans).

The fact that the advent and proliferation of the moving picture in America coincided with Irish emigration to America has offered the appearance of support for notions of an Irish-American film audience. Indeed, Desmond Bell articulated this argument in an Arts and Humanities Research Council (AHRC)-funded research network project entitled *Early Cinema and the Diasporic Imagination: The Irish in America, 1890–1930*.[26] However, this argument has severe limitations, if not problems. Irish emigration to America had existed long before the rise of the moving picture; in fact, the period from 1890 to 1900 saw those emigration numbers shrink from what they had been in any previous decade from 1840 to 1890; similarly, the Irish also decreased in terms of their percentage of total arrivals into the United States during 1890–1900.[27] More generally, however, it is important to iterate the fact that two events occuring parallel to one another does not automatically speak to issues of causality or significant intersection.

Other arguments about an Irish-American film audience rely on the working-class status of Irish-Americans, rather than the era of their emigration. For example, in his essay 'The Irish Migrant and Film', Rockett argues that, while Irish-Americans during the 'silent era' represented only 'six percent of the American population, they were apparently concentrated in urban areas, and being overwhelmingly working class, were proportionately more important to film exhibitors than their numbers might suggest. It is this Irish-American constituency which the early cinema sought to bring to the cinema with images of themselves.'[28] Here Rockett presumably refers to the nickelodeon era and to the geographical location and economic status of nickelodeon audiences. While there is no doubt that large numbers of nickelodeons existed in cities like New York, historians such as Robert C. Allen have offered evidence that working-class neighbourhoods had fewer nickelodeons than in middle-class neighbourhoods.[29] This is to say nothing of the sheer numbers of both Americans and nickelodeons that existed outside of urban areas like New York City. More important, perhaps, is the fact that various scholars have debated the extent to which the working class comprised the majority of nickelodeon audiences.[30]

Speaking on the issue of Irish-American audiences, Barton claims: 'Working class Irish audiences congregated in neighbourhood clubs and picture houses and by the teens were being catered for by filmmakers with a different agenda.'[31] While she mentions 'filmmakers' in the plural, her only evidence is mention of a single film-maker, Walter MacNamara, and her only evidence of 'Irish audiences' is a single New York theatre that premiered MacNamara's film, *Ireland a Nation*. However, the venue she cites (New York City's 'Forty-Fourth Street Theatre') was certainly not a neighbourhood theatre; moreover, primary sources suggest quite clearly that Irish-American attendance for at least some screenings of *Ireland a Nation* was bolstered by promotion in the Irish-American press and by organized attendance from Irish societies, rather than by coherent and ritualistic 'working class Irish audiences'.[32]

Following from Rockett and Barton, Denis Condon's *Early Irish Cinema, 1895–1921* (2008) promotes a similar theory about an alleged Irish-American film audience. He claims: 'Given that it was the diasporic Irish in the United States to whom these Irish dramas were primarily addressed, it is hardly surprising that they should flatter their audience by endorsing their decision to leave Ireland, a country of acknowledged beauty but with serious economic and political difficulties.'[33]

In other words, Irish-Americans were the target audience for films with plots designed for them. However, the very films he mentions, such as *The Colleen Bawn* (1911) and *Arrah-na-Pogue* (1911), were adaptations of Dion Boucicault stage plays that had played at theatres frequented by *general* audiences, rather than specifically Irish-American audiences, in small towns and large cities across America for well over a generation before being adapted into films.[34]

The narrative of an Irish-American audience, at least as it has been suggested in existing literature, is problematic for many reasons. Rockett, Barton and Condon speak as if a monolithic Irish-American audience existed, as they make no attempt to address differences that existed between Irish-Americans of different ages, genders, religions, economic groups, and so forth. Nor do they acknowledge the Irish-Americans living outside of urban areas like New York City. However, another key issue is the fact that these Irish-themed films were screened at hundreds of venues across the United States: the audience for them was without doubt the general audience that consumed non-Irish-themed films as well. Indeed, the Irish-themed films were themselves usually programmed on bills that included non-Irish-themed entertainment, meaning other moving pictures and illustrated songs.

I believe that these three narratives used to place Irish-themed early American films into the categories of Irish Cinema and/or Irish-American Cinema have been repeated in part because existing literature in this area has not engaged in any in-depth conversation with historical studies on early American cinema. For example, in his monumental work, *The Emergence of Cinema: The American Screen to 1907* (1990), Charles Musser discusses the first moving picture to include an Irish character, *Chinese Laundry Scene* (1894).[35] Musser, one of the key historians of early American cinema, also mentions the film and the Irish character it contains in his essay 'Ethnicity, Role-Playing, and American Film Comedy: From *Chinese Laundry Scene* to *Whoopee* (1894–1930)'.[36] However, scholars of Irish Cinema have never discussed or catalogued the very first film produced in America (or anywhere else, for that matter) to depict an Irish character, even though information about it appears in highly important secondary sources on early American cinema.[37]

Contemporary scholars of Irish film have also made little use of primary materials when discussing early Irish-themed American cinema. In those instances when figures such as Gibbons and Barton do use primary documents in writing about these films, their citations reveal that the primary sources they quote are in fact refracted through secondary sources.[38] Indeed, even Gillespie, whose book is little concerned with early cinema, confidently suggests that 'one would be hard-pressed to find significant formal differences between [the indigenous Irish films produced by the Film Company of Ireland and the O'Kalem films]'.[39] However, he offers no evidence to support his claim, which would require the analysis of some films that do not survive to be plausibly accepted.

Only Rockett and Condon have made much use of primary materials. Condon constructs a history of Ireland and early cinema that draws on many exciting and important primary sources, but his subject is indeed Ireland and early cinema, not the Irish-themed films produced by American companies that are the focus of my book; for him, the matter of American cinema emerges centrally due to the Kalem Company. By contrast, Rockett lists an impressive array of citations for primary sources on Irish-themed American films in *The Irish Filmography*, but those citations – much like the films he lists and the formatting of the same – draw quite heavily on citations offered in catalogues published by the American Film Institute.[40] They do not constitute a rigorous engagement with the vast archive of sources available in the United States.

# Research Methodology and Sources

To redress the concerns I have identified, I have adopted a research methodology borne out of recent film historiography. For example, I have attempted to avoid the pitfall of first developing an argument and then finding a small number of films or other sources to buttress an over-simplified conclusion. Rather, I began by making an exhaustive search of every relevant primary source that I could uncover. For many reasons, including gaps in the historical archive, no such investigation could ever hope to be complete. At the same time, a key goal of my research methodology was not to be intentionally *incomplete*. An avoidance of studying all possible primary sources or adopting a shoddy research ethic would have meant, among other problems, that so many important films, lantern slides and other relevant issues would have been left undis-covered. To offer but one example of hundreds, *Caught by Wireless* – arguably one of the most important Irish-themed films in early American cinema – would have continued to languish in obscurity. Missing data on this scale is enough to have skewed prior theories and conclusions.

A crucial primary resource for this project has been the surviving films of the period under consideration, ranging from those Irish-themed films examined by previous scholars to those films that, like *Caught by Wireless*, have not been. Moreover, my study has been informed by viewing a large array of early American films that are not Irish-themed, as they often feature important links and similarities to those that are, such as the use of the same basic plotline or the same comic situation. As a result, I have viewed the Irish-themed films under consideration through the lens of what I believe them to be: functions of early American cinema, not components of a distinctive 'Irish-American cinema'. However, given the fact that so many early American films no longer exist, the use of moving pictures cannot alone suffice in the construction of the kind of film history I propose.

Related to my use of films as primary documents is my use of surviving pre-cinema entertainment, including the scripts for theatrical plays and vaudeville acts, as well as extant lantern slides and lectures. In the case of slides, the effort to provide an exhaustive examination has been particularly important and particularly challenging. Some public archives and museums in America house collections of fiction and non-fiction lantern slides produced in the nineteenth and twentieth centuries, such as those slides released by the Keystone View Company now housed at both the California Museum of Photography at the University of California/Riverside and at the Johnson-Shaw Stereoscopic Museum in Meadville, Pennsylvania. However, the bulk of surviving lantern slides reside in the hands of private collections. For example, the Marnan Collection in Minneapolis, Minnesota, proved to be an invaluable resource for illustrated song slides of both the nineteenth and twentieth centuries.

I have also tried to examine an array of relevant paper sources from the period under consideration. Promotional materials for moving pictures and for its pre-cinema contexts have proven to be very important. These include advertisements, playbills, programmes and posters. Other kinds of primary documents have also shed important light on these Irish-themed films. First-hand accounts of the period by such people as Gene Gauntier, for example, and surviving letters written by employees of the Kalem Company, have helped me to reconstruct events important to the production of some of the films I examine.

This book has also made extensive use of relevant publications printed during the nineteenth and early twentieth centuries. These include a wide range of stereopticon and moving picture catalogues, as well as of theatre, photography and lantern slide trade publications. I undertook an exhaustive search through those industry publications that covered the emergent moving picture, including *The New York Clipper*, *The Phonoscope*, *The New York Dramatic Mirror*, *The Billboard* and *Variety*, as well as those trade publications devoted more specifically to the cinema, such as *Views and Film Index* (later known as *The Film Index*), *Moving Picture World*, *Moving Picture News*, *Motion Picture News*, *The Nickelodeon*, *Motography* and others. I have also conducted similar research into those periodicals published by film manufacturing companies (i.e. 'house organs'), such as the *Kalem Kalendar* and the *Vitagraph Bulletin* (aka *Vitagraph Life Portrayals*). The lack of useful indexing for such publications required my examination of every page of these publications from their first issues to 1915. While that proved to be quite a lengthy process, it has also proven very fruitful for understanding the period, for rediscovering relevant films, and for finding important data about the production and release of those Irish-themed films already catalogued by modern scholars. The use of so many publications – rather than, for example, an examination of only *Moving Picture World* – has been necessary, given that each publication chronicled unique data. For example, much significant information about the Irish-themed films produced by the Kalem Company was published only in *The Film Index*.

However, to rely only on film-related print publications was not possible for the kind of exhaustive historical inquiry I envisioned. As a result, I also undertook a major excavation of various general audience newspapers that published reviews, articles, editorials and advertisements of relevant pre-cinema and early cinema entertainment. These ranged from major urban newspapers like the *New York Times* to such small-town newspapers as the *Indiana Progress*, published in Indiana, Pennsylvania. Such general newspapers were in addition to my study of the seven major Irish-American newspapers published during the early cinema period. These publications included: *The Advocate* (aka the *Irish-American Advocate*), the *Gaelic American*, *The Irish-American*, the *Irish World* (aka the *Irish World and American Industrial Liberator*), the *Kentucky Irish-American*, the *National Hibernian*, and *The Pilot* (aka the *Boston Pilot*). Unlike many of the city and town newspapers I used, which have been digitized and are thus keyword searchable, these Irish-American newspapers are neither digitized nor indexed, thus requiring a page-by-page search for the whole of the early cinema period.

While much of my emphasis has been on reclaiming information from primary sources, I have also engaged with relevant secondary sources. Whereas I perceive a myriad of problems in existing literature on 'Irish Cinema' and 'Irish-American Cinema', I have found much important assistance and data in secondary literature on early American cinema. Many scholars working in that area have produced extremely important texts in an effort to illuminate the origins of American cinema, as well as the production, distribution and reception of the same. Here I would suggest yet another way in which my research has attempted to realign the study of these Irish-themed films with the discipline of Film Studies, as the work of previous film historians – rather than, say, cultural theorists – has proven critical in my understanding of early American cinema.

My research on this topic has required much work over the period of several years at a range of institutions, archives and museums, including (but not limited to) the Free Library of Philadelphia; the George Eastman House in Rochester, New York; the Library of Congress in Washington, DC; the Lincoln Centre for the Performing Arts in New York City; the Margaret Herrick Library of the Academy of Motion Picture Arts and Sciences in Beverly Hills, California; the New York Public Library; the University of California/Los Angeles; the University of Oklahoma in Norman, Oklahoma; and the University of Southern California in Los Angeles. It has also led me to work with a wide range of collectors of primary sources across the United States, as well as my own accumulation of primary sources from eBay and other auctions.

Such research led to my obtaining copies of literally thousands and thousands of primary documents, as well as copies of a large number of films, lantern slides, posters, sheet music and other film-related ephemera. That was in addition to a wide-ranging use of secondary sources in the area of American film history. These materials have formed a very substantial corpus from which I have been able to construct a history of Irish-themed films in early American cinema and their pre-cinema contexts.

# Book Contents

The problems I have identified with existing literature on Irish-themed early American cinema have created an urgent need for the historical research I have undertaken. My exhaustive primary research does not support notions of a distinct 'Irish-American Cinema' and instead forces consideration of another narrative: these Irish-themed films functioned as an inseparable component of the broader category of American entertainment, and, more specifically, of American cinema. Such films operated within emergent film genres and bore the influence of nineteenth-century live entertainment and magic lantern slides.

A key recurrent issue that arises in the historical record of these films is that of 'authenticity', or – as it was often termed in the nineteenth and early twentieth centuries – the 'genuine' and the 'real'. For Irish-themed entertainment, the questions revolved around which entertainment was perceived to be authentically Irish and which was not, as well as who was the proper judge of the same. Such concerns were problematic for many reasons. As Mark Phelan has noted, 'authenticity is never stable or fixed, but is rather, capriciously chimerical and in flux'.[41] He adds that any theatrical 'reproduction of authenticity' is an oxymoron.[42] Ascertaining the 'genuine' qualities of Irish-themed American entertainment of the nineteenth and early twentieth centuries was a task that faced many specific challenges, including the fact that, for example, some performers without Irish heritage became, for the sake of the stage, 'Irish comedians'. Additionally, people who had Irish heritage commonly wrote, directed and/or acted in non-Irish themed stage productions and films.

However problematic it was and remains, the question of 'authenticity' – and its apparent opposite, the 'stage Irish' – pervaded Irish-themed entertainment of the nineteenth and early twentieth centuries. Rather than serve to distinguish Irish-themed entertainment in America, such concerns instead connected it to the broader American entertainment industry. Arguments over what was or was not 'genuine' were a regular concern of nineteenth-century theatre and vaudeville acts in America, ranging from similar questions about other ethnicities to issues of the believability of story-lines, costumes and sets. Such questions became crucial to early American cinema as well. Many 'non-fiction' films were faked, and some of them created controversies as a result. By contrast, other films, including many fictional films, consciously strove for what was called 'realism' or the 'real'.

To organize and consolidate my primary research and the key issues aris-
ing from it, I have organized this book into three sections, 'Pre-Cinema
Contexts', 'Genre Formations' and 'Film Audiences'. Together, these
sections cover a span of fifty years: 1866–1915. These time markers were
selected because of the historical importance that they hold. The year 1866
was the first full year following the end of the US Civil War, and the year
1915 is generally understood to be the point at which the early cinema
period came to an end. The half-century under review thus allows for a
thorough investigation of the decades leading up to the advent of the
cinema, as well as its progress through the nickelodeon period and to the
dawn of the feature film era.

'Pre-Cinema Contexts' constructs a history of Irish-themed live entertainment in America from 1866 to 1915, the entirety of the historical
period that this book encompasses. Such entertainment did not end with
either Edison's first public demonstration of moving pictures in 1893 or his
first publicly projected films in 1896. Instead, it continued parallel to the
rise of the moving picture, the result of which meant that early American
cinema was not only heavily influenced by pre-cinema contexts, but also
existed in an exchange of ideas with it.

Chapter 1, 'Theatre and Events', investigates the history of live Irish-
themed entertainment on the American stage; it examines not only
Broadway plays, but also touring stage productions, variety shows, live
sketches and vaudeville acts. The enormity of this topic has led me to
isolate five incremental years as representative case studies: 1866 (the year
after the US Civil War ended), 1876, 1886, 1896 (the year of the first
publicly projected films in America) and 1906 (the beginning of the nickelodeon era). Importantly, this chapter reveals the deep historical roots and
ongoing popularity of Irish-themed entertainment with general audiences
across the United States for the period of history under review, which
ranged from simple 'stage Irish' performances to elaborate attempts to
produce 'genuine' Irish productions. As previously suggested, such entertainment was part of the broader American entertainment industry, in
which, for example, ethnic humour was central and the parodying of various nationalities was commonplace.

Chapter 2, 'Lantern Slides', investigates a crucial form of projected,
visual entertainment that has been noticeably absent from secondary literature on Irish-themed American cinema: the magic lantern slide. This
chapter chronicles the growth of Irish-themed lantern slides in the nineteenth century and early twentieth century, as well as the public forums at
which they were projected, such as public 'travelogue' lectures. Important
to this discussion is the proliferation of both non-fiction slides of Ireland

(and, as the nineteenth century progressed, ethnographic images of the Irish) and fictional Irish-themed slides, which often featured ethnic stereotypes, usually for comedic purposes. While these two categories existed, the historical archive reveals that the boundary between them was hardly fixed. It is worth bearing in mind that a concept of early cinema that excludes pre-cinema and the ways in which films and other visual entertainment converged and overlapped during this period may be convenient for a theorist of Irish-American culture, but it is problematic for the film historian.

'Genre Formations', the second section of this book, builds a history of the three major genres in which the Irish-themed American film participated: Non-fiction, Comedy and Melodrama. These genres emerged from and were shaped by nineteenth-century entertainment of the type explored in 'Pre-Cinema Contexts'. This section also underscores the fact that these Irish-themed films were *not* 'Irish' (or, for that matter, 'Irish-American'), but were instead American films. Due to that fact, they were subject to broader trends that affected non-fiction, comedy and melodrama in early American cinema. Collectively, the four chapters in this section also reveal how porous generic boundaries could be in early American cinema.

Chapter 3, 'Non-Fiction', highlights the fact that Irish-themed non-fiction films were a component of the broader non-fiction genre prevalent in early American cinema. Such films were in large measure born out of the nineteenth-century lantern slide and the travel lecture, and could in fact depict more than one kind of non-fiction subject within a single film. For example, some Irish-themed non-fiction films presented images of trains, roiling waters, and parades, all three of which represented popular topics commonly featured in non-Irish-themed moving pictures. Other generic issues surround the intent of these non-fiction films. At times – dependent on their images or the verbal commentary that accompanied them – such moving pictures attempted to be humorous, a goal they shared with fictional comedy films. Here again, the boundary between fiction and non-fiction was porous.

Chapter 4, 'Comedy', contextualizes Irish-themed comedies within the larger category of American film comedy, in which various ethnic stereotypes were common and in which many of the same gags, storylines and 'trick' cinematographic effects were repeated in moving pictures both with *and* without Irish characters. Chapter 3 also interrogates some comedic film characters that may or may not have been read as 'Irish'. Finally, this chapter explains the various ways in which early film comedies attempted to be seen as 'genuine', including their use of current events as the basis for storylines.

Chapter 5, 'Melodrama', examines the rise of the Irish-themed melo-drama film in the nickelodeon era. These melodramas made overt attempts to achieve the appearance of authenticity. Such efforts culminated in the Kalem Company shooting various Irish-themed melodramas on location in Ireland, an approach that the same company also used to shoot, for example, German stories in Germany, or Egyptian stories in Egypt. The result yielded American films shot overseas and intended largely for release in America. This drive towards the 'genuine' was not at all dissimilar to the intentions of early non-fiction cinema.

The final chapter comprising 'Genre Formations' is Chapter 6, 'Film Characters'. Drawing at times on pre-cinema influences and at times on previous moving pictures, American films regularly deployed a number of Irish film characters in narratives set not in Ireland, but in the United States. These include the Irish boxer, the Irish policeman, the Irish gangster and the Irish priest. Such characters represent another way in which generic boundaries were porous, as these characters appeared in various kinds of films ranging from non-fiction to comedies and melodramas. Moreover, these characters were not uniquely Irish; non-Irish boxers, policemen, gangsters and priests proliferated in early American cinema as well. In addition, while many film characters of this period had Irish names, their ethnicity often had little or no impact on their character traits or appearance. A number of film heroes in westerns and action/adventure films bore Irish names, for example, but their heritage had little if any impact on the narratives in which they appeared. More than Irish film characters, they were American film characters who happened to have Irish names.

Section Three of this book, 'Audiences', is comprised of one chapter on that topic. The use of the grammatical plural is key to this chapter, as there was no single audience for Irish-themed American films and illustrated songs in the early cinema period. People who viewed these films did so in virtually every city and town in America, and they were marked by various demographic and psychographic differences. They included Irish-Americans, but those Irish-Americans did not represent a monolithic group. Balanced film programmes, publicity materials and various audience reactions reveal the complexities of film viewers and their relationship to the cinema in this period.

# Conclusion

*Emerald Illusions: The Irish in Early American Cinema* represents an apt title for the history I have written. There can be no doubt that a large number of Irish-themed films were produced during the period of early American cinema, and that those same films drew upon a range of nineteenth-century influences, particularly live entertainment and the lantern slide. Such films and their pre-cinema contexts engaged in an ongoing dialogue about the illusory nature of reproducible authenticity. Some films were quite exacting in their efforts to be perceived as 'genuine', while others revelled in the inauthentic world of the 'stage Irish'. In the end, however, all of them were illusions on the screen, presenting cinematic simulacra to general audiences across the United States.

Another reason I believe the title *Emerald Illusions* properly represents the contents of this book is the fact that it eschews the prevailing interpretation of these films in existing literature, which I view as little more than a convenient invention, an illusion of an 'Irish/Irish-American Cinema'. This has been a subject area fraught with unsupported assertions and over-simplifications. By contrast, this book reframes these films as what I believe they were, first and foremost: American moving pictures produced for American film audiences.

In *Caught by Wireless*, the villainous landlord receives a degree of come-uppance at the hands of Paddy, who thrashes him after finding him in his home. However, the landlord is permanently dispelled not by fisticuffs, but instead by technology. The 'efficacy of the marconigram' allows police on two continents to work to achieve their goal by using accepted, modern methods. One century later, I have attempted to construct the first history of the Irish in early American cinema and pre-cinema using accepted, modern historiographic methods and rigorous, in-depth research.

# Notes

1. Advertisement, *Moving Picture World*, 21 March 1908, p.251.
2. D. Pierce, 'The Legion of the Condemned: Why American Silent Films Perished', *Film History*, 9, 1 (1997), pp.5–22.
3. *Caught by Wireless* is available on the DVD entitled *D.W. Griffith as an Actor* (Phoenix, AZ: Grapevine Video, 2008).
4. '*Caught by Wireless*', *Moving Picture World*, 21 March 1908, p.241.
5. Quoted in D.N. Doyle, 'Cohesion and Diversity in the Irish Diaspora', *Irish Historical Studies*, 31, 123 (May 1999), pp.411–34.
6. K. Miller, *Emigrants and Exiles: Ireland and the Irish Exodus to North America* (New York: Oxford University Press, 1985).
7. K. Miller, *Ireland and Irish America: Culture, Class, and Transatlantic Migration* (Dublin: Field Day Publications, 2008).
8. K. Moss, 'St Patrick's Day Celebrations and the Formation of Irish-American Identity, 1845–1875', *Journal of Social History*, 29, 1 (Autumn 1995), pp.125–48; P. Darby, 'Gaelic Sport and the Irish Diaspora in Boston, 1879', *Irish Historical Studies*, 33, 132 (November 2003), pp.387–403.
9. P. O'Sullivan, 'Developing Irish Diaspora Studies: A Personal View', *New Hibernia Review*, 7, 1 (Spring 2003), pp.131.
10. Ibid., p.132. O'Sullivan also notes: 'There is considerable literature on cinematic representations of Ireland. I say to students: Do not expect to learn much about Ireland and the Irish; do expect to learn about the demands of genre' (p.135).
11. K. Rockett, *The Irish Filmography: Fiction Films 1896–1996* (Dublin: Red Mountain Media, 1996).

12. R. Barton, 'Introduction', in R. Barton (ed.), *Screening Irish-America: Representing Irish-America in Film and Television* (Dublin: Irish-American Press, 2009), p.1.
13. M. McLoone, *Irish Film: The Emergence of a Contemporary Cinema* (London: British Film Institute, 2000).
14. R. Barton, *Irish National Cinema* (London: Routledge, 2004). Similarly, the cover of Denis Condon's book *Early Irish Cinema* (Dublin: Irish Academic Press, 2008) features a still from Kalem's *The Colleen Bawn* (1911), which was an early American film, not an early Irish film.
15. M.P. Gillespie, *The Myth of an Irish Cinema: Approaching Irish-Themed Films* (Syracuse, NY: Syracuse University Press, 2008), p.xii.
16. Gillespie, pp.xii-xiii.
17. Ibid., pp.xiii-xiv.
18. Barton, *Irish National Cinema*, pp.13–33.
19. K. Rockett, L. Gibbons and J. Hill, *Cinema and Ireland* (London: Croom Helm, 1987), p.7.
20. Ibid., p.9.
21. Ibid., p.7.
22. Ibid., p.12.
23. Barton, *Irish National Cinema*, p.19.
24. Ibid.
25. Rockett, Gibbons and Hill, *Cinema and Ireland*, p.9.
26. D. Bell, 'The Lads and Lasses from Ould Ireland: The Irish and the Silent Screen', *Film Ireland* (March/April 2007), p.31.
27. D.H. Akenson, 'An Agnostic View of the Historiography of the Irish-Americans', *Labour/Le Travail*, 14 (Fall 1984), pp.123–59.
28. K. Rockett, 'The Irish Migrant and Cinema', in P. O'Sullivan (ed.), *The Creative Migrant* (London: Leicester University Press, 1994), p.171.
29. R.C. Allen, 'Motion Picture Exhibition in Manhattan, 1906–1912', *Cinema Journal*, 18, 2 (Spring 1979), pp.2–15.
30. For example, questions over exactly who attended nickelodeon theatres resulted in the 'Singer–Allen' debate, which is recounted in M. Stokes, 'Introduction: Reconstructing American Cinema's Audiences', in M. Stokes and R. Maltby (eds), *American Movie Audiences: From the Turn of the Century to the Early Sound Era* (London: British Film Institute, 1999), pp.1–11.
31. Barton, *Irish National Cinema*, p.18.
32. See, for example, 'To See *Ireland a Nation*', *Gaelic American*, 24 October 1914, p.5. The numbers of Irish-Americans in attendance for screenings of *Ireland a Nation* at the Forty-Fourth Street Theatre in New York City are also in question. One review of the film ('*Ireland a Nation*', *Variety*, 10 October 1914, p.716) suggested that 'In New York, the audiences that have been viewing the picture are almost wholly Irish. One night late last week the big 44th street auditorium was practically sold out at 25 and 50 cents.' However, another review (R.C. McElvary, '*Ireland a Nation*', *Moving Picture World*, 3 October 1914, p.67) wrote of the film's 'first view' at the same theatre, claiming more modestly that 'there was a happy sprinkling of folks from the "ould sod"' in an audience that also included 'a host of moving picture people and friends of the producers'. In addition to the possible discrepancy, which could in fact have resulted from observations of different audiences attending different screenings, it is important to note that the theatre charged between twenty-five and fifty cents per ticket, which was well over two (and upwards of five, in the case of fifty cents) times the cost of a ticket for a typical neighbourhood film theatre in New York City at the time. Such ticket prices thus call into question the extent to which those who did attend the film were 'working class'.
33. Condon, *Early Irish Cinema*, p.127.
34. See Chapter 1 of this book for information on the touring versions and revivals of Boucicault's Irish-themed plays.
35. C. Musser, *The Emergence of Cinema: The American Screen to 1907* (Berkeley, CA: University of California, 1990), p.86.
36. L.D. Friedman, *Unspeakable Images: Ethnicity and the American Cinema* (Urbana, IL: University of Illinois, 1991), pp.39–81.
37. For example, *Chinese Laundry Scene* is not catalogued in Rockett's *Irish Filmography* or, as of May 2010, on *Irish Film & TV Research Online*, accessible at www.tcd.ie/irishfilm.

38. Here I am thinking specifically of Gibbons's 'Romanticism, Realism, and Irish Cinema', in Rockett, Gibbons and Hill, *Cinema and Ireland*, pp.194–257; Barton's 'A Silent Revolution' in her *Irish National Cinema*, pp.13–33; and Barton's 'Introduction', in Barton (ed.), *Screening Irish-America*, pp.1–16.
39. Gillespie, *Myth of an Irish Cinema*, p.12.
40. E. Savada (ed.), *American Film Institute Catalog of Motion Pictures Produced in the United States: Film Beginnings, 1893–1910* (Lanham, MD: Scarecrow Press, 1995); P.K. Hanson (ed.), *The American Film Institute Catalog of Motion Pictures Produced in the United States: Feature Films, 1911–1920* (Berkeley, CA: University of California Press, 1988).
41. Mark Phelan, ' "Authentic Reproductions": Staging the "Wild West" in Modern Irish Drama', *Theatre Journal*, 61, 2 (2009), p.236.
42. Ibid., p.237.

# Chapter One

# *Theatre and Events*

Writing about the development of Irish-American theatre, Maureen Murphy divided its history into five periods: pre-1830, 1830–60, 1860–90, 1890–1918 and 1918-present.[1] The 'stage Irishman' appeared in the years before 1830; the stage Irishman and his counterpart, the 'stage immigrant', proliferated during the period 1830–60. Murphy also suggests that an 'original comic character, based on an Irish immigrant type' emerged in 1848: 'Mose, the Bowery B'hoy', who was a 'boaster and brawler, heroic fire fighter, and guardian angel of the greenhorns'.[2]

Murphy also argues that the theatre of 1860–90 reflected the fact that Irish immigrants were taking 'their places in American life among its leading citizens'. She believes this manifested in two major comic forms: 'the romantic nationalism of Dion Boucicault's Irish melodramas, particularly *The Colleen Bawn* (1860), *Arrah-na-Pogue* (1864), and *The Shaughraun* (1874), and in the realistic sketches of Edward Harrigan's urban Irish immigrants in the Mulligan cycle (1878–1884)'.[3]

This period was followed by the era of 1890–1918, in which the theatre responded to the growth of Irish political power. For example, many productions featured the Irish as politicians or candidates for elective office.[4]

Murphy's historical epochs are helpful in understanding some depictions of the Irish in American theatre. However, her work features an emphasis on legitimate theatre productions in New York City. What has been absent from much scholarship in this area is a consideration of the many forms that Irish-themed live entertainment took. For various reasons, ranging from financial to geographical, most Americans did not attend Broadway plays. However, many of them did attend variety programmes that included Irish-themed entertainment at such venues as opera houses and, later, vaudeville theatres. Many others saw touring versions or revivals of Irish-themed plays.

It is important to underscore the fact that Irish-themed entertainment was staged in cities and towns across America during the post-Civil War era, just

**1.1** The cover of Harry L. Newton's *Killarney Blarney* (1905).

as it had been during the antebellum period. For example, E.F. Niehaus has chronicled the history of Irish-themed entertainment on the New Orleans stage from 1830 to 1862.[5] Many Irish performers appeared in minstrel shows during roughly the same time period.[6] Furthermore, as Carl Wittke has noted, Irish-American comedy of the sort offered by actor Barney Williams was 'as popular on the Pacific Coast [in the 1850s] as in the large eastern cities'.[7] Irish-themed entertainment varied from three-act plays to sketch comedy, all of which featured evolving content. By the end of the Civil War, for example, William H.A. Williams claims, 'there was, besides the negative aspects, a more positive side to the stereotype of the Irish'.[8]

As both Kathleen Heininge and John P. Harrington have suggested, questions about authenticity were asked of much Irish-themed live entertainment in the post-Civil War era.[9] The debate over what was and what was not 'genuinely' Irish came in the form of publicity, as well as in responses given to such entertainment from journalists and from audience members. Indeed, this emphasis on promoting and judging the authenticity of Irish-themed entertainment was not unique to live theatre. For example, Sister Mary Francis Clare's novel *From Killarney to New York; or, How Thade Became a Banker* (1877) promised that it would 'typify an incident in Irish-American life'; it was, so its title page claimed, 'a story of real life'.[10]

Dion Boucicault's highly popular Irish-themed plays represent a key component of the discussion over authenticity. As Deirdre McFeely has noted, a group of Irish-Americans congratulated Boucicault in 1875 for 'elevating the stage representation of the Irish character'. McFeely adds: 'The mainstream, or Anglo-American, audience equally approved of Boucicault's representation of the Irish. The theatre critics of the mainstream New York daily newspapers welcomed Boucicault's portrayal of what they considered to be the real Irish of Ireland.'[11] Such sentiments appeared numerous times in the nineteenth-century press. An 1874 article published in the *New York Times* claimed that Boucicault had 'created an Irish drama, and almost driven the old-fashioned rough-and-tumble Irishman from the stage. The caricature is gone. The portrait from nature has been substituted in its stead.'[12]

However, questions of authenticity hardly resulted in unanimous answers. Comedian Barney Williams, who, like Boucicault, had been born in Ireland, provides an example of the lack of agreement that arose over exactly who and what was authentic. Even as early as the 1850s, Williams had been decried as a crude 'imitator' of the Irish.[13] However, such criticisms hardly kept him and others from suggesting the opposite.[14] In 1869, an advertisement publicized the 'genuine Irish acting' in *The Emerald Ring*, which was due to 'Mr and Mrs Barney Williams in their famous characters of Mike and Maggie Macarty'.[15] Over a decade later, the *New York Herald* praised Williams for his work in *Innisfallen, or the Men in the Gap*, claiming it offered 'real, genuine Hibernian warmth'.[16] In some ways, Williams had inherited the mantle of the Irish comedian Tyrone Power (1795–1841), who himself had been viewed as 'genuine' in the antebellum era.[17]

Such discussions did not centre only on famous comedians like Williams and famous playwrights like Boucicault. Less renowned actors and plays participated in the conversation as well. According to his publicity in 1882, comedian Joseph Lewis (in his guise of 'Barney O' Toole') represented 'real, original Irish wit and humor'.[18] In 1908, an Indiana newspaper proclaimed Tom Waters and his musical skit *The Mayor of Laughland* to be 'real Irish comedy'.[19] As for plays and sketches, the *San Francisco Chronicle* claimed in 1888 that *The Ivy Leaf* was 'genuine Irish drama of the school that Boucicault has made familiar'.[20] Then, in 1910, the *Oakland Tribune* favourably reviewed the vaudeville act *A Romance of Killarney*, reassuring readers that it was 'genuine Irish comedy'.[21]

Proclamations of authenticity were not only linked to performers and to the plays and sketches in which they starred, but also to very specific aspects of these productions. For example, elaborate sets for Boucicault's *The Colleen Bawn* attempted to 'represent "picturesque" Killarney'.[22] Advertisements for *True Irish Hearts* in 1890 promised a 'genuine Irish bag pipe player', as well as 'songs in the real Irish language'.[23] The following year, publicity for *The Ivy Leaf* heralded its use of 'genuine Irish pipes'.[24] Even ads in 1886 for the equestrian drama *The Bandit King* heralded the use of a 'genuine Irish donkey'.[25]

Judgments on exactly what play or performer was 'genuine' could create controversies. Debates emerged, and conclusions reached at any given point were hardly fixed; they could evolve over time. According to Heininge, 'By the end of the nineteenth century, Boucicault was accused of creating a new stage Irish figure rather than eradicating the previous ones.'[26] As Gwen Orel has noted, questions over the authenticity of Boucicault's plays erupted in the Irish-American press in the late nineteenth and early twentieth centuries.[27] That said, however, the *National Hibernian* praised Boucicault in 1904 for having 'shed luster on [his] profession, and through it on the country that gave [him] birth'.[28] Then, in 1915, *The Irish Monthly* heralded Dion Boucicault as being an important Irish playwright in America.[29]

Whatever constituted the 'genuine' to an individual participant in, or a viewer of, Irish-themed live entertainment, its opposite was the 'stage Irishman'. As drama historian Margaret G. Maryoga claimed in 1943, 'The stage Irishman is as old as American drama itself.'[30] However, the use of the grammatical singular poses historical problems; there were various kinds of

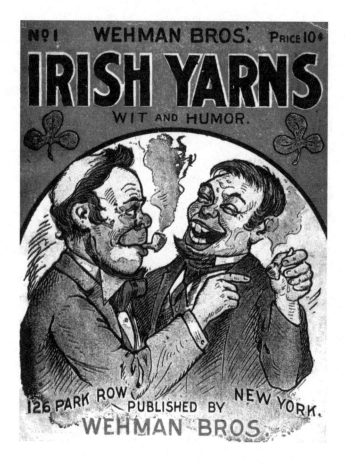

**1.2** The cover of the Wehman Brother's *Irish Yarns* (1907).

'stage Irishmen'. For example, the style and approach of Irish comedians differed greatly in the post-Civil War period. Nowhere are these differences more clear than in comparing the Irish 'romantic singing comedians', as they were called, who acted and sang in lavish, three-act stage plays and who were at times applauded by the Irish-American community, and those rough 'knockabout Irish comedians' who appeared in sketch comedy at vaudeville theatres. Moreover, Irish-themed vaudeville acts were not necessarily static; their content and approach changed over time.[31]

Variances also occurred in print cartoons of the Irish during the second half of the nineteenth century. Thomas Nast, who drew cartoons for *Harper's Weekly* from the 1860s to the 1880s, depicted Irishmen with what *Puck* magazine described as an 'ourang-outang Celt' who was 'all jaw and no brain'; such artwork echoed the Hibernian ape-men drawn by George Cruikshank and Sir John Tenniel in England in the nineteenth century.[32] Despite their indictment of *Harper's* cartoons, *Puck* also published cartoons featuring stereotypical Irish characters, which were drawn by such artists as Frederick Burr Opper. These cartoons depicted Irishmen (like 'Pat') and women (like 'Bridget') who bore stereotypical 'Irish' appearances, including large jaws, dirty physical presentation, clay pipes, and clothing that featured shamrocks; these characters also possessed stereotypical character traits, such as being stupid, lazy and/or violent. However, by the 1890s, *Puck's* treatment of the Irish changed in both frequency and tone.[33] That was in addition to the fact that artists at other publications also began to treat Irish characters differently, such as Richard Outcault in his serialized newspaper cartoon strip *Hogan's Alley*, which ran from 1895 to 1898. In it, Outcault created a character known as the 'Yellow Kid', who, as David Nasaw has noted, 'looked Asiatic, was bald like the poor European kids whose heads were shaved to prevent lice, had an Irish name, Mickey Duggan, and an Irish girlfriend'.[34] Duggan was thus an immigrant living in the slums, creating comedy based on the problems of acculturation, rather than exemplifying one of the 'stage Irish' variants or even a specifically Irish character.

Despite such variations, many people in the late nineteenth and early twentieth centuries did perceive the issue as a singular and offensive 'stage Irishman'. A 1903 editorial in the *Atlanta Constitution* described the caricature as one that tried to 'out-favor the chimpanzee' with stage gimmicks that were anything but realistic. These included 'green whiskers and the kind of hair that seems to bleed', as well as 'bizarre' costumes comprised of 'Scotch plaid trousers, a vest of wall-paper pattern, and a green or red coat'.[35] Speaking of the stage Irishman's 'wife', the newspaper added: 'If what seems bad in a man seems doubly so in a woman, it seems trebly so in a stage Irishman's wife. She defies the conventionalities – in fact [she] defies anything and everything in sight, even common decency.'

It is regrettable that scripts for many Irish-themed comedy acts of the late nineteenth and early twentieth centuries no longer exist. However, a number of phonograph recordings of the period shed light on the kinds of 'Irish' humour that gained popularity. Russell Hunting's 'Casey' skits – such as *Casey as Hotel Clerk* (1895), *Casey as Judge* (1896), *Casey at the Telephone* (1896), *Casey as a Doctor* (1897), *Casey Putting His Baby to Sleep* (1897), *Casey as Umpire at a Ball Game* (1898) and *Casey Listening to a Phonograph* (1905) – provide some insight into the performance of Irish-themed vaudeville humour, as do some of his other recordings, such as *Reilly as a Policeman* (circa 1895–96), *Mr Finnegan and Mr Flanigan* (1897) and *Murphy's Phonograph* (1897). Hunting was not alone, as several others recorded similar comedic sketches and songs, including James White's *Michael Casey Exhibiting His Panorama* (circa 1896–99) and *Dennis Reilly at Maggie Murphy's Home after Nine O'Clock* (circa 1896–99), Len Spencer's *Clancy's Prize Waltz Contest* (1904), John Kaiser's *Casey Courting His Girl* (1904), and Edward M. Favor's *Who Threw the Overalls in Mrs Murphy's Chowder* (1901), *The Mick That Sent the Pick* (1902), *O'Brien Has No Place To Go* (1908) and *Mary Ann O'Houlihan* (1909). Favor's *McGinty at the Living Pictures* was popular enough that he recorded it on at least three occasions (1897, 1901 and 1904).

Of the scripts for Irish-themed acts that do exist, some have survived because they were published and widely distributed at the time. These include the works of Harry L. Newton, who wrote a large number of one-act comedies in the early twentieth century. Among his many efforts was the monologue *Killarney Blarney* of 1905, which featured the character Barney McGoogen, a 'Corker from Cork', who was supposed to wear 'red wig and fringe whiskers' and a 'suit of clothes several sizes too large'. His commentary, which Newton wrote in 'Irish' dialect, included anecdotes about an 'Englishman' and such friends as 'Clancy', who suffers marital troubles.[36] Newton also published *The Recruiting Office: An Irish Rapid-Fire Comedy Act* in 1905, and *Mrs Clancy's Confession* in 1911, a monologue that included humour about a Dutchman and the subject of marriage.[37] Newton instructed actresses in the latter to wear a 'green dress' and a 'small green bonnet' and to have their 'face made up red'.[38]

In addition to such scripts, many vaudeville jokes and short sketches were published and distributed to the public in the nineteenth century.[39] For example, the 1891 booklet *Cooper's Irish Dialect Readings and Recitations* featured stories about such characters as 'Pat', 'Kitty', 'Muldoon', 'O'Rafferty' and others.[40] These tales included anecdotes and poems about Irish love and domestic strife, as well as such stories as *Shamus O'Brien* and *Paddy and His Pig*, the latter offering a story of the cohabitation of the Irish and farm animals. The 1898 book *Irish Wit and Humor* catalogued tales of 'Paddy' and 'Biddy' and other Irish characters in short monologues and brief jokes about Irish politics, Irish domestic life and the Irishman in America. Its introduction claimed that Irish-themed humour was 'a factor in human experience which the world can ill afford to lose'.[41]

Many people in 1898, particularly in the Irish-American community, would have disagreed with that declaration. By 1906, one newspaper review noted: 'The true Irish spirit came in with the Gaelic revival, and Irish comedy everywhere is outgrowing the monkey-faced Pat of the cartoon.'[42] The foundation of the Gaelic League in 1893 and a concentration on the revival of the Irish language helped forge that 'true Irish spirit', which was

The Latest Emanation of "The Mind of Ireland."

THE "PLAYBOY" AND HIS PROTECTORS.

**1.3** A cartoon decrying *The Playboy of the Western World*.
Published in the *Gaelic American* on 2 December 1911.

promoted by the Irish-American press and various Irish societies and organizations.[43] In the early twentieth century, one of the stated goals of the
Gaelic League of America was to 'banish such monstrosities as the stage
Irishman'.[44] Similarly, the United Irish Societies waged a bitter fight against
the Russell Brothers, who had gained fame in the late nineteenth century by
appearing in drag in their comedy sketch *Irish Servant Girls*.[45]

The struggle against the inauthentic was hardly restricted to New York
City or Boston, or other urban areas. By 1905, James E. Dolan, National
President of the Ancient Order of Hibernians, waged a war against the
stage Irishman in the American Midwest. One newspaper account claimed:
'Dolan's chief object of attack is the long-lipped apeish looking freaks who
appears in melo-drama [*sic*] and farces as the "Irish comedian". He claims
that, with one or two exceptions, there are no persons at present on the
stage who can imitate the Irish brogue with anything like reality.'[46] Writing
of Dolan's efforts, the *National Hibernian* told readers that such plays and
sketches survived by touring 'out-of-the-way sections' of the country, but
that the 'avenging hand . . . raised against them' was 'bound, sooner or later,
to banish them forever from the public gaze'.[47]

Noting that Irish audience members had pelted 'stage Irishmen' with overripe eggs and vegetables at theatres in New York and Philadelphia, the *Atlanta Constitution* editorialized that the offensive caricature should be 'punished as well as suppressed'.[48] Irish performers also offered their own views, perhaps to distinguish themselves from the inauthentic. Daniel Sully, a popular Irish comedian, complained in 1903, 'Why, when I see some of the fellows who claim to be Irish comedians, giving impersonations of Irishmen, who look as much like monkeys as one looks like another, I'm reminded of the song, *Johnny, Get Your Gun*, or *Rouse mit 'Em*.'[49]

By 1908, one attendant at an Ancient Order of Hibernians' conference announced: 'I am very pleased to state that "the stage Irish man" [*sic*] has been almost entirely driven from the American stage except for a few rare instances which show that the evil still exists in a few sections, but our crusade has met with practically complete success.'[50] 'Practically complete success' is an important phrase. Some people bemoaned the potential disappearance of the stage Irishman. An editorial comment in the *Atlanta Constitution* advised readers in 1903 that 'there is another side to this war on the stage Irishman – when we get rid of him, we shall have nothing but $2 shows left to us'.[51] Vaudeville continued to feature 'stage Irish' comedians, and H.P. Kelly's 1906 book *Gems of Irish Wit and Humor* distributed stage Irish jokes about 'Pat and Mike', 'Murphy', 'Casey', 'Bridget' and others.[52]

Such vaudeville humour appeared in many other subsequent books. In 1908, Wehman Brothers offered a range of joke books for aspiring vaudeville comedians, including *Irish Jokes*, *Irish Wit and Humor* and *Combination Irish, Hebrew, and Dutch Jokes*. Those specific books were in addition to more general manuals like *Choice Vaudeville Jokes*, *Vaudeville Gags and Jokes* and *New Book of Monologues, No. 1*, which also included Irish jokes as a component of the broader spectrum of vaudeville humour. For example, *New Book of Monologues, No. 1* offered nearly sixty pages of anecdotes, one involving 'Pat', one involving 'Casey' and one involving 'O'Brien'.[53] Even if in retreat, the stage Irishman had not been eradicated.

Controversies over the stage Irishman as well as the overall issue of authenticity generally dealt with issues of actor costumes and make-up, as well as their style of humour; some stage Irish comedians specialized in rough, 'knockabout' comedy, for example.[54] However, the issue of the ethnic origins of these performers was at best secondary. Nora Bayes gained much fame with her Irish-themed novelty songs in the early twentieth century, including the famous *Has Anybody Here Seen Kelly?*[55] Bayes was Jewish, but the fact that she was singing Irish-themed music was not seen as problematic or offensive.

The most famous case in which ethnic origins were viewed as unimportant came in the negative reaction of the Irish-American press (particularly the *Gaelic American*) to J.M. Synge's play *The Playboy of the Western World* in New York in 1911, despite the fact that the same company of Irish players had earlier performed the same at the Abbey Theatre in Dublin.[56] Indeed, Synge was renowned for what Mark Phelan has called his 'scrupulous attention to details', which included making certain that props used at the Abbey Theatre were authentic.[57] *The Playboy of the Western World* did not represent crude vaudeville comedy of the Russell Brothers sort, nor did it represent the 'stage Irishman' as the character was described in the early twentieth century. However, one performance in New York in November 1911 caused a 'riot'; *The Billboard* reported that 'much refuse was thrown at the actors and the police reserves were called. Ten prisoners were taken.'[58] No other live entertainment in the period from 1866 to 1915 provoked such a barrage of negative responses and challenges to its authenticity from the Irish-American press as did *The Playboy of the Western World*.

Such issues of authenticity would play an important role in the rise of the Irish-themed moving picture, which was heavily influenced by Irish-themed live entertainment of the post-Civil War era. Regrettably, few secondary sources exist on this subject, and – as stated previously – much of what has been written tends to concentrate on legitimate theatre in New York City. To examine such a lengthy period of time effectively and efficiently, this chapter offers five case studies, beginning in 1866, the first year after end of the Civil War. Subsequent case studies investigate 1876, 1886 (the year in which Harry W. French introduced his pivotal tourist-based approach to illustrated travel lectures of Ireland), 1896 (the year in which Edison first publicly projected moving pictures) and 1906 (the year in which the nickelodeon saw crucial growth). While dense, these case studies attempt to paint a detailed picture of a period much in need of further research.

These case studies underscore the ongoing concerns over authenticity, but they also reveal other patterns. By 1896, the *Salt Lake Tribune* claimed, 'Boucicault's Irish dramas have been a God-send [*sic*] to more than one American company, their perpetual popularity carrying them when all else fails.'[59] This chapter makes clear that Boucicault's 'Irish dramas' found enormous popularity across the United States, from their initial productions to the early years of the twentieth century. Other Irish-themed plays became quite popular as well, but only Fred Marsden's *The Kerry Gow* seems to have achieved the kind of ongoing success of Boucicault's plays.

The fifty years between 1866 and 1915 also show an increasing emphasis on stories about Irish characters in America. John Brougham wrote

32

plays about Irish-Americans in the mid-nineteenth century, rather than focus on Ireland; beginning in the 1870s, Edward Harrigan would do the same.[60] Similarly, sketch comedy and vaudeville acts regularly featured American settings as well, often combining Irish characters with other ethnicities. For example, in 1879, a variety show entitled *Mary Fiske's English Blondes* featured a courtroom sketch called *Dutch Justice*, which included both Irish and German comedians. That same year, the play *The Emigrant Train; or, Go West* featured Irish, Dutch and Italian dialect comedians; the cast also included four blackface performers.[61] That was in addition to the famous Jewish comedian George Fuller Golden, whose monologues in the late nineteenth and early twentieth centuries often recounted tales of 'his blundering friend, Casey'.[62]

These five case studies also highlight the deep roots that Irish-themed moving pictures had in American popular entertainment. Such entertainment predates the wave of Irish-American immigration that occurred at the end of the nineteenth century. It was not dependent on Irish-American audiences of any era, and it was not at all confined to New York City or even American cities. Audiences in small towns and large cities across the United States witnessed similar kinds of Irish-themed live entertainment from the end of the Civil War to the early years of the twentieth century, all of which functioned as part of the broader American entertainment industry.

# Case Study, 1866

Based upon surviving press accounts, Dion Boucicault was clearly the key figure in Irish-themed entertainment in America in 1866. For example, in February of that year, the 'celebrated Irish comedian' T.H. Glenney appeared as 'Shaun the Post' in Boucicault's *Arrah-na-Pogue* at the Bowery Theatre in New York City.[63] The 'new play' was also staged in various other cities, including Milwaukee, Wisconsin, where it was 'well-received'.[64] That same year, a syndicated newspaper article detailed Boucicault's use of the song *The Wearing of the Green* in the play, and Piano Forte Manufacturers of New York City sold sheet music of the *Arrah-na-Pogue March*.[65]

Boucicault's play *The Colleen Bawn, or the Brides of Garryowen* also appeared on numerous stages in 1866. As one newspaper critic noted, 'Many of the scenes make an impression on the mind which can never be obliterated, and it is unquestionably one of the most attractive and fascinating dramas ever witnessed.'[66] While versions of the play were staged in various cities, including Janesville, Wisconsin, and Dubuque, Iowa, the most notable production that year occurred at Wallack's Theatre in New York City.[67] It ran at least seven weeks and starred Dan Bryant, an Irish comedian and singer; Bryant had earlier gained a degree of fame working in minstrel shows.[68]

That same year, Dan Bryant also played the title role in *Shamus O'Brien, the Bould Boy of Glengall* for at least eleven weeks at Wallack's Theatre.[69] Reviewing the play, the *New York Times* noted that the 'very old and entirely familiar' story told the 'tale of England's tyranny and Ireland's hopeless fighting for independence'.[70] While *The Times* claimed that 'Mr Bryant is by no means a great delineator, neither is he a pleasing singer', the newspaper did admit that Bryant possessed much 'personal magnetism'.[71] In a subsequent review, the *New York Times* was more kind, suggesting that Bryant was 'worthy of being ranked beside those who have so long held a monopoly of the low Irish comedy business'.[72] Bryant's popularity meant that he starred in other Irish-themed productions at Wallack's in New York in 1866, including Tyrone Power's *Born to Good Luck*, J.H. Amherst's *Ireland As It Was* and John Brougham's *The Irish Emigrant*.[73]

While the *New York Times* described Bryant as a comedian, he was in fact a versatile actor who appeared in comedies, dramas and 'comedy dramas'. In that way, Bryant was similar to the Irish comedian Barney Williams, who was the more famous of the two. Williams and his wife Maria Pray hired James Pilgrim, a British playwright, to write plays for them that featured melodrama and Irish-themed comedy; such a combination echoed Boucicault's approach.[74] Williams became famous thanks to such 'Irish' plays, after having earlier appeared in minstrel shows. By 1866, New York's Winter Garden promoted Williams as 'The True Type and Embodiment of Irish Character, Irish Gaiety, and Irish Wit'.[75]

On a single evening at that venue in 1866, Williams appeared in 'three glorious pieces': *Fairy Circle, or, Con O'Carglan's Dream* (a 'drama'), *In and Out of Place* (a 'comedy') and *The Happy Man* (a 'roaring farce' with Williams playing 'Paddy Murphy').[76] That same year, Williams and his wife starred in such plays as *Rory O'More, Connie Soogah, or, the Wearing of the Green* and *All Hallow Eve; Or, Snap-Apple Night* (a 'beautiful Irish drama').[77] They also portrayed 'Lanty McLoughlin' and 'Kate Kearney' in the play *The Lakes of Killarney*. Advertisements not only emphasized Barney Williams's name, but also the play's use of 'new and beautiful scenery' to convey the setting named in its title.[78]

A number of other 'Irish comedians' also attracted attention in 1866, including G.C. Davenport and S.W. Bradshaw.[79] One touring company managed by Charles Plunkett offered *Robert Emmet*, the 'romantic Irish drama', on the same bill with *Handy Andy*, a 'roaring Irish comedy'.[80] Julia Daly appeared as 'Kate O'Brian' in a 'popular comedy' entitled *The Maid of Munster*.[81] Sam Ryan starred in a travelling version of the play *Ireland*

**1.4** Artwork depicting one scene in Boucicault's *The Colleen Bawn*.

*As It Is*.[82] However, next to Barney Williams, the most popular Irish comedian in 1866 may well have been John Dillon, who toured in such sketches as *Barney the Bawn*, *Irish Mesmerism* and *Our Irish Relations*.[83] One newspaper article claimed, 'Any one [*sic*] who has ever witnessed Mr Dillon's personation [*sic*] of an Irish character need not be told that he has few superiors on the American stage for such delineations, and there is no disputing his great abilities in the line of his profession.'[84]

In addition to Irish comedy, the *New York Times* noted that, in 1866, the 'city has been surfeited with the old school Irish drama', causing them to herald John Brougham's *O'Donnell's Mission*, which was set in France and Spain and featured an heroic Irish character exiled by William of Orange.[85] The newspaper declared that the drama was 'a refreshing oasis in the desert of so-called Irish comedy'.[86] Other Irish dramas that year included a revival of James Pilgrim's 1851 *Shandy Maguire; or the Bould Boy of the Mountain, Kate of Killarney, or, the Fairy of the Lakes* and *Inshavogue*. Unique among these was a version of J.B. Buckstone's *Green Bushes; or, The Huntress of the Mississippi*, which focussed not on Ireland, but on Irish (and non-Irish) characters in the United States.[87]

# Case Study, 1876

Analysing the state of Irish drama in 1876, the *Brooklyn Daily Eagle* bemoaned a 'sameness', claiming:

> All recent Irish dramas have depended upon the priest, the colleen, the informer, the gallant young Irish gentleman, the pretty lady with the red cloak (she always has a red cloak) and the saucy, good for nothing fellow in shapely gray stockings, who is more than a match at repartee for all of them put together, and makes love like a house afire. There is always, too, a suspicion of a whiskey still, and not infrequently a kitchen scene in which an immense jug of punch is brewed.

Whatever similarities may have existed in Irish-themed entertainment at that time, it appears that audiences perceived at least some differences. In particular, Dion Boucicault's Irish-themed plays remained the most popular.

By 1876, Boucicault's fame was so great that the American press covered not only his plays, but also his personal life. For example, newspapers across the United States printed articles that year about the deaths of his son and his daughter.[88] Boucicault's plays also continued to make much news, including those with Irish storylines. One syndicated newspaper article reported that he had received 'over $250,000' in proceeds from *The Colleen Bawn*.[89] Revivals of *Arrah-na-Pogue* were staged in 1876, but the most talked-about Boucicault play that year was *The Shaughraun*, which had just experienced 'an unprecedented run of one hundred and fifty nights' in New York City during the 1874–75 season.[90] It was staged in various American cities in 1876.[91]

The year 1876 also saw the first production of Fred Marsden's play, *The Kerry Gow-Dhuv*, the title of which was quickly shortened to *The Kerry Gow*.[92] In an apparent effort to draw upon the reputation of Boucicault's work, some publicity touted it as a 'companion piece' to *Arrah-na-Pogue*.[93] Advertisements also referred to it as 'an entire[ly] new Irish drama, of intense interest, abounding in wit, pathos and music, [with] beautiful scenery, realistic effects, and [the] engagement of the popular Irish comedian, Joseph Murphy'.[94] Thanks to *The Kerry Gow* – which Marsden wrote specifically for him, apparently at his request – Murphy would become far more popular than he had previously been; he received favourable reviews that year in cities ranging from Oakland, California, to Milwaukee, Wisconsin.[95]

Marsden was not alone in an effort to combine the humour and drama that Boucicault had so effectively managed in his plays. A touring version of

ACADEMY OF MUSIC.

# LAST NIGHT

Of Milwaukee's Favorite Comedian

MR. JOS.

# MURPHY

## MATINEE AT 2-30

BY SPECIAL REQUEST

# KERRY GOW !

AFTERNOON AND EVENING.

Matinee prices, 25 and 50 cents.

Next week FURBISH'S FIFTH AVE-
NUE Company.

1.5 Advertisement published in the *Milwaukee Daily News*
on 16 September 1876.

*Kathleen Mavourneen* starring Alice Vane offered a similar approach in
1876, with Vane singing such music as the title song and *The Wearing of the
Green*.[96] Edward Harrigan's play *Iascaire* offered the story of an Irish
fisherman. A revival of Edward Stirling's play *Aline, or the Rose of Killarney*
toured the US in 1876.[97] The same was true of W.J. Florence's *Inshavogue, or
The Hero of 1798*, a story of the Irish rebellion. Edwin Clifford's company
mounted a touring version of *Inshavogue* in the autumn of 1876; it starred
the 'Irish comedian' Felix A. Vincent, who appeared in a production of
*Arrah-na-Pogue* the same year.[98] Colonel Thomas Shiel Henderson's play
*Tullamore* offered yet another tale based on the rebellion of 1798, again
combining comedy and drama.[99] The *Brooklyn Daily Eagle* praised its 'fine
portraiture of Irish character and presentation of Irish scenery'.[100]

Playwright and actor Edward Harrigan also mounted 'comedy drama'
productions, such as his 1876 play *The Grip*, which was a story not of
Ireland, but instead focussed on the 'Five Points' area of New York City.[101]
In it, Harrigan portrayed Irish-American Patrick Reilly in what advertisements called 'a truly natural piece of character acting'.[102] During the 1870s,

37

Harrigan became famous as an actor, singer, songwriter and playwright. Among his greatest successes that decade were a number of humorous plays about the 'Mulligans' that he produced with his partner Tony Hart.[103]

Writing about the state of Irish comedy in 1876, the *Brooklyn Daily Eagle* ignored Harrigan, instead declaring: 'There is really no Irish comedian worthy to the name in America. Dion Boucicault is in England. John Brougham – is it *scandulum magnatum* to say so? – is growing too old to play the rollicking Irish characters he has himself created, and poor Barney Williams, the most popular but least capable of them all, is dead.'[104]

Whether or not there were Irish comedians 'worthy to the name' in America in 1876, it is clear that a great number of them attempted to claim the place held by Barney Williams, who died in April of that year.

Among the most noted Irish comedians that year were Hugh Fay, Patrick Maglone, William Wylie ('The Man from Ireland') and John Reilly ('The famous sensational and eccentric Irish comedian').[105] Frank George presented his touring act of 'Irish Opinions, Sayings, Songs, etc'.[106] Publicity touted the 'very celebrated Hibernian impersonator' Harry Kernell as the 'Merry Son of the Little Green Isle'.[107] A number of Irish comedy teams (or 'double Irish' acts, as they were called) also toured America in 1876, including Hurley and Marr ('The Irish Comedians'), Scanlan and Cronin ('Hibernian Character Performers') and Rickey and Barney ('The Greatest of Irish Comedians and the Master Character Comedians').[108] Those duos were all in addition to the 'The Fieldings', an act comprised of John and Maggie Fielding. Referring to themselves as 'Irish sketch artists', The Fieldings enacted such comical sketches as *The Irish Soldier*.[109]

Irish comedian John Dillon also continued to command a great amount of attention in 1876. His major appearance that year came in Bartley Cambell's society comedy *Risks*, which toured the country after appearing in New York.[110] In it, Dillon played Pemberton Pembroke. While Dillon was known as an Irish comedian, Pembroke was not specifically coded as Irish.[111] By 1876, Pat Rooney had also become a famous performer. He was publicized as 'the greatest of all Irish comedians', though – like Dillon – Rooney's comedy (and the songs that he sang) were not strictly Irish in theme.[112]

Other comedians also offered sketch comedies and acts that combined Irish comedy with other types of humour, including other ethnic humour. In 1876, for example, Charles and Marian Young promoted themselves as 'Dialect Artists and Vocalists, Scotch and Irish'.[113] Similarly, the 'celebrated Irish comedian' Frank Drew toured in *Mixem Getherem; or, Many Faces Under a Hood*. In it, Drew offered 'the peculiarities of all nations – England, Ireland, Scotland, France, Germany, and America' and also sang 'a number of songs in all languages'.[114]

Irish-themed comedy appeared in other types of productions as well. Various acts attempted to connect Irish comedy with non-fiction Irish-themed entertainment, particularly those shows that claimed to offer audiences a 'tour' of Ireland. Such non-fiction entertainment attempted to provide the other acts with the veneer of authenticity; the result underscores the porous boundary between fiction and non-fiction entertainment. For example, Frank MacEvoy's *New Hibernicon and Irish Comedy Company* offered comedy, particularly in the form of W.F. Lawler and his character 'Barney the Guide'.[115] The travelling show also featured the *Hibernian Minstrels* which included vocalists, dancers and other artists who attempted to give audiences an authentic depiction of Irish talent.[116] Similarly, in 1876, *Healy's Hibernian Gems* toured first with *Jerry Cohan's Irish Comedy Company* and then with *Dan Morris' Irish Comedy Company* to give – in both cases – a 'great pictorial, musical, and national exhibition, representing a tour in Ireland, accompanied by vocal and instrumental music'.[117] One review praised the '70 magnificent views' of Ireland that were projected; these 'views' – presumably lantern slides – included the 'River Shannon, Lakes of Killarney' and many other 'localities and subjects'.[118]

Such combinations of Irish-themed comedy and non-fiction entertainment seem to have achieved some degree of success, as is evident by their sheer numbers. In addition to the shows already mentioned, *Burke's Tableaux of Erin and Comedy Company* toured in 1876 with John M. Burke starring in the comic sketch *Shaun O'Reilly, or the Folks We Meet in Ireland*.[119] The comedy depicted Ireland from a tourist's point of view, and it was complemented with non-fiction images. As one newspaper described, 'the panoramic portion of the exhibition consists of a series of beautiful and truthful representations of the cities, towns, and picturesque and historic spots of old Ireland'.[120] Yet another such company was McGill and Strong's *Emerald Minstrels Comedy and Mirror of Ireland*. A description of the show suggested that the 'music, songs and dances, the Irish wit and the pleasing scenes of the *Mirror of Ireland* form a variety that is quite diverting'.[121] The 'accomplished Boston soprano' Kate O'Laughlin received much promotion in McGill and Strong's advertisements, which ironically promised an 'Entire New Programme' featuring 'All the Old Favorites!'[122]

# Case Study, 1886

As in 1866 and 1876, Dion Boucicault continued to tower over Irish-themed entertainment in 1886. While the press that year covered such topics as Boucicault's genealogy and his marital status (specifically, whether or not he was a bigamist), four of his Irish-themed plays were staged in

**1.6** Advertisement published in the 16 January 1886 issue
of the *New York Clipper*.

various cities across America.[123] In January of 1886, Harry M. Williams
produced a *Colleen Bawn Company* with Jessie Lee Randolph in the lead
role of Eily O'Connor; the *New York Clipper* praised the actors and the
scenery after a performance in Brooklyn that same month.[124] By March, the
*Clipper* noted that audiences in New York City 'bestow[ed] liberal
applause' on the same company.[125]

Harry M. Williams also produced a touring version of Boucicault's *The
Shaughraun* during the first half of 1886. It appeared in such cities as

Washington, DC, Boston, Brooklyn and Troy, New York.[126] Williams's company would probably have staged the play at many more venues had Boucicault not obtained an injunction against him. The two had made a contractual agreement allowing Williams to produce the two plays in 'dime museums', but Boucicault learned that Williams had also 'made preparations to bring them out in cheap theatres'. That fact led Boucicault to take legal action, which brought a rapid end to the tour.[127]

Williams was not alone in his efforts to bring Boucicault's Irish-themed plays to the stage in 1886. Two different companies produced versions of Boucicault's 1884 play *Robert Emmet*.[128] Other companies produced touring versions of *The Colleen Bawn* and *The Shaughraun*, which appeared in such cities as Newark, Ohio, and Eau Claire, Wisconsin.[129] By August 1886, H.J. Sargent announced new touring companies of what he titled *Boucicault's Shaughraun* and *Boucicault's Colleen Bawn*.[130] A version of Boucicault's *Arrah-na-Pogue* starring Kate Claxton also toured, appearing in such cities as Hoboken, New Jersey.[131] The *Boston Journal* claimed that 'abundant laughter... and more decided expressions of approval by the audience' met the Claxton version when it appeared at the Boston Museum.[132]

Aside from Boucicault's work, the most popular Irish-themed plays in 1886 might well have been Fred Marsden's *The Kerry Gow* and *Shaun Rhue*, both of which were staged repeatedly that year. While Boucicault's plays featured different actors in different productions, the two Marsden plays became completely dependent on the appearance of the 'distinguished Irish comedian and vocalist' Joseph Murphy for their success, to the extent that when Murphy's brother appeared in the lead role of *The Kerry Gow* in Decatur, Illinois, in 1886, rather than Murphy himself, a minor controversy erupted.[133] Joseph Murphy's affiliation with the play became so well known that some newspapers even referred to *The Kerry Gow* as 'his' play and did not even mention Marsden.[134]

Overall, *The Kerry Gow* was more popular than *Shaun Rhue*, and it achieved some of its renown due to perceptions that it was authentic. For example, in 1886, the *Fort Wayne Sentinel* (Fort Wayne, Indiana) described it as 'a drama portraying Irish life in a realistic manner'.[135] The *Mitchell Republican* (Mitchell, South Dakota) went even further, claiming that 'realism [was] carried to its limit' in the play.[136] That same year, the *Pittsburgh Dispatch* promised: 'There is none of Irish burlesque or alleged funny business about it.'[137] The *Philadelphia North American* noted much the same in 1886, reminding readers that humour in *The Kerry Gow* was 'never coarse'.[138]

The Boucicault and Marsden plays were thus important not only in terms of their widespread popularity in America, but also in terms of their ability to blend humour and drama into a formula that many audience members in 1886 took to be authentic, rather than as offensive 'stage Irish' comedy. Not surprisingly, many other plays attempted to duplicate the same formula. In 1886, for example, Edward Harrigan's 'comic play' entitled *The O'Reagans* offered elements of drama as well.[139] The play featured Harrigan as 'Barney O'Reagan' and Joseph Sparks as 'Bernard O'Reagan' ('from Ireland'); though set in America, it did feature an allusion to 'Home Rule for Ireland'.[140]

By contrast, the bulk of Irish-themed entertainment in 1886 focussed on comedy rather than on a combination of comedy and drama. Such plays and sketches also suggest the public may have been weary of overtly political Irish plays. For example, the 'Great Irish Comedian' W.J. Scanlan appeared in a 'new Irish play' entitled *Shane-na-Lawn*, which was advertised in Galveston, Texas, as a 'true picture of Irish life, without priest, red coat, or political allusions'.[141] A review in the *New York Times* noted that 'not one reference to English "oppression" or Irish suffering is made in the text'.[142] Instead, the show was a simple comedy, keeping the audience in 'roars of laughter from beginning to end'.[143]

Numerous other Irish comedians travelled throughout the United States that same year in short acts and sketches, many of them appearing in vaudeville theatres of the type that Tony Pastor made profitable in the early 1880s. Such comedians included Joe J. Sullivan, Herbert Cawthorn (as 'Barney O'Brady'), John T. Kelly (formerly of 'Kelly and Ryan') and John Kernell (the 'King of Irish Comedians').[144] There were also numerous teams offering Irish-themed comedy, such as 'Murphy and Mack', 'Maloney and Gray', 'O'Brien and Morris', 'Sheridan and Flynn', the 'Devere Sisters', 'Leonard and Mullen' (the 'Irish Character Comedians') and 'Needham and Kelly' ('The Original Hibernian Twins').[145]

Some comedy performances relied upon famous characters already known to audiences; for example, Charles E. Verner played *Shamus O'Brien* at numerous theatres in 1886.[146] Others attempted to merge Irish comedy with non-Irish-themed entertainment, as in *The Irish Mikado*, which starred Edwin Joyce, 'The Greatest Irish Comedian'.[147] The play combined Japanese sets with Joyce's 'Irish' singing and dancing.[148] A third approach was to create acts or sketches that were highly unique. In 1886, the 'Irish comedians' known as 'Dolan and McCarthy' introduced their *Burlesque Wrestling Match*.[149]

While the specific jokes and humour employed by some of these comedians is difficult to analyse, given a lack of surviving scripts, it is clear that some acts that year specialized in 'stage Irish' stereotypes. For example, Belle Dolan was billed as the 'Rough Irish Character-Vocalist'.[150] Pat Rooney's 'New Comedy Company' offered *Pat's Wardrobe*, a 'broad farce'

**NOVELTIES OF ALL KINDS**
WANTED AT ALL TIMES.
**WANTED.**
For the Stock Company,
a good Negro - comedian,
Irish - comedian. Dutch -
comedian, Dashing Sou-
brette and twenty - five
handsome young ladies for
Burlesque and the Cafe,
Everybody write. All let-
ters will be answered.
ADDRESS
WILEY HAMILTON,
CASINO THEATRE, ST. LOUIS, MO.

1.7 Advertisement from the 14 August 1886 issue of the *New York Clipper*.

written by Elliot Barnes.[151] In it, Pat is mistaken for a missing 'Wild Man from Borneo', thus drawing on stereotypes of the Hibernian ape-man.[152] Such comedy was in addition to the appearance of 'stage Irish' representations of clichéd Irish names, such as 'Casey' in 'Casey the Fiddler', and 'Bridget' in *My Aunt Bridget*, which George W. Monroe (in drag, as the title character) and John E. Rice performed across the United States, ranging from Trenton, New Jersey to San Antonio, Texas.[153]

Irish caricatures not only appeared in short sketches, but also in full-length productions. The team of Barry and Fay starred in a travelling company of the variety programme *Irish Aristocracy* in 1886, which was replete with 'their inimitable Irish absurdities', most famously in the comical *Muldoon's Picnic*.[154] Two years earlier, the *New York Times* had decried Barry and Fay as being 'well-worn specimens of stage Irishmen'.[155] Similarly, the team of Murray and Murphy toured in *Our Irish Visitors*, which one newspaper account claimed was 'full of [comedy that] is technically called "business"', suggesting rough, stage Irish comedy.[156] At the same time, however, the *Cedar Rapids Evening Gazette* promised theatregoers that 'it is not offensive to any class, and no person, however nice or proud, can take umbrage at a single event or saying' in the play.[157]

Another important concern for such entertainment was narrative setting. A number of Irish-themed comedies in 1886 were set in the United States, as opposed to Ireland. For example, the 'Eminent Irish Comedian' T.J. Farron appeared with Gracie Emmett in the 'farce comedy' *The Soap*

**1.8** Advertisement published in the 27 November 1886 issue of the
*New York Clipper*.

*Bubble*, which was set in America.[158] Irish comedian Daniel E. Ryan appeared in Daniel Sully's *Corner Grocery*, an Irish-themed comedy set in New York.[159] Sully appeared in a version of *Corner Grocery* himself that year, as well as in his 'new play' *Daddy Nolan*, a three-act comedy also set in New York.[160] The success of Sully's plays and his character 'Daddy Nolan' brought forth a number of imitators, such as *A Box of Cash*, in which Edward M. Favor starred as the character 'Timothy O'Hara'; it too featured an American setting.[161]

As had been the case a decade earlier, numerous travelling companies continued to combine Irish-themed comedy with non-fiction entertainment. For example, *McAvoy's Double Hibernicon* promoted itself as an 'Irish and American Tourist Company and Mirror of Ireland'. Audience members who attended its 1886 shows would have seen onstage 'the finest street parade on Earth, an Irish Brigade Brass Band, and a Genuine Irish band of pipers, drawn in an Imported Irish Jaunting car'.[162] The show also included a 'vocalist and descriptive lecturer, portraying vividly the beautiful scenery of Ireland', as well as a range of singers, and an Irish comedian who 'don't [sic] have to use a red wig'.[163] One newspaper review proclaimed that it was a 'true mirror of Ireland in her present condition, and should be attended by everybody, especially Irishmen'.[164]

The phrase 'Mirror of Ireland' was hardly unique that year. Dan Morris Sullivan had his own touring show entitled *Mirror of Ireland!* which featured, 'new songs, dances, duets, jigs, reels, and comedic Irish and Dutch plays'. It also included a 'very comical play' entitled *Sight Seeing in the Emerald Isles*, as well as '80 beautiful scenes, with magnificent, moonlight effects'.[165] One newspaper review noted that Dan and Josie Morris Sullivan were the cornerstone talent.[166] Another description referred to the 'panorama part' of the show, claiming it was 'very beautiful and realistic'.[167] The '80 beautiful scenes' in the 'panorama' were presumably lantern slides.

Similarly, *Harrigan's Hibernian Tourists*, also known as *Harrigan's Double Irish and American Tourists*, offered a 'first-class' combination of Irish singers, bagpipe players, comedians, two small ponies, an Irish jaunting car and at least one ventriloquist.[168] One advertisement promised a 'panoramic of cities and scenery in Ireland'.[169] It also promoted the show's authenticity, claiming 'It's Irish You Know.' [170] Reviews of the show, which was produced by Edward Harrigan, were generally favourable. One of them drew particular attention to 'Jerry Cohan as a rollicking Irishman and clog dancer' and 'his sister Nellie as Nora', who was 'well, simply irresistible'.[171]

The most famous of these kinds of travelling shows was *Howorth's Hibernica*. In 1886, *Howorth's* made its 'twenty-fifth annual tour', which featured 'beautiful landscape paintings of noted places and scenes in Ireland' as part of its tourist-based entertainment.[172] That same year, the *New York Clipper* listed travelling shows entitled *Howorth's Irish Tourists*, *Howarth's Hibernica* and *Howarth's Hibernian Tourists*.[173] It is possible these were all the same show, or different travelling companies produced by the same 'Howorth', but it is also possible that the different spellings of the name ('Howarth') might have been another company attempting to trade on Howorth's name.

Rather than promote comedy, either by itself or as combined with other entertainment, some Irish-themed entertainment in 1886 presented dramatic storylines. For example, Paddy Ryan, the Irish-American boxer and former world heavyweight champion, starred in a touring version of *Terry the Fox*, a 'romantic Irish drama'.[174] The first act of the play 'shows the persecution endured by suffering tenants at the hands of unfeeling land agents', whereas the second act revolves around the visit of the title character's brother 'who is coming all the way from America to visit the home of his childhood'.[175] A key feature of the play was the opportunity to see Ryan in person; theatrical appearances of Irish-American boxers became highly popular in the late nineteenth century.

The emphasis on Ireland's troubles in plays like *Terry the Fox* was cause for many to celebrate the occasions when other Irish-themed plays eschewed them. One newspaper in 1886 happily announced the fact that 'an Irish drama, without the usual accompaniment of red-coated soldiers, oppressed tenants, and tyrannical landlords, is actually to be produced soon in New York'.[176] That was in addition to W.H. Power's touring melodrama *The Ivy Leaf*, in which a 'shrewd' Irish lad thwarts the 'machinations of a jealous and designing villain'.[177] The *Louisville Times* noted:

> The scene is laid in Ireland and the characters are all Irish, but only the brightest and best side of life in the Emerald Isle is shown. There is no suggestion of the squalor, distress, or misfortune so generally associated with the conceptions of Ireland's condition. There is no gloomy background of 'Ireland's woes', no vociferous declamation about patriotism, oppression or land laws.[178]

The same reviewer drew attention to *The Ivy Leaf*'s 'striking' scenery, which included 'a view of the Lakes of Killarney'. Another critic praised the play for being a 'noted and laudatory departure from the caricatures that are usually presented as Irish to American audiences, and which are a reproach to and calumny on the Irish name and people'.[179]

Despite the predominance of Irish-themed comedy and – to a lesser extent – drama in 1886, some 'Irish' acts concentrated on other forms of entertainment. 'Miles, Ireland and McHugh' were a musical trio touted as 'the Gems of Ireland'; their slogan was 'Tis Irish, You See'.[180] Also, famed Irish-American boxer and then-world heavyweight champion John L. Sullivan, who had wrested his title from Paddy Ryan, toured in 1866 with *Lester and Allen's Big Minstrels*. The novelty was little more than the chance to see Sullivan in person, another example of the box-office appeal of the Irish-American boxer on the stage.[181]

# Case Study, 1896

As in previous years, Dion Boucicault's plays continued to be a prominent feature of Irish-themed entertainment in America in 1896. Both *The Colleen Bawn* and *The Shaughraun* were revived at the American Theatre in New York City that year, with Aubrey Boucicault portraying lead roles in both.[182] A touring version of *The Colleen Bawn* directed by W.L. Gleason appeared in various theatres across the US, including the Lyceum in Salt Lake City, Utah.[183] That was in addition to the 'Nickerson Comedy Company', which offered *The Colleen Bawn* as one of its various touring productions.[184] Amateur productions of Boucicault's plays were also staged, including a version of *Arrah-na-Pogue* produced by the Ancient Order of Hibernians in Logansport, Indiana; one newspaper review applauded its 'genuine wit'.[185]

Joseph Murray also continued to be an important presence, specifically in his ongoing tours of *Shaun Rhue* and *The Kerry Gow*.[186] The same was not true of the much-admired W.J. Scanlan. Newspapers across America reported that Scanlan, 'who was probably the most popular romantic Irish comedian and vocalist the American stage has ever known', was dying in an insane asylum in New York.[187] His death left a void, as Scanlan was not in fact an 'Irish comedian', but rather an Irish 'romantic singing comedian'. A number of others attempted to inherit his position. For example, Charles Horne was the 'inimitable Irish comedian and sweet singer'.[188] And Tony Farrell, the 'Sweet Singer and Irish Comedian', toured in a production of *Garry Owen*.[189]

Chauncey Olcott – who was praised for his talent and for being an Irish-American – commanded much more attention than either Farrell or Horne in 1886.[190] As one article claimed, 'Mr Olcott has become very popular with the public. His fine stage presence, his delightful singing and his majestic acting make him the leading Irish comedian of the day.'[191] In 1896, he appeared in travelling productions of Fred Marsden's *The Minstrel of*

*Clare*, Augustus Pitou's *Mavourneen*, and Augustus Pitou and George Jessop's *The Irish Artist*.[192] One review praised the latter not only for Olcott's performance, but also the 'realistic and beautiful' scenery that depicted Ireland.[193]

However, as the *Waterloo Daily Courier* noted in May 1896, 'Andrew Mack [rather than Olcott] is now universally considered to be the successor' to W.J. Scanlan.[194] Another newspaper suggested Mack had 'a voice that greatly resembles Scanlan'.[195] Scanlan's wife even presented her husband's green velvet cap to Mack, which Mack wore in a touring version of Jessop and Townsend's *Myles Aroon* in 1896.[196] The play was a 'romantic Irish comedy' that featured numerous songs and cast Mack in an 'Irish heroic role'; Scanlan had earlier starred in the same play.[197] An article in the *Syracuse Daily Standard* promised readers that *Myles Aroon* was 'one of the truest pictures of Irish home life' ever presented on the stage.[198]

In 1896, the Irish 'romantic singing comedian' was only one type of 'Irish comedian', just as had been the case in 1886 and earlier. Others did not sing, or they sang in sketch comedies in vaudeville that attracted less attention than Mack or Olcott's work in three-act plays. Many of these kinds of 'Irish comedians' – at least some of whom were 'stage Irish' comedians – toured in 1896, including Ed J. Heffernan, George Gorman, James F. Post, Tom Killeen, Tom Flynn, Matt Farnan, James Bowman and W.C. Davis.[199] One 'Irish Comedian', known simply as 'Evans', received billing using just a single name.[200] Others tried to promote their uniqueness, such as 'Kittie Burke, the Irish Thrush' and 'Major Doyle, the Liliputian Irish Comedian'.[201] That same year, Katie Rooney tried to carve out a niche by offering impressions of such famous people as her father, Pat Rooney.[202]

Daniel Sully continued to be a major presence in Irish-American comedy, with one newspaper heralding him as 'the most original and artistic Irish comedian on the stage today'.[203] In the spring of 1896, he toured in *A Social Lion* and in *A Bachelor's Wives*; in the autumn, he toured in *The Millionaire* and in *O'Brien, the Contractor*. The *Titusville Herald* touted the latter as being a 'realistic' play that 'shows the son of the Emerald Isle rounded out by a residence in this free country'.[204] Another newspaper suggested that, when Sully appeared in San Francisco in *A Social Lion*, representatives from the local Irish societies attended in order to determine whether or not his work was an 'offensive caricature'. Their verdict was positive, and so they proclaimed: 'Let every Irishman go and see Dan Sully.'[205]

By contrast, some Irish-themed comedy plays and sketches received less favourable press. Edward Harrigan's *Marty Malone* featured a 'rough sailor' (played by Harrigan) who befriends a young lady who eventually inherits money and marries an important aristocrat.[206] Reviews bemoaned

1.9 Advertisement published in the 30 October 1886 issue
of the *New York Clipper*.

the fact that Harrigan's plays – which, like Sully's sketches, were often set
in America – were weaker than they had been in previous years, attributing
his declining popularity to the decreasing quality of his work.[207] By the
1890s, Harrigan no longer worked with his former partner Tony Hart,
another reason that 'old audiences' found his work less satisfying.[208]

Much Irish-themed comedy in 1896 occurred in the form of travelling
comedy duos appearing in vaudeville acts and sketches. These included
Murphy and Mack, Fisher and Carroll, Thomas and Quinn, Sheehan and
Lacy ('The Best Irish Talking Act in the Country'), Leslie and Tenley
('America's Favorite Irish Comedians'), Dave Murphy and Tom McCoy
('The Irish Ambassadors'), Scanlon and Perry ('The Irish Comedy
Boomers'), and The Rays ('The Heavy and Light Weight Champions of

Irish Comedy').[209] Some of these acts also attempted to promote their uniqueness. For example, the Russell Brothers repeatedly appeared in drag as the title characters of their popular sketch *Irish Servant Girls*.[210]

However, the most popular Irish comedy duo in 1896 was without doubt Charlie Murray and Ollie Mack, who had become famous in previous years thanks to such comedy farces as *Irish Neighbors*. Among Murray and Mack's specialties was 'their burlesque on skirt dancing and glove contests' and 'their original sidewalk talk'.[211] In the spring of 1896, Murray and Mack toured in *Finnegan's Ball*, which featured Murray as 'Casey', a 'keen conception of the humorosities [sic] of the Irish character', and Mack as the title character.[212] Promotional materials for the show depicted both of them in typical 'stage Irish' make-up and costumes. George H. Emerick, the author of *Finnegan's Ball*, appeared in drag in the role of 'The Widow Gallagher'.[213] Then, in the autumn of 1896, Murray and Mack toured in *Finnegan's Courtship*, which one critic praised for its 'well defined plot'.[214] Another newspaper claimed it was 'the best comedy [Murray and Mack] ever had'.[215]

An array of other Irish-themed comedy plays and vaudeville sketches appeared on stages across the US in 1896, including *McCarthy's Mishaps*, *McSorley's Twins*, *Maloney's Troubles*, *O'Houlihan's Serenade*, *O'Brady's Wedding* and *Lannigan's Ball*.[216] In some cases, the lack of surviving scripts or in-depth critical reviews makes it difficult to discern precise narrative information about them. However, it is clear that a number of these plays and sketches featured Irish characters in American settings. For example, the three-act comedy *The Irish Greenhorn* featured Irish comedian and playwright Dan McCarthy as 'Casey', a character who flees Ireland for America and then returns to Ireland.[217]

Others plays and sketches offered stories that took place entirely in America, such as a touring version of *Chimmie Fadden*, which adapted Edward W. Townsend's literary character for the stage.[218] America also seems to have provided the setting for *Teaching Hogan's Kid* (starring Carr and McLeod) and *The Irish Tenants* (starring James Casey and Maggie Le Clair).[219] More notably, at least in terms of their ongoing success, *Hogan's Alley* and *McFadden's Row of Flats* were set in America and featured Irish-American characters. In 1896, advertisements promoting both comedies appeared in the *New York Clipper*, each carrying strict legal warnings against unauthorized performances.[220]

It is also clear that 'stage Irish' comedians and comic sketches featured an increasing emphasis on other ethnic groups. For example, in 1896, the 'Versatile Singing Comedy Team' of Seeker and Wilkes called themselves the 'Dutch Ace' and 'Irish Queen', offering humour based upon both

**1.10** Advertisement published in the 20 March 1886 issue of the *New York Clipper*.

**1.11** Advertisement published in the 25 July 1896 issue of the *New York Clipper*.

nationalities and their interaction with one another.[221] Much the same was true of John T. Kelly and Gus Williams, who – while touring in the *20th Century Girl* – were promoted as the 'best known Irish and Dutch character impersonators on the American stage to-day [*sic*]'.[222] Individual comedians also promoted their ability to offer comedy based on more than one ethnicity. Billy Farrell was an 'Irish and Dutch comedian', offering humour and dialects in his act associated with both nationalities.[223] The same was true of Charles Jones and Lew Ellis.[224] John R. Burke took their approach even further, as he promoted himself as a 'Dutch, Irish, and blackface comedian'.[225]

Other Irish comedians promoted their use of 'stage Irish' stereotypes and 'rough' Irish humour. For example, Larry McCale and Ed B. Daniels billed themselves as 'America's Leading Knockabout Irish Comedians'.[226] Ferguson and Mack toured in 1896 claiming to be the 'originators' of 'Knockabout Irish Comedy'.[227] Such comedy seems to have been popular with many audiences that year. For example, when reviewing their performance at the Orpheum Theatre, the *Oakland Tribune* wrote, 'the Irish comedy of Ferguson and Mack won...demonstrative signs of approval from the audience'.[228]

Given the range of different kinds of 'Irish comedians' on the stage, issues of authenticity often arose in the press. At times the emphasis was on a play or sketch. For example, when the 'Ideal Irish Comedian' Edwin Hanford starred in *The Shamrock*, it was promoted as 'the modern Irish play'.[229] Dan McCarthy appeared in a touring version of *Cruiskeen Lawn*, a 'pretty story, unfolding [in] a series of pictures of the "Ould Sod"'.[230] In other cases, discussion centred on the comedian's talent. For example, the *Trenton Evening Times* proclaimed that William Barry, a 'favorite Irish comedian', did 'not [have] an equal in the field' in terms of his 'perfection of dialect'.[231]

As in previous years, some companies continued to combine Irish comedy with non-fiction entertainment in an effort to be perceived as genuine. In 1896, *Howorth's Hibernica* made yet another annual tour, featuring a 'farcical comedy' entitled *The 2 Dans*, as well as various music and other comic skits.[232] The *Connecticut Catholic* also noted: 'The beautiful landscape paintings of noted places and scenes in Ireland are certainly admired by lovers of true art, but are more fully appreciated by the natives of the Emerald Isle, who gave with fond delight and unspeakable emotion on the familiar scenes of their early childhood.'[233] Other articles and advertisements that year drew attention to *Howorth's* use of 'panoramic views', which was probably a reference to the projection of lantern slides.[234]

Other Irish-themed entertainment in 1896 focussed on music rather than comedy or drama. For example, the 'Irish Opera' *Bryan Born* was staged in Washington, DC.[235] George H. Timmons, an 'Irish Singer and Harpist', toured in a 'new' vaudeville act.[236] Annie Buckley performed Irish songs 'in character'.[237] Polly Holmes, billed as 'The Irish Duchess', offered 'New Songs'.[238] Describing her act, the *New York Clipper* said: 'Decked in a handsome costume, she sang an attractive list of exhilarating Irish ditties, which were applauded with much vigor, and resulted in a hit of a most noticeable sort.'[239]

Irish-American boxers also continued to be an important aspect of Irish-themed entertainment in 1896. John L. Sullivan toured in conjunction with Eugene O'Rourke's play *The Wicklow Postman*. For at least part of the tour, Sullivan's old boxing rival Paddy Ryan assisted him.[240] Irish-American James J. Corbett, who had won the World's Heavyweight Boxing Championship by knocking out John L. Sullivan in 1892, also toured in 1896, starring in the play *A Naval Cadet*.[241] A review in the *New Brunswick Daily Times* noted the play was 'the best opportunity he has yet had to display his abilities as an actor'.[242]

# Case Study, 1906

By 1906, Dion Boucicault's work had attained great respect from the mainstream American press. As the *New York Times* wrote that year:

> Dion Boucicault, it must be remembered, was, so to speak, the Thomas A. Edison of the American drama. He actually made so many theatrical inventions that even innovations for which he was not directly responsible were ascribed to him... [Among his innovations was the fact that he] was the first man to take a single production on the road, and the first play to be so presented was *The Colleen Bawn*, with the late John Drew as the star.[243]

As of 1906, Boucicault's 'Irish comedy dramas' (as they were called that year) were controlled by Louise Thorndyke Boucicault, who gave permission that autumn for a major revival of *Arrah-na-Pogue* starring Andrew Mack as 'Shaun the Post'.[244] Publicity claimed that 'A complete scenic and electric production is carried, and it said that the organization is the largest that has ever toured in an Irish play.'[245]

Andrew Mack remained extremely popular in 1906, just as he had been ten years earlier. In the spring of that year, he toured in *The Way to Kenmare*, portraying a character born in Ireland who grows up in America only to return to Ireland as an adult.[246] Publicity for the play promoted the fact that the 'versatile Irish comedian' would sing such songs as *The Rose of Kenmare* and *The Legend of the Maguires*.[247] The *New York Dramatic Mirror* wrote that Mack was 'every inch as much of the melodious hero as he used to be'.[248] *The Billboard* also noted that audiences in Chicago responded to his performance with 'enthusiastic applause'.[249]

By 1906, Mack was one of the most respected Irish 'romantic singing comedians'.[250] However, Chauncey Olcott continued to be quite popular as well. In the spring of 1906, for example, Olcott toured in Theodore Sayre's play *Edmund Burke*, in which he sang a number of new songs.[251] As its title suggests, the play revolved around the life of Edmund Burke, concentrating biographically on the year 1750.[252] In the autumn, Olcott toured in another Sayre play, *Eileen Asthore*, which was set in the Dublin of circa 1804.[253] In it, Olcott's character 'Richard Temple' suffers under much financial debt. He plans to leave Ireland, but then decides to stay after meeting a character named 'Eileen O'Donnell'.[254] Both plays received strong reviews in the *New York Dramatic Mirror*.[255]

Mack and Olcott were not the only 'romantic singing comedians' that

**1.12** Artwork promoting a Daniel Sully sketch comedy.

year. In 1906, the *Washington Post* wrote: 'Fiske O'Hara. Good name for a new Chauncey Olcott or Andrew Mack, eh? And its owner is already as fat as Chauncey or Andrew at half their age.'[256] Another review placed Fiske O'Hara in the tradition of Mack, Olcott and W.J. Scanlan.[257] The *New York Dramatic Mirror* called him 'a fine, jovial specimen of vigorous youth ... he has [an] abundance of hearty goodwill, he has considerable talent, he has an agreeable voice, and he sings with somewhat unusual technical skill'.[258] While reviews of his travelling play *Mr Blarney of Ireland* – an 'Irish-American musical comedy drama' set in New York – were not always favourable, critics of 1906 ranked O'Hara 'high among Irish singers'.[259]

Along with Fiske, the 'natural singing Irish actor' Barney Gilmore also gained much attention in 1906. Gilmore toured that year in Daniel L.

Hart's 'new comedy drama', *A Rocky Road to Dublin.*[260] Newspaper reports noted enthusiastic audience reaction to Gilmore and praised the three-act play as being a 'pleasing change from the rough and tumble exhibition of ordinary "Irish shows" '.[261] The *Syracuse Post-Standard* drew particular attention to the play's inclusion of a 'real Irish dance' and offering the 'real thing in a jaunting car'.[262]

Unlike O'Hara and Gilmore, the Irish 'romantic singing comedian' Allen Doone chose not to tour in a new play, but instead opted to star in an old favourite. One newspaper wrote: 'A few years ago it was said that Joseph Murphy and *The Kerry Gow* could not be distinctly separated... some argue that Murphy made the play, while others testify that the play made Murphy. Which of the arguments is correct is hard to say.'[263] In 1906, Murphy personally selected Doone 'from a thousand' possibilities to take his place in productions of *The Kerry Gow*, which had – according to one newspaper account – experienced 'three decades of continuous prosperity'.[264] As the lead character 'Dan O'Hara', Doone quickly received strong reviews.[265] The transition was not complete, however, as Murphy himself continued to appear in a condensed, vaudeville version of *The Kerry Gow* that same year.[266]

A large array of other Irish comedians – those who generally would not have been publicized as 'romantic singing comedians' – toured vaudeville theatres in 1896. These included Tom Killeen, Bert Baker, Tom Kennette, Pat White, J.H. Ferguson, Bobby Mack, Teddy Pierce, T.F. Diamond, Jimmy Ray, Billy Gross ('The Entertaining Irish Comedian') and Ben Dillon ('The Eccentric Irish Comedian').[267] Katie Rooney, daughter of Pat Rooney, continued to appear in vaudeville in what one newspaper described as 'exceptionally clever Irish character imitations, including that of her father'.[268] Similarly, James Francis Sullivan offered imitations of Irish comedians such as Pat Rooney, the Russell Brothers, Harry Kernell and others, in addition to playing 'eccentric' Irish characters in his vaudeville acts.[269]

Other Irish comedians were noted for the particular sketches in which they appeared. For example, Pat Rooney remained extremely popular. In 1906, he toured with Marion Brent in *Make Yourself at Home* and *The Busy Bell Boy.*[270] Daniel Sully toured in such plays as *Our Pastor*, in which he played the pastor of a church in Idaho.[271] Tom Waters ('The Irish Comedian') starred in such sketches as *Neighborly Neighbors* and *The Mayor of Laughland.*[272] Tom Nawn played an Irishman in the sketch *A Touch of Nature*, as did Bert White in *A Day at Niagara Falls.*[273] Other sketches that year included Edwin Keough in *A Bit of Blarney*, Marty O'Neil in *The Arrival of Kitty McCarthy*, Larry McCale in *An Irish Admiral* and William Inman in *Recognition.*[274]

A large number of Irish comedy teams played vaudeville in 1906, including Callahan and Mack, Miles and Nitram, West and Sawyer, Corbley and Burke, Earl and Bartlett, Burns and Morris, Halliday and Leonard, Madden and Jess, Murphy and Magee, and Sprague and Mack ('The Irish Aldermen').[275] Some of these comedy teams appeared in rather elaborate sketches. For example, Gallagher and Barrett, who by 1906 had spent fourteen years on the stage portraying various Irish characters, presented a new comedy that year entitled *The Battle of Too Soon*. In it, Barrett portrayed the 'low comedy part' of 'Careless Casey'.[276]

The Russell Brothers also presented a sketch that year, *The Great Jewell Mystery*, featuring themselves in numerous roles. Among other parts, James Russell appeared in drag as an Irish domestic, thus echoing the brothers' famous *Irish Servant Girls* sketch. Indeed, the final act of *The Great Jewell Mystery* drew heavily on *Irish Servant Girls*. However, both brothers dressed in drag for a number of non-Irish roles in *The Great Jewell Mystery*, ranging from a 'French woman' and a 'Russian actress' to a 'palmist' and a 'lady of fashion'.[277] Other Irish comedians also appeared in drag that year. The 'Irish comedian' Larry McCale appeared in a 'comedy female part' in the sketch *For Girls Only*, and James Hennessey dressed as an 'Irish girl' for his vaudeville act.[278] *Variety* even noted that Louise Arnot – of the comedy team of Gunn and Arnot – had a deep enough voice to suggest that she was an 'impersonation by a man'.[279]

As had been the case in 1896, Murray and Mack were the most popular Irish comedy team in show business. After concluding their work in the play *A Night on Broadway*, Murray and Mack returned to vaudeville with more 'Irish comedy'.[280] In the spring, they toured in a sketch entitled *Around the Town*, which the *Oakland Tribune* called a 'clever and diverting satire on certain phases of New York life'.[281] It was the seventh sketch that Murray and Mack had produced in their fourteen years together.[282] While praising the duo, the *Atlanta Constitution* described them as 'the proverbial stage Irishmen with a lot of horse play and rough house thrown in'.[283] Given their popularity, they operated a second 'Murray and Mack Company' in the autumn of 1906, offering a 'first-class' organization that toured with such plays as *Robert Emmet*.[284]

Setting remained an important factor in many of these sketches, some of which took place in Ireland. Callahan and Mack's sketch *The Old Neighborhood* was apparently set in Ireland; the *New York Dramatic Mirror* noted that it 'brought a furtive tear to the eye of many an Irishman in the audience'.[285] More notably, the Rogers Brothers – who were not Irish comedians – appeared in their comedy sketch *The Rogers Brothers in Ireland*, which featured them as German-American tourists abroad, a

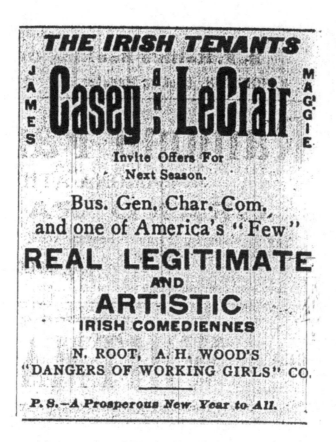

1.13  Advertisement published in the 13 January 1906 issue of the
*New York Dramatic Mirror*.

gimmick that they had used in previous sketches in which they 'visited' London, Paris, and other locations.[286] Much of the humour revolved around their attempt to purchase the Blarney Stone for exhibition in America.[287] Newspaper reviews praised not only the Rogers Brothers, but also the sketch's scenery, which included images of the Lakes of Killarney and Blarney Castle.[288]

Most Irish-themed sketches and plays of 1906 seem to have been set in America, such as *The Irish Tenants* and *Irish Pawnbrokers*.[289] The same also seems to have been true of *Mrs Murphy's Second Husband* and *Mrs McFudd at the Phone*, both of which starred Gracie Emmett.[290] Similarly, James B. Donovan ('The King of Ireland') and Rena Arnold starred in *Twenty Minutes on Broadway*, with Donovan portraying an Irish character and Arnold presenting her 'inimitable brogue'.[291] Perhaps most famous of these were the ongoing productions of *McFadden's Flats* produced by Gus Hill, who had apparently shortened its title from *McFadden's Row of Flats*. Hill's production – which had been 'rotten-egged' the year before in New York for its stage Irish caricatures – toured much of the United States, presenting the show that had 'made millions laugh'.[292]

Of those productions set in America, some featured storylines that proved important to early Irish-themed moving pictures. For example, Martin and Buckley offered the comedy *An Irish Christening*.[293] The Quigley Brothers appeared in their 'original satirical farce' entitled *Election Day*, in which Bob Quigley played an Irish ward boss in America; Raymond Merritt's monologue *Irish Politicians* covered similar ground, as did the play *A Tammany Tiger*, written by A. Gratton Donnelly.[294] Booker and Corbley's *The Walking Delegate* featured 'knockabout' humour involving a non-union Irish hod carrier.[295] Those were all in addition to Arnot and Gunn's sketch *Regan's Luck*, in which a poor Irishman and his wife receive a letter informing them of a large inheritance. They proceed to make extravagant purchases until a second letter arrives announcing the first was a joke.[296] Such storylines had deeper roots than 1906. Representations of the newly rich Irish experiencing troubles had already been well explored, including in the circa-1901 sketch *Mag Haggerty's Father*.[297]

As in previous years, some Irish comedies with American settings built humour out of the Irish interacting with other nationalities. For example, the musical comedy *Me, Him, and I* offered a story set in America about a tramp, a German and an Irishman.[298] The three-act story also included a character touted as 'the only Irish Indian in captivity'.[299] But the greatest concentration of these stories came in vaudeville sketches. The comedy team of McFarland and McDonald played Irish and German characters in their act; similarly, Markey and Moran offered a sketch in which one was Irish and the other Scottish.[300] Fred Irwin's *Big Show* included a trio of comedians, one being Jewish, one being Dutch and one being Irish; the same combination also appeared in a burlesque show entitled *The Golden Crook*.[301] Such an approach was taken even further with the October 1906 announcement of Mark Murphy's new 'comedy drama'; titled *The Irish Jews*, its lead character was named 'Moses McGinnis'.[302]

Other Irish-themed entertainment concentrated on music rather than comedy. Numerous singers featured Irish songs as part of their repertoire in 1906, including Virginia Earl, Mayme Barnes, Mayme Queenig and the '4 Singing Colleens', who offered songs of 'the old and new world'.[303] Polly Holmes, the 'Irish Duchess', attempted to make a comeback in 1906.[304] John Morrison, originally of Saginaw, Michigan, made a speciality of singing Irish songs. He was generally billed as 'The Irish Singer', rendering such tunes as *My Wild Irish Rose* and *My Yankee Irish Girl*.[305] Singer Eva Thatcher also focussed on Irish songs in her monologue *The Irish Lady*.[306] The same was true of 'Little Amy Butler', though she received poor reviews in comparison to Morrison and Thatcher.[307]

Irish-American boxers also continued to be a draw in the entertainment world. For example, John L. Sullivan appeared at various vaudeville theatres that year.[308] James J. Corbett began 1906 by appearing as the title character in George Bernard Shaw's play *Cashel Byron's Profession*.[309] The play's lack of success resulted in Corbett starring in a comic vaudeville sketch entitled *A Thief in the Night*.[310] Its reviews were mixed. One complained that Corbett failed to 'get out [the] full humor of his lines', while another praised him for causing 'laughs without noise or clowning'.[311]

More clearly than in 1896 or earlier, the issue of authenticity became important in 1906. For example, the *New York Dramatic Mirror* heralded a group of Irish plays staged in Boston.[312] However, that did not mean that critics welcomed tales of Ireland that focussed on issues such as British oppression and/or poverty. Edwin Hanford's play *The Kerry Fair* was praised for avoiding 'evictions, red-coats, landlords, etc., which have long ere this become irksome to all patrons of Irish drama'.[313] Similarly, *The Belle of Killarney* was described as 'bright' and 'sparkling' when it played Dallas, Texas, that year.[314]

Questions over authenticity arose more commonly with comedians and whether or not they offered genuine Irish humour. For example, James Casey and Maggie LeClair promoted themselves as 'Real, Legitimate, and Artistic Irish Comedians'.[315] Similarly, Maggie Weston claimed to be a 'Real Irish Comedienne', and *Variety* declared that singing comedian Irene Jermon was a 'real Irish girl'.[316] However, it is difficult to discern the intended meaning of the word 'real'. For example, *Variety* also suggested that Halliday and Leonard presented a 'real old-time Irish act', which may well have been a reference to the team's use of long-standing 'stage Irish' stereotypes, rather than to their perceived authenticity.[317]

In other cases, it is quite clear that the discussion centred on whether or not the comedian was himself 'stage Irish' or 'genuine'. For example, Irish comedian John T. Kelly appeared in both *Finnigan's Finish* and *A Game of Con* in 1906.[318] The *New York Dramatic Mirror* praised the latter, noting: 'In delineating the character of Dan O'Rourke, Mr Kelly was not obliged to resort to the eccentricities of make-up or costume that have characterized some of his work in the past. He was simply the average Irishman: natural, full of humor, and effective at all times.'[319] Similarly, a newspaper article in Salt Lake City, Utah, suggested that 'When [comedian Roger] Imhof depicts an Irishman, it is

**1.14** Artwork used
to publicize
Murray and Mack
in 1896.

genuinely Irish. If he makes a move, a gesture, or takes a stop, it is Irish to the minutest detail.'[320] *Variety* said much the same, claiming Imhof was 'true to life in make-up and manner of speech'.[321]

By contrast, *Variety* claimed that the 'stage Irish' make-up in an act presented by Wallace and Beech ('comedy acrobats and contortionists') was 'not funny'; however, rather than having taken offence at the make-up, their review suggests instead that they thought the make-up was not necessary for an acrobatic act.[322] They also derided one of the Mahoney Brothers for wearing make-up of 'the most exaggerated type of an "Irish character"'. They viewed him as 'too aggressive in his ambitious attempt to be funny', including his knockabout humour with his brother.[323] Once again, rather than having necessarily been offended by Mahoney's make-up, it seems that *Variety* viewed it as simply inappropriate for the act. In these cases, the entertainment industry reacted negatively, but with a different set of priorities from those held by the Irish-American press.

More than anyone else, the entertainment industry fixed on Nora Kelly ('The Dublin Girl') as the key example of the inauthentic in 1906. Initially, while *Variety* believed that she was 'not strong vocally', they did not question the fact that she was 'from Ireland', in part because she sang 'only those melodies dear to the Hibernian'.[324] The *New York Dramatic Mirror* believed much the same, telling readers that Kelly was an 'Irish' singer whose voice achieved 'indifferent success'.[325] Within two weeks of these pronouncements, however, *Variety* recanted, admitting that 'Nora Kelly' was 'probably the best hoax perpetrated in some time'.[326] They learned that 'Kelly' was not 'fresh from the "ould sod" '. Nor did she have a 'brogue of unmistakable genuineness', as her publicity claimed.[327] In reality, she was an American who had spent the previous seven years as an unknown chorus girl in a burlesque show. She was, in short, a fraud.

# Conclusion

Irish-themed entertainment in America of the nineteenth and early twentieth centuries is a subject area that has been largely ignored by modern scholars. To the extent that it has been examined, the emphasis has generally been on New York productions of stage plays written by important figures like Dion Boucicault and Edward Harrigan. Much more work needs to be undertaken in order to unearth and to understand the sheer number of Irish-themed plays, variety shows and vaudeville acts that were staged, and how they functioned as a component of the broader American entertainment industry. Irish-themed melodrama was a type of American melodrama, just as stage Irish comedy was one of the many forms of ethnic humour on the American stage.

However, the case studies offered herein prove that Irish-themed entertainment was ubiquitous throughout the United States, holding appeal for general audiences in both small towns and large cities. While such entertainment (and reactions to it) evolved over time, various patterns emerged, such as the ongoing popularity of the Irish 'romantic singing comedian', of Irish boxers-turned-actors, and of 'tourist' shows like *Howarth's Hibernica*. Cataloguing these repetitions illustrates how embedded they were in the American entertainment industry – and how familiar audiences were with them – prior to the advent of the cinema.

Irish-themed entertainment on the American stage proved to be a major influence on the narratives and the visuals of the Irish-themed film in early American cinema. For example, stage Irish comedies and Irish-themed melodramas provided important narrative inspiration for early moving pictures. The same was true of specific elements of nineteenth-century Irish-themed entertainment, meaning that the cinema would incorporate particular character names and traits (such 'Pat', 'Casey' and 'Bridget'), particular storylines (such as those written by Boucicault and Marsden), particular settings (such as Killarney) and even particular words (such as 'Mavourneen') that had already become well known to American audiences. Those influences were all in addition to the ongoing and often complicated debates over authenticity that would become important to Irish-themed moving pictures.

Thus, Section One of this book – meaning this chapter and Chapter 2 – not only attempts to redress the lack of historiographic practice in the area of Irish-themed entertainment of the nineteenth and early twentieth centuries, but also to reconnect the Irish-themed moving picture with its pre-cinema influences.

# Notes

1. M. Murphy, 'Irish-American Theatre', in M.S. Seller (ed.), *Ethnic Theatre in the United States* (Westport, CT: Greenwood Press, 1983) pp.221–237.
2. Ibid., pp.223–4.
3. Ibid., p.224.
4. Ibid., p.227.
5. E.F. Niehaus, 'Paddy on the Local Stage and in Humor: The Image of the Irish in New Orleans, 1830–1862', *Louisiana History: Journal of the Louisiana Historical Association*, 5, 2 (Spring 1964), pp.117–34.
6. R. Nowatzki, 'Paddy Jumps Jim Crow: Irish-Americans and Blackface Minstrelsy', *Éire Ireland*, 41, 3 and 4 (Fall/Winter 2006), pp.162–84.
7. C. Wittke, 'The Immigrant Theme on the American Stage', *Mississippi Valley Historical Review*, 39, 2 (September 1952), p.216.
8. W.H.A. Williams, *'Twas Only an Irishman's Dream: The Image of Ireland and the Irish in American Popular Song Lyrics, 1800–1920* (Urbana, IL: University of Illinois Press, 1996), p.88.
9. See, for example, Heininge's chapter on 'Authenticity' in her monograph *Buffoonery in Irish Drama: Staging Twentieth-Century Post-Colonial Stereotypes* (New York: Peter Lang Publishing, 2009), pp.15–30, as well as Harrington's essay 'Synge's *Playboy*, The Irish Players, and the Anti-Irish Irish Players' in his anthology, *The Irish Play on the New York Stage, 1874–1966* (Lexington, KY: University of Kentucky, 1997), pp.55–74.
10. M.F. Clare, *From Killarney to New York; or, How Thade Became a Banker* (New York: Irish National Publishing House, 1877).
11. D. McFeely, 'Between Two Worlds: Boucicault's *The Shaughraun* and its New York Audience', in J.P. Harrington (ed.), *Irish Theatre in America: Essays on Irish Theatrical Diaspora* (Syracuse, NY: Syracuse University Press, 2009), p.55.
12. 'Amusements', *New York Times*, 15 November 1874, p.7.
13. Niehaus, 'Paddy on the Local Stage and in Humor', p.126.
14. Williams, *'Twas Only an Irishman's Dream*, pp.86–7.
15. Advertisement, *New York Herald*, 14 April 1869, p.14.
16. 'Amusements', *New York Herald*, 22 February 1870, p.4.
17. Williams, *'Twas Only an Irishman's Dream*, p.86.
18. 'Local Briefs', *Dubois Weekly Courier* (Dubois, PA), 2 February 1882, p.3. To preserve the integrity of primary sources, I will maintain American spellings, e.g. 'humor' throughout this book when offering quotations in which they appear.
19. *'The Mayor of Laughland* Sunday Evening', *Fort Wayne Journal-Gazette* (Fort Wayne, IN), 12 February 1908, p.5.
20. Quoted in *'The Ivy Leaf*', *Reno Evening Gazette*, 7 March 1888, p.3.
21. 'Here Is Genuine Irish Comedy', *Oakland Tribune* (Oakland, CA), 24 June 1910, p.9.

22. Daly, p.12.
23. Advertisement, *Logansport Journal* (Logansport, IN), 23 March 1890, p.5.
24. Advertisement, *Logansport Reporter* (Logansport, IN), 22 December 1891, p.3.
25. Advertisement, *New York Times*, 7 February 1886, p.11.
26. Heininge, *Buffoonery in Irish Drama*, p.8.
27. G. Orel, 'Reporting the Stage Irishman', in J.P. Harrington (ed.), *Irish Theatre in America: Essays on Irish Theatrical Diaspora* (Syracuse, NY: Syracuse University Press, 2009), pp.66–7.
28. 'The Lingering Stage Irishman', *National Hibernian*, 15 January 1904, p.4.
29. 'The Stamp of the Irish Race', *Irish Monthly*, 43, 509 (November 1915), p.731.
30. M.G. Maryoga, *A Short History of the American Drama* (New York: Dodd, Mead & Co., 1943), p.247.
31. For a discussion of some of the changes that occurred in Irish-themed entertainment and vaudeville acts, see S. Staples, *Male–Female Comedy Teams in American Vaudeville, 1865–1932* (Ann Arbor, MI: UMI Research Press, 1984), pp.85–9.
32. J.J. Appel, 'From Shanties to Lace Curtains: The Irish Image in *Puck*, 1876–1910', *Comparative Studies in Society and History*, 13, 4 (October 1971), pp.372–3.
33. Ibid., pp.369, 371–2.
34. D. Nasaw, *The Chief: The Life of William Randolph Hearst* (New York: First Mariner, 2000), p.109.
35. 'War on the Stage Irishman', *Atlanta Constitution*, 4 April 1903, p.6.
36. H.L. Newton, *Killarney Blarney* (Chicago, IL: T.S. Denison, 1905).
37. H.L. Newton, *The Recruiting Office* (Chicago, IL: T.S. Denison, 1905); H.L. Newton, *Mrs Clancy's Confession* (Chicago, IL: T.S. Denison, 1911).
38. Newton, *Mrs Clancy's Confession*, p.2.
39. In addition to the kinds of publications cited in the main text, comical stories and jokes about the Irish were also occasionally published in American newspapers. See, for example, 'Have a Laugh with Us', *Belleville Telescope* (Belleville, KS), 1 November 1907, p.16.
40. G. Cooper, *Cooper's Irish Dialect Readings and Recitations* (New York: Wehman Brothers, 1891).
41. W.H. Howe, *Irish Wit and Humor* (Philadelphia, PA: George W. Jacobs, 1898), p.3.
42. 'Kerry Gow', *Racine Daily Journal* (Racine, WI), 6 November 1906, p.4.
43. Ú. Ní Bhroiméil, 'The Creation of an Irish Culture in the United States: The Gaelic Movement, 1870–1915', *New Hibernia Review* (Autumn 2001), pp.87–100.
44. Ibid., p.99.
45. G. Maschio, 'Ethnic Humor and the Demise of the Russell Brothers', *Journal of Popular Culture*, 26, 1 (Summer 1992), pp.81–92.
46. 'To Fight Stage Irishmen Here', *Logansport Journal*, 23 November 1905, p.7.
47. 'The Lingering Stage Irishman', p.4.
48. 'War on the Stage Irishman', p.6.
49. 'Daniel Sully on Stage Irish', *Eau Claire Leader* (Eau Claire, WI), 8 February 1903, p.14.
50. 'Middlesex Co. A. O. H.' *Lowell Sun* (Lowell, MA), 12 October 1908, p.31.
51. [Untitled], *Atlanta Constitution*, 4 April 1903, p.6.
52. H.P. Kelly, *Gems of Irish Wit and Humor* (New York: George Sully & Co., 1906).
53. *New Book of Monologues, No. 1* (New York: Wehman Brothers, 1908).
54. A discussion of such 'knockabout' comedy appears in 'Oneida County', *National Hibernian*, 15 April 1904, p.5.
55. P.B. Lavitt, 'First of the Red Hot Mamas: "Coon Shouting" and the Jewish Ziegfeld Girl', *American Jewish History*, 87, 4 (December 1999), pp.253–90.
56. Harrington, 'Synge's *Playboy*, The Irish Playboy, and the Anti-Irish Irish Players', pp.55–74.
57. Phelan, p.237.
58. 'Riot in Theatre', *Billboard*, 2 December 1911, p.40.
59. 'Drama and Music', *Salt Lake Tribune* (Salt Lake, UT), 3 May 1896, p.11.
60. P.M. Ryan, 'The Hibernian Experience: John Brougham's Irish-American Plays', *MELUS*, 10, 2 (Summer 1983), pp.33–47.
61. Wittke, 'Immigrant Theme', p.225.
62. 'Stage Notes of the Week', *New York Times*, 14 August 1898, p.6.
63. Advertisement, *New York Times*, 6 February 1866, p.7.
64. 'Theatre', *Daily Milwaukee News* (Milwaukee, WI),17 March 1866, p.5.

65. [Untitled], *Fort Wayne Daily Gazette* (Fort Wayne, IN), 21 September 1866, p.3; advertisement, *New York Times*, 17 April 1866, p.7.
66. 'Theatre', *Janesville Gazette* (Janesville, WI), 3 August 1866, p.1.
67. Advertisement, *Dubuque Daily Herald* (Dubuque, IA), 10 March 1866, p.5.
68. Advertisement, *New York Times*, 22 July 1866, p.7.
69. Advertisement, *New York Times*, 23 August 1866, p.7.
70. 'Amusements', *New York Times*, 1 August 1866, p.4.
71. Ibid.
72. 'Wallack's Theatre', *New York Times*, 20 August 1866, p.5.
73. Advertisement, *New York Times*, 12 June 1866, p.7; advertisement, *New York Times*, 16 July 1866, p.7; advertisement, *New York Times*, 13 July 1866, p.7.
74. Williams, *'Twas Only an Irishman's Dream*, p.98.
75. Advertisement, *New York Times*, 24 April 1866, p.7.
76. Ibid.
77. Advertisement, *New York Times*, 16 April 1866, p.7; advertisement, *New York Times*, 19 May 1866, p.7.
78. Advertisement, *New York Times*, 10 April 1866, p.7.
79. 'Amusement', *Titusville Herald* (Titusville, PA), 28 November 1866, p.3; advertisement, *Brooklyn Daily Eagle*, 25 April 1866, p.1.
80. Advertisement, *Dubuque Democratic Herald* (Dubuque, IA), 8 February 1866, p.1.
81. [Untitled], *Dubuque Daily Herald*, 4 April 1866, p.2.
82. Ibid.
83. 'John Dillon', *Daily Milwaukee News*, 29 September 1866, p.5; 'Theatrical', *Dubuque Daily Herald*, 7 November 1866, p.4.
84. 'Theatre', *Janesville Gazette*, 4 October 1866, p.1.
85. 'Amusements', *New York Times*, 18 August 1866, p.4.
86. 'Winter Garden', *New York Times*, 30 August 1866, p.5.
87. Advertisement, *Brooklyn Daily Eagle*, 20 September 1866, p.1.
88. [Untitled], *Atlanta Constitution*, 30 January 1876, p.4; 'Foreign', *Palo Alto Reporter* (Emmetsburg, IA), 4 March 1876, p.3.
89. 'Current Items', *Palo Alto Pilot* (Emmetsburg, IA), 23 November 1876, p.3.
80. 'Amusements', *Morning Oregonian* (Portland, OR), 27 October 1876, p.3; 'Amusements', *Burlington Hawk-Eye* (Burlington, IA), 23 November 1876, p.1.
91. 'News in Brief', *Indiana Progress* (Indiana, PA), 26 October 1876, p.2.
92. See, for example, advertisement, *Milwaukee Daily News*, 16 September 1876, p.4.
93. Advertisement, *Brooklyn Daily Eagle*, 22 May 1876, p.1.
94. Advertisement, *Brooklyn Daily Eagle*, 26 May 1876, p.1.
95. 'Wade's Opera House', *Oakland Tribune*, 23 March 1876, p.3; 'Murphy at the Academy', *Milwaukee Daily News*, 13 September 1876, p.4.
96. 'The Opera House', *Galveston Daily News* (Galveston, TX), 8 February 1876, p.4.
97. 'Aline at the Atheneum', *Dubuque Herald*, 7 September 1876, p.4.
98. 'Edwin Clifford's Troupe', *Janesville Gazette*, 2 September 1876, p.4; 'Inshavogue', *Janesville Gazette*, 7 September 1876, p.4; advertisement, *Janesville Gazette*, 9 September 1876, p.1.
99. 'Dramatic', *Brooklyn Daily Eagle*, 2 May 1876, p.2.
100. 'Dramatic', *Brooklyn Daily Eagle*, 3 May 1876, p.3.
101. 'Gossip from Gotham', *Yates County Chronicle* (Penn Yan, NY), 3 February 1886, p.4.
102. Advertisement, *New York Times*, 30 January 1886, p.7.
103. 'Edward Harrigan, Old Comedian, Dead', *New York Times*, 7 June 1911, p.9.
104. 'Park Theatre', *Brooklyn Daily Eagle*, 1 May 1876, p.1.
105. Advertisement, *Brooklyn Daily Eagle*, 12 May 1876, p.1; 'Olympic Theatre', *Brooklyn Daily Eagle*, 25 September 1876, p.4; advertisement, *Brooklyn Daily Eagle*, 8 November 1876, p.3; advertisement, *Brooklyn Daily Eagle*, 30 August 1876, p.1.
106. Advertisement, *Brooklyn Daily Eagle*, 28 August 1876, p.1.
107. Advertisement, *Brooklyn Daily Eagle*, 20 March 1876, p.1.
108. Advertisement, *Brooklyn Daily Eagle*, 26 August 1876, p.1; advertisement, *Brooklyn Daily Eagle*, 12 February 1876, p.1; advertisement, *Brooklyn Daily Eagle*, 14 October 1876, p.1.

109. 'Musical and Dramatic', *Brooklyn Daily Eagle*, 29 February 1876, p.3.
110. Advertisement, *Janesville Gazette*, 26 June 1876, p.4.
111. 'Dillon Last Night', *Janesville Gazette*, 27 June 1876, p.4.
112. Advertisement, *Brooklyn Daily Eagle*, 24 April 1876, p.1; 'Hooley's Opera House', *Brooklyn Daily Eagle*, 1 May 1876, p.2.
113. Advertisement, *Brooklyn Daily Eagle*, 8 April 1876, p.4.
114. Advertisement, *Brooklyn Daily Eagle*, 4 August 1866, p.1.
115. [Untitled], *Portsmouth Times* (Portsmouth, OH), 8 January 1876, p.3.
116. Advertisement, *Athens Messenger* (Athens, OH), 6 January 1876, p.5.
117. Advertisement, *Oshkosh Daily Northwestern*, 10 June 1876, p.4.
118. 'Healy's Hibernicon', *Milwaukee Daily News*, 7 May 1876, p.1.
119. Advertisement, *Daily Kennebec Journal*, 30 August 1876, p.3.
120. 'Burke's Comedy Company', *Bangor Daily Whig and Courier* (Bangor, ME), 26 July 1876, p.6.
121. 'Emerald Minstrels', *Titusville Herald*, 26 February 1876, p.3.
122. Advertisement, *Hornellsville Tribune* (Hornellsville, NY), 31 March 1876, p.3.
123. [Untitled], *Butte Daily Mirror* (Butte, MT), 25 April 1886, p.2; 'Dion Boucicault's Divorce', *Decatur Daily Republican* (Decatur, IL), 14 January 1886, p.2.
124. [Untitled], *New York Clipper*, 9 January 1886, p.676; 'Brooklyn', *New York Clipper*, 9 January 1886, p.678.
125. 'New York', *New York Clipper*, 13 March 1886, p.822.
126. 'Dramatic Companies', *New York Clipper*, 15 March 1886, p.134; 'Dramatic Companies', *New York Clipper*, 15 May 1886, p.134; 'Dramatic Companies', *New York Clipper*, 10 June 1886, p.214; 'New York', *New York Clipper*, 13 March 1886, p.822.
127. 'Dramatic Injunctions', *New York Times*, 2 April 1886, p.8.
128. 'Pennsylvania', *New York Clipper*, 19 June 1886, p.218; 'Indiana', *New York Clipper*, 13 March 1886, p.820.
129. 'Fanchon the Cricket', *Newark Daily Advocate* (Newark, OH), 9 December 1886, p.1; advertisement, *Eau Claire Daily Free Press* (Eau Claire, WI), 9 April 1886, p.3. *The Colleen Bawn* appeared in Newark, OH; *The Shaughraun* was staged in Eau Claire, WI.
130. Advertisement, *New York Clipper*, 7 August 1886, p.335.
131. 'New Jersey', *New York Clipper*, 23 October 1886, p.503.
132. Quoted in 'Kate Claxton', *Fitchburg Sentinel* (Fitchburg, MA), 27 August 1886, p.3.
133. Advertisement, *Cedar Rapids Evening Gazette* (Cedar Rapids, IA), 3 December 1886, p.3; 'A Card', *Decatur Daily Republican*, 23 November 1886, p.3.
134. See, for example: 'Local Paragraphs', *Decatur Daily Review* (Decatur, IL), 16 November 1886, p.4.
135. [Untitled], *Fort Wayne Sentinel* (Fort Wayne, IN), 12 January 1886, p.4.
136. 'Realism on the Stage', *Mitchell Daily Republican* (Mitchell, SD), 18 November 1886, p.4.
137. Quoted in [untitled], *Cedar Rapids Evening Gazette* (Cedar Rapids, IA), 3 December 1886, p.2.
138. 'Joe Murphy in *Kerry Gow* at Music Hall, Saturday, May 15', *Newark Daily Advocate*, 11 May 1886, p.2.
139. 'Mr Harrigan's New Piece', *New York Times*, 12 October 1886, p.5; 'Park Theatre', *New York Clipper*, 23 October 1886, p.502.
140. 'Park Theatre', *New York Clipper*, 23 October 1886, p.502.
141. Advertisement, *Galveston Daily News*, 22 February 1886, p.1.
142. 'General Mention', *New York Times*, 22 September 1885, p.5.
143. 'W.J. Scanlan', *Fort Wayne Sentinel*, 20 January 1886, p.4.
144. Advertisement, *Chester Times* (Chester, PA), 24 December 1886, p.5; advertisement. *Newark Daily Advocate*, 11 October 1886, p.4; 'A Star Company', *Reno Evening Gazette* (Reno, NV), 5 January 1886, p.3; advertisement, *New York Clipper*, 16 January 1886, p.704; 'At the Playhouses', *Syracuse Standard* (Syracuse, NY), 26 December 1886, p.7.
145. 'Circus, Variety, and Minstrel', *New York Clipper*, 13 February 1886, p.756; [untitled], *Newark Daily Advocate*, 11 May 1886, p.4; 'Opening Announcement', *Daily Times* (New Brunswick, NJ), 14 May 1886, p.3; advertisement, *New York Clipper*, 9 October 1886, p.477; advertisement, *New York Clipper*, 24 July 1886, p.303; advertisement, *New York Clipper*, 18 December 1886, p.640; advertisement, *New York Clipper*, 4 December 1886, p.606.
146. 'Local News', *Lowell Sun*, 18 September 1886, p.8.

147. Advertisement, *New York Clipper*, 20 March 1886, p.15; advertisement, *Chester Times*, 29 September 1886, p.2.

148. Advertisement, *New York Clipper*, 20 March 1886, p.15.

149. Advertisement, *New York Clipper*, 16 January 1886, p.701.

150. Advertisement, *New York Clipper*, 23 January 1886, p.720.

151. [Untitled], *Tyrone Daily Herald* (Tyrone, PA), 25 November 1886, p.8.

152. Advertisement, *New York Clipper*, 11 September 1886, p.413.

153. 'New York', *New York Clipper*, 9 January 1886, p.678; 'New York', *New York Clipper*, 18 December 1886, p.630; advertisement, *Trenton Times* (Trenton, NJ), 30 October 1886, p.4; advertisement, *San Antonio Light* (San Antonio, TX), 13 September 1886, p.1.

154. 'Pennsylvania', *New York Clipper*, 15 May 1886, p.138.

155. 'Amusements', *New York Times*, 6 May 1884, p.4.

156. 'Amusements', *Newark Daily Advocate*, 25 September 1886, p.2.

157. 'Gilhooley and McGinnis', *Cedar Rapids Evening Gazette*, 30 March 1886, p.1.

158. Advertisement, *New York Clipper*, 8 May 1886, p.127; 'Comedy Fun Saturday Night', *Decatur Republican*, 4 February 1886, p.3; advertisement, *Piqua Daily Call* (Piqua, OH), 25 September 1886, p.3.

159. Advertisement, *Yates County Chronicle*, 3 February 1886, p.2; advertisement, *Lebanon Daily News* (Lebanon, PA), 8 March 1886, p.4.

160. Advertisement, *New York Clipper*, 3 July 1886, p.255.

161. [Untitled], *Fort Wayne Sentinel*, 7 May 1886, p.1.

162. Advertisement, *New York Clipper*, 30 October 1886, p.326.

163. Ibid.

164. [Untitled], *Newark Daily Advocate*, 1 November 1886, p.1.

165. 'Street Gossip', *Mitchell Daily Republican*, 2 May 1886, p.3; advertisement, *Mitchell Daily Republican*, 4 May 1886, p.3.

166. 'The Weekly Pick-Up', *Upper Des Moines* (Algona, IA), 14 April 1886, p.4.

167. [Untitled], *Northern Vindicator* (Esterville, IA), 23 April 1886, p.5.

168. Advertisement, *New York Clipper*, 30 October 1886, p.527; 'Local and Personal', *Huntingdon Journal* (Huntingdon, PA), 29 January 1886, p.3.

169. Advertisement, *New York Clipper*, 23 October 1886, p.511.

170. Ibid.

171. 'Harrigan's Hibernians', *Titusville Herald*, 19 February 1886, p.4.

172. 'Howorth's Hibernica', *Huntingdon Journal* (Huntingdon, PA), 26 November 1886, p.3.

173. 'Indiana', *New York Clipper*, 9 January 1886, p.677; 'Kentucky', *New York Clipper*, 17 April 1886, p.7; 'Miscellaneous', *New York Clipper*, 20 November 1886, p.563.

174. Advertisement, *New York Clipper*, 20 March 1886, p.12.

175. 'Paddy Ryan on the Stage', *Fitchburg Sentinel*, 17 April 1886, p.3.

176. 'Dramatic World', *Fort Wayne Gazette* (Fort Wayne, IN), 19 December 1886, p.3.

177. 'The Ivy Leaf', *Cedar Rapids Evening Gazette*, 18 December 1886, p.4.

178. Ibid.

179. 'Next Friday Night', *Logansport Journal*, 16 November 1886, p.3.

180. Advertisement, *New York Clipper*, 21 August 1886, p.364; advertisement, *New York Clipper*, 25 December 1886, p.652.

181. Advertisement, *New York Clipper*, 6 February 1886, p.751; 'Chicago Worships John L. Sullivan As He Stalks Its Highways', *New York Clipper*, 17 April 1886, p.66; 'John L. Sullivan Still Finds Profit in Minstrelsy', *New York Clipper*, 1 May 1886, p.102.

182. 'Boucicault in *The Colleen Bawn*', *New York World*, 17 March 1896, p.8; 'Combination Houses', *New York World*, 22 March 1896, p.45.

183. Advertisement, *Salt Lake Tribune*, 7 May 1896, p.4.

184. Advertisement, *Bath Independent* (Bath, ME), 14 March 1896, p.3; advertisement, *Fitchburg Sentinel*, 27 January 1896, p.2.

185. 'Arrah Na Pogue', *Logansport Journal*, 18 March 1896, p.4; [untitled], *Logansport Reporter*, 12 March 1896, p.6.

186. [Untitled], *Alton Evening Telegraph* (Alton, IL), 23 April 1896, p.3; 'Standard Theatre', *New York Clipper*, 10 October 1896, p.505.

187. 'News in a Nutshell', *North Adams Transcript* (North Adams, MA), 25 January 1896, p.3.
188. 'Amusements', *Dubuque Daily Herald*, 9 September 1896, p.8.
189. Advertisement, *Middletown Daily Argus* (Middletown, NY), 21 February 1896, p.3.
190. 'Olcott's Adieu Tonight', *Oakland Tribune*, 26 August 1896, p.15.
191. Amusements', *Dubuque Daily Herald*, 20 October 1896, p.8.
192. Advertisement, *Salt Lake Tribune*, 12 September 1896, p.4.
193. 'The Irish Artist', *Dubuque Daily Herald*, 18 October 1896, p.8.
194. [Untitled], *Waterloo Daily Courier* (Waterloo, IA), 21 May 1896, p.6.
195. 'Amusements', *Trenton Evening Times*, 17 March 1896, p.2.
196. 'Curtain Raisers', *Racine Daily Journal* (Racine, WI), 30 November 1896, p.2.
197. 'Andrew Mack in *Myles Aroon*', *Syracuse Herald* (Syracuse, NY), 27 January 1896, p.4; 'Amusements', *Trenton Evening Times*, 14 March 1896, p.2.
198. 'Amusements', *Syracuse Daily Standard*, 29 January 1896, p.11.
199. Advertisement, *New York Clipper*, 12 December 1896, p.659; 'At the Bijou', *North Adams Transcript*, 15 September 1896, p.3; advertisement, *Salt Lake Tribune*, 12 June 1896, p.4.
200. Advertisement, *Des Moines Daily News*, 9 September 1896, p.2.
201. 'Last Night's Shows', *Davenport Daily Leader* (Davenport, IA), 18 December 1896, p.6; 'At the Burtis,' *Davenport Daily Leader*, 23 December 1896, p.3.
202. 'Music Hall Notes', *New York Times*, 5 April 1896, p.10.
203. 'Amusements', *Cedar Rapids Evening Gazette*, 29 January 1896, p.7.
204. 'O'Brien, the Contractor', *Titusville Herald*, 15 December 1896, p.4.
205. 'Dan Sully in *A Social Lion*', *Colorado Springs Gazette* (Colorado Springs, CO), 3 January 1896, p.5.
206. 'Marty Malone', *New York Clipper*, 3 October 1896, p.491.
207. 'A Night of New Plays', *New York Times*, 1 September 1896, p.5; 'Harrigan's Latest Play', *Ironwood News Record* (Ironwood, MI), 14 November 1896, p.13.
208. 'Edward Harrigan, Old Comedian, Dead', p.9.
209. 'A Rattling Good Comedy', *Logansport Journal*, 4 October 1896, p.4; advertisement, *Salt Lake Tribune*, 7 June 1896, p.10; 'Massachusetts', *New York Clipper*, 15 August 1896, p.375; 'New York', *New York Clipper*, 10 October 1896, p.506; 'New York,' *New York Clipper*, 22 August 1896, p.392; 'New York', *New York Clipper*, 29 August 1896, p.408; advertisement, *New York Clipper*, 12 December 1896, p.659; advertisement, *New York Clipper*, 6 June 1896, p.222; 'Hyde and Behmans', *New York Clipper*, 18 April 1896, p.104; advertisement, *New York Clipper*, 13 June 1896, p.242; advertisement, *New York Clipper*, 4 April 1896, p.77.
210. Advertisement, *New York World*, 17 Feb. 1896, p.7; 'Proctor's Theatre', *New York Clipper*, 23 May 1896, p.184.
211. 'The Opening Night', *Logansport Reporter*, 12 September 1896, p.3.
212. 'News of Plays and Players', *Syracuse Herald*, 26 January 1896, p.8.
213. 'Murray and Mack', *Daily Leader* (Eau Claire, WI), 26 February 1896, p.4.
214. 'Murray and Mack', *Logansport Pharos*, 8 September 1896, p.3.
215. 'Murray and Mack Again', *Sterling Standard* (Sterling, IL), 10 December 1896, p.14.
216. 'On the Road', *New York Clipper*, 7 March 1896, p.2; 'On the Road', *New York Clipper*, 17 October 1896, p.518; 'On the Road', *New York Clipper*, 12 December 1896, p.648; advertisement, *New York Clipper*, 15 August 1896, p.386.
217. 'Amusements', *Fort Wayne News*, 22 October 1896, p.2; 'The Irish Greenhorn', *New York Clipper*, 5 December 1896, p.637.
218. 'Stage Glints', *Newark Daily Advocate*, 29 May 1896, p.3; 'Theatrical Stars Shine', *Oakland Tribune*, 28 November 1896, p.3; 'A New York Boy,' *Daily Times* (New Brunswick, NJ), 24 January 1896, p.5.
219. Advertisement, *New York Clipper*, 26 September 1896, p.478; advertisement, *New York Clipper*, 24 October 1896, p.548.
220. Advertisement, *New York Clipper*, 7 November 1896, p.576; advertisement, *New York Clipper*, 7 November 1896, p.579.
221. Advertisement, *New York Clipper*, 4 July 1896, p.289.
222. 'Coming Attractions', *Burlington Hawk Eye*, 16 April 1896, p.3.
223. 'Miscellaneous Shows', *New York Clipper*, 16 May 1896, p.169.

224. Ibid.

225. 'Miscellaneous Shows', *New York Clipper*, 31 October 1896, p.555.

226. Advertisement, *New York Clipper*, 1 August 1896, p.354.

227. Advertisement, *New York Clipper*, 25 July 1896, p.337.

228. 'The Orpheum', *Oakland Tribune*, 8 September 1896, p.13.

229. Advertisement, *Middletown Daily Argus*, 9 October 1896, p.3; 'Amusements', *Trenton Evening Times*, 7 November 1896, p.2.

230. Advertisement, *Syracuse Daily Standard*, 2 March 1896, p.9.

231. 'Amusements', *Trenton Evening Times*, 28 January 1896, p.1.

232. Advertisement, *Stevens Point Daily Journal* (Stevens Point, WI), 6 March 1886, p.9.

233. Quoted in 'Howorth's Hibernica', *Huntingdon Journal*, 26 November 1886, p.3.

234. 'Amusements', *Daily Herald* (Delphos, OH), 1 February 1896, p.8; 'The Play House', *Daily Herald*, 3 February 1896, p.8; advertisement, *Daily Chronicle* (Marshall, MI), 19 March 1896, p.2.

235. 'District of Columbia', *New York Clipper*, 25 July 1896, p.327.

236. 'Proctor's Pleasure Palace', *New York Clipper*, 29 August 1896, p.408.

237. 'Tony Pastor's Theatre', *New York Clipper*, 18 July 1896, p.312.

238. Advertisement, *New York World*, 5 January 1896, p.15.

239. 'Tony Pastor's Theatre', *New York Clipper*, 4 September 1896, p.424.

240. 'The Wicklow Postman', *Ironwood News Record* (Ironwood, MI), 25 April 1896, p.10; 'Pittsburgh', *New York Clipper*, 13 June 1896, p.230.

241. 'Corbett in *A Naval Cadet*', *New York World*, 1 December 1896, p.9.

242. 'Corbett Coming', *Daily Times* (New Brunswick, NJ), 15 January 1896, p.5.

243. [Untitled], *New York Times*, 21 October 1906, p.22.

244. 'Andrew Mack', *Trenton Times*, 18 September 1906, p.11.

245. 'Andrew Mack Here To-Night [*sic*]', *Syracuse Post-Standard*, 22 October 1906, p.3.

246. 'The Way to Kenmare', *Des Moines Daily News* (Des Moines, IA), 14 January 1906, p.10.

247. 'Andrew Mack, Jan. 8th', *Eau Claire Leader*, 7 January 1906, p.14.

248. 'The Way to Kenmare', *New York Dramatic Mirror*, 26 May 1906, p.3.

249. W. Patrick, 'Pat-Chats', *Billboard*, 24 February 1906, p.11.

250. Use of this term appears, for example, in [untitled], *San Antonio Gazette*, 10 February 1906, p.14.

251. 'The Events Next Week', *Fort Wayne News*, 3 March 1906, p.3.

252. 'Notes on the Coming Week at the Playhouse', *New York Times*, 21 October 1906, p.22; 'Coming to the Theatres', *Washington Post*, 18 January 1906, p.19.

253. 'Notes on the Coming Week at the Playhouse', *New York Times*, 21 October 1906, p.22.

254. 'Olcott's New Play', *New York Times*, 18 August 1906, p.5.

255. 'Chicago', *New York Dramatic Mirror*, 24 March 1906, p.14; 'St Louis', *New York Dramatic Mirror*, 21 April 1906, p.15; 'St Louis', *New York Dramatic Mirror*, 29 September 1906, p.14.

256. 'New Plays in New York', *Washington Post*, 7 January 1906, p.7.

257. 'Fiske O'Hara Makes Friends', *Syracuse Post-Standard*, 30 March 1906, p.4.

258. 'Mr Blarney of Ireland', *New York Dramatic Mirror*, 13 January 1906, p.3.

259. 'Stage Talk', *Des Moines Daily News*, 22 October 1906, p.2.

260. 'Barney Gilmore Next Week', *Atlanta Constitution*, 30 March 1906, p.8.

261. 'Theatres', *Atlanta Constitution*, 4 April 1906, p.5; 'Popular Comedians at the Bastable', *Syracuse Post-Standard*, 22 December 1906, p.16.

262. 'Barney Gilmore in Congenial Role', *Syracuse Post-Standard*, 25 December 1906, p.3.

263. 'Theatrical Notes', *New Brunswick Times* (New Brunswick, NJ), 20 October 1906, p.3.

264. 'Kerry Gow, Sept. 18', *Daily Kennebec Journal*, 12 September 1906, p.2; 'Stage Talk', *Des Moines Daily News*, 22 October 1906, p.2.

265. See, for example: *Oshkosh Daily Northwestern* (Oshkosh, WI), 12 February 1906, p.4; 'Theatrical Notes', *Lake County Times* (Hammond, IN), 1 November 1906, p.5; 'It Made Joe Murphy Rich', *Anaconda Standard* (Anaconda, MT), 12 December 1906, p.5.

266. 'Murphy Will Not Retire', *Billboard*, 13 January 1906, p.3; 'Murphy Has 12 Weeks', *Variety*, 27 October 1906, p.6.

267. 'Pawtucket, R. I.', *Variety*, 31 March 1906, p.16; 'Toledo, Ohio', *Variety*, 28 April 1906, pp.14–15; 'Bowery', *Variety*, 14 April 1906, p.12; 'Pittsburg [*sic*], PA', *Variety*, 27 February 1906, p.12; 'Worcester, Mass,' *Variety*, 14 July 1906, p.16; advertisement, *Oshkosh Daily Northwestern*, 13

February 1906, p.8; 'Amusements', *Logansport Chronicle*, 29 September 1906, p.8; advertisement, *Oshkosh Daily Northwestern*, 28 July 1906, p.8; 'Bell Theatre', *Oakland Tribune*, 29 May 1906, p.4; advertisement, *Reno Evening Gazette*, 8 June 1906, p.3; 'John Drew Tonight', *Fort Wayne News*, 30 March 1906, p.14.

268. 'Our Amusement Bulletin', *Altoona Mirror* (Altoona, PA), 8 December 1906, p.8.
269. 'James Francis Sullivan', *New York Dramatic Mirror*, 26 May 1906, p.2.
270. 'Keith's', *Variety*, 3 February 1906, p.7; 'Worcester, Mass', *Variety*, 12 December 1906, p.13.
271. 'Dan Sully in *Our Pastor*', *Portsmouth Herald*, 16 January 1906, p.4.
272. 'Neighborly Neighbors', *Evening Times* (Cumberland, MD), 24 September 1906, p.5; '*The Mayor of Laughland*', *Frederick News* (Frederick, MD), 6 December 1906, p.3.
273. 'The Colonial', *Variety*, 13 January 1906, p.8; 'The Moonlight Maids', *Variety*, 25 August 1906, p.9.
274. 'Out of Town', *Variety*, 7 April 1906, p.6; 'Comedy Featured on Valley Bill', *Syracuse Post-Standard*, 30 June 1906, p.10; 'McCale Will Leave Burlesque', *Variety*, 27 October 1906, p.5; 'Twenty-Third Street', *Variety*, 8 December 1906, p.9.
275. 'Last Week's Bills', *New York Dramatic Mirror*, 20 January 1906, p.18; advertisement, *San Antonio Light* (San Antonio, TX), 15 July 1906, p.4; 'Newark, NJ', *Variety*, 24 March 1906, p.16; 'Pottstown, PA', *Variety*, 17 March 1906, p.15; 'Baltimore, MD', *Variety*, 3 March 1906, p.11; 'Hoboken, NJ', *Variety*, 17 February 1906, p.12; 'Baltimore, MD', *Variety*, 27 January 1906, p.13; 'Philadelphia', *Variety*, 12 May 1906, p.15; 'Last Week's Bills', *New York Dramatic Mirror*, 3 March 1906, p.18; advertisement, *Variety*, 22 December 1906, p.27.
276. 'Gallagher and Barrett', *New York Dramatic Mirror*, 22 December 1906 [n.p.].
277. 'Era of Hilarity on at Bastable', *Syracuse Post-Standard*, 31 August 1906, p.4.
278. 'Circle', *Variety*, 28 April 1906, p.8; 'Pawtucket, R. I.', *Variety*, 19 May 1906, p.12.
279. 'Family', *Variety*, 3 March 1906, p.8.
280. 'Murray and Mack', *Variety*, 19 May 1906, p.7.
281. 'Grand Opera House', *Oakland Tribune*, 17 February 1906, p.18.
282. 'Next Thursday Night', *Hutchinson News* (Hutchinson, KS), 31 December 1906, p.7.
283. 'At the Grand', *Atlanta Constitution*, 20 September 1906, p.4.
284. 'Murray and Mack No. 2', *Billboard*, 21 April 1906, p.14.
285. 'Last Week's Bills', *New York Dramatic Mirror*, 3 February 1906, p.18.
286. 'Theatres', *Syracuse Herald*, 24 September 1906, p.5.
287. 'St Louis', *New York Dramatic Mirror*, 20 January 1906, p.15.
288. 'Cute Colleens Please the Eye', *Syracuse Post-Standard*, 26 September 1906, p.4.
289. 'Bell Theatre', *Oakland Tribune*, 4 November 1906, p.13; 'Routes', *Billboard*, 27 October 1906, p.18.
290. 'Hyde & Behman's', *Variety*, 21 April 1906, p.9; advertisement, *Variety*, 4 August 1906, p.20.
291. 'Merrymeeting Park', *Bath Independent and Enterprise* (Bath, ME), 11 July 1906, p.2.
292. Advertisement, *New York Dramatic Mirror*, 12 May 1906, p.17; 'Musical', *Billboard*, 22 September 1906, p.31; 'Advertising That Doesn't Pay', *Gaelic American*, 13 January 1912, p.4.
293. 'Mt. Vernon, NY', *Variety*, 8 September 1906, p.15.
294. Advertisement, *Washington Post*, 30 December 1906, p.4; 'Union Square', *Variety*, 17 November 1906, p.10; 'Utica, N.Y', *Variety*, 10 March 1906, p.12.
295. 'Amphion,' *Variety*, 10 March 1906, p.8; 'Pastor's', *Variety*, 12 May 1906, p.9.
296. 'Arnot and Gunn', *Variety*, 5 May 1906, p.6.
297. William H.A. Williams, 'Green Again: Irish-American Lace-Curtain Satire', *New Hibernia Review*, 6, 2 (Summer 2002), pp.14–15.
298. '*Me, Him and I* Draws Well at the Majestic', *Washington Post*, 2 January 1906, p.35.
299. '*Me, Him, and I*, Musical Comedy at the Majestic', *Washington Post*, 22 April 1906, p.37.
300. 'The Avenue Girls', *Variety*, 3 November 1906, p.12; 'Twenty-Third Street', *Variety*, 11 August 1906, p.9.
301. 'Irwin's Big Show', *Variety*, 1 September 1906, p.9; '*The Golden Crook*', *Variety*, 24 November 1906, p.10.
302. 'The Murphys Featured', *Variety*, 6 October 1906, p.6.
303. 'Pastors', *Variety*, 11 August 1906, p.8; 'Nightingales', *Variety*, 1 September 1906, p.9; 'St Louis', *New York Dramatic Mirror*, 11 August 1906, p.13; advertisement, *Variety*, 28 July 1906, p.17.

304. 'The Irish Duchess Returns', *Billboard*, 4 August 1906, p.8.
305. 'Saginaw, Mich.', *Variety*, 3 February 1906, p.13; 'Last Week's Bills', *New York Dramatic Mirror*, 26 May 1906, p.16.
306. Advertisement, *Billboard*, 6 January 1906, p.32.
307. 'Amusements', *Oshkosh Daily Northwestern*, 20 February 1906, p.4; 'Providence, R. I.', *Variety*, 1 September 1906, p.15
308. [Untitled], *Variety*, 19 May 1906, p.3.
309. 'The Drama in New York,' *Salt Lake Tribune*, 14 January 1906, p.10; [untitled], *Variety*, 17 February 1906, p.3.
310. 'Orpheum', *Variety*, 12 May 1906, p.8.
311. 'James J. Corbett', *Variety*, 10 March 1906, p.6; 'Novelty', *Variety*, 21 April 1906, p.8.
312. 'Boston', *New York Dramatic Mirror*, 3 February 1906, p.14.
313. '*The Kerry Fair*', *Logansport Pharos*, 28 March 1906, p.3.
314. 'Amusements', *Dallas Morning News*, 18 May 1906, p.4.
315. Advertisement, *New York Dramatic Mirror*, 13 January 1906, p.18.
316. Advertisement, *New York Dramatic Mirror*, 26 May 1906, p.15; 'Wilmington, Del.', *Variety*, 10 March 1906, p.13.
317. 'Shows of the Week', *Variety*, 10 March 1906, p.9.
318. 'John T. Kelly and Company', *Variety*, 13 January 1906, p.4; 'John T. Kelly', *Variety*, 27 October 1906, p.8.
319. 'Last Week's Bills', *New York Dramatic Mirror*, 20 October 1906, p.16.
320. 'Amusements', *Salt Lake Tribune*, 25 April 1906, p.7.
321. 'Empire Burlesquers', *Variety*, 27 October 1906, p.10.
322. 'Correspondence', *Variety*, 3 February 1906, p.12.
323. 'Correspondence', *Variety*, 22 September 1906, p.11.
324. 'Nora Kelly', *Variety*, 4 August 1906, p.8.
325. 'Last Week's Bills', *New York Dramatic Mirror*, 11 August 1906, p.16.
326. 'Nora Kelly Never Saw Dublin', *Variety*, 18 August 1906, p.7.
327. Ibid.

# Chapter Two
# *Lantern Slides*

While Ireland and the Irish were common topics in American stage plays, variety shows and vaudeville acts during the nineteenth century, such entertainment usually faced severe visual limitations. At most, a stage backdrop might depict an urban or rural Irish landscape. Similarly, books, magazines and the covers of sheet music offered line drawings and paintings of something that most Americans had never seen: Ireland and its citizens. The advent of photography allowed for authentic images of Ireland to be acquired, but the distribution and display of such photographs relied heavily on another entertainment form: the magic lantern.

Various kinds of phantasmagoria and lantern shows had been staged in America throughout the first half of the nineteenth century. However, it was not until 1850 that the Langenheim brothers presented the first photographic glass slide.[1] As Charles Musser has noted:

> Photography provided the first key element of standardization in screen practice. With the ability to make multiple copies of a single image, slide producers now had a process of manufacture that was much more efficient than hand painting, and this development was accompanied by corresponding advances in lithography, which was also used to make lantern-slide images. Multiple photographic images could be smaller than painted slides yet provided greater detail and were much cheaper to produce. Lanterns could be scaled down, made more portable, and sold for less. Screen practitioners had begun to adopt methods of industrial manufacture.[2]

Photographic slides experienced gradual growth during the 1850s and 1860s.[3] However, their numbers increased greatly during the 1880s and beyond, as did their appearances at various kinds of public events.

2.1  The Chicago Transparency
Company's *Road Scene,*
*County Galway.*

2.2  Underwood and Underwood's
*Harvesting on the Island*
*of Achill, Ireland.*

From the end of the US Civil War to the early twentieth century, slide manufacturers produced a large number of non-fiction slides of Ireland. In keeping with other 'foreign views', as they were often called, most of these slides featured expeditionary images, offering rural and urban landscapes to audiences who became tourists travelling through Ireland by means of lantern projections. A smaller number of non-fiction slides offered ethnographic images of Irish people at work or in social settings like marketplaces; here again the slides attempted to convey authentic visual information to the eyes of American tourists. While such non-fiction slides appeared at various venues, they were most commonly projected in illustrated travel lectures.

By contrast, fictional Irish-themed slides of the nineteenth century generally relied on cartoon artwork to create what in most cases were stereotypical images for comedic purposes. Slide manufacturers also produced fictional slides to function as illustrated songs. While illustrated song slides emerged in the nineteenth century, they experienced their peak of popularity during the nickelodeon era. In the same way that the words spoken during illustrated travel lectures helped audiences to interpret the non-fiction slides they viewed, music lyrics interacted with song slide visuals, thus framing their meaning.

In some cases, the boundaries between non-fiction and fiction lantern slides became blurred. During the early years of Irish non-fiction lantern slides, numerous lecturers and slide presenters regularly integrated them into fictional entertainment. For example, *Howarth's Hibernica* projected non-fiction slides of Irish landscapes in 1883; one period account noted that 'as the panorama and lecture progress, stage performances take place illustrating life and character on the "auld sod" '.[4] A review of the show in Tyrone, Pennsylvania, suggested it was 'so funny that the whole opera house shook with laughter and everybody went home smiling'.[5] Rather than fulfilling a strictly educational remit, the non-fiction slides participated in entertainment that included fictional elements.

More commonly, the effort to combine non-fiction slides with fictional entertainment involved music. In 1870, *MacEvoy's New Hibernicon* featured 'brilliantly illuminated transparent pictures' of rural and urban Ireland, as well as slides depicting the 'life of St Patrick'. Professor Currier gave a 'descriptive and historical lecture', but the *Hibernicon* also featured 'immortal Irish melodies'. The singers included two women and one man, 'Barney, the Guide', who offered 'illustrations of Irish wit and song'.[6] The use of such music continued at lantern performances in subsequent years. In 1886, the 'Morrisseys' offered a *Panorama of Ireland* that featured Miles Morris, a 'patriotic Irish vocalist as lecturer'.[7] Professor Snider's 'Lecture Concert' on Ireland in 1892 and Professor Allen's *A Bicycle Trip Through Ireland* in 1897 also featured music.[8] Perhaps the most elaborate of these musical performances was Professor Morrow's 1895 *Photorama of Ireland and Scotland*, featuring as it did 'a choir of twenty voices ... to sing the national airs as the various scenes are displayed'.[9]

In other cases, manufacturers prepared sets of lantern slides that combined non-fiction and fiction images. In an effort to tell a single, visual narrative, the ten-slide series *Killarney* – created by the Briggs Company and sold by Kleine Optical in 1905 – included some slides featuring artwork of fictional scenes and some slides featuring hand-coloured authentic photographs. For Slides 2 (*Bounteous Nature Loves All Land*), 4 (*Innisfallen's Ruined Shrine*), 5 (*Still At Muckross You Must Pray*) and 10 (*Wings of Angels So Might Shine*), Briggs used photographs of relevant scenery; for example, Slide 10 is a photograph of the Lakes of Killarney. By contrast, Slides 3 (*Angels Fold Their Wings*), 7 (*Angels Often Pausing There*), 8 (*Music There for Echo Dwells*) and 9 (*Tinge the Cloud Wreaths in the Sky*) were relevant artwork. Slide 7, for example, is an illustration of an angel playing a harp.[10] Thus, from slide to slide, an audience would have witnessed a regular shift between fiction and non-fiction visuals.

Catalogues published by American slide manufacturers generally attempted to draw distinctions between non-fiction Irish-themed slides, which represented 'genuine' views of a foreign country, and fictional Irish-themed slides, which usually depicted stereotypical characters through artwork. Many of the people who projected these slides would have placed faith in the same categories. For example, travel lecturers usually screened authentic images of actual sites; by contrast, singers using illustrated song slides offered fictional narratives through music and projected images. However, the boundaries between the two kinds of Irish-themed slides continued to be porous throughout the nineteenth and early twentieth centuries for numerous reasons, as non-fiction slides often attempted to be entertaining and fictional slides often attempted to be viewed as authentic.

## Non-fiction Lantern Slides

Non-fiction lantern slides of Ireland appeared in the United States at least as early as 1864, but their numbers increased greatly during the 1880s and 1890s, as catalogues for various lantern slide manufacturers and distributors attest. Such growth suggests the popularity not only of Irish-themed slides, but also of the larger category known as 'foreign views'. As Jens Ruchatz has noted, 'The latter half of the nineteenth century saw travel as an overriding subject in projection practice.'[11] Many of these foreign views originated from French and English lantern suppliers. For example, the US company Benerman & Wilson acquired a large number of slides depicting various countries of the world from the American agency of the French firm of Levy & Company.[12] In other cases, American slide manufacturers employed their own photographers to take needed images. While these slides could be screened at homes or other private settings, their projection at theatres resulted in an enormous size; as Ruchatz has noted, 'the projected travel photograph seemed to transport its audience to the very spot where it had been recorded'.[13]

As with other travel slides, the Irish-themed lantern slide initially concentrated solely on urban and rural landscapes and showed no people. However, that changed during the final decades of the nineteenth century. Advances in photographic technology resulted in faster shutter speeds, which meant that it became easier to obtain quality images of people and other objects that were moving. That allowed for the creation of expeditionary images that depicted on-screen tourists visiting notable Irish locations, as well as for ethnographic images that depicted Irish citizens at work. The result of these advancements can be seen in such late-nineteenth- and early-twentieth-century slides as the Chicago Transparency Company's *Road Scene, County Galway*, which shows an Irish jaunting car in motion, and Underwood & Underwood's *Harvesting on the Island of Achill, Ireland*, which shows two women working in a field. Along with these kinds of rural views, many slides offered urban images of people walking through streets and markets. Even people or horses moving in the background of a location no longer resulted in flawed or blurred images, as a slide of Cork's statue of Father Mathew (released by George Kanzee of San Francisco) attests.

**2.3** Underwood and Underwood's *A Fireside Scene, County Kerry, Ireland*.

With the growing number of ethnographic slides came an increase in the number of slides that show people and/or animals deliberately posed by a photographer for particular reasons, including images that fitted certain nineteenth-century stereotypes. For example, Moore, Bond & Company sold a slide entitled *Irish Pig – A Favored Boarder*, which featured staged imagery of Irish cohabitation with farm animals. Similarly, an Underwood & Underwood slide entitled *A Fireside Scene, County Kerry, Ireland* shows an obviously posed couple seated in front of a fireplace inside a cottage; two pigs inhabit the same space.[14] These images call into question the authenticity of at least some non-fiction slides.

Much the same could be said of some hand-coloured slides. Locations depicted in these slides were authentic and their photographic quality was usually quite professional, meaning that their images feature precise focus and skilled visual composition. Hand colouring added beautiful tints to these slides, resulting in increased prices from their manufacturers and – at least at times – increased publicity for those who projected them. However, such colour tints were not authentic. Some companies like Underwood & Underwood – a company formed in 1880 in Ottawa, Kansas and then relocated to New York City in 1887 – had artists who used muted shades and colours that would appear realistic, whereas others used garish and vibrant colours that created a distinctly unnatural appearance. For example, L.J. Marcy's slide *The Giant's Gate – The Giant's Causeway* has a sky that features layers of blue, purple and green; the same company's *Upper Lakes*

**2.4** L. J. Marcy's *The Giant's Gate –*
*The Giant's Causeway*; its sky features
layers of blue, purple, and green
colour tints.

**2.5** T. H. McAllister's
*Ireland–Panorama of Donegal.*

*of Killarney* offers a similarly bizarre blend of colours in the sky, as well as an inordinate amount of bright purple foliage.

Whether or not they used hand-tinted colours or posed models, some Irish-themed lantern slides could be viewed without need of a lantern or even a slide. For example, Underwood & Underwood released numerous lantern slides depicting Irish landscapes and Irish citizens. In 1896, the company began selling many of its slide images to newspapers and magazines. By 1901, the key component of Underwood & Underwood's sales had become stereoscopic photographs (or 'stereo views', as they were often called) for use in home stereoscopic viewers. In fact, the company chose to concentrate on stereo views after the success of *Tour of the World*, a set of seventy-two stereo views released in 1897.[15] Stereo views had already gained popularity with upper-income families during the post-Civil War era; by the 1880s, competition, price reductions and widespread availability (including through door-to-door sales) meant that members of other economic classes purchased them.[16] As with the newspaper and magazine licences, these stereo views allowed for the images on Irish-themed lantern slides to appear in other media.

## Lantern Slides for Sale

The rise of Irish-themed lantern slides in the United States was hardly immediate. For example, W. Langenheim did not sell any Irish slides in an 1850 catalogue, or in an 1861 catalogue, the latter of which did offer glass slides of Egypt, Italy, Germany, Switzerland, France, England and

Scotland.[17] It would not be until after the end of the US Civil War that slides of Ireland were readily available from US companies. During the last twenty-five years of the nineteenth century, the number of such slides increased exponentially. By 1894, for example, William H. Rau's catalogue offered over 130 different slides of Ireland.[18] Such increased numbers were hardly unique to the topic of Ireland and the Irish, as the lantern slide business had grown during those same years, as had the number of slides they sold of all 'foreign views'.

Using T.H. McAllister's company as an example, it is possible to see that two approaches emerged for the sale of non-fiction lantern slides. In 1865, T.H. McAllister – a member of a family that had sold optical goods in the United States since 1796 – opened a business in New York City that sold slides and lanterns. By 1890, his catalogue claimed to offer the 'largest assortment' of optical and lantern supplies in America.[19] The evolution of his business included an evolution in the numbers and kinds of Irish-themed slides that he sold. For example, in his 1867 catalogue, McAllister offered 'foreign views' of nine different countries, including England and Scotland. However, at that time, he did not sell any non-fiction slides of Ireland.[20]

By the time of his November 1882 catalogue, McAllister offered fifty-eight different slides of Ireland as part of his *Places of Interest – Foreign* series, a larger number than he offered of China, Japan or India, but eleven fewer slides than he sold of Scotland, and only one third as many as he sold of England.[21] The Irish slides – available for individual purchase – included images of Belfast, Dublin, Cork, Waterford, Galway, Limerick and Killarney; their content included such man-made structures as castles, abbeys, colleges and cathedrals, as well as such natural scenery as the Cliffs of Moher, the Giant's Causeway and the Gap of Dunloe. In addition, he sold *Lakes of Killarney – View of the Lakes*, a slide that featured a proto-moving picture: by use of a lever on the side of the slide, a moon would rise over the lakes.[22] While these slides could be used in the home, their general audience seems to have been lecturers who would use them to construct their own public presentations.

McAllister's second approach was to offer slides that had to be purchased in sets. Each set was accompanied by its own printed lecture, allowing the buyer to give public presentations without having to programme slides or write speeches. In the case of Ireland, McAllister offered two different sets in 1882. *Ireland, the North and the West* included fifty views of such cities as Belfast, Derry, Galway and Limerick, with individual slides depicting such sites as Dunluce Castle and the Giant's Causeway.[23] The second set, *Ireland, the South*, consisted of sixty slides depicting Dublin, Kilkenny, Cork and Killarney, with individual slides showing such images as *The Colleen Bawn Rock and Cave*, the *Glengariff Waterfall* and *Ross Castle*.[24] Based upon their titles, it seems that the lectures addressed audience members as tourists who were hurriedly shown site after site with brief spoken comments on each. Moreover, the titles of individual slides suggest the possibility that some of them duplicated those slides sold individually in the *Places of Interest – Foreign* series.

McAllister's slides of foreign countries apparently sold quite well during the rest of the nineteenth century. By 1898, he had greatly enlarged his *Places of Interest* series, so much so that each country received a separate series name (for example, *Places of Interest – Scotland*, *Places of Interest – France*, and so forth).[25] In his catalogue that year, he offered nearly 750 different non-fiction slides of Ireland, all of which could be bought in black-and-white or in hand-tinted colour. Given their sheer numbers, McAllister categorized the slides by county name (with twenty-five of Ireland's thirty-two counties represented); these categories were then subdivided by the name of the city, town or region. Such numbers meant that McAllister greatly expanded the number of slides depicting sites that he had covered in previous years; in 1898, he offered thirty-eight different slides of the *Giant's Causeway and Vicinity*, as opposed to four in 1882. In addition, he also offered slides on many regions and towns that had not been represented in his 1882 catalogue, such as, for example, six different slides of the small Irish town of Ardmore.

*Places of Interest – Ireland* also illustrates a growth in photographic content. To be sure, many of the new slides seem similar to those sold in 1882. They represent landscapes and panoramas of cities, as well as such sites as ancient crosses, round towers, abbeys, cathedrals and bridges. However, a number of the slides McAllister sold in his 1898 catalogue included ethnographic content, focussing on Irish people and various aspects of their daily lives. These included images of rural life, such as *Farm on Carlingford Bay* (County Louth), *Typical Irish Home* (Donegal), *Digging Potatoes on a Hillside* (Glendalough), *Making Hay* (Achill Island) and *Killarney Boatmen*, as well as of urban life, such as *Grand Parade* (Cork), *Fish Market* (Youghal), *Baker* (Newry) and *Going Shopping* (Kildare). Other slides in the 1898 catalogue were propagandistic. Some of them depict Irish nationalists, such as *Parnell Addressing the People, Westport* (County Mayo) and *The People Cheering Parnell, Westport* (County Mayo); others reflect economic woes in scenes that may well have been staged, such as *Police Returning from an Eviction* (Cork), *An Evicted House* (Glendalough) and *Beggar Women* (Queenstown).

Whereas McAllister's individual slides of Ireland had increased heavily in number, his slide sets with prepared lectures on the subject had decreased.

Rather than continue to sell *Ireland, the North and West* and *Ireland the South*, McAllister offered only one non-fiction slide set in 1898. Written by Fitzgerald O'Cavan in 1885 and illustrated by sixty-one slides, *Our Tour in Ireland* was intended to be an approximately one-hour lecture. Its title was apt, as the lecture quickly moved from Queens-town Harbour (depicted on the first slide, as if the audience is a tourist who

2.6 T. H. McAllister's *Ireland – Queen's College, Belfast.*

has just arrived in Ireland) to Cork, Killarney, Tipperary, Limerick, Galway, Sligo, Donegal, Derry, the Giant's Causeway, Belfast, Tara and Dublin. The lecture included images of *An Irish Jaunting Car* and *Railway Travel*, which served not only to explain Irish modes of transportation (particularly the requisite jaunting car), but also to simulate the audience's geographical movements. The tour came to a conclusion with a *Portrait of Edmund Burke* (slide 59), *Portrait of Robert Emmett* (slide 60) and *Erin go bragh* (slide 61), which, unlike the first fifty-eight slides, were topics depicted by artwork rather than photography.[26] At any rate, the structure of O'Cavan's text would prove highly influential on professional lecturers.

Other manufacturers continued to sell new lantern slides and slide sets during the early years of the twentieth

2.7 T. H. McAllister's *Shetland Ponies.*

century. In 1905, for example, the L. Manasse Company offered a 'short lecture set' on Ireland that consisted of a brief lecture and twelve slides available in either black-and-white or hand-tinted colour.[27] In keeping with the parallel approach of selling both lecture sets and individual slides, L. Manasse also offered eighty non-fiction Irish slides for individual purchase. While most of those slides depicted landscapes, a small number were ethnographic, such as *Peasant and Donkey Cart, Killarney* and *Natives of Mourne, County Down*.[28] Despite the influx of such new slides, however, many of those from the 1870s and 1880s continued to be sold into the twentieth century. While McAllister had ceased offering *Ireland, the North and West* and *Ireland the South*, both slide sets appear for sale in L. Manasse's 1905 catalogue; these featured the same lectures, as well as the same slides listed in the same order as they had nearly twenty-five years earlier in McAllister's catalogue.[29]

While it is difficult to discern the sales numbers for such lantern slides, they continued to be sold during the nickelodeon era. In 1906, for example, the Lantern & Film Exchange offered 254 different slides of Ireland; the following year, Moore, Bond & Company offered the same 254 slides in their own catalogue.[30] These included expeditionary images (including those sites that had already appeared in non-fiction cinema, such as *Shooting the Rapids, Killarney*), as well as ethnographic images. The final twenty-nine slides in the group of 254 were categorized separately as 'Irish Scenes and Characters', which included such slides as *Wild Irish Rose (Girl), Gathering Sea-weed, Irish Peasant Farmer, Irish Carrying Home Turf For Fuel* and three versions of *Irish Woman Spinning Flax*. Rather than capture the daily life and work of the Irish people, *Bothering a Tourist* attempted to be humorous. Others in the group of twenty-nine depicted economic troubles, such as *An Evicted Tenant and Family, Battering Down an Irish Home* and *Evicted Widow and Orphans at Cross*.

Slides also continued to be sold during the nickelodeon era in sets of ready-made lectures. In 1908, *Moving Picture World* wrote about the 'Cult of the Travelogue', in which they noted the 'increasing demand from theatre managers for some interesting and instructive feature to introduce into the regular moving picture entertainment'. They announced that Williams, Brown & Earle was the 'first in the field' with short 'lecturette[s]' that consisted of 'beautifully colored slides' accompanied by 'printed lectures'. Subjects ranged from 'Lincoln' and 'art, statuary' to 'travelogues' on a large number of countries, including the 'beauty spots of Scotland, England, Ireland, etc'.[31] Most of the slides in their Irish lecture were non-fiction, hand-tinted photographs of landscapes, but one image was a cartoon drawing of a man attempting to kiss the Blarney Stone. That same

2.8 A slide from Williams, Brown, and Earle's 1908 prepared 'lecturette'
*Picturesque Emerald Isle*, which was intended for use in nickelodeons.

year, *Moving Picture World* reported on the release of 'Ingram's
Lecturettes', which consisted of 'twelve beautifully colored slides and a
written lecture of about twenty minutes'. The subjects ranged from travelogues of *The Hudson River* and *Egypt and the Egyptians* to *Glimpses of
Spain and Morocco* and *The Lakes of Killarney*.[32]

## The Irish-Themed Illustrated Lecture

With the rise of lantern slides featuring 'foreign views' came a rise in the
number of illustrated travel lectures, which proved extremely popular in the
years following the American Civil War. Some audience members saw images
of places where they had once travelled, or where they might hope to travel in
the future. Others witnessed scenes of countries that they would have never
seen, countries that they could never afford to visit. As one American poster
promoting an illustrated travelogue in the 1880s proclaimed: 'No railway or
steamboat fares; no hotel expenses; no harpy waiters and guides to fee; no
peril to life or limb; no sea-sickness; in short, the pleasure of travelling and
"sight-seeing" without the annoyance and expense.'[33]

Lecturers at such events not only projected lantern slides as a visual aid,
but in many cases they also verbally interacted with images, suggesting
possible interpretations to the audience ranging from empirical data to

anecdotal stories. While many lecturers wrote their own lectures, others used prepared text sold by slide manufacturers or available in books. Written by Edward L. Wilson, *Wilson's Lantern Journeys* offered text for illustrated lectures on a large array of countries, including (in his 1888 edition) Ireland.[34] The Irish lecture included text for 108 slides that began with an approach of the coastline, continued with Dublin, Cork, Galway, Derry and Belfast, and included such famous spots as Blarney Castle, the Lakes of Killarney, the Gap of Dunloe, Muckross Abbey, Kate Kearney's Cottage, the Giant's Causeway and – with a written reference to Boucicault – the Colleen Bawn Rock. Wilson wrote most of the text with a formal tone, though for Slide 39, *Paddy and His Pigs*, he offered quotations from a character named 'little Mickey', who speaks with a stereotypical dialect while driving his pigs to market.[35]

During the late nineteenth and early twentieth centuries, lecturers who used lantern slides presented various kinds of public talks on Irish topics. Some of these covered Irish art and culture. For example, in Hartford, Connecticut, in 1905, Father Flanagan presented his lecture *Irish Art*.[36] Then, in Massachusetts in 1909, Reverend Thomas H. O'Connor projected fifty slides during his lecture *Ancient Celtic Art, Ancient Language, and Cult of the Celtic People*.[37] Other illustrated lectures covered Thomas Moore's poetry, as occurred in Lowell, Massachusetts, in 1894, and in Boston in 1906 and 1907.[38]

Historical lectures using lantern slides were also popular. In 1900, the Reverend Father Sheehy delivered a talk on Irish history in Washington, DC.[39] In 1906, Patrick J. Haltigan, editor of the *National Hibernian*, lectured in New York City on *Irishmen in the American Revolution and Their Early Influences in the Colonies*; the following year, he presented *Historic Ireland, Its Music, Soldiers are Statesmen*, which used 150 slides.[40] Illustrated lectures were also given on such topics as the life of Robert Emmet, as occurred in New York City in 1915.[41]

Even more common were illustrated lectures on the subject of Saint Patrick. In 1899, for example, the Reverend Dr Green gave a talk in Cedar Rapids, Iowa, on *The Life and Times of St Patrick*.[42] Then, in 1907, the Reverend T.P. Hurley delivered an illustrated lecture entitled *Ireland and St Patrick*.[43] Three years later, the Brayton Manufacturing Company of Chicago created and offered for sale a 'special lecturette' entitled *Life of St Patrick*. The set included twelve hand-coloured slides and text for a short lecture, allowing speakers with little or no knowledge of the subject to present the topic at nickelodeons.[44]

Politics and propaganda, which usually promoted Irish freedom, consti-tuted another form of the illustrated lecture. Some of these addressed the

**2.9** *O'Connell Monument in Glasnevin Cemetery, Dublin,*
from John L. Stoddard's first illustrated lecture on Ireland.

issue within broad parameters, such as a 1904 lecture on *Hibernianism* given in New York that was 'filled with beautiful and pathetic pictures of the past, realistic descriptions of the present, and inspiring predictions of the future'.[45] Two years later, the Reverend Father Hurley's 1906 lecture in Boston covered Irish 'military, ecclesiastical, political, and social history'; William E. Curtis and the 'Honorable' Michael J. Ryan's lecture *Ireland's Past and Present*, presented in Washington, DC, in 1909, also offered a broad approach to the subject.[46] Other lectures focussed more specifically on freedom in Ireland, such as the Reverend Michael J. Mitchell's 1904 lecture in New York; titled *Ireland a Nation*, it concluded with 'lantern views of scenes in Ireland'.[47]

However, the dominant form of illustrated lecture on Ireland was the travel lecture. In these cases, the bulk of the lantern slides offered scenic, expeditionary views of Ireland; as the nineteenth century progressed, ethnographic slides were incorporated, though generally in much smaller numbers than the expeditionary slides. The lecturers not only projected these images, but also commented on them, usually interpreting them as if the audience members were tourists abroad, rather than Irish immigrants watching slides of their homeland. As a review of the Morrissey's *Panorama of Ireland* suggested in 1886, one could see Ireland 'without experiencing the sea

**2.10** *Site of the Banquet Hall, Tara Hill*, from John L. Stoddard's
second illustrated lecture on Ireland.


sickness'.[48] Such lectures on Ireland were popular, but represented only one
topic within the larger and popular category of illustrated travel lectures.

Indeed, some slides and discussions of Ireland occurred within lectures
that also discussed other countries. Some of these provided visual tours of
the world, such as M.M. Ballou's 1887 lecture *Round the World in One
Evening* and Professor Rue's 1894 lecture on the same subject.[49] In other
cases, tour lectures covered a smaller number of countries. For example, a
'Mr Bolton' offered a 'tour through Ireland, Scotland, and England' in
1884 with a series of 'fine views'; three years later, John L. Barbour gave
illustrated lectures on the *British Isles*, which included a section on
Ireland.[50] Others lectured on even more specific geography. In 1882, Harry
W. French presented *Over the Ocean: Ireland and Scotland*.[51] Using
coloured slides and a thirty-foot screen, French combined 'humor and
poetry' into a lecture that took the audience 'to Blarney Castle in a jaunting car, a tour among the Lakes of Killarney, Dublin, [and] the Giant's
Causeway and its legendary origin' before then shifting to Scotland.[52]

In most cases, however, illustrated travel lectures covering Ireland
focussed on that country alone. Shortly before the US Civil War ended,
H.B. McKeon, manager of the Hope Chapel on Broadway in New York
City, booked *The Mammoth Stereoscopticon [sic], Or, [A] Mirror of the
Universe*. As part of a lecture series entitled *Tour of the World*, an

individual performance was devoted to *Scenes from Ireland*. To build interest in the lecture, McKeon claimed that his show had 'never before [been] exhibited in any part of the world' and that his lantern slides depicted 'many local scenes of thrilling interest'. The appearance of lectures on Ireland within a larger series of travel lectures continued for decades thereafter.[53]

However, it would only be after the Civil War that his travel lectures on Ireland proliferated. These subsequent lectures sometimes featured sophisticated linguistic and visual devices to give the audience members a sense that they were tourists in foreign lands. Describing Harry W. French's lecture *Ireland and the Irish* in 1886, the *Boston Globe* wrote:

> Starting from New York, Mr French took his listeners, in imagination, on board of a big Cunarder out upon the waters of the Atlantic, across the sea to Dublin Bay, which he calls the distinct and appropriate entrance to Ireland. As the ship entered the harbor, the different points of interest and beautiful scenery were finely depicted upon the large canvas, while Mr French described everything so minutely as to leave a lasting impression upon the minds of his listeners, and almost make a person believe that he was really in the country so described.[54]

Though it owed a debt to Fitzgerald O'Cavan, French's lecture took the tourist-based approach to a greater extreme and would have a crucial influence on future lecturers. For example, Francis Dillon-Eagan used a similar approach in 1889 when he gave a two-part lecture entitled *A Picturesque Tour Through Ireland* at the Atheneum in Brooklyn, New York. With the aid of approximately 100 slides, Dillon-Eagan began by projecting a slide of a steamship at New York's harbour. He then described the 'trials and pleasures' of life aboard ship before arriving at Queenstown Harbour and then beginning a journey around Ireland.[55]

Such tourist-based lectures on Ireland continued well into the twentieth century. In 1902, for example, Garrett P. Serviss gave his lecture *Ireland, From Killarney's Lakes to the Giant's Causeway* at the Brooklyn Institute; he developed the talk after travelling to Ireland himself, an experience that the *Brooklyn Daily Eagle* described as 'love at first sight'.[56] In 1907, *Views and Film Index* reported that several lantern lectures on Ireland were underway, such as the Reverend George W. Reynolds *Ireland and the Irish People* and the Reverend George Worrall's *Auld Ireland*.[57] Five years later, Mary Meyers lectured in Boston on *Picturesque Ireland*.[58] Then, in New

York in 1915, Frank W. McGurk gave an illustrated lecture called *A Junket through Ireland*.[59] A number of these lectures incorporated Harry W. French's basic approach to the subject, such as depicting the ocean voyage to Ireland and/or the tourists' landing at either Cork or Dublin.[60]

The tone of these lectures varied from the serious to the humorous. For example, in 1890, the Reverend Lindsay Parker offered his *Pictorial Tour through the Emerald Isle*, which used approximately sixty slides. In addition to describing various locations in Ireland, Parker offered 'English, Irish, and Dutch dialect stories' that 'delight[ed] his listeners'.[61] Similarly, in Maryland in 1892, Dr C.N. Whitney attempted to infuse his *A Trip to Ireland* with both lantern slides and 'humorous' stories.[62] Years later, in 1913, the 'Irish orator' Mr Corkey attempted to do the same at a lecture in Michigan.[63] In such cases, non-fiction slides were combined with overt attempts to entertain, rather than merely educate; in some cases, such entertainment as 'dialect stories' may well have been fictional tales told with affected, 'stage Irish' accents and mannerisms.

While most of these lectures were intended for the general public, a much smaller number in the early twentieth century were sponsored by Irish-American organizations. In 1904, for example, the Ancient Order of Hibernians opened a lecture bureau that was promoted in the *National Hibernian*; their lecturers included Robert Turner, whose 1906 lectures included an *Evening in Ireland* (featuring 150 slides) and *Picturesque Ireland* (featuring 220 slides).[64] The following year, the *National Hibernian* promoted Professor Michael G. Rohan's talk *Beautiful Ireland*, which was 'illustrated with 100 handsomely colored lantern views'.[65] Some of these lectures occurred as part of St Patrick's Day celebrations in such cities as Boston, Chicago and New York City.[66] The extent to which these lectures differed from those given to general audiences is difficult to discern. In some cases, if lecturers such as Robert Turner purchased slides from companies such as T.H. McAllister, they could have projected many of the same images as, say, a lecturer such as George Worrall. Instead, the key differences probably occurred in the verbal presentation and interpretation of the images. Among other variances, lectures presented to Irish-American audiences may have emphasized themes like nostalgia rather than tourism.

Regardless of their intended audience, lecturers often used some of the same slides of Ireland over a period of decades, in part because dealers continued to sell the same slides; indeed, some audiences who attended more than one lecture on Ireland might have viewed some of the same slides on more than one occasion. As late as 1903, Thomas A. Curry presented *Our Tour of Ireland*, using the same slides and reading the same O'Cavan text that had been sold since 1885.[67] By contrast, to give the appearance of

**2.11** *The Keel Constabulary*, from one of Burton Holmes'
illustrated lectures on Ireland.

being more unique than their competition, other lecturers tried to distinguish themselves by publicizing the sheer number of slides that they
projected; for example, W.J. Walsh promoted the fact that he would screen
200 slides of Ireland in his 1904 lecture in Connecticut, as opposed to the
mere fifty or sixty slides that some of his competition used.[68] The following
year, publicity for J.P. O'Mahoney's lecture in Indianapolis, Indiana, highlighted the fact that he projected 150 slides and that among them could be
found images of every Irish county.[69]

Other lecturers promoted the quality of their slides. When giving a tour
lecture in Ironwood, Michigan, in 1899, Father Sheehy claimed 'to possess
the finest collection of Irish views in the world'.[70] More often, the emphasis on quality translated into publicity that promoted 'new' slides of
Ireland.[71] Some lecturers underscored the fact that they had taken their own
photographs in Ireland and thus projected unique slides. For example, in
Los Angeles in 1896, the Reverend William Horace Day's lecture included
photographs he had recently taken on a 'go-as-you-please' bicycle tour of
Ireland.[72] The following year, Frank C. Davis gave a similar lecture in Los
Angeles entitled *A Trip through Ireland on a Bicycle*; in it, he featured
approximately 100 'lantern views' that, with the exception of four
portraits, he had shot himself.[73]

While the popularity of such lectures seems clear, given the sheer number
of them that occurred from the end of the US Civil War until 1915, some

2.12 *Selling Mountain Dew*, from one of Burton Holmes' illustrated lectures on Ireland.

newspaper accounts recorded audience responses that further substantiate that fact. Speaking of an 1895 lecture on Ireland, the *Boston Globe* noted the 'appreciative eyes of the thoroughly delighted audience'.[74] The *Chicago Tribune* noted an even more excited audience in 1910. The newspaper claimed the lecturer 'practically abandoned talking to allow his enthusiastic "hearers" to enjoy and cheer the lantern views of Erin's Isle'.[75]

However, negative responses could occur if audiences believed the lecturer was ill-informed or biased, particularly if audience members were Irish-American. In 1910, the *Gaelic American* complained of a 'silly [illustrated] lecture on Ireland' given by the Board of Education in New York City, which they believed was 'an insult to the intelligence of the serious minded people of Irish or any other extraction'.[76] The newspaper concluded by suggesting that 'not only in New York, but elsewhere, should these tour lectures die a sudden death', adding that representatives of Irish societies should keep 'a watchful eye out for the ignoramus who tackles an Irish subject' in order to be 'rid of all this class of entertainer'.[77]

## The Lecturers

Between 1865 and 1915, a large array of people gave lectures on the subject of Ireland. Some of them, such as the aforementioned Garrett P. Serviss, maintain an important place in the history of illustrated lectures, with Ireland being only one of many topics on which they lectured. Others, such as the aforementioned Reverend William Horace Day, were amateur lecturers who possessed a particular interest in Ireland. Examining these people reveals what is hardly surprising: they exemplify a wide diversity of backgrounds and wide array of reasons for giving their lectures.

Most of the lecturers were men, though a small number of the lecturers who presented tours of Ireland were women. In 1889, Sarah D. Hamlin lectured on *Picturesque Ireland* with a series of 'exceptional views'.[78] Nearly two decades later, the Hibernian Lecture Bureau promoted Mrs

Katharine A. O'Keefe-O'Mahoney's illustrated lecture on *Famous Irish Women*.[79] However, the most famous woman to lecture on Ireland was Kathleen Mathew, touted in advertisements as 'Erin's Gifted Daughter'. She presented 'pictorial reviews' for numerous years, ranging from at least as early as 1907 to as late as 1917.[80] Mathew appeared at many of these lectures wearing 'Irish costume', and sometimes giving an 'exhibition of Irish step dancing'.[81] She also offered 'dramatic impersonations of great Irishmen at their best'.[82] A 1914 review of her lecture claimed that her 'recitals are very much out of the ordinary... it is said [she] completely captivates an audience'.[83]

Of the men who lectured on Ireland, some of them were not professionals in the field, but instead were associated with other careers. In 1881, a Judge Bick utilized the 'Euryscope' to illustrate his 'rambles taken through Ireland'.[84] Then, in 1888, the Honourable E.S. Taylor, secretary of the Lincoln Park Board in Chicago, gave illustrated lectures entitled *Ireland* after completing his own 'extensive' travels in the country.[85] Many others were either priests or preachers. In Boston in 1887, for example, Father O'Callaghan 'commenced to describe his travels in Ireland, illustrating his topics with 120 views'.[86] Two years later in Lowell, Massachusetts, the Reverend D.M. Burns offered an Irish lecture 'spiced with humorous references', but which also included a 'serious side'; the lecture was 'finely illustrated by the lantern'.[87] Then, in 1895, the Reverend J.J. McNulty offered his *Scenes and Scenery of Ireland* at the Grand Opera House in Boston.[88]

However, many of these lecturers attempted to make their living from the magic lantern. Some were self-appointed 'professors' who travelled from town to town and city to city. These included 'Professor Latham', who lectured on Ireland in New York in 1886.[89] To maintain bookings each season, such professional lecturers had to develop new lectures with some regularity. Harry W. French, who figures so importantly in the history of the Irish-themed lecture, continued to craft new lectures on the subject in the years following his 1886 *Ireland and the Irish*; for example, in 1890, he offered *Scenes of Ireland*.[90] The extent to which such new lectures represented new slides and verbal accompaniment is unknown; it is possible that, outside of the new lecture title, the changes were minimal.

As for those professional speakers who focussed solely on Ireland, the most notable was Seamus MacManus, the Irish-born author, poet and folklorist who gained fame in part by writing for Irish-American newspapers in the 1890s. He began extensive lecture tours in 1906, offering such subjects as *The Glories, the Sorrows, and the Hopes of Ireland*, *Irish Fairy and Folk-Lore* and *A Rollicking Ramble in Ireland*, the latter of which was illustrated with 100 slides.[91] MacManus presented his lectures to Irish-

American organizations, as well as to general audiences across the United States. Reviewing one of his talks, the vice-president of the National Geographic Society said:

> Rarely has a lecturer captured a National Geographic Society audience as did Seamus MacManus, the audience over which I presided in November [1909], with his *Rollicking Ramble in Ireland*. The large lecture hall of the society was crowded, and several hundred members were turned away. Mr MacManus' pictures were unusually good, but far more potent was his own personality, which breathes the spirit of Ireland itself, with its humor, its naivete, and its mysticism.[92]

MacManus continued to give a variation of the lecture, which he retitled *A Merry Ramble 'Round Ireland*, in 1911. By that time, he used 150 lantern slides, all of them 'exquisite panoramic illustrations' incorporated into a 'superbly entertaining monotravelogue'.[93] A review of the lecture as given in Los Angeles in 1913 noted that he created a 'colorful word picture' by accompanying his slides with 'humorous, fanciful, [and] pathetic' tales.[94]

Others gained notoriety by lecturing on Ireland and other subjects: for example, Professor A.S. Bickmore, who offered illustrated lectures on Ireland during the 1890s. His other lecture topics ranged from *North Atlantic Ocean – The Bermudas* to *Human Anatomy and Physiology*. The *New York Times* once suggested that 'there is nothing inexplicable about Professor Bickmore's popularity as a lecturer to one who has never heard him. His minute knowledge of every detail of his subject, combined with an animated delivery, is bound to capture any audience.'[95] Though he apparently confined his lectures to New York, he gave dozens of lectures on numerous topics, often presenting them to groups of educators. Having travelled extensively in Ireland, Bickmore built a reputation on the uniqueness of his slides. Speaking of his 1894 lecture on Ireland, the *New York Times* noted his success with his audience, which they believed was 'due to the professor's chatty descriptions and to his happy choice of the order in which the illustrations were shown'.[96] Two weeks later, Bickmore offered a follow-up lecture entitled *Northern Ireland – The Giant's Causeway*, featuring slides made from photos he had taken on a trip to Ireland earlier that same year.[97]

Another notable lecturer was Professor Donald Downie, whom the *Atlanta Constitution* described as a 'versatile and entertaining Scotch barrister'; though he spoke on a variety of subjects, he was perhaps best known for his lecture *Napoleon Bonaparte*.[98] In 1889, Downie offered a lecture entitled *Ireland*, during which he exhibited 'nearly a hundred colored pictures'.[99] Four years

**2.13** *Paddy Makin' Love*, a surviving slide from T. H. McAllister's 'Economic Series' entitled *Irish Characters*.

later, he gave a talk entitled *Through the British Isles with a Camera*, during which he covered 'Scotland, Ireland, and England'.[100] He then returned to an Ireland-only lecture in 1894, during which he projected what were called 'original photographs', the implication being that he had taken them himself.[101] That same year, he also offered what was one of the more unique travel lectures on the subject, *Ireland and Japan*.[102]

However, the travelling public lecturer who presented the largest number of different lectures on the subject might well have been Professor A.G. Cromwell, who gave his talk *Ireland and the Lakes of Killarney* in 1886; the *New York Times* claimed it featured some of the 'most interesting' slides in his 'large collection'.[103] The following year, he offered *Ireland and the Irish* and *A Tour of Ireland* at the Grand Opera House in New York City.[104] He then returned to the subject in 1889 with both *Ireland* and a repeat of *Ireland and the Irish*.[105] In 1891, he once again gave a lecture entitled *Ireland*.[106] Whether such lectures were exactly the same as in prior years or not is unknown. At any rate, in 1892, he crafted yet another lecture, *Ireland, the Emerald Isle*.[107] That same year, he also included Ireland as part of his 'world tour' lecture presented at the Pittsburgh Exposition.[108]

## John L. Stoddard and E. Burton Holmes

While numerous people became well-known professional lecturers, the pre-eminent American travel lecturer of the nineteenth century was John L. Stoddard. Born in 1850, Stoddard began giving travel lectures as a teacher at the Boston Latin School in the 1870s. His lectures proved popular enough with students that he was soon asked to deliver them to public audiences.[109] By 1878, he was lecturing professionally and using what he called his 'Phaedroscope', a dissolving-view limelight lantern.[110] Later, Stoddard had a dissolving-view lantern built to his specifications by the C.T. Milligan company.[111] With it, Stoddard's operator could have:

> two identical lenses...focused on precisely the same area of the screen... each contained one view and were placed consecutively behind the left and right lenses. By turning a stop-cock, the operator gradually diverted the light from one lantern into another. The result on the screen was that the first picture faded from view while the next was emerging into complete clearness...The pictures projected by this new method took on astounding reality; they appeared as if from nowhere and dissolved into space.[112]

According to Stoddard's biographer, the dissolving views 'delighted' audiences, who 'flocked to his lectures'.[113]

For the next two decades, Stoddard became nationally famous, lecturing on various travel subjects to audiences often as large as 2,000 people.[114] His retirement in 1897 at the age of 47 coincided with the rise in popularity of a new travel lecturer.[115] In 1898, the *Syracuse Evening Herald* wrote:

> The announcement that John L. Stoddard, the eminent lecture, had retired from the field was a cause of great regret to many thousands throughout the country. Already, however, E. Burton Holmes, whose fame as a lecturer has been a well-established fact in the West for several seasons, seems to have most successfully assumed the mantle of his illustrious predecessor in Boston, New York, and other Eastern cities.[116]

Born in 1870, E. Burton Holmes – or Burton Holmes, as he would commonly be called in his publicity – began giving public travel lectures in 1893. An avid traveller, Ireland was the first country he visited on his many voyages around the world.[117] At any rate, the *Herald* was soon proven correct in its assessment, as during the twentieth century Holmes became even more famous than Stoddard. He would later be given credit for inventing the term 'travelogue', as well as for being the 'first lecturer to introduce an entire program of colored views'.[118] Holmes would go on to lecture for over five decades.[119]

Many reasons account for the Stoddard and Holmes's success. Both were good-looking and both were great orators. They travelled the world in pursuit of first-hand information, which set them apart from many other lecturers who simply purchased slides and spoke about countries they had never visited. Another key to their success was the fact that both men used slides in their lectures that were not purchased from American slide manufacturers; most of their images were unique to their lectures. Initially, Stoddard purchased his images from 'an agent in Paris who sent his photographers to practically every European country'.[120] He also relied on photographers in the areas he visited for supplementary photographs. Stoddard claimed that he later 'gave up this method and took all of his own views in order to have them up to the minute'.[121] Holmes took a slightly different approach. While at times he did obtain images from companies based in other countries, he generally relied on Oscar B. Depue, his photographer and lantern operator, to take photographs on their trips.[122]

Both Stoddard and Holmes lectured on a wide array of countries, including Ireland. Most of the texts used in nineteenth- and early-twentieth-century public lectures on Ireland no longer exist. Fortunately, both Stoddard and Holmes published their lectures in book form. In his first lecture on Ireland, John L. Stoddard took a very different approach from Fitzgerald O'Cavan and Harry W. French. He began with a prologue that was in part autobiographical:

> My first trip through Ireland was like the tour usually made by those who, in their eagerness to reach Great Britain and the continent, rush through the Emerald Isle as though the shabby, insignificant portal of a splendid palace. My recent tour convinced me that on the first occasion I had ignorantly passed by objects of transcendent value, as one unskilled in mineralogy might live above the fields of South Africa, yet die in poverty. The fact is, that for certain forms of natural scenery, memorials of Druid paganism, wonderful prehistoric relics, and priceless souvenirs or primitive Christianity, Ireland has no equal in the world. If one begins by pitying her, one ends by loving her.[123]

He then concluded his prologue with a lengthy discussion about British involvement in Ireland, claiming that 'England's mode of ruling Ireland in the past finds little justification either in common sense or in the laws of God and Man.'[124] Unlike many other travel lecturers, Stoddard actively took a position on the issue of Irish freedom.

Stoddard's lecture then shifted to his images of his own arrival at Dublin Bay, followed by a detailed tour of Dublin's major streets, bridges, cathedrals, museums and monuments. He spoke at length about Trinity College and the

Book of Kells held in its library, which provided the transition to his discussion of Christian and pagan sites and relics elsewhere in Ireland. That allowed him the opportunity not only to show relevant slides of such places as *Cong's Deserted Cloisters*, but also such landscapes as the *Entrance to Baltimore Harbor, County Cork*.[125] He concluded the lecture by drawing a brief connection between ancient Celtic and Egyptian civilizations, a comparison made perhaps due to widespread public interest in Egypt.[126]

In terms of style, Stoddard's text features occasional use of first-person and personal anecdotes, often in an effort to emphasize the fact that he was a world traveller and had personally visited the sites he discussed. For example, when speaking of 'Ogham stones', Stoddard told his audience:

> As I stood looking at the strange incisions, carved in the twilight of the Irish dawn on these rough monoliths, as messages to posterity, I thought of the stupendous temple-palaces at Thebes which I had seen but a few months before; and more than ever was I impressed with the mysterious law that seems to regulate the rise and fall of nations.[127]

Stoddard also used first person to advance his views, such as when he claimed the Irish needed to be 'lifted from the bestiality of drunkenness to a higher plane of self control'.[128] He did much the same in his continued commentary on the British, as when he notes his dismay that three 'educated' Englishmen were unable to tell him the distance between the English and Irish coasts.[129]

Unlike some of his other travel subjects, such as Denmark and Sweden, Stoddard created a second lecture on Ireland, which suggests his continued interest in the country, as well as the topic's popularity. In the second lecture, he complained that the 'tour of the average traveller in Ireland comprises Killarney, Blarney Castle, Dublin, and the Giant's Causeway, with scarcely more than a day allowed for each'.[130] Those words also act as an indictment of the O'Cavan–French style of Irish lecture, which rapidly showed audience members slides of important sites with little time to linger on them before moving onto yet another location.

Stoddard's second lecture discussed the fact that Ireland was a seat of learning in the sixth and seventh centuries, and he used that history to conduct a different kind of tour of Ireland, one that examined such sites as Newgrange, St Columba's home and a range of historic round towers, castles and standing stones. At the same time, Stoddard's second lecture incorporated a range of slides that were similar to those sold by various American companies. For example, he screened a slide of *An Irish Jaunting*

**2.14** Slide 4 from the illustrated song *They've Won Every Nation's Battles But Their Own* (DeWitt C. Wheeler, 1910).
*(Courtesy of the Marnan Collection, LLC, Minneapolis, Minnesota)*

*Car, Beautiful County Wicklow* and *A Bit of Galway Bay*; he also included a small number of ethnographic images, such as *Cutting Peat* and *An Exile's Mother*.

Once again, Stoddard used the first person and a range of anecdotes to emphasize his own travels. He also used at least one slide of himself, pictured in an extreme long shot entitled *Site of the Banquet Hall, Tara Hill*.[131] However, the second lecture operated differently from the first in that Stoddard incorporated more humour; when he recounted the words spoken to him by various Irish persons, he attempted to mimic their dialect.[132] He also used wit to address the issue of English rule, as when he recalled an English tourist asking an Irish guide about the prevalence of 'localities under the names of "The Devil's Glen", "The Devil's Bridge", and similar Satanic titles'. Stoddard recalled that the English tourist said, 'the devil seems to own a good deal of property around here', to which the Irish guide replied, 'Yes, sor [*sic*], but he's an absentee landlord, and lives in England.'[133]

Another key difference between the first and second lectures is the fact that the second included no prologue. Stoddard chose to end, rather than begin, his lecture with his personal reaction to Ireland and its history:

> 'Poor Ireland', I murmured, 'would that this harmony of cloudless firmament and tranquil sea might be symbolic of thy future, as the departed storm is emblematic of the past.' At present I believe that wish is likely to be realized. A brighter sky than ever yet made luminous this emerald of the northern seas is dawning on her happier, hope inspired children. The melancholy years of her heart-breaking history, dark with innumerable clouds of misery, have sunk below the horizon of the Past. Heaven forbid that any child of Albion or Erin should seek to resurrect the ghosts of those crime-blackened centuries! Let them remain, amid the countless other wrecks of poor humanity, forever buried in the ocean of oblivion.[134]

To illustrate his concluding thoughts on the subject, Stoddard offered a slide of an Irish-made anchor.

In his own lecture on Ireland, Burton Holmes adopted a tone similar to that of Stoddard's second lecture. While he mentioned such events as the Battle of the Boyne, Holmes avoided political comments about the British. Instead, he concentrated on tourist information, often conveyed with a sense of humour; for example, he noted that 'any traveller who has been rash enough to lean over the parapet of the O'Connell Bridge and take "a sniffy of the Liffey" will agree that it can never be mistaken for a field of new mown hay'.[135] In recounting his own experiences with the Irish, Holmes also attempted to convey their dialects. He went so far as to tell his audience: 'I defy anyone to travel along Irish roads and talk with the people and not acquire a temporary brogue; you feel peculiar and pedantic and unpleasantly superior if you continue to speak in your usual way.'[136]

Holmes borrowed Stoddard's device of being a tour guide who takes his audience from England to Dublin Bay, rather than by ocean voyage from America. Also like Stoddard, Holmes lingered on Dublin before moving onto such sites as Newgrange and various round towers and Celtic crosses. However, by incorporating fewer personal anecdotes than Stoddard, as well as by spending less time on individual sites, Holmes did take his audience on a more geographically encompassing tour of Ireland. For example, he included slides of Achill Island, Connemara, Limerick, Tipperary, Killarney, Cork and Belfast.

Holmes's lecture thus situated itself between Stoddard's two Irish lectures and the O'Cavan–French tradition. Where it created a unique place for itself was in its greater emphasis on ethnography. For example, Holmes included such slides (and accompanying commentary) as *Dublin Darlings, Colleens – Young and Old, The Keel Constabulary, Likeable Lads, Two Old Boys of Dooagh, Children of the Old Sod, Singing of Ireland's Woes, The Hillside Hermit* and *Selling Mountain Dew*.[137] With these images, Holmes avoided propaganda or personal judgments (as opposed to Stoddard's stated disdain for alleged Irish drunkenness), opting instead to fulfil the obligation he stated within the lecture: 'Travel and Learn.'[138]

That credo also led Holmes to incorporate another unique component into his lecture. The Stoddard and O'Cavan–French lectures generally avoided images of Irish modernity, but Holmes took a different approach. He quite noticeably featured images of automobiles, trams and trains. Such an interest in modes of travel is not surprising, nor is his interest in new technologies. After all, in the late 1890s, Holmes would gain his greatest fame by merging his travelogues with moving pictures.

# Fictional Slides

Companies producing and/or distributing Irish-themed lantern slides in America sold many that featured openly fictional content. During the nineteenth century, the number of fictional Irish-themed slides was quite small as compared to the number of non-fiction Irish-themed slides sold by the same manufacturers. Such slides were also quite different initially, given the fact that they generally featured cartoon artwork rather than photographs. However, that began to change with the rise in popularity of illustrated song slides during the nickelodeon era in which hundreds of Irish-themed song slides were produced using photographs of live models.

To examine the history of fictional Irish-themed slides, the T.H. McAllister company can once again serve as an example. While he sold no non-fiction slides of Ireland in his 1867 catalogue, McAllister did offer two fictional slides: *The Irish Flute Player (The Melody)* and *The Irish Flute Player (The Jig)*. These slides – like so many that would be sold in the year that followed – depicted stereotypical Irish characters for comical purposes. In addition, he offered various slides featuring comical images of African-Americans, Mexicans, the Chinese, the British and the Scottish.[139]

**2.15**  Slide 7 of Scott and Van Altena's 1911 illustrated song
*She's Never Been in Ireland, But She's Irish Just the Same.*
(*Courtesy of the Marnan Collection, LLC, Minneapolis, Minnesota*)

In his November 1882 catalogue, by which time the non-fiction Irish-themed slides vastly outnumbered the fictional Irish-themed slides, McAllister offered *The Jig, St Patrick's Day* as a 'dissolving view'.[140] He also sold two Irish-themed *Movable Comic Views*: *Irishman Dancing* and *Irishman Driving Pig*. These hand-coloured slides were a kind of proto-moving picture, thanks to a portion of the character being painted on a glass plate that moved when the projectionist pulled a small lever on the side of the wooden frame. Both were included in a series that depicted other nationalities in comic poses, such as *Turk's Head*, *Scotchman Dancing*, *Scotchman Taking Snuff* and *London Porter*.[141] The series was apparently successful, as some of the same slides were still being sold in McAllister's April 1898 catalogue, as were a large array of new entries, such as *Irish Stew*.[142]

In addition to his *Movable Comic Views*, McAllister also included fictional Irish topics in two other series offered in his 1898 catalogue. In a 'new' series entitled *Silhouettes*, McAllister offered 150 different comic views of various topics and nationalities, ranging from the Chinese to Haitians.[143] Among these were two Irish-themed slides, *Mrs MacSweeney* and *Scotch or Irish*, the latter being a comic 'whiskey' slide. Whereas these slides were cheaper in cost than his 'Movable Comic Views', McAllister intended another group titled *Humorous Transformations* to be 'of finer execution' than any of his other comic series. *Humorous Transformations* consisted of 100 slides, all of them being 'brilliantly colored ... movable pictures'.[144] The series included two Irish-themed slides, one of which was the darkly comic *Pat's Visit to the Tower of London (He Loses His Head)*. The other slide was *Irish Scenery*, featuring 'Paddy and the pig', which returned to the same kind of humour as *Irishman Driving Pig*.

By 1898, McAllister had also introduced his *Economic Series*, a 'special line of colored slides, consisting of popular subjects at popular prices'.[145] The subjects ranged from *Religious Subjects* and *Comic Subjects* to *Naval Vessels, U.S.* and *Irish Characters*, the latter category consisting of seventeen different slides. Using artwork rather than photographs, the Irish series was wholly comic in tone, with many of their titles attempting to mimic stereotypical Irish dialects, such as *The Onconvaynience of Married Life* and *'Aisy, Acushlaw, while I hoist my ould coat forninst the haste'*. Two slides in the group focussed on the kissing of the Blarney stone, and another depicted an Irish character driving some pigs. Others offered a character named 'Pat' (or, on some slides, 'Paddy') either drinking or fighting, or courting a woman and then suffering the fate of married life.

A surviving slide from the series, *Paddy Makin' Love*, depicts an Irish man with whiskers sitting in a pub holding hands with an Irish woman. As he looks at her, both of them smile. In the background is a heavy-set barmaid pouring a glass of whiskey; she too is smiling, and her cheeks are coloured with more red than either the man or the woman. On the floor near the man's feet are three dogs, as well as what appears to be the head of a pig. While the caricatures do not feature the grotesque physical features of some stage Irish cartoons, *Paddy Makin' Love* does play on ethnic stereotypes, including an illusion to the cohabitation of the Irish with animals.[146]

Though the predominant number of these fictional slides presented ethnic stereotypes, at least one exception occurred. In 1908, W. Stephen Bush, who wrote for *Moving Picture World*, advertised his services for lectures on 'dramatic, historic, or classic' subjects in 1908; in addition to prepared talks entitled *Othello*, *Enoch Arden* and *Washington at Valley*

*Forge*, Bush gave a lecture entitled *Shamus O'Brien*, apparently built around the nineteenth-century opera.[147] While this seems to have been a rare occurrence, the Bush example shows that at least some Irish-themed fictional slides depicted subjects other than wholly comic caricatures, even if such slides do not seem to have been widely distributed or offered for retail sale.

## Illustrated Song Slides

While it is certain that the illustrated song slide was invented in the nineteenth century, controversy surrounds its inventor. One account suggests that Tony Pastor created the illustrated song slide for use at a New York vaudeville theatre/music hall in the 1860s.[148] In other cases, credit for its invention went to Philip Phillips, a Methodist minister who used slides to accompany his singing in church, or to Bernard Covert, who allegedly introduced the song slide into popular music and venues.[149] Whoever deserves credit, it is clear that the use of a performer singing a song accompanied by lantern slides projections became a popular attraction after the end of the US Civil War.

It is also clear that the Irish-themed illustrated songs were being performed as early as the 1870s. During that period, a singer named James Holbrook toured the United States with illustrated Irish 'love ballads'.[150] In 1908, *Views and Film Index* recalled:

> Holbrook sang his ballads and they were illustrated by lantern, the first dissolving machine the writer ever saw, and were presented while the curtain was down and the stage being set for the next act. Holbrook sang such songs as *Killarney, Mary, the Rose of Tralee, Kathleen Mavourneen*, and other Irish ballads of the better class. They were illustrated from nature and life.[151]

Unfortunately, it is unknown as to what these slides of 'nature and life' depicted; while it is possible that Holbrook screened some non-fiction slides of Ireland, it is equally possible that his slides featured artwork or even photographs of non-Irish locations.

Holbrook certainly had a range of possibilities for his act. As William H.A. Williams has noted, American music companies published sheet music for a large number of Irish-themed songs in the 1850s and 1860s, many of them featuring titles that named an Irish man or woman; a number of them combined a woman's name and a Gaelic term of endearment, such as

**2.16** Slide 12 from the illustrated song
*A Wee Drop O' the Cruiskeen Lawn* (A. L. Simpson, 1912)
*(Courtesy of the Marnan Collection, LLC, Minneapolis, Minnesota)*

'Mavourneen', 'Astore', 'Aroon' and 'Machree'.[152] The lyrics of these songs conveyed love stories, as well as tales of Ireland and of migration from it. In his research, Williams found that only 10 per cent of those Irish-themed songs from 1800 to 1870 were comic.[153]

With regard to the post-Civil War period, Williams notes that immigration continued to be a recurrent topic for Irish-themed sheet music; however, his study claims that such songs decreased in number from approximately 32 per cent of Irish-themed songs to about 20 per cent. He suggests the possibility that the decrease came about in part because of the 'dramatic growth in comic songs (36 percent of all Irish-themed songs in the 1880s and 1890s)'.[154] He also asserts that a number of Irish-themed songs of the 1880s and 1890s dealt with issues such as 'Making It in America', and that an increased use of shamrock imagery appears on sheet music covers during those same years.[155] Such music and imagery proved important to the emergent illustrated song slide.

Live acts featuring illustrated songs became common during the 1890s, and they remained popular attractions at vaudeville theatres during the early years of the twentieth century. Singers of illustrated songs presented popular new music with lantern slides that were usually relevant to the lyrics they sang. These acts generally travelled with their own lanterns and lantern operators, and a number of them – such as Ada Jones and the team of Maxwell and Simpson – achieved some degree of fame.[156]

During this period, the initial heyday of the illustrated song, a large number of Irish-themed illustrated songs emerged. One of the most popular was *Why Did They Sell Killarney?*, which was performed in theatres across America in 1904.[157] Some songs focussed on nostalgia for Ireland, whereas many others were simple comedy numbers. However, at least one of the illustrated comic songs included an underlying political commentary. Surviving slides for *The Mick Who Threw the Brick* (circa 1899) depict cartoon artwork of an Ancient Order of Hibernians parade passing in front of 'O'Hoolihan's' pub. Lyrics tell the audience: 'The Mick Who Threw the Brick/Will Never Throw Another/For Calling Me an "A.P.A"/He now lies undercover.' The 'Mick's' invocation of the anti-Catholic American Protective Association results in him being pummelled, which is represented by cartoon artwork in the slides.[158]

In addition to vaudeville theatres, singers featured Irish-themed illustrated songs at a number of other events, some of which presented inoffensive lyrics and images to what may have been predominantly Irish-American audiences. For example, some performances occurred as part of St Patrick's Day celebrations, as happened in Fitchburg, Massachusetts, in 1898.[159] They also occurred as part of an illustrated lecture entitled *Beautiful Ireland*, which was given in Hartford, Connecticut, in 1906; for that event, rather than simply providing music at a lantern performance, a woman specifically sang 'songs appropriate to the pictures on the canvas, such as *Killarney, Bells of Shandon, Meeting of the Waters*, and *My Pretty Irish Maid*'.[160] Illustrated songs also occurred at such recitals as *The Music of Ireland*, which was presented in Syracuse, New York in 1910. At that event, William Snyder sang *Killarney*, which was 'illustrated with lantern slides, showing the Lakes of Killarney and other views of Ireland'.[161]

Despite its appearance at so many venues, the illustrated song slide would find its greatest success in the nickelodeon theatre. During the period from 1906 to 1913, the illustrated song achieved the height of its popularity. Managers of nickelodeon theatres could rent song slides from film exchanges along with their moving pictures, or they could purchase sets of slides to keep.[162] In some cases, prominent music publishers (rather than slide manufacturers) even gave away song slides or sold them at heavily reduced prices.[163] By hiring a local singer – or 'illustrator', as they were sometimes called in publicity, a term which linked the performer to the on-screen visuals – nickelodeon exhibitors could offer the public the latest popular songs at an affordable rate. In some cases, these singers achieved a degree of local fame; at least one of them – Mike Scott, 'the man from Dublin' who sang in Hartford, Connecticut, in 1907 – was Irish.[164] In other instances, non-Irish singers affected Irish accents when performing Irish-themed songs; for example, the *New York Dramatic Mirror* applauded George S. Skipper for doing just that at a 1909 nickelodeon performance of *My Irish Queen*.[165]

The use of illustrated songs at nickelodeon theatres had various benefits. They added variety to nickelodeon shows. They increased the running time of a nickelodeon programme, while simultaneously giving the film projec-tor a rest; given the risk of fires, some cities and states required intermittent usage of film projectors. They also gave projectionists time to thread up the next moving picture.[166] The fact that sheet music – and, in some cases, phonograph recordings – became 'illustrated' added another dimension to their popularity.

Demand for song slides grew quickly during the early nickelodeon period, causing many companies that had sold them in the pre-nickelodeon era to continue offering some of their old titles. For example, in 1904, Lubin had sold a set of slides for *Why Did They Sell Killarney?*; he contin-ued selling the same set in his 1906 catalogue. However, Lubin added new titles in 1906, presumably to meet growing demand from exhibitors for more titles. These included *My Wild Irish Rose* and *It's Only a Letter from Ireland*.[167] Demand continued to grow, in part due to nickelodeon exhibitors changing their programmes three or more times a week, which meant that individual songs often had little time to become hits, much to the chagrin of music publishers.[168]

By the autumn of 1906, a number of other companies were selling song slides to exhibitors and to film exchanges, including the Boswell Manufacturing Company (who were based in Chicago), Eugene Cline & Company (Chicago), Harstn & Company (New York), the McIntosh Lantern Company (Chicago) and the Selig Polyscope Company (Chicago); the T.H. McAllister company also distributed song slides during this period.[169] As the nickelodeon era progressed, others became important in this field, such as Alfred L. Simpson and the Excelsior Slide Company. However, due to the popularity and numbers of their releases, three song slide manufacturers emerged as the most important: Scott & Van Altena

**2.17** Slide 14 from the illustrated song *Kate Killarney*
*(I'll Put Away a Kiss for You)* (Excelsior Slide Co., 1910).
*(Courtesy of the Marnan Collection, LLC, Minneapolis, Minnesota)*

and DeWitt C. Wheeler (both located in New York City) and the Chicago
Transparency Company (located in Chicago).

With minimum orders of at least fifty sets, such companies prepared
illustrations for new songs. In addition to an occasional use of artwork,
that meant shooting photographs at either sets or existing locations with
models dressed in attire appropriate to the song's lyrics. Among those who
appeared in song slides were such future film stars as Francis X. Bushman,
Mabel Normand, Priscilla Dean and Alice Joyce.[170] They also included the
Irish-American actor Edward O'Connor, who was later noted for his work
in moving pictures at the Edison Manufacturing Company.[171] These actors
were generally unknown at the time that they posed for song slides. By
contrast, the 'famous Irish comedian' Dan Sully – who had toured exten-

sively throughout the US in various productions – was already extremely popular when he began posing for song slides at the Seminary Publication Company in 1908.[172]

Song slide sets usually resulted in 16 slides per song, although sometimes the number was 14 or more than 16.[173] The first slide presented the song's title, usually by showing the cover of its sheet music. The next fourteen slides offered images usually comprised of models in costumes and at locations/on sets appropriate to the song's narrative. More specifically, their actions and expressions in each slide usually accompanied the song's first verse (four slides), its first chorus (three slides), its second verse (four slides), and its second chorus (three slides). In some cases, the image commented upon or added narrative information to the lyrics, interacting with them rather than being merely a visual representation of them.[174] The final slide in the set then printed the words to the chorus in order for the audience to sing along, something which they did not do during the bulk of the song, which was generally sung by a single, professional performer.[175]

The illustrated song slide was thus a projected visual narrative accompanied by music. In 1917, Charles K. Harris called the song slide the 'little father of photodrama', claiming that the scenes they included created stories told through careful attention to choice of models, costumes, locations and lighting. He added that the 'same methods that were used in making song slides are now being used by the greatest moving picture directors in making their scenarios'.[176] Harris himself was a testament to the narrative and aesthetic link between song slides and the moving picture, as he began writing film scenarios after the song slide era ended. That link extended to the fact that early film projectors also had the capacity to project slides, or, perhaps more accurately, magic lanterns of the era had the ability to project films.[177]

However, film historians have generally overlooked the crucial importance of the illustrated song in the nickelodeon era. As Rick Altman has suggested: 'Even the best histories consider nickel theatres primarily in the context of early cinema, and thus explain their existence and growth primarily through developments specific to the film industry. A more satisfactory approach to the nickelodeon phenomenon would recognize the fundamentally multimedia nature of the storefront theatre program.'[178] Altman continues by suggesting that the illustrated song was important in 'setting standards for matching music to the moving picture'.[179] Given the comments made by Charles K. Harris, it is possible to extend Altman's argument and note the fact that historians have also generally ignored the illustrated song's interaction with, and possible influence upon, the narrative structure and visual style of nickelodeon-era moving pictures.

In terms of Irish-themed illustrated songs, a large number of them became quite popular. For example, music publishers Francis Day & Hunter advertised the song *Miss Killarney* on many occasions during the autumn of 1907 in the pages of the *New York Dramatic Mirror*; their ads claimed that the 'Great Irish Song Hit' was the 'Season's Sensation', adding that 'Beautiful Slides' could be purchased for five dollars per set from DeWitt C. Wheeler.[180] However, perhaps more important than the popularity of a specific illustrated song is the fact that literally hundreds of Irish-themed song slides were produced and distributed during the nickelodeon era, far more than the number of fictional Irish-themed moving pictures produced during the same time period.[181]

## Song Slide Narratives and Genres

By the time of the nickelodeon era, the Irish-themed songs of Tin Pan Alley focussed on a range of topics, from descriptions of Ireland to specific characters like the Irish mother and the Irish colleen. Some songs offered love stories, some addressed the 'American Dream', and others described the interactions of the Irish with other nationalities.[182] The Irish-themed comic song continued to be popular as well. Williams notes that:

> some of the urban Paddy songs, so popular in the 1870s and 1880s, were still being written in the late 1890s and early 1900s...However, the old knock-about Paddy songs were passing in favor of 'novelty' songs, which were comic, but in a very special sense. They embraced the new, the improbable, the eccentric, the nonsensical, and the unexpected... The fact that telephone, itself a novelty to many people, rhymed with an Irish name, was enough to generate *Cordelia Malone* by Billy Jerome and Jean Schwartz (1904). Similarly, there is *Nora Malone, Call Me by Phone* (1909), which includes an example of Tin Pan Alley Gaelic: 'mushawurra, wurra, wurra, wurra/Old Erin's Isle could not make me smile/Without Nora Malone'.[183]

While Williams acknowledges that Irish stereotypes continued in American popular music, he suggests that they were in a process of change, and that the Irish fared better in early-twentieth-century music than such ethnicities as the Jews and Italians.[184]

As for those Irish-themed songs that were 'illustrated', it is apparent that many offered stories that became Irish thanks only to the inclusion of Irish

**2.18** Slide 15 of the illustrated song *Pots and Pans* (DeWitt C. Wheeler, 1911), which features actress Anita Stewart.
*(Courtesy of the Marnan Collection, LLC, Minneapolis, Minnesota)*

names or recurrent Irish words, such as 'Acushla' and 'Mavourneen'. Others even inadvertantly included words or ideas associated with other countries. For example, *Arrah Wanna (An Irish Indian Matrimonial Venture)* (A.L. Simpson, 1906) features Barney Carney playing Scottish bagpipes, and *Bess Machree* (company unknown, 1909) includes the Scottish word 'bonnie'.

Rarely did politics or current events enter into the Irish-themed illustrated song during the nickelodeon period. A key exception was *They've Won Every Nation's Battles But Their Own*, released by DeWitt C. Wheeler in 1910.[185] Written by Ren Shields, John Nestore and George Christie, its lyrics offer the first-person views of an Irish-American who tells the story of the 'home of [his] forefathers'. He suggests that every 'Paddy' is a fighter possessing 'neither fear or fright', but that, despite their successes in a range of battles and wars, they have not won the freedom of their own country. To illustrate the tune, Wheeler drew heavily on artwork to depict the kinds of wars suggested in the lyrics; for Slide 4, a green-tinted Irish flag was superimposed over artwork of American soldiers fighting the British in the Revolutionary War. Wheeler also included artwork of people not mentioned in the song, including Robert Emmett (Slide 10) and Edmund Burke (Slide 14), as well as a photograph of the O'Connell statue in Dublin (Slide 7).

A number of other illustrated songs did address a general sense of pride and patriotism for Ireland. For example, the character in *I Love to Hear an Irish Band Upon St Patrick's Day* (DeWitt C. Wheeler, 1912) proudly announces 'My daddy's land was Paddy's land.' Similar sentiments are heard in such illustrated songs as *You Will Have to Sing an Irish Song* (DeWitt C. Wheeler, 1908), *The Home of the Celt and the Gael* (DeWitt C. Wheeler, 1907), *The Hat My Father Wore Upon Saint Patrick's Day* (DeWitt C. Wheeler, 1909), and *I'm Glad I'm Irish* (Manhattan Slide Company, 1910). Other illustrated songs spoke of pride in particular aspects of Irish culture, such as music in *The Song that Reaches Irish Hearts* (A.L. Simpson, 1911). However, these illustrated songs were in the minority of those released during the nickelodeon era.

In terms of sheer numbers, the dominant genre to emerge was the Irish love story, which included such efforts as *Under the Maples with Molly O* (Solar Slide Company, 1909) and *Her Name Is Mary Donahue* (DeWitt C. Wheeler, 1910).[186] Many of these were set in Ireland, the most famous perhaps being *A Colleen Bawn* (G.W. Bond, 1906); the slides for the song offer a three-act storyline depicting the young couple together, then separated, and then reunited. Other illustrated songs featured more simple tales of love that did not require the characters to separate. In *A Bushel O'Kisses* (Scott & Van Altena, 1909), a 'shamrock queen' named Mollie gives her heart to the 'finest boy in Paddy's land'. In *Under the Irish Moon* (A.L. Simpson, 1909), the moon 'turned to green' in honour of the 'Irish queen'. Similar lyrics appear in *Nora, My Irish Queen* (Scott & Van Altena, 1911). By contrast, *As Long as the Shamrock Grows Green* (Scott & Van Altena, 1912) offers a story of a male character who must patiently wait for the 'love knot [with his sweetheart] to tie'.

Many of these Irish love stories were set in America, and some of them – such as *My Irish Prairie Queen* (North American Slide Company, 1909) – were comical in tone. The couple in *My Irish Dearie* (DeWitt C. Wheeler, 1910) meet on St Patrick's Day, with Slide 3 showing a parade marked by American and Irish flags. In *Go Find a Sweetheart from the Emerald Isle*

**2.19** Slide 16 from the illustrated song *Love Me to a Yiddisha Melody (Oh! You Kiddisha!)* (Excelsior Slide Co., 1911).
*(Courtesy of the Marnan Collection, LLC, Minneapolis, Minnesota)*

(A.L. Simpson, 1908), Barney, whose grandparents emigrated from Dublin, plans not to 'do a thing [his] father wouldn't do', and so he must find a 'colleen', rather than a non-Irish wife. Similarly, *The Girl I'll Call My Sweetheart Must Look Like You* (DeWitt C. Wheeler, 1911) mentions that the male character's 'sweet colleen' must have 'eyes of Irish blue'. Even more overtly comical was the romance between Bertie McClore and Mildred Moore in *Make a Noise Like a Hoop and Roll Away* (A.L. Simpson, 1908); Bertie loves his Irish sweetheart dearly, even though she uses 'the worst kind of slang'.

A *Wee Drop O' the Cruiskeen Lawn* (A.L. Simpson, 1912) features an even more complicated love story. In it, the son of an Irish policeman meets Rosie, the 'daughter of the widow Grady', whom he calls his 'Dublin Daisy' and 'sweet Colleen Bawn'. Their growing love necessitates that their parents meet, though each of them has only one parent. Thanks in part to drinking the alcohol named in the title, their parents also fall in love. The positive effects of the drink are visualized in Slide 8, which has the young couple in a vignette comprised of whiskey bottles, and Slide 11, which mattes the older couple inside of a whiskey bottle. As with so many other Irish-themed illustrated songs, the set of slides for this song exemplifies a clear, three-act storyline.

At times immigration became an important narrative component of the Irish love story. In one case – Scott & Van Altena's *I've Got Rings on My Fingers; or Mumbo Jumbo Jijjiboo J. O'Shea* (Scott & Van Altena, 1909) – the Irish character is 'cast away' to an East Indian island. After he achieves success and becomes a tribal chief, O'Shea invites his sweetheart Rose McGee from Dublin Bay to join him. In *Come Kiss the Blarney, Mary Darling* (DeWitt C. Wheeler, 1911), the lead character moves to London where he meets Mary. When she refuses to kiss him, he invites her to Ireland to kiss the Blarney stone.

However, rather than set such songs in countries like London, the bulk of the immigration love stories told of lovers separated by the Atlantic Ocean, one of them having moved to the United States. Unrequited love marked many of these sad stories, as geography (and sometimes the passage of time) becomes too great an obstacle for those in love. Such illustrated songs included *Katie Darling, I Am Waiting* (Van Allin, 1907), *Bess Machree* (company unknown, 1909), *For Killarney and You* (DeWitt C. Wheeler, 1910), *Killarney, My Home O'er the Sea* (DeWitt C. Wheeler, 1911) and *When I Dream of Erin (I'm Dreaming of You)* (A.L. Simpson, 1912).

Other tales of separation feature couples who intend to reunite in Ireland. This separation is treated with humour in *Kate Killarney, I'll Put A Kiss Away For You* (Excelsior, 1910), in which the male character is an 'Irish rover, flirting the whole world over', but his favoured 'colleen is Killarney's Queen', and so he will return to her someday. The male character of *In Old Ireland Where the River Kenmare Flows* (Scott & Van Altena, 1911) speaks of his 'winsome colleen', his 'Kathleen Mavourneen' who is actively waiting for him to return to Ireland. In *My Killarney Rose* (Levi, 1911), the male character announces he will 'go back to paddy's land' to 'win the heart and hand' of his 'shamrock dearie'. Similarly, the young man in *My Rose of Old Kildare* intends to return to County Kildare to the girl he 'left behind'; the male lead in *Tipperary* (DeWitt C. Wheeler, 1907) plans much the same, with Slide 9 depicting the ocean liner he uses for that purpose.

In other cases, the couple plan to reunite in America. In *Sweet Eileen Asthore* (DeWitt C. Wheeler, 1912), the male character sails from the

**2.20** Slide 11 of A. L. Simpson's 1907 illustrated song, *Since Arrah Wanna Married Barney Carney* features a misspelling in the phrase 'Erin Go Bragh'.
*(Courtesy of the Marnan Collection, LLC, Minneapolis, Minnesota)*

United States to the land of 'lassies and ladies, Rosies and Paddies' in order to bring his sweetheart back to his new home. The lead character of *Since I Fell in Love with Mary* (Scott & Van Altena, 1910) tries to save money so that he can send for his 'Mary from Killarney'. Other illustrated songs featured couples who managed to overcome the financial cost of ocean passage. In *My Irish Mary* (Harstn, 1909), Mary McCue travels across the ocean to be with Dennis McGuire; much the same happens in *My Irish Maid* (DeWitt C. Wheeler, 1908), in which the male character's 'Irish Queen' of Kenmore is at long last 'sailing over' to be with him.

Much the same kind of story appeared in *Where's Kitty O'Brien?* (Genre Transparency Company, 1910), though that song features a sad ending for the man in love with her. The lyrics speak of 'Mike M'Gown from Dublin town' who moved to America and began sending half of his wages to Ireland every week so that his sweetheart Kitty O'Brien could eventually afford to make the voyage herself. When the day for her ocean passage finally came, she 'met one Mike O'Shay' at Dublin bay and soon fell in love with him. Slides for the song show M'Gown's desperate search for O'Brien at the ship when it docks in America; the tragedy is amplified by O'Brien's appearance in Slides 6 and 13, the latter of which pictures her holding up a round life preserver.

Many other immigration stories addressed life in America, though such lives could be spent pining for other countries. A number of illustrated songs feature homesick characters whose hearts remain in Ireland. These included *Killarney, My Home O'er the Sea* (DeWitt C. Wheeler, 1911), *Ireland Never Seemed So Far Away* (Scott & Van Altena, circa 1911–12), *In the Shadow of the Dear Old Blarney Stone* (DeWitt C. Wheeler, 1913) and *The Bells of Killarney* (Scott & Van Altena, 1913). Similarly, the Irish-American character in *Dublin Daisies* (DeWitt C. Wheeler, 1909) wonders about 'Daddy's land'; he dreams of Ireland, because he has heard that nowhere are the 'daisies half so fair' as in Dublin.

Other illustrated songs discussed the 'American Dream'. *Hello Miss Liberty* (Scott & Van Altena, 1913) claimed success was possible for Irish immigrants (Slide 12), as well as for the British, Germans, French and Italians. By contrast, other stories told of the hard work that awaited many immigrants. DeWitt C. Wheeler's 1911 illustrated song *Pots and Pans* addressed the issue through comedy. In it, Mary Ann Gilhooley is a 'roguish Irish belle' who decides she is 'through with Paddy's land' and leaves for America. Rather than find success as an actress on Broadway, Gilhooley is reduced to washing pots and pans and thus becomes the 'queen of dishes and tins and cans'. The song – which had been featured by Fannie Brice in the *Ziegfeld Follies of 1911* – was translated into slides with model Anita Stewart portraying Gilhooley. In the illustrated song, Gilhooley is an Irish domestic who not only washes pots and pans (Slides 4 to 7), but also – in visuals that supplement the limited narrative described in the lyrics – scrubs the floor (Slide 9), does laundry (Slide 10) and sweeps leaves (Slide 11). The comical side of Gilhooley's plight is emphasized in Slide12, in which she is matted inside a huge pot cooking on a stove, as well as in Slide 14, in which she wears a pot on her head like a hat.

A genre related to the immigration story is what might be called the 'Meeting of Nationalities', tales that hinged on the interactions between the Irish and other nationalities. These illustrated songs took place in various countries. For example, *Kerryana* (Scott & Van Altena, 1910) tells the story of a 'highland laddie' from Scotland named Andy McNab who meets a 'colleen' from Killarney and wants to take her 'back to old Dun-dee'. In *My Irish Caruso*, (DeWitt C. Wheeler, 1909) an Irish woman sings about a man who is both Irish and Italian; she met him in Tipperary, and 'perhaps you've heard his name/For it's James Caruso Murphy/and his voice has brought him fame.' Because he uses the 'Dago language', she can't understand him, but that is one of the reasons that he becomes her beloved 'Irish Caruso'.

In other cases, the setting of these stories is less clear. In *Santiago Flynn* (A.L. Simpson, 1908), which was subtitled *A Spanish–Irish Episode*, Molly does not want to hear the title character's Spanish music, ordering him to 'change your blarney/play Killarney'. He soon wins her heart by announcing his father was named 'Paddy Flynn'. While the outdoor locations were probably shot in New York, the song lyrics note that the character Flynn is Mexican; the lyrics also mention the Rio Grande, suggesting the setting is Texas or Mexico. Four years later, *My Turkish Opal From Constantinople* (Scott & Van Altena, 1912) had an 'Irish Turk named Pat McGirk' sent to the 'Turkish war', where he meets his love in the form of a harem dancer. While the song explicitly claims that the couple end up living in Cork, Ireland, the lyrics also curiously refer to the American holiday of Thanksgiving, for which McGirk 'brought home a Turkey and a Stork'.

Many of these 'Meeting of Nationalities' illustrated songs clearly indicate that they are set in the United States. For example, *You Will Have to Sing an Irish Song* (DeWitt C. Wheeler, 1908) features a woman who leaves Ireland for America, where she meets a 'Dutch man who won't leave [her] alone'. He serenades her with Dutch songs, but ' "Ich lie-be dich"…makes [her] sick', and so he will have to learn the *'Wearing of the Green'*. Other song slides have Irish and Jewish characters interacting, thus advancing a narrative that would become common in moving pictures. Such slides included *O'Brien Has No Place to Go* (DeWitt C. Wheeler, 1908) and *'Tis Tough When Issie Rosenstein Loves Genevieve Malone* (Excelsior, 1910).[187] Excelsior's 1911 *Love Me to a Yiddisha Melody (Oh! You Kiddisha!)* explored the subject of love between ethnicities at length. The male character Patrick J. O'Brien is a policeman who marries Sadie Katzenstein. He had mistakenly 'thought that Sa-die was an I-rish queen/Just be-cause her cos-tume was green/Oy! Oy! Oy!' He serenades her with Irish songs, which gave Excelsior the opportunity to picture the covers of various Irish-themed sheet music on Slide 7. Sadie represents an inversion of the woman in *You Will Have to Sing an Irish Song*, as she insists that Patrick sing a 'yiddisha melody'; Slide 8 shows her holding Yiddish sheet music as an example. Her needs in this regard are underscored later in the song when Patrick accidentally discovers that 'his captain Ikey Rubinstein' visits her at home while he is at work.

**2.21** Slide 10 of Scott and Van Altena's 1913 illustrated song
*The Kelly's Are at It Again* relies heavily on offscreen space.
*(Courtesy of the Marnan Collection, LLC, Minneapolis, Minnesota)*

However, the most popular 'Meeting of Nationalities' illustrated songs would not be Irish–Jewish, as would later be the case on stage and in the cinema, but rather Irish–Native American. Scott & Van Altena's 1908 slides for *Minnie-Ha-Ha Donahue* pictured model Beatrice Madison Barber as an 'Indian maiden of long ago' who 'stopped wearing feathers for the wearing of the green' after meeting an 'Irish cowboy' named Donahue. The chorus switches from third person to Donahue's first person, with him promising, 'Sure mavourneen, I'll be true/Be my squaw achushla do.' In keeping with the artwork on the cover of F.B. Haviland's sheet music, the model portraying Donahue in Scott & Van Altena's slides wears cowboy attire and in no way is depicted as an Irish caricature.

The most popular love story between an Irishman and a Native American came in A.L. Simpson's 1906 *Arrah Wanna (An Irish Indian*

*Matrimonial Venture).*[188] According to the song, each night Barney Carney
'from Killarney' would visit the prairies with a wedding ring, in hopes of
convincing Arrah Wanna, an 'Indian maid', to marry him. Scott & Van
Altena's slides for the song represent an example of a slide manufacturer
adding much narrative information to a song's lyrics, as Carney is much
more persistent and creative than in the lyrics. In Slide 6, for example, he
hangs a large shamrock on Arrah Wanna's tepee; by Slide 12, the tepee is
covered with shamrocks. The narrative then culminates in Slide 18, in
which Carney wears war paint and a Native American headdress with
green-tinted feathers.

Given the success of *Arrah Wanna*, in 1907 an illustrated song was
released of its sequel, *Since Arrah Wanna Married Barney Carney*. Its lyrics
announce that Carney's influence on the tribe have all their 'wig-wams all
full of Irish Blarney'. The Native Americans now 'celebrate on each St
Patrick's Day' and their 'pipe of peace is made of Irish clay'. To illustrate
the narrative, Scott & Van Altena's slides show Native American characters
smoking clay pipes and wearing green-tinted feathers. One tepee is covered
with shamrocks, while another offers the phrase, 'Erin Go Brah'[sic]. The
links between the two peoples are even addressed in the chorus slide, which
was tinted green and depicted artwork of a Native American.

Humour informed many of these genres, but in some cases the illustrated
songs seemed to exist for little purpose other than comedy. The most
famous example was *Has Anybody Here Seen Kelly?*, originally written by
C.W. Murphy and Will Letters, but adapted with new lyrics for American
audiences by William McKenna in 1909. In it, Michael Kelly and his
'sweetheart' came from County Cork 'on a holiday to New York'. On the
'Great White Way', Kelly 'lost his little girl', whose first-person question
results in the song's title and chorus. DeWitt C. Wheeler's 1910 illustrated
song offers numerous images of the female model matted into non-fiction
photographs of New York City, some of which show street parades; in one
rather self-reflexive slide, she looks at the very New York theatre in which
singer Nora Bayes introduced the song *Has Anybody Here Seen Kelly?* to
American audiences. While it is likely that few audiences would have probably not noted that fact, they might well have found Slide 12 curious. In a
departure from every other slide in the set, Slide 12 mattes a photograph of
Kelly's sweetheart into cartoon artwork of a group of men who hear her
question; the result is a use of mixed media of a type that would later be
explored by the moving picture.

The success of the song *Has Anybody Here Seen Kelly?* led to other
comic songs using the same character name, such as *Kelly's Gone to
Kingdom Come!*, which featured lyrics by Sax Rohmer. As with so many

others in the comedy genre, A.L. Simpson's 1910 illustrated song unfolds very much like a film narrative.[189] The title character, 'Pat O'Hara Connemara Palestine O'Guggenheim Li Hung Dooley Ballyhooley J. Columbus Kelly', has travelled to 'ev'ry spot of ground that dots old Mother Earth'. Purchasing an 'aeroplane', Kelly attempts to fly the English Channel, but his trip ends in failure. 'Now he's below where the dead ones go', the lyrics announce. The first slides in the set show photographs of Kelly and his plane, but then Slides 12 through 14 offer cartoon artwork that shows Kelly falling into the water where a large whale (which is not mentioned in the song's lyrics) eagerly awaits him.[190]

The character name returned again in Scott & Van Altena's 1913 illustrated song, *The Kellys Are At It Again*. In it, Michael Kelly and his wife move into a 'Harlem flat' where they spend each evening calling each other by pet names while he bounces her on his knee. They make so much noise that nearby 'Missus Flynn' calls the police, but as soon as the authorities leave, the Kellys are 'at it again'. In the second verse, months have passed and Kelly returns home late on a payday. His wife throws an iron at him, which causes him to bounce her up and down again on his knee, but he does not call her by any pet names. She hits the ceiling, which falls down and once again disturbs 'Missus Flynn'. Scott & Van Altena's slides depict the key actions described by the lyrics, but also add other comic visuals. For example, Slide 12 shows Kelly's wife threatening to hit him with a bottle, Slide 13 shows her pulling his tie, and Slide 14 shows the couple through a cracked glass window, each holding a clump of the other's hair.

Battling spouses are only one example of the stereotypical fighting Irish in the illustrated song. Genre Transparency's 1910 *What's the Matter With Reilly (He's All Right!)* offered a fight between Irish-American men. In Slides 1 through 8, we see a family at home enjoying themselves; one of them plays a fiddle. Then, in Slide 9, one man hits another on the nose, which causes an Irish policeman to arrive on the scene. He soon restores order, as Slides 11 through 13 depict peace breaking out among friends. The final image in the illustrated song depicts a young man and woman together at home for a requisite happy ending (though curiously they are posed in a different apartment from the one seen in the first thirteen slides).

In addition to these specific genres, the illustrated song of the nickelodeon era also included Irish characters in non-Irish-themed stories. These usually feature a character with a name coded as Irish, even though the lyrics do not describe his or her national origin. The most famous of these would be the character Casey in *Take Me Out to the Ballgame* (DeWitt C. Wheeler, 1908), but there were numerous others. The young man in DeWitt C. Wheeler's 1908 *Take Me Out to the End of the Pier* (who

**2.22** Slide 14 of Scott and Van Altena's 1908 illustrated song
*Don't Take Me Home.*
*(Courtesy of the Marnan Collection, LLC, Minneapolis, Minnesota)*

was modelled by Francis X. Bushman) has a 'steady' named Maggie McGee, and Archibald Nugent, the male lead in the Chicago Transparency Company's 1908 *Roll on the Rollaway (The New Roller Skate Craze)*, takes his sweetheart Kate Rooney roller skating.

Similarly, the male lead in *Take Me Up With You Dearie* (DeWitt C. Wheeler, 1909) gives his 'sweet Molly Ryan' rides in his airplane. The female character in *Sing, Kate, Sing* (DeWitt C. Wheeler, 1909) is 'Miss Katie O'Shane', and the female character in *Dora Dooley* (Stereopticon & Film Exchange, 1909) is named in the song's title. The chauffeur in *Take Me Out for a Joy Ride* is Rudolph O'Neill (Scott & Van Altena, 1909), and the bowler in *Set 'Em Up in the Alley* (A.L. Simpson, 1909) is Louis O'Malley. The piano player in *Oceana Roll* (DeWitt C. Wheeler, 1911) is Billy McCoy, and the young man in *He'd Have to Get Under – Get Out and Get Under (to Fix Up His Automobile)* (Scott & Van Altena, 1913) is Johnny O'Connor.

That these characters are Irish is incidental; outside of their names, their ethnic heritage is not particularly relevant to the lyrics and narratives of these illustrated songs. At the same time, slide manufacturers did occasionally try to emphasize their Irish heritage through visuals. For example, the comical *Don't Take Me Home* (Scott & Van Altena, 1908) tells the story of 'Augustus J. McCann...a henpecked married man', whose wife makes him do various chores. Slides 6 and 7 picture him doing housework in a green-tinted skirt. In *He'd Push It Along* (Scott & Van Altena, 1914), the lead character 'Mister McNally' regrets married life as he pushes a baby carriage; the slides tint his clothing green.

## Song Slide Images

While illustrated song slides were dependent upon sheet music companies for their titles, lyrics and melodies, slide manufacturers maintained control over their visual content and style. Sometimes they departed from the specifics described in the lyrics of songs they depicted; in other cases, as already suggested, they added unique narrative information. For example, the lyrics of *Won't You Come Over to Philly, Willie* never mention Ireland or anything Irish; however, the images in A.L. Simpson's 1907 slides make clear that the character Willie starts out in Ireland.

As Williams notes, sheet music for Irish-themed songs increasingly featured illustrated covers during the late nineteenth century and beyond.[191] Between 1900 and 1920, approximately one third of such illustrated sheet music covers featured photographs of performers. However, in those cases when sheet music covers offered artwork depicting the narratives told in their lyrics, song slide manufacturers did not feel obliged to use such images as a guide for their slides, even though those sheet music covers generally constituted the first slide in their song slide sets.

Beyond an ability to circumvent or add to narrative information contained in sheet music, an individual illustrated song could feature an array of complicated visuals. Altman has noted that song slide visuals featured multimedia images (given that title slides usually reprinted pre-existing sheet music covers), and that subsequent slides at times featured images of 'borrowed arts', such as artwork and cartoons. He also suggests that it was not uncommon for slide-makers to produce 'surreal' images featuring 'multiple planes, unexpected matches, and contrasting scales' by means of post-production work on photographs taken by the slide manufacturers.[192] Various examples of such surrealistic images occurred in the

**2.23** Slide 15 of the illustrated song *Kelly's Gone to Kingdom Come!* (A. L. Simpson, 1910) combines cartoon artwork and a photograph of the title character.

*(Courtesy of the Marnan Collection, LLC, Minneapolis, Minnesota)*

Irish-themed song slide. In Slide 12 of *My Irish Dearie* (DeWitt C. Wheeler, 1910), a cartoon shamrock is superimposed onto the face of its female model. Slide 15 of Excelsior's 1911 *Love Me to a Yiddisha Melody (Oh! You Kiddisha!)* matted its young couple on top of an enormous police hat, allowing them to 'sit' on a symbol of the male lead's career.

Despite surrealistic images, as well as the repetitive use of Irish stereotypes, song slide manufacturers often tried to promote the authenticity of their slides. For example, DeWitt C. Wheeler claimed his *Mother Machree* (1911) featured 'native costumes', adding, 'many of the scenes represented were actually taken on the Emerald Isle'.[193] The same company promoted the fact that *For Killarney and You* (1911) was set in 'Irish costume', and

**2.24**  Slide 1 of the illustrated song *The Colleen Bawn* (G. W. Bond, 1906)
mattes its models into an authentic photograph of Killarney.
*(Courtesy of the Marnan Collection, LLC, Minneapolis, Minnesota)*

that *Killarney, My Home O'er the Sea* (1911) was 'remarkable for its realism and for the preservation throughout of the atmosphere in which the
story of the song is laid'.[194] Similarly, Scott & Van Altena announced that
slides for *Nora, My Irish Queen* (1911) pictured 'characteristic Irish scenes
that are at once recognized as such'. They also stated that *The Dublin Rag*
(1911) featured 'the quaint old Irish costume amid scenery that takes you
right to the old country'.[195]

In addition to such publicity, many song slide manufacturers regularly
incorporated non-fiction images of Ireland into their fictional illustrated
songs. Authentic and untouched Irish landscapes (save for hand-tinted
colour) appeared as individual slides within such illustrated songs as *The*

*Home of the Celt and the Gael* (DeWitt C. Wheeler, 1907), *Katie Darling, I am Waiting* (Van Allin, 1907), *Under the Irish Moon* (A.L. Simpson, 1909), *In the Shadow of the Dear Old Blarney Stone* (DeWitt C. Wheeler, 1913) and *In the Valley of the Shannon* (Scott & Van Altena, 1914). Surveying these images, it seems likely that song slide manufacturers obtained these non-fiction images from such companies as Underwood & Underwood.

Rather than transport their American models to Ireland, which does not seem to have ever occurred, song slide manufacturers occasionally matted their posed photographs into pre-existing non-fiction photographs of Ireland. In at least one case, *The Bells of Killarney* (Scott & Van Altena, 1913), this is not an attempt to situate the characters in Ireland, but rather to suggest (in Slides 9 and 13) that they are in America thinking about Killarney, which is pictured above their heads as if they are daydreaming. However, in most cases, such matting was an attempt to make it appear that the song's characters – and, by extension, its models – were actually in Ireland. For example, the models in *The Colleen Bawn* (G.W. Bond, 1906) are matted into an actual photograph of Killarney. The models for *In Old Ireland Where the River Kenmore Flows* (Scott & Van Altena, 1911) are matted into a photograph of an Irish river (Slide 9) and into a photograph of the exterior of an Irish cottage (Slide 13). Slides 2 and 3 of *The Dublin Rag* (Scott & Van Altena, 1911) features its young couple matted into photos of Irish landscapes. Slide 8 of Excelsior's *Roses of Erin* (1911) matted its female model into an image of Blarney Castle. DeWitt C. Wheeler's *Come Kiss the Blarney Mary Darling* (1911) matted its male and female models against Blarney Castle in Slides 5 and 12; Scott & Van Altena did the same in Slide 13 of *A Little Bunch of Shamrocks* (1913).

The purpose of these slides was to convey a sense of authenticity. At times, as in Excelsior's slides, the fact that one photograph has been matted into another is fairly obvious due to poor post-production work, the results undermining the attempt to be perceived as genuine. In other cases, the matting is less noticeable; sometimes photographers knew that such matting would happen when they shot the models, and quite skilfully found methods to add to their believability. For the illustrated song *In the Shadow of the Dear Old Blarney Stone* (1913), DeWitt C. Wheeler matted its young couple onto an image of Blarney Castle for three slides. For one of them (Slide 4), the models were seated on top of a stone wall; the models and the stone wall were then matted onto the photograph of the castle. The wall offers a smooth form of matting, and the fact that it reappears throughout the slide set further adds to its verisimilitude.

By contrast, exteriors that appear in many other illustrated songs are not Ireland, even though the lyrics of those songs would suggest that they are. These include *Eileen My Own* (Van Allin, 1907), *Miss Killarney* (DeWitt C. Wheeler, 1907), *Shamrock* (DeWitt C. Wheeler, 1907), *Only a Shamrock* (Boswell, 1908) and *Mother Machree* (DeWitt C. Wheeler, 1910). The same is true of A.L. Simpson's *Go Find a Sweetheart from the Emerald Isle* (1909), though the inaccuracy of its location is only noticeable under scrutiny. The photographer shot the song's models in a very shallow depth of field, which causes the backgrounds to fall out of focus. It is unknown as to whether or not the depth of field was intended to disguise the locations, but that is the result.

In other cases, song slide photographers chose American locations – most of them in New York – that were evocative of Irish landscapes, such as hills that, once they were tinted, could appear bright green. Photographers also chose to pose their models at or on structures that appeared Irish. For example, stone walls appeared in numerous slide sets, particularly those manufactured by Scott & Van Altena. These include Slide 11 and 16 of *Katie Darling, I am Waiting* (Van Allin, 1907), Slide 7 of *Top O' the Mornin' Bridget McCue* (Scott & Van Altena, 1907), Slide 13 of *I'm Awfully Glad I'm Irish* (Scott & Van Altena, 1909), Slides 4 and 5 of *The Dublin Rag* (Scott & Van Altena, 1911) and Slide 10 of *In Old Ireland Where the River Kenmore Flows* (Scott & Van Altena, 1911). The combination of such structures with models costumed in Irish attire was another attempt at simulating Irish settings in America.

At times, the noticeably authentic and inauthentic intermingled within a single illustrated song. For example, most slides for DeWitt C. Wheeler's *Farewell Killarney* (1906) featured its models set against obviously painted backgrounds; however, one slide depicts the actual Carrick-a-Rede rope bridge, which had appeared in numerous non-fiction slides. The Levi Company's *Blarney Kate* (1911) matted its models into a photograph of Ireland for Slide 3, but landscapes in its other slides are obviously not of Ireland. The same was true of the Chicago Transparency Company's *Where the River Shannon Flows* (1905); Slide 2 pictures Blarney Castle, whereas Slide 7 features the models situated in a landscape that is clearly not Ireland. Similarly, DeWitt C. Wheeler's *My Rose of Old Kildare* (1912) matted its models into images of Ireland for Slides 6 and 11, but for most others – such as Slides 5, 7, 12 and 14 – they used a stage with curtain backdrops. These instances suggest that song slide manufacturers had commitments to authenticity, but that such commitments only went so far.

At least two illustrated songs of the period featured even more complicated approaches to the issue of setting. Slide 1 of Scott & Van Altena's *Kerryana*

**2.25** Slide 11 of Van Allin's 1907 illustrated song *Katie Darling,
I Am Waiting* was photographed in America, but made to look like
Ireland thanks to a stone wall.
*(Courtesy of the Marnan Collection, LLC, Minneapolis, Minnesota)*

(1910) is an image of Killarney, and Slide 3 is an image of an Irish cottage. Other images matted the models into actual Irish landscapes, such as Slides 2 and 5. However, Slides 4, 9, 11 and 14 feature the models in a studio set, resulting in a mix of three different kinds of settings. Much the same could be said of DeWitt C. Wheeler's *Sweet Eileen Asthore* (1912), which featured its models in three distinct situations: an indoor studio set with a curtain backdrop, outdoor locations in America, and outdoor locations in Ireland (such as Blarney Castle) against which its models were matted.

Issues of authenticity also arose when selecting the models who portrayed the characters in each song. Aside from the question of whether

**2.26** Slide 14 of the illustrated song *Where's Kitty O'Brien?*
(Genre Transparency Co., 1910) depicts actors wearing stage Irish makeup.
*(Courtesy of the Marnan Collection, LLC, Minneapolis, Minnesota)*

the models were or were not themselves Irish (and it seems that most were not), their on-screen representation through make-up and costume is something that varied. In a small number of cases, such representations were not ethnic stereotypes. For example, the cowboy Pat O'Day in *Sante Fe* (A.L. Simpson, 1910), which used members of the 101 Ranch for its models, is not depicted as a caricature. Moreover, nothing about the character Maggie McGee or her attire in DeWitt C. Wheeler's *Take Me Out to the End of the Pier* (1908) appears stereotypical. Rather than the requisite green-tinted clothing, for example, she wears a purple skirt. Much the same could be said of *Blarney Kate* (Levi, 1910), in which the model's dress is also purple.

However, 'stage Irish' caricatures dominated many illustrated song slides. Some of this stereotyping occurs through the saturated colour tints. The female model in *Since Cohan Wrote 'Mary Was a Grand Old Name'* wears a bright green dress (Premo, 1909), as do the models in *Shamrock* (DeWitt C. Wheeler, 1907) and *I'm On Agen* [sic] *With Monaghan, and Off Agen* [sic] *With You* (T.H. McAllister, 1910). Similarly, the male lead in *Arrah Wanna* wears an Irish hat and stockings that are tinted bright green, the male lead in *Miss Killarney* (DeWitt C. Wheeler, 1907) wears a jacket tinted bright green, and the male lead in *Come Kiss the Blarney Mary Darling* (DeWitt C. Wheeler, 1911) wears a cape and hat tinted bright green. The boxer in *Oh! You! Jeffries!* (Genre Transparency Company, 1910) wears green-tinted shorts, and the male characters in *That Little Bit of Green* (Harry F. Stains, 1910) all wear green-tinted suits. Such a use of the colour green may have received various responses, but at least one unfavourable comment was recorded in a 1909 issue of the *New York Dramatic Mirror*, which complained about A.L. Simpson's slides for *Under the Irish Moon*. Along with noting that the slides did not have 'the faintest atmosphere of Ireland', the trade declared the use of a moon coloured green was 'grotesque'.[196]

Other potentially offensive caricatures appeared in other slides due to 'stage Irish' make-up, including exaggerated wigs, whiskers and beards that were usually tinted bright red. For example, the old man in *Go Find a Sweetheart from the Emerald Isle* (A.L. Simpson, 1909) has fake whiskers and beard. The musician in *The Tipperary Twirl* (A.L. Simpson, 1910) wears fake whiskers, which are coloured bright red. Similarly, all four characters at the harbour scenes of *Where's Kitty O'Brien?* (Genre Transparency Company, 1910) have obviously fake hair and whiskers that are tinted bright red.[197] Other illustrated songs combined the use of such make-up with green-tinted apparel. In *Won't You Come Over to Philly, Willie?* (A.L. Simpson, 1907), the character has a fake beard and hair tinted bright red, as well as also a bright green suit and socks. The lead in A.L. Simpson's *Kelly's Gone to Kingdom Come!* (1910) wears fake hair, whiskers and a beard, all tinted bright red, as well as clothes tinted green; similarly, Scott & Van Altena's *Finnegan Gave It To Me* (circa 1912) has its title character wearing a green-tinted vest and red-tinted hair.

Stereotypical props can also be seen in many illustrated songs. Irish clay pipes appeared prominently in *Since Arrah Wanna Married Barney Carney* (Scott & Van Altena, 1907), *Santiago Flynn* (A.L. Simpson, 1908), *Where's Kitty O'Brien?* (Genre, 1910), *The Tipperary Twirl* (A.L. Simpson, 1910), *A Wee Drop O' the Cruiskeen Lawn* (A.L. Simpson, 1912), *My Turkish Opal From Constantinople* (Scott & Van Altena, 1912) and *Finnegan Gave It To Me* (Scott & Van Altena, circa 1912). The same was true of stereo-typical Irish hats, which appeared in *My Irish Caruso* (DeWitt C. Wheeler, circa 1909), *The Dublin Rag* (Scott & Van Altena,1911), *Mother Machree*

(DeWitt C. Wheeler, 1910) and *Come Kiss the Blarney, Mary Darling* (DeWitt C. Wheeler, 1911). Such props and sets were often tinted green, ranging from the walls and carpet of a home's interior – as in Genre's 1910 *What the Matter With Reilly (He's All Right!)* – to the shutters on the exterior of a house – as in DeWitt C. Wheeler's 1907 *Shamrock*.

Presumably to save money, some of the same stereotypical props and costumes reappeared in various illustrated songs. For example, Excelsior used the same models and costumes in *Roses of Erin* (1911) as they had in *Kate Killarney* (1910). Slides for DeWitt C. Wheeler's *Dublin Daisies* (1909) used painted flats that had been previously seen in *Farewell Killarney* (1906). The exterior of the home used for *Mother Machree* (DeWitt C. Wheeler, 1910) also appeared in *My Irish Dearie* (DeWitt C. Wheeler, 1910). The same Irish harp appears in both Scott & Van Altena's *I'm Awfully Glad I'm Irish* (1909) and *The Dublin Rag* (1911). At times, even the exact same slides were repeated. Slide 15 of G.W. Bond's *The Colleen Bawn* (1906) was a close-up of a group of green-tinted shamrocks. The identical photograph later became Slide 14 of Genre's *We'll Go Back to Erin Someday, Mavourneen* (1909), as well as Slide 13 in Genre's *Oh! You! Jeffries!* (1910).

In most cases, however, Irish-themed song slides used stereotypical colours and props as vignettes for important characters in the song. *The Dublin Rag* (Scott & Van Altena, 1911) vignettes its young couple through what appears to be torn green fabric; in *The Kellys Are At It Again* (Scott & Van Altena, 1913), the male and female characters burst through a wall with green wallpaper. Harp vignettes appear in both *The Song That Reaches Irish Hearts* (A.L. Simpson, 1911) and *The Bells of Killarney* (Scott & Van Altena, 1913). An enormous Irish whisky bottle and an Irish clay pipe form vignettes in *A Wee Drop O'the Cruiskeen Lawn* (A.L. Simpson, 1912); an Irish clay pipe vignette also appeared in Slide 12 of *The Song that Reaches Irish Hearts* (Simpson, 1911). Such examples were in addition to an Irish flag and harp appearing inside a vignette of green-tinted shamrocks for Slide 4 of *That Tumble Down Shack in Athlone* (Scott & Van Altena, 1918), a post-nickelodeon organist slide set that combined live models and captioned lyrics.

Use of a single, large green-tinted shamrock was the most common of these vignettes. Slide 2 of *Ireland Never Seemed So Far Away* (Scott & Van Altena, circa 1911–12) uses a shamrock vignette for its male and female lead characters; the same is true of Slides 2 and 14 of *In Old Ireland Where the River Kenmore Flows* (Scott & Van Altena, 1911) and Slide 12 of *Killarney* (Scott & Van Altena, 1912). In other cases, the shamrock vignette was reserved solely for the female lead, as in *Nora, My Irish Queen* (Scott

**2.27** Slide 13 of the illustrated song *As Long as the Shamrock Grows Green* (Scott and Van Altena, 1912) features a shamrock border.

& Van Altena, 1913). The Chicago Transparency Company had earlier used a similar vignette for the female lead for Slide 16 of *Where the River Shannon Flows* (1905).

In some cases, these vignettes could convey important narrative and/or thematic information. For example, in Slide 3 of *Finnegan Gave It To Me* (Scott & Van Altena, 1912), the lead male character arrives in New York City. He steps out of a torn shamrock, a visual sign of his sadness at having departed Ireland. Slide 5 of DeWitt C. Wheeler's *Katie O'Sullivan* (1911) features a non-fiction photograph of an Irish waterfall. On top of it is matted a shamrock; the song's young couple appear inside the shamrock, which – in combination with the waterfall – underscores the geographical location of their relationship.

Vignettes were not the only way that song slide manufacturers used post-production to add stereotypical Irish props to their images. For example, shamrock borders appear on five slides of *As Long as the Shamrock Grows Green* (Scott & Van Altena, 1912), as well as on Slide 7 of *The Girl I'll Call My Sweetheart Must Look Like You* (DeWitt C. Wheeler, 1911). Scott & Van Altena used them for *In the Valley of the Shannon* (1914) and for *In Old Ireland Where the River Kenmore Flows* (1914). Rather than create a shamrock border, Slide 12 of *Peg O' My Heart* (Scott & Van Altena, 1913) features an entire background consisting of many small shamrocks.

However, the Irish-themed song slide was not solely dependent on the use of stereotypical visuals. Indeed, many vignettes in such illustrated songs are props that have nothing to do with Ireland or the Irish, but instead are relevant to particular lyrics. For example, Slide 15 of Excelsior's 1911 *Love Me to a Yiddish Melody (Oh! You Kiddisha!)* matted its male and female leads into a huge pocket watch, and Slide 8 of *As Long as the Shamrock Grows Green* (Scott & Van Altena, 1912) vignetted its young couple inside a pearl necklace. Such vignettes could just as easily be found in any non-Irish-themed song slides, many of which also employed surrealistic imagery.

# Conclusion

The decline of the illustrated song slide may well have started in some sections of the United States as early as 1911, but it is clear that the era had largely come to an end by 1913.[198] Certainly a number of different companies continued to produce and distribute Irish-themed song slides until that time. For example, as late as May 1912 the British slide manufacturer Bamforth opened offices in New York City in an attempt to enter the American market. One of their trade advertisements promoted 'Lantern Slides Illustrating Standard English, Scotch, and Irish Songs'. Of the five song slide sets they listed for sale, four were Irish.[199]

In a minor way, the song slide returned in the silent feature film era, with various manufacturers creating slides that could be projected while movie theatre organists played. A small number of these were Irish-themed, such as the Standard Slide Corporation's *Abie's Irish Rose* in 1925. Inspired by the Broadway stage play of the same name, its lyrics claimed: 'May-be Abie was a Jew-ish ba-by/But he's got an I-rish nose/I-rish smell-er on a Jew-ish fell-er/He knows how to pick an I-rish Rose.' Rather than picturing live models as in the heyday of the illustrated song slide, *Abie's Irish Rose* used cartoon characters and artwork that featured shamrocks.

However, the illustrated song slide had clearly given way to movies, a fact underscored by James A. Fitzpatrick's 1926 Pathé short subject, *Songs of Ireland*. Released as part of a 'Famous Melody Series' that also included *Songs of Italy*, *Songs of England* and *Songs of Scotland*, the film offered 'picturesque scenes of Old Erin accompanied by the various melodies pictured'.[200] Those melodies, many of which focussed on Killarney, were heard thanks to an 'orchestra score...which makes the synchronizing of the picture and music perfect'.[201] Movies had fully subsumed the functions of the illustrated song slide.

In terms of non-fiction slides, illustrated lectures on Ireland continued throughout the twentieth century; for example, as late as 1979, Eloise and Earl Dibble gave an illustrated lecture entitled *Welcome to Ireland* in Harrison, New York.[202] However, whereas the emphasis in the late nineteenth and early twentieth centuries had been on public lectures, the key appearance of non-fiction slides of Ireland after 1915 came in school classrooms.

Beginning in 1906, the Keystone View Company of Meadville, Pennsylvania, marketed its '600 Set' to schoolteachers. Various editions of the company's '600' catalogue listed a thirty-six-slide set entitled *The British Isles*, which included nine images of Ireland.[203] A 1938 Keystone publication indicates that the company had continued to market a *British Isles* lecture that included slides of Ireland.[204] During the 1940s and 1950s, Keystone sold similar slide sets, which in some cases drew on negatives from earlier decades, including images that Keystone had purchased in 1912 from Underwood & Underwood.[205] One of Keystone's arguments was that the 'use of motion pictures does not displace the use of lantern slides', though that is in fact what occurred during the twentieth century.[206]

However, from the end of the US Civil War until 1915, the Irish-themed lantern slide was crucial in constructing an 'Irish' visual culture in America, bringing images of Ireland, the Irish and the 'stage Irish' to widespread audiences. Illustrated song slides were a component of a larger industry in American entertainment, as were other, non-musical fictional Irish-themed slides. Similarly, non-fiction slides of Ireland participated in the broader category of travel and tourist-based non-fiction slides. In many respects, non-fiction and fiction slides existed in distinct categories, one representing efforts towards the 'authentic' and one representing its apparent opposite in the 'stage Irish'. Nonetheless, the line between them was porous, under-scoring the problems of representing 'genuine' Irish-themed entertainment on the screen, problems that would also manifest in the American moving picture.

Together, these slides proved crucial in the development of Irish-themed early cinema. Non-fiction slides had a profound effect on early travelogue films, guiding the locations and topics that were filmed and the manner in which they were depicted. Similarly, fictional lantern slides – particularly illustrated song slides and their accompanying lyrics – had a major influence as well, specifically on many of the narratives explored by fictional moving pictures, as well as, to a lesser degree, their visual style. Indeed, much of the content in early Irish-themed films was a direct outgrowth of the Irish-themed lantern slide.

# Notes

1. J. Ruchatz, 'Travelling by Slide: How the Art of Projection Met the World of Travel', in R. Crangle, M. Heard and I. van Dooren (eds), *Realms of Light: Uses and Perceptions of the Magic Lantern from the 17th to the 21st Century* (London: Magic Lantern Society, 2005), p.35.
2. C. Musser, *The Emergence of Cinema: The American Screen to 1907* (Berkeley, CA: University of California, 1990), p.32.
3. S. Herbert, 'Photographic Slides', in D. Robinson, S. Herbert and R. Crangle (eds), *Encyclopaedia of the Magic Lantern* (London: Magic Lantern Society, 2001), p.232.
4. 'Amusements', *Oshkosh Daily Northwestern* (Oshkosh, WI), 17 April 1883, p.4.
5. 'Local Department', *Tyrone Daily Herald* (Tyrone, PA), 25 January 1883, p.3.
6. Advertisement, *New York Herald*, 17 March 1870, p.2.
7. Advertisement, *New York Clipper*, 25 September 1886, p.445.
8. 'Neighboring News', *Hamilton Daily Democrat* (Hamilton, OH), 4 April 1892, p.2; advertisement, *Fitchburg Sentinel* (Fitchburg, MA), 13 March 1897, p.2.
9. 'Notes of the Stage', *New York Times*, 6 October 1895, p.11.
10. Slides 1 (*Emerald Isles and Winding Bays*) and 6 (*No Place Else Can Charm The Eye*) have not been examined, as they are not contained in the otherwise complete set housed at the George Eastman House in Rochester, New York.
11. Ruchatz, 'Travelling by Slide', p.40.
12. Musser, *Emergence of Cinema*, p.36.
13. Ruchatz, 'Travelling by Slide', pp.35–6.
14. Underwood & Underwood also released *A Fireside Scene, County Kerry, Ireland* as a stereo view in 1901.
15. J. Waldsmith, *Stereo Views: An Illustrated History and Price Guide* (Iola, WI: Krause Publications, 2002), p.10.
16. Ibid., p.7.
17. *Catalogue of Langenheim's New and Superior Style Colored Photographic Magic Lantern Pictures and for the Dissolving View & Lantern Apparatus, Carefully Selected from the Best Pictures of the Old and New Masters for Education, Private, and Public Exhibition; Also, a Catalogue of Langenheim's Stereoscopic Pictures on Glass and Paper, and Microscopic Photos of a Superior Quality* (Philadelphia, PA: American Stereoscopic Company, 1861), pp.29–30.
18. *Illustrated Catalogue: Lantern Slides and Photographs, Views in All Parts of the World* (Philadelphia, PA: William H. Rau, 1894), pp.116–19.
19. Musser, *Emergence of Cinema*, p.32, quoted in D. Rossell, 'McAllister', in Robinson, Herbert and Crangle (eds), *Encyclopaedia of the Magic Lantern*, p.181.
20. *Catalogue and Price List of Stereopticons, Dissolving View Apparatus, Magic Lanterns, and Artistically Coloured Photographic Views* (New York: T.H. McAllister, 1867), pp.29–30.
21. *Catalogue and Price List of Lanterns, Dissolving View Apparatus, Magic Lanterns, and Artistically-Colored Photographic Views on Glass* (New York: T.H. McAllister, 1882), p.77.
22. Ibid., p.60.
23. Ibid., p.89.
24. Ibid., p.90.
25. *Catalogue of Lanterns, Dissolving View Apparatus, and Magic Lanterns with Extensive Lists of Views for the Illustrator of All Subjects of Popular Interest* (New York: T.H. McAllister, 1898), p.203.
26. Ibid.

27. Ibid., p.59.
28. Ibid., p.109.
29. *Stereopticons and Slides* (Chicago, IL: L. Manasse Co., 1905), p.110. Available in *A Guide to Motion Picture Catalogs by American Producers and Distributors, 1894–1908: A Microfilm Edition* (New Brunswick, NJ: Rutgers University Press, 1985), Reel 5.
30. *Lanterns, Lantern Slides, Moving Picture Machines* (Chicago, IL: Lantern & Film Exchange, 1906), pp.428–30; *Lanterns, Lantern Slides, Moving Picture Machines* (Chicago, IL: Moore, Bond & Co. [circa. 1907]). Available in *Guide to Motion Picture Catalogs ... 1894–1908: Microfilm Edition*, Reel 5.
31. 'The Cult of the Travelogue', *Moving Picture World*, 16 May 1908, p.438.
32. 'Lecturettes', *Moving Picture World*, 14 November 1908, p.380.
33. Quoted in Ruchatz, 'Travelling by Slide', p.37.
34. Edward L. Wilson, *Wilson's Lantern Journeys* (New York: E.L. Wilson, 1888), pp.232–72.
35. Ibid., p.244.
36. 'Irish Art and Music', *Hartford Courant* (Hartford, CT), 17 May 1905, p.7.
37. 'St Patrick's Celebration', *North Adams Evening Transcript* (North Adams, MA), 13 March 1909, p.6.
38. 'Poems of Moore Illustrated', *Lowell Sun* (Lowell, MA), 14 December 1894, p.4. Information concerning Michael Dwyer's lectures on Moore's poetry appears in 'Hibernians', *Kentucky Irish-American*, 13 January 1906, p.3, as well as in 'Mr Dwyer's Lectures', *Boston Globe*, 24 June 1907, p.14.
39. 'Lectured on Ireland', *Washington Post*, 30 April 1900, p.4.
40. 'Grand Illustrated Lecture', *Gaelic American*, 22 December 1906, p.6; 'The Hibernian Lecture Bureau', *National Hibernian*, 15 January 1907, p.8; 'Hibernian Lecture Bureau', *National Hibernian*, 15 October 1907, p.3.
41. Information on Thomas Tuite's lectures on Robert Emmett appears in 'Emmet's Life in Pictures', *Gaelic American*, 15 November 1913, p.3; 'Mr Tuite Will Show Many Rare Emmet Pictures', *Gaelic American*, 11 December 1915, p.8; and 'Thomas P. Tuite Delivers Lecture on Robert Emmet', *Gaelic American*, 18 December 1915, p.5.
42. 'Dr Green to Lecture', *Cedar Rapids Evening Gazette* (Cedar Rapids, IA), 16 March 1899, p.8.
43. 'St Patrick Celebration', *New York Times*, 15 March 1907, p.16.
44. Advertisement, *Moving Picture World*, 12 March 1910, p.397.
45. 'Dr Shahan's Brilliant Lecture', *National Hibernian*, 15 December 1904, p.4.
46. 'Lecture by Rev. Fr Hurley', *Boston Globe*, 16 December 1906, p.24; advertisement. *Washington Post*, 5 February 1909, p.4.
47. 'An Irish Nation', *New York Times*, 16 May 1904, p.6.
48. Advertisement, *New York Clipper*, 25 September 1886, p.445.
49. 'The Star Course', *Newport Mercury*, 31 December 1887, p.1; 'At the Theatre', *Salt Lake Tribune* (Salt Lake City, UT), 12 July 1894, p.5. Lectures on world tours were not restricted to theatres and lecture halls. For example, a world tour lecture that depicted Ireland was given at the First Congregational Sunday School of Racine, Wisconsin, in 1911. See 'Church Gives Entertainment', *Racine Daily Journal*, 23 December 1911, p.5.
50. [Untitled], *Elyria Weekly Republican* (Elyria, OH), 10 January 1884, p.5; 'Entertainments', *Hartford Daily Courant*, 9 March 1885, p.2. Professor H.H. Ragan offered a similar lecture – entitled *England, Scotland, Ireland, and Wales* – with slides projected by a 'powerful lantern' in Chautauqua, New York, in 1884 ('The Chautauqua Assembly', *New York Times*, 21 July 1884, p.5). Then, in 1891, a lantern lecture on the subject of Scotland, Ireland and England was given at the Burtis Opera House in Davenport, Iowa ('Brevities', *Davenport Daily Tribune*, 11 March 1891, p.4).
51. Advertisement, *Fitchburg Sentinel* (Fitchburg, MA), 23 February 1882, p.3.
52. 'Ireland and Scotland', *Boston Daily Globe*, 22 September 1882, p.2. French also presented the same lecture in Hartford, Connecticut. See 'Interesting Lecture', *Hartford Daily Courant*, 26 July 1882, p.2.
53. As an example, Dr C.H. Steele presented five different lectures on five different days in Oakland, California, in 1891: *The Highlands and Lowlands of Scotland, London, the World's Metropolis, Picturesque Ireland, Paris, the Beautiful*, and *Mountains and Lakes of Switzerland* (advertisement, *Oakland Tribune*, 18 April 1891, p.7).

54. 'Ireland and the Irish', *Boston Daily Globe*, 18 October 1886, p.5. A 'Mr Bolton' offered a similar approach two years earlier in a lecture on Ireland, Scotland and England by giving his audience 'a graphic description of a trip across the Atlantic, a tour through Ireland, Scotland, and England, the points of interest being well portrayed by the fine views exhibited'. See [untitled], *Elyria Republican* (Elyria, OH), 10 January 1884, p.5.

55. 'Francis Dillon-Eagan's Lecture', *Brooklyn Daily Eagle*, 14 November 1889, p.3; 'Pictures of Ireland', *Brooklyn Daily Eagle*, 15 November 1889, p.3.

56. 'Brooklyn Institute News', *Brooklyn Daily Eagle*, 30 January 1902, p.11. That same year, Joseph Martin gave an illustrated lecture in New York City entitled *Ireland*. See 'Lecture on Ireland', *The Irish-American*, 15 February 1902, p.4.

57. 'Lantern Lectures', *Views and Film Index*, 23 March 1907, p.4; 'Lantern Lectures', *Views and Film Index*, 4 May 1907, p.4.

58. 'Gave Travelogue', *The Pilot* (Boston, MA), 27 January 1912, p.3.

59. 'City Brevities', *New York Times*, 28 February 1915, p.13.

60. For example, the lecture *Ever Green Isle* – which was presented in Hartford, Connecticut, in 1903 – had the 'traveller' land at Queenstown before moving onto Irish scenery. See 'Tour through Ireland', *Hartford Courant*, 9 February 1903, p.9.

61. 'A Tour of the Emerald Isle', *Brooklyn Daily Eagle*, 22 January 1890, p.1.

62. 'Della – August 22', *Daily News* (Frederick, MD), 23 August 1892, p.3.

63. 'Irish Oratory at Chautauqua', *Evening Statesman* (Marshall, MI), 21 August 1913, p.1.

64. 'Our New Lecture Bureau', *National Hibernian*, 15 November 1904, p.4; 'The A. O. H. Lecture Bureau', *National Hibernian*, 15 March 1906, p.3.

65. 'The Hibernian Lecture Bureau', *National Hibernian*, 15 April 1907, p.8.

66. For example, illustrated tour lectures of Ireland occurred as part of St Patrick's Day celebrations in Boston in 1890 ('Scenes in Ireland', *Boston Globe*, 17 March 1890, p.5), Chicago in 1909, 1910 and 1913 ('Ireland's Patron Saint Is Honored', *Chicago Tribune*, 18 March 1909, p.5; 'Songs of Ireland for Patron Saint', *Chicago Tribune*, 18 March 1910, p.11; 'Irish Celebrate St Patrick's Eve', *Chicago Tribune*, 17 March 1913, p.5) and New York City in 1898 and 1899 ('Mayor Grant's Quest', *New York Times*, 18 March 1898, p.1; 'St Patrick's Day Events', *New York Times*, 17 March 1899, p.3).

67. 'Tour of Ireland', *Hartford Courant*, 9 February 1903, p.9.

68. 'An Evening in Ireland', *Hartford Courant*, 18 April 1904, p.7. The *Illustrated Lecture on Ireland Concert and Dance* made a similar claim, suggesting the talk would feature 'the most beautiful and varied collection of pictures of Ireland ever seen here. Over 200 scenes illustrating delightfully the serene beauties of the Emerald Isle.' See advertisement, *Irish-American Advocate*, 23 July 1921, p.8.

69. 'A Gaelic Entertainment', *Gaelic American*, 30 December 1905, p.2.

70. 'Illustrated Lecture', *Ironwood Times* (Ironwood, MI), 5 August 1899, p.1.

71. For example, when Dr J.J. Landers gave a lecture on Ireland in Dunkirk, New York, in 1888, he promoted the fact that he used 'many beautiful new lantern views'. See 'The Yellow Fever Entertainment', *Dunkirk Observer* (Dunkirk, NY), 5 October 1888, p.4.

72. 'Scenes in Ireland', *Los Angeles Times*, 20 June 1896, p.5.

73. 'A Trip Through Ireland', *Los Angeles Times*, 13 January 1897, p.7.

74. 'Scenes of Ireland', *Boston Daily Globe*, 29 April 1895, p.12.

75. 'Songs of Ireland for Patron Saint', *Chicago Daily Tribune*, 18 March 1910, p.11.

76. 'Silly Lecture on Ireland', *Gaelic American*, 10 December 1910, p.3.

77. Ibid.

78. 'Local Matters', *Fitchburg Daily Sentinel*, 13 March 1889, p.3.

79. 'Hibernian Lecture Bureau', *National Hibernian*, 15 October 1907, p.3.

80. The *Gaelic American* noted that Mathew had made her first trip to America in 1907. 'She made her first public appearance in New York City and scored an unqualified success', the newspaper wrote. See 'Miss Kathleen Mathew', *Gaelic American*, 5 December 1908, p.8. See also advertisement, *Irish-American Advocate*, 28 November 1908, p.5; advertisement, *Gaelic American*, 3 January 1914, p.8.

81. 'Miss Mathew's Coming Lecture', *Irish-American Advocate*, 13 February 1909, p.2; 'Briefs', *Naugatuck Daily News* (Naugatuck, CT), 22 September 1913, p.3.

82 . 'Miss Mathew Will Appear on Sunday Evening', *Irish-American Advocate*, 20 February 1909, p.1.

83. 'Where to Go Today', *Washington Post*, 17 May 1914, p.2.

84. 'Amusements', *Oshkosh Daily Northwestern* (Oshkosh, WI), 7 May 1881, p.4.

85. 'Brieflets', *Janesville Daily Gazette* (Janesville, WI), 14 March 1888, p.4.

86. 'Travels in Ireland', *Boston Daily Globe*, 6 December 1887, p.6.

87. 'Church News', *Lowell Sun*, 11 May 1889, p.5.

88. 'Scenery of Ireland', *Boston Daily Globe*, 29 April 1895, p.12.

89. 'Notes of the Week', *New York Times*, 31 January 1886, p.7.

90. 'Scenes in Ireland', *Boston Daily Globe*, 17 March 1890, p.5.

91. 'Seamus MacManus to Lecture in America', *The Pilot*, 6 October 1906, p.5; 'Seamus MacManus at Manhattan College', *The Pilot*, 8 December 1906, p.4; 'Mac Manus [sic] in New York', *Gaelic American*, 12 December 1908, p.8; 'Mac Manus [sic] on the Road', *Gaelic American*, 19 December 1908, p.5; 'Mac Manus [sic] Lecture Tour', *Gaelic American*, 30 April 1910, p.5; 'MacManus' Lecture Tour', *Gaelic American*, 14 January 1911, p.3; 'M'Manus' Lecture Tour', *Gaelic American*, 20 May 1911, p.7; 'Seamus McManus [sic] Goes on a Lecture Tour', *The Irish-American*, 9 November 1912, p.1; 'Seamus MacManus in Minnesota', *The Irish-American*, 14 December 1912, p.1.

92. 'Mr MacManus' Lectures', *Gaelic American*, 15 October 1910, p.7.

93. Advertisement, *Irish-American Advocate*, 23 February 1918, p.6.

94. 'Tour Ireland in Ireland', *Los Angeles Times*, 11 February 1913, p.II8.

95. 'With Prof. A.S. Bickmore', *New York Times*, 20 January 1895, p.23.

96. 'Scenes in the Green Isle', *New York Times*, 14 October 1894, p.9.

97. 'Ireland on Lantern Slides', *New York Times*, 28 October 1894, p.16.

98. 'Donald Downie', *Atlanta Constitution*, 8 April 1893, p.O5.

99. 'Amusements', *New York City*, 15 December 1889, p.12.

100. 'Donald Downie', p.O5.

101. 'Illustrated Lecture on Ireland', *Washington Post*, 8 January 1894, p.5.

102. 'Illustrated Lecture', *Daily News* (Frederick, MD), 23 January 1894, p.3.

103. 'Notes of the Week', *New York Times*, 24 October 1886, p.9.

104. 'Notes of the Week', *New York Times*, 2 January 1887, p.7; 'Amusements', *New York Times*, 13 March 1887, p.2.

105. 'Amusements', *New York Times*, 17 March 1889, p.3; 'Theatrical Gossip', *New York Times*, 22 October 1889, p.8.

106. 'The Theatrical Week', *New York Times*, 15 November 1891, p.13.

107. 'The Theatrical Week', *New York Times*, 14 February 1892, p.13.

108. 'Pittsburg [sic] Exposition', *Indiana Progress* (Indiana, PA), 14 September 1892, p.1.

109. D.C. Taylor, *John L. Stoddard: Traveller, Lecturer, Litterateur* (New York: P.J. Kennedy & Sons, 1935), pp.114–15.

110. X.T. Barber, 'The Roots of Travel Cinema: John L. Stoddard, E. Burton Holmes, and the Nineteenth-Century Illustrated Travel Lecture', *Film History*, 5, 1 (March 1993), p.70.

111. Ibid., p.73.

112. Taylor, *John L. Stoddard*, pp.125–6.

113. Ibid., p.126.

114. Barber, 'Roots of Travel Cinema', p.72.

115. Ibid., p.73.

116. 'At the Theatres', *Syracuse Evening Herald*, 31 December 1898, p.4.

117. Barber, 'Roots of Travel Cinema', p.79; E.B. Holmes, *The World Is Mine* (Culver City, CA: Murray & Gee, Inc., 1953), p.46.

118. 'Fruits of 2, 500, 000 Mile Journeys for Film Public', *Logansport Journal-Tribune* (Logansport, IN), 12 January 1916, p.8.

119. Barber, 'Roots of Travel Cinema', p.82.

120. Taylor, *John L. Stoddard*, p.126.

121. Ibid.

122. Barber, 'Roots of Travel Cinema', p.81.

123. J.L. Stoddard, *John L. Stoddard's Lectures, Supplementary Volume* (Boston, MA: Balch Brothers Co., 1901), pp.8–9. While they certainly read as if they are speeches, it is possible that Stoddard reworked the text of his two Irish lectures for print publication. However, his biographer implies that they are an accurate representation of lectures he offered to the public. See Taylor, *John L. Stoddard*, pp.46–7.

124. Stoddard, *John L. Stoddard's Lectures, Supplementary Vol.*, p.22.
125. The titles I use for Stoddard's slides reflect the captions he gave them in *John L. Stoddard's Lectures, Supplementary Vol.* He did not sell retail copies of his slides or necessarily announce their titles during his lectures.
126. Ibid., pp.107–8.
127. Ibid., p.107.
128. Ibid., pp.59–62.
129. Ibid., pp.32, 35.
130. Ibid., p.125.
131. Ibid., p.133.
132. Ibid., pp.120–1, 168, 191–2.
133. Ibid., p.168.
134. Ibid., pp.213–14.
135. E.B. Holmes, *England, Scotland, Ireland: Burton Holmes Travelogues* (Chicago, IL: White House, 1922), p.230. In this book, Holmes's lecture on Ireland is presented as if it was the same lecture he had given publicly many years earlier. While it does read as if it is a speech, it is possible that Holmes made some modifications for print publication.
136. Ibid., p.276.
137. The titles I use for Holmes's slides reflect the caption titles that he gave them in *England, Scotland, Ireland: Burton Holmes Travelogues*.
138. Ibid., p.256.
139. *Catalogue and Price List of Stereopticons ... Photographic Views* (1867), pp.28–9, 33.
140. *Catalogue and Price List of Lanterns ... Photographic Views on Glass* (1882), p.59.
141. Ibid., p.67.
142. *Catalogue of Lanterns ... Subjects of Popular Interest* (1898), p.93.
143. Ibid., p.95.
144. Ibid., p.94.
145. Ibid., p.98.
146. These same same slides were offered for sale over a period of years. For example, the Kleine Optical Company sold them as a series of 'Irish Characters' in their 1905 catalogue (p.19).
147. Advertisement, *Moving Picture World*, 11 July 1908, p.32.
148. 'Tony Pastor and His Sixty Years on the Stage', *New York Times*, 16 August 1908, p.SM3.
149. 'The Song Slide Situation: An Interview with the "Daddy" of the Song Slide', *Views and Film Index*, 7 March 1908, p.14.
150. Ibid., p.13.
151. Ibid.
152. W.H.A. Williams, *'Twas Only an Irishman's Dream: The Image of Ireland and the Irish in American Popular Song Lyrics, 1800–1920* (Urbana, IL: University of Illinois Press, 1996), pp.34–5.
153. Ibid., pp.71–2.
154. Ibid., p.102.
155. Ibid., pp.106–8, 110–11.
156. J.W. Ripley, 'All Join in the Chorus', *American Heritage*, 10, 4 (June 1959), p.53.
157. For example, the song was performed in Ogden, Utah, in 1904: see 'Random References', *Standard* (Ogden, UT), 8 July 1904, p.5. That same year, Peter Dunsworth – the 'new illustrated song singer'– became an 'instantaneous success' when he sang the song at the Bell Theatre in Oakland, California ('Bell Theatre', *Oakland Tribune*, 1 October 1904, p.15). Sheet music for *Why Did They Sell Killarney?* had been sold as early as 1901. See advertisement, *New York Clipper*, 2 November 1901, p.783.
158. The original slides for this illustrated song exist in the Marnan Collection in Minneapolis, Minnesota. Unless otherwise noted, my comments on the visuals of Irish-themed illustrated songs stem from an examination of the original slides in the Marnan Collection.
159. 'Illustrated Song and Story', *Fitchburg Sentinel*, 18 March 1898, p.5.
160. 'Panorama of Ireland', *Hartford Courant*, 3 March 1906, p.7.
161. '20 Harpists on the Stage', *Post-Standard* (Syracuse, NY), 14 March 1910, p.6.
162. See, for example: advertisement, *Moving Picture World*, 20 March 1909, p.1909; advertisement, *Moving Picture World*, 9 April 1910, p.572.

163. 'Good News for Slide Makers', *Views and Film Index*, 9 February 1907, p.2; 'Destroying the Lantern Slide Business', *Moving Picture World*, 3 October 1908, p.253.
164. 'Souvenirs at the Scenic', *Hartford Courant*, 19 December 1907, p.12.
165. 'Moving Picture Notes', *New York Dramatic Mirror*, 10 July 1909.
166. E. Bowser, *The Transformation of Cinema, 1907–1915* (Berkeley, CA: University of California, 1990), p.15.
167. *Illustrated Song Slides* (Philadelphia, PA: S. Lubin, 1905); ibid. Available in *Guide to Motion Picture Catalogs ... 1894–1908: Microfilm Edition*, Reel 2.
168. 'Not a Song Hit on the Market', *Moving Picture World*, 4 July 1908, p.6.
169. 'Our Commercial Index', *Views and Film Index*, 22 September 1906, p.7.
170. Ripley, 'All Join in the Chorus', p.52.
171. For example, O'Connor was a model in DeWitt C. Wheeler's illustrated song slides for *Why Don't They Set Him Free?* (1913).
172. 'Trade Notes', *Moving Picture World,* 15 May 1908, p.438.
173. Ripley, 'All Join in the Chorus', p.51.
174. All that said, some nickelodeon theatre managers tried to save money by reusing slides from previous songs, including in those instances when a slide, or slides, for another song had been broken ('Destroying the Lantern Slide Business', *Moving Picture World*, 3 October 1908, p.253). Moreover, lantern operators occasionally projected the correct slides out of order. For example, one nickelodeon theatre manager in a small town used a noticeably incorrect slide during a performance of *Way Down Upon the Swanee River* ('Things the Audiences Miss', *New York Times*, 8 December 1912, p.X11).
175. Bowser, *Transformation of Cinema, 1907–1915*, p.15.
176. C.K. Harris, 'Song Slide the Little Father of Photodrama', *Moving Picture World*, 10 March 1917, p.1520.
177. As Rick Altman has said, 'it is a distortion of history to label these machines film projectors, for they are simply magic lanterns (light source and slide transport) to which moving picture capability had been added'. See R. Altman, *Silent Film Sound* (New York: Columbia University Press, 2004), p.183.
178. Ibid., p.182.
179. Ibid., p.192.
180. Advertisement, *New York Dramatic Mirror*, 19 October 1907, p.17.
181. Illustrated song collector and historian John W. Ripley made these calculations, notes of which exist in the Marnan Collection of Minneapolis, Minnesota.
182. Williams, *'Twas Only an Irishman's Dream*, pp.192–7, 216–33.
183. Ibid., p.189.
184. Ibid., p.197.
185. 'Song Slide Releases', *The Film Index*, 31 December 1910, p.30.
186. Advertisement, *Moving Picture World*, 14 August 1909, p.230; advertisement, *Moving Picture World*, 12 March 1910, p.348.
187. Advertisement, *Moving Picture World*, 19 February 1910, p.271.
188. Another indication of *Arrah Wanna*'s popularity was the fact that A.L. Simpson was not the only company to release a set of illustrated song slides for it. In 1907, Harstn & Company promoted a set ('Illustrated Songs', *Views and Film Index*, 9 February 1907, p.5), as did the F.B. Haviland Publishing Company ('Song Slides', *Views and Film Index*, 4 May 1907, p.5). These might have been comprised of different slides from the A.L. Simpson slides, or they might have been the same, thus exemplifying its widespread distribution and popularity.
189. 'Song Slide Releases', *The Film Index*, 31 December 1910, p.30.
190. Influenced by *Has Anybody Here Seen Kelly?*, the third verse of *Kelly's Gone to Kingdom Come* features 'Missus Kelly,' who travels to consult with Sherlock Holmes as to Kelly's whereabouts; she believes he may have left her for a mermaid.
191. Williams, *'Twas Only an Irishman's Dream*, p.183.
192. Altman, *Silent Film Sound*, section entitled 'Color Plates' [n.p.].
193. 'Song Slide Releases', *The Film Index*, 24 June 1911, p.30.
194. 'Song Slide Releases', *The Film Index*, 4 February 1911, p.30; 'Song Slide Releases', *The Film Index*, 11 February 1911, p.30.

195. 'Song Slide Releases', *The Film Index*, 18 March 1911, p.30.

196. 'A Few Recent Slides and Songs', *New York Dramatic Mirror*, 17 July 1909.

197. 'Song Slide Releases', *The Film Index*, 31 December 1910, p.30.

198. G.F. Blaisdell, 'From the Observatory', *Moving Picture News*, 25 November 1911, p.38. In this article, Blaisdell congratulated the 'picture theatre proprietors in Quincey, Ill.' for eliminating sold slides from their film programmes.

199. Advertisement, *Moving Picture News*, 11 May 1912, p.41. The four Irish song slide sets were *Kathleen Mavourneen*, *The Irish Emigrant*, *The Dear Little Shamrock*, and *Killarney*.

200. 'The Movies', *Hamilton Evening Journal* (Hamilton, IN), 17 March 1926, p.11.

201. 'At the Orpheum', *Oelwein Daily Register* (Oelwein, IA), 2 April 1926, p.5.

202. 'This Week', *New York Times*, 11 March 1979, p.ADZ10.

203. *Visual Education: Teacher's Guide to Keystone's 600 Set* (Meadville, PA: Keystone View Company, 1922), p.20–1.

204. Zoe A. Thralls, *Unit XXVI: The British Isles* (Meadville, PA: Keystone View Co., 1938).

205. Karen Martin, *A Short History of the Keystone View Company* (Meadville, PA: Johnson-Shaw Stereoscopic Museum, 2006), p.10.

206. G.E. Hamilton, *The Stereograph and the Lantern Slide in Education* (Meadville, PA: Keystone View Co., 1946), p.44.

# Chapter Three

# *Non-Fiction*

Published in the September 1911 issue of *Motion Picture Story Magazine*, Lizzie Pinson's poem *A Motion Picture Traveller* described an American named Bill who could:

> Tell of the Orient, France, and the Nile,
> Of Great Britain and Africa, too;
> He'd climb the Alps where he lingered a while
> To enjoy the magnificent view.
> On the various industries, customs, and dress
>
> Of countries both near and afar,
> He'd declaim in a manner that needs must impress –
> He'd met Emp'ror, King, Sultan, and Czar.[1]

The poem ends by admitting the man had never 'been out of his own native State'. Moving picture travelogues, rather than personal experience, had 'taught Bill all he knows'.

As Charles Musser has noted, the moving picture 'travelogue' (a term invented by travel lecturer E. Burton Holmes) was a direct outgrowth of lantern slide travel lectures given by such people as Holmes and John L. Stoddard, and it emerged as 'one of the most popular and developed' genres in early American cinema.[2] Indeed, during the late 1890s, moving pictures shot in other countries quickly became a component of travel lectures in the United States, where they functioned alongside the continued use of lantern slides. In addition, moving picture travelogues were regularly screened at film exhibitions in programmes that also featured fictional films.

In Pinson's poem, 'Bill' experiences both major categories of non-fiction travelogue that appeared in early cinema. The first of the categories could be called the expeditionary film, which focussed on landscape 'panoramas', as they were often described in their titles and catalogue descriptions.[3] In

**3.1** Advertisement published in the 15 August 1903 issue of the
*New York Clipper*.

addition to those images, Bill also sees 'various industries, customs, and dress' of people living outside of the United States; in other words, he also watches the ethnographic moving picture, which concentrated on the people and culture of a given region or country.[4] Together these films became part of the larger genre of 'foreign views', a category that, as Tom Gunning has noted, adopted a 'particular point of view, one from outside the land viewed'.[5] In Pinson's poem, Bill experiences a tourist-based point of view, a point of view that dated to travel lectures of the nineteenth century.

At times these two categories could overlap, as expeditionary and ethnographic images could occur in the same moving picture travelogue, just as they had within travel lectures illustrated by lantern slides; the commonality of such images was that both generally adopted a touristic point of view. Indeed, Gunning sees these films as part of the larger context of travel images of the late nineteenth and early twentieth centuries (which also included postcards, for example) and suggests that such images 'cannot be understood' without consideration of the 'development of mass tourism'.[6] He adds: 'Images of foreign lands took on a more tangible quality when audiences knew it was possible to travel to them, even if they did not undertake the journey themselves.'[7]

In Pinson's poem, 'Bill' also meets various world leaders, who were chronicled in yet another category of early non-fiction cinema, the current events film. As with the expeditionary and ethnographic travelogues, the current events film emerged in the 1890s. Such moving pictures offered non-fiction images of other countries or regions, but their focus was on newsworthy events. The primary influence on them was not the travel lecture (though some travel lecturers had incorporated current events into their talks), but instead newspapers and photojournalism. After the introduction of *Pathe's Weekly* in America in 1911, the earlier current events films transformed into the newsreel (and, to a lesser extent, the propaganda film), which then became the dominant form of non-fiction film at US theatres.[8]

From at least as early as 1900, Ireland became the topic of many different expeditionary, ethnographic and current events films screened in the United States as part of the broader category of 'foreign views'. As Jeffrey Ruoff has suggested, 'the educational impulse of the travelogue is one of its defining characteristics, even when it is a pretext for other, less edifying pleasures'.[9] Indeed, other visual pleasures were present, as these travelogues and current events films – which would often be screened as part of programmes that also included fictional films – attempted to provide entertainment as well as education. In 1909, for example, travelling exhibitor Lyman H. Howe promoted the dual purpose of early travelogues in publicity for his show: 'To the World, the World we show/We make the World to laugh/And teach each Hemisphere to know/How lives the Other Half.'[10]

Musser has noted that the early fiction film adopted aspects of the travelogue genre, but it is also true that the early non-fiction film appropriated elements of the fictional film. As Alison Griffiths has written:

> Oppositions between real and faked, authentic and fabricated, and genuine and imitation were ... subject to flexible interpretation in this period. In addition, the problem of 'authentic' travel films from reconstructions and re-enactments, which were the bedrock of countless popular films portraying ethnographic subjects as well as coronations, executions, military campaigns, boxing matches, and safaris in the pre-1905 period, blurs the boundaries between fact and fiction.[11]

In one or more cases, non-fiction films of Ireland and the Irish were mired in a problem that pervaded much non-fiction film of the early cinema period: they were faked. For example, according to a catalogue summary, Edison's 'realistic' *Boers Bringing in British Prisoners* (1900) showed 'a mixed company of Gordon Highlanders, Irish Fusilliers, and English lancers, as a group of prisoners taken to the rear by a troop of Boer cavalry'.[12] In reality, the film was shot in New Jersey, and it includes no footage of Irish troops.[13]

As a result of the proliferation of such faked 'non-fiction' moving pictures, such as faked versions of famous boxing matches, some film companies often attempted to underscore the authenticity of their own images. For example, an American Mutoscope & Biograph catalogue summary of Gaumont's *Kissing the Blarney Stone* (1904, aka *Blarney Castle and Stone*) pronounced: 'This is the Genuine thing. There has been an imitation of this famous scene, but this is the first time the quaint ceremony has been shown in motion pictures just as it occurs at Blarney Castle.'[14] Here the term 'actuality', as the non-fiction film was often called at the time, resonates with particular meaning. *Kissing the Blarney* Stone offered something that actually happened in the actual location as stated, as opposed to a previous 'imitation'.

Despite the fact that the boundary between fiction and non-fiction moving pictures in the early cinema period was porous, the history of Irish-themed non-fiction of that era would be marked by an emphasis on authenticity and consistency. This was due in part to the fact that such non-fiction films about Ireland were in most cases actually shot on location in Ireland. In terms of consistency, these non-fiction films often revisited particular locations (the Lakes of Killarney and the Giant's Causeway, for example) or particular kinds of ethnographic scenes (such as workers in peat bogs, or Irish citizens in urban market scenes) that had been depicted in earlier non-fiction films, as well as in lantern slides and stereo views; the same sites had also been heralded in popular music and live entertainment of the nineteenth century.

## The Travel Lecturer and the Moving Picture

As already noted, illustrated travel lectures of the nineteenth century heavily influenced moving picture travelogues. More specifically, it is important to understand that, as early as the spring of 1897, various public speakers in America were considering the use of moving pictures as a supplement to their lectures.[15] In many cases, such lecturers would use film footage in addition to lantern slides, thus creating an interplay between both media forms. Many lecturers purchased their moving pictures from companies that sold films; during the pre-nickelodeon and nickelodeon eras, companies like Lubin sold both non-fiction lantern slides and non-fiction moving pictures within the same catalogue. However, other lecturers would shoot their own footage while travelling, thus obtaining images that were both relevant and unique to their lectures.

The first American lecturer to screen moving pictures at public lectures was E. Burton Holmes. After purchasing a moving picture camera in France in 1897, Holmes and his pioneering travel cinematographer Oscar Depue immediately began shooting their own footage. Unfortunately, the precise details of their travel movements in 1897 are unknown, but it is clear, for example, that they shot some footage in Italy that year, and that they also travelled to England. Those details – as well as the fact that Holmes and Depue regularly visited many countries on their European trips – suggest that they could well have undertaken filming in England and Ireland in 1897. Holmes did not lecture on Ireland during his 1897–98 season, but that would not have prohibited his shooting in the country. Nor would it have prohibited him screening footage of Ireland if he had acquired it, as his initial use of moving pictures in 1897–98 represented an added attraction to his lectures. Such images, which were projected by Depue, covered a range of travel subjects outside of the specific topic of his lectures.[16] One journalist in Fort Wayne, Indiana, described the selection as offering '*A Polo Game at Lake Forest, Cyclists Coasting on Sheridan Road, Fire Alarm, Gondola Scene*, etc'.[17]

It is also quite possible that Holmes and Depue visited Ireland in the summer of 1898. For his 1898–99 season, Holmes's moving pictures included 'several glimpses of the Queen's jubilee celebration in London' along with a 'number of [other] motion pictures'.[18] And, while they probably did not travel to Europe on their 1899 trip – having opted instead to shoot footage in China, Japan and Manila that year – they may well have filmed in Ireland in 1900, 1901 and/or 1902.[19] In his memoirs, Charles Urban, the managing director of Warwick Trading Company, noted:

> The Paris Exposition of 1900 brought over Mr Burton Holmes, the eminent American world traveller and writer, who added the cinema to his illustrated lantern slide lectures, for which he became very popular. As Warwick films were principally of a travel character, Mr Holmes visited us twice-a-year and view[ed] the series of films of countries our men had taken views of. We supplied him with extracts of scenes from these films, so as to enable his cameraman Depue to take snap shots of Holmes in identical surroundings to those shown in the film.
>
> These snap shots he made into lantern slides, which were interspersed with the films when showing as he lectured. This

conveyed to people that he also took the cinema pictures. This had two advantages. First, many of the film scenes could only be procured in certain seasons and many events and fete days on religious days in many countries were only enacted on specific dates, which may not have coincided with the time of Mr Holmes' visit. Weather conditions also had much to do with securing good photographic results.

Second, as one cameraman sometimes spent six months in a country to make a representative series, illustrating the scenic beauties, peculiarities of architecture, etc. etc. that it became much cheaper to Mr Holmes in thus adapting ready-made pictures for his lectures.[20]

As Urban resigned from Warwick in February 1903, his mention of Holmes's 'twice-a-year' visits would probably have referred to the years 1900–02, a period during which Holmes and Depue could also have filmed in Ireland. While they did obtain some lantern slides and moving pictures from Warwick, it does seem that they acquired most of their footage themselves.

What is certain is that Holmes spent several weeks in Ireland in the summer of 1904, where he was 'charmed' by the 'island itself and with its hospitable, witty people'.[21] During that trip, Depue shot footage in Ireland and England.[22] After returning to the US, Holmes readied five lectures for his 1904–05 touring season: *In London, Round About London, Beautiful Ireland, The Russian Empire* and *Japan*, the last two of which he had given in previous seasons.[23] In Chicago, one of the first cities on the tour, a newspaper review described *Beautiful Ireland* as:

a travelogue in three scenes and thirty-two motion pictures ... A wealth of colored views [of Ireland] were the result of his photographic achievements and an interesting and varied series of motion pictures also were taken by him and his associates. A number of 'crazy' motion pictures – crossing from Holyhead to Dublin, Cruise from Bangor to Belfast, Cook's Tourists in Killarney, Town, and the 'crazy' rowboats – will be shown.[24]

Details are scant, but the 'thirty-two motion pictures' may have indicated the number of individual shots of Ireland that were projected.

After finishing what was 'by far the most successful' reception Holmes had ever experienced in Chicago, he travelled to the west coast, where he gave his lectures (including *Beautiful Ireland*) in San Francisco, Los Angeles

3.2 Advertisement published in the 1 October 1904 issue of the *New York Clipper*. Given the length and title of *Shooting the Killarney Rapids, Ireland*, it is possible that this film represents a different version of the subject than both the Warwick and the Gaumont.

and 'vicinity', before then heading east to Philadelphia, Washington, DC, Pittsburgh and Detroit.[25] A newspaper review of *Beautiful Ireland* in Washington, DC, noted that Holmes proclaimed: 'To appreciate an Irishman's love for his country, one must see its beauties.' The newspaper added:

> Mr Holmes showed the wonders of the Giant's Causeway, one of the greatest examples of volcanic architecture, and his pictures gave up a most vivid impression of Killarney's charm. That Ireland is not wholly dependent upon her scenic wonders was shown by the life and fashion which the horse show brings together at Dublin. On the other hand, the lecturer told of the sadness and hopelessness of the peasants' life.[26]

In mentioning the 'peasants' life', this account underscores the power the lecturer held over how an audience might interpret individual images; 'sadness and hopeless' mitigated the 'scenic wonders'.

In the spring of 1905, Holmes gave his five different lectures in New York, Brooklyn and Boston. Speaking of *Beautiful Ireland*, the *New York Times* described, 'pictures of Cork, Belfast, and Dublin', and noted that 'historic and beautiful spots in various sections of Ireland provoked much applause'.[27] A review in the *Boston Globe* provided more detail, claiming the 'peculiarities' of the Giant's Causeway were 'clearly depicted', and that Killarney's beautiful scenes were shown to excellent advantage, and the famous Blarney castle was also presented. Various cities with their bustling activity were illustrated, as well as the quiet villages, presenting a marked contrast. In addition to the regular views, a number of moving pictures were shown, many of them so arranged that they supplied the humorous side of the lecture capitally.

Mention of the lecture's 'humorous side' reiterates the fact that such lectures and travelogue films emphasized entertainment as well as education. In *Beautiful Ireland*, the entertainment value may well have been strong, as Holmes repeated the lecture on one or more occasions in 1907.[28]

The American Film Institute has catalogued some seventeen films shot in Ireland by Holmes and Depue; given the fact that these films are dated 1905 and that three of them were shot at the Dublin horse show, they probably constitute seventeen of the thirty-two 'films' – which, as already suggested, might have been only brief shots or short scenes – that Holmes and Depue filmed in 1904.[29] Among the other films they catalogue are a trio of railway films shot in Ireland and a film of an Irish jaunting car in Dublin, the latter being shot from a moving train.[30] Some of the catalogued films seem to be expeditionary in content, showing an 'Old Spinning Wheel' at Dooagh, as well as on-screen tourists at the Gap of Dunloe and the Cliffs of Moher.[31] Based upon their titles, others seem to have been ethnographic, showing such scenes as *Irish Kiddies Coming Out of School*, *Market Women Leaving the Railway Station*, *The Old Boys of Dooagh*, *Achill Island* and a *Squad of Seaforth Highlanders Leaving [the] Bank of Ireland*.[32] Two films showed Irish dancing, and two more depicted the *Irish Constabulary* at Achill Island and a *Battery of Artillery Crossing Ball's Bridge* at Limerick.[33]

Holmes and Depue returned to Ireland and England in the summer of 1914, shooting an array of moving pictures and photographs for use in a new lecture. Holmes gave the talk, which was simply titled *Ireland*, in Chicago in November 1914 before presenting it and several other lectures in such cities as New York, Washington, DC, and Boston.[34] The *Washington Post* noted that the then-current troubles in Ireland created an additional level of interest among audiences.[35] Another article suggested that *Ireland* included 'stirring motion pictures of scenes [of] the great struggle for home rule in Ireland, the Ulster crisis, and the mobilization and departure for the firing line of some well-known Irish regiments'.[36] Whereas Holmes's previous films focussed on the expeditionary and ethnographic, his 1914 films included current events.

However, while the lecture did feature such images as the 'drums and colors of the Ulster volunteers', the bulk of *Ireland* did focus on what the *Washington Post* called the 'wild and rugged beauty of the little island that is always green'.[37] The *Boston Globe* reported:

> Several hundred new colored views and more than two dozen motion pictures gave a satisfying insight into the ever-increasing characteristics of the land, its inhabitants, and its industries... Of course the motion pictures took one on the famous jaunting cars – with the accent on the jaunt – and into the bogs, the castles, to the Blarney Stone, on the 'Ballybunion limited' and to many another 'bally' place.[38]

*Ireland* presented, at least in part, a continuation of what so many lantern slide lectures of the nineteenth century had offered: a touristic point of view in which audience members 'travelled' throughout the island thanks to his words and moving pictures.

Burton Holmes was not alone in his use of moving pictures for public lectures on Ireland. Dwight Elmendorf, the famous travel lecturer of the late nineteenth century and an expert on the colouring of stereopticon slides, screened moving pictures at least as early as 1899 for such lectures as *The Yellowstone Park*, *The Santiago Campaign and the Destruction of Cervera's Fleet* and *Old Mexico and Her Pageants*.[39] Then, in May and June of 1900, Elmendorf travelled to Ireland, England and France. One newspaper account wrote: 'He was aided in his work by a new cinematographic apparatus which he has used with very great success in procuring moving pictures.'[40] Unlike Holmes, who relied on Oscar Depue as cinematographer, Elmendorf seems to have shot his own footage in Ireland.[41]

During May and June 1900, Elmendorf became the first documented American to shoot moving pictures in Ireland. Elmendorf's footage would also constitute the earliest known films of Ireland to be screened in the United States; the images became a key component in Elmendorf's lecture *Ireland from the Giant's Causeway to Glengariff*, which he delivered in the autumn of 1900. Among the locations he discussed were Belfast, Portrush and Dunluce Castle, all of which were shown in lantern slides. A review in the *Brooklyn Eagle* described his moving pictures in brief, saying: 'The cinematograph effects were... very amusing, particularly that of a cock fight in the barnyard of an Irish farm house, and all of them were wonderfully realistic in their effects.'[42]

After giving another lecture in 1902 entitled *Sunny Days in Ireland*, Elmendorf later returned to Ireland in order to gather more footage for yet

| We are the Only Manufacturers Prepared to Supply ALL Demands for | |
|---|---|
| **TOURS OF THE WORLD CARS.** | Trip through Ireland................................................. 4,000 feet<br>Trip through Switzerland.......................................... 6,000 feet<br>Trip through Italy.................................................. 2,500 feet<br>Trip through Canada............................................... 3,000 feet<br>Trip through England.............................................. 4,000 feet<br>Trip through Transvaal............................................ 2,000 feet<br>Trip through India................................................ 2,000 feet<br>Trip through Abyssinia............................................ 2,000 feet<br>Trip through South Africa......................................... 3,000 feet<br>Trip through Australia, N. Z...................................... 3,000 feet<br>Trip through America.............................................. 4,000 feet<br>Trip through France............................................... 1,000 feet<br>Trip through Germany.............................................. 3,000 feet<br>Railway Panoramas from Every Part of the World.................. 10,000 feet<br>Naval Subjects, Merchant, Marine and from All Over the World.... 8,000 feet<br>Fishing Pictures................................................. 2,000 feet<br>Turbulent Seas, Waterfalls and Streams........................... 2,000 feet<br>Steamship Panoramas.............................................. 3,000 feet<br>A Transatlantic Trip of the S. S. Kronprinz Wilhelm, from Bremen to<br>New York...................................................... 2,000 feet<br>Cruise of the Steamer Ophir, with Prince and Princess of Wales on board. 23,000 feet<br>And others from all the countries of the world.  Can be had in any length. |

3.3 Lubin advertisement promoting the 4,000 foot long *Trip Through Ireland*, published in the 14 April 1906 issue of the *New York Clipper*.

another lecture.[43] In May 1906, the *New York Times* noted that Elmendorf was sailing 'for Ireland, where he will take additional motion pictures on that subject'.[44] For his 1906–07 season, Elmendorf featured *Ireland* among his lectures, which was apparently built on footage he obtained on the 1906 trip. His season also included lectures on England and Scotland, to which he had travelled in addition to Ireland.[45]

That Elmendorf's lecture on Ireland contained unique footage was important, as Burton Holmes was lecturing on Ireland that season as well. In fact, Elmendorf gave his Ireland lecture in Washington, DC, on 22 February 1907, only one month after Holmes had offered his own lecture in the same city.[46] In describing Elmendorf's *Ireland*, the *Boston Globe* noted:

> Mr Elmendorf's wonderful moving pictures and colored slides add a charm to his vivid descriptions of people and places that make his talks unusually interesting and valuable from an educational standpoint. He is not only a traveller, but an artist, and he never misses a beautiful effect, his views showing his audiences the best of everything worth seeing.
>
> Belfast to Derry, Dublin, Lough Erne, Tara's hill, and the Lakes of Killarney. No phase of Irish life, either pathetic or comic, was slighted. Cities [sic] busy market places, beautiful country homes, Blarney castle, the water courses, and different types of Irish character being reproduced accurately.[47]

Their review added that Elmendorf showed the 'true Celtic sportsman, horseman and fisherman; the legends of the land; the shrewdness of the country folk, and many characteristics of the denizens of the Emerald Isle'.

However, which of these images were shown through moving pictures and which through lantern slides is unknown.

Elmendorf returned to Ireland as a topic for his 1915–16 season, perhaps due to the attention given to Ireland in the US press at that time.[48] However, he did combine his discussion of the country into a lecture referred to in the *Chicago Tribune* as *The British Isles*; shortly thereafter, the *Washington Post* announced the lecture as *Ireland, Scotland, and England*, suggesting that a change of title might have occurred.[49] Comparing him favourably to Burton Holmes, the *Chicago Tribune* noted:

> He started last night from Queenstown, pausing there long enough to tell a story, and a minute or two later was showing us how an obese friend of his tried to buss the Blarney stone. Bantry Bay, the lakes of Killarney, Peat Digging, salmon fishing, a litter of Irish pigs, Hurdle Races, the Streets of Dublin, a Robin Eating Cherries, and The Giant's Causeway were a part of the edifying loot of his cinema.[50]

Whether or not these were in part or in whole new moving pictures, or were recycled from his 1906 trip is unknown, but the *Chicago Tribune* did record that he probably reused at least some footage from his 1900 trip, noting: 'He had a story and a reflection for each picture, and even the scene of an amateur Irish cockfight moved him to remarks of a contemplative nature.' The same newspaper also underscored Elmendorf's efforts to entertain as well as educate, adding: 'At one point he sang, in his rich baritone, the lullaby with which his old Irish nurse was wont to soothe his boyhood ills, and he showed the photograph of the cottage wherein she passed in her declining years.'[51]

Elmendorf and Holmes were not alone in using moving pictures as part of travel lectures on Ireland. As the *Educational Screen* wrote:

> One lecture specialist, who let no grass grow under his feet in keeping up with the times, was Ernest M. Newman of Chicago. In 1908 he had been a member of Theodore Roosevelt's party in Africa – a distinction which no doubt helped greatly to develop his long-maintained personal lecture circuits in fifteen leading American cities, and to establish the Newman Lecture Company in his home metropolis.[52]

Newman, who was generally credited as 'E.M. Newman' in advertisements, had earlier been an associate of Holmes before branching off on his own.[53]

He covered a range of topics in his 1912 'Traveltalks' lecture tour, ranging from lectures on countries like Scotland, Wales and Germany to more specific topics like *Rural England and the Coronation of George V.*[54]

His 1912 lecture on Ireland included an array of stereopticon slides and moving pictures. Reviewing it, the *Washington Post* noted that:

> The Giant's Causeway, Blarney castle, with its famous kissing stone, the seaside resorts, wild and rugged coast scenery, and excellent moving pictures indicate the large extent of the little, green-carpeted island over which Mr Newman carried his tourists last night. Among the moving pictures was one displaying a close view of Richard Croker and his magnificent home, and a remarkable production of a steeplechase, with many falling horses and daring riders. Specimens of Cromwell's destructiveness, pre-Christian ruins, and early Irish architecture were of great interest to those who like to dig deep into the history of countries they visit.[55]

Reviewing the same lecture in Boston, one newspaper noted that it included other 'scenes', including 'pretty scenes in County Wicklow'.[56] While Newman did travel abroad, it is difficult to determine whether he shot his own footage of Ireland, obtained footage from others, or screened some combination of the two.

While Holmes, Elmendorf and Newman represent the best known of the travel lecturers who used moving pictures, many others presented lectures throughout the United States. In 1912, *Moving Picture World* wrote of the growing demand for 'competent lecturers':

> To-day in almost every large city there is at least one house, often the best house in the place, which has its lecturer. In nine cases out of ten he is a man of some education and some gift of speaking and thoroughly alive to the obligations and possi- bilities of his task... A lecture on a subject illustrated by motion pictures is far more interesting and far more difficult than the talks on still slides, which are going out of fashion as an independent form of amusement.[57]

Such lecturers gave talks on various kinds of topics, though travel subjects remained popular, including lectures on Ireland.[58] For example, R.G. Knowles, a humorist and vaudevillian, became a well-known travel lecturer, presenting many of his talks with a humorous slant; he referred to these as 'travelaughs'.[59] In 1908, he opened his third US lecture series with *Ireland As It Is*, which featured 'colored and motion pictures'. The *New York Times* announced that Knowles had 'lately returned from another tour of the world and personally photographed historic and unique places not generally seen and not on the beaten track of the regular tourist'.[60]

Less well known was Kate Crary and her 'Crary Lecture Co.' of Iowa, which had begun touring in the 1880s. Crary's husband, who was variously referred to as 'Mr Crary' and 'Dr Crary' in the press, operated the magic lantern and, later, film projector for her lectures.[61] Crary not only spoke at her lectures, but also sang songs at them.[62] Unlike many other lecturers, she usually lectured at churches in smaller cities, such as Oshkosh, Wisconsin, and Decatur, Illinois. However, she did incorporate moving pictures into her talks at an early stage. In 1899, at least one of her lectures, *Paris and the Alps*, featured moving pictures in tandem with lantern slides.[63]

After covering Ireland briefly in an 1885 lecture on Europe, she offered *Art Tours of the British Isles: Ireland, England, and Scotland* in 1889.[64] Then, in 1895, Crary lectured more generally on *England, Scotland, and Ireland*.[65] When she repeated the lecture in 1898, the *Syracuse Standard* noted that it was 'brilliantly illustrated by stereopticon views'.[66] By September 1901, Crary offered the lecture *England, Scotland, and Ireland* with '150 stereopticon views and a fine series of moving pictures'. It was one of a number of lectures she offered that year with moving pictures, which included *Paris and the Alps*, *Italy and Rome*, *Yosemite and Yellowstone* and the *Pan-American Exposition*. A 1901 newspaper in Indiana wrote, 'Mr and Mrs Crary have recently added new features to these tours, consisting of wonderful moving pictures and popular illustrated songs. The moving pictures given each evening illustrate scenes in the actual life of the peoples and countries visited.'[67] Kate Crary continued to give the *England, Scotland, and Ireland* lecture for several years, presenting it, for example, at the Trinity M.E. Church in Lima, Ohio, in 1906 and at the Presbyterian Church in Austin, Minnesota, in 1907, where 'standing room only' crowds meant that it became the 'most popular' lecture she gave in the town.[68]

Though at least one account from the 1880s suggested Crary's lectures resulted from her 'travels in Europe and America', there is no record that she travelled to Ireland to shoot her own moving pictures.[69] Given that she also screened such images as *Battle Scenes in Our Late War*, it is apparent she obtained some, if not all, of her footage from others.[70] Holmes and Elmendorf were probably protective of their footage when it came to other lecturers, as at least some of their images were unique. After all, it was not just that they screened moving pictures, but that they screened some moving pictures that could not be seen elsewhere. However, Kate Crary apparently had to look to others to fulfil her moving picture needs. In most cases, that meant relying on emergent film companies that sold prints of their moving pictures to exhibitors.

## The Pre-Nickelodeon Era

During the pre-nickelodeon era, a number of film companies offered Irish-themed non-fiction films; however, they very definitely concentrated on Ireland rather than Irish-America. Perhaps a person or people from Ireland can be seen in the Edison Manufacturing Company's film *Emigrants Landing at Ellis Island* (1903, aka *Immigrants Landing at Ellis Island*), or in American Mutoscope & Biograph's *Arrival of Emigrants, Ellis Island* (1906, aka *Arrival of Immigrants, Ellis Island*). However, the identification of the Irish or Irish-Americans is mere guesswork; neither of these films were promoted as Irish or Irish-American moving pictures.

Only a very small number of non-fiction moving pictures of the early and silent period were promoted for their Irish-American content, at least three of them being military films. Released in June 1898, American Mutoscope's *Irish Volunteers* depicted the First Regiment of the Irish Volunteers, led by Colonel James Moran, at the Decoration Day parade on 30 May 1898, as they passed a reviewing stand at Madison Square Garden. According to the *New York Times*, the regiment – who made an 'admirable showing' – marched with the Veteran Corps of the Sixty-Ninth Regiment and Bayne's Sixty-Ninth Regiment Band.[71] That same year, American Mutoscope also released *69th Regiment Passing in Review* (1898), which depicted the 'Fighting 69th' in Tampa, Florida; a 1902 catalogue description claimed the film was an 'excellent picture photographically', and showed the regiment 'awaiting [their] order to go to Cuba'.[72]

Five years later, Edison released *69th Regiment, N.G.N.Y.* (1903); their catalogue summary noted that the film showed 'the famous Irish regiment marching up Fifth Avenue at 26th Street, while taking part in the Decoration Day parade.[73] They pass platoon front, close to the camera, at a swinging gait.'[74] Though *Irish Volunteers* (by its very title) and *69th Regiment, N.G.N.Y.* (through its catalogue summary, as well as thanks to ongoing press coverage of the 'Fighting Irish') drew attention to Irish heritage of the two different regiments, they constituted military parade films rather than ethnographic studies of Irish-Americans; for example, American Mutoscope also released such military parade films as *65th Regiment at Double Time* (1898), which depicted a non-Irish regiment.[75]

**3.4** Advertisement published in the 7 September 1907 issue of the *Moving Picture World*.

*Dick Croker Leaving Tammany Hall* (Edison, 1900) captured the famous Irish politician on a Sunday afternoon, but it was generally alone in depicting current events in Irish-America. The only other non-fiction film of this era that included obvious images of Irish-Americans was an Edison film that is now catalogued by the Library of Congress as *St Patrick's Day Parade, Lowell, Mass*. No copyright was registered for it, and no film catalogues or publications from the pre-nickelodeon era list it, which calls into question the extent to which it might have been sold or screened. The Library of Congress received their original 35mm nitrate circa 1959 from the George Kleine Collection.[76] They have dated the film as 'ca. 1905', as no records seem to indicate when the film was shot. The *Lowell Sun* did not report on any St Patrick's Day parade in 1905 or the years immediately before and after it, though at least one Irish-American newspaper account clearly suggests that such a parade did occur in Lowell in 1906.[77]

Regardless of the exact year, the film was definitely shot in Lowell, as the visible buildings and street scene make clear that the parade processes up the city's Central Street. Running three minutes, twenty-one seconds at a projection speed of sixteen frames per second, the film features two edits, the first of which results only in a minor change of camera angle. Two marching bands are seen during the procession, as are what seems to be a variety of politicians, policemen, an armed, uniformed regiment, and various other people, including some children. Among those represented could be area divisions of the Ancient Order of Hibernians (including the Ladies' Auxiliary), members of the Irish Benevolent Society, the Wolfe Tone Guards and/or members of area temperance societies, all of which had marched in a previous St Patrick's Day parade in Lowell.[78] The second and final edit on the Library of Congress print then offers a pan from right to left, catching the appearance of a priest, who might be Father William Joyce, Oblates of Mary Immaculate. The pan stops as he descends the steps of a church (which appears to be Lowell's Immaculate Conception Parish Church) and begins strolling down a sidewalk that extends from screen left to screen right. Just before he disappears from frame, the priest smiles at the camera and lifts his hand to remove his hat. In order to avoid missing the action, the cinematographer then improvises a pan to the right to keep him in the frame. Overall, the film's images are similar to many other parade films of the period.

Rather than focussing on Irish-America, film companies instead concentrated on Ireland, either filming their own non-fiction subjects or importing and distributing non-fiction subjects created by companies based in England. Travel lecturers who did not shoot their own footage purchased and screened some of these films. However, the key customers for such moving pictures in the pre-nickelodeon era were likely to be travelling exhibitors who purchased and screened them alongside non-Irish-themed films. For example, in April 1905, 'Shepard's Motion Pictures' appeared in

Washington, DC, to screen a programme that included (in their order of billing): *The Prodigal Son, A German Hunting Scene, The Girl and the Wolf, Scenes from Killarney* and *Out in the Streets*.[79]

Only three of the films marketed to exhibitors in the United States in the pre-nickelodeon period addressed current events in Ireland, all of them covering the presence of British royalty on Irish soil. Curiously, both of the first two of these films carried the same title, *Queen Victoria's Last Visit to Ireland*. They were shot by the British Mutoscope & Biograph Company in Dublin in April 1900 and were presumably released later that same year, though the earliest published reference to them in the United States seems to have been in American Mutoscope & Biograph's *Picture Catalogue* of November 1902. One of the two films (catalogue number 603 E) showed the Queen being cheered by 'thousands of people, as she passes through an arch of welcome', whereas the other (catalogue number 605 E) offered a 'very close view of the Queen' as she received a basket of flowers from 'a deputation of little girls'.[80] Then, in August 1903, the Edison Manufacturing Company offered *King Edward's Visit to Ireland*, which they promoted in an advertisement with *Rube and Mandy at Coney Island* as one of their two 'latest' titles.[81] A subsequent Edison catalogue description claimed that the 100-foot film depicted the 'King and Queen landing at Queenstown' and provided a 'close and clear view of their Majesties' during their procession.[82]

Various American film companies distributed a large array of expeditionary and ethnographic non-fiction films about Ireland in this period, though not until 1903. By contrast, images of numerous other countries were sold in America as early as the autumn of 1897.[83] One of the key Irish-themed non-fiction films to appear was *The Vitagraph in Ireland*, sold in a circa-1903–04 Vitagraph catalogue. Offering 'glimpses of the Emerald Isle', its running time was approximately twenty minutes, making it the most in-depth film on the subject released in America in this era.[84] In terms of numbers of film releases, however, the key company responsible for non-fiction films about Ireland in the pre-nickelodeon era was the Warwick Trading Company, a firm based in England that had been formed from the British branch of the American company Maguire & Baucus.

Warwick shot numerous films in Ireland in 1900, though none of them seems to have been distributed in the United States.[85] The company then shot another group of non-fiction films in Ireland in 1903. A number of those 1903 films became available for purchase to US exhibitors through such companies as Lubin, the American Mutoscope & Biograph Company, and the Kleine Optical Company, and continued to be sold into the nickelodeon era by such companies as the Chicago Projecting Company and the

Amusement Supply Company.[86] Those films released in America (followed by the year of their American release) were as follows:

*At Work in a Peat Bog* (1903, aka *Working in a Peat Bog*)[87]

*Irish Peasants Bringing Their Milk to a Cooperative Creamery* (1903)

*Panorama of Queenstown* (1903)[88]

*Scenes in an Irish Bacon Factory* (1903)

*Scenes in an Irish Market Place* (1903)[89]

*Scenes of Irish Cottage Life* (1903)

*A Trip Through the Gap of Dunloe* (1903)

*Patrick Street, Cork* (1904, aka *Patrick Street at Cork, Ireland*)[90]

*Arrival of the Mail Steamer at Larne* (1905)

*Getting the Hay* (1905)

*Market Street at Kenmare* (1905, aka *Market Day at Kenmare*)

*Milking Time: A Kerry Herd* (1905)

*Potter at Work (Cork Exhibition)* (1905, aka *Potters at Work (Cork Exhibition)*)

*Rock Scene at Ballybunion* (1905)

Such films, which collectively offered both expeditionary and ethnographic footage, echoed images that had long been captured in lantern slides; in a 1894 catalogue, for example, William H. Rau offered two 'Panorama' slides of Queenstown, three slides of 'Cottages' in Ireland, a slide of 'St Patrick Street' in Cork, as well as a slide taken in Killarney entitled '*Will ye have ony [sic] milk?*'[91]

Four of these Warwick films survive at the George Eastman House in Rochester, New York, including *Potters at Work*, which shows four men and one woman painting and moving pots in a serious moving picture comprised of a single shot. *At Work in a Peat Bog* and *Getting the Hay* also offer films built on a single shot, both showing adults and children working together. However, both films also illustrate a sense of humour, in part due to dogs playing nearby and in part due to children whimsically looking into the camera in each film. More cinematically advanced is *Scenes in an Irish Market Place*, which features a pan shot of a street scene and then an edit to another, albeit similar, shot that also features a pan. The images are reminiscent of the Underwood & Underwood stereo view *Market Day in Killarney* (1901), but at the same time they are more self-reflexive and humorous. For example, several smiling children look into the camera during the first image and then keep moving to stay in the shot as the camera pans.

The extent to which the Warwick films were screened in America is unknown, but the fact that more films followed the initial 1903 releases, as well as the fact that all of them were available for sale for some three to five years after their initial release, suggests that they sold well. That is all in addition to the fact that the Warwick films were not the only non-fiction films of Ireland to be released in America. Another example was the Gaumont film *Dunloe Women*, sold in the US first by Kleine Optical and the American Mutoscope & Biograph Company in 1904, and, three years later, by the Chicago Projecting Company; one catalogue entry suggested the film included both expeditionary and ethnographic images, claiming it offered a 'panorama of an interesting bit of Irish scenery, with Irish cottages, etc., giving a close view of a couple of merry Irish lasses'.[92]

Some of these films were probably those screened as part of 'Sherman's Moving Pictures' at the Parsons Theatre in Hartford, Connecticut, in 1905. The *Hartford Courant* promised that a 'special feature' would be 'a series portraying life in Ireland with views of famous spots on the beautiful isle'.[93] Such a description might refer in part to the type of Irish non-fiction film that became the most prevalent during the pre-nickelodeon period in the US, the expeditionary film. At least a few of these films – such as Warwick's *A Trip to the Giant's Causeway* (1903), *A Trip Through the Gap of Dunloe* (1903) and *The Waterfalls of Glengariffe* (1905) – seem to have pictured little other than topography of the sort that had long appeared in lantern slides.[94] The same was probably true of *The Lakes of Killarney* (1903, aka *Panorama of the Lakes of Killarney From Hotel/Panorama of Lakes of Killarney From Lake Hotel*) and *River Shannon* (1903).[95] However, an American Mutoscope & Biograph Company catalogue in April 1903 indicates that *River Shannon* included an image of a hotel; *The Lakes of Killarney* had itself been shot at a hotel.[96] These two films implicitly suggest what would be more explicit in the other Irish expeditionary films of the period: picturesque views as experienced by on-screen tourists.

For example, that same April 1903 catalogue describes Warwick's *Coaching in Ireland* (1903) as 'showing tourists' on the 'romantic pass of Keim-an-eigh on the route to Killarney'.[97] Warwick's *Coaching Through the Tunnel on the Kenmere Road* (1903) pictured 'coaches of tourists passing through the picturesque tunnels which connect County Cork and County

Kerry', and *On Horseback, Killarney* (1903) depicted 'a party of tourists on horseback and foot proceeding through the picturesque gap of Dunloe'.⁹⁸ An emphasis on tourism was also present in Warwick's *Leaving the Lake Hotel, Killarney* (1905); given their titles, the same was likely true of *Coaching from Glengariffe to Kenmore* (1903, aka *A Coach Drive from Glengariffe to Kenmore*), *Coaches Starting from Larne and Passing Through the Tunnel on the Antrim Coast* (1905) and *Through Tunnel on the Antrim Coast* (1905). These films offered on-screen tourists who acted as representatives for their eventual audience members. Warwick was not alone in this approach. Gaumont's *Blarney Castle and Stone* (1904, aka *Kissing the Blarney Stone*), which was released in the US by Biograph, began 'with a panoramic view of the castle grounds, and ends with a close view of tourists being held by the heels over the wall in that they may kiss the Blarney Stone'.⁹⁹

In other cases, film companies combined non-fiction films of Ireland with other topics that held perceived value for audiences of early cinema. For example, Edison's *Automobile Race at Ballyshannon, Ireland* (1904) was one of a number of early films concentrating on automobile races, others without Irish settings being Lubin's *The Automobile Race* (1904), and American Mutoscope & Biograph's *Automobile Races at Ormond, Fla.* (1904) and *Automobile Race for the Vanderbilt Cup* (1904). When screened by the Hadley Moving Picture Company in February 1904, *Automobile Race at Ballyshannon, Ireland* was heralded by one newspaper review as one of the 'triumphs of the program'.¹⁰⁰ Its success might have been due at least as much to its being a part of the automobile race genre as to having been shot in Ireland.

Warwick's *Mono Railway Between Listowel and Ballybunion, Ireland* (1903), *Railway Panorama Between Green Island and Kilroot* (1905) and *Railway Panorama Between Kilroot and Whitehead* (1905) not only offered images of tourists moving across Ireland by rail, but also fitted into the larger category of non-fiction train films. Of *Mono Railway*, for example, a 1908 Lubin catalogue described it as 'the only railway in the world which runs on a single rail. It has a double engine of a most peculiar construction. The picture is exceedingly interesting, and will be appreciated by every audience.'¹⁰¹

Similarly, Warwick's *A Rough Sea on the Derry Coast* (1905) offered Ireland in tandem with images of rough waters. Films of crashing waves, 'surf scenes', and the like had achieved popularity with audiences since 1896.¹⁰² The same was true of Warwick's *Cliff Scenery at the Gobbins* (1903, aka *Cliff Scenery at the Gobbins, Ireland/Cliff Scenery at the Fabbins*), which a 1908 Lubin catalogue described as 'a series of pictures illustrating the extraordinarily beautiful spot, with numerous tourists passing over the bridge spanning the chasms. The rough sea lends variety to this most interesting picture.'[103]

Given the relatively limited amount of surviving business data on pre-nickelodeon cinema, as well as the fact that early moving pictures were screened on programmes with a variety of films, it is difficult to establish how much financial success individual titles attained. However, some indicators would suggest that one of, if not the, most successful Irish non-fiction film of the period was Warwick's *Shooting the Rapids at Killarney* (1903, aka *Shooting the Rapids of Killarney*). A Lubin catalogue of 1908 described the film as:

> A most interesting picture, showing several boards laden with passengers passing through the rapids and waving their hats to the audience. In the foreground we see the old wire bridge, well known to every Irish born and visited by everybody who travels through Ireland. The scenery is one of the most beautiful ever seen, and will be a great hit wherever shown.[104]

Warwick created a 100-foot expeditionary film of Ireland that would appeal to those from Ireland or who had toured the country, as well as the broader public, due in part to the fact it was yet another film that featured rough waters. In that respect, it fitted into a group of films that included American Mutoscope & Biograph's *Shooting the Long Sault Rapids* (1898), and that would continue into the nickelodeon era with such films as *Shooting the Rapids* (Gaumont, 1911), *The Biwa Canal and Shooting the Rapids at Katsuragawa, Japan* (Selig, 1912), *Shooting the Rapids of the Pagsanjan River in the Philippines* (Selig, 1913) and *Shooting the Famous Hozu Rapids of Japan* (Méliès, 1913).[105] *Shooting the Rapids at Killarney* also drew on images of the Killarney rapids that had previously appeared on picture postcards and lantern slides.

Catalogue and trade advertisements promoting *Shooting the Rapids at Killarney* attest to its popularity, but another indicator of its success was the fact that one – and possibly two – films with nearly the same titles appeared in the US shortly after its release.[106] For example, Gaumont released a film with essentially the same title within the space of a single year.[107] Their *Shooting the Rapids, Killarney* (1904, aka *Shooting the Rapids of Killarney/Shooting the Rapids*) offered in 160 feet of film what were similar images to the Warwick, save for perhaps one unique feature; according to a *Biograph Bulletin* that described the film for its US release, 'In one scene the camera is placed in a boat, and the spectator enjoys the sensation

**3.5** Vitagraph's *Cork and Vicinity* (1912).

of shooting the rapids himself.'[108] Reviewing the film in 1904, the *Optical Lantern and Cinematograph Journal* proclaimed it was the 'gem of the whole collection [of recent Gaumont films] ... This is a picture that has a most pleasing effect.'[109]

A few years later, a 1907 Edison catalogue lists a film entitled *Shooting Rapids, Killarney, Ireland*, which suggests – given that it was listed next to their *King Edward's Visit to Ireland* – that it might date to the pre-nickelodeon era; its length was listed as 155 feet, which suggests it was either different from the Warwick and Gaumont films or an altered version of one of them.[110] A Sears, Roebuck & Company catalogue of 1907 describes what – given that it lists an identical title and a length of 155 feet – is probably the same film as listed in the Edison catalogue. The description claims:

> Taken after a series of heavy showers, this picture shows the world-famed rapids at a moment when they are really dangerous. After seeing the interesting and arduous operation of getting a boat up the rapids against the stream and under the picturesque old ruined bridge, we take our stand at one side of the Rapids, looking towards the bridge, and see boat after

boat come rushing and twisting under the bridge and whirling past the camera upon the tumbling, eddying waters. Then we have the actual Shooting of the Rapids as seen from the boat. A complete illusion for the audience has the same effect as if they were actually undergoing the risk of being in the same boat. In the foreground are the anxious faces of the boatmen, straining every nerve to keep the boat straight and steady, and prevent her being tossed against the bridge or the boulders of rock on either side.[111]

Rather than the expeditionary film that merely showed scenery, or the expeditionary film that offered on-screen tourists as filmic representatives of the audience, this final version of *Shooting the Rapids* continued what Gaumont had attempted in 1904: creating the illusion that the audience was actually part of the expedition.

The idea of placing the spectator into the action of expeditionary films manifested in a more extreme form in Hale's Tours, developed by George C. Hale and Fred W. Gifford and patented by them in 1904.[112] In an effort to combine moving pictures with amusement park rides, they used a Pullman railroad car for audience seating, stretching a curtain across one open end and projecting travel footage shot from moving trains on the reverse side. To complete the effect, a system of 'levers, pulleys, wheels and sound-making devices' (the latter including a locomotive whistle) added a sense of motion, as if the car was moving.[113] By 1905, Hale's Tours had achieved enough success in Kansas City for rights to be sold elsewhere across the US; other companies quickly appropriated the idea, such as White & Langever's Steamboat Tours of the World, which were 'reproduced by a marine illusion, boat, and moving pictures'.[114]

A 1906 Selig Polyscope catalogue supplement promoted films for use in Hale's Tours, with the topics ranging from the Black Hills to Arkansas and from Chicago to Tampa. They also offered expeditionary films of countries other than the United States, including Switzerland, England and Ceylon. The same catalogue promoted the film *Trip Through Ireland*, which offered:

a trip from Glenbrook to Monkstown, giving a very pretty view of the country on one side and the water on the other, a short stop is made showing a splendid panoramic view of the Giant's Causeway with hundreds of tourists arriving at the station, clambering over the irregular heights of the Columnar Bassalt. Then closing the journey in the lovely little railway from Glenwood to Drake's Pool.[115]

As Selig apparently sold the film to any buyer, exhibitors competing against Hale's Tours could purchase the film. In New York in 1905, one of them projected *Trip Through Ireland* at a St Patrick's Day event using the 'Hibernianscope', though no description of the device was given.[116] Another exhibitor invited audiences at an Irish Fair to see the film by sitting in an automobile, a 'clever mechanical invention by which the observer is led to imagine that he is being whisked along at the rate of forty miles an hour, while biographs on either side unroll realistic scenes'.[117]

Whereas the pre-1906 films had generally ranged from 50 feet to 150 feet in length, *Trip Through Ireland* was 615 feet in length, signalling a shift in the film industry that would be most pronounced in the transition to the emergent nickelodeon era. Individual films would grow in length, which in some cases would bring them greater attention. However, in terms of the Irish-themed non-fiction film, in many respects there was a clear continuity from the pre-nickelodeon to the nickelodeon era.

## The Nickelodeon Era

Between 1906 and 1912, moving picture companies produced and/or distributed a number of non-fiction films about Ireland, though such films were increasingly screened at nickelodeons, rather than by travelling exhibitors or by travel lecturers, even though both of those professions continued to exist. In 1910, for example, the *Nickelodeon* claimed: 'We can no longer sit through an hour's lecture without getting quite tired, even when the lecture is beautifully illustrated by pictures that do or do not move; consequently, fifteen minutes of pictures is a most pleasing way of getting our ideas of foreign countries.'[118] Given that the running times of such moving pictures about Ireland in the nickelodeon period were sometimes five or ten or more times longer than, say, the Warwick films released in America during 1903–05, they often combined expeditionary and ethnographic images into the same film; current events, however, remained a rare topic.

Overall, the country of Ireland dominated the Irish-themed non-fiction film, as only one major non-fiction film examined Irish-America during this period. In 1908, Urban-Eclipse released *St Patrick's Day in New York* (1908). Of the film, *Moving Picture World* noted that 'Erin's proud and respected subjects do homage to their revered patriarchal saint on American soil.' Along with showing Broadway and the general parade procession, the trade also mentioned that 'various orders and societies are represented – children and adults take part and Erin's emblems float proudly in the breezes abreast of Old Glory'.[119] Based upon its description, the film was not dissimilar to *St Patrick's Day Parade, Lowell, Mass.*, or, for that matter, many other non-Irish-themed parade films released in the early twentieth century.

Of the many non-fiction films about Ireland in the nickelodeon era, some represented the continued sale of moving pictures produced before 1906. For example, the *American Film Institute Film Catalog: Film Beginnings, 1893–1910* suggests there was a 1906 film entitled *Irish Reel*, but it is likely that it is the same film issued with the same title by Warwick in 1903.[120] Similarly, the film *Ireland's Giant's Causeway*, advertised at a screening in Washington, DC, in January 1908, was probably Warwick's *Trip to the Giant's Causeway* (1903), which Edison had offered for sale from 1904 to at least as late as 1907.[121] All of the other Warwick films about Ireland that had been sold in America before 1906 were still readily available in 1908, if not later.

However, many new non-fiction films about Ireland screened in the nickelodeon era were produced after 1905. In March 1907, for example, the *Optical Lantern and Kinematograph Journal* described new British-made films about Ireland, which were produced in part for release in the United States:

> Following on the successful Scotch series, the Urban Trading Co. will shortly issue a number of films of Irish life and scenery. They have already shown a part of the series at the Alhambra, under the title of *From Euston to Erin*, in which the whole of the journey from London is shown, including some delightful glimpses of the scenery of North Wales... Where the English maker appears to have a distinct advantage is in the fact that he can produce, and does produce, subjects which the American cannot find time to put his hand to – series such as those of Scottish and Irish scenes made by the Urban Co., that of *Diamond Mining in South Africa* by the Warwick Trading Co., and so on.[122]

Their journalist then proceeded to ask the question: 'Why should not English makers have more of that [American] trade, which cannot all be satisfied by themselves?'

In this case, the 'English maker' was in fact Charles Urban, an American working in England, who, as previously stated, had been a manager at Warwick when their Irish travelogues had been produced in 1900; though he had left the company in February 1903, he may have played a role in the planning stages for Warwick's 1903 Irish travelogues. Urban and the Urban Trading Company were probably driven to create films in 1907 with the

American market in mind, due at least in part to a shortage of US films during 1906 and the first part of 1907.[123] He was also spurred by the fact that *Bonnie Scotland*, part of his 'Scotch' series, had 'made bigger sales in America than anywhere else'; shooting in Ireland created a logical companion to that series, as well as a return to a topic that had provided some success for Warwick.[124]

Urban's advertisement in the March 1907 issue of the *Optical Lantern and Kinematograph Journal* announced the series as 'Beautiful Erin', and was followed by a description of films that attempted to capture both expeditionary and ethnographic topics:

> [in a] unique sequence of animated pictures of the principal places of interest in Ireland, its natural and historic beauties, and the habits, customs, pleasures, and industries of its people.
>
> The pictures, with complete novelty and exquisite beauty, interpret the various aspects of river, mountain, lake and sea, of bog, valley, cover, and island so fully and artistically as to leave little to be desired. Only the most absolutely perfect film subjects have been chosen, from a whole season's negative exposures, and these form an enlightening *and entertaining series of great interest and value* [emphasis in original].
>
> Sections of the series, which have been exhibited at the Alhambra, London, were not merely approved, but *thoroughly appreciated by the vast audiences* [emphasis in original]. They appealed to every class of the crowded and critical house, and professional men, travellers, critics, soldiers, sailors, and the public generally greeted most enthusiastically every subject introduced.[125]

The 'Beautiful Erin' series consisted of seven films, including two that were over 600 feet in length: *Irish Scenes and Types* and *Glimpses of Erin*. Others in the series ranged from 150 feet to 445 feet, and included such titles as *Irish Life and Character* and *Features of Ireland*, as well as a trio of films that repeated the earlier cross-genre formula employed by Warwick. For example, *Transferring Mails at Queenstown to the White Star S. S. Baltic* was a 'grand marine subject', and *Railway Run from Waterford to Wexford* and *Euston to Erin* were train films, the latter being advertised as a 'delightful Railway Panorama which is in itself an education'.[126]

For reasons that are difficult to discern, the 'Beautiful Erin' series did not appear in America until approximately August 1907, and when it did,

# TAKE A TRIP TO IRELAND !

On **Thursday Evg., Jan. 19,** The IRISH-AMERICAN ADMOCATE will exhibit at **American Theatre Hall**

### EITHTH AVENUE AND 42d STREET.

## A Series of Views of Ireland

### By means of the wonderful Vitagraph Process of Moving Pictures.

These pictures of the most natural and interesting places in Ireland were taken this Summer, and many of the places and scenes will be familiar to every reader of this paper. The entire series of 30 odd views will be equal to a tour of Ireland.

The show will commence at 9 P. M. and will last an hour and 20 minutes. A reception and dance will follow. **General Admission, 25 Cents.**

BEAR IN MIND that these views are NOT merely photographs or stereoptican views, but they are, as an Irish Journal has described, THE REAL THING. In other words, the outdoor life of the people is shown in the figures of persons moving about in their ordinary, e eryday course; jaunting cars, steam and electric trams, coaching parties, horses, sheep and the faithful little donkies, moving about in the busy towns on market days, or in the pastoral quiet of the country-side, are all shown with startling perfection in their natural and active settings of valley and mountain, lake, river and shore of the sea. Some of the industries, some of the troubles, some of the traditions are pictured with life-like accuracy. These pictures will teach you, in addition to many other things, that Ireland as a picture land is inexhaustible. A partial description of some of the places and things shown in the present series are as follows:

1. Glengarriff, as seen last July with its castle, coast scenery and tourists scanning the scenery along the mountain side.

2. DUBLIN FAIR GROUNDS, judging the sturdy cart horses.

3. KILLARNEY LAKES, CO. KERRY, boating parties shooting the rapids.

4. FAMOUS BLARNEY CASTLE, Co. Cork. This fine old Blarney stone is shown to perfection with a party of travelers who put aside their dignity hoping to be benefited by the magic of the celebrated stone; great fun; a prize picture.

3. SHEEP HERDING. Large flocks of sheep, with shepherd and his dog very busy; property of the rich landlord farmers.

6. CROSS ROADS AND CROSS PURPOSES. More fun and trouble; blessed are the peace makers.

7. TRANSFORMATION OF THE FAT PORKERS. The pig might be termed the staple live stock of the poorer tenant farmers of Ireland.

8. TYPES OF THATCHED COTTAGES, to be found all over the land. The tenant did not dare to improve his house or his little bit of land for the moment he did his rent would be arbitrarily raised, generally beyond his ability to pay, and if he resisted eviction, the agents and bailiffs and constables would make short work of the cottage. Many a man now wealthy and prosperous in this and other lands first saw God's sunlight in one of these same cottages.

9. In the Turf Bogs of Ireland. A familiar scene to all who have "been there."

10. Market Day at Kenmore, Co. Kerry. A fair type of such "festive" occasions.

11. Rough on the "Agent." A case of mistaken identity.

12. Mono, or Single Rail Railway, Ballybunion, Co. Kerry. A curious railroad, believed to be the only one of its kind in the world. Complete operation including switching and a full view of the neat little town and summer resort.

13. The wise little donkey gets more wisdom. Side-splitting with humor.

14. The Giant's Causeway, Co. Antrim. One of the world wonders; a fine picture.

15. Picturesque Scenery, south Coast. A rapid ride on the mail train from Limerick Junction to Dublin; quick succession of towns and villages, rivers, roads and valleys. Hold on tight.

16. An eviction scene in which the occupiers successfully resist the evicting force and battering ram. A prize picture.

17. Shearing the sheep; showing the modern method of gathering some of the famous Irish wool.

18. Coaching party, Killarney, Glengarriff, Kenmare. The celebrated Tourist Route.

19. An Irish Home. Another real one.

20. The Strenuous Life. A lucky strike of the moving picture market, Clonmel, Co. Tipperary.

21. A poaching scene in Co. Galway. Great fun in which the party were chased over hedges and ditches and ponds of water by gamekeepers and police.

22. The Goblins, Coast of Derry. One of the finest scenes in Ireland.

23. Dublin during the royal visit, military pageant passing through the principal streets.

24. Leaving Queenstown for America. Emigrants getting on the tender for the big ship.

25. Leaving New York for a visit to Ireland. What New York Harbor looks like when on an ocean liner.

**3.6** Advertisement published in the 31 December 1904 issue of the *Irish-American Advocate.*

Urban-Eclipse (the US distributor) offered only three of the seven films. Contractually, in an early example of region-based restrictions on film releases, Urban could only sell *Features of Ireland*, *Irish Life and Character*, *Railway Run from Waterford to Wexford* and *Transferring the Mails at Queenstown* to non-US exhibitors.[127] Despite the *Optical Lantern*'s pronouncement that the 'Beautiful Erin' series represented an example of films by an 'English maker' who had the 'time' to create such subjects, the four films not available for sale by Urban-Eclipse were in fact created and copyrighted by American lecturer E. Burton Holmes and American cinematographer Oscar Depue.[128] They generated money by selling the films to Urban, but prohibited US sales of the same, presumably to keep the footage unique to Holmes's lectures in America and whatever other purposes he may have had for them.[129]

Of the three Urban films that were released in America, Urban-Eclipse offered *Irish Scenes and Types* first.[130] Descriptions in US trade publications suggest that the title of the 717-foot long film was apt: composed of five major sequences, it oscillated between emphases on the expeditionary and the ethnographic. It began with images of Dublin, including O'Connell Bridge, Sackville Street, and the Phoenix Park barracks of the Royal Irish Constabulary, before moving to a rural setting in order to show the Irish peat industry in what *Views and Film Index* reported to be 'great minuteness'.[131] The rural footage also included images of 'children-drivers and their donkeys' delivering peat to Castlebar.[132] Another section of the film depicted Blarney Castle, Limerick and the River Shannon.

*Irish Scenes and Types* then shifted to Cork, where 'countless children are thrust aside [at the coal market] by a cheerful woman who wishes to monopolize the camera – and nearly succeeds'.[133] Another shot captured an 'Irish colleen' who helps rescue a girl and boy with a car who are stuck in a ditch, and yet another showed 'eleven girls of various ages' living in a 'congested district'. Then, for its final section, the film revealed life in rural Ireland, with images ranging from the milking of a family cow and a 'rural Irishman at work – smoking' to the gathering of kindling and two men 'discussing tobacco and national affairs'. It concluded with 'old peasants calmly enjoying their leisure', and 'eventide, rest'.[134] Such accounts of *Irish Scenes and Types* suggest that it recalled images (as well as the humorous tone) depicted in previous Irish-themed films, lantern slides and stereo views, as well as the tourist-based structure of nineteenth-century lectures on Ireland.

Describing the film's production, *Moving Picture World* noted the difficulty that Urban's crew had in persuading an 'Irish town crier' to pose, finally convincing him based upon on an 'assurance that the American public would appreciate the result'. They also described the impact that a rural 'Irish beauty' had on the film-makers:

> Shy, sedate, and modest, it is only by an evident exercise of self control that she preserves a grave demeanor, and even so a glimpse of Irish humor is apparent through the studied

decourousness [*sic*]. The expert who secured this picture has a
large experience of the charmers of many countries, but this
Irish girl dwells in his grateful memory as a sweet experience.[135]

These words represent the earliest published production tales of the travails
of shooting in Ireland, a topic that would later factor into the publicity for
the filming expeditions undertaken by such companies as Kalem. Moreover,
the publicity seems to have anticipated successful screenings that occurred
in various US cities. A brief review in the *Boston Globe* referred to *Irish
Scenes and Types* as the 'most important motion picture' of the week.[136]
When the film played New York shortly thereafter, it was the main film
attraction at the Eden Musée.[137]

Approximately one month after releasing *Irish Scenes and Types* for sale
to US exhibitors, Urban-Eclipse offered the 347-foot long film *Conway to
Dublin*, which was probably a retitled and shortened version of the 445-
foot long *Euston to Erin*, perhaps by eliminating the London sequence and
beginning with North Wales. Headlining the same trade publication advertisements was *Glimpses of Erin*, announced as a 'companion picture to
*Irish Scenes and Types*'.[138] The film began its on-screen tour at the Giant's
Causeway, then shifted to Achill Island and the Gap of Dunloe before
concluding with Killarney.[139] Once again, Urban constructed a film that
echoed previous slides, stereo views and lecture topics, focussing in this
case on a few specific locales like Killarney that had proven to be popular
in previous years.

*Glimpses of Erin* included some ethnographic scenes, ranging from the
'peasants' at Achill Island to an 'Irish jig danced by a young peasant
couple'. The latter was an 'energetic performance, which is evidently a great
event to the dancers and fiddlers. Unusual seriousness and earnestness are
apparent, and the face of the male dancer in particular is a study in phys-
iognomy.' However, the bulk of the film featured expeditionary images,
returning to the Warwick approach of showing on-screen tourists – in this
case both American and English, depending on the scene – navigating various landscapes; the film even showed them having a 'halt for luncheon. As
this was one of Ireland's rainy days, it will be noticed that the travellers are
appropriately clad in waterproofs and sou'-westers.'[140]

As with *Irish Scenes and Types*, though perhaps with even greater
complexity, *Glimpses of Erin* attempted to do more than just combine
ethnographic and expeditionary footage. It tried to evoke various and
perhaps shifting emotions in its audience by including humour, as well as
the kind of thrills that had earlier marked such films as Warwick's *Shooting*

*the Rapids at Killarney* (1903) and its imitators. *Moving Picture World* suggested that:

> The humor conveyed by many of the pictures in this series is of that quaint and subtle Irish character which is almost as undescribable [sic] as a fragrance, while in others are delight-fully whimsical subjects which are certain of a hearty welcome. Others again, are portrayed with a realism and vividness little short of magical, while all are as refreshing as a breeze from Old Ireland to an emigrant in a man-stifled foreign town.[141]

The 'realism and vividness' extended to the inclusion of footage of 'shoot-ing the rapids which connect the Lakes [of Killarney]', resulting in what *Moving Picture World* proclaimed to be a 'thrilling scene ... as boat after boat is cleverly brought down'.[142]

   Though it is difficult to discern how much financial success this trio of 'Beautiful Erin' films achieved in America, at least one of them may have been shown under a different title.[143] In 1907, travelling exhibitor Lyman H. Howe – who had earlier shown images of Ireland during his 1905 season – screened a film in Trenton, New Jersey, entitled *Ireland and Its People*.[144] He also projected the film in Detroit, Milwaukee and Boston; in the latter city, the film was incorrectly promoted as being the 'first time in the history of Ireland' that footage had been taken of the country and its people.[145] Of his moving pictures of Ireland, the *Boston Globe* noted:

> most of [the images were] located about Cork, Dublin, and Limerick. There are pretty characteristic bits of each of these three old cities. A view of Blarney castle is of exceptional interest and gives one a better idea of this famous structure than any number of single photographs. Pictures showing the industries of the country are instructive and lifelike. The peas-ant life of the Irish people is shown in a way that leaves little to the imagination...The peat fields and many other typical bits of Irish scenery were also shown.[146]

The description is close to the contents of *Irish Scenes and Types*, and it is very possible that *Ireland and Its People* was either a retitled version of it, or a unique film edited from footage used in *Irish Scenes and Types* and perhaps *Glimpses of Erin* and/or *Conway to Dublin*. It is clear that Howe had obtained many films from Urban over a period of several years, and that he had earlier screened *The Unseen World* (1903), which was crafted out of four of Urban's science films.[147]

No further non-fiction films about Ireland were released to US exhibitors until 1908, when the French-produced Pathé Frères film *In Ireland – An Excursion to Killarney* was screened in what seems to have been a limited release. At 692 feet, the film – which concentrated on the Lakes of Killarney – was not covered by US trade publications of the time; however, it was listed in advertisements in San Antonio, Texas, where it was projected in both April and July.[148] Then, in 1909, *Moving Picture World* offered a description of British film-maker R.W. Paul's 276-foot-long *Killarney's Lakes*, which was retitled *Lakes of Killarney* for its American release. While it was likely that Paul created the film from wholly original footage, *Moving Picture World*'s description makes it sound almost as if it was crafted from a few of the Warwick Irish-themed films or even *In Ireland – An Excursion to Killarney*; its contents also echoed many previous lantern slides. It featured images of tourists on horseback, riding around Irish villages and the lakes, as well as images of the Gap of Dunloe and – in yet another version of the old favourite – of 'shooting the rapids'. To create a sense of originality, Paul's film offered two boats, rather than one, for a climax 'in which a crash is narrowly averted'.[149]

Approximately two years passed before any new non-fiction films about Ireland were released in America. The next to appear were a group of films produced by the American company Kalem, which – as will be discussed in Chapter 5 – sent a film crew and actors to Ireland to produce fictional films on three occasions. While in the country for that purpose, they accumulated footage for what became a number of non-fiction film releases in the United States. It is unknown whether they began with the intention of shooting these four particular films, whether they decided to make them after reaching Ireland, or whether their stories crystallized after the crew left the country with large amounts of non-fiction footage. At any rate, such activity fits a pattern, as Kalem also shot non-fiction footage for travelogue releases while on location shoots in other countries such as Egypt and England.[150] What is important about their three Irish releases is that the films were ethnographic, and – rather than being repetitions of earlier lectures, slides, stereo views, or prior films – they represented largely unique stories for American audiences.

Kalem released the first two films together on one split reel in late 1911, which suggests that both were shot on the second trip that Sidney Olcott made to Ireland. The first film on the reel was *The Franciscan Friars of Killarney, Ireland* (advertised in some cities simply as *The Franciscan Friars of Killarney*); the trade publication *Motography* noted that the film showed

**3.7** Advertisement published in the 8 May 1909 issue
of the *Irish-American Advocate*.

a 'benediction on the feast of Corpus Christi, a most interesting and impressive outdoor ceremonial'. *Moving Picture World* added that 'it contains a long procession of Irish folk led and conducted by the Killarney friars'.[151] A newspaper review offered a different, though not necessarily contradictory, description, claiming the film chronicled 'a typical Irish gathering, showing people of prosperous and up-to-date appearance. Verily the Ireland of today is not the Ireland of a half a century ago.'[152]

The second film on the split reel was *Among the Irish Fisher Folk*.[153] *Motography* claimed it depicted the Howth quays at low tide, as well as the departure of a fishing fleet who set their nets and then return with a 'big catch'. The fish are 'sold at auction by samples. The cargo is then unloaded and the fish are counted.' The film concluded with images of the fish being 'cleaned by Irish girls and the mackerel is washed, boxed, and iced'.[154] *Moving Picture World* praised its photography and its 'intimate' portrait of 'Irish fishermen and maidens'.[155]

Kalem's next non-fiction Irish-themed release, *The O'Kalems Visit Killarney* (aka *The O'Kalems Visit to Killarney*) came approximately one month later, in January of 1912; it also probably stems from footage shot on the second O'Kalem trip to Ireland. The *New York Dramatic Mirror* described it as an 'interesting travel picture [that] shows the Kalem players when in Ireland visiting points of interest around the delightful lakes of song and poetry'.[156] Unlike their other non-fiction Irish films, it used the by-then familiar formula of depicting on-screen tourists at what had become the most often filmed region of Ireland; indeed, *Moving Picture World* noted that it 'not only shows instructive pictures, [but it also] has much holiday trip atmosphere, which makes it doubly pleasing'.[157] In this case, however, the on-screen tourists were notable film actors such as Sidney Olcott and Gene Gauntier. Given the use of the production company nickname, 'O'Kalem's', the film was also in some respects a behind-the-scenes story.[158]

By contrast, *Conway, the Kerry Dancer* – probably filmed on Olcott's third trip to Ireland and released in late 1912 – offered Kalem's third ethnographic moving picture of Ireland.[159] In an advertisement for the film, the company described it as 'a remarkable exhibition of Ireland's famous terpsichorean artist'.[160] Their synopsis of the film, published in *Moving Picture World*, added, 'our picture shows him in one of his many characteristic dances'.[161] Concentrating as it did on Irish dancing, the film repeated a formula that had appeared in such previous moving pictures as *Irish Couple Dancing Breakdown* (1903) and *Irish Reel* (1903). However, the key difference was that those earlier films were apparently shot in the United States and featured dancers who may not even have been Irish. Rather than representing stage Irish caricatures, *Conway, the Kerry Dancer* offered US audiences what seems to have been a depiction of an authentic Irish dancer.

The Kalem Company's Irish-themed films spurred other American filmmakers to shoot on location in Ireland during the late nickelodeon era. In 1912, for example, Vitagraph released three short Irish non-fiction films, all paired on split-reels with non-Irish-themed moving pictures. *Scenes of Irish Life in Dublin*, released in October of 1912, was the first of the group, all of which would be directed by Larry Trimble. According to the *Vitagraph Bulletin*, the film did not limit itself to depicting the famous sites in the city centre, opting instead to concentrate on:

> the outskirts, [where] we get an idea of life among the poorer tenants of the metropolis. We see the people as they live on their small estates, and recently built tenements. An occasional interview with some of the older inhabitants are very interesting studies. On our way we stop at the Glondalkin Inn, the oldest in Ireland, and meet the prettiest barmaid in all Ireland, who entertains us with her winning smile and her Irish wit. All the inhabitants seem to be blessed with good health and happy hearts. They are a treat to behold and a pleasure to meet.[162]

*Moving Picture World* evidently agreed, claiming that the 'photographs were perfect'.[163] *Scenes of Irish Life in Dublin* was the second film on a 'two on one' reel with *An Expensive Shine*, a fictional film starring Flora Finch about the disappearance of a diamond necklace hidden in the toe of a shoe.[164] In contrast to Kalem's *Among the Irish Fisher Folk* and the *Franciscan Friars of Killarney*, this Vitagraph release represents the standard film industry approach to split reels, in which a non-fiction film was usually paired with a fiction film.[165]

Released in December 1912, *Cork and Vicinity* became Vitagraph's second Irish non-fiction release; it focussed on images of Blarney Castle, Queen's College and the Cork stockyards, as well as 'some of the old ruins'. It also included images of film comedian John Bunny 'at the Black Pool'. Bunny, who was associated with fictional films, had travelled to Ireland in September 1912 to make the Vitagraph comedy *Bunny Blarneyed, or, The Blarney Stone*, which would be released on a split reel with *Scenes of Japan* in March 1913. Vitagraph's plot summary suggested that 'we can almost imagine he is trying to fathom some of the traditions connected with its depths', though the company did not mention whether he appeared in other sequences or simply appeared randomly in one scene.[166] At any rate, his appearance meant the film bore some similarities to *The O'Kalems Visit Killarney*. Vitagraph suggested that exhibitors accompany *Cork and Vicinity* with such music as *The Song that Reaches Irish Hearts* or *Killarney, My Home Over the Sea*.[167] Both of those popular music tunes featured fictional stories, and in 1911 both had become illustrated Irish song slides featuring images of actors in sets. The on-screen appearance of John Bunny and Vitagraph's suggestions for musical accompaniment blurred the lines between fiction and non-fiction.

Vitagraph's third release was *Views of Ireland*, which they advertised in February 1913 as being 'full of beautiful scenery'; it appeared on the same reel as *Mr Ford's Temper*, a fictional story of a man who is his 'own worst enemy' until he 'reforms'.[168] The *Vitagraph Bulletin* promised exhibitors that *Views of Ireland* would have widespread appeal, claiming that its 'magnificent scenes [were] brought within the reach of all'.[169] Noting that it included images of Kerry and Muckross Abbey, *Moving Picture World* claimed the film's photography was 'good enough'.[170] For reasons that are unknown, Vitagraph publicized the film less than its two predecessors; furthermore, it is difficult to establish exhibitions of the film at specific venues. Even less attention came to Gem's film *Dublin*, released in mid-1913, which *Moving Picture World* dismissed in only two sentences: 'Glimpses of Ireland's famous old city. The photos are not overly clear in places.'[171]

# The Non-fiction Film in the Irish-American Community

Based upon a survey of six Irish-American newspapers from 1896 to 1915, it does not seem that moving pictures represented a particularly important aspect of their interests.[172] To the extent that limited coverage was given to any Irish-themed films, it was generally to non-fiction films, rather than fictional films. Even then, as Chapter 7 will discuss, very limited reportage occurred on the subject, and most of it was printed during the nickelodeon era.

However, one particular newspaper did briefly discuss Irish non-fiction films shortly before the nickelodeon era began. In December 1904, the *Irish-American Advocate* described an event held by the United Irish League in New York City that showed a 'portrayal of... Irish scenery by means of moving pictures', adding 'the pictures were the real thing'.[173] The moving pictures were not described, so it is difficult to determine whether or not they were Warwick film releases. Then, perhaps inspired by that event, the same newspaper promoted its own screening programme in 1905, which first appeared on 19 January of that year as *Take a Trip Through Ireland!* The newspaper repeated the screening a few more times that spring, as well in December 1905, though they had changed its title to *A Trip Through Ireland*.[174] One advertisement promised:

> Plenty of Fun and amusing incidents in the trip that are side splitting with humour. These pictures are faithful reproductions of live and interesting places in Ireland. They were taken last summer and many of the places and scenes will be familiar to every reader of this paper. The entire series of thirty odd views will be equal to a tour of Ireland.[175]

The same advertisement listed descriptions of the 'views' in question, some of which seem quite similar to descriptions of Warwick's Irish series, such as *Mono Railway Between Listowel and Ballybunion, Ireland* (1903). However, other 'views' (like '*An Irish Home.* Another real one') are more mysterious in terms of their origin.

Some two years later, in 1907, the *Irish-American Advocate* promoted yet another event entitled *A Trip to Ireland*, which was 'a three-hour tour ... shown in motion pictures of the very latest films. Some taken last summer will be exhibited, and all places of interest will be shown... [It] will be positively the most up to date exhibition of Irish scenes ever offered in New York.'[176] The origin of these films is difficult to ascertain. The Hale's

Tours film *Trip Through Ireland* had been released in 1906, though it scarcely would have lasted three hours, unless some of the event's running time was devoted to slides or other entertainment. In 1906, Lubin advertised a film that was also titled *Trip through Ireland*, released as part of a series of 'trip through' films for 'Tours of the World Cars'. Their publicity claimed that their *Trip Through Ireland* ran a rather astounding 4,000 feet in length (as opposed to the 615 feet of the Hale's Tours film, which suggests that they were indeed different films).[177] Perhaps this event screened the Lubin film, or perhaps it screened images from various releases, including repurposing footage from the 1905 screenings. Regardless, the 1907 event drew on a tradition that dated from at least as early as 1886 with travel lecturer Harry W. French; the *Advocate* noted: 'It will be just like a four-weeks' vacation, starting from New York to Queenstown, all through Ireland, and back to New York again for the St Patrick's Day parade.'[178]

Two years later, the *Irish-American Advocate* promoted a similar event titled *A Holiday Trip Through Ireland*. Despite the similarity of titles, they promised 'two hours of the latest and most fascinating' motion pictures of Ireland, including 'tramway rides through Dublin, Belfast, Limerick, Cork, and other Irish cities, getting a full view of public buildings, monuments, shops, and open thoroughfares'. The films also included:

> The outdoor life of the people...shown in the figures of persons moving about in their ordinary, everyday course; at the races, fairs, dances, sports, hunts, cross-roads, bogs, fields, in the busy towns on market days, or in the pastoral quiet of the country-side, are all shown with startling perfection in their natural and active settings of valley and mountain, lake, river, and shore of the sea. Some of the industries, some of the troubles, some of the traditions, are pictured with life-like accuracy.[179]

These were allegedly the 'latest views of the old land now shown for the first time in New York'. If true, that again begs the question of which company produced these films.

# The Post-Nickelodeon Era

The arrival of the feature film did not yield feature-length film travelogues of Ireland. In fact, the production of short films decreased, which probably caused the number of 'travel pictures' to decrease. On the one hand, the fan publication *Motion Picture Story Magazine* published an article praising travelogues in 1911.[180] On the other hand, that same year, *Motography* – while acknowledging a 'public preference for travel pictures' – noted that they had 'almost disappeared from the screen'. They blamed exhibitors for failing to book such films, but added:

> there is little new to take in travel pictures. Urban and Pathe, not to list practically all the other makers, have visited every corner of the globe and made travels and scenics from Boston to Thibet [*sic*] and from Greenland to the South Pole. Of course, that doesn't do us any good, for most of us never saw any of these pictures. But they have been taken, and so no maker wants to take them again, and they are too old to release.[181]

The following year, *Moving Picture World* decried the poor visual quality of many then-current travelogues, as well as the 'comparatively little judgment exercised in selecting what is most enjoyable [for an audience to view]'.[182]

Instead, the current events film of Ireland – which had earlier represented such a small number of moving picture releases – came to dominate the non-fiction market. Charles Urban's company Kinemacolor was responsible for the first of these films in the feature era, *The Royal Visit to Ireland*; it also became the first colour moving picture shot in Ireland. Filmed in July 1912, it was not released in the United States until April 1913.[183] *The Royal Visit to Ireland* echoes many of the same images seen in both versions of *Queen Victoria's Last Visit to Ireland* (1902) and *King Edward's Visit to Ireland* (1903). For example, the Kinemacolor film included images of the arrival of the royal party, their reception in various locations, and the presentation of floral bouquets to the Queen and Princess Mary. Kinemacolor also promised that they had obtained a particularly 'excellent view of the Royal Party' while it passed in front of the camera.[184] Consideration of *The Royal Visit to Ireland* along with the Urban 'Beautiful Erin' series and the earlier Warwick Irish travelogues suggests that Charles Urban was the leading figure in the production of non-fiction films about Ireland during the early cinema period.

In late 1913, Kalem released two current events films, both of which were apparently filmed on Olcott's third trip to Ireland. The first was *Ulster Day in Belfast*. *Moving Picture World*'s synopsis claimed that the film showed a 'number of interesting views' of the celebration, culminating in images of the 'famous leaders of the Ulster men, reviewing the various organizations as they march by'. They added that the same film featured other 'topical views', including a 'thrilling lumberyard fire in London, the Brooklands Race Meeting, an English classic; the Czarevitch Stakes, an exciting English auto race; [and] the annual fair at Stratford-on-Avon, the birthplace of Shakespeare'.[185] Both the *New York Dramatic Mirror* and *Motion Picture News* praised the film's cinematography, with *Motography* adding a positive note about its 'timely' and 'interesting views'.[186] Kalem did not promote the non-Irish aspects of *Ulster Day in Belfast*, and the *Kalem Kalendar*'s description of the film does not even mention them; as a result, it seems likely that the Irish footage dominated the running time. However, it is also possible that their exclusive promotion of the Irish content came as a result of the success of their previous Irish-themed films; perhaps it was also because of the fact that *Ulster Day in Belfast* was released on a split reel with *Frayed Fagin's Adventures* (1913), a comedy short subject starring Irish actor John E. Brennan as a comedic Irish character. Moreover, the *Kalem Kalendar* might well reveal the key reason to highlight the Ulster Day footage: the fact that it was current. The publication drew attention to the fact that the film was 'timely in view of the present conditions in Ulster, Ireland'.[187]

Shortly thereafter, in November 1913, Kalem released *The Dublin Horse Show* (1913) on a split reel with the film *Laundress and the Lady*, starring John E. Brennan in drag as 'Bridget, the Cook' and Phyllis Daniels as 'Mary Flannagan, the laundress'.[188] Once again, Kalem linked the Irish non-fiction and fiction film – the ostensibly authentic Irish and the stage Irish – on the same reel, thus blurring the lines between the two. Also, Kalem once again included other, non-Irish scenes within an Irish current events film. Of *The Dublin Horse Show*, the *Kalem Kalendar* announced: 'Other scenes show sports in England and France. A unique picture is that of the water-cycling contest at Nogent-sur-Marne, France.'[189] The *New York Dramatic Mirror* noted that these other events were equally important aspects of the film; the *Motion Picture News* – which listed its title as *The Dublin Horse Show and Other Events Across the Water* – even suggested that the result was 'a sort of Kalem Weekly', thus likening it to the emergent newsreel.[190] As for the horse show, the film featured the 'opening of the famous event in the Royal Dublin Society's grounds at Balls Bridge, Ireland. The parade of the contestants shows some of the finest horses in the world.'[191]

The final film in this group of current events films was the most ambitious. On 29 December 1912, A. Blinkhorn issued *The First Irish National Pilgrimage to Lourdes*, produced by the General Film Agency Ltd of London. Rather than contain footage of other events and/or be released on a split reel with another film, the film's running time was apparently long enough that it had to be released in two parts. Blinkhorn had lengthened the title, which had been released in Great Britain simply as *Pilgrimage to Lourdes*. *Moving Picture World* noted that the film chronicled the journey of 3,000 Irish citizens, covering each major stage of their trip, from the stops in London and France to the 'Procession of the Blessed Sacrament'. Though they wrote about the concluding sequence in which some of the sick were cured, *Moving Picture World* drew particular attention to one of the travel sequences:

> Some of the most affecting scenes shown in the film are those at Victoria Station at Folkstone. The pilgrims had left Dublin the night before, and are breaking their journey in London for a hurried breakfast, which is snatched on the station itself. London policemen are carrying littlers, and cheerful porters, having turned nurses for the time being, are tenderly rendering invaluable assistance. The station is shrouded in the peculiar gloom of a London morning, and yet the blend of Celtic cheerfulness and Saxon readiness for emergencies, renders the atmosphere far from oppressive.[192]

*The First Irish National Pilgrimage to Lourdes* thus managed to cover a current events topic in which the Irish on screen were themselves the tourists, rather than being, as had so often been the case in the past, local citizens in Ireland visited by on-screen tourists from England or the United States.

# Conclusion

With a narrative built around a journey and the use of the Irish as characters, *The First Irish National Pilgrimage to Lourdes* focussed not only on current events, but also on expeditionary and ethnographic concerns. These three topic areas had guided the production of Irish-themed non-fiction films from the pre-nickelodeon era to the emergence of the feature film. Such narrative and cinematic emphases were shared by the broader category of non-fiction film-making, which focussed on authenticity as a key goal. However, other factors – including the need to entertain viewers – meant that the non-fiction film, whether Irish-themed or not, bore some commonalities to the fiction film.

The boundaries between the fiction and non-fiction film had been in flux throughout the early cinema period, often calling into question what was 'authentic', 'genuine' or 'real'. After all, only months after the release of

*The First Irish National Pilgrimage to Lourdes*, the weekly serial *Our Mutual Girl* (1914) offered yet another example of the complicated interplay between fiction and non-fiction. In fifty-two weekly one-reel episodes, Margaret, the 'Mutual Girl' (Norma Phillips) combated fictional villains, but she also conferred with famous political and theatrical personalities who portrayed themselves. She visited noted fashion stores in Manhattan and attended important functions in the city. An episode released in April 1914 found the character appearing at the St Patrick's Day parade, with images of it echoing earlier non-fiction actualities of the same event.[193]

However, the pilgrimage to Lourdes and the St Patrick's Day parade bring another issue into focus as well: the increasing emphasis on current events that marked the non-fiction film at the end of the early cinema period. The newsreel releases of Pathé, Mutual, Universal, Selig and others came to the fore by 1915, largely replacing the earlier expeditionary and ethnographic travelogues with weekly current events footage. Ireland and the Irish would remain a recurrent feature of the American non-fiction film during the silent era that followed, but such topics would generally appear as one story of many, in regular newsreel releases.

# Notes

1.  L. Pinson, 'A Motion Picture Traveller', *Motion Picture Story Magazine* (September 1911), p.83.
2.  C. Musser, 'The Travel Genre in 1903–1904: Moving Towards Fictional Narrative', in T. Elsaesser (ed.), *Early Cinema: Space, Frame, Narrative* (London: British Film Institute, 1990), p.123.
3.  Tom Gunning discusses such 'panoramic views' in ' "The Whole World Within Reach": Travel Images Without Borders', in J. Ruoff (ed.), *Virtual Voyages: Cinema and Travel* (Durham: Duke University Press, 2006), pp.27–8.
4.  For more information on these kinds of early non-fiction films, see Ruoff (ed.), *Virtual Voyages*.
5.  Gunning, ' "Whole World Within Reach" ', p.25.
6.  Ibid., pp.27–8. Alison Griffiths also discusses the relationship between postcards and travelogue cinema. See ' "To the World the World We Show": Early Travelogues as Filmed Ethnography', *Film History*, 11, 3 (1999), pp.289–90.
7.  Gunning, ' "Whole World Within Reach" ', p.27.
8.  For a history of the early current events films, and the introduction and proliferation of the newsreel in the United States, see R. Fielding, *The American Newsreel, 1911–1967* (Norman, OK: University of Oklahoma, 1972).
9.  J. Ruoff, 'Introduction: The Fourth Filmic Dimension', in Ruoff (ed.), *Virtual Voyages*, pp.1–24, at p.3.
10. Quoted in Griffiths, ' "To the World the World We Show" ', p.282.
11. Griffiths, ' "To the World the World We Show" ', p.291.
12. Advertisement, *New York Clipper*, 21 April 1900, p.184. As of May 2010, a copy of *Boers Bringing in British Prisoners* is available at the Library of Congress's 'American Memory' website, http://memory.loc.gov.
13. C. Musser, *Edison Motion Pictures, 1890–1900* (Washington, DC: Smithsonian Institute, 1997), pp.586–7.
14. K.R. Niver and B. Bergsten (eds), *Biograph Bulletins, 1896–1908* (Los Angeles, CA: Locare Research Group, 1971), p.133. It is likely that the 'imitation' of the kissing of the Blarney stone to which they referred was *European Rest Cure* (Edison, 1904).
15. 'Institute's Work Extended', *Brooklyn Daily Eagle*, 19 March 1897, p.16.

16. After a lecture on 'Cities of the Barbary Coast' in Chicago in November 1897, Holmes offered 'a special series of motion pictures ... projected by the chronomatographe, including this year's championship matches in golf, polo, and football'. See 'Dramatic Notes', *Chicago Tribune*, 21 November 1897, p.41. Speaking of Holmes's lectures in Boston in 1898, the *Boston Globe* noted: 'At the conclusion of each of [Holmes's] lectures, new groups of "motion pictures" will be shown.' See 'Burton Holmes' Lectures', *Boston Globe*, 16 January 1898, p.18.

17. 'E. Burton Holmes', *Fort Wayne Daily Gazette* (Fort Wayne, IN), 21 December 1897, p.5.

18. 'Burton Holmes's Lectures', *New York Times*, 12 March 1899, p.17.

19. 'Simple at First', *Boston Globe*, 7 May 1899, p.23; 'Burton Holmes Will Lecture', *Chicago Tribune*, 1 October 1899, p.44.

20. L. McKernan (ed.), *A Yank in Britain: The Lost Memoirs of Charles Urban* (Hastings, East Sussex: Projection Box, 1999), pp.60–1.

21. 'Playbills', *Chicago Tribune*, 27 November 1904, p.C1.

22. 'Burton Holmes at the Columbia', *Washington Post*, 5 February 1905, p.6.

23. 'Amusement Notes', *Boston Globe*, 27 September 1904, p.8.

24. 'Playbills', p.C1.

25. 'Lectures', *Chicago Tribune*, 11 December 1904, p.C2.

26. 'Burton Holmes on Ireland', *Washington Post*, 1 March 1905, p.9.

27. 'Beautiful Ireland the Topic', *New York Times*, 3 April 1905, p.9.

28. 'The Week at Local Theatres', *Washington Post*, 20 January 1907, p.FP2. *Views and Film Index* referred to Holmes's 1907 lecture by the title *Ireland the Beautiful*. See 'Stereopticon Lectures', *Views and Film Index*, 16 March 1907, p.4.

29. E. Savada (ed.), *The American Film Institute Catalog of Motion Pictures Produced in the United States: Film Beginnings, 1893–1910* (Lanham, MD: Scarecrow Press, 1995). The three films of the Dublin horse show are catalogued as: *Irish Hunters Taking the Stone Wall, Dublin Horse Show*; *Jumping by Irish Hunters, Dublin Horse Show*; and *Lord Lieutenant of Ireland and Escort, Dublin Horse Show*.

30. These films are catalogued in ibid. as: *Passing Train, Balleybunion Railway, Ireland*; *Passing Train, Balleybunion Railway, Ireland, No. 2*; *Turntable of the Balleybunion Railway, Ireland*; and *Retrogressive Jaunting Car, Reverse Panorama from Moving Train, Dublin, Ireland*.

31. These films are catalogued in ibid. as: *Old Spinning Wheel, Dooagh, Achill Island, Ireland*; *Tourist Party in the Gap of Dunloe*; *Tourists [sic] Party near Kate Kearney's Cottage, Gap of Dunloe*; and *Tourists En route to the Cliffs of Moher, Ireland*.

32. These films are catalogued in ibid. as: *Irish Kiddies Coming Out of School, Achill Island*; *Market Women Leaving the Railway Station at Galway*; and *Squad of Seaforth Highlanders Leaving Bank of Ireland, Dublin*. The other film I describe in the main text is *The Old Boys of Dooagh, Achill Island, Ireland*; Savada, in ibid., mistakenly catalogues it as having been shot in Iceland.

33. The two films featuring Irish dancing are catalogued in ibid., as: *An Irish Jig at Dooagh, Achill Island, Ireland* and *Servant's Dance, Lake Hotel, Killarney, Ireland*. The other two films I mention are catalogued as: *Irish Constabulary, Keel, Achill Island, Ireland* and *Battery of Artillery Crossing Ball's Bridge, Limerick, Ireland*.

34. 'Playbills of the Week', *Chicago Tribune*, 1 November 1914, p.F2.

35. 'Columbia – Burton Holmes in Ireland', *Washington Post*, 3 December 1914, p.14.

36. 'Burton Holmes in "Ireland" ', *New York Times*, 31 January 1915, p.X6.

37. 'Where To Go Today', *Washington Post*, 6 December 1914, Pp.3; 'Holmes' Dream Country', *Washington Post*, 7 December 1914, p.4.

38. 'Trip to Ireland', *Boston Globe*, 30 January 1915, p.4.

39. 'The Yellowstone Park', *Brooklyn Daily Eagle*, 8 April 1900, p.20; 'The Santiago Campaign', *Brooklyn Daily Eagle*, 4 April 1899, p.3; 'Bull Fight in Old Mexico', *Brooklyn Daily Eagle*, 25 April 1899, p.12.

40. 'Lectures on Geography', *Brooklyn Daily Eagle*, 20 September 1900, p.14.

41. 'Dwight Elmendorf, Lecturer, Dead', *New York Times*, 28 May 1929, p.26. This is not to say that Elmendorf did not procure some footage for his lectures from other people, as Burton Holmes did. However, Elmendorf (even if he was working with an unnamed cinematographer) did shoot footage in Ireland, which calls into question Charles Musser and Carol Nelson's assertion that 'Unlike Holmes, Elmendorf did not have the capability to take his own films but used pictures that were

readily available from American producers and sales agents.' See C. Musser and C.S. Nelson, *High-Class Moving Pictures: Lyman H. Howe and the Forgotten Era of Traveling Exhibition, 1880–1920* (Princeton, NJ: Princeton University Press, 1991), p.83.

42. 'Renaissance Sculpture', *Brooklyn Daily Eagle*, 29 October 1900, p.11.
43. 'Institute Program Has Some New Features', *Brooklyn Daily Eagle*, 19 October 1902, p.22.
44. 'Dwight Elmendorf's Plans', *New York Times*, 27 May 1906, p.X5.
45. Ibid., p.X5.
46. Advertisements, *Washington Post*, 20 January 1907, p.8.
47. 'Fair Erin's Isle', *Boston Globe*, 10 February 1907, p.2.
48. 'Elmendorf's Lectures This Week in Symphony Hall', *Boston Globe*, 31 October 1915, p.50.
49. P. Hammond, 'Mr Elmendorf and the British Isles', *Chicago Tribune*, 13 January 1916, p.17; 'News and Gossip of the Theatrical World', *Washington Post*, 23 January 1916, p.3.
50. Hammond, 'Mr Elmendorf and the British Isles', p.17.
51. Ibid.
52. A.E. Krows, 'Motion Pictures – Not for Theatres: Part IV', *Educational Screen* (December 1938), p.326.
53. 'E.M. Newman', *New York Times*, 19 April 1953, p.91.
54. 'Beautiful Rural England', *Washington Post*, 22 January 1912, p.6; 'Traveltalks in Jordan Hall by E.M. Newman', *Boston Globe*, 18 February 1912, p.50.
55. 'Picturesque Ireland', *Washington Post*, 29 January 1912, p.10.
56. 'Newman Travel Talk', *Boston Globe*, 6 March 1912, p.20. This review used the words 'scenes' and 'views' to describe the images that Newman projected, thus making it difficult to discern exactly which images were moving pictures and which were lantern slides. The entire text of the review notes: 'The first part of the lecture was devoted to descriptions and views of some of the larger and more famed cities and towns, including interesting and familiar scenes in the counties of Wicklow and Waterford, County Kerry, the Lakes of Killarney, the River Shannon, scenes in County Limerick, antiquated castles, views and descriptions of lace and butter making and potato raising, scenes representing National pastimes and enchanting scenery. Wild and rugged coast scenery and waterfalls, salmon fishing and inspiring scenes of ruins and early Irish architecture contributed to the second half of the lecture. Other scenes, with descriptive talks, included the launching of a ship, a view of Richard Croker's home, a remarkable picture of a steeplechase race, and pretty scenes in County Wicklow.'
57. 'Facts and Comments', *Moving Picture World*, 18 May 1912, p.604.
58. For example, Hugh O'Donnell gave a lecture in Boston in 1913 entitled *Ireland*, in which he screened various images: 'Interesting types of persons and street scenes were shown from Dublin, Killarney, and other noted places. One of the features was an action picture showing a storm on the coast, the waves dashing high on the shore. The trooping of the colors, a church ceremony, the Dublin Horse Show, the Series Regatta, and Irish Derby were shown. The visit to the Zoo in motion, Warren Point Gaelic football game, and the trip to Kerry and Louth also brought out warm applause. The inspection of the Orangemen by Sir Edward Carson and the pilgrimage to the Wolf Tone's graves were shown in motion and color.' See 'Lectures on "Ireland" ', *Boston Globe*, 8 November 1913, p.2.
59. 'R.G. Knowles at Weber's', *New York Times*, 5 December 1909, p.X10.
60. 'The R.G. Knowles Pictures', *New York Times*, 21 February 1909, p.SM14.
61. 'Paris and the Alps', *Daily Northwestern* (Oshkosh, WI), 19 December 1899, p.2.
62. 'Trip to the Alps', *Steubenville Herald* (Steubenville, OH), 20 April 1897, p.6.
63. 'Paris and the Alps', p.2.
64. 'Town and County News', *Spirit Lake Beacon* (Spirit Lake, IA), 13 March 1885, p.5; 'Local Brevities', *Perry Chief* (Perry, IA), 15 November 1889, p.5.
65. 'Pictorial Records', *Cedar Rapids Evening Gazette* (Cedar Rapids, IA), 24 December1895, p.5. Crary also presented the same lecture in Steubenville, Ohio, in 1897. See 'Trip to the Alps', *Steubenville Herald*, 20 April 1897, p.6.
66. 'Oneida', *Syracuse Standard* (Syracuse, NY), 13 April 1898, p.7.
67. 'The Crary Tours', *Logansport Daily Pharos* (Logansport, IN), 21 September 1901, p.4.
68. [Untitled], *Lima Daily News* (Lima, OH), 7 February 1906, p.3; 'Crary Tours', *Austin Daily Herald* (Austin, MN), 7 December 1907, p.2.

# Non-Fiction

69. 'All About Wright', *Cedar Rapids Evening Gazette*, 25 September 1889, p.2.
70. 'Crary Tours', p.4.
71. 'Decoration Day Parade', *New York Times*, 29 May 1898, p.13; 'Decoration Day Parade', *New York Times*, 31 May 1898, p.12.
72. *Picture Catalogue* (New York: American Mutoscope & Biograph Company, November 1902), p.168. Available in *A Guide to Motion Picture Catalogs by American Producers and Distributors, 1894–1908: A Microfilm Edition* (New Brunswick, NJ: Rutgers University Press, 1985), Reel 2.
73. A copy of *69th Regiment, N.G.N.Y.* exists at the Library of Congress in Washington, DC.
74. Savada (ed.), *American Film Institute Catalog ... Film Beginnings, 1893–1910*, p.984.
75. Other examples of non-Irish-American military parade films include: *7th and 71st Regiment, New York* (Edison, 1897); *71st Regiment, New York* (Edison, 1897); *71st Regiment, N.G.S.N.Y.* (American Mutoscope & Biograph, 1897); and *Sev. Regiments Passing the Monument* (Lubin, 1899).
76. '*St Patrick's Day Parade, Lowell, Mass.*', Library of Congress, 'American Memory', [online] available at http://memory.loc.gov/ammem/index.html.
77. 'New Hampshire', *National Hibernian*, 15 April 1906, p.1.
78. 'St Patrick's Day Parade', *Lowell Sun* (Lowell, MA), 1 March 1895, p.5.
79. 'Shepard's Motion Pictures at the Academy To-Night', *Washington Post*, 9 April 1905, p.A2.
80. *Picture Catalogue* (November 1902), p.104. Available in *Guide to Motion Picture Catalogs ... 1894–1908: Microfilm Edition*, Reel 2.
81. Advertisement, *New York Clipper*, 15 August 1903, p.596.
82. *Edison Catalogue* (Orange, NJ: Edison Manufacturing Co., October 1903), p.13.
83. For example, in their autumn 1897 catalogue, Maguire and Baucus offered moving pictures taken in Germany, England, Spain, Russia, Switzerland, Mexico and Egypt. See *Lumière Films, Edison Films, and International Films, Fall Catalogue 1897* (New York: Maguire & Baucus Ltd, 1897), pp.4–5. Available in *Guide to Motion Picture ... 1894–1908: Microfilm Edition*, Reel 1.
84. *Managers Read This Great List of New Vitagraph Features! All of Which Are Long Subjects, Can Be Billed as Headline Attractions! And Are Guaranteed Money-Makers* (New York: American Vitagraph Company [ca. 1903–04]), p.9. Available in *Guide to Motion Picture Catalogs ... 1894–1908: Microfilm Edition*, Reel 4.
85. See D. Gifford, *The British Film Catalogue, Volume Two: Non-Fiction Film, 1888–1994* (London: Fitzroy Dearborn, 2000), pp.58, 59.
86. All of these films are listed for sale in the *Chicago Projecting Co's Entertainers Supplies, Catalogue No. A123* (Chicago: Chicago Projecting Company, 1907), p.273, as well as in *Amusement for Profit* (Chicago: Amusement Supply Co. Incorporated, 1908), p.421. Available in *Guide to Motion Picture Catalogs ... 1894–1908: Microfilm Edition*, Reel 6.
87. A copy of *At Work in a Peat Bog* exists at the George Eastman House in Rochester, New York.
88. *Panorama of Queenstown* included shots of 'the harbor, city front, cathedral, etc.' See *Film Catalogue Supplement No. 1* (New York: American Mutoscope & Biograph Company, April 1903), p.17. Available in *Guide to Motion Picture Catalogs ... 1894–1908: Microfilm Edition*, Reel 2.
89. A copy of *Scenes in an Irish Market Place* exists at the George Eastman House in Rochester, New York.
90. Warwick released a film entitled *Patrick Street, Cork* in 1900, and a film with the same title in 1903. It is possible that these two films are in fact the same, which would mean that the US release that carried that same title in 1904 was in fact shot some four years earlier. However, as Warwick apparently did re-shoot some of the same Irish topics they filmed in 1900 again in 1903, it is also possible that there were two different films entitled *Patrick Street, Cork*. See Gifford, *British Film Catalogue, Vol. 2*, pp.58, 103.
91. *Illustrated Catalogue: Lantern Slides and Photographs, Views in All Parts of the World* (Philadelphia, PA: William H. Rau, 1894), pp.116–19.
92. *Chicago Projecting Co's Entertainers Supplies, Catalogue No. A123*, p.273.
93. 'The Parsons Theatre', *Hartford Courant* (Hartford, CT), 8 April 1905, p.7.
94. *A Trip Through the Gap of Dunloe* is listed in both *Chicago Projecting Co's Entertainers Supplies, Catalogue No. A123*, p.273, as well as in *Amusement for Profit*, p.421. Both sources list it as being a Warwick film, and they list it as a distinct film from *On Horseback, Killarney* (which also included one or more shots of the Gap of Dunloe), a fact underscored by their different lengths (125 feet versus 150 feet).

95. For example, in 1894, William H. Rau sold such slides as *Gap of Dunloe, Lakes of Killarney* (and eleven other variants of the same) and some nineteen different slides of the Giant's Causeway. See *Illustrated Catalogue: Lantern Slides and Photographs, Views in All Parts of the World*, pp.118–19.
96. *Film Catalogue Supplement No. 1*, p.18.
97. Ibid., p.17.
98. Ibid.
99. 'New English Subjects in Standard Gauge', *Biograph Bulletin 34*, 17 October 1904, which is reprinted in Niver and Bergsten (eds), *Biograph Bulletins, 1896–1908*, p.133.
100. 'Grand – Moving Pictures', *Syracuse Herald*, 14 February 1904, p.19.
101. *Lubin Films* (Philadelphia, PA: S. Lubin, 1908), p.67; *Picture Catalogue* (November 1902), p.168. Available in *Guide to Motion Picture Catalogs...1894–1908: Microfilm Edition*, Reel 3. A copy of *Mono Railway Between Listowel and Ballybunion, Ireland* exists at the George Eastman House in Rochester, New York.
102. Examples of such films include: *Surf at Long Branch* (Edison, 1896), *Sad Sea Waves* (American Mutoscope & Biograph, 1897), *Surf Scene at Monterey* (Edison, 1897), *Sea Waves* (Edison, 1898), *Surf Dashing Against England's Rocky Coast* (British Mutoscope & Biograph), *A Storm at Sea* (Edison, 1900), *Surf Scene* (Edison, 1904), *Surf Scene on the Pacific* (Selig Polyscope, 1904) and *Surf Scene, Waikiki, Honolulu* (Edison, 1907).
103. *Lubin Films* (Philadelphia: S. Lubin, 1908), p.66.
104. Ibid.
105. '*The Biwa Canal and Shooting the Rapids at Katsuragawa, Japan*', *Moving Picture World*, 9 November 1912, p.552; '*Shooting the Rapids of the Pagsanjan River in the Philippines*', *Moving Picture World*, 28 June 1913, p.1358; '*Shooting the Famous Hozu Rapids of Japan*', *Moving Picture World*, 22 November 1913, p.906.
106. It would seem that Warwick's *Shooting the Rapids at Killarney* was a new version of a topic that they had filmed three years earlier. In 1900, they released a film called *Shooting the Rapids at Killarney*, which – given the fact it was fifty feet in length as opposed to the 100-foot length of their 1903 film – does seem to be a different film with the same title and topic, rather than a reissue. As with the other Warwick Irish films of 1900, there seems to be no record that the 1900 version of *Shooting the Rapids at Killarney* was ever sold or screened in America. See Gifford, *British Film Catalogue, Vol. 2*, p.58.
107. In addition to catalogue entries for Warwick's *Shooting the Rapids at Killarney*, the film was featured in a Lubin advertisement in the *New York Clipper*, 21 January 1905, p.1143.
108. 'New English Subjects in Standard Gauge', which is reprinted in Niver and Bergsten (eds), *Biograph Bulletins, 1896–1908*, p.133. In an advertisement in the *New York Clipper*, 1 October 1904, p.739, the New York offices of Georges Méliès purported to be the 'sole and exclusive agent' for *Shooting the Rapids, Killarney*. However, the film was also sold by American Mutoscope & Biograph, Edison, and Kleine Optical.
109. 'New Films', *Optical Lantern and Cinematograph Journal* (November 1904), p.20.
110. *Edison Films for Edison Projecting Kinetoscopes* (Orange, NJ: Edison Manufacturing Company, January 1907), p.55. Available in *Guide to Motion Picture Catalogs...1894–1908: Microfilm Edition*, Reel 1.
111. *Motion Picture Machines and Stereopticons* (Chicago, IL: Sears, Roebuck & Co., 1907), p.143. Available in *Guide to Motion Picture Catalogs...1894–1908: Microfilm Edition*, Reel 5.
112. R. Fielding, 'Hale's Tours: Ultrarealism in the Pre-1910 Motion Picture', *Cinema Journal*, 10, 1 (Autumn 1970), pp.34–47.
113. 'Hale's Tours and Scenes of the World', *Moving Picture World*, 15 July 1916, p.372.
114. Advertisement, *Billboard*, 22 September 1906, p.44.
115. *Supplement No. 44* (Chicago, IL: Selig Polyscope Company, 1906) [n.p.]. Available in *Guide to Motion Picture Catalogs...1894–1908: Microfilm Edition*, Reel 2.
116. 'Sunday Concerts', *New York Times*, 12 March 1905, p.X5.
117. 'To Give an Irish Fair', *New York Times*, 5 June 1905, p.14.
118. A. Benedict, 'A Plea for Open Sundays', *Nickelodeon*, 1 February 1910, p.76.
119. '*St Patrick's Day in New York*', *Moving Picture World*, 16 May 1908, p.444.
120. Savada (ed.), *American Film Institute Catalog...Film Beginnings, 1893–1910*, p.534.

121. Advertisement, *Washington Post*, 12 January 1908, p.3; *Edison Films for Edison Projecting Kinetoscopes* (Orange, NJ: Edison Manufacturing Company, July 1904), p.55; *Edison Films for Edison Projecting Kinetoscopes* (Orange, NJ: Edison Manufacturing Company, January 1907), p.55.

122. 'The Month's New Films', *Optical Lantern and Kinematograph Journal* (March 1907), pp.117, 121.

123. C. Musser, *The Emergence of Cinema: The American Screen to 1907* (Berkeley, CA: University of California Press, 1990), p.488.

124. 'The Month's New Films', p.121. Other Scottish-themed films produced by Urban continued to be released in the US, including *Scotland* (see '*Scotland*', *Moving Picture World*, 16 May 1908, p.444) and *A Trip Through Scotland* (see '*A Trip Through Scotland*', *Moving Picture World*, 26 November 1910, p.1236).

125. Advertisement, *Optical Lantern and Kinematograph Journal* (March 1907) [n.p.]

126. Ibid.

127. Ibid.

128. Ibid.

129. In January 1906, the *Optical Lantern and Cinematograph Journal* noted: 'The Urban Trading Company have certainly made a capture in their arrangements with the Vitagraph Company, of America, and Burton Holmes, of Travelogue fame...Those who attended Burton Holmes' Travelogues will remember the splendid pictures of far away countries, which illustrated his interesting lectures. The Urban Trading Company will now be in a position to sell these wonderful films, and we can predict a big demand for them' (p.62).

130. Though descriptions of individual scenes indicate that Urban's *Irish Scenes and Types* was the same film released as *Irish Scenes and Types* by Urban-Eclipse, Kleine Optical Company advertisements for the American release (*Moving Picture World*, 7 September 1907, p.427; *Views and Film Index*, 7 September 1907, p.9) claimed the Urban-Eclipse release was 717 feet in length, as opposed to the 685 feet that constituted the Urban release. It is possible that there were minor differences between the two films.

131. [Untitled], *Views and Film Index*, 7 September 1907, p.6.

132. Ibid.

133. '*Irish Scenes and Types*', *Moving Picture World*, 7 September 1907, pp.426, 428.

134. Ibid., p.428.

135. Ibid.

136. 'Theatre Premiere', *Boston Globe*, 10 September 1907, p.2.

137. 'Vaudeville', *New York Times*, 3 November 1907, p.X1.

138. Advertisement, *Views and Film Index*, 21 September 1907, p.9; advertisement, *Moving Picture World*, 28 September 1907, p.1.

139. '*Glimpses of Erin*', *Views and Film Index*, 28 September 1907, p.6.

140. '*Glimpses of Erin*', *Moving Picture World*, 21 September 1907, p.458.

141. Ibid.

142. Ibid.

143. As Griffiths has observed, 'Idiosyncratic re-titling and creative re-purposing of [travelogue] film footage [during the early cinema period] makes it difficult to identify films and to say with certainty who shot them, when, and with what precise purpose.' (See ' "To the World the World We Show",' p.295).

144. Advertisement, *Trenton Evening Times* (Trenton, NJ), 15 May 1907, p.10. In terms of Howe's 1905 season, an advertisement in the *Stevens Point Daily Journal* (Stevens Point, WI), 5 April 1905, claimed that he would screen 'Intensely interesting American Pictures...Also scenes in Russia, France, Scotland, Wales, Ireland, Norway, and Manchuria' (p.1).

145. Musser and Nelson, *High-Class Moving Pictures*, pp.174–5. Musser and Nelson refer to the film as *Ireland and Her People*. However, some newspaper advertisements use the word '*Its*' rather than '*Her*'. See, for example, advertisement, *Boston Globe*, 13 March 1907, p.17; advertisement, *Gettysburg Compiler* (Gettysburg, PA), 3 April 1907, p.4; advertisement, *Trenton Evening Times*, 15 May 1907, p.10. With regard to claims that *Ireland and Its People* represented the first time footage had ever been filmed in Ireland, see 'Lyman Howe's Pictures', *Boston Globe*, 10 March 1907, p.38.

146. 'Fine Moving Pictures', *Boston Globe*, 16 March 1907, p.11. Another description of the film suggested that it included 'the habits, customs, and industries of Ireland in town and country'. See 'Lyman Howe Moving Pictures', *Fitchburg Daily Sentinel* (Fitchburg, MA), 9 March 1907, p.6. Yet another description noted: 'Ireland has long been enshrined in song and story, but for the first time in its history it has now been enshrined in enduring moving pictures. Splendid animated pictures of its principal places of interest; the habits, customs and industries of its people as well as its historic and natural beauties will be shown.' The description then suggested that specific film images featured Dublin (including the Bank of Ireland, the 'imposing O'Connel [sic] and Nelson monuments', the Post Office and Trinity College), the 'zig-zag streets of Cork', Blarney Castle and Limerick. That was all in addition to the 'vivacity and happy-go-lucky temperament of the easy-going Celt', depicted through 'typical Irish characters of the Old Clothes Market; an Irish "Suffragette", and the town crier'. See 'Historic Ireland', *Gettysburg Compiler*, 3 April 1907, p.1.
147. Musser and Nelson, *High-Class Moving Pictures*, p.148. Additional details of Howe's acquisition of films from Charles Urban can be found in ibid., pp.99, 131, 152, 164, 177–8, 198, 217, 227, 229–30.
148. Advertisement, *San Antonio Light* (San Antonio, TX), 20 April 1908, p.8; advertisement, *San Antonio Light*, 27 July 1908, p.8.
149. '*Lakes of Killarney*', *Moving Picture World*, 12 June 1909, p.809.
150. Such non-fiction films resulting from Kalem trips to Egypt and England include: *Ancient Temples of Egypt* (1912), *Egypt As It Was in the Time of Moses* (1912), *Egyptian Sports* (1912), *Sports in Merrie [sic] England* (1913) and *The Lord Mayor of London* (1914).
151. '*The Franciscan Friars of Killarney*', *Moving Picture World*, 16 December 1911, p.904.
152. '*The Pastime Theatre*', *Sheboygan Journal* (Sheboygan, WI), 26 February 1912, p.7.
153. 'Current Educational Releases', *Motography*, December 1911, p.267.
154. Ibid.
155. '*Among the Irish Fisherfolk* [sic]', *Moving Picture World*, 16 December 1911, p.904. See also '*Among the Irish Fisher Folk*', *Moving Picture World*, 25 November 1911, p.656.
156. 'O'Kalems Visit Killarney', *New York Dramatic Mirror*, 10 January 1912, p.32.
157. '*The O'Kalems' Visit to Killarney*', *Moving Picture World*, 20 January 1912, p.202.
158. Speaking about a children's matinee of the film, the *Oakland Tribune* suggested: 'Few children have not heard of this famous place [Killarney, Ireland], and will therefore appreciate the coming of the *Kalem [sic] Visit to Killarney*.' See 'To Show Views of Famous Killarney', *Oakland Tribune* (Oakland, CA), 14 June 1912, p.7.
159. '*A Race with Time*', *Kalem Kalendar*, 15 November 1912, p.9. As this article indicates, *Conway, The Kerry Dancer* was released on a split reel with the fictional, non-Irish-themed film *A Race with Time*.
160. Advertisement, *Moving Picture World*, 30 November 1912, p.854.
161. '*Conway, the Kerry Dancer*', *Moving Picture World*, 2 December 1912, p.1002.
162. '*An Expensive Shine* and *Scenes of Irish Life in Dublin*', *Vitagraph Bulletin*, 17–31 October 1912, p.13.
163. '*Scenes of Irish Life*', *Moving Picture World*, 9 November 1912, p.553. *Moving Picture World* referred to the film as *Scenes of Irish Life*, rather than as *Scenes of Irish Life in Dublin*. However, it is clear that the publication was speaking about the same film. Not only do they identify the film as a Vitagraph release, they speak about it alongside *An Expensive Shine*. See also '*Scenes of Irish Life at Dublin*', *Moving Picture World*, 19 October 1912, p.266.
164. Such a combination of a non-fiction and a fiction film on the same split reel was certainly not unique to Irish-themed films. For example, Éclair released the 'comedy' *A Criminal in Spite of Himself* on the same reel with the non-fiction film *Oporto, Portugal, and Its Harbor* in 1912. See '*Oporto, Portugal and Its Harbor*', *Moving Picture World*, 30 November 1912, p.878.
165. Krows, 'Motion Picture – Not for Theatres', p.212.
166. '*Too Many Caseys* and *Cork and Vicinity*', *Vitagraph Bulletin*, 2–31 December 1912, p.13.
167. 'Music Suggestions', *Vitagraph Bulletin*, 2–31 December 1912, p.16.
168. Advertisement, *Moving Picture World*, 22 February 1913, p.753.
169. '*Views of Ireland*', *Vitagraph Bulletin*, 1–28 February 1913, p.37.
170. '*Views of Ireland*', *Moving Picture World*, 15 March 1913, p.996. See also '*Views of Ireland*', *Moving Picture World*, 15 February 1913, p.698.

171. '*Dublin*', *Moving Picture World*, 19 July 1913, p.321.
172. The publications examined were: *The Gaelic American* (New York), *The Irish-American* (New York), *The Irish-American Advocate* (New York, aka *The Advocate*), *The Irish World and American Industrial Liberator* (New York, aka *The Irish World*), *The Pilot* (Boston, MA, aka *The Boston Pilot*), and *The National Hibernian*.
173. 'Seeing Ireland in Moving Picture', *Irish-American Advocate*, 3 December 1904, p.1.
174. 'Seeing Ireland in Moving Pictures', *Irish-American Advocate*, 14 January 1905, p.4; 'A Trip to Ireland', *Irish-American Advocate*, 21 January 1905, p.1; 'A Trip Through Ireland', *Irish-American Advocate*, 4 February 1905, p.4; advertisement, *Irish-American Advocate*, 11 February 1905, p.4; advertisement, *Irish-American Advocate*, 25 February 1905, p.4; advertisement, *Irish-American Advocate*, 18 March 1905, p.8; advertisement, *Irish-American Advocate*, 1 April 1905, p.4; 'A Trip Through Ireland', *Irish-American Advocate*, 20 May 1905, p.1.
175. Advertisement, *Irish-American Advocate*, 11 February 1905, p.4.
176. 'A Trip Through Ireland on St Patrick's Day', *Irish-American Advocate*, 8 March 1913, p.1. Though it seems to have been used in a general sense, rather than as company identification for the films, the word 'vitagraph' (with a lower-case 'v') does appear in 'Two Exhibitions of *A Trip Through Ireland*', *Irish-American Advocate*, 25 May 1907, p.8.
177. Advertisement, *New York Clipper*, 14 April 1906, p.240. Lubin's other 'Trip Through' films were also lengthy. For example, their *Trip through Switzerland* was 6,000 feet, their *Trip through England* was 4,000 feet, and their *Trip through Germany* was 3,000 feet. It is quite possible that some of the Irish footage in their *Trip through Ireland* was repurposed for their 10,000-foot film *Railway Panoramas from Every Part of the World*, which was also advertised in the 14 April 1906 issue of the *New York Clipper*.
178. 'Two Exhibitions of *A Trip Through Ireland*', p.1.
179. Advertisement, *Irish-American Advocate*, 27 February 1909, p.8.
180. F. Starr, 'The World Before Your Eyes', *Motion Picture Story Magazine* (May 1911), p.57.
181. 'Travel Pictures Again', *Motography* (September 1911), pp.105–6.
182. L.R. Harrison, 'Photoscenes of Travel', *Moving Picture World*, 5 October 1912, p.21.
183. 'Current Educational Releases', *Motography*, 5 April 1913, p.231.
184. '*The Royal Visit to Ireland*', *Moving Picture World*, 5 April 1913, p.90.
185. '*Ulster Day in Belfast*', *Moving Picture World*, 13 December 1913, p.1316.
186. '*Ulster Day in Belfast*', *New York Dramatic Mirror*, 17 December 1913, p.38; '*Ulster Day in Belfast, Ireland*', *Motion Picture News*, 3 January 1914, p.42; '*Ulster Day in Belfast*', *Motography* 25 December 1913, p.488.
187. '*Ulster Day in Belfast*', *Kalem Kalendar*, 1 December 1913, p.15.
188. The *Kalem Kalendar* ('*The Laundress and the Lady*', 15 November 1913, p.3) spells the character name as 'Flannagan' in a list of credits, but then spells the character name 'Flannigan' in its plot summary.
189. '*The Dublin Horse Show*', *Kalem Kalendar*, 15 November 1913, p.3. The same description appears in '*The Dublin Horse Show*', *Moving Picture World*, 22 November 1913, p.894, as well as in '*The Dublin Horse Show*', *Motography*, 13 December 1913, p.443.
190. '*The Dublin Horse Show*', *New York Dramatic Mirror*, 10 December 1913, p.41; '*The Dublin Horse Show*' and *Other Events Across the Water*', *Motion Picture News*, 6 December 1913, p.44.
191. 'Current Educational Releases', *Motography*, 13 December 1913, p.443.
192. '*The First Irish National Pilgrimage to Lourdes*', *Moving Picture World*, 3 January 1914, p.98.
193. Advertisement, *Evening Gazette* (Cedar Rapids, IA), 17 April 1914, p.15.

AMERICA'S REPRESENTATIVE COMEDIANS

# MURRAY AND MACK

## CREATORS OF THE LAUGHING HABIT

Charlie Murray (left) exemplifies the transition between Irish-themed comedy on the stage, where he became famous, and the screen, where he forged a successful career that lasted from the early cinema period to the talkies.

# Chapter Four

# *Comedy*

The 1894 Edison film *Chinese Laundry Scene* depicts a Chinese man who evades an Irish police officer by means of various acrobatic tricks. The film was the first American moving picture to depict an Irish character; it also illustrates the influence of pre-existing forms of American entertainment on the emergent moving picture. While *Chinese Laundry Scene* eschews certain kinds of authenticity (such as the fact that its characters were played by Italian actors), it attempts to recreate ethnic caricatures well known to audiences in the 1890s.[1]

Early cinema regularly employed various ethnic stereotypes for comedic purposes. For example, in addition to their Irish-themed comedies, Lubin's 1903 catalogue of moving pictures also sold such films as *Snickelfritz Has a Hot Time*, *Why Krausemeyer Couldn't Sleep*, *Mrs Sneider's First Pinch of Snuff* and *Butcher Shop, Nos. 1 and 2* (featuring the characters Hans Pumpernickel and Hiney Dingelspiel).[2] The use of Irish and Irish-American characters occurred as part of a larger movement within early American film comedy in which caricatures of Germans, Dutch, Jewish, Italian and other nationalities were common.[3]

In addition to the use of recognizable stereotypes, early Irish-themed comedy films looked to specific vaudeville acts and popular music for inspiration. For example, the fifty-foot film *McGinty Up to Date* (distributed by Montgomery Ward & Company, circa 1899) 'shows McGinty's skeleton at the bottom of the sea. He sits on a large bull frog and moves his head from side to side. Fishes, waving seaweed, etc.'[4] The film appropriated its narrative and character's name from Joseph Flynn's 1888 song, *Down Went McGinty*, in which McGinty ends up at the bottom of the sea, 'foolishly' jumping into it after his wife 'skipp'd away and took along the child'. *McGinty Up to Date* is thus an example of what Jonathan Auerbach has called the 'relentlessly intermedial' nature of early cinema, which drew 'on their spectators' foreknowledge of prior cultural forms and practices – newspapers, still photographs, vaudeville routines, magic lantern shows – as well as the specific cultural content contained by these precursor practices'.[5] To understand the film *McGinty Up to Date*, or at least to understand it with any depth, an audience needed to remember the song that inspired it.

Moving pictures also influenced subsequent moving pictures, resulting in various forms of repetition. At times, such repetitions occurred in the form of direct remakes. In 1903, Lubin released *A Wringing Good Joke*, in which character Patsy Casey is physically pulled towards a washtub because a 'bad boy' has tied his coat to Mrs Casey's wringer; he 'falls over backwards much to the amusement of the boy'.[6] Two years later, Lubin released *Wash Day at Casey's* (1905). Once again, the same basic story appeared on screen, this time with the 'contents of the wash tub' soaking Casey's head.[7] Such film remakes were similar to retellings of the same jokes that occurred on the vaudeville stage.

However, in this case the cinematic joke was hardly Irish. As early as 1899, Edison released a version of *A Wringing Good Joke* in which the character who falls over ('Grandpa') was not coded as Irish.[8] A year later, Edison released another version of the story, known both as *A Wringing Good Joke* and *New 'Wringing Good Joke'*; once again, the character was not Irish. Then, in 1903, American Mutoscope & Biograph offered their own version of the story as *Tommy's Ringing Good Joke on Dad*, in which the characters were not Irish. Other non-Irish-themed comedies also featured similar comic situations, including *Mischievous Willie's Rocky Chair Motor* (American Mutoscope & Biograph, 1902), *How Tommy Got a Pull on Grandpa* (American Mutoscope & Biograph, 1903), *Poor Old Fido!* (American Mutoscope & Biograph, 1903) and *Why Foxy Grandpa Escaped a Ducking* (American Mutoscope & Biograph, 1903). Those films are all in addition to the broader category of moving pictures featuring children pulling pranks on their elders.[9]

The Irish-themed comedy film operated not only as a subcategory of the American comedy film, but also of the broader American moving picture industry. For example, *How Murphy Paid His Rent* (circa 1899), *How Bridget Served the Salad Undressed* (American Mutoscope & Biograph, 1898) and *How the Dutch Beat the Irish* (Edison, 1901) represent three Irish-themed moving pictures that featured titles beginning with the word 'How'. These film titles act as the first component of a form of cinematic joke in which the on-screen action provides the punchline. Many other American films of the time offered similar titles for the same purpose, meaning that the trio of Irish-themed examples were a small part of a larger trend within the American cinema.[10]

Importantly, Irish-themed comedies also participated in the American film industry's drive towards moving pictures that were – or at least appeared to be – 'realistic' or 'genuine'.[11] At times, this approach meant casting Irish actors or embedding Irish characters into fictional stories drawn from current, non-fiction events. In other cases, specifically Edison's *European Rest Cure* (1904), this approach meant incorporating non-fiction footage into fictional films.[12] However, such efforts towards the 'genuine' were at odds with the exaggerated ethnic stereotypes that appeared in many Irish-themed comedies. An ongoing tension between these two forces marked the Irish-themed comedy in the early cinema period. As a result, these films constitute a lengthy, complicated and, at times, repetitious history, but one that deserves to be explored thoroughly.

## The Pre-Nickelodeon Era

The issue of narrative setting was of great consequence to the Irish-themed comedy. In the aforementioned film *The European Rest Cure* (Edison, 1904), an American travels to France, Italy, Germany and Ireland in hopes of a relaxing vacation. His comical trip is hardly restful, however; for example, in Ireland he visits Blarney Castle and falls while attempting to kiss the Blarney Stone. The sequence represents a humorous account of a tradition that had earlier been depicted in many travel lectures on Ireland. However, in terms of the Irish-themed comedy film, *The European Rest Cure* is a rare exception: the overwhelming majority of such comedies were not only shot in America, but they were also set in America instead of Ireland.

These American settings did not prohibit film companies from attempting to promote the authenticity of their Irish-themed comedies. For example, according to an 1899 F.M. Prescott catalogue description, *Christening Murphy's Baby* was a 'real Irish christening' featuring a 'genuine ruction' after the characters 'imbibe too much of the flowing bowl'. The rest of the synopsis – which concludes by promising that the film is a 'corker' – reveals that *Christening Murphy's Baby* is a fictional comedy.[13] The film was neither 'real' nor 'genuine', but that hardly prevented Prescott from claiming otherwise.

Similarly, in 1903, Lubin distributed *Biddy's Day Off* and *Irish Couple Dancing Breakdown*; catalogue descriptions for both suggest that they featured fictional characters who engage in dancing, but both descriptions use the same identical phrase to describe the on-screen action: 'real, old Irish breakdown'.[14] Lubin also promised that *Irish Reel*, with its apparently fictional characters Biddy Murphy and Mickey Roach, included a 'real Irish reel'.[15] In actuality, these films were apparently shot in America and may well have used non-Irish actors in their casts. As a result, the two films bore more in common with American Mutoscope & Biograph's *Why Mrs*

## Latest Moving Picture Films.

**THE BEWITCHED BARBER SHOP**
(Magic subject). Full of Fun and mysterious changes. About 100ft. long. Price, $14.00.

## FINNEGAN'S FINISH.

Mrs. Finnegan objects to the tobacco Finnegan smokes and proceeds to do him up proper with soap suds, stove etc. Extremely funny. About 75ft. long. Price, $10.50.

## THE MAGICIAN

Shows Audience, who appreciate the many tricks performed. A sure favorite; 70ft. long. Price, $10.00.

**A NIGHT IN THE COUNTRY.**
City girls have a pillow fight at the expense of the Landlady's pillows. Landlady objects, disperses the girls with a shingle properly applied.

## MY NEW HYDROGEN GAS OUTFIT.

No Saturator to explode. Hydrogen Tank, complete, $30.00. Can be used with any make of Portable Oxygen Outfit Complete outfit, Oxygen and Hydrogen Tanks, $60.00.

**E. H. AMET, Waukegan, Ill.**

**4.1** Advertisement from the 27 May 1899 issue of the *New York Clipper*.

*McCarthy Went to the Ball* (1900), in which the title character 'drops into a jig' at a dance, than they do with non-fiction cinema.[16]

Other films attempted to build a degree of authenticity by adapting pre-existing fictional works that had attained credibility with audiences. For example, the Gaumont-British film *Murphy's Wake* was released in the United States in late 1903.[17] It was an adaptation of a sequence from Dion Boucicault's 1874 play *The Shaughraun*. The film was the first effort at adapting a noted and – at least in some quarters – respected Irish-themed stage play for the screen, an approach for which the Kalem Company would later become famous. At the same time, the film drew upon the larger culture of Irish wake humour that had appeared in a large number of vaudeville acts, in comical lantern slides and in comical stereo views, most of which could hardly be viewed as 'genuine', the result illustrating the tension between that goal and the use of ethnic stereotypes.[18]

The appearance of authenticity came in other forms as well, such as the use of current events as a source of comedy. Indeed, two of the first Irish-themed fictional films released in America had then-current political subtexts. Edison's *Irish Way of Discussing Politics* (1896, aka *Irish Political Discussion* and *Irish Politics*) parodied Democrats at Tammany Hall.[19] Released the same year, Edison's *Pat and the Populist* (1896, aka *Pat Vs. Populist*) features Pat climbing a ladder with a load of bricks; after a 'populist politician' begins to speak, Pat 'shows his displeasure by dropping bricks' on him.[20] Channelling news stories into comedy meant these films had their basis in non-fiction, exemplifying again the struggle between recycled stereotypes and efforts towards the 'genuine'.

Current events also very much informed the humour of Edison's *City Hall to Harlem in 15 Seconds, Via the Subway Route* (1904), in which an Irish labourer named Casey attempts to detonate a bomb at City Hall. When at first the fuse fails to go off, Casey approaches it and is blown through the tunnel at tremendous speed when it does explode. An advertisement for the film announced 'Rapid Transit is no longer a dream', which referred not only to the comical speed of Casey's movement after the explosion, but also to the fact that the first underground line of the New York subway system had just opened in October 1904.[21]

Edison's comedy *Kansas Saloon Smashers* (1901) built its humour out of current events by lampooning a famous individual. Temperance advocate Carrie Nation had begun her crusade of 'smashing' saloons in Kansas in June 1900, a practice that she continued in other states. Given her use of axes and bricks to destroy saloons, Nation gained much fame, which was at its height in 1901.[22] The Edison film – which was being screened by March 1901, shortly after Nation gave a nationally publicized lecture in Kansas City – featured an 'Irishman' entering a bar:[23]

> [He] sets a huge pail on the bar to be filled, and while he is drinking a glass of foaming beer, Mrs Nation and her followers enter with their hatchets. One of the women jams the Irishman's stiff hat down over his eyes and another one douses him with his own pail of beer. They then wreck the saloon and smash the mirrors, bottles, cash register and bar fixtures. The bartender plays a stream of seltzer water on Mrs Nation, and as she backs away from behind the counter, a policeman enters and hustles everybody out.[24]

Nation was also lampooned in American Mutoscope & Biograph's *Carrie Nation Smashing a Saloon* (1901), Lubin's *Mrs Nation and Her Hatchet Brigade* (1901), and Edison's *Why Mr Nation Wants a Divorce* (1901) and *An Educated Chimpanzee* (1901). In the latter film, a chimpanzee changes into an Irishman smoking a pipe; the Irishman then takes a drink, 'after which Carrie Nation and her little hatchet is [sic] portrayed to perfection'.[25]

## The 'Stage Irishman'

The stage Irishman and Irish woman made numerous appearances in early US cinema. In *Levi and Cohen, the Irish Comedians* (American Mutoscope & Biograph, 1903), the title characters, who are Jewish, appear onstage to perform their act.[26] Both wear fake hair with receding hairlines, fake beards and fake whiskers in the stage Irish tradition. One repeatedly knocks the other's hat off his head. The unseen audience quickly tires of the act and pelts them with eggs and tomatoes. A catalogue description called the film 'very funny', apparently because the unfunny Irish stereotypes as depicted by Jewish comedians are on the receiving end of the audience's wrath. The film thus echoes the backlash that Irish stereotypes in the theatre received from the Irish-American press in the late nineteenth and early twentieth centuries.

Despite such occasional insight into their offensive qualities, stage Irish stereotypes proliferated in the cinema. Noticeably fake whiskers and beards appear in many other films, including *Casey's Christening* (American Mutoscope & Biograph, 1905) and *A Coal Strike* (American Mutoscope & Biograph, 1906).[27] At times, the make-up was less overt, as in American Mutoscope & Biograph's *Lady Bountiful Visits the Murphys on Wash Day* (1903); however, that film was also one of several that used the Irish clay pipe as a form of on-screen identification of a character's ethnicity; the same was true of *A Pipe for a Cigar* (American Mutoscope & Biograph, 1904).[28]

In addition to stereotypical make-up and props, some Irish-themed comedy films featured clichéd Irish character names, such as Pat in the aforementioned *Pat and the Populist*. Others drew upon stereotypical Irish character traits, such as fighting. Within its fifty feet of footage, for example, the aforementioned *Irish Way of Discussing Politics* features 'two Sons of Erin', complete with stage Irish make-up and clay pipes, who fight and then make friends, thanks to a glass of beer. According to one Edison catalogue entry, it was a 'typical Irish argument', a suggestion that it could easily be viewed as simple stage Irish comedy, rather than as a form of political commentary.[29]

Such stereotypical character actions as fighting became common, though sometimes imprecise, markers of ethnicity. For example, a German husband and wife argue at the beginning of American Mutoscope & Biograph's *Our Deaf Friend, Fogarty* (1904). When Fogarty arrives, the trio begin to drink beer. The German pours soot in Fogarty's hat, but when Fogarty leaves, the soot ends up on the German.[30] The film's basic joke existed outside of stage Irish humour. Non-Irish characters dumped soot on one another's heads in such films as *The Black Storm* (American Mutoscope & Biograph, 1900) and *The Lovers, Coal Box, and Fireplace* (Edison, 1901). More generally, drinking and fighting also appeared in films featuring non-Irish characters, including *Champion Beer Drinker* (American Mutoscope & Biograph, 1900) and *Drunken Scene* (Lubin, 1903). Indeed, the nebulous qualities of ethnicity extended even to the catalogue description for Fogarty, which begins by claiming the husband is German and ends by claiming he is a 'Dutchman'.[31]

**4.2** *Levi and Cohen, the Irish Comedians*
(American Mutoscope and Biograph, 1903).

However, as much as early American cinema incorporated such pre-existing stage Irish stereotypes, it could also provide new possibilities for them. Along with fighting and drinking, for example, the Irish-themed fictional film of this period could create humour by employing cinematic techniques impossible to duplicate on the stage. 'Trick' films, as they were called, meant a new chapter for the stage Irish. For example, American Mutoscope & Biograph's *The Barber's Queer Customer* (1900) featured a man who, thanks to a cinematic trick, 'appears first to be an Irishman; then an Italian with a heavy moustache', and then eventually an African-American.[32] The transformation of the chimpanzee to an Irishman in *An Educated Chimpanzee* (Edison, 1901) is another example of the reliance on a cinematic trick to create humour, combining new technologies with old stereotypes of the Hibernian ape-man.

In these cases – the more traditional stage Irish film comedies and the new stage Irish 'trick' films – repetition was important, both in the adaptation of pre-existing jokes and stories and in the production of more than one film on the same subject. For example, *O'Finnegan's Wake* (circa 1899) drew on the aforementioned brand of humour associated with Irish wakes. In the film, 'O'Finnegan, who is supposed to be dead, is carried in and laid in his coffin. His wife is weeping bitterly. Several men are present at the wake, smoking and drinking. Finally O'Finnegan rises in his coffin and takes a drink himself. Everyone becomes frightened, and they fall on the floor.'[33] Approximately one year later, in July 1900, American Mutoscope & Biograph released *A Wake in 'Hell's Kitchen'*.[34] It was a retelling of the same story, with a slightly altered ending. Rather than fall onto the floor, the mourners flee from the tenement apartment. They return soon thereafter, and, 'seeing that the beer is gone, engage in a controversy over it. During the scrap, the corpse jumps out of the coffin and takes part in the melee.'[35]

Another example of such repetition came in films featuring Irish characters harmed by explosions. American Mutoscope & Biograph's *'Drill Ye Tarriers, Drill'* (1900) – which took its title and storyline from a popular 1888 American song, as underscored by the use of the quotation marks – features an Irishman with a fake beard and whiskers who is blown into the air when some dynamite explodes. In the form of a dummy stand-in, the character falls back to the ground; thanks to a careful edit, the actor replaces the dummy and then stands up.[36] Cinematographic tricks thus allowed for film-makers to bring the 1888 song lyrics to life on the screen in a way that would have been difficult, if not impossible, on the stage. Here the pre-cinema story and the use of film editing are co-dependent.

One year later, Edison's *The Finish of Michael Casey; or, Blasting Rocks in Harlem* (1901) repeated the same basic storyline. Five Irishmen are 'hard at work drilling' until their lunch break. One of them sits on a dynamite keg, which explodes when he drops a lit match into it. The resultant explosion sends him 'into the air like a shot out of a gun'.[37] His body then drops back to the ground. Five years later, American Mutoscope & Biograph returned to the same basic joke and camera trick in *Brannigan Sets off a Blast* (1906), which the company promoted for its 'remarkable realism'.[38] These repeated stories are akin to the retellings of the same joke, though not a joke necessarily dependent on Irish characters. Comedic explosions appeared in various non-Irish-themed moving pictures, such as *Catastrophe in Hester Street* (American Mutoscope & Biograph, 1904), in which a 'Dago puts his push car in front of a dynamite storage shed, and the whole business blows up.'[39]

Repetition came in other forms as well. For example, Edison's *Fun in a Bakery Shop* (1902) features a baker fashioning busts of famous celebrities, such as Buffalo Bill, and then making 'a very comical Irishman with cocked hat, clay pipe, and Donegal whiskers'.[40] Two Irish bakers then appear and 'dip [the baker] into a barrel of flour. When drawn out, he is completely covered with the white meal, but having filled his mouth with flour, he blows it into the eyes of the two bakers, who fall to the floor.'[41] While the film incorporated an ethnic stereotype of an Irishman, it was related to a range of comedy films without Irish stereotypes that featured similar titles beginning with the word '*Fun*', much like the aforementioned '*How*' moving pictures.[42]

As had already occurred on stage and in popular music, humour was also born out of the clash between different nationalities. In *How Murphy Paid His Rent* (circa 1899), Patsy Murphy's Dutch landlord arrives at his apartment to collect the rent. Murphy leaves the room and returns with two pairs of boxing gloves. Murphy bests the landlord, and then he and his wife kick him out of their home. 'The same old story,' an 1899 catalogue description read, 'the Dutch and Irish won't mix.'[43] Edison's *How the Dutch Beat the Irish* (1901) inverted the 'same old story' so that an Irish policeman admonishes a Dutch cook for leaving a barrel on the pavement.[44] The cook later replaces the barrel, having hidden a bulldog underneath it. When the policeman later picks it up, the dog 'wrecks his brand new uniform'.[45]

By contrast, many other Irish-themed comedy films were hardly dependent on their characters' ethnicity. For example, in *Finnegan's Finish* (a seventy-five-foot film distributed by E.H. Amet in 1899), 'Mrs Finnegan objects to the tobacco Finnegan smokes and proceeds to do him up proper with soap suds.'[46] The short comedy was based on marital strife, a factor that had appeared in Irish-themed entertainment in the pre-cinema period, but the use of other character names or ethnic affiliations would scarcely have limited the potential for comedy or changed the narrative substantively. Indeed, marital strife was the basis for many such non-Irish-themed comedies of the period, including *Breaking Up Housekeeping* (Lubin, 1897), *Not the Man She Waited For* (American Mutoscope & Biograph, 1900), *Shut Up!* (American Mutoscope & Biograph, 1902), *Such a Quiet Girl, Too!* (American Mutoscope & Biograph, 1903) and *True Love Never Runs Smooth* (Lubin, 1903). In the end, the fact that Finnegan and his wife are Irish is incidental to the story.

Similarly, Lubin's *Target Practice, and What Happened to Widow Flaherty* (1902) is a simple tale of the title character who is accidentally hit by a young man shooting at a target; in turn, she and her dog attack the young man.[47] The title character is washing clothes, which might call to mind the Irish domestic servant, but no particular visual cues draw attention to her being Irish. Without the name 'Widow Flaherty', the Irish content of the film is somewhat in question. The same was also apparently true of American Mutoscope & Biograph's *Why Mrs Murphy Takes Her Meals Standing* (1899, aka *A Good Shot*), in which 'Willie' shoots at Mrs Murphy, the washerwoman, as well as of a number of other films. For example, according to a catalogue description, the film *Fun on the Joy Line*

(Lubin, 1905) featured an Irish woman as a character. While she does take a drink, the character looks essentially the same as the other non-Irish characters; nothing is particularly distinctive about her appearance or costume.

While the lack of available prints for many films makes it difficult to address this problem conclusively, it does seem that, at least in some cases, character names were the key referent to an ethnicity that may not otherwise have been visually pronounced. Lubin's catalogue description of *Washerwoman's Mistake* (1903) refers to the title character as 'Mrs O'Toole', but probably nothing inside the film's running time did, meaning that she may or may not have been read as Irish by some viewers. The same was true of American Mutoscope & Biograph's *Firing the Cook* (1903); a catalogue description refers to her as an 'Irish cook', though whether that was reinforced visually in some way is hard to determine.[48] At any rate, it is clear that viewers in the early cinema period did occasionally misunderstand the ethnicity of the characters that they saw on screen.[49]

Nowhere was this reliance on character names more important than in American Mutoscope & Biograph's *Nora's 4th of July* (1901, aka *Nora's Fourth of July* and *How Nora Entertained Officer Duffy*). Without the name(s) in the title of the film, the narrative – in which a boy named Willie sets off a firecracker – hardly suggests anything Irish or Irish-American, let alone an example of the stage Irish. Indeed, the actress in *Nora's 4th of July* was not full-figured in the manner of the stage Irish maid/laundress stereotype. She could well have been a maid of any ethnicity existing in yet another moving picture about a troublesome child.

Such unstable ethnic identification may have been furthered by the fact that some comedies with Irish characters commonly bore narrative similarities to those without Irish characters. Edison's *Beauty Show* (1903) features an 'aged and quite stout Irish woman' who receives the consolation prize, thus causing 'the audience to screech with laughter'.[50] The film was much the same as Lubin's *The Beauty Show* (1903) and American Mutoscope & Biograph's *A Joke on the Old Maid* (1900), neither of which included Irish characters. Similarly, a catalogue synopsis of *Love Me Little, Love Me Long* (Lubin, 1903) suggested:

> Show dis picture to de 'tuff Guys. This is how Patsy Mulligan makes love to his own Maggie Murphy and is up-to-date. The amorous Patsy kisses his lady-love in every conceivable manner and some of you will probably learn a trick or two from this loving couple. It is by no means a 'Club Picture' – you can show it anywhere. It merely depicts a love scene between two of the lower class.[51]

Based upon the description, the fact that the two lovers are Irish is incidental; if anything, it seems that Patsy and Maggie's class affiliation is more important than their ethnicity. Rather than drawing on the tradition of comical romance tales told in popular Irish-themed plays and popular music, *Love Me Little, Love Me Long* is part of a cinematic tradition that began with *The May Irwin Kiss* (Edison, 1896) and continued with such 'kissing' films as *The Bowery Kiss* (Edison, 1901), *In a Massage Parlor* (American Mutoscope & Biograph, 1902), *Love at 20 and 40 Years After* (Lubin, 1902) and *New Colored Kiss, No. 2* (Lubin, 1903).

### 'Comic' Irish Characters in the Pre-Nickelodeon Era

To build links to pre-existing vaudeville acts and popular songs, some film companies created moving pictures featuring characters with recognizable Irish names. Four recurrent character names were used in numerous films made at various companies, three of which were men who often bore similar character traits: Murphy, Pat and Casey. Bridget, the fourth character, was the only female; however, as with the trio of male character names, her appearance and actions varied from film to film. With the exception of five of the 'Murphy' films, none of these characters appeared in a coherent series of films in the pre-nickelodeon era; as a result, their names usually offered little more than the potential for ethnic identification and tenuous links to prior entertainment forms.

By the end of 1899, at least three comic films had used the character name Murphy, though these were not part of the same series. For example, catalogue descriptions claim the character in *How Murphy Paid His Rent* was 'Patsy Murphy', whereas *Murphy's Surprise* featured 'Dennis Murphy', who 'drop[s] dead on the floor' after learning his wife has had twins.[52] Those two films were in addition to *Christening Murphy's Baby*, though the catalogue description gives the lead character no first name.[53] It was not until 1903 that Selig Polyscope used the 'Murphy' name for what they announced to be a 'series' of comic films. Importantly, it was the first 'Irish' film series in the history of American cinema. Though it is difficult to know for certain, given the lack of surviving prints, it seems likely that this series, released as it was in such a short time frame, featured the same actor as Murphy in each film.

The first of the Selig films was *Murphy's Trouble with the Photographer*, in which Murphy is ejected from a photographic studio following some 'comical mishaps'.[54] Another was *Murphy and the Midget*, in which 'words lead to blows' and result in a fight that Murphy loses. Two other films were built on domestic strife. One of them was *Murphy's Jealousy*, in which

**4.3** In this 4 February 1905 advertisement, published in the New York Clipper, Paley and Steiner offered *Bridget in Trouble* and *Bridget Has Her Photo Taken* for sale.

Murphy uses several weapons against a man 'making love' to his wife before accidentally turning a hose on himself. The other was *Murphy Has Troubles with His Wife*, in which the couple fight one another with boxing gloves; given that Mrs Murphy wins the battle, the Selig catalogue referred to the film as a 'fine object-lesson for young wives in the proper management of their husbands'.[55] The series concluded with *Murphy Returns from a Masquerade*. In it, Murphy's wife becomes enraged after Murphy falls to the floor, a victim of 'dancing and drinking'.[56] The series thus included some stereotypical stage Irish character traits and acts, as well as – particularly in the case of *Murphy's Trouble with the Photographer* – some narrative situations that were hardly unique to Irish-themed comedy.

Characters named 'Pat' or 'Paddy' also appeared in numerous films of the pre-nickelodeon era. Six years after releasing *Pat and the Populist* (1896), Edison distributed the British-produced *Hod Carrier's Ping Pong*, in which 'Paddy and Mike', two 'sons of Erin', play a game of ping-pong with trowels after they finish their lunch. Mike 'endeavors to explain the rules of the game to Paddy, but Paddy won't have it, and biff; the fight begins'. The two men fall into mortar, with their boss having to stop their argument.[57] In 1904, American Mutoscope & Biograph

released *And Pat Took Him at His Word* (1904), in which the title character misreads an advertisement sign and starts a fight; similar situations
had earlier appeared in such non-Irish comic films as *Hot Mutton Pies*
(American Mutoscope & Biograph, 1901) and *The Reversible Sign
Painter* (Edison, 1901).[58] Characters named Pat made other appearances
in early cinema, as in *Rushing the 'Growler'* (circa 1899), *Uncle Reuben
Lands a Kick* (1900) and *There Is No Fool Like an Old Fool* (1903).
However, in these cases, the name 'Pat' appears only in film company
catalogue descriptions, not in the film titles or – presumably, given the
era – in their running times.[59] As a result, even if viewers understood the
characters to be Irish, they may or may not have understood them to be
named Pat unless they heard the catalogue descriptions read aloud before
or during projection.

Appearing on screen more often in the pre-nickelodeon period than
either Murphy or Pat were a number of characters named Casey. The first
instance came in Edison's *Casey at the Bat* (1899).[60] The film's title was
inspired by Ernest Thayer's famous 1888 poem, though its brief narrative
has little to do with it. The 'umpire makes a decision that Casey don't like,
and argument follows, during which Casey deftly trips him up, and continues the argument on the ground'. Edison's catalogue description called the
film 'a solemn warning to all rotten umpires'.[61] In the film, Casey appears
without stage Irish make-up.

Edison then shot a number of 'Casey' films, though not as a consistent
series. The aforementioned film *The Finish of Michael Casey; or, Blasting
Rocks in Harlem* (1901) was the first of these.[62] It was followed by *Michael
Casey and the Steamroller* (1902), in which a steamroller flattens the title
character. One of his co-workers hits his head with a 'great mallet until he
has driven him down his proper height and circumference'.[63] Rather than
create comedy from stage Irish stereotypes, these are trick films, reliant
upon editing and the replacement of the actor's body with fake stand-ins
for their humour. Indeed, the same basic joke in *Michael Casey and the
Steamroller* had appeared the year before in *Soot Versus Suds* (American
Mutoscope & Biograph, 1901), and would appear subsequently in
*Washerwomen and Chimney-Sweep* (Edison, 1903), neither of which seems
to have featured Irish characters.

Without using the name 'Michael', Edison then proceeded to promote
*What Casey Won at the Raffle* and *Casey's Twins* in February 1903. Here
the film-makers eschewed film tricks, opting instead to build humour out
of the cohabitation of the Irish and animals. In *Raffle*, Casey returns home
drunk with a pig; it sucks from the bottle belonging to Casey's baby while
Casey and his wife argue.[64] In *Twins*, which operates as something of a

sequel, Casey gives his baby a bottle when it cries, then lifts a pig out of the cradle; the pig, which is dressed in baby clothes, fights with the baby over the bottle. To make matters worse, a 'small dog runs in and takes part in the fight'.[65] Such films followed in the tradition of a large number of depictions of the Irish living with farm animals that had appeared in vaudeville acts, lantern slides and stereo views.

Later that year, Edison released *Casey's Frightful Dream* (1903), one of its final four Casey films.[66] In it, the title character, sporting a stereotypical beard and whiskers,

> [gets] out of bed while asleep, walks to the window, raises the sash and steps out on the sill. The scene changes and Casey is seen walking along the edge of the roof. He finally loses his balance and rolls over the side of the roof. The climax of this picture is reached when Casey is seen rolling from his bed onto the floor.[67]

Casey awakens and realizes that drinking whiskey caused his 'frightful dream'. He then kneels and says a thankful prayer. In this case, alcohol and the use of a minor stunt – Casey walking on a set painted to look like a roof – are the source of the intended humour.

For three of their final four Casey films, however, Edison returned to cinematic tricks as the basis of the comedy. Though still not using the first name 'Michael', two of the films returned to the basic explosion gag used in *The Finish of Michael Casey*. *Casey and His Neighbor's Goat*, which first appeared for sale in Edison's October 1903 catalogue, features Casey – wearing a fake beard and whiskers – returning home to find a goat eating his corn. In retaliation, he 'proceeds to tie several sticks of dynamite to the cornstalks'.[68] The goat returns, causing an explosion that 'wrecks the house and blows Casey into the clouds. When the smoke clears, Casey is seen to fall into the yard.'[69] Similarly, as has already been mentioned, *City Hall to Harlem in 15 Seconds, Via the Subway Route* (1904), features an explosion that blows Casey through a subway tunnel and then into the air, which causes him to fall through the roof of his own home, 'landing on top of Mrs Casey and upsetting her and the tub of water'.[70]

*Casey's Nightmare* (1903) was another of the trick Casey films. After a night drinking, Casey decides to sleep at a hotel and 'sober up before facing his wife at home'. After a case of mistaken identity in which Casey hugs a butler whom he believes is the maid, the film shifts not into stage Irish comedy, but instead into the kinds of tricks associated with the films of Georges Méliès. A candle rises into the air and is soon swallowed by a 'demon picture'. Casey's boots run up the wall, and the 'demon picture' eats his nightshirt. Then the bed 'seems also to come to life and gives Casey a severe shaking up, turning over on him, and doing all sorts of strange tricks'. An imp appears in the room, but in an effort to hit it, Casey strikes a tray held by the butler. The proprietor and his servants then attempt to remove Casey, who proves extremely agile in eluding them. He eventually disappears 'up a chimney'.[71]

The next appearance of Casey characters came in two 1905 films, both of which avoided cinematic tricks, opting instead for physical comedy. One of them was American Mutoscope & Biograph's film *Casey's Christening*, which has a wrapped dog being placed in a cot and mistaken for a baby; after a mother mistakes it for her child, a fight occurs, with Casey – wearing a fake beard and whiskers – knocking another man out.[72] The other film, Lubin's *Wash Day at Casey's*, drew heavily on Lubin's previous film *A Wringing Good Joke* (1903) and the other, aforementioned 'wringing' films.[73]

Like Pat, the Casey of *Wash Day at Casey's* and the other Casey moving pictures was little more than a repeated character name that was reused for different films at different film manufacturing companies. As a result, the character was really plural, as it was portrayed differently by different actors in moving pictures that at times drew on stage Irish traditions, but at times drew on other, non-Irish-themed comedies, as well as on the new possibilities provided by cinematic tricks. In some cases, on-screen visual cues like make-up, costume and props may have presented stage Irish traditions. However, surviving films like *Casey at the Bat* make clear that not all of these films employed such make-up and costumes. Thus, it is difficult to speak of Casey (or Pat, for that matter) as a singular, codified character. And, with the exception of the Selig film series, the same would be true of the Murphy films.

The other recurrent 'Irish' character name in the pre-nickelodeon era was Bridget, who had her roots in *Puck* magazine cartoons and in American vaudeville acts, most famously embodied in George W. Monroe's 'grotesque farce' *My Aunt Bridget*.[74] Appearing in drag, Monroe had starred as the title character for years in the late nineteenth and early twentieth centuries.[75] These depictions were in addition to popular jokes featuring a character named Bridget, which usually described her as a maid in Harlem. Such jokes were occasionally syndicated in newspapers, as in 'How Bridget Prepared Crabs' in 1894 and 'How Bridget Spoiled Things' in 1901.[76] The Bridgets of early cinema were usually domestic servants with little intelligence; at times, these characters engaged in working-class love with policemen or firemen.

Unlike Selig's five Murphy films, it is not possible to suggest that the Bridget films as produced by various companies constituted anything like a coherent series or even featured a singular character with the same attributes. The first of the Bridget films, American Mutoscope & Biograph's *How Bridget Served the Salad Undressed* (1898), illustrates the amorphous quality of the character. Catalogue entries suggested the tale was the 'old and popular story, told by motion photography'; the simple joke featured Bridget mistaking the dinner order and bringing in the salad in a state of undress 'hardly allowable in polite society'.[77] However, the 'old and popular' story was also screened under such titles as *No Salad Dressing Wanted*. The removal of the name Bridget from the title thus removed her from the story, leaving instead what could have been perceived simply as a comical domestic servant who may or may not have been seen as Irish. At a minimum, some audiences would have needed either verbal information about the film (such as from a catalogue description) or prior knowledge of the particular 'old and popular story'. Much the same could be said of the film *Serving Potatoes Undressed* (circa 1899), which seems to have been a different film with a similar storyline; a Prescott catalogue description refers to its servant as Bridget, but the lack of her name in the film title may have obscured that fact to at least some audiences.[78]

The nebulous qualities of the character are also apparent in American Mutoscope & Biograph's next four Bridget films: *Mysterious Disappearance of a Policeman* (1899), in which Bridget's employer catches her with an amorous 'copper'; *Spirits in the Kitchen* (1899), in which Bridget and her policeman drink beer and then witness various cinematic tricks, including a tramp that turns into a stove and a chair that turns into a tub of water; *Reginald's First High Hat* (1899), in which Bridget dumps a pail of water on a 'dude' who is beneath the window where she is cleaning; and *Little Willie in Mischief Again* (1899), in which the title character fills a pan with water so that it will later soak Bridget.[79] Comedic situations between Bridget and her romantic policemen invoked the pre-existing Bridget stereotype and thus might have been readily recognizable to many audiences. However, it is possible that some audiences would not have automatically perceived the maid in *Little Willie in Mischief Again* to be either Bridget or even Irish. While many Irish women were maids in New York City at the turn of the century, that fact would have been less known to many audiences elsewhere in America, who would have been more likely to have recognized the caricature from *Puck* magazine or from vaudeville. The lack of an Irish/Bridget connection might have been particularly pronounced in *Little Willie in Mischief* because 'Little Willie' was a prankster character who appeared in – and was named in the titles of – several other American Mutoscope & Biograph films that included no Irish characters.[80]

Edison's *Buster's Dog to the Rescue* (1904) used the character Bridget in a manner similar to *Little Willie in Mischief*.[81] It was one of several 'Buster

**4.4** In Edison's *Happy Hooligan Surprised* (1901), the title character (centre) wears a thick beard (rather than the cartoon character's thinner beard) and a crushed hat (rather than the cartoon character's trademark tin can).

Brown' films produced by Edison, each based upon Richard Felton Outcault's popular newspaper cartoon that began in 1902 and featured Buster and his dog Tige.[82] In the film, Bridget cooks some pastries, places them in the cupboard and leaves the room. Buster tries to get them by use of a ladder, though his mother enters and chastises him. After she departs, Tige retrieves the pastries and bounds down the stairs. Once again, as Bridget was apparently not named within the film's running time, some audiences may have perceived her as nothing more than a generic cook.

Characters named Bridget also appeared in numerous other pre-nickelodeon films, including Paley and Steiner's *Bridget Has Her Photo Taken* (1905), Paley and Steiner's *Bridget's Troubles* (1905), and Lubin's *A Catching Story* (1905) and *Policeman's Love Affair* (1905).[83] In some respects, the Lubin films more clearly invoked the nineteenth-century Bridget stereotype, thanks to using particular character actions that went beyond, for example, her simply cooking food in *Buster's Dog to the Rescue. A Catching Story* features Bridget doing the laundry; she accidentally 'pulls her mistress, who is caught by her dress, into the washtub full of water. A hair pulling match is the result of this catching story.'[84] In *Policeman's Love Affair*, Bridget the cook flirts with the policeman Michael

McGinnis, thus returning to a recognizable narrative situation that had already been explored in *Mysterious Disappearance of a Policeman* and *Spirits in the Kitchen*.[85]

Of all the Bridget films of the pre-nickelodeon era, emphasis on the character Bridget and her name was perhaps most pronounced in two Edison films. By April 1901, Edison had released *Why Bridget Stopped Drinking* (aka *Why Bridget Gave Up Drinking*).[86] In it, Bridget secretly takes a drink from a professor's 'spirit closet'. After he later discovers the bottle is empty, the professor plants a bucket of water and a skeleton in the closet. When she next opens the door, the water spills on her head and the skeleton, which holds a sign warning readers to 'Beware of Rum', falls out and 'pushes her violently to the floor'.[87] The film's title not only clearly enunciated Bridget's name, but was also phrased in a similar way to the Bridget jokes of the period.

That same year, Edison's *The Finish of Bridget McKeen* (1901) offered a more elaborate retelling of American Mutoscope & Biograph's *How Bridget Made the Fire* (1900).[88] As in its predecessor, Bridget uses kerosene in the stove, which causes an explosion; her body 'goes up through the ceiling. In a few seconds, her body comes down in piecemeal. First an arm, then a leg, then her head, then another arm, and then the trunk.'[89] The film then cuts to a cartoon of her tombstone, which fulfils the punchline of the film's title and reiterates Bridget's name. A male actor in drag portrayed the character Bridget McKeen, thus echoing George W. Monroe and other stage actors like the Russell Brothers. As a result, this particular incarnation invoked the Bridget stereotype from vaudeville more clearly than any other film of the pre-nickelodeon era.[90]

In the pre-nickelodeon period, the Bridget films culminate in *How Bridget's Lover Escaped* (1905), which was similar to *Policeman's Love Affair*. In it, dinner party guests wait for their food while Bridget and a fireman 'make love to one another in the kitchen'.[91] The impatient diners eventually invade the kitchen to find Bridget feigning unconsciousness, with her lover hidden in the icebox. Soon they learn the truth and phone the police while the fireman flees the scene. The policemen have no luck in catching him, however, which allows the fireman and Bridget to reunite at the end of the film. The film, which was produced by Georges Méliès's Star Films, was released in America at least as early as 1905.[92] It would later reappear during the nickelodeon era, as a lengthy review in a 1907 issue of *Views and Film Index* indicates.[93]

Surveying all of the films in which they appeared, Bridget, Murphy, Pat and Casey were not particularly distinct characters, and the comedic situations in which they appeared were often similar to one another, as well as to other, non-Irish-themed comedies. *The Finish of Bridget McKeen* might have more clearly invoked the pre-existing vaudeville stereotype than any other Bridget film of the period, but even its storyline of someone causing an explosion by lighting kerosene or other gases appeared in non-Irish comedies, including *Another Job for the Undertaker* (Edison, 1901) and *Mary Jane's Mishap; or Don't Fool with the Paraffin* (American Mutoscope & Biograph, 1903), which featured a 'typical Hinglish girl', rather than an Irish woman.[94] Moreover, the Bridget moving pictures were part of a much broader category of comedy films produced and/or distributed in America that featured domestic servants, many of whom were apparently not coded as Irish. Some of these characters were cooks.[95] Others were maids or laundry women.[96] Such comedies told stories similar to the Bridget films, ranging from the travails of domestic servants who were fired, as in *'I Had to Leave a Happy Home for You'* (American Mutoscope & Biograph, 1900) to those who had romances and/or jealous affections for policemen, as in *Policemen Play No Favorites* (American Mutoscope, 1898), *Jealous Cook and Policeman* (American Mutoscope & Biograph, 1899), *Off His Beat* (American Mutoscope & Biograph, 1903), *A Trick on the Cop* (American Mutoscope & Biograph, 1904) and *How the Cook Made Her Mark* (American Mutoscope & Biograph, 1904). The domestic servant and her on-screen exploits were hardly unique to Bridget or even to characters coded as Irish.

## Happy Hooligan

Character names and the national origins they implied could be imprecise, if not problematic. A name like 'Murphy' might well have been immediately identifiable to most audiences as Irish, but such was not the case with all comic names, particularly that of Happy Hooligan. In 1900, Frederick Burr Opper created the character as a newspaper cartoon strip for William Randolph Hearst's *New York Journal*. It quickly became a hit with readers and appeared in many newspapers across the United States.[97] Describing Happy Hooligan in 1903, the *New York Times* said he was a 'good-hearted tramp, who tries to do all he can for others, but always gets "done" himself'.[98]

Recognizing his popularity, various people adapted the Hooligan character for use in entertainment and products outside of newspapers. In 1901 and 1902, for example, Ross Snow appeared as the character in *Happy Hooligan*, a live action musical farce that toured various cities.[99] Two years later, Billy Howard and Katherine Harris starred in a vaudeville act entitled *The Adventures of Happy Hooligan*.[100] Songwriters Victor Vogel and Bryan

4.5 *The Line at Hogan's* (Biograph, 1912).

Stillman wrote a 1902 song entitled *Happy Hooligan*. Children's 'funny books' of Hooligan appeared in stores by 1902, and Hooligan Easter eggs were sold in 1903.[101] In 1904, Emporia, Kansas even held a 'Happy Hooligan' dance.[102] As a result, Opper's character helped bring the word 'hooligan' into common usage in American English.[103]

The use of the term may not have been particularly common throughout America before the newspaper strip began. For many Americans in the early years of the twentieth century, 'hooligan' may have had little meaning outside of Opper's character. It is likely the name sounded Irish to some audiences. For example, Lubin's film *Boy and Hod-Carrier* (1903) included a character named Patsy Hooligan who engages in a 'hot scrap' with a boy who causes him to fall off his ladder. Though he was not meant to be Happy Hooligan, the hod-carrier was meant to be Irish.[104] However, other Americans might well have associated the word 'hooligan' specifically with tramps, rather than specifically with the Irish, an example of which is depicted in the non-Happy Hooligan film *The Hooligan Idea* (1907).[105]

In addition to questions about the word 'hooligan', there are also questions about whether or not the specific character Happy Hooligan was ever intended to be Irish. It is true that Opper had previously drawn Irish caricatures for *Puck* magazine, though he chose the name Happy Hooligan in part for its alliterative qualities, something that he also did with Hooligan's brother in the cartoon strip, Gloomy Gus. Neither of them spoke in an Irish brogue; instead, the cartoon strip features Hooligan speaking with a Brooklyn accent, using such repeated phrases as 'youse guys'. Hooligan's apparel was rather expected for a tramp, tattered clothes and shoes with holes in them; he also wore an old tin can for a hat. In some of the colour strips, Hooligan wears a green jacket, but in others the same jacket appears red. It could be argued that his facial features suggest an Irish caricature, but at the same time it could also be argued that his features resemble other Opper characters who are not at all meant to be Irish, including those who appeared in his 'Maud' and 'Alphonse and Gaston' cartoon strips. Hooligan's brother Gloomy Gus does not at all appear to be Irish; the same is

204

true of Hooligan's other brother Montmorency, who wears a monocle and speaks with a British accent. When Hooligan travelled to Europe in cartoon strips in 1904 and 1905, he was called a 'Yankee' on more than one occasion, rather than any word(s) suggesting the Irish. In 1910, Happy Hooligan the character claimed in print that he was born in Germany.[106] Two years later, artwork of Happy Hooligan used to promote a stage play even depicted him as African-American.[107] Such variances indicate that Happy Hooligan was not universally considered to be Irish, and that even Frederick Burr Opper may have not perceived him as such. Indeed, the aforementioned variations echo the multi-ethnic qualities of Outcault's 'Yellow Kid' character in the 1895–98 newspaper cartoon strip *Hogan's Alley*.

At any rate, Happy Hooligan was extremely popular. Between 1900 and 1903, the Edison Manufacturing Company produced approximately thirteen Happy Hooligan films.[108] In at least one of them, *The Bull and the Picnickers* (1902), Hooligan appeared on screen with his brother Gloomy Gus. Beginning in mid-1903, after the release of the final entry in the Edison series, American Mutoscope & Biograph produced approximately thirteen Happy Hooligan films; Gloomy Gus appeared in at least two of them, *Happy Hooligan in a Trap* (1903) and *Gloomy Gus Gets the Best of It* (1903).[109] Those moving pictures were in addition to *Two of a Kind*, a Happy Hooligan film sold by Selig in 1903.[110] These films became part of a larger tradition of moving picture companies adapting popular newspaper cartoons, which included American Mutoscope's 'Katzenjammer Kids' films in 1898 and continued with American Mutoscope & Biograph's 'Foxy Grandpa' and 'Alphonse and Gaston' films in 1902.

As much as anything else, it is likely that audiences of the time understood the film version of Happy Hooligan to be a tramp.[111] His on-screen actions and narrative exploits bear far more relation to the many other tramp films of the time as they do to stage Irish caricatures.[112] In writing about ethnicity and early cinema, Charles Musser has noted that the 'tramp had a nonethnic identity determined by other traits – notably his socioeconomic status'.[113] American Mutoscope & Biograph, Lubin, and Edison made numerous tramp films, including Edison's popular 'Weary Willie' series, which was an outgrowth of a British cartoon character created by Tom Browne.[114] Nowhere is this more 'nonethnic identity' pronounced than in Edison's *The Twentieth Century Tramp; or, Happy Hooligan and the Airship*, copyrighted under that title in January 1902.[115] A catalogue synopsis describe the tramp in the film – who flies over New York City in a 'flying machine' before it explodes and he falls into the river – as 'Weary Willie', not Happy Hooligan, who is named in its title.[116] The same film was also listed in another catalogue simply as *The Twentieth Century Tramp* with

'Weary Willie' named in its plot synopsis. As a result, *The Twentieth Century Tramp* could well have been screened on some occasions as a Weary Willie film rather than a Hooligan film.[117] It was as if the Edison Manufacturing Company saw the two tramps as essentially the same character, rather than one of them being distinctly Irish.

The Happy Hooligan of the screen was thus engaged in a battle for his own authenticity. The narrative hallmark of the cartoon strip was Hooligan trying to help someone else, only to end up accidentally at fault, and – by extension – in trouble with police. Police did trouble Hooligan in *Hooligan Visits Central Park* (1901), *Happy Hooligan's Interrupted Lunch* (American Mutoscope & Biograph, 1903) and *Hooligan's Roller Skates* (American Mutoscope & Biograph, 1903), but the brevity of the Hooligan films did not usually allow for the newspaper cartoon's narrative formula to be adapted. Moreover, Hooligan's appearance in moving pictures did not always resemble the newspaper cartoon. In a film like Edison's *Happy Hooligan Surprised* (1901), for example, the character wears a thick beard (rather than the cartoon character's thinner beard) and a crushed hat (rather than the cartoon character's trademark tin can). As a result, he appears quite similar to tramps in such non-Hooligan films as *Stop Thief!* (Edison, 1904).

# The Nickelodeon Era

During the nickelodeon era, stereotypical Irish characters proliferated in American cinema, which may not be surprising, given the growing number of film releases. Increased running times and the increased use of intertitles meant that such characters were more clearly named than they were during the pre-nickelodeon era. Conversely, however, the names themselves became less meaningful; for example, 'Pat' and 'Bridget' become attached to various kinds of characters in various kinds of films, including dramatic characters. Moreover, in many cases, as in *Mulcahey's Raid* (Essanay, 1910, aka *Mulcahy's Raid*), *Logan's Babies* (Edison, 1911) and *Murray, the Masher* (Méliès, 1912), the indication of Irish heritage suggested by a character's name seems not to have factored into plotlines of their films.[118] For example, though it was advertised as an 'Irish comedy', nothing in the surviving synopses of *Kelly, USA* (Atlas, 1911) suggests that the title character or the film's comedic situations drew upon Irish stereotypes.[119]

That said, attempts to increase the perceived realism and authenticity in Irish-themed comedies continued during the nickelodeon era. 'Sure it's Irish', promised Vitagraph's advertisements for *Michael McShane, Matchmaker* (1912) with John Bunny, offering little evidence other than the

4.6 *Pat's Breeches* (Champion, 1912).

fact that the film was set in Ireland, rather than the more common American setting.[120] Based upon surviving films and surviving images from lost films, it seems that the use of stage Irish make-up on film actors diminished during the period, but did not disappear. For example, surviving frames of *Finnigan's Initiation* (Lubin, 1909) suggest that the actor playing the title role donned the typical stage Irish make-up. Also in 1909, the *New York Dramatic Mirror* complained that the title character of *Mulligan's Waterloo* (1909) was 'an overdrawn stage Irishman, outrageously made up'.[121] However, that was not the case in other films of the same year, such as *Dope Head Clancy* (Phoenix, 1909), in which the actor wears make-up and clothing resembling a typical film tramp.[122] The decrease in the usage of stage Irish make-up – specifically the noticeably fake beards and whiskers – is tied at least in part to larger trends in the American film industry, in which the use of heavy stage make-up slowly gave way to more subtle make-up styles which themselves were an attempt to be more 'genuine' in appearance.

However, while Irish characters became – if viewed over a range of films – more complicated and less likely to feature stage Irish make-up, they continued to be influenced by pre-existing entertainment like popular music and vaudeville. The same was true of other ethnic film characters. For example, American Mutoscope & Biograph's *Fights of Nations* (1907) featured various scenes of characters representing such nationalities as the Irish, the Scots, the Jews and the Spanish; all of these unfold as if they are vaudeville acts.[123] Characters of the same nationalities fight with one another until Uncle Sam offers 'Peace' at the conclusion. In the film's 'Sons of the Ould Sod' section, Haggerty and Fogarty 'battle furiously' until Mrs Haggerty brings them the 'soothing balm' of beer.[124] The film repeated the basic action of Edison's *Irish Way of Discussing Politics* (1896), one example of the narrative repetition that occurred in the nickelodeon era.

## Recurrent Storylines in the Nickelodeon Era

A number of pre-nickelodeon films continued to be sold during the nickelodeon period, in part due to the fact that the early nickelodeon era was marked by a shortage of new films.[125] In their 1907 catalogue, for example, Selig Polyscope sold *Murphy's Troubles with the Photographer* (1903).[126] That same year, Lubin's catalogue included *Irish Politics* (1896), *Rushing the 'Growler'* (circa 1899) and *Policeman's Love Affair* (1905).[127] Repetition came in other forms as well, as some films reworked storylines and jokes that had appeared on screen in prior years. Vitagraph's film *The Death of Michael Grady* (1910) and Lubin's *The Widow Casey's Return* (1912) were more elaborate versions of the basic joke told in *O'Finnegan's Wake* (circa 1899) and *A Wake in 'Hell's Kitchen'* (1900), both concluding as they did with mourners frightened by a presumed corpse.[128]

Similarly, *McGinty's Sudden Rise* (Edison, 1909) drew on the explosion gag seen in American Mutoscope & Biograph's *'Drill Ye Tarriers, Drill'* (1900) and *The Finish of Michael Casey; or, Blasting Rocks in Harlem* (1901); in the 1909 film, foreman McGinty physically scolds a mischievous boy for dropping his drink; in retaliation, the boy sets off the powder keg that acts as McGinty's chair. The blast sends McGinty high into the sky. On his fall back to earth, he hits a church steeple and then, finally, the ground.

When his workmen find him, he is missing an arm and a leg. They take him to a doctor 'of the occult variety' who makes 'a few mysterious passes with his supple hands and arms', thus causing McGinty's missing limbs to return.[129] Once again, cinematographic tricks provide much of the humour in an effort to visualize a plotline that stems back to the 1888 song, *Drill Ye Tarriers, Drill*.

The use of cinematographic 'tricks' decreased in nickelodeon-era Irish-themed comedies, though they did not disappear, as two films with characters named Casey attest.[130] *When Casey Joined the Lodge* (1908) has the title character fighting with lodge member Riley.[131] A stick of dynamite then causes an African-American character to fly 'through the ceiling and into the clouds'. Riley later throws dynamite at some policemen, causing them to 'fly skyward' as well.[132] The following year, *Casey's Jumping Toothache* (Edison, 1909) featured a dentist who resorts to the use of gas in order to extract the title character's tooth.[133] Casey 'floats upwards, breaking a hole in the ceiling, and drifts away', at least until he is awakened from his dream.[134] Both films used special effects not dissimilar to *McGinty's Sudden Rise*.

Selig Polyscope's *Mike, the Model* (1907) and Lubin's *After the Celebration* (1908) also used 'tricks' in their own efforts to recycle old film jokes. Both retell the basic plotline of *Casey's Nightmare* (1903): an Irishman's drinking becomes the excuse for trick photography. In *Mike, the Model*, a 'typical Irishman', in the words of Selig's catalogue, portrays Julius Caesar for a sculptor. Mike drinks some of the sculptor's alcohol, which causes him to 'violently' assault a clay statue before sinking into a sound sleep; then, the sculptor's statues seem to come to life. When Mike tries to destroy two of them, they change into 'demons armed with tridents' before disappearing in a 'cloud of fire'.[135] *After the Celebration* presented a less elaborate narrative, probably because it was only 165 feet long as compared to the 600 feet of *Mike, the Model*. In it, Mike celebrates St Patrick's Day by drinking. When he returns home, he sees a beer barrel 'change into his mother-in-law', who is then 'replaced by a shamrock, the shamrock by a pitcher, the pitcher by two of his friends, these turn into a snake, the snake into a block of ice'.[136]

However, most Irish-themed films of this period eschewed such tricks, drawing instead on pre-cinema narratives that had appeared in vaudeville, popular music, and other entertainment forms. For example, a number of stories returned to the Irish fighting each other or battling other economic classes. In *The Line at Hogan's* (Biograph, 1912), Hogan and McNabb are 'rivals for the hand of the Widow O'Shaughnessy', and in *Dooley's Scheme* (Biograph, 1911), Officer Dooley competes with plumber Mike Doyle to win the heart of a housemaid.[137] Lubin's *Lunch Time* (1910) features a fight that

4.7 *Pat the Soothsayer* (Kalem, 1912).

begins when Mike drops a brick on Pat's head, but their anger is quickly redirected to a tramp who steals Mike's lunch.[138] The same year, Edison's *Pat and the 400* (1910) presented the story of Pat Murphy, a happy family man who lives in the slums. Some representatives of the upper class visit their home to bring charitable gifts, but they reprimand Pat for drinking and his wife for poor housekeeping. In order to exact revenge, Pat, his wife and his friends crash a musical event at the wealthy family's home.[139]

Conflicts between Irish-Americans and other nationalities also continued in a number of films during the nickelodeon period, probably inspired as much by the plethora of illustrated song slides on that topic as by any other kind of entertainment form. While it is difficult to know the reason, Lubin explored this storyline far more than any other film manufacturing company of the period. In 1908, Lubin's *Two Little Dogs* featured the Irish 'Pat' Clancy and Dutch 'Henry' Dietrich, who work together as labourers. Both purchase dogs, and, after their dogs start fighting, so do Clancy, Dietrich and their families.[140] *Hogan Versus Schmidt* (Lubin, 1912), *Riley and Schultz* (Keystone, 1912) and *Hogan's Alley* (Edison, 1912) addressed conflicts between the Irish and the Dutch, the latter film relying on stage Irish make-up.[141] Lubin also released *Becky Gets a Husband* (1912), which featured the first major example of the Irish–Jewish storyline on film. Much like Excelsior's 1911 illustrated song *Love Me to a Yiddisha Melody (Oh! You Kiddisha!)*, *Becky Gets a Husband* offered a love story about a young Jewish woman and a young Irish man. However – in a plot device that anticipated later stage plays and films built on the same conflict – their fathers, who are neighbours, disagree with their planned marriage.[142] The result causes chaos and some 'rough business', meaning knockabout physical comedy of the type that had been seen in vaudeville.[143]

Numerous moving pictures also connected current events to humour, as was the case in American Mutoscope & Biograph's *A Coal Strike* (1906).[144] While its story involved little more than the accidental dumping of coal on an Irish laundress, its title echoed newspaper headlines at the end of 1905 and the beginning of 1906. During that time, the United Mine Workers threatened to strike on more than one occasion, causing coal prices to rise. The problem grew to the extent that President Theodore Roosevelt personally intervened in February 1906.[145]

At least three films of 1907 also built comedy out of current events. Selig Polyscope's *The A.P.A. and the Irishman* (1907) invoked the American Protective Association's anti-Catholic stance for the sake of knockabout humour none too different from the illustrated song *The Mick Who Threw the Brick* (circa 1899).[146] Lubin's *Smuggled into America* (1907) featured a Chinese-American attempting to smuggle two Chinese friends into the United States by dressing them as an Irish man and woman; that same year, a debate raged in Washington, DC, about immigration laws and the so-called 'Chinese exclusion policy'.[147] And Lubin's *When Women Vote* (1907) offered a comedy about the suffrage movement with its characters Mr and Mrs O'Brien; the fact that they are Irish has little to do with its storyline.[148]

The reuse of old ideas and the retelling of old storylines did not go unnoticed in the film industry press. For example, of *McNabb Wants to Get Arrested* (Raleigh and Robert, 1910), the *New York Dramatic Mirror* said, 'this story has been done before at least twice, and truth requires the admission that it was better done'.[149] Two years later, *Moving Picture World* warned readers that *O'Brien's Busy Day* (Imp, 1912) was 'not very original'.[150] Such criticism had little impact on film manufacturing companies, as they continued to return to previous moving pictures and pre-cinema entertainment for narrative source material.

### 'Comic' Irish Characters in the Nickelodeon Era

Nickelodeon-era film companies often relied on some of the same Irish character names that had been used in earlier moving pictures. However, in most cases, the purpose was not to create film series featuring a repetitive character. Rather, film-makers simply chose names already long associated with comedy. Thus, ill-defined characters bearing names like Pat and Casey appeared in different moving pictures at different companies. In some cases, their appearance and/or character traits were coded as Irish, but in other cases their ethnicity was less clearly pronounced.

Consider, for example, a film like Vitagraph's *Too Many Caseys* (1912), which offered the story of two families named Casey who live side by side and constantly argue with one another. At one point, they jointly catch a burglar, but their continued fighting allows him to escape. A policeman arriving at the scene arrests both Caseys for wielding firearms. Eventually, the authorities catch the burglar and release the Caseys, who are so happy that 'a truce is declared'.[151] Here the characters bear a name that had long been used in Irish-themed jokes in vaudeville and other comedic forms, including pre-nickelodeon era films, and they engage in knockabout stage Irish character actions. *Moving Picture World* even declared that actor William Shea offered the characterization of a 'real Irisher'.[152]

By contrast, *Dope Head Clancy* (1909) illustrates the looseness with which such Irish names were used. In it, Clancy is a tramp wearing trousers that are too short, a jacket that is too tight and a hat that is too small. His lack of intelligence, as noted in the film's title, causes him to experience four misadventures, ranging from wrecking a fruit cart and being thrown out of a baseball stadium to becoming quickly unpopular at a wrestling match and on a film set. Nothing about Clancy suggests the stage Irish; instead, he is yet another film tramp with little in the way of distinguishing features, and his comedic misadventures do not borrow from Irish stereotypes.

Two years later, Edison released *Pat Clancy's Adventure* (Edison, 1912, aka *Pat Clancy's Adventures*), which was based on O. Henry's short story *The Shamrock and the Palm*. The film told the story of Pat's problems with a Spaniard when he leaves America to work in Guatemala.[153] Though the Spaniard tricks him, Pat eventually receives 'satisfaction' when they return to a US port and authorities sentence the Spaniard for vagrancy, making him clean the streets for ten days.[154] The *New York Dramatic Mirror* noted that 'the story has been carefully and effectively managed to express this humour with the capable Irish comedian, Edward O'Connor, in the leading role'.[155] Its 'Clancy' was vastly different from the one seen in *Dope Head Clancy*, indicating that these character names did not have fixed meanings.

Nowhere is this lack of character definition more evident than in examining other characters named Pat. One of the first films of the nickelodeon era to feature a 'Pat' character was Essanay's *Breaking Into Society* (1908), which starred Ben Turpin as hod-carrier Pat O'Brien.[156] He receives a letter informing him that his uncle has died and left him a fortune. After reading the letter, Pat quits his job and rushes home to his wife, Bridget, who demolishes all of the furniture after learning they have entered 'high society'. They change the spelling of their name to 'O'Breean', they purchase a mansion and they attend a ball at the wealthy Vandepool's home. However, Pat is soon informed that the inheritance was 'all a mistake', causing them to return to their 'old shanty'.[157] The film's narrative fitted within a tradition of inheritance films that dated at least to *The Legacy* (Lubin, 1903) and continued with *The Hobo's Dream* (Lubin, 1908), both of which apparently featured non-Irish characters.[158] However, *Breaking into Society* introduced that storyline into Irish-themed film comedy for the first time on film, simultaneously signalling what would become a new narrative trend and the redeployment of long-standing stage Irish stereotypes.

Characters named Pat then appeared in a number of 1912 films produced by five different companies. *Pat's Breeches* (Champion, 1912) was a simple comedy in which some children soak the title character's trousers by turning a hose on him; thanks to his girlfriend Nora, Pat ends up wearing a doctor's trousers, thus causing the doctor to wear Pat's.[159] Two other films – *Pat's Day Off* (Keystone, 1912) and *Pat the Soothsayer* (Kalem, 1912) – told stories of marital strife. The former features a Pat who pretends to commit suicide as a form of revenge on his wife Bridget.[160] In the latter, Pat leaves his wife to become a fortune-teller's assistant. When she goes to the fortune-teller to learn what has become of him, Pat (in disguise) describes his own 'death'. He then returns home with her after she sees through the ruse.[161]

Problems with women also plagued Pat in Edison's *How Patrick's Eyes Were Opened* (1912), which starred Edward O'Connor in the title role. Rather than being a poor construction worker, Pat is a 'wealthy contractor'.[162] He is also enamoured of an attractive young woman, though his untrustworthy friend Mike has designs on her as well. Thanks to an invention called the 'projecto-optician', Pat 'discovers his rival' with the young woman, causing him to 'bow gracefully out' in what Edison promised was a 'bright and novel comedy'.[163] Here again it becomes necessary to view the character Pat as plural. Competing with another man for the attention of a lady was a storyline that had indeed appeared in previous Irish comedies, but the addition of technology as a narrative topic and the avoidance of a fight scene were contrary to the narratives of earlier films.

Characters named Bridget also appear in a number of films during the nickelodeon era, as well as in at least one notable vaudeville act of the period, and she too was hardly codified or singular.[164] The first of these films was probably Vitagraph's *At the Stage Door; or, Bridget's Romance* (1908). Its Bridget is Bridget O'Hooligan, a 'horrible looking old scrub woman' who mistakenly believes that a character named Johnny has sent her flowers. When she learns that he has no interest in her, she tries to 'drown her disappointment by frequent draughts from a "black bottle" '.[165] That same year, Lubin's *The Washerwomen's Revenge* (1908) was reminiscent of earlier films that featured single punchline humour, although Bridget is not the butt of the joke; instead, Bridget and an unnamed cook give the iceman 'a good drenching'.[166] Those two films were in addition to *Bridget's Dream* (Bush, 1908), which was, according to *Moving Picture World*, 'laughable from start to end'.[167] Three years later, in *Fickle Bridget* (Solax, 1911), the title character leaves her job as a cook after inheriting a fortune; she marries a Count rather than the Irish policeman or German iceman who previously vied for her attentions.[168]

By 1909, some of these Bridgets exemplified intelligence and common sense, becoming something of working-class victors against upper-class employers. They did not conform to the character's 'stereotypical stupidity', as Musser has called it.[169] Lubin's *A Servant's Revenge* (1909) has Bridget dismissed from her position. In retaliation, she returns to the house in disguise, placing cascarets in various pots and pans, and switches the gas hose supplying light to the dining room for a water hose. The result brings 'complete revenge'.[170] Vitagraph's *Bridget on Strike* (1909) features a smart, capable Bridget, whose employers beg her to return after having fired her for requesting a salary increase.[171] Nowhere is this different kind of Bridget more pronounced than in *The Maid's Strategem* (Imp, 1912). In it, Bridget Kelly is a 'very pretty Irish girl, accomplished, and with a good education. She is maid to Mrs Warner, an arrogant society widow, who is hated by all her servants.'[172] Borrowing one of her employer's gowns, Bridget wins the favour of a wealthy young man at a society party. Though she is later exposed as a maid, he still loves her. She has won a husband, thanks to her stratagem. 'Good for her', *Moving Picture World* proudly declared.[173] Characters of this type were dramatically different from, say, the one depicted in *The Finish of Bridget McKeen*.

Other Bridget films drew on the nineteenth-century stereotype, even while adding variations that complicated both her and the narratives in which she appeared. Solax's *Bridget, the Flirt* (1911) features the character as a cook who engages in 'lovemaking' with Hans, a barber's assistant, before then flirting with two other men. Hans threatens suicide, causing Bridget 'to mend her ways'.[174] Then, in Lubin's *Bridget and the Egg* (1911), a young boy named Willie substitutes a china egg for a real egg. Bridget cannot break it and informs Willie's mother of her troubles. By the time the two women go into the kitchen, Willie has replaced the china egg with a real one. When Bridget breaks it with great force, both women – not merely

**4.8** In *The Maid's Strategem* (Imp, 1912), Bridget Kelly is a 'very pretty Irish girl, accomplished, and with a good education'.
*(Courtesy of the Free Library of Philadelphia)*

Bridget – are splashed by it. When they learn that Willie is the culprit, he is 'punished as a result'.[175]

*Bridget's Sudden Wealth* (Edison, 1912), along with the non-Bridget film *An Accidental Millionaire* (Lubin, 1912), repeated the basic narrative of *Breaking into Society* (Essanay, 1908) and *Fickle Bridget* (Solax, 1911), thus helping to concretize a new narrative typology for the Irish-themed film comedy. Both films feature working-class characters – Bridget in *Sudden Wealth* and Michael Duggan in *An Accidental Millionaire* – who inherit fortunes and experience an array of problems. Bridget mistreats the policeman she loves, only later to learn the error of her ways.[176] Duggan has problems fitting into high society until he learns that his inheritance must go to someone else who was presumed lost at sea; Duggan is 'happy to get away from it all, and back to his overalls and corned beef and cabbage'.[177] As with *Breaking into Society*, the two films feature an immediate escalation of social status. They are 'American Dreams' that transform into comedic nightmares.

The immediate influence of *Bridget's Sudden Wealth* can be seen in an Éclair film released a few months later, *Aunt Bridget* (1912). For some audiences, the title would have evoked memories of George W. Monroe's vaudeville performances as *My Aunt Bridget*, even if the depictions were different. In the film, poor Aunt Bridget lives with her nephew and niece. The young couple grow tired of her and eventually put her on a train to another city without realizing that she has just won the lottery. Curiously, however, they put her on a train to Paris, the film apparently being set in France. Here again is an example of the nebulous aspects of the Bridget character, which extended in this film to her geographical location.[178]

As with the earlier period, it is also important to note that various nickelodeon-era films featured domestic servants like cooks and laundresses who were apparently not coded as Irish, including *The New Maid* (Pathé Frères, 1908), *The Servant's Good Joke* (Pathé Frères, 1909), *The Cook Makes the Madeira Sauce* (Vitagraph, 1910), *Discharging the Cook* (Selig Polyscope, 1911) and *Getting Rid of Trouble* (Biograph, 1912).[179] Moreover, some period discussions of 'Bridget' films did not even bother to mention the character's name or ethnicity, as was the case in the *New York Dramatic Mirror*'s review of *A Servant's Revenge* (Lubin, 1909).[180] Conversely, there were domestic servants who were coded as Irish, but who were not named Bridget. For example, Essanay's *The Laundry Lady's Luck* (1911) featured 'Mrs O'Brien' as a laundress who loses her rent money.[181] Pathé Frères' *Pots, Pans, and Poetry* (1911) featured an unnamed 'Irish cook' who believes she has a special ability to 'make poetry or music at will. Some fun is extracted from the experience through which she goes in discovering her mistake.'[182] The following year, *Nora, the Cook* (Lubin, 1912) was an 'Irish girl' who threw 'several households into discord'.[183]

Despite the variety of Bridget characters and the changes that could be noted from the pre-nickelodeon era, no overall chronological evolution took place. For example, one of the final nickelodeon films featuring a Bridget character returned to the old stereotype for inspiration. While cleaning a professor's home in *Bridget's Explanation* (Lubin, 1912), Bridget breaks one of his two priceless Phoenician bowls. He and his guests rush into the room, demanding an explanation. Bridget pantomimes the accident for them, during which she breaks the second bowl. Here she is depicted as a simple, stupid domestic servant. Though the film was 321 feet long, contemporary descriptions suggest it was built on a single punchline, another way in which it was similar to some of the pre-nickelodeon films.[184]

Kalem's *Queen of the Kitchen*, released in September 1912, illustrates how the old stereotypes and new narratives could interact with ease in a single film. Its storyline was in some ways similar to Vitagraph's *Bridget on Strike* (1909). Bridget 'objects' to Mr Clark, her employer, entering her kitchen 'sanctum', and so – after a 'disturbance' – he fires her. But Clark and his wife are 'proverbial newlyweds' and come to appreciate Bridget's 'sterling' qualities while preparing dinner for some guests. They beg Bridget to come back to work, which she does after obtaining a 'substantial increase in salary'. This was not the stupid Bridget of the nineteenth century, but rather a savvy character who bests her employers. However, echoing *The Finish of Bridget McKeen* and nineteenth-century vaudeville performers like George W. Monroe, Bridget in this film was portrayed by the noted male actor John E. Brennan.[185] He was not alone in his drag performance that year. John Bunny played the title character in Vitagraph's *Doctor Bridget* (1912), in which 'Biddy' throws out a spoiled, 'sick' boy's medicine, curing his problems with a prescription of hard labour.[186] By that time, Bunny was already 'well known' for his 'role of [an] Irish cook' in drag, having performed it in such prior films as *Teaching McFadden to Waltz* (Vitagraph, 1911).[187]

# The Post-Nickelodeon Era

Taken as a whole, the Irish-themed comedies of the post-nickelodeon era largely followed the pattern established by earlier films. These moving pictures employed a range of different kinds of humour, some inspired by nineteenth-century caricatures and some liberated from them.[188] Familiar Irish character names continued to be the source of ethnic humour, but some of the very same names increasingly became attached to characters who hardly exemplified stage Irish stereotypes, as was the case in films like *Nora's Boarders* (Edison, 1913).[189] The emphasis on authenticity also continued. For example, in 1913, *Moving Picture World* complained that *Finnegan* (Essanay, 1913) was a 'comedy of Irish characters that might have been more amusing if it had been made more convincing'.[190] Together the post-nickelodeon era comedies represent a complicated picture, but one that was little changed from the nickelodeon era.

Stage Irish make-up and costumes decreased in usage, but they certainly did not disappear. For example, *Moving Picture World* claimed that Mr Casey in *Mrs Casey's Gorilla* (Biograph, 1913) 'was more like a gorilla without his gorilla costume'.[191] *Motion Picture News* noted much the same, claiming 'the names and make-up of the various characters are sufficient to arouse humour without action'.[192] Surviving images also suggest that *Hogan's Alley* (Pathé Frères, 1914, aka *In Hogan's Alley*) employed heavy make-up.[193] The following year, *He Wanted Work* (Lubin, 1914) featured an example of similar make-up as worn by a non-Irish character. *Moving Picture World* wrote: 'There is a lot of fun in this offering, if it does bear the brand of inconsistency. A colored man makes up as an Irishman to obtain a job. He gets it and also several other things.'[194]

**4.9** *Hogan's Alley* (Pathé Frères, 1914, aka *In Hogan's Alley*).

However, in most cases, such make-up was avoided. This change was not necessarily part of an enlightened evolution. After all, much emphasis remained on stereotypical stage Irish character traits and acting, including drinking and fighting. For example, the drunken Casey of *Casey's Birthday* (Lubin, 1914) brawls with his friends who hide in the darkness at his surprise party; some of the problems result from the letter 'P' being knocked off a birthday cake, leaving 'APA' in yet another reference to the American Protective Association.[195] Thus, the move away from stage Irish make-up was likely to have been part of a continuing industry move towards more subtle, and thus more authentic, make-up for all actors in all films. Here again the Irish-themed comedy was connected to trends in the larger American film industry.

### Recurrent Storylines in the Post-Nickelodeon Era

Films of this period drew on earlier entertainment forms for narrative inspiration. For example, *Pat's Idea* (Heron, 1913), *Kelly's Ghost* (Crystal, 1914) and *When Dooley Passed Away* (Lubin, 1914) returned to Irish wake humour, with all three featuring characters who are wrongly presumed to be dead.[196] *Dan Greegan's Ghost* (Biograph, 1913) and *Finnigan's Bomb*

(Keystone, 1914) had plots that hinged on explosives, drawing yet again on the song *Drill Ye Tarriers, Drill.*[197] *Kelly Goes to War* (Universal, 1912) combined an explosion with the title character visiting the bottom of the sea, echoing the lyrics of Joseph Flynn's *Down Went McGinty.*[198] *Casey at the Bat* (Vitagraph, 1913) returned to the famous poem for inspiration, offering a more faithful adaptation than the 1899 film.[199]

Marital strife continued to provide comedic potential as well. Henpecked Irish husbands appeared in such films as *At the Telephone* (Lubin, 1913), *Finnegan* (Essanay, 1913), *The Henpecked Hod Carrier* (Thanhouser, 1913), *Long May It Wave* (Lubin, 1914) and *Casey's Tribulations* (Royal, 1915).[200] In *Hannigan's Harem* (Pathé Frères, 1913), an 'Irishman' dreams that he becomes a sultan's gardener, but his wife 'Biddy' causes him grief for working so near the sultan's wives.[201] Similarly, husband Pat in *Biddy Brady's Birthday* (Falstaff, 1915) receives three wishes from a genie in a lamp; foolishly, he transforms one of his wife's rooms into an Egyptian harem.[202] Four other Irish-themed comedies – *Married Men* (Lubin, 1914), *Murphy and the Mermaids* (Biograph, 1914), *Pat Casey's Case* (Essanay, 1914) and *They Loved Him So* (Vitagraph, 1915) – even featured conclusions in which angry wives chased their husbands.[203] Such 'chase' endings were common in American film comedy of the period.

Humorous troubles between suitors appeared in other films as well. *Kitty's Knight* (Vitagraph, 1913) told the story of rival Irish-American characters attempting to win the love of an Irish-American woman.[204] A similar story appeared in *The Courtship of the Cooks* (Edison, 1914) in which two chefs (one an Italian and one a German) compete for the affections of a laundress named O'Hara.[205] Kalem's *For the Love of Mike* (1914) inverted the story, having three women – Bridget, Maggie and Mary – vying for the affections of policeman Mike McCarthy (John Bunny); none of them succeed, as Mike is already married, with seven children.[206]

Male Irish characters fought for other reasons too. In *Riley's Decoys* (Biograph, 1913), two Irishmen operate competing boarding houses, though Riley wins all the business after two stranded women stand at his front door and attract potential customers.[207] The following year, *A Tango Tragedy* (Lubin, 1914) had father Pat Muldoon trying to shoot his daughter's sweetheart for dancing with her; by the end of the film, however, Pat relents and even tangos with his wife.[208] Characters Mike Clancy and Pat Murphy wage an ongoing war with one another in *Fire! Fire!* (Lubin, 1914); that same year, the Sweeneys and Clancys did battle in *Sweeney's Christmas Bird* (Vitagraph, 1914).[209]

Conflicts between the Irish and other ethnicities continued in moving pictures as well, probably influenced by the ongoing release of illustrated song slides on the same topic. Surprisingly, given the success of such illus-trated songs as *Arrah Wanna*, it seems that no films of the period depicted Irish characters interacting with Native American characters (though Crystal's 1913 *Clancy the Model* did feature its title character wearing Native American attire before becoming drunk and changing clothes with a member of the town militia).[210]

Though they did not encounter Native Americans, Irish characters did meet many other ethnicities. *Rafferty's Raffle* (Apollo, 1914) featured Fred Mace portraying the title role in a comedy that had an Irish neighbourhood 'come to blows' with an African-American neighbourhood.[211] Italians plagued Irish characters in *Dan Greegan's Ghost* (1913), *Brannigan's Band* (Lubin, 1914), *Casey's Vendetta* (Komic, 1914) and *McGinty and the Count* (Edison, 1915).[212] *A Dollar Did It* (Keystone, 1913) and *The Rival Barbers* (Majestic, 1914) featured the Irish fighting the Dutch.[213] The same was true of *A Sprig o' Shamrock* (Imp, 1913), in which a Dutchman tries to marry an Irishman's daughter, but then finds himself thrown out the window after salting, peppering and eating their precious shamrocks from Ireland.[214]

In *The Rivals* (Majestic, 1913), *The Rival Pitchers* (Majestic, 1913) and *Friendly Neighbors* (Powers, 1913), Irish and German characters vie for the affections of the same women.[215] Two years later, Patsey and Fritz fought over the same woman ('Mamie') in *The Perfumed Wrestler* (Selig Polyscope, 1915).[216] Those films were in addition to *Heinze's Resurrection* (Keystone, 1913) in which a German character bothers O'Brien, and in *Just Like Kids* (Lubin, 1915) in which a German and Irishman fight after their children do the same.[217] The German storylines are particularly interesting in view of the close relationship – at least as depicted in the Irish-American press – between some Irish-Americans and German-Americans during the First World War.

Certainly the key 'Meeting of Nationalities' story to proliferate in the post-nickelodeon era was one that had not been as prominent in previous years: the Irish–Jewish story. In 1913, Mack Sennett directed *The Riot*, featuring Fatty Arbuckle as a Jewish father and Mabel Normand as his daughter; Charles Inslee and Alice Davenport played an Irish couple who squabble with them.[218] That same year, in *Murphy's I.O.U.* (Keystone, 1913), the title character owes money to Cohen and pays him with his wife's jewellery.[219] McGann, in *McGann and His Octette* (Biograph, 1913), has worse problems over his financial debt to Ikey Goldstein, who has him imprisoned; Ikey has his own troubles when Judge O'Reilly makes him support McGann's family while McGann is in jail.[220] By contrast, the title character of *Murphy and the Mermaids* (Biograph, 1913) forces a Jewish peddler to chop wood so that he

**4.10** *When Hooligan and Dooligan Ran for Mayor* (Vitagraph, 1915).

can go to the beach.[221] *Levi and McGuiness Running for Office* (Independent Moving Pictures, 1913) has its title characters vie for the position of a city alderman; they are arrested after they and their sons fight.[222] *Moving Picture World* expressed concern about the film's 'race rioting between the Irish and the Jews', but admitted that some of the characterizations were 'genuinely amusing'.[223] Together, such films paved the way for the many subsequent Irish–Jewish stage plays and films.

The reuse of storylines like the 'Meeting of Nationalities' illustrates the reliance on pre-cinema entertainment, sometimes as refracted through earlier moving pictures that had already adapted the same material. Other recurrent storylines were more specifically tied to the cinema, offering tales that were less dependent on other kinds of entertainment. For example, *Traffickers in Soles* (Feature Photoplay Co., 1914, aka *Traffickers on Soles*) with Levy and McGuiness spoofed the feature film *Traffic in Souls* (1913); it was one of two different moving picture parodies of that melodrama.[224]

Film history thus represented an ever-growing body of narratives that could be repurposed. Naughty children of the type that had appeared in many earlier films provided humour in *Poor Finney* (Punch, 1912) and *Where's the Baby* (Biograph, 1913).[225] *Murphy's New High Hat* (1913) concluded with Irish music and dance reminiscent of such films as *Irish Couple Dancing Breakdown* (1903).[226] *The Mix-Up at Murphy's* (Biograph, 1914) offered comedy based upon a case of mistaken identity, a topic that had informed many previous films.[227] The title characters in *When Hooligan and Dooligan Ran for Mayor* (Vitagraph, 1915) sabotage each other's campaigns, though in the end both of them lose to – in another nod to current events – 'Straightwater, the Prohibition Candidate'.[228]

Other repeated narratives built on the use of insurance policies for comedic purposes. Both *Mulligan's Ghost* (Columbus, 1914) and *Pat Hogan, Deceased* (Vitagraph, 1915) told stories of wives collecting life insurance on husbands who were not dead.[229] *Gilliagan's Accident Policy* (Biograph, 1914) also told a tale using insurance as the key joke. In it, a 'henpecked Irishman buys an accident policy and tries to get hurt... he does not succeed until he has surrendered the policy'.[230]

**4.11** *Frayed Fagin's Adventures* (Kalem, 1913).

Nowhere did this reuse of previous film stories occur more commonly than with inheritance comedies. The title character of *The Dream of Dan Maguire* (Selig, 1913) is a hod-carrier who falls asleep on the job. During a dream, money left to him by a rich uncle causes him to have various troubles with his wife and servants. He then runs for political office, but never wins because a fellow worker wakes him up.[231] In *Spending It Quick* (Biograph, 1914), Pat and his wife invest a $500 inheritance from an uncle's estate in a new car and nearly kill themselves after going over a cliff in the 'ride of their lives'; after brushing himself off, Pat announces he is happy the car 'was not [worth] $1000, as he would have lost more money'.[232] Then, the title character of *Mrs Maloney's Fortune* (Vitagraph, 1914), portrayed by Kate Price, inherits a large estate. She drops her lover Michael Finnegan (William Shea) and attempts to move into high society. After getting drunk, she comes to her senses and tours a slum. She finds an orphan who is in fact the rightful heir of the fortune. Maloney takes him home and then agrees to marry Finnegan.[233] Similarly, Riley in *This Isn't the Life* (Lubin, 1915) inherits money and unhappily lives in a new neighbourhood. He pretends to be insane, hoping his legal fees at court will deplete his wealth.[234] The newly rich title character of *Food for Kings and Riley* (Edison, 1915) so desires corned beef and cabbage that his socialite wife refuses to cook that he begins to eat with a poor 'widder woman'.[235]

Of all these films, the most unique approach to the familiar storyline came in *Rooney's Sad Case* (Vitagraph, 1915), in which the title character does not actually inherit money, but instead enacts a bizarre plan to marry into it. In a newspaper, Rooney reads about someone who lost his memory and then married a 'beautiful heiress'. He plans to do the same, renting a nice suit from a Jewish storeowner so that he will appear wealthy. He tries the scheme on a busy road, pretending to have hit his head when a rich man passes. The man takes Rooney home, and a doctor bandages his head. The wealthy man's daughter speaks to Rooney, who imagines that she is beautiful. However, when the gauze is removed and he finally sees her face, he 'nearly faints and regains his memory in a hurry'.[236]

## 'Comic' Irish Characters in the Post-Nickelodeon Era

As in the nickelodeon era, the use of Irish character names did not necessarily indicate a use of stage Irish stereotypes. In *Feeney's Social Experiment* (Reliance, 1913), for example, the title character is not stupid; instead, he outwits the wealthy millionaires who once employed him in a tale that *Moving Picture World* called 'well pictured and worthwhile'.[237] In some cases, the Irish heritage of a given character had little or nothing to do with the comedic stories in which they were involved, as was the case with *Bound to Occur* (Essanay, 1913, featuring characters named Carney), *Finney's Luck* (Punch, 1913), *Frayed Fagin's Adventures* (Kalem, 1913), *Actor Finney's Finish* (Essanay, 1914), *McBride's Bride* (Kalem, 1914), *A Quiet Day at Murphy's* (Joker, 1914), *Mrs Murphy's Cooks* (Selig, 1915), *Finn and Haddie* (Lubin, 1915), *Borrowing Hogan* (Santa Barbara, 1915) and *Rooney, The Bride* (Edison, 1915).[238] The narratives of such films would scarcely have been different if the ethnic identification of the title characters had been changed.[239] Indeed, it is worth noting that many similar comedy films of the period featured characters of other ethnicities.

Names that had long been used in Irish-themed film comedies also continued to be given to a vast array of different characters. For example, the Casey of *The Pennant Puzzle* (Selig, 1912) causes comedy by trying to solve a puzzle for a $1,000 prize.[240] The following year, in the title role of *Pat, the Cowboy* (Kalem, 1913), John E. Brennan 'cause[s] amusement' due to an 'unfamiliarity with the ways of the country' when he moves west.[241] Based upon surviving plot synopses and images, there is no indication that this film portrays Pat as inherently dim-witted or that it used stage Irish make-up or costumes. Rather, Pat is simply a stranger in a strange land in a 'fish out of water' comedy.

Bridget also continued to be a name attached to various kinds of characters who oscillated between the old stereotype and derivations from it. In 1913, a cook named Bridget O'Hoolihan loves policeman Pat Flaherty, the 'cop on the beat' in the Lux film *The Cook's Revenge*.[242] In *The Surrender* (Powers, 1913), a rural cook named Bridget rudely awakens a sleeping society woman visiting the farm where she works.[243] In Kinemacolor's *Love and Laundry* (1913), a laundress named Bridget is the accidental recipient of a love letter meant for another.[244] The title character of *Bridget Bridges It* (Essanay, 1914) also appears in a story of mistaken identities, as she has received a party invitation instead of an intended offer of laundry work. This Bridget is smart enough to win the prize of an automobile, but also too 'inept' to drive it home properly.[245] In *The Cook's Mistake* (Edison, 1915), Bridget attends a masquerade ball brandishing two revolvers, planning to

**4.12** *Pat the Cowboy* (Kalem, 1913).

shoot a policeman whom she believes has betrayed her love. She ends up chasing a crook wearing the policeman's costume down the street and into a restaurant that she 'shoots up'. Eventually Bridget and a group of policemen end up inside a tank of water.[246]

The nineteenth-century Bridget stereotype was most clearly exemplified by two other films of the period. In *The Laundress and the Lady* (Kalem, 1913), Bridget is a cook who mistakes the sweetheart of her boss's son for a newly hired laundress.[247] The fact that a male actor (John E. Brennan) portrays Bridget echoed prior films like *The Finish of Bridget McKeen* (1901) and the George W. Monroe tradition.[248] Two years later, Edison's *Curing the Cook* (1915) also featured a male actor (William Fables) in drag playing Bridget. In this film, the character works at a students' boarding house. Because she is lazy and drinks so much, the students play a joke on her by placing a skeleton in the coal bin to scare her.[249] The film borrowed its key joke from Edison's 1901 film *Why Bridget Stopped Drinking* (aka *Why Bridget Gave Up Drinking*).

However closely those films followed long-standing stereotypes, others offered quite different depictions. In *That Heavenly Cook* (Edison, 1915), Bridget's employer fires her, though she is eventually rehired at an increased salary. Though still a domestic servant, in this case the character is 'impertinent' rather than stupid.[250] That same year, a very different Bridget appears in *Mike's Elopement* (Reliance, 1915) as the girlfriend of a 12-year-old boy. The two decide to elope, though various troubles result in Bridget literally carrying Mike back to his home. She is coded as Irish, but she is not stupid or ugly. Nor is she a domestic servant.[251] The same was true of Bridget (spelled 'Bridgett') as portrayed by Kate Price in the Vitagraph comedy *The Conquest of Constantia* (1915).[252] Similarly, the Bridget Clancy of the Selig comedy *Wipe Yer Feet* (1915) was not a servant, but rather a mother insistent on cleanliness.[253]

Such examples were all in addition to the fact that other domestic servants in the cinema were not coded as Irish, including the comical Swedish cook in *Found Out* (Essanay, 1913), the title character of *Sally Scraggs, Housemaid* (Red, 1913) and 'Vivian' in *An Up-To-Date Cook* (Universal, 1914).[254] Furthermore, in 1914 and 1915, Wallace Beery appeared as 'Sweedie', a Swedish maid, in a series of approximately thirty Essanay comedies. Their numbers dwarf the number of Bridget films in the post-nickelodeon period, and they represent a male actor in drag portraying a non-Irish domestic servant.[255]

## The Film Series

Except for Selig Polyscope's five 'Murphy' moving pictures in 1903, Irish-themed comedies were not generally produced in codified film series until the late nickelodeon period.[256] The emergence of these film series, which continued into the post-nickelodeon period, provided the potential for clearly defined characters to emerge over a number of moving pictures. Their approaches to comedy drew not only on previous forms of entertainment, but also on previous entries in the very same series, their characters being the culmination of a group of films. The rise of the Irish-themed film series also coincided with the rise of the American film star, the result being that the two intersected, as some notable actors repeatedly portrayed the same (or similar) comic Irish characters.

The Reliance Film Company produced the first major Irish-themed comic film series, which featured the Irish domestic servant 'Bedelia'.[257] However, they were not the first to bring a Bedelia character to the screen. In a November 1905 catalogue, the Kleine Optical Company offered a 'trick' film entitled *Bedelia and the Witch*. In it, Bedelia: 'got a notion that she would do the family washing at night. We see her at the wash-tub when the milkman comes in with bottles of milk. Then they make love to each other. Bedelia resumes her work. A witch appears riding a broom, but disappears shortly. Next Bedelia's tub vanishes, and a series of mystifying happenings bewilder her.'[258] Though it would not generally be considered an Irish name, Bedelia would have had particular resonance in America in the early twentieth century. In 1903, sheet music for *Bedelia: An Irish Coon Song* (written by William Jerome and Jean Schwartz, who attained fame with songs like *Chinatown, My Chinatown*) sold over one million copies. At least three phonograph records of the song were released shortly thereafter, one of them featuring Billy Murray. The song's lyrics tell the story of 'a charming Irish lady with a roguish winning way'. Bedelia is a 'flower from Killarney with a Tipperary smile/She's the best that ever came from Erin's Isle.' *Bedelia*'s enormous success inspired another song, recorded in 1904, *The Wedding of Barney and Bedelia*.

Drawing on the song's fame, Reliance produced nine Bedelia moving pictures in 1912.[259] Anthony O'Sullivan starred in drag as the title character, a stout and bossy Irish cook. The *New York Dramatic Mirror* noted that he played the role in his 'inimitable style'.[260] The same publication described Bedelia as a 'buxom Irish cook of uncertain and erratic temper'.[261] A 1912 newspaper column called her 'the Irish cook-lady', while *Moving Picture World* once referred to her as 'the autocratic kitchen queen'.[262] On another occasion, the trade claimed that 'every one [sic] will remember Bedelia, who nevertheless doesn't appear often enough to be tiresome', a comment that suggests audience familiarity with the character (presumably dating to the song) as well as with the previous films in the series.[263] After all, Reliance released their Bedelia films over the space of just eleven months, beginning with the first entry, *Bedelia's Busy Morning* (1912), and ending with *Trying to Keep Bedelia* (1912).

Those same nine Bedelia films clearly drew on Irish comic traditions from the stage and screen. Bedelia has troubles with the milkman, on whom she 'vents her wrath' in *Bedelia's Busy Morning* (1912); in the same film, echoing *The Finish of Bridget McKeen*, she also 'starts a fire in the kitchen using kerosene'.[264] *Bedelia's 'At Home'* (1912) revived Irish wake humour, with Bedelia's husband Mike Clancy mistakenly believed to be dead.[265] In *Bedelia and Mrs Busybody*, Bedelia has troubles with both her intoxicated husband and a 'busybody', on whom she exacts 'punishment' for 'prying into other people's affairs'.[266] In *Bedelia and Her Neighbor*, she fights with an African-American woman who lives nearby.[267] Current events provided an opportunity for *Bedelia and the Suffragette* (1912), in which Bedelia cooks for a 'modern' family in which the wife works and the husband – whom Bedelia bullies – stays at home.[268] She also 'bosses' the husband and wife who employ her in *Bedelia and the Newlyweds* (1912) and *Trying to Keep Bedelia* (1912).[269]

**4.13** The sheet music cover for the hit song *Bedelia* (1903), the 'Irish Coon Song Serenade'.

Collectively, the Bedelia films not only constitute the first major Irish-themed comedy series of the nickelodeon era, but also represent a more consistent and sustained depiction of the Irish domestic servant stereotype than do any other films of the early cinema period. Indeed, while she may have gained her name from the 1903 song, Reliance's Bedelia had little in common with the character depicted in its lyrics. Instead, she was in fact an incarnation of the stereotypical Bridget of the nineteenth century, more so than most of the characters in early American cinema who were actually named Bridget.

By contrast, the next Irish film series to appear on American screens was far less consistent. The French company Lux released at least eleven 'Pat' comedies in the US from December 1912 to February 1914. One trade publication spoke of Pat as the 'Lux comedian', though surviving synopses suggest that the character varied greatly from film to film.[270] For example, Pat stupidly wrecks a large house that he nearly burns down in *Pat, the Electrician* (1913); similarly, in *Pat Wishes to Economize* (1913), the title character tries to hang some pictures, thus creating what *Moving Picture World* called a 'comedy of [the] furniture breaking, house destroying sort'.[271] That same year, the Pat in *Pat as a Bird Fancier* (1913) opens a cage that he thinks contains a bird, but flees when the animal it contains has four legs.[272] Then, in 1914, *Pat's Motor* returned to explosion gags in an effort to create humour, with Pat using a match to search for a problem with an automobile engine.[273]

However, the Pat of *Pat's Fancy Dress* (1913) builds comedy not out of Pat's stupidity, but instead out of a leopard costume that he wears to a masked ball; he succeeds in frightening several women until a real leopard appears.[274] The film *Pat Moves to Diplomatic Circles* (1913) was a comedy of mistaken identities, and both *Tickets, Please* (1913) and *Pat Gets on the Trail* (1913) created humour from romantic situations and – in the case of the latter film – a rivalry for the same woman.[275]

Some of the Pats in the Lux film series may well not have emphasized comedy. Their first Pat release had been *Pat and the Milliner* (1913), in which Pat is a 'young man-about-town' who takes a job simply to be near a 'charming young lady' who works at the same establishment.[276] That same year, *Pat's Busy Day* (1913) offered a rural Pat who achieves the 'American Dream' after he moves to the city; this Pat bears no apparent relationship to the 'stage Irish' Pat. Instead, it relied on such 'trick' photography as a 'triple exposure'.[277] The following year, *Pat Fannagan's Family* (1914, aka *Pat Flannagan's Family*) featured a serious tale of a Pat who is a department story deliveryman. He purchases a steamship ticket to go to Ireland, but gives up his 'cherished plans' to adopt some young children.[278] Given that these films were apparently made in France, it is possible that – rather than having been originally envisioned as a codified series of Irish-themed comedies – the name Pat was simply appended to them for their American release.

Though comprised of only three films, Selig's 'Sweeney' series in 1913 featured, like Bedelia, a coherent character, far more so than Lux's Pat. On the one hand, the films recycled plots and comedic situations that had been used in many previous moving pictures, something that may well have prevented the series from becoming more popular. On the other hand, the first and second films in the series bore a narrative link, the second building on the storyline of the first. That approach was largely new to Irish-themed comedy, as it was something that was usually dependent on a film series. The first entry, *Sweeney and the Million* (1913), featured the title character, a hod-carrier portrayed by John Lancaster, inheriting a fortune. However, he quickly loses it after some bad investments and 'rash' gambling at a card game.[279] *Moving Picture World* praised the film for adding 'one or two new incidents' to the increasingly clichéd inheritance storyline.[280] The second film, *Sweeney and the Fairy* (1913), had the long-suffering hod-carrier fall asleep during lunch. In his dream, a fairy returns to him all the affluence he lost in the prior film; however, his wealth evaporates when he awakes.[281] The connection between it and the first film did not go unnoticed by the industry trade publications.[282] Then, in the final film, *Sweeney's Dream* (1913), the hod-carrier has yet another dream, this time becoming 'president of a republic' until being stirred from his slumber.[283]

By 1914, the year after the Sweeney films, the Irish-themed comedy series became increasingly dependent upon star talent. For example, Charlie Murray, who had been famous as one half of the Murray and Mack comedy team, appeared in four 'Skelley' comedies at Biograph in 1914.[284] The character was not particularly developed, and varied from film to film. In *Skelley's Birthday* (1914), he is married and has a home; by contrast, after reviewing *Skelley and the Turkey* (1914), *Motion Picture News* described Skelley and his pal as 'Irish hoboes'.[285] However, the fact that the popular and recognizable Murray was the star gave the films a coherence that they would not otherwise have had. For example, *Moving Picture World* believed *Skelley's Birthday* offered Murray an opportunity to 'get in some of his "old time" stunts'.[286] The Skelley character was thus subservient to Murray's own well-developed persona that dated to the nineteenth century.

At some point in mid-to-late 1914, Murray left Biograph for Keystone, where he appeared in a similar series, though the new character's name was Hogan.[287] In some cases, the Hogan films drew on stage Irish character traits. For example, Hogan gets into a brick-throwing fight with other Irish labourers in *Hogan's Mussy Job* (1915). Hogan also drinks too much in some of the films, including *Hogan the Porter* (1915). After battling a female pickpocket at a moving picture theatre in *Hogan's Wild Oats* (1915), he gives up drinking. In all, there were at least eight Hogan films,

**4.14** *Bedelia's Busy Morning* (Reliance, 1912) featured actor Anthony O'Sullivan (left) starring in drag as the 'buxom Irish cook of uncertain and erratic temper'.

but the character was not particularly distinct, and in some cases the films did not rely on ethnic stereotypes. Once again, the lack of character definition was offset by Murray's own presence. For example, originally the name 'Hogan' appeared in the working title of the film *Beating Hearts and Carpets* (1915); by the time of its release, Murray's character was simply listed as 'Sewing Machine Demonstrator'.[288] Hogan had been dependent on Murray, but Murray was not dependent on either Hogan or Skelley.

Similarly, the 'Kate' series at Vitagraph in 1914 and 1915 featured Kate Price, who was born in Ireland and became noted in America over a period of many years for her Irish characterizations. In at least six comedy films, Price played a character named 'Kate' who – like Murray's Skelley and Hogan – was coded as Irish.[289] These films generally offer her character name simply as 'Kate', though *Strictly Neutral* (1915) credits her as 'Kate, the Irish Cook'. Surviving prints of *Officer Kate* (1914) show a character who drinks beer and fights with her husband. In *Cabman Kate* (1915), she is a washerwoman who smokes a cigar and who speaks – thanks to the intertitles – in an Irish dialect and uses such words as 'Begorrah'.[290]

The dependence of Skelley, Hogan and Kate on the actors who portrayed them brings another important matter into focus. Skelley and Hogan were not particularly different from many of the other characters that Charlie Murray portrayed on screen at the end of the nickelodeon era and beyond. The same was true of the character Kate and many of Kate Price's other roles. Both actors played other, similar comical characters on screen who had different Irish names.[291] Murray and Price also portrayed characters who had no names, but were simply identified by their jobs (such as 'The Janitor' or 'The Cook'), though some of these seem to have had Irish traits.[292] Additionally, they also portrayed similar characters on screen who had distinctly non-Irish names.[293] Surviving films and images suggest that – in addition to their own recognizable faces – Murray and Price often wore similar costumes and make-up in many of these different films. As a result, the Skelley, Hogan and Kate series were rather porous and could have been easily confused/conflated with other Murray and Price films.

Indeed, the emergence of Irish film stars, as well as film stars touted for portraying Irish roles, complicates further the already diffuse Irish-themed film comedy. When praising the 'amusing' qualities of *Rooney's Bad Case* (Vitagraph, 1915), *Moving Picture World* noted that star Sidney Drew's 'grandfather was celebrated for his acting of Irish character parts' and that the 'grandson...inherited much of his grandsire's skill'.[294] Such a comment was not particularly different from, say, Charlie Murray – whose work on the stage was still remembered – portraying an Irish comic role in the cinema. Once again, the past encroached on the present; pre-cinema entertainment influenced the cinema. But then there are less clear situations, such as the case of the famous film comedian Augustus Carney, who was born – as his publicity sometimes noted – in Ireland.[295] Carney starred in three successful film series: Hank and Lank at Essanay from 1910 to 1911, Alkali Ike at Essanay from 1911 to 1914, and Universal Ike at Universal in 1914. Nothing about any of those characters was coded as Irish, let alone stage Irish. However, there exists the possibility that audiences familiar with his biography might still, as a result have read his characters as 'Irish'.

The producers of the final Irish film series of the early cinema sought to avoid such vagueness by highlighting their own authenticity. In promoting the new company All Celtic Film, Inc., producer Charles O'Hara touted his Irish background and that of all of his co-workers, 'even the man that does the printing and developing of the films'.[296] *Motography* assured readers that the people behind the scenes had 'real' Irish names, thus suggesting that they could produce authentic Irish-themed comedies.[297] For the All Celtic film series, O'Hara chose the character name Rafferty, which had previously been used for the unrelated comedies *The Ups and Downs and*

**4.15** Actress Kate Price (seated, left) in *Mrs Maloney's Fortune* (Vitagraph, 1914).

*Rafferty* (Comet, 1911) and *Rafferty's Raffle* (Apollo, 1914).[298] Joe Sullivan assumed the role of the lead character, with Peggy Shannon cast as his co-star.[299] To the press, O'Hara promised that the 'Adventures of Peaceful Rafferty' series was 'high class, refined, and [does] not at any time descend to scenes of vulgarity'.[300] By referring to 'vulgarity', O'Hara might have meant the use of stage Irish stereotypes, but it is likely that he also might have meant other types of 'low' comedy that were not specifically ethnic.

All Celtic released four Rafferty films in 1915, the first being *Rafferty Settles the War* (1915, aka *Rafferty Stops the War*), in which Rafferty dreams that he brings peace to the war in Europe after having stopped the fighting between various ethnicities in his own neighbourhood.[301] In *Rafferty Stops a Marathon* (1915, aka *Rafferty Stops a Marathon Runner*), Rafferty incorrectly believes a marathon runner is an escaped lunatic from a local asylum.[302] The final two films in the series seem to have featured narratives that were connected.[303] In *Rafferty at the Hotel de Rest* (1915), Rafferty becomes infatuated with a young lady while waiting to see a doctor. After being consigned to the hotel named in the film's title, Rafferty vies for the young lady's attentions amid many other suitors.[304] Then, in *Rafferty Goes to Coney Island* (1915), Rafferty follows the same young lady and the other suitors to Coney Island. All of the rivals give up after a fortune-teller advises the young lady to scorn them.[305] Reviewing the films, *Motography* believed that they featured a 'slapstick' approach to comedy.[306]

While at least one surviving still suggests that the lead character wore fake Irish whiskers, the Rafferty films offered a somewhat fresh approach to the Irish-themed comedy. For example, one trade publication noted that the films were: 'primarily, of course ... Irish comedies, dwelling at length upon the adventures of ... a financially comfortable son of Erin, who, despite his old age, has a half-grown boy's propensity for getting into trouble. His readiness at paying for the damages involved and his willingness to forgive, earn for him the name of "Peaceful Rafferty".'[307] As with so many of the films discussed in this chapter, the Rafferty films regrettably do not survive. However, even if Rafferty was as 'high class' and 'refined' as Charles O'Hara claimed, the character remained but one component of a

Like the Rays of the Sun Peaceful Rafferty Is Everywhere, for He Is the Greatest
Irish Comedian on the Screen Today, and the Biggest Box Office Winner of the
Age. Play His Pictures if You Want Something New, Refined, Funny, and Good. We
Lead in Comedy Making, and the Others Follow. Book These and See for Yourself.

## "Rafferty Stops The War"
## "Rafferty Stops A Marathon Runner"
### COMING
## "Rafferty At The Hotel De Rest" and
## "Rafferty Goes To Coney Island"

*Released Through*

### The World Film Exchanges

**A NEW RAFFERTY PICTURE EVERY WEEK– GET THEM ALL**

Created by Charles C. O'Hara          Directed by J. A. Fitzgerald

# ALL CELTIC FILM, Inc., 1400 Broadway, N. Y. Chas. C. O'Hara, President

**4.16** Advertisement published on 17 July 1915 in the *Motion Picture News*.

larger, complicated group of Irish-themed comedies, some of which continued to rely on long-standing stereotypes.

# Conclusion

In 1915, Vitagraph released the film *No Tickee – No Washee*, which starred William Shea, who had appeared in numerous Irish-themed films, as 'Mike Callahan' and Kate Price as 'Mike's Wife'.[308] A synopsis in *Moving Picture World* noted:

> Mike Callahan has but one collar, and that soiled, to attend the annual outing of the Bricklayer's Union with, so he sends it to Wing Lee, the Chinaman's, to have it done up in a rush. [Mike's son] loses the very important half ticket; consequently, when Mike calls for his collar he is told with many gestures, 'No tickee – no washee!' Mike gets mad and gives battle to the Chinks, but they are too many for him and he has to run for his life, pursued by the whole crowd of Chinamen. An exciting chase follows, and the police force are dragged from their various pursuits of fishing, sleeping and guiding schooners

over the bar to join in the chase, and they finally succeed in corralling the pursuers and the pursued.[309]

While its running time featured a more developed plotline, *No Tickee – No Washee* is little different from *Chinese Laundry Scene* of 1894. Here the Irish and Chinese are involved in a comedic chase that mirrored their earliest depictions in the American cinema.[310] Much the same could be said of Edison's 1915 film *Curing the Cook* (1915), in which a male actor once again played Bridget in a tale that was essentially a remake of *Why Bridget Stopped Drinking* (Edison, 1901, aka *Why Bridget Gave Up Drinking*).

*No Tickee – No Washee* and *Curing the Cook* were released at the end of the early cinema period, as was the Rafferty series. It would be tempting to argue that the Irish-themed comedy was evolving at that moment, moving from stereotypes entrenched from the advent of the cinema to newer, more 'refined' depictions. To be sure, the Irish-themed comedy did experience various changes from 1894 to 1915. Longer running times allowed for somewhat more complicated storylines to emerge. As time progressed, films increasingly borrowed from the ever-growing history of American cinema, thus seeing the proliferation of, for example, Irish-themed inheritance comedies. Trends towards more subtle film make-up meant a decrease in the use of heavy stage Irish make-up. Irish-themed comedies also became less dependent on cinematographic tricks in the nickelodeon and post-nickelodeon eras.[311] Conversely, they became more reliant on recognizable on-screen talent, particularly in the final years of the early cinema period.

All of those changes suggest the many ways in which the Irish-themed comedy participated in the broader, evolving category of early American film comedy, which drew on an array of ethnic stereotypes and comic routines borrowed from popular music, vaudeville and other live entertainment. However, those changes did not involve a simple, linear evolution from more grotesque ethnic stereotypes as seen in the *Curing the Cook* to the more refined world of Rafferty. After all, those films were released the very same year. *No Tickee – No Washee* was indeed similar to *Chinese Laundry Scene*, even though it was produced two decades later. Whatever evolutions occurred, the dependence on previous films and pre-cinema influences meant that, however much had changed, much also remained the same. Various kinds of Irish-themed comedies existed in a genre that was both dense and complicated, ranging from those films that revelled in the 'stage Irish' traditions to those that sought to offer a greater sense of authenticity.

# Notes

1. C. Musser, *The Emergence of Cinema: The American Screen to 1907* (Berkeley, CA: University of California Press, 1990), p.86.

2. *Complete Catalogue of Lubin's Films* (Philadelphia, PA: S. Lubin, 1903), pp.21, 23, 27, 33. Available in *A Guide to Motion Picture Catalogs by American Producers and Distributors, 1894–1908: A Microfilm Edition* (New Brunswick: Rutgers University Press, 1985), Reel 3.

3. Many ethnic stereotypes appeared in early American cinema. For example, German stereotypes appeared in such films as: *Bologna Eating Contest* (Edison, 1902), *Two Germans in a Theatre* (Edison, 1902) and *Such a Good Joke, But – Why Don't He Laugh?* (Lubin, 1908). As another example, Dutch stereotypes appeared in such films as: *The Baldheaded Dutchman* (American Mutoscope & Biograph, 1898), *Accidents Will Happen* (American Mutoscope & Biograph, 1902), *A Dutchman Shaving* (Edison, 1902), *The Dutchman's Interrupted Dinner* (Edison, 1902), *A Bucket of Cream Ale* (American Mutoscope & Biograph, 1904) and *Three Jolly Dutchmen* (Paley and Steiner, 1905).

4. *Catalog of Magic Lanterns, Stereopticons, and Moving Picture Machines* (Chicago, IL: Montgomery Ward and Co. [circa 1899]), p.39. (The Magic Lantern Society of the United States and Canada reprinted this catalogue in 1996.)

5. J. Auerbach, 'Chasing Film Narrative: Repetition, Recursion, and the Body in Early Cinema', *Critical Inquiry*, 26, 4 (Summer 2000), p.801.

6. *Complete Catalogue of Lubin's Films*, p.49.

7. *Lubin's Films* (Philadelphia: S. Lubin [circa 1905–06]) [n.p.]. Available in *Guide to Motion Picture Catalogs... 1894–1908: Microfilm Edition*, Reel 3.

8. A copy of the 1899 film *A Wringing Good Joke* exists at the George Eastman House in Rochester, New York.

9. Such films include, for example: *The Bad Boy and Poor Old Grandpa* (American Mutoscope, 1897), *A Close Shave* (American Mutoscope & Biograph, 1901), *The Bad Boy's Joke on the Nurse* (Edison, 1901), *Grandma and the Bad Boys* (Lubin, 1902), *The Lovers' Knot* (American Mutoscope & Biograph, 1902), *Krousemeyer Kids* (Selig Polyscope, 1903), *Mischievous Boys* (Lubin, 1903), *Bad Boy's Joke on the Nurse* (Edison, 1904), *The Bad Boy and the Grocery Man* (American Mutoscope & Biograph, 1905) and *A Jilted Suitor* (Lubin, 1905).

10. Such films include: *How a Rat Interrupted Afternoon Tea* (American Mutoscope, 1897), *How the Athletic Lover Outwitted the Old Man* (American Mutoscope, 1898), *How the Ballet Girl Was Smuggled into Camp* (American Mutoscope, 1898), *How a Bottle of Cocktails Was Smuggled into Camp* (American Mutoscope, 1898), *How the Dressmaker Got Even with a Dead Beat* (American Mutoscope, 1898), *How Farmer Jones Made a Hit at Pleasure Bay* (American Mutoscope, 1898), *How the Gobbler Missed the Axe* (American Mutoscope, 1898), *How She Gets along without a Maid* (American Mutoscope, 1898), *How Uncle Reuben Missed the Fishing Party* (American Mutoscope, 1898), *How Bill the Burglar Got a Bath* (American Mutoscope & Biograph, 1899), *How Little Willie Put His Head on His Pa* (American Mutoscope & Biograph, 1899), *How Mamie Had Her Leg Pulled* (American Mutoscope & Biograph, 1899), *How N. Y. Society Girls Take to the Fad of Tattooing* (American Mutoscope, 1899), *How Papa Set Off the Fireworks* (American Mutoscope & Biograph, 1899), *How the Medium Materialized Elder Simpkin's Wife* (American Mutoscope & Biograph, 1899), *How the Porto [sic] Rican Girls Entertain Uncle Sam's Soldiers* (American Mutoscope & Biograph, 1899), *How the Tramp Lost His Dinner* (American Mutoscope & Biograph, 1899), *How Tottie Coughdrops Summer Suit Was Spoiled* (American Mutoscope & Biograph, 1899), *How Charlie Lost the Heiress* (American Mutoscope & Biograph, 1900), *How He Saw the Eclipse* (American Mutoscope & Biograph, 1900), *How the Artist Captured the Chinese Boxers* (American Mutoscope & Biograph, 1900), *How the Farmer Was Bunchoed* (American Mutoscope & Biograph, 1900), *How the Magician Got the Best of the Installment Man* (American Mutoscope & Biograph, 1900), *How the Old Maid Got a Husband* (American Mutoscope & Biograph, 1900), *How the Young Man Got Stuck at Ocean Beach* (American Mutoscope & Biograph, 1900), *How They Fired the Bum* (American Mutoscope & Biograph, 1900), *How They Got Rid of Mama* (American Mutoscope & Biograph, 1900), *How They Rob Men in Chicago* (American Mutoscope & Biograph, 1900), *How the Lover Squared Himself with Papa* (Edison, 1902), *How Uncle Josh Defeated the Badgers* (Edison, 1902), *How Buttons Got Even with the*

*Butler* (American Mutoscope & Biograph, 1903), *How He Missed His Train* (Méliès, 1903), *How Mike Got the Soap in His Eyes* (American Mutoscope & Biograph, 1903), *How Rube Stopped the Trolley Car* (Lubin, 1903), *How a Wife Gets Her Pocket Money* (Lubin, 1903), *How the Valet Got Into Hot Water* (Edison, 1903), *How a French Nobleman Got a Wife through the New York Herald 'Personal' Columns* (Edison, 1904), *How Jones Lost His Roll* (Edison, 1905) and *How Willie Got the Eggs* (American Mutoscope & Biograph, 1905).

11.  Such descriptions appeared, for example, in the moving picture catalogue synopses for such films as: *Caught in the Undertow* (1902), *The Prodigal Son* (Selig Polyscope, 1902), *Chariot Race* (Lubin, 1903) and *The Poachers* (Edison, 1903).

12.  As of May 2010, a copy of *European Rest Cure* is available at the Library of Congress's 'American Memory' website, http://memory.loc.gov.

13.  *Catalog of New Films for Projection and Other Purposes* (New York: F.M. Prescott, 1899), p.70. Available in *Guide to Motion Picture Catalogs...1894–1908: Microfilm Edition*, Reel 1.

14.  *Complete Catalogue of Lubin's Films*, pp.52, 68.

15.  Ibid., p.68.

16.  *Picture Catalogue* (New York: American Mutoscope & Biograph Company, November 1902), p.35. Available in *Guide to Motion Picture Catalogs...1894–1908: Microfilm Edition*, Reel 1.

17.  Advertisement, *New York Clipper*, 21 November 1903, p.944. This film should not be confused with the Walturdaw Company's film *Murphy's Wake*, which was released in England in September 1906. For more information on that film, see [untitled], *Optical Lantern and Kinematograph Journal* (September 1906), p.201.

18.  Such stereo views include: *The Wake* (James M. Davis, 1888), *By the Howly* [*sic*] *St Patrick* (Strohmeyer & Wyman, 1894), *Mickie O'Hoolihan's Wake* (Strohmeyer & Wyman, 1894), *McCarthy's Wake* (C.H. Graves/Universal Photo Art Company, 1897), *Patrick Brannigan's Wake* (Keystone, late nineteenth/early twentieth century), *By the Holy St. Patrick! There's Brannigan's Ghost* (Keystone, late nineteenth/early twentieth century) and *McGinty's Wake* (Canvassers, late nineteenth/early twentieth century).

19.  C. Musser, *Before the Nickelodeon: Edwin S. Porter and the Edison Manufacturing Company* (Berkeley, CA: University of California Press, 1991), p.69. Trade publications listings for *Irish Way of Discussing Politics* (under the title *Irish Political Discussion*) and *Pat and the Populist* appeared in 'New Films for "Screen" Machines', *Phonoscope*, November 1896, p.16.

20.  *No. 94, Edison Films* (Orange, NJ: Edison Manufacturing Company, March 1900), p.36. Available in *Guide to Motion Picture Catalogs...1894–1908: Microfilm Edition*, Reel 1.

21.  Advertisement, *New York Clipper*, 5 November 1904, p.872.

22.  'Carrie Nation Dead', *New York Times*, 10 June 1911, p.13.

23.  'Mrs Nation a Lecturer', *New York Times*, 9 February 1901, p.2; [untitled], *Wellsboro Gazette* (Wellsboro, PA), 29 March 1901, p.5.

24.  *No. 288, Edison Films* (Orange, NJ: Edison Manufacturing Co., July 1906), p.15. Available in *Guide to Motion Picture Catalogs...1894–1908: Microfilm Edition*, Reel 1.

25.  Quoted in E. Savada (ed.), *The American Film Institute Catalog of Motion Pictures Produced in the United States: Film Beginnings, 1893–1910* (Lanham, MD: Scarecrow Press, 1995), p.298.

26.  As of May 2010, a copy of *Levi and Cohen, the Irish Comedians* is available at the Library of Congress's 'American Memory' website, http://memory.loc.gov.

27.  Copies of *Casey's Christening* and *A Coal Strike* exist at the Library of Congress in Washington, DC.

28.  Copies of *Lady Bountiful Visits the Murphys on Wash Day* and *A Pipe for a Cigar* exist at the Library of Congress in Washington, DC.

29.  No. 288, *Edison Films*, p.36.

30.  K.R. Niver and B. Bergsten (eds), *Biograph Bulletins, 1896–1908* (Los Angeles, CA: Locare Research Group, 1971), p.204.

31.  Ibid.

32.  *Picture Catalogue*, p.39. A copy of *The Barber's Queer Customer* exists at the George Eastman House in Rochester, New York.

33.  *Catalog of New Films for Projection and Other Purposes*, p.6. (As this catalogue indicates, *O'Finnegan's Wake* was sold as early as 1899.)

34.  A copy of *A Wake in 'Hell's Kitchen'* exists at the Library of Congress in Washington, DC.

35. *Picture Catalog*, p.39. (American Mutoscope & Biograph did not copyright *A Wake in 'Hell's Kitchen'* until June 1903.)
36. A copy of *'Drill Ye Tarriers, Drill'* exists at the Library of Congress in Washington, DC.
37. *No. 288, Edison Films*, p.18.
38. Niver and Bergsten (eds), *Biograph Bulletins, 1896–1908*, p.263. A copy of *Brannigan Sets Off the Blast* exists at the Library of Congress in Washington, DC.
39. Savada (ed.), *American Film Institute Catalog... Film Beginnings, 1893–1910*, p.160. Other comedic explosions with non-Irish characters occur in such films as *Saved!* (American Mutoscope & Biograph, 1904) and *Impatient Customer* (Pathé Frères, 1905).
40. A copy of *Fun in a Bakery Shop* exists at the Library of Congress in Washington, DC.
41. *No. 288, Edison Films*, p.21. (By the time of *No. 288, Edison Films*, the company had retitled the film *Fun in a Bakery*.)
42. Such films included: American Mutoscope & Biograph's *Fun in a Harlem Flat* (1898), *Fun in the Barn* (1898) and *Fun in a Photograph Gallery* (1900); Edison's *Fun in a Butcher Shop* (1901) and *Fun in a Chinese Laundry* (1901); and Lubin's *Fun in a Spanish Camp* (1898), *Fun in a Chinese Laundry* (1901) and *Fun at a Children's Party* (1901).
43. *Catalogue of New Films for Projection and Other Purposes*, p.6. *How Murphy Paid His Rent* later appeared for sale in the *Complete Catalogue of Lubin Films*, p.47, which has caused the incorrect assumption that the film dates from that year. Subsequently, as a 1907 Lubin catalogue indicates, the film was retitled *How Murphy Paid Rent*.
44. A copy of *How the Dutch Beat the Irish* exists at the Library of Congress in Washington, DC.
45. *No. 288, Edison Films*, p.17.
46. Advertisement, *New York Clipper*, 27 May 1899, p.259.
47. *Catalog No. 3, New Films* (Philadelphia: S. Lubin, 1902), p.5. Available in *Guide to Motion Picture Catalogs... 1894–1908: Microfilm Edition*, Reel 3. A copy of *Target Practice, and What Happened to Widow Flaherty* exists at the George Eastman House in Rochester, New York.
48. The same argument could be made of such films as *Why Mrs Jones Got a Divorce* (Edison, 1900). A copy of it, as well as *Firing the Cook*, exist at the Library of Congress in Washington, DC.
49. For example, in 1909, a journalist for the *Woodland Daily Democrat* of Woodland, California, wrote about the film *The King's Pardon* (Edison, 1908), claiming that it was adapted from a 'great Irish drama'. However, the journalist was incorrect, as the film was not adapted from an Irish drama and it did not feature Irish characters; the film was, in fact, set in England and its characters were English. See *'The King's Pardon'*, *Woodland Daily Democrat* (Woodland, CA), 19 February 1909, p.1; advertisement, *Moving Picture World*, 28 November 1908, p.430; *'The King's Pardon'*, *Moving Picture World*, 5 December 1908, p.448; *'The King's Pardon, New York Dramatic Mirror*, 5 December 1908, p.8.
50. Savada (ed.), *American Film Institute Catalog... Film Beginnings, 1893–1910*, p.84.
51. *Complete Catalogue of Lubin's Films*, p.34.
52. *Catalog of New Films for Projection and Other Purposes*, p.7. (As this catalogue indicates, *How Murphy Paid His Rent* was sold as early as 1899.)
53. Ibid.
54. *1903 Complete Catalog of Films and Moving Picture Machines* (Chicago, IL: Selig Polyscope Co., 1903), p.21. Available in *Guide to Motion Picture Catalogs... 1894–1908: Microfilm Edition*, Reel 2.
55. Ibid., pp.21–2.
56. Ibid., p.22.
57. *No. 135, Edison Films* (Orange, NJ: Edison Manufacturing Co., September 1902), p.120. Available in *Guide to Motion Picture Catalogs... 1894–1908: Microfilm Edition*, Reel 1.
58. A copy of *And Pat Took Him at His Word* exists at the Library of Congress in Washington, DC.
59. The version of *Rushing the 'Growler'* in question was sold by Lubin in their January 1903 catalogue. However, the same film title with the same catalogue entry appears in *Catalog of New Films for Projection and Other Purposes*, p.35.
60. A copy of *Casey at the Bat* appears on *Reel Baseball*, DVD (New York: Kino International, 2007).
61. *No. 94, Edison Films*, p.35.
62. *No. 288, Edison Films*, p.18.
63. *No. 135, Edison Films*, p.122.

64. *Supplement 168, Edison Films* (Orange, NJ: Edison Manufacturing Co., February 1903), p.8. Available in *Guide to Motion Picture Catalogs . . . 1894–1908: Microfilm Edition*, Reel 1.
65. *Supplement 168, Edison Films*, p.8.
66. A copy of *Casey's Frightful Dream* exists at the Library of Congress in Washington, DC.
67. *No. 288, Edison Films*, p.18.
68. A copy of *Casey and His Neighbor's Goat* exists at the Library of Congress in Washington, DC.
69. *No. 185, Edison Films* (Orange, NJ: Edison Manufacturing Co., October 1903), p.12. Available in *Guide to Motion Picture Catalogs ... 1894–1908: Microfilm Edition*, Reel 1.
70. *No. 288, Edison Films*, pp.33–4.
71. *No. 185, Edison Films*, p.16.
72. K.R. Niver, *Motion Pictures from the Library of Congress Paper Print Collection 1894–1912* (Berkeley, CA: University of California Press, 1967), p.21.
73. While sometimes dated as 1900, Edison's film *A Wringing Good Joke* appears for sale in Prescott's 1899 catalogue, *New Films Supplement No. 3* [n.p.].
74. J.J. Appel, 'From Shanties to Lace Curtains: The Irish Image in *Puck*, 1876–1910', *Comparative Studies in Society and History*, 13, 4 (October 1971), p.367.
75. 'Amusements', *New York Times*, 4 August 1889, p.3; 'The Century Players', *New York Times*, 15 March 1904, p.9; 'George W. Monroe, Actor Dies at 70', *New York Times*, 30 January 1932, p.17. For more information on the character Bridget in nineteenth-century entertainment, see Chapter 1.
76. 'How Bridget Prepared Crabs', *Frederick News* (Frederick, MD), 30 June 1894, p.6.
77. *Picture Catalogue*, p.14; 'How Bridget Spoiled Things', *Des Moines Daily Capital* (Des Moines, IA), 29 March 1901, p.12.
78. *Catalog of New Films for Projection and Other Purposes*, p.16.
79. *Picture Catalogue*, p.25. Copies of *Spirits in the Kitchen* and *Reginald's First High Hat* exist at the Museum of Modern Art in New York City.
80. These include American Mutoscope & Biograph's *Little Willie and the Minister* (1898), *Little Willie and the Burglar* (1899), *Little Willie in Mischief Again* (1899) and *How Little Willie Put a Head on Pa* (1899). Edison also made a film with the character, entitled *Little Willie's Last Celebration* (1902).
81. A copy of *Buster's Dog to the Rescue* exists at the George Eastman House in Rochester, New York.
82. These include: *Buster and Tige Put a Balloon Vendor Out of Business* (1904), *Buster Brown and the Dude* (1904) and *Buster Makes Room for His Mama at the Bargain Counter* (1904).
83. Paley and Steiner advertised the film *Bridget Has Her Photo Taken* in the *New York Clipper* on 4 February 1905. They listed the running time at forty feet. In the same ad, they also listed (at seventy-three feet) a film titled *Bridget in Trouble*, which is probably by the same film, *Bridget's Troubles*, which had been released circa January 1905.
84. *Lubin's Films, 1907*, p.31. Available in *Guide to Motion Picture Catalogs, 1894–1908: Microfilm Edition*, Reel 3.
85. *Lubin's Films* [circa 1905–06] [n.p.].
86. Advertisement, *New York Clipper*, 20 April 1901.
87. *No. 105, Edison Films, Complete Catalog* (Orange, NJ: Edison Manufacturing Co., July 1901), pp.77–8. Available in *Guide to Motion Picture Catalogs . . . 1894–1908: Microfilm Edition*, Reel 1.
88. Copies of *How Bridget Made the Fire* and *The Finish of Bridget McKeen* exist at the Library of Congress in Washington, DC.
89. *No. 288, Edison Films*, p.15.
90. A similar story appeared in *The Smoky Stove* (American Mutoscope & Biograph, 1903), with a kitchen maid 'blown to the ceiling' after a stove mishap. 'She arises, however, not much the worse for her experience, making a very laughable finish to the scene.' It is difficult to determine if this maid was coded as Irish. See Niver and Bergsten (eds), *Biograph Bulletins, 1896–1908*, p.197.
91. *Complete Catalog of Genuine and Original 'Star' Films (Moving Pictures)* (New York: George Méliès of Paris, 1 June 1905), p.129. Available in *Guide to Motion Picture Catalogs . . . 1894–1908: Microfilm Edition*, Reel 4.
92. As accessed on 1 August 2009, Trinity College Dublin's *Irish Film & TV Research Online* (http://www.tcd.ie/irishfilm/index.php) suggests the film was released in 1907 and may have been a retitled version of *Le Mariage de Victorine* (1907) or *Le Mariage de Victoire* (1907). Given the film's appearance for sale in the *Complete Catalog of Genuine and Original 'Star' Films (Moving*

*Pictures)*, 1 June 1905, such speculation cannot be accurate. Moreover, it is in fact possible that *How Bridget's Lover Escaped* was shot in the United States, as by 1905 Méliès's brother Gaston had already moved to America.

93. '*How Bridget's Lover Escaped*', *Views and Film Index*, 15 June 1907, p.6.
94. Savada (ed.), *American Film Institute Catalog... Film Beginnings, 1893–1910*, p.656.
95. Such films include, for example: *Teasing the Cook* (American Mutoscope, 1899), *The Cook's Revenge* (Lubin, 1901), *Meandering Mike* (American Mutoscope & Biograph, 1901), *Pie, Tramp and the Bulldog* (Edison, 1901), *Why Mrs Jones Wants a Divorce* (Edison, 1901), *Why the Cook Was Fired* (1902), *The Cook's Revenge* (Méliès, 1903), *The Cook Visits the Parlor* (American Mutoscope & Biograph, 1903), *Making a Welsh Rabbit* (American Mutoscope & Biograph, 1903), *The New Cook* (American Mutoscope & Biograph, 1903), *The Cook in Trouble* (Méliès, 1904) and *Mind! Madame Is Coming* (Pathé Frères, 1904).
96. Such films include, for example: *The Washerwoman's Troubles* (Edison, 1897), *The Quarrelsome Washerwoman* (American Mutoscope & Biograph, 1903), *A Shocking Accident* (Lubin, 1903), *Washerwomen and Chimney Sweep* (Edison, 1903), *Washerwoman and Buss* (Edison, 1904) and *Gay Washerwoman* (Pathé Frères, 1905).
97. J. Lindenblatt, *Frederick Burr Opper's Happy Hooligan* (New York: Nantier, Beall, Minoustchine, 2008), pp.13, 15.
98. 'At Other Houses', *New York Times*, 3 May 1903, p.22.
99. 'Happy Hooligan at Hartford', *Hartford Courant*, 1 November 1901, p.3.
100. 'Vaudeville at Keiths', *New York Times*, 27 October 1903, p.7.
101. Advertisement, *Lincoln Evening News* (Lincoln, NE), 16 December 1903, p.4; advertisement, *Oakland Tribune*, 7 April 1903, p.9.
102. [Untitled], *Emporia Gazette* (Emporia, KS), 12 November 1904, p.1.
103. For an example, see ' "Happy Hooligan" in Real Life', *Boston Globe*, 13 November 1901, p.8.
104. A character named 'Mrs Hooligan' appeared in the film *The Fox-Hunt* (American Mutoscope & Biograph, 1906), though both she and the story had nothing to do with Opper's character. See Niver and Bergsten (eds), *Biograph Bulletins, 1896–1908*, p.274.
105. '*The Hooligan Idea*', *Views and Film Index*, 22 June 1907, p.6.
106. Lindenblatt, *Frederick Burr Opper's Happy Hooligan*, p.111.
107. 'The Drama', *Suburbanite Economist* (Chicago, IL), 27 December 1912, p.10.
108. These films include: *Hooligan Assists the Magician* (aka *Happy Hooligan Assists the Magician*, 1900), *Happy Hooligan April-Fooled* (1901), *Happy Hooligan Has Troubles with the Cook* (1901), *Happy Hooligan Surprised* (aka *Happy Hooligan's Surprise*, 1901), *Hooligan Visits Central Park* (1901), *Hooligan Takes His Annual Bath* (1901), *Hooligan Causes a Sensation* (1901), *Hooligan and the Summer Girls* (1901), *Hooligan at the Seashore* (1901), *Hooligan's Narrow Escape* (1901), *Happy Hooligan Turns Burglar* (1902), *The Bull and the Picnickers* (1902) and *Hooligan's Fourth of July* (1903). Copies of the films *Happy Hooligan April-Fooled*, *Happy Hooligan Surprised* and *Happy Hooligan Turns Burglar* exist at the Library of Congress in Washington, DC.
109. These films include: *Gloomy Gus Gets the Best of It* (1903), *Happy Hooligan Earns His Dinner* (1903), *Happy Hooligan in a Trap* (1903), *Happy Hooligan Interferes* (1903), *Happy Hooligan's Interrupted Lunch* (aka *Happy Hooligan Breaks into Society*, 1903), *Hooligan as a Safe Robber* (1903), *Hooligan in Jail* (1903), *Hooligan to the Rescue* (1903), *Hooligan's Christmas Dream* (1903), *Hooligan's Roller Skates* (1903), *Hooligan's Thanksgiving Dinner* (1903), *Poor Hooligan, So Hungry Too!* (1903) and *An Unprotected Female* (1903). Copies of the films *Happy Hooligan Earns His Dinner*, *Happy Hooligan in a Trap*, *Happy Hooligan Interferes* and *Happy Hooligan's Interrupted Lunch* exist at the Library of Congress in Washington, DC.
110. *1903 Complete Catalog of Films and Moving Picture Machines*, p.23.
111. K.L. Kusmer, *Down and Out, On the Road: The Homeless in American History* (New York: Oxford University Press, 2001), p.186.
112. Kusmer (in ibid., pp.187–8) discusses the relationship between Hooligan and other tramp characters in the cinema.
113. C. Musser, 'Ethnicity, Role-Playing, and American Film Comedy: From *Chinese Laundry Scene* to *Whoopee*', in L. Friedman (ed.), *Unspeakable Images: Ethnicity and the American Cinema* (Urbana, IL: University of Illinois Press, 1991), p.47.
114. American Mutoscope & Biograph made such tramp films as: *The Tramp and the Bather* (1897),

*Tramp in a Millionaire's Bed* (1897), *A Tramp's Dinner* (1897), *The Tramp and the Giant Firecracker* (1898), *The Tramp and the Muscular Cook* (1898), *The Tramp Trapped* (1898), *The Tramp and the Burglar* (1900), *Tramp in the Haunted House* (1900), *The Tramp Gets Whitewashed* (1900) and *A Tramp in the Well* (1900). Lubin produced such films as: *Tramp's Nap Interrupted* (1901), *Almost a King* (1903), *The Tramp in the Barber Shop* (1903), *Tramping on a Rolling Glove* (1903), *The Tramp's Dream* (1903), *The Tramp's First Bath* (1903), *The Tramp's Surprise* (1903) and *Tramp's Revenge* (1905). Edison's tramp films included: *The Tramp in the Kitchen* (1898), *The Astor Tramp* (1899), *Pie, Tramp and the Bulldog* (1901), *The Tramp Cyclist* (aka *The Trick Cyclist*, 1901), *The Tramp's Strategy That Failed* (1901) and *A Scarecrow Tramp* (1903). Edison also produced several films featuring a tramp character named 'Weary Willie', including *The Tramp and the Crap Game* (1900), *The Tramp and the Nursing Bottle* (1901), *The Tramp's Dream* (1901), *The Tramp's Miraculous Escape* (1901), 'Weary Willie' and the Gardener' (1901), 'Weary Willie' Kidnaps a Child* (1904) and *'Weary Willie' Kisses the Bride* (1904).

115. A copy of *Twentieth Century Tramp; or, Happy Hooligan and His Airship* exists at the Cineteca del Fruili in Germona, Italy.

116. Savada (ed.), *American Film Institute Catalog... Film Beginnings, 1893–1910*, p.1111.

117. *No. 135, Edison Films*, p.72.

118. 'Mulcahey's Raid', *New York Dramatic Mirror*, 5 March 1910, p.19; 'Logan's Babies', *Moving Picture World*, 4 November 1911, p.410; 'Murray, the Masher', *Moving Picture World*, 22 June 1912, p.1156.

119. 'Kelly, U.S.A.', *Moving Picture World*, 4 February 1911, p.268; 'Kelly, U.S.A.', *Moving Picture World*, 25 February 1911, p.431.

120. Advertisement, *Moving Picture World*, 9 November 1912, p.525. See also 'Michael McShane, Matchmaker', *Moving Picture World*, 2 November 1912, p.476; 'Michael McShane, Matchmaker', *New York Dramatic Mirror*, 20 November 1912, p.34.

121. 'Mulligan's Waterloo', *New York Dramatic Mirror*, 7 August 1909, p.16.

122. *Lubin Films Released from November 15th to 25th, 1909* (Philadelphia, PA: Lubin Manufacturing Co., 1909) [n.p.]. Available in *Guide to Motion Picture Catalogs... 1894–1908: Microfilm Edition*, Reel 3. See also 'Finnegan's Initiation', *Moving Picture World*, 27 November 1909, p.721; 'Finnegan's Invitation' [sic], *New York Dramatic Mirror*, 4 December 1909, p.17; 'Dope Head Clancy', *Moving Picture World*, 6 November 1909, p.661. A copy of *Dope Head Clancy* exists at the George Eastman House in Rochester, New York.

123. Niver and Bergsten (eds), *Biograph Bulletins, 1896–1908*, p.290. A copy of *Fights of Nations* exists at the Library of Congress in Washington, DC.

124. 'Fights of Nations', *Moving Picture World*, 9 March 1907, pp.9–10.

125. Musser, *Emergence of Cinema*, pp.449–51.

126. *1907 Catalogue of the Selig Polyscope and Library of Selig Films* (Chicago, IL: Selig Polyscope, Co., Inc., 1907), p.65.

127. *Lubin's Films, 1907*, pp.33, 20.

128. 'The Widow Casey's Return', *Moving Picture World*, 15 June 1912, p.1058. The same could be said of the Walturdaw Company's film *Murphy's Wake*, which was made in England in 1906 and released in the United States the following year. See [untitled], *Optical Lantern and Kinematograph Journal* (September 1906), p.201.

129. 'McGinty's Sudden Rise', *Moving Picture World*, 17 July 1909, p.97.

130. *McNabb Visits the Comet* (Lux, 1910) also relied on special effects, with the title character – who is 'comet mad' – dreaming an 'enchanting fairy vision'. See 'McNab Visits the Comet', *Moving Picture World*, 2 July 1910, p.26.

131. 'When Casey Joined the Lodge', *New York Dramatic Mirror*, 20 June 1908, p.6.

132. 'When Casey Joined the Lodge', *Views and Film Index*, 13 June 1908, p.10.

133. 'Casey's Jumping Toothache', *New York Dramatic Mirror*, 31 June 1909, p.16.

134. 'Casey's Jumping Toothache', *Moving Picture World*, 17 July 1909, p.97.

135. *Supplement No. 72* (Chicago, IL: Selig Polyscope, Co., Inc., November 1907) [n.p.]. Available in *Guide to Motion Picture Catalogs... 1894–1908: Microfilm Edition*, Reel 2.

136. 'After the Celebration', *Moving Picture World*, 4 April 1908, p.298.

137. Niver and Bergsten (eds), *Biograph Bulletins, 1896–1908*, p.445; 'Dooley's Scheme', *Moving Picture World*, 11 November 1911, p.494.

138. 'Lunch Time', *Moving Picture World*, 7 November 1908, p.366.
139. 'Pat and the 400', *Moving Picture World*, 2 July 1910, p.37; 'Pat and the 400', *New York Dramatic Mirror*, 9 July 1910, p.20.
140. 'Two Little Dogs', *Moving Picture World*, 20 June 1908, p.532.
141. 'Hogan Vs. Schmidt', *Moving Picture World*, 14 December 1912, p.1106; 'Riley and Schultz', *Moving Picture World*, 12 October 1912, p.144; 'Hogan's Alley', *Moving Picture World*, 10 February 1912, p.510; 'Hogan's Alley', *Moving Picture World*, 2 March 1912, p.780.
142. 'Becky Gets a Husband', *Moving Picture World*, 1 April 1912, p.158.
143. 'Becky Gets a Husband', *Moving Picture World*, 27 April 1912, p.329.
144. *A Coal Strike* was reminiscent of the film *A Boarding School Prank* (American Mutoscope & Biograph, 1903), in which schoolgirls devised a trick in which soot covered a schoolmistress, who was not coded as Irish.
145. 'Mine Lock-Out Plan to Avoid Coal Strike', *New York Times*, 25 September 1905, p.2; 'President Intervenes to Avert Coal Strike', *New York Times*, 27 February 1906, p.1.
146. *1907 Catalogue of the Selig Polyscope and Library of Selig Films*, p.68.
147. See, for example, 'Straus Champions Federal Control', *New York Times*, 9 December 1907, p.3.
148. 'When Women Vote', *Views and Film Index*, 6 July 1907, p.4.
149. 'McNabb Wants to Get Arrested', *New York Dramatic Mirror*, 1 January 1910, p.18.
150. 'O'Brien's Busy Day', *Moving Picture World*, 10 February 1912, p.482. See also 'O'Brien's Busy Day', *Moving Picture News*, 20 January 1912, p.44.
151. 'Too Many Caseys', *Moving Picture World*, 30 November 1912, p.906.
152. 'Too Many Caseys', *Moving Picture World*, 21 December 1912, p.1184.
153. 'Pat Clancy's Adventure', *Moving Picture World*, 16 December 1912, p.922; 'Pat Clancy's Adventure', *Moving Picture World*, 6 January 1912, p.40.
154. 'Pat Clancy's Adventure', *Edison Kinetogram*, 1 February 1913, p.12.
155. 'Pat Clancy's Adventures', *New York Dramatic Mirror*, 3 January 1912, pp.30–1. (Though copyrighted in late 1911 and reviewed in January 1912, the film was then re-released in February 1913; the *Kinetogram* announced the official release date as 26 February 1913.)
156. An advertisement in the *Des Moines Daily News*, 15 April 1908, promotes a comedy film entitled *Pat and His Battery*. It is difficult to determine whether this is a film which has not been catalogued, or whether it might be a retitled version of another comedy.
157. 'Breaking into Society', *Moving Picture World*, 12 September 1908, p.11; 'Breaking into Society', *Views and Film Index*, 12 September 1908, p.10.
158. 'The Hobo's Dream', *New York Dramatic Mirror*, 12 December 198, p.6.
159. 'Pat's Breeches', *Moving Picture World*, 29 June 1912, p.1269; 'Pat's Breeches', *Universal Weekly*, 29 June 1912, p.13.
160. 'Pat's Day Off', *Moving Picture World*, 30 November 1912, p.916; 'Pat the Soothsayer', *Kalem Kalendar*, 1 October 1912, p.13; 'Pat the Soothsayer', *Moving Picture World*, 26 October 1912, p.376.
161. 'Pat the Soothsayer', *Moving Picture World*, 26 October 1912, p.l376.
162. 'How Patrick's Eyes Were Opened', *Moving Picture World*, 13 April 1912, p.160.
163. 'How Patrick's Eyes Were Opened', *The Kinetogram*, 1 July 1912, p.10.
164. The vaudeville act was Daly and Devere's routine, which was known both as *The Janitress* and *Bridget's Word Goes*. It was apparently performed as late as 1907. See S. Staples, *Male–Female Comedy Teams in American Vaudeville, 1865–1932* (Ann Arbor, MI: UMI Research Press, 1984), p.84.
165. 'At the Stage Door', *Moving Picture World*, 14 March 1908, p.219.
166. 'The Washerwomen's Revenge', *Moving Picture World*, 12 September 1908, p.201; 'The Washerwomen's Revenge', *Views and Film Index*, 12 September 1908, p.10.
167. 'A Child's Prayer – Bridget's Dream – He Is a Jolly Good Fellow', *Moving Picture World*, 12 December 1908, p.478.
168. 'Fickle Bridget', *Moving Picture News*, 9 December 1911, p.7; 'Fickle Bridget', *Moving Picture World*, 16 December 1911, 928.
169. Musser, 'Ethnicity, Role-Playing, and American Film Comedy', p.45.
170. 'A Servant's Revenge', *Moving Picture World*, 27 November 1909, p.769. See also 'Servant's Revenge', *New York Dramatic Mirror*, 27 November 1909, p.13.

171. 'Bridget on Strike', *Moving Picture World*, 22 May 1909, p.676; 'Bridget on Strike', *New York Dramatic Mirror*, 29 May 1909, p.15.
172. 'The Maid's Strategem', *Moving Picture World*, 18 May 1912, p.662.
173. 'The Maid's Strategem (Imp)', *Moving Picture World*, 25 May 1912, p.736.
174. 'Bridget, the Flirt', *Moving Picture World*, 17 June 1911, p.1388.
175. 'Bridge [sic] and the Egg', *Moving Picture World*, 25 March 1911, p.663; 'Bridget and the Egg', *Moving Picture World*, 8 April 1911, p.780.
176. 'Bridget's Sudden Wealth', *Moving Picture World*, 31 August 1912, p.904; 'Bridget's Sudden Wealth', *Moving Picture World*, 21 September 1912, p.1175.
177. 'An Accidental Millionaire', *Moving Picture World*, 2 November 1912, p.476.
178. 'Aunt Bridget', *Moving Picture World*, 2 November 1912, p.490; 'Aunt Bridget', *Motion Picture News*, 19 October 1912, p.26; 'Aunt Bridget', *Universal Weekly*, 2 November 1912, p.26.
179. 'The New Maid', *Moving Picture World*, 20 June 1908, p.532; 'Servant's Good Joke', *New York Dramatic Mirror*, 9 October 1909, p.16; 'The Cook Makes the Madeira Sauce', *New York Dramatic Mirror*, 1 January 1910, p.16; 'Discharging the Cook', *The Film Index*, 13 May 1911, p.25; 'Getting Rid of Trouble', *Moving Picture World*, 31 August 1912, p.908; 'Getting Rid of Trouble', *Moving Picture World*, 21 September 1912, p.1175.
180. 'Servant's Revenge', *New York Dramatic Mirror*, 27 November 1909, p.13.
181. 'The Laundry Lady's Luck', *Moving Picture World*, 6 May 1911, p.1025; 'The Laundry Lady's Luck', *Moving Picture World*, 20 May 1911, p.1141.
182. 'Pots, Pans, and Poetry', *Moving Picture World*, 11 March 1911, p.542.
183. 'Nora, the Cook', *Moving Picture World*, 14 December 1912, p.1106; 'Nora, the Cook', *Moving Picture World*, 4 January 1913, p.51.
184. 'Bridget's Explanation', *Moving Picture World*, 22 June 1912, p.1156.
185. 'Queen of the Kitchen', *Kalem Kalendar*, 1 September 1912, p.5.
186. 'Doctor Bridget', *Moving Picture World*, 7 December 1912, p.1000; 'Doctor Bridget', *Moving Picture World*, 7 December 1912, p.1185.
187. 'Teaching McFadden to Waltz', *Moving Picture World*, 8 July 1911, p.1584. *Motography* noted that 'one of the funniest scenes was that which disclosed Mr Bunny in his well-known role of [an] Irish cook'. See 'Teaching McFadden to Waltz', *Motography*, July 1911, p.39.
188. Some films of this era used Irish characters, though their ethnicity does not seem to have been particularly important to the stories in which they appeared, as in the case of *How Mrs McFadden Looked Out* (Thanhouser, 1913). See 'How Mrs McFadden Looked Out', *Moving Picture World*, 15 February 1913, p.681.
189. 'Nora's Boarders', *Moving Picture World*, 15 November 1913, p.762; 'Nora's Boarders', *Moving Picture World*, 29 November 1913, p.1007; 'Nora's Boarders', *Motion Picture News*, 29 November 1913, pp.46-47.
190. 'Finnegan', *Moving Picture World*, 5 April 1913, p.47.
191. 'Mrs Casey's Gorilla', *Moving Picture World*, 29 November 1913, p.1007.
192. 'Mrs Casey's Gorilla', *Motion Picture News*, 29 November 1913, p.38.
193. 'Hogan's Alley', *Pathé Fortnightly Bulletin*, 3–14 March 1914 [n.p.]. See also 'Hogan's Alley', *Moving Picture World*, 29 February 1914, p.1152; 'In Hogan's Alley', *Moving Picture World*, 21 March 1914, p.1524.
194. 'He Wanted Work', *Moving Picture World*, 29 August 1914, p.1240.
195. 'Casey's Birthday', *Moving Picture World*, 23 May 1914, p.1116.
196. K. Rockett, *The Irish Filmography: Fiction Films 1896–1996* (Dublin: Red Mountain Media, 1996) p.266, 'Kelly's Ghost', *Motion Picture News*, 7 March 1914, p.44; 'Kelly's Ghost', *Moving Picture World*, 7 March 1914, p.1300; 'Kelly's Ghost', *Moving Picture World*, 14 March 1914, p.1385; 'When Dooley Passed Away', *Moving Picture World*, 28 February 1914, p.1146; 'When Dooley Passed Away', *Moving Picture World*, 21 March 1914, p.1524; 'When Dooley Passed Away', *Motion Picture News*, 14 March 1914, p.48.
197. 'Dan Greegan's Ghost', *Moving Picture World*, 27 September 1913, p.1392; 'Dan Greegan's Ghost', *New York Dramatic Mirror*, 1 October 1913, p.35. A copy of *Dan Greegan's Ghost* exists at the Museum of Modern Art in New York City, New York.
198. 'Kelly Goes to War', *Universal Weekly*, 26 October 1912, p.37; 'Kelly Goes to War', *Moving Picture World*, 26 October 1912, p.388.

199. 'Casey at the Bat', *Moving Picture World*, 28 December 1912, p.1324; 'Casey at the Bat', *Moving Picture World*, 18 January 1912, p.263.

200. 'At the Telephone', *Moving Picture World*, 21 June 1913, p.1278; 'Finnegan', *Moving Picture World*, 15 March 1913, p.1128; 'Finnegan', *Moving Picture World*, 5 April 1913, p.47; 'The Henpecked Hod Carrier', *Moving Picture World*, 6 December 1913, p.1208; 'Long May It Wave', *Moving Picture World*, 20 June 1914, pp.1728, 1748; 'Casey's Tribulations', *Moving Picture World*, 8 May 1915, p.980; 'Casey's Tribulations', *Moving Picture World*, 15 May 1915, p.1072. (The character in *The Henpecked Hod Carrier* is named 'Mr Henpeck', so it is difficult to ascertain whether or not he was intended to be Irish.)

201. 'Hannigan's Harem', *Moving Picture World*, 5 July 1913, p.78; 'Hannegan's [sic] Harem', *Moving Picture World*, 26 July 1913, p.428.

202. 'Biddy Brady's Birthday', *Motography*, 11 September 1915, p.544.

203. 'Married Men', *Moving Picture World*, 3 January 1914, p.76; 'Murphy and the Mermaids', *Biograph*, 12 September 1914, p.9; 'Murphy and the Mermaids', *Moving Picture World*, 31 October 1914, p.64; 'Pat Casey's Case', *Moving Picture World*, 23 May 1914, p.1142; 'Pat Casey's Case', *Moving Picture World*, 13 June 1914, p.1540; 'They Loved Him So', *Moving Picture World*, 3 April 1915, p.111.

204. 'Kitty's Knight', *Moving Picture World*, 29 November 1913, p.1040; 'Kitty's Knight', *Moving Picture World*, 20 December 1913, p.1411.

205. 'Courtship of the Cooks', *Moving Picture World*, 16 January 1915, p.368.

206. 'For the Love of Mike', *New York Dramatic Mirror*, 23 September 1914, p.34; 'For the Love of Mike', *Kalem Kalendar*, October 1914, p.2; 'For the Love of Mike', *Moving Picture World*, 30 November 1912, p.912.

207. 'Riley's Decoys', *Moving Picture World*, 13 December 1913, p.1326; 'Riley's Decoys', *Moving Picture World*, 3 January 1914, p.48.

208. Rockett, *Irish Filmography*, p.277.

209. 'Fire! Fire!', *Moving Picture World*, 6 June 1914, p.1442; 'Sweeney's Christmas Bird', *Vitagraph Life Portrayals*, 1–31 December 1914, p.47; 'Sweeney's Christmas Bird', *Motography*, 26 December 1914, p.910; 'Sweeney's Christmas Bird', *Moving Picture World*, 9 January 1915, p.220; M.C. Rask, 'Sweeney's Christmas Bird', *Photoplay*, January 1915, pp.28–34.

210. 'Clancy the Model', *Moving Picture World*, 24 May 1913, p.844.

211. 'Rafferty's Raffle', *Motion Picture News*, 14 March 1914, p.48; 'Rafferty's Raffle', *Moving Picture World*, 21 March 1914, p.1525.

212. 'Brannigan's Band', *Moving Picture World*, 19 December 1914, p.1752; 'Brannigan's Band', *Moving Picture World*, 9 January 1915, p.220; 'Casey's Vendetta', *Moving Picture World*, 7 November 1914, p.834; 'McGinty and the Count', *New York Dramatic Mirror*, 6 January 1915, p.35; 'McGinty and the Count', *Moving Picture World*, 9 January 1915, p.251; 'McGinty and the Count', *Moving Picture World*, 30 January 1915, p.671.

213. 'A Dollar Did It', *Moving Picture World*, 21 April 1913, p.206; 'The Rival Barbers', *Moving Picture World*, 28 February 1914, p.1164; 'The Rival Barbers', *Moving Picture World*, 7 March 1914, p.1238. Here I would note that American films of the early cinema period are sometimes vague when it comes to characters who were Dutch and who were Germans ('Deutsch').

214. 'A Sprig o' Shamrock', *Moving Picture World*, 19 April 1913, p.308; 'A Sprig o' Shamrock', *Moving Picture World*, 26 April 1913, p.382.

215. 'The Rivals', *Moving Picture World*, 15 November 1913, p.782; 'The Rivals', *Moving Picture World*, 22 November 1913, p.869; 'The Rival Pitchers', *Moving Picture World*, 13 December 1913, pp.1334, 1336; 'Friendly Neighbors', *Moving Picture World*, 14 June 1913, pp.1138, 1176.

216. 'The Perfumed Wrestler', *Moving Picture World*, 6 February 1915, p.878.

217. 'Heinze's Resurrection', *Moving Picture World*, 8 March 1913, p.890; 'Just Like Kids', *Moving Picture World*, 19 June 1915, p.1987.

218. B.E. Walker, *Mack Sennett's Fun Factory* (Jefferson, NC: McFarland & Co., 2010), p.281; 'The Riot', *Moving Picture World*, 16 August 1913, p.745.

219. 'Murphy's I.O.U.', *Moving Picture World*, 12 April 1913, p.206; 'Murphy's I.O.U.', *Moving Picture World*, 19 April 1913, p.282.

220. 'McGann and His Octette', *Moving Picture World*, 1 November 1913, p.495; 'McGann and His Octette', *New York Dramatic Mirror*, 5 November 1913, p.342. A copy of *McGann and His*

*Octette* exists at the George Eastman House in Rochester, New York.

221. 'Murphy and the Mermaids', *Moving Picture World*, 26 September 1914, p.1809. A copy of *Murphy and the Mermaids* exists at the George Eastman House in Rochester, New York.

222. 'Levi and McGuiness Running for Office', *New York Dramatic Mirror*, 5 November 1913, p.40. A copy of *Levi and McGuiness Running for Office* exists at the British Film Institute in London.

223. 'Levi and McGuiness Running for Office', *Moving Picture World*, 15 November 1913, p.738.

224. 'Traffickers in Soles', *Moving Picture World*, 28 February 1914, p.1168. The other parody was Joker's *Traffic in Soles*, also released in 1914. See 'Traffic in Soles', *Motion Picture News*, 7 March 1914, p.44, as well as 'Traffic in Souls', *Moving Picture World*, 7 March 1914, p.1238.

225. 'Poor Finney', *Moving Picture World*, 23 November 1912, p.816; 'Poor Finney', *New York Dramatic Mirror*, 27 November 1912, p.31; 'Poor Finney', *Moving Picture World*, 7 December 1912, p.977; 'Where's the Baby', *Moving Picture World*, 1 November 1913, p.522.

226. 'Murphy's New High Hat', *Moving Picture World*, 29 November 1913, p.1009.

227. 'Murphy's New High Hat', *Moving Picture World*, 15 November 1913, p.782; 'Murphy's New High Hat', *Moving Picture World*, 29 November 1913, p.1009; 'The Mix-Up at Murphy's', *Moving Picture World*, 15 August 1914, p.1000; 'The Mix-Up at Murphy's', *Moving Picture World*, 29 August 1914, p.1240. A copy of *The Mix-Up at Murphy's* exists at the George Eastman House in Rochester, New York.

228. 'When Hooligan and Dooligan Ran for Mayor', *Vitagraph Bulletin* (January 1916), p.33.

229. 'Mulligan's Ghost', *Moving Picture World*, 24 October 1914, p.534; 'Pat Hogan, Deceased', *Vitagraph Life Portrayals*, 1–31 August 1915, p.9; 'Pat Hogan, Deceased', *Motography*, 7 August 1915, p.273.

230. 'Gilligan's Accident Policy', *Moving Picture World*, 9 May 1914, p.854; 'Gilliagan's Accident Policy', *Moving Picture World*, 23 May 1914, p.1116.

231. 'The Dream of Dan Maguire', *New York Dramatic Mirror*, 22 October 1913, p.36; 'The Dream of Dan Maguire', *Moving Picture World*, 25 October 1913, p.380.

232. 'Spending It Quick', *Moving Picture World*, 21 September 1914, p.1512.

233. 'Mrs Maloney's Fortune', *Vitagraph Bulletin*, 1–31 March 1914, p.25; 'Mrs Maloney's Fortune', *Moving Picture World*, 7 March 1914, p.1280; 'Mrs Maloney's Fortune', *Motion Picture News*, 28 March 1914, p.46.

234. 'This Isn't the Life', *Moving Picture World*, 18 December 1915, p.2235.

235. 'Food for Kings and Riley', *Motion Picture News*, 14 August 1915; 'Food for the Kings and Riley', *Motography*, 14 August 1915, p.326. (*Motography*'s review used the word '*the*' in listing the film's title.)

236. 'Rooney's Sad Case', *Vitagraph Life Portrayals*, December 1915, p.39. See also 'Rooney's Sad Case', *Moving Picture World*, 4 December 1915, p.1894.

237. 'Feeney's Social Experiment', *Moving Picture World*, 6 September 1913, p.1069; 'Feeney's Social Experiment', *Moving Picture World*, 6 September 1913, p.1108.

238. 'Bound to Occur', *Moving Picture World*, 15 February 1913, p.698; 'Finney's Luck', *Moving Picture World*, 18 January 1913, p.300; 'Finney's Luck', *Moving Picture World*, 11 January 1913, p.160; 'Frayed Fagin's Adventures', *Moving Picture World*, 13 December 1913, p.1316; 'Frayed Fagin's Adventures', *New York Dramatic Mirror*, 17 December 1913, p.38; 'Actor Finney's Finish', *New York Dramatic Mirror*, 27 May 1914, p.41; 'Actor Finney's Finish', *Moving Picture World*, 6 June 1914, p.1408; 'McBride's Bride', *Kalem Kalendar*, 1 April 1914, p.15; 'McBride's Bride', *Moving Picture World*, 23 May 1914, p.1116; 'A Quiet Day at Murphy's', *Moving Picture World*, 13 June 1914, p.1542; 'Mrs Murphy's Cooks', *Moving Picture World*, 17 April 1915, p.450; 'Mrs Murphy's Cooks', *Moving Picture World*, 1 May 1915, p.727; 'Finn and Haddie', *Motography*, 11 September 1915, p.542; 'Borrowing Hogan', *Motion Picture News*, 2 October 1915, p.84; 'Rooney, the Bride', *Edison Kinetogram*, 1 March 1915, p.13; 'Rooney, the Bride', *Moving Picture World*, 6 March 1915, p.1496.

239. I would also note the use of concocted names that might have sounded Irish to some viewers. For example, the lead character of *Swat the Fly* (Essanay, 1911) was 'McSwatt', and the professor in *Slim and the Petticoats* (Frontier, 1913) was named 'McNutt'. See 'Swat the Fly', *Moving Picture World*, 22 July 1911, p.123; 'Slim and the Petticoats', *Moving Picture World*, 13 December 1913, p.1334.

240. 'The Pennant Puzzle', *Moving Picture World*, 13 July 1912, p.176.

241. 'Pat, the Cowboy', *Moving Picture World*, 31 May 1913, p.920.

242. 'The Cook's Revenge', *Moving Picture World*, 30 August 1913, p.988.
243. 'The Surrender', *Moving Picture World*, 30 August 1913, p.990.
244. 'Love and Laundry', *Moving Picture World*, 17 May 1913, p.746.
245. 'Bridget Bridges It', *Moving Picture World*, 21 March 1914, p.1570.
246. 'The Cook's Mistake', *Moving Picture World*, 10 April 1915, p.282.
247. 'The Laundress and the Lady', *Moving Picture World*, 22 November 1913, p.894; 'The Laundress and the Lady', *Moving Picture World*, 6 December 1913, p.1151.
248. 'The Laundress and the Lady', *New York Dramatic Mirror*, 10 December 1913, p.41.
249. 'Curing the Cook', *Kinetogram*, January 1915, p.14; 'Curing the Cook', *New York Dramatic Mirror*, 6 January 1915, p.35.
250. 'That Heavenly Cook', *Moving Picture World*, 27 February 1915, p.1333; 'The [sic] Heavenly Cook', *Motography*, 6 March 1915, p.375.
251. 'Mike's Elopement', *Moving Picture World*, 15 May 1915, p.1158.
252. 'The Conquest of Constantia', *Vitagraph Life Portrayals*, December 1915, p.33.
253. 'Wipe Yer Feet', *Moving Picture World*, 9 January 1915, p.268; 'Wipe Yer Feet', *Moving Picture World*, 16 January 1915, p.368.
254. 'Found Out', *Moving Picture World*, 26 April 1913, p.379; 'Sally Scraggs, Housemaid', *Moving Picture World*, 16 August 1913, p.745; 'An Up-To-Date Cook', *Moving Picture World*, 11 April 1914, p.266. Other examples of cooks and maids who do not seem to have been Irish appeared in such films as: Kalem's The 'Fired' Cook, *Moving Picture World*, 22 March 1913, p.1249; Imp's The Magnetic Maid, *Moving Picture World*, 7 June 1913, p.1033; Solax's Cooking for Trouble, *Moving Picture World*, 12 July 1913, p.206.
255. 'The Laundress', *Moving Picture World*, 14 November 1914, p.932. An earlier example of a male actor in drag portraying a non-Irish-coded domestic servant probably occurred in *The New Cook* (Kalem, 1911), in which Fred Santley played 'The Cook'. Period reviews, synopses and advertisements do not suggest that the cook was Irish. See 'The New Cook', *Moving Picture World*, 1 July 1911, p.1524; advertisement, *Moving Picture World*, 1 July 1911, p.1489; 'The New Cook', *Moving Picture World*, 22 July 1911, p.124.
256. Here I am not considering the Happy Hooligan moving pictures as an Irish comic film series for reasons outlined in the main text with regard to the character's unclear ethnicity. I am also hesitant to consider Bison's trio of 'Dooley' films as an Irish comedy film series. In 1909, Bison released *Dooley's Thanksgiving Dinner* (aka *Dooley's Thanksgiving Turkey*). The following year, the same company released *Dooley's Holiday* (1910) and *Dooley Referees the Big Fight* (1910). All three films starred Charles Avery as the title character; Avery did portray an Irish character in Mack Sennett's *The Riot* (Keystone, 1913), but he also played various ethnicities during his career. Despite the Irish-sounding name, surviving plot synopses suggest that none of the three drew on particularly 'Irish' or 'Irish-American' comedy. Moreover, a review of *Dooley's Holiday*, in *Moving Picture World* (5 March 1910) seemed uncertain as to whether the character in this film was even the same as the character in the earlier film, *Dooley's Thanksgiving Holiday*. The publication noted: 'Perhaps this is the same Dooley who had a remarkable experience with a turkey at Thanksgiving' (p.339). It seems that these three films were hardly perceived to be a series of any kind, let alone to be an Irish-themed series. With regard to another Irish-themed comedy series, see Chapter 6 for a discussion of the 'One Round O'Brien' films produced in 1913 and 1914.
257. The nine Bedelia films produced by Reliance were, in order of their release dates, as follows: *Bedelia's Busy Morning* (1912), *Bedelia and Mrs Busybody* (1912), *Bedelia and the Suffragette* (1912), *Bedelia's 'At Home'* (1912), *Bedelia as a Mother-in-Law* (1912), *Bedelia and Her Neighbor* (1912), *Bedelia and the Newlyweds* (1912), *Bedelia Has a Toothache* (1912) and *Trying to Keep Bedelia* (1912). A copy of *Bedelia and the Newlyweds* (1912) exists at The Library of Congress in Washington, DC.
258. *Complete Illustrated Catalog of Moving Picture Machines, Stereopticons, Slides, Films* (Chicago, IL: Kleine Optical Company, November 1905), p.323.
259. After the Reliance series ended, Vitagraph produced *Bedelia Becomes a Lady* (1913), casting Mary Charleson (Kate Price's niece) as Bedelia; the film had a rural setting and was not affiliated with the Reliance films. See 'Bedelia Becomes a Lady', *Vitagraph Life Portrayals*, 1–31 March 1913, p.55; 'Bedelia Becomes a Lady', *Moving Picture World*, 29 March 1913, p.1354; 'Bedelia Becomes a Lady', *Moving Picture World*, 12 April 1913, p.165.

260. 'Bedelia and Mrs Busybody', *New York Dramatic Mirror*, 28 February 1912, p.37.

261. 'Bedelia's Busy Morning', *New York Dramatic Mirror*, 21 February 1912, p.31.

262. [Untitled], *Evening Tribune* (Albert Lea, MN), 15 June 1912, p.3; 'Bedelia and the Suffragette', *Moving Picture World*, 2 March 1912, p.804.

263. 'Bedelia Has a Toothache', *Moving Picture World*, p.1294. Similar comments appear in 'Bedelia as a Mother-in-Law', *Moving Picture World*, 4 May 1912, p.427.

264. 'Bedelia's Busy Morning', p.31; advertisement, *Daily News* (Frederick, MD), 8 March 1912, p.3.

265. 'Bedelia's "At Home" ', *Moving Picture News*, 24 February 1912, p.46; 'Bedelia's "At Home" ', *Moving Picture World*, 16 March 1912, p.1000.

266. 'Bedelia and Mrs Busybody', *Moving Picture World*, 24 February 1912, p.716; 'Bedelia and Mrs Busybody', *New York Dramatic Mirror*, 28 February 1912, p.37; 'Bedelia and Mrs Busybody', *Moving Picture World*, 2 March 1912, p.782.

267. 'Bedelia and Her Neighbor', *Moving Picture World*, 21 September 1912, p.1208; 'Bedelia and Her Neighbor', *Moving Picture World*, 5 October 1912, p.43.

268. 'Bedelia and the Suffragette', *Photoplay*, March 1912, p.56; 'Bedelia and the Suffragette', *Moving Picture World*, 2 March 1912, p.804; 'Bedelia and the Suffragette', *Moving Picture World*, 9 March 1912, p.867.

269. 'Bedelia and the Newlyweds', *Moving Picture World*, 2 November 1912, p.486; 'Trying to Keep Bedelia', *Moving Picture World*, 4 January 1913, p.90.

270. 'Pat's Motor', *Moving Picture World*, 27 February 1914, p.1166.

271. 'Pat, the Electrician', *Moving Picture World*, 30 May 1913, p.960; 'Pat Wishes to Economize', *Moving Picture World*, 22 March 1913, p.1260; 'Pat Wishes to Economize', *Moving Picture World*, 5 April 1913, p.49.

272. 'Pat as a Bird Fancier', *Moving Picture World*, 8 March 1913, p.932.

273. 'Pat's Motor', p.1166.

274. 'Pat's Fancy Dress', *Moving Picture World*, 19 July 1913, p.360.

275. 'Pat Moves to Diplomatic Circles', *Moving Picture World*, 17 May 1913, p.742; 'Tickets, Please', *Moving Picture World*, 8 February 1913, p.616; 'Pat Gets on the Trail', *Moving Picture World*, 5 July 1913, p.88.

276. 'Pat and the Milliner', *Moving Picture World*, 27 December 1912, p.1332; 'Pat and the Milliner', *Moving Picture World*, 4 January 1913, p.52.

277. 'Pat's Busy Day', *Moving Picture World*, 8 March 1913, p.997; 'Pat's Busy Day', *Moving Picture World*, 8 March 1913, p.1030.

278. 'Pat Fannagan's Family', *Moving Picture World*, 14 February 1914, p.876.

279. 'Sweeney and the Million', *Moving Picture World*, 1 February 1913, p.494.

280. 'Sweeney and the Million', *Moving Picture World*, 22 February 1913, p.779.

281. 'Sweeney and the Fairy', *Moving Picture World*, 7 June 1913, p.1050.

282. In 'Sweeney and the Fairy', *Moving Picture World*, 21 June 1913, used the phrase 'it will be remembered' (p.1252) to refer to the continued narrative action from *Sweeney and the Million* to *Fairy*.

283. 'Sweeney's Dream', *Moving Picture World*, 12 July 1913, p.226.

284. The four Skelley films produced by Biograph and starring Charlie Murray are, in order of their release: *Skelley's Skeleton* (1914), *Skelley Buys a Hotel* (1914), *Skelley and the Turkey* (1914) and *Skelley's Birthday* (1914).

285. 'Skelley and the Turkey', *Motion Picture News*, 7 March 1914, p.43.

286. 'Skelley's Birthday', *Moving Picture World*, 18 April 1914, p.360.

287. The Hogan films produced by Keystone and starring Charlie Murray are, in order of their release: *Hogan's Annual Spree* (1914), *Hogan's Wild Oats* (1915), *Hogan's Mussy Job* (1915), *Hogan, the Porter* (1915), *Hogan's Romance Upset* (1915), *Hogan's Aristocratic Dream* (1915), *Hogan Out West* (1915) and *From Patches to Plenty* (1915). The film *Borrowing Hogan* (Santa Barbara Films, 1915) was not part of this series.

288. For more information on the Hogan films, see Walker, *Mack Sennett's Fun Factory*.

289. The Vitagraph films starring Kate Price as 'Kate' included, in order of their release: *Officer Kate* (1914, July), *Fisherman Kate* (1914), *Cabman Kate* (1915), *Whose Husband?* (1915), *Strictly Neutral* (1915) and *Get Rid of Aunt Kate* (1915).

290. A copy of *Officer Kate* (1914) exists at the UCLA Film and Television Archive. Copies of *Cabman Kate* (1915) circulate among collectors of silent film.

291. For example, Charlie Murray portrayed 'Knock-Out McDoo' in *The Rise and Fall of McDoo* (Biograph, 1913), 'O'Brien' in *Never Known to Smile* (Biograph, 1913) and *McGann and His Octette* (Biograph, 1913), and 'Mr Hennessy' in *The Somnambulists* (Biograph, 1913). Similarly, Kate Price portrayed 'The Widow McCarthy' in *The Widow's Might* (Vitagraph, 1913), 'Mrs McGee' in *Tim Grogan's Foundling* (Vitagraph, 1913), 'Mrs Sullivan' in *O'Hara's Godchild* (Vitagraph, 1913), 'Mrs Maloney' in *Mrs Maloney's Fortune* (Vitagraph, 1914), 'Mrs Clancy' in *Sweeney's Christmas Bird* (Vitagraph, 1914), 'Bridget' in *Chiefly Concerning Males* (Vitagraph, 1915) and 'Mrs McCarty' in *They Loved Him So* (Vitagraph, 1915).

292. For example, at Biograph in the single year of 1912, Charlie Murray portrayed 'The Cook' in *Getting Rid of Trouble*', 'The Husband' in *Love's Messenger*, 'The Policeman' in *A Mixed Affair*, 'The Traveling Salesman in *A Disappointed Mama*, 'The Town Bully' in *A Ten-Karat Hero*, 'The Police Commissioner' in *Like the Cat, They Came Back*, 'The Pastor' in *At the Picnic Basket*, 'A Tramp' in *His Auto Maiden's Trip* and the 'First Crook' in *An Absent-Minded Burglar*. Similarly, at Vitagraph in the single year of 1912, Kate Price portrayed 'A Widow' in *Captain Barnacle's Messmates*, 'The Cook' in *The Great Diamond Robbery*, 'The Housekeeper' in *Red Ink Tragedy*, 'A Domestic Servant' in *Her Old Sweetheart*, 'The Housekeeper' in *A Lively Affair*, 'The Cook' in *Father's Hot Toddy*, 'The Cook' in *The Professor and the Lady*, 'A Pupil' in *In the Flat Above*, and 'The Cook' in *All for a Girl*. The cook in *How Mr Bullington Ran the House* (1912), also portrayed by Kate Price, seems to have had stereotypical Irish traits. See L.R. Harrison, 'How Mr Bullington Ran the House', *Moving Picture World*, 26 October 1912, p.327.

293. For example, Charlie Murray portrayed 'Schmaltz' in *Their Idols* (Biograph, 1912), 'Henrico' in *Hoist on His Own Petard* (Biograph, 1912), 'Samuel Johnson' in *Highbrow Love* (Biograph, 1913), 'Red Hicks' in *Red Hicks Defies the World* (Biograph, 1913), a 'Male Apache Dancer' in *The Mothering Heart* (Biograph, 1913), 'Deacon Hicks' in *The Winning Punch* (Biograph, 1913), 'U.R. Dunn' in *He's a Lawyer* (Biograph, 1913), 'Mr Binks' in *Binks Vacation* (Biograph, 1913) and 'Count de Beans' in *Her Friend the Rabbit* (Keystone, 1914). Similarly, Kate Price portrayed 'Mrs Brown' in *Stenographers Wanted* (Vitagraph, 1912), 'Mrs Humph' in *The Jocular Winds of Fate* (Vitagraph, 1912), 'Sarah Simmonds' in *The Old Kent Road* (Vitagraph, 1912), 'Mrs Briggs' in *Who's to Win?* (Vitagraph, 1912), 'Amanda Witherspoon' in *Pandora's Box* (Vitagraph, 1912), 'Jaspar's Wife' in *A Juvenile Love Affair* (Vitagraph, 1912), 'Bertha le Noir' in *The Bond of Music* (Vitagraph, 1912), 'Markham's African Wife' in *Captain Barnacle's Legacy* (Vitagraph, 1912), Mrs Binks in *Wanted, a Strong Hand* (Vitagraph, 1913), 'Mrs Simpson' in *Jerry's Uncle's Namesake* (Vitagraph, 1914), 'Mrs Flivver' in *Mr Bingle's Melodrama* (Vitagraph, 1914), 'Mrs Whippem' in *Lillian's Dilemma* (Vitagraph, 1914), 'Mrs Edwards' in *A Horseshoe–For Luck* (Vitagraph, 1914) and 'Mrs Eaton' in *Fair, Fat and Saucy* (Vitagraph, 1914).

294. '*Rooney's Sad Case*', *Moving Picture World*, 18 December 1915, p.2202.

295. See, for example, 'Alkali Ike on His Way to Paris', *Moving Picture World*, 8 November 1913, p.598.

296. 'All Celtic's Clean Films', *Motography*, 29 May 1915, pp.886–7.

297. 'All Irish Film Company', *Motography*, 17 July 1915, p.108. For more information on All Celtic Films, Inc., see also: 'All Celtic Takes Larger Offices', *Motography*, 5 June 1915, p.937; 'Rafferty Series Making Good', *Motography*, 26 June 1915, p.1040; 'O'Hara Talks of Comedy Films', *Motography*, 10 July 1915, p.74.

298. '*The Ups and Downs of Rafferty*', *Moving Picture World*, 9 December 1911, pp.840, 842; '*The Ups and Downs of Rafferty*', *Moving Picture World*, 23 December 1911, p.990.

299. Various secondary sources claim that Charles O'Hara portrayed Rafferty, but that is contradicted by numerous primary sources, including ' "Peaceful Rafferty's" Creator Talks about the Film's Success', *Motography*, 24 July 1915, p.147; and C.R. Condon, 'Two New Rafferty Pictures', *Motography*, 26 June 1915, pp.1060–1.

300. ' "Peaceful Rafferty's" Creator', p.147.

301. '*Rafferty Settles the War*', *Moving Picture World*, 3 July 1915, p.144. See also C.R. Condon, 'First All Celtic Releases', *Motography*, 22 May 1915, pp.839–40.

302. '*Rafferty Stops a Marathon Runner*', *Motography*, 22 May 1915, p.858.

303. Condon, 'Two New Rafferty Pictures', p.1060.

304. '*Rafferty at the Hotel de Rest*', *Motography*, 10 July 1915, p.48.

305. '*Rafferty Goes to Coney Island*', *Motography*, 10 July 1915, p.48.

306. L. Denig, 'All Celtic Features', *Moving Picture World*, 19 June 1915, p.1949.

307. Condon, 'Two New Rafferty Pictures', p.1060.

308. *'No Tickee – No Washee'*, *Vitagraph Life Portrayals*, November 1915, p.35.

309. *'No Tickee – No Washee'*, *Moving Picture World*, 30 October 1915, p.1017.

310. *'No Tickee – No Washee'*, *Motion Picture News*, 20 November 1915, p.86. (This review notes that 'much is made of a humorless chase'.)

311. A notable exception would be *Knockabout Kelly, A Magician in Spite of Himself* (Méliès, 1914, aka *Knockabout Kelly, Magician*), whose title character steals a magic wand. The ensuing antics build humour out of cinematographic tricks. See *'Knockabout Kelly, A Magician in Spite of Himself'*, *Moving Picture World*, 2 May 1914, p.706; *'Knockabout Kelly, Magician'*, *Moving Picture World*, 8 May 1914, p.820.

# Chapter Five

# *Melodrama*

While the pre-nickelodeon era was rife with examples of comic fictional films featuring Irish stereotypes, it was not until the nickelodeon era began – approximately ten years after the first public US film screenings in 1896 – that American moving picture companies produced serious Irish-themed fictional films that eschewed ethnic caricatures. Such films even attempted to re-inscribe character names associated with the earlier comedies. For example, Vitagraph's *A Brave Irish Lass: The Story of an Eviction* (1909) featured characters named 'Pat' and 'Bridget' in a dramatic storyline.

The appearance of these kinds of Irish-themed films coincided with an array of other major changes in the film industry. As Charles Musser has suggested: 'The year 1907 was pivotal for the institution of American cinema. While crisis and fundamental changes occurred at almost every level of the industry, perhaps the most important transformation involved the interrelated modes of production and representation.'[1] According to Tom Gunning, this transformation, which began in 1907 and continued through 1913, 'represents the true *narrativization* of the cinema' (emphasis in original).[2] The moving picture was no longer as dependent on audience awareness of pre-existing vaudeville acts, stage plays, novels or music, as it increasingly told stories with narrative and visual devices that resulted in an increasingly closed – rather than open and intermedial – experience.

One of the many issues that affected the nickelodeon-era American film was an increasing drive towards what many industry trade publications called 'realism', by which they generally meant verisimilitude. As Charlie Kiel has noted:

> the issues of realism that had informed discussions of photography persisted in the criticism of narratives, suggesting that the fundamental question remained one of believability; the oft-repeated phrase 'truthfulness to life' demonstrates the centrality of verisimilitude to the trade press aesthetic. Trade

249

press critics understood that audience comprehension and involvement go hand in hand, always predicated on a film's sustained cultivation of verisimilitude.[3]

In a 1911 issue of *Moving Picture World*, C.H. Claudy spoke of the matter more bluntly, claiming, 'we don't thank you, Mr Producer, we motion picture audiences, for forcing down our throats, the knowledge that this is only a screen and a picture – we want to think it's the real thing'.[4]

Moving picture companies wishing to create 'real' Irish-themed films usually sought to adapt pre-existing works. Non-'stage Irish' music of the nineteenth century provided one source; poetry and non-fiction historical subjects were others. However, the most common resource for 'genuine' Irish film narratives were nineteenth-century stage plays that had achieved ongoing popular success in America, such as those written by Dion Boucicault. However, the gulf between the stereotypical comedies of the pre-nickelodeon era and the serious fictional films of the nickelodeon era is not as great as it might at first seem. Boucicault's *The Shaughraun* provided source material for such comic films as Gaumont's *Murphy's Wake* (1903) and Walturdaw's *Murphy's Wake* (1906), both of which were produced in England and then released in the United States. The two films offered comic stereotypes that easily fitted into the tradition of Irish wake humour present in American vaudeville acts and in stereo views.

However, the treatment of such adaptations changed in the nickelodeon era. The intermedial quality of pre-nickelodeon Irish-themed films, which depended on the audience's knowledge of a given tradition such as vaudeville humour, became less important to these 'genuine' Irish-themed films, as they featured story structures founded, at least in some cases, upon the idea of unity, which, as Keil has noted, 'would bind together the stages of the narrative's progress'.[5] Titles and inserts aided the narration of these films, allowing audience members to understand them without necessarily having seen and remembered the stage plays upon which they were based.

At the same time, moving picture companies in the nickelodeon era adapted Boucicault's Irish-themed stage plays for two reasons that were inextricably tied to one another. The fact that many of his plays had achieved popular successes throughout the United States during the final decades of the nineteenth century meant that, even by the time of the nickelodeon era, their titles and stories remained well known. Film versions of them drew on their long-standing fame; it mattered less whether or not an audience member had seen the stage plays on which these films had been based than the fact that they had heard of them, a factor of much impor-

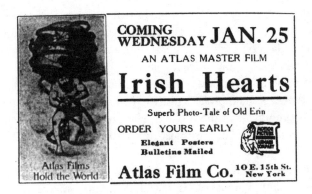

**5.1** Advertisement published in the *Moving Picture World* on 21 January 1911.

tance to their publicity. Secondly, the film adaptations attempted to draw upon the long-standing respectability of these plays that had been embraced by at least some critics and audience members. The desired result was films that would be seen as authentic; the fact that Boucicault was Irish and that his plays often featured Irish words and names in their titles and dialogue added to the perception of general audiences that they were 'real'.

These Irish-themed fictional films also marked a change in that their narratives were often set in Ireland, whereas the earlier fictional films were comedies set in America. The Irish setting became a regular feature in publicity that promoted the authenticity of these films. For example, Selig Polyscope promised that *The Irish Blacksmith* (1908) possessed 'scenery marvellously faithful to the locality in which the dramatic events take place'.[6] Such settings often featured locations that had long been depicted in non-fiction lantern slides, such as Blarney Castle, which factored heavily into the narrative of Powers' *Come Back to Erin* (1911).[7] Film companies like Kalem tried to add greater 'realism' to the use of Irish settings by shooting on location in Ireland. One newspaper review of Kalem's *The Shaughraun* (1912) announced the fact that the film was shot 'upon Irish soil', and was, as a result, 'accurate in every detail'; such claims distanced the film from earlier adaptations like the 1903 and 1906 versions of *Murphy's Wake*.[8]

Even the choice of cast members became important. Rolinda Bainbridge added authenticity to *Irish Hearts* (Atlas, 1911) because she had 'played with Chauncey Olcott in all his productions, as leading woman, and has appeared to advantage in many other Irish plays and pictures'.[9] Film actors Mary Pickford, Henry B. Walthall and Robert Harron added credibility to

D.W. Griffith's *Wilful Peggy* (Biograph, 1910), due to the fact that so many audience members recognized them.[10] These examples are all in addition to stars like Gene Gauntier, whose general renown was complemented by the fact that she repeatedly played Irish roles.

In each of these respects, including the participation in the emergent star system and the overall impetus towards 'realism', the Irish-themed melodrama was a component of the broader genre of American film melodrama and, by extension, in the larger project of the American cinema. These films are examples of what Rick Altman has termed the 'Americanization' of US cinema, a process by which the prominence of foreign films (such as those produced by Pathé) diminished at nickelodeons as American-made films increased in number and popularity.[11] As a result, the Irish-themed melodramas shared various goals with non-Irish themed films produced in America.

## *Kathleen Mavourneen* and the Irish-Themed Melodrama in the Cinema

The William Travers stage play *Kathleen Mavourneen* – first presented in New York City in 1863, but seen in revivals as late as 1905 – inspired various songs and poems in the nineteenth century. The Travers stage play also inspired variations of itself. As Musser has noted, theatrical 'reworkings' of *Kathleen Mavourneen* during the nineteenth century avoided charges of copyright infringement, allowed various theatrical troupes a degree of creativity, and 'attracted audiences already familiar with the basic storyline but ready to be entertained by new variations on a familiar theme'.[12] Yet another such variation came in the form of the moving picture. The Edison Manufacturing Company's *Kathleen Mavourneen* inaugurated the Irish-themed melodrama in the early nickelodeon period.[13]

Directed by Edwin S. Porter and released in August 1906, the film eschewed the make-up and humour of the stage Irish, opting instead for a serious attempt to convey its storyline in seventeen distinct scenes with nine different characters.[14] As Musser has argued, 'audiences would have had difficulty sorting out the narrative unless they already knew the play and/or received assistance from missing intertitles or a lecture'.[15] Thus, the film's mode of representation remained tethered to the pre-nickelodeon era, its narrative structure dependent on the spectator's foreknowledge of the play. In this respect, *Kathleen Mavourneen* was very much a transitional film.

At the same time, the film's visual style is linked to what Thomas Elsaesser has called the cinema's 'drive for realism and verisimilitude'.[16] While it was not shot in Ireland, *Kathleen Mavourneen* illustrates a conscious attempt to secure locations that are evocative of Ireland, ranging

CLASS A FILMS, 15 CENTS PER FT.          CLASS B FILMS, 12 CENTS PER FT

# EDISON

## Films and Projecting Kinetoscopes

Exhibition Model Kinetoscope, $115.00. Universal Model Kinetoscope, $75.00

### ARE THE RECOGNIZED STANDARDS THROUGHOUT THE WORLD

OUR LATEST DRAMATIC SUCCESS,

## THE FIRST AND ONLY IRISH PICTURE.

# KATHLEEN MAVOURNEEN,

### A THRILLING IRISH MELODRAMA IN SEVENTEEN SCENES.

CAST OF CHARACTERS.

**KATHLEEN,**                                         **KITTY O'NEIL**

TERENCE O'MORE, Kathleen's Lover......................WALTER GRISWOLD
CAPTAIN CLEARFIELD, an Irish Landlord.................H. L. BASCOM
DUGAN, Clearfield's Willing Tool......................W. R. FLOYD
DAVID O'CONNOR, Kathleen's Father.....................E. M. LESLIE
FATHER O'CASSIDY, the Parish Priest...................N. B. CLARKE
DANNY KELLY, Friend of Terence........................J. McDOVALL
KITTY O'LAVERY, an Odd Irish Character................JENNIE CLIFFORD
BLACK RODY, the Robber Chief..........................C. F. SEABERT
RED BARNEY                                          } D. R. ALLEN
DARBY DOYLE  ·Of the Robber Band......................D. J. McGINNIS
DENNIS O'GAFF,                                       } W. F. BORROUGHS

Soldiers, Constables, Robbers, Peasants, etc.

The Insult—The Hold Up—The Robbers' Cave—Serving the Papers—The Chase—Kathleen's Home—The Fire (Beautifully hand painted)—The Abduction—Kathleen in the Robbers' Cave—The Drugged Whisky—The Rescue—The Angelus—The Village Dance—The Wedding. SEND FOR ILLUSTRATED DESCRIPTIVE CATALOGUE No. 302.

No. 6266.  Code VECHTVAAN.  Length, 1,000 ft.  Class A.  $150.

## AN INSTANTANEOUS SUCCESS.

### TELL ITS OWN STORY—PLAINER THAN WORDS.

**To Our Friends and the Public:**
We take this opportunity to heartily thank you for your generous appreciation and many complimentary notices and kind expressions for our humble efforts.

EDISON MANUFACTURING CO.

5.2  Advertisement published in *The Billboard* on 15 September 1908.

from outdoor hills to a cottage and a rock fence; costumes used in the film also suggest a conscious effort to achieve historical accuracy. *Kathleen Mavourneen* thus adopts visual strategies similar to those used by manufacturers of illustrated song slides. In these respects, it is very much a nickelodeon-era film striving to be seen as 'genuine'. Indeed, publicity for the film in the *New York Clipper* claimed that the film featured a 'real Irish jaunting car' and 'real champion reel dangers'.[17] A review in the *Oakland Tribune* went even further, incorrectly claiming that the 'pictures were taken in Ireland'.[18]

The Edison Manufacturing Company definitely viewed *Kathleen Mavourneen* as an important and unique moving picture, taking the highly unusual step of advertising it in one entertainment trade publication with a full cast list, naming each actor and the role that he or she portrayed.[19] *Views and Film Index* even published paragraph-length descriptions on each one of the film's seventeen scenes.[20] Speaking of the film in 1906, *The Billboard* wrote:

> In *Kathleen Mavourneen*, the Edison Mfg. Co. have turned out a film which is a distinct novelty among motion photographs. The film represents a skillfully acted representation of one of the most popular Irish melodramas ever seen upon the stage, and the instantaneous success which the film has attained speaks in substantial praise of the clever idea, and the firm which invented the new style of film. It is sure to be only a forerunner of other pictures planned along the same successful line.[21]

The discussion of a 'new style of film' probably refers to the successful adaptation of a stage play to the screen, a factor reinforced by publication of the cast list.[22] However, the comment also might well have meant that *Kathleen Mavourneen* was the first Irish-themed fictional film to be produced in America. Indeed, in another trade advertisement, Edison heralded *Kathleen Mavourneen* as 'the first and only Irish picture'.[23]

*The Billboard* was not alone in its assessment. The *Optical Lantern and Kinematograph Journal*, published in England but read by many Americans in the film industry, asserted that the film's sequences were 'vividly shown in a series of exciting episodes, and the subject ends up prettily with a wedding'.[24] Positive reactions also appeared in numerous American newspapers. In Indiana, for example, the *Logansport Journal* wrote: 'nothing like [*Kathleen Mavourneen*] was ever seen in Logansport'.[25] In Utah, the *Salt Lake Tribune* called it 'one of the most realistic pictures that flashes across the screen'.[26] The film's popular success even prompted Edison to reissue the film in 1908.

In August 1911, the Yankee Film Company released its own version of *Kathleen Mavourneen*, which maintained much of the narrative action of the Edison film. However, the Yankee version has Kathleen's harrowing near-death experience take place in the form of a 'horrible dream', from which she awakes with an understanding that she should marry her sweetheart of many years, rather than the squire who tries to kill her in her dream. Like the Edison version, the film concludes with a wedding. In the Yankee film, however, the 'squire takes his defeat manfully and makes the couple a substantial wedding present, sufficient to give them a start in life'.[27] While it was an attempt to construct a happier ending to the same story, the Yankee film shared the Edison film's efforts at being seen as authentic.

Foregoing the title and character name *Kathleen Mavourneen*, the Powers Motion Picture Company produced their own version of the story, which they released as *Sogarth Aroon* in March 1912. In it, the lead character, Kitty O'Toole, wins the affections of a young lord and a peasant.[28] She dreams that she marries the lord, who 'hires men to try and kill her, but she is rescued by her faithful peasant lover'.[29] As a result of the dream and some advice from her priest, Kitty is 'led to choose the humbler path and remain within her own proper sphere'.[30] The *New York Dramatic Mirror* noted that 'this film has received careful and consistent treatment, and is acted with both understanding and conviction in representing Irish life'.[31] The use of the Irish language in the title was an apparent attempt to add verisimilitude to the film.

Two subsequent versions appeared in 1913. On 17 March of that year, Imp released a three-reel version of *Kathleen Mavourneen* directed by the Irish director Herbert Brenon and starring Jane Fearnley and King Baggott. In reviewing the film, the *San Antonio Light* – which quoted critics who said the film would send audiences 'home in a happy frame of mind' – mistakenly claimed that Dion Boucicault was the author, perhaps because by that time his name had been so often associated with other Irish-themed films.[32] In *Moving Picture World*,[33] George Blaisdell praised the sets, claiming that 'A bit of lane, with the low-roofed white buildings, mentally removes you to a little Irish village. And there you will remain until the end of the play.'

The Edison Manufacturing Company then released a new version of *Kathleen Mavourneen* just over one month later, on 19 April 1913, which starred Mary Fuller and Marc McDermott.[34] Advertisements touted Fuller's name, as well as the fact that the 'great dramatic offering was set in a truly Irish atmosphere'.[35] The *Oakland Tribune*'s review claimed: 'It has remained for the Edison company to present the dramatic story in magnificent detail upon the screen.'[36] In reality, it was the fifth film version of the story produced in America; the Edison Manufacturing Company had in fact produced the first version.

However, Thanhouser would produce the final film version of the story during the early cinema period. Their two-reel moving picture *Kathleen, the Irish Rose* (1914) borrowed some elements from the 1911 Yankee version, with Kathleen dreaming much of the narrative action. In the Thanhouser film, an old Squire who loves Kathleen wrongly accuses her beloved Terrence of a crime. She awakens from her terrible dream just as he is about

**5.3** Actress Jane Fearnley in the title role of *Kathleen Mavourneen* (Imp, 1913).

to be hanged.[37] *Moving Picture World* called the film an 'Irish love story with very little that is fresh or new in it'.[38] Given that the variations of the story had appeared on the screen six times in the space of eight years, it is easy to understand their complaint. At the same time, the repetitions are not unlike the many revivals of the stage play in the nineteenth and early twentieth centuries, with the same Irish-themed story told and retold to general audiences.

## 'Genuine' Irish Films of the Nickelodeon Era

As Musser has noted, the 1906 version of *Kathleen Mavourneen* 'helped lead to the adaptation of theatrical material that became common in later years'.[39] Its influence was widespread, but it specifically affected the Irish-themed film of the nickelodeon era, which would commonly adapt stage plays. Such adaptations drew on the fame of their source material, but – as opposed to *Kathleen Mavourneen* (1906) – offered narratives that were understandable without foreknowledge of their source material. Such films exemplify the narrativization of the American cinema during the nickelodeon period. Here is another reason why they must be considered American films, even if they were set in Ireland.

The reliance on pre-existing stage plays can be seen in Vitagraph's *The Shaughraun* (1907, aka *The Shaughraun, An Irish Romance*), based on Dion Boucicault's play of the same name.[40] Approximately two years later, Vitagraph produced another version of the same play under the title *An Irish Hero* (1909).[41] Released on a split-reel with a comedy entitled *Lost in a Folding Bed* (1909), *An Irish Hero* was shorter than *The Shaughraun*, but Vitagraph promoted it heavily, particularly the fact that prints were 'hand colored'.[42] As with the various versions of *Kathleen Mavourneen* of the nickelodeon era, both *The Shaughraun* and *An Irish Hero* were set in Ireland.[43]

Similarly, in 1908, Selig Polyscope released *A Daughter of Erin* (1908), which they promoted as a 'Great Irish Drama'.[44] Though they had changed the title and the character names, Selig based their story on Boucicault's play *The Colleen Bawn*.[45] Three years later (in the same month that they released their *Kathleen Mavourneen*), the Yankee Film Company released their own version of the story, retaining the title *The Colleen Bawn*. *Moving Picture World* noted:

> The English-speaking theatre-going public are well acquainted with this beautiful Irish tale made famous by song and story ... The story is too well known to need repeating, for where can you find a man, woman, or child who does not know dear... Myles na-Copaleen, Hardress Creegan, Danny Mann, Eily O'Connor, Anne Chute, Sheelah, or any of the other well-beloved characters.
>
> After months of untiring labor, study and effort, the Yankee Film Co. have produced a masterpiece of which they may justly be proud. An effort has been made to adhere as closely as possible to the original play by Dion Boucicault and Laura Keene, and the result is a magnificent production that will recall pleasant memories to the old-timers and delight the eyes of all who see it.[46]

The trade publication also noted that 'proper scenery and costumes of the period of 1792 were procured only by having them specially made, and then began the long journey to the beautiful Emerald Isle with a selected company of players, where the most magnificent scenery in the world was obtained'.[47] While there is no record that Yankee actually did journey to Ireland in order to shoot on location, some publicity claimed that they had in fact done so.

Pre-existing narratives also provided the impetus for Selig's 1908 version of *Shamus O'Brien*. The story originated as J. Sheridan Le Fanu's poem, to which Samuel Lover added some additional lines during a lecture tour of America in 1840. In 1867, Will S. Hays published his song *Shamus O'Brien*, which would be reprinted numerous times, including in a 1901 songbook.[48] Then, in 1897, an opera entitled *Shamus O'Brien* premiered on Broadway in New York City. George H. Jessop based his libretto on the poem; the opera also featured music by Dr Charles Villiers Stanford. As the *New York Times* noted, '[Jessop] has taken the good old story of *Shamus O'Brien*, familiar to every schoolboy who has had to deliver declamations, and made of it an opera comique book that is absolutely unique in the quality of its excellence.'[49]

Selig's publicity in 1908 for *Shamus O'Brien* attempted to draw on the long-standing fame of the story, claiming that 'the subject is made famous by the celebrated poem of that name, and a dramatic company which toured this and other countries some years ago'. To heighten the authenticity of its adaptation, Selig added: 'It is one of the most worthy of Irish dramas, and certainly our reproduction of this historical play eclipses all former film subjects of this nature. The scenes are of exceptional beauty, and the costumes are lavish, both conforming to the time and place of the story's origin.'[50] Those same words would later appear in newspaper advertisements promoting the film.[51] Their mention of 'former film subjects' probably referred to such films as *Kathleen Mavourneen* (1906).

In 1912, Imp released another film version of the story, which was also titled *Shamus O'Brien*.[52] Pronouncing that it was the 'grandest picture ever produced by the "Imp" ', one of the company's trade advertisements heralded the fact that 'It's Irish through and through! Adapted from a Classic Irish Poem by an Irishman! Leading Performers are Irish. Producer Also an Irishman!'[53] *Moving Picture World* offered similar details: 'The Imp Films Company, their directors and acting staff have seized upon this fine theme to produce a magnificent two-reel subject full of atmosphere – it is an Irish play produced under Irish direction and acted by Irish men and women, who all entered into the very marrow of the theme.'[54] In judging its authenticity, the *New York Dramatic Mirror* noted the film's fidelity to its original source material, claiming 'the picture...follows very closely with requisite dramatic amplification the lines of J.S. La [*sic*] Fanu's outlaw'.[55]

Other films were influenced by different kinds of pre-existing narrative and visual sources. For example, Vitagraph's *A Brave Irish Lass: The Story of an Eviction* (1909) drew upon a broad array of eviction stories that had appeared in non-fiction literature like newspapers, as well as such non-fiction lantern slides as *Police Returning from an Eviction* and *An Evicted House*, both of which had been sold by T.H. McAllister in his 1898 catalogue. The film's story – in which a 'gentlemanly-looking villain' attempts to displace the O'Malleys from their home until they are saved at the last minute – also bore the influence of Fred Marsden's nineteenth-century stage play *The Kerry Gow*.[56] However, it is important to note that many moving picture melodramas not set in Ireland featured similar narratives; in other words, despite its attempts to be viewed as an authentic Irish story, *A Brave Irish Lass* was also influenced by a range of non-Irish-themed American melodramas.

Rather than depend on previous works of fiction, some American moving picture manufacturers relied on non-fiction history tales of Ireland for narrative content. For example, Edison's *Peg Woffington* (1910) starred

**5.4** A scene from *Shamus O'Brien* (Imp, 1912).

Florence Turner in a fictionalized account of the life of a famous Dublin-born actress of the eighteenth century.[57] The following year, Thanhauser released *Robert Emmet*; the company's synopsis made no reference to Boucicault's stage play, but referred instead to general historical data.[58] *Moving Picture World* proclaimed that *Robert Emmet* was 'a well acted and well staged and worthy picture in every sense'.[59] By contrast, a critic for *Moving Picture News* noted 'that a student of history learns enough lessons to remember an old proverb – audi alteram partem. I have with deep regret noticed that this firm has of late given indications of "taking sides" in matters theological and national. The film must neither be an advertisement of sects nor of political opinions.'[60] *Robert Emmet* was not only the first major American film to offer a fictional retelling of a non-fiction tale of Irish history, but it was also at the vanguard of perceived propaganda films. Much the same charge could well have been made against *Irish Hearts* (1911), which attempted to show the 'malice, treachery, and greed' of the British soldiers and their 'persecution of God-fearing Irish peasants'.[61] In such cases, *Moving Picture News* equated 'taking sides' with a lack of objectivity, and, by extension, a lack of authenticity.

While not directly based on Irish history, Yankee's *For the Wearing of the Green* (1911) – which was released only two weeks after *Robert Emmet* – told a similar story of an Irish patriot named Neil O'Connor, who was

**5.5A and 5.5B** In *Caught by Wireless* (Biograph, 1908) D.W. Griffith plays 'Paddy'.

'feared by the British, and loved by the Irish'.[62] O'Connor hides in the hills 'to avoid being captured, and probably hung, as a traitor'.[63] After he is arrested, his beloved Lady Broughton secures a written pardon. The villainous Sir James threatens to burn the pardon unless Broughton becomes his wife. She refuses, but cannily replaces the pardon with another piece of paper. At the last minute, O'Connor is saved when the real pardon is produced. Given its fictional characters, Yankee – in what was their third Irish-themed film of 1911 – was able to mediate history with fictional devices that were standard in American film melodramas of the nickelodeon era. Such liberties allowed Yankee to offer a happy ending of the sort that *Robert Emmet* could not.[64]

Certainly there were exceptions to the general practice of adapting particular Irish-themed literature and stage plays. For example, Vitagraph's *The Gambler and the Devil* (1908) drew on previous literary sources, though none that were specifically Irish-themed. Set in nineteenth-century Ireland, the young squire Barry Kilgowan develops a 'craving' for gambling, so much so that he pulls a revolver to kill himself. 'At that moment, there is a puff of smoke from the fireplace and a devil appears', according to the studio's synopsis. The devil gives Barry the wealth he needs, but their agreement requires that the two play cards one year later, the stake being Barry's wife, Moira. Barry loses, though Moira 'eludes' the devil and dispels him by holding up a cross.[65]

That same year, Edison's *The Leprechawn* (1908) also invoked the supernatural. It featured the familiar eviction story with the cruel landlord, but added a 'heavy load' of leprechaun's gold that solves all financial woes.[66] Thanks to a charm from a local witch, the leprechaun not only helps a young woman and her widowed mother financially, but he also transforms into a 'mounted gentleman'. *Moving Picture World* believed the film accurately 'caught the witchery of Ireland'.[67] The *New York Dramatic Mirror* largely agreed, claiming the film was one of the 'prettiest picture-stories' it had ever reviewed; however, the publication was troubled by the appearance of 'two telegraph poles' in one scene, a 'modern detail hardly in keeping with the remote period when the events are supposed to have occurred'.[68] The inauthentic had frustrated the film-makers' best efforts.

Another example of a tale created for the cinema would be Biograph's *Wilful Peggy* (1910), which the company announced as 'A Story of the Early Days in Ireland'.[69] The film was directed by D.W. Griffith, shot by G.W. 'Billy' Bitzer, and starred Mary Pickford in the title role. *Moving Picture World* described the film as:

> A most delightful romantic comedy of the early days in Ireland...It shows the true Irish traits of candor and truth. Peggy, though a peasant girl, is self-willed and afraid of no one. Her spunky, pugnacious nature, which tends to empha- size her beauty, impresses the lord of the manor to the extent of proposing marriage. The marriage takes place and after a tumultuous honeymoon, he finds he is in possession of a rare jewel of womanhood.[70]

Some of the film's humour arises from Peggy's lack of familiarity with 'court manners and etiquette' and her rage at those ladies around who cannot conceal their amusement.[71]

However, films like *Wilful Peggy* and *The Leprechawn* were exceptions. Most Irish-themed films of the period made repeated use of characters like Con, the Shaughraun, Shamus O'Brien and Robert Emmet, which suggests various possibilities, including the fact that films about them were appar- ently popular with general audiences in America and thus inspired remakes. However, such repetitions can also be read as another way in which the 'genuine' Irish-themed film was not so dissimilar to its apparent opposite, the Irish-themed comedy. Such comedies also repeatedly reused the same characters and comical situations over and over again. In both cases, such Irish-themed melodramas and comedies again participated in the process of repetition common in the broader spectrum of American cinema.

# Immigration Narratives

Another key group of Irish-themed films to emerge during the nickelodeon period were those that attempted to build 'realism' through stories about immigration, which was a recurrent theme in illustrated song slides of the same period. Their narratives address issues that were standard features of moving picture melodramas, ranging from economic problems with stock characters like villainous landlords to economic successes, in which the young male character moves to an American city in order to achieve the 'American Dream' and marry the woman he loves.

Biograph's *Caught by Wireless* (1908) was the first fictional American moving picture to offer a story of Irish migration to America.[72] Directed by Wallace McCutcheon and shot by G.W. 'Billy' Bitzer, the film starred D.W. Griffith as Paddy, who returns home one day to find his wife being terrorized by the rent collector (Edward Dillon). Paddy thrashes the villain, who in turn threatens revenge. Paddy then leaves his wife and children in Ireland and journeys to America. Once settled, Paddy joins the New York City police force and is soon able to pay for his family's voyage. Travelling with them on the same ocean liner is the rent collector, fleeing to America after having stolen money from his employer's safe. Scotland Yard uses the 'mercurial celerity of the Marconi contrivance' to telegraph a message to the New York police force, who arrest the rent collector when he sets foot upon American soil. Paddy is able to reunite with his family.[73]

*Caught by Wireless* is economical in its sets and storyline; in a way, its storytelling approach – which includes no intertitles – is vague, suggestive of a film made as much as two years earlier. The appearance of the rent collector is shown only from the interior of Paddy's cottage; no exterior or establishing shot indicates the Irish setting, though it is suggested by Paddy's costume and a map of Ireland hanging in the Irish police station. The fragmented narrative offers only a single exterior of 'Ireland', which was shot in America; it depicts Paddy in a forest saying goodbye to his wife and two children.

*Caught by Wireless* offers an important example of the fact that these Irish-themed melodramas functioned within broader narrative strategies of the American moving picture. For example, the film's title does not specify any Irish content, but rather the technology by which the villain is captured. *Moving Picture World* noted the same in their review of the film, which suggested that the 'Marconi device...is accurately reproduced.'[74] Judgments about authenticity in this case had little to do with the Irish setting or costumes.

5.6 Advertisement published in the 19 March 1910 issue of the
*Moving Picture World*.

Two years later, Lubin released *The Irish Boy* (1910), with Howard
Mitchell playing the title role. Its narrative chronicled a young immigrant
from Ireland who 'finds fortune through hard work and wins a home for the
girl he loves and the dear old folks from over the seas'.[75] The reunification of
the Irish immigrant and his lover echoes stories told in numerous Irish-
themed illustrated song slides. According to Lubin, the Irish setting was
based on a 'famous painting'. A review of the film in *Moving Picture World*
claimed: 'Here is a realistic picture that tells a real heart story…very
graphically, with a wealth of adequate stage settings and sympathetic acting.
It is neither mawkish nor silly. It is sentimental, but the sentiment is the real
heart sort that adds to the interest and holds the attention unbroken from
first to last.'[76] Lubin made similar pronouncements in their advertisements

5.7  Actor Harry T. Morey (right) in *Wild Pat* (Vitagraph, 1912).

for *The Irish Boy*, underscoring the fact that the film made 'no cheap appeal to false sentiment'.[77] Here the perceived 'realistic' qualities of the film thus had at least as much, or more, to do with a sophisticated handling of melodrama as a narrative form as with anything perceived to be 'Irish'.

The final key effort to convey an immigration narrative during the nickelodeon period came in the form of Vitagraph's *Wild Pat* (1912). In this film, a priest instructs Wild Pat to move to the United States in order to escape the 'bad influences about him', meaning alcohol and his 'hard drinking' friends. Leaving his wife in Ireland, Pat finds work in the boiler room of an American factory. After some drunken men stoke too much coal into the furnaces, Pat realizes that an explosion is imminent; nevertheless, he charges into the boiler room to turn the safety valve. His actions avert a catastrophe, but Pat is so badly scalded that he dies. His priest in Ireland soon receives the news of his heroic death, which he then conveys to Pat's widow.[78]

*Wild Pat*, which *Moving Picture World* praised for its 'commendable' acting, offered a darker version of the 'American Dream' as depicted in *Caught by Wireless* and *The Irish Boy*.[79] Rather than achieve financial success with relative ease, Pat's occupation is a difficult and dangerous working-class position. However, he does gain something from his American experience: a new opportunity to prove himself in a new land.

It is also possible to view *Wild Pat* as another example of the porous boundaries between the Irish-themed melodrama and the Irish-themed comedy. Though *Wild Pat* was a dramatic story with no apparent attempt to promote 'stage Irish' caricatures, the story, hinging as it does on an explosion, returns to the 'explosion' narrative exploited in such Irish-themed comedies as *'Drill Ye Tarriers, Drill'* (1900), *How Bridget Made the Fire* (1900), *The Finish of Michael Casey; or Blasting Rocks in Harlem*, (1901), *The Finish of Bridget McKeen* (1901), *Casey and His Neighbor's Goat* (1903) and *Brannigan Sets Off a Blast* (1906). That is in addition to the fact that Vitagraph produced four fictional Irish-themed moving pictures in 1912; one of the others was the comedy *Doctor Bridget*, which very much drew upon ethnic stereotypes.

# The Kalem Company

At the end of 1908, the Kalem Company released their film *The Molly Maguires, or, Labor Wars in the Coal Mines*; the title referred to a covert organization of Pennsylvania coal miners, who took their name from a 'secret political society' in Ireland.[80] A review in *Moving Picture World* claimed the film 'created no strong impression' due to its unrealistic scenes, which included a 'ridiculous conclusion'. The critic went so far as to pronounce that the burning of a cottage 'shows too much smoke for such a small cabin'.[81] For the company, which had only been organized the year before, such accusations of being inauthentic were problematic.[82] Kalem took pride in having rapidly developed a reputation for producing 'real pictures'.[83] Their emphasis on the 'genuine' grew during 1909 and 1910. In May 1910, for example, *Moving Picture World* offered a very different reaction to Kalem's film *The Cliff Dwellers*, claiming:

> The Kalem Company have left nothing to chance in the archaeology of the subject. It is too often the case nowadays that in Western pictures and also in historical pictures, inaccuracies and anachronisms occur. The Kalem Company have prevented this by preparing the costumes and scenes of the pictures from plates and drawings in the possession of the American Museum of Natural History... We think the care which the Kalem Company have taken to make this picture accurate as well as pictorial and dramatic, deserves a warm word of acknowledgment.[84]

Kalem, which would sometimes release as many as five films per week, had by that time earned respect for their 'real' moving pictures, a respect that they hoped would grow during the summer and autumn of 1910.

It was during those months that they shot and released their first moving picture set in Ireland. By the time of its release, the film (which at

times during its production had been referred to *The Irish Lad's Return*)
was titled *The Lad from Old Ireland*, and – at least in some publicity –
bore the subtitle *A Romance of Erin*.[85] *The Lad from Old Ireland* told the
story of Terry (played by Sidney Olcott, who also directed the film), who
leaves his sweetheart Aileen in Ireland and immigrates to America, where
he soon becomes an important alderman at Tammany Hall and thus
achieves the 'American Dream'. However, when he learns that Aileen's
landlord plans to evict her from her cottage, Terry returns to Ireland,
arriving just in time to pay the overdue rent. Terry and Aileen then
marry.[86] The story bore the influence of *Caught by Wireless*, as well as a
range of illustrated song slides in which two lovers separated by the
Atlantic are reunited (or intend to reunite), as in *Tipperary* (1907).
Indeed, the second shot of the young couple has them posed on a fence
made of stones with a cottage in the distance, the same kind of image seen
repeatedly in such illustrated songs as *Katie Darling, I Am Waiting*
(1907), *Top O' the Morning Bridget McCue* (1907), *I'm Awfully Glad
I'm Irish* (1909) and *Kitty* (1909).

   However, *The Lad From Old Ireland* distinguished itself by shooting its
Irish exteriors on location in Ireland, an effort at increasing the authenticity of the film. Given that by 1910 itinerant lecturers and non-fiction
cinematographers had filmed images throughout the globe, it is in some
ways surprising that it had taken so long for an American company to
shoot a fictional film on location in another country.[87] William Wright,
Kalem's treasurer, explained the origins of their trip to Ireland:

> Mr [Frank] Marion [one of the three men who started Kalem]
> startled us one morning by announcing he was going to send
> a company to make Irish pictures on Irish soil. A small party
> was formed under the lead of Sidney Olcott [who had headed
> the first stock company at Kalem]. Mr Olcott selected
> Beaufort for his headquarters. Pictures were made on and
> around the Lakes of Killarney and in the Gap of Dunloe...In
> our first year in Ireland...all sites were exteriors.[88]

The crew had left New York on 6 August 1910, shooting some footage
aboard their ocean liner during the trip to Queenstown. Gene Gauntier,
who played the female lead in the film, noted that Irish 'peasants' appeared
in the film in small roles and as extras, which may have occurred out of
necessity (given that Olcott's cast from America was too small to have
included extras), but that as a result added another layer of authenticity to
the film.[89]

5.8 Two images that Kalem used to publicize *The Lad from Old Ireland* (1910).

While staying in Ireland, Olcott and Gauntier also starred in *The Irish Honeymoon* (1911), in which they played Larry Malone and Maggie McClusky, newlyweds who visit Ireland on their honeymoon. Olcott doubled as director for a film that would be touted as a comedy. Eschewing ethnic stereotypes, *The Irish Honeymoon* offered a new kind of Irish-themed comedy, which was more authentic, partly because of its location shoot.[90] In addition, the film constructed the appearance of authenticity by incorporating former Tammany Hall politician Richard Croker as a character, with Croker – by then retired in Ireland – portraying himself.[91] His previous film credit had been in the non-fiction moving picture *Dick Croker Leaving Tammany Hall* (Edison, 1900).

Frank J. Marion's plans for Olcott and Gauntier were not limited to Ireland, however. According to *The Film Index*, 'from Ireland the party went to London, Berlin, Raddusch, Elberfield, Antwerp, and Paris, returning home October 6th after covering a distance of 10,000 miles'.[92] The publication also spoke of Kalem's overseas filming plans in the collective, stating:

> 'A feature of these pictures, and one which is carried through each subject, is the linking of the old and the new world. In each picture the scenes shift to and from America and Ireland or the Continent, and is the first instance in the making of the photoplay in which anything of this character has been attempted.'[93] The industry press noted more specific similarities between the Kalem films that Olcott shot overseas after

5.9 A publicity postcard of Gene Gauntier.

the first two of them were released. The Film Index suggested that *The Little Spreewald Maiden* (1910), shot in Germany and starring Gene Gauntier, was 'built on a similar plan as the Irish picture [*The Lad from Old Ireland*], only it is the girl that is the heroine this time'.[94]

*The Film Index* also told readers that 'it should be remembered that these pictures will not be scenic subjects, but will be story pictures giving glimpses of out of the way places and phases of real life at home and abroad'.[95] Their comment agreed that films like *The Lad from Old Ireland* and *The Little Spreewald Maiden* possessed ethnographic value, not unlike some non-fiction moving pictures and lantern slides. For example, *The Lad from Old Ireland* shows Terry working in a peat bog, work that had been depicted in non-fiction Irish-themed lantern slides and in non-fiction Irish-themed moving pictures, such as *At Work in a Peat Bog* (1903, aka *Working in a Peat Bog*) and *Irish Scenes and Types* (1907).

Others did not agree with that ethnographic assessment, perhaps because the narratives of *The Lad from Old Ireland* and *The Little Spreewald Maiden* were fictional and their characters were not played by indigenous actors. For example, a critic in *Moving Picture World* noted *The Lad from Old Ireland*'s 'chief interest lies in the scenery'.[96] Kalem may well have agreed. The location scenery became pivotal in their publicity for the film; in the *Kalem Kalendar*, they highlighted the fact that the film was 'Produced on the "Ould Sod" '. Exhibitors then reiterated the same to potential patrons, with newspaper advertisements informing the public that the film featured 'actual scenes in Ireland'.[97]

Scenery was even more crucial to the threadbare storyline of *The Irish Honeymoon*. The first scene in the film was titled 'They're off!' and the second was 'S. S. Baltic'. Subsequent scenes focussed on Cork, on travelling in a jaunting car, on Blarney Castle, on the Gap of Dunloe, on the Lakes of Killarney, on the Colleen Bawn Rock, on shooting the rapids and on Dublin 'from a bus'. *The Irish Honeymoon* thus repeated the formula used by Harry W. French and others in illustrated travel lectures of the nineteenth century, transporting the audience from New York to various locations in Ireland and then back to America. Individual scenes, such as the Gap of Dunloe and the rapids at Killarney, also returned to non-fiction images that appeared in numerous non-fiction Irish-themed lantern slides and moving pictures.

Kalem advertisements called *The Irish Honeymoon* 'a bridal tour through the beautiful scenic sections of the Emerald Isle', specifically telling readers they would 'See the actual feat of kissing the Blarney Stone', promoting the same kind of authenticity as had Gaumont's non-fiction *Kissing the Blarney Stone* (1904). Kalem even appended *A Trip through Ireland* as a subtitle to *The Irish Honeymoon*, the name echoing the titles of numerous lectures, as well as such moving pictures as *Trip through Ireland* (Hale's Tours, 1906) and *Trip through Ireland* (Lubin, 1906).[98]

Of the films that Olcott and Gauntier shot on location in Ireland and Germany in 1910, Kalem released *The Lad from Old Ireland* first. It became the most successful film of the group.[99] As a result, it retained an important place in Kalem's history.[100] The fact that Kalem even sold a 'record-breaking' 160 prints of the film in London meant that they were 'afraid the English producers would flock to Ireland to make pictures, but not a soul did'.[101] They might also have been concerned that another American company would do the same. To pre-empt such competition, Kalem quickly planned another location shoot in Ireland.

Kalem announced the trip in March 1911, noting that 'only Ireland' would be visited, due to the 'enthusiastic reception' given to *The Lad from Old Ireland*.[102] At that time, Kalem suggested the company would spend 'several months working in various parts of the Island', but remained 'undecided upon the question of subjects', short of the hope that they could film several 'popular Irish dramas with the scenes taken in the localities made famous by these plays'.[103] Kalem's hesitation about which dramas to film may well have resulted from the fact that they were at that time defendants in a copyright infringement lawsuit over their 1907 version of *Ben Hur*. Kalem lost the suit, which would be decided at the US Supreme Court in November 1911.[104]

By the following month, *The Film Index* noted that Kalem chose to dispatch a company of players led by Gene Gauntier (which included Sidney Olcott) to Ireland, presumably because of their involvement with *The Lad from Old Ireland* the year before; at that time, Kalem had two other working companies of players, one headed by Alice Joyce and one headed by Frederic Santley. For the first time, the Gauntier company – the bulk of its members having just constituted Kalem's 'Southern Stock company' – took the nickname 'The O'Kalems', a name which originated at Kalem and which was quickly adopted by film industry trade publications.[105]

In May 1911, *The Film Index* noted that the O'Kalem's principal production would be Boucicault's *The Colleen Bawn*, which would be 'taken amid the scenes around which the original play was written'.[106] By the time the O'Kalems departed for Ireland on 3 June 1911, *Moving Picture World* added that they would also produce a film version of Boucicault's play *Arrah-na-Pogue*.[107] Other plans included a film 'dealing with the Irish home rule question in which Mr Redmond, the great Irish leader, will cooperate'.[108] The impetus to use Redmond may have been an outgrowth over the publicity Kalem received from Richard Croker's appearance in *The Irish Honeymoon*; at any rate, the Redmond film idea was apparently abandoned.

The O'Kalems landed in Ireland on 10 June 1911, after which they erected a temporary studio in Beaufort in County Kerry.[109] According to *Motion Picture Story Magazine*, the 'extra people' who would appear in films on the second trip were 'engaged in London', though it seems possible that at least some extras were cast in Ireland.[110] At any rate, by the time the O'Kalems

**5.10** A scene from *The Colleen Bawn* (Kalem, 1911).

returned to America on 7 October 1911, they had shot approximately eight fictional films in Ireland, though some of them required additional scenes that were filmed in a New York studio.[111] These films included: *Arrah-na-Pogue* (1911), *The Colleen Bawn* (1911), *The Fishermaid of Ballydavid* (1911), *Rory O'More* (1911), *Far from Erin's Isle* (1912), *His Mother* (1912), *The O'Neill* (1912) and *'You Remember Ellen'* (1912).[112]

The first of these films to be released – which occurred on 16 October 1911 – was also the one that received the most publicity: *The Colleen Bawn*.[113] As one advertisement noted, the film was 'a powerful Irish drama familiar to everyone', adding 'every scene in this Irish production was made in Ireland'.[114] A review in Mansfield, Ohio, heralded the fact that 'it illustrates to the letter a world's [sic] famous author', with 'every scene ... taken on the exact spot described'.[115] Other publicity drew attention to the film's 'scenic wonders', which includes 'the beautiful lakes of Killarney' and the 'Colleen Bawn rock', which had earlier been depicted in numerous lantern slides and picture postcards.[116] The industry publication *Motography* even suggested that 'the beauties of Ireland form such a charming background that the release might well be considered a scenic, were it not for the fact that the intensity of the action keeps our mind focussed on the players'.[117]

*The Billboard* also drew attention to the location cinematography, as well as to the authenticity of the props that Kalem used:

> The furniture [in many scenes] is the identical stuff supposed
> to have been used by the participants in the real tale and

271

borrowed from the owners to be used in the picture. Anne Chute's castle is likewise reproduced in structure and the furniture and contents taken from the real castle moved to the studio for the purpose of staging the scenes occurring in one of the rooms. The Colleen Bawn rock and Myles na Coppaleen's still are two of the scenes in the picture staged in the real rock and still as they are preserved today.[118]

The publication concluded by suggesting that the combination of the story and locations culminated in a 'realistic view', one in which a 'glimpse of Irish life is given excellent opportunity to present itself'.[119]

A surviving print of *The Colleen Bawn* reveals the extent to which Kalem perceived authenticity as one of the key goals of the film.[120] In addition to a large array of long shots situating characters within the Irish landscape, the film's intertitles constantly underscore the genuine locations seen on screen and their connection to the play. One tells the viewer the scene: 'Show[s] the identical landing described by Boucicault in his play'; in a manner similar to nineteenth-century travel lectures, another draws attention to 'the celebrated Gap of Dunloe'. Many of these operate on screen parallel to story dialogue or information. For example, a single intertitle informs: 'Eily keeps her tryst, little thinking of the harm about to befall her', as well as '(Showing the real Colleen Bawn Rock and Cave)'. Another announces: 'Danny confesses to the murder of the Colleen Bawn' and '(The bed used in this scene belonged to Daniel O'Connell and was occupied by him)'. A single line separates the fiction from the non-fiction words, thus creating parallel stories, one being the Boucicault drama and the other being an ongoing narrative (though presumably a secondary one, given the parentheticals) about the film's 'real' locations and props.

Kalem's *Arrah-na-Pogue* (1911) was also promoted for its association with Boucicault and for its having been shot in Ireland; *Moving Picture World* touted the fact that 'thanks to the careful work of the producer [who filmed on location], those scenes and characters [from the play] have been preserved in all their primitive quaintness and simplicity'.[121] The film also became notable because it was possibly the first US moving picture for which a complete musical score was written.[122] A reliance on the fame of pre-existing sources was also responsible for *Rory O'More* (1911) and '*You Remember Ellen*' (1912). A 1911 newspaper article claimed that Gene Gauntier based her scenario for *Rory O'More* 'on the famous poetic narrative of *Shamus O'Brien*'.[123] Much publicity also surrounded the film's location shooting, with one newspaper article promising images of

'Killarney' and the 'Gap of Dunloe'.[124] *Moving Picture World* cited a connection between Samuel Lover's poem and the landscapes, noting:

> The purpose of the Kalem Company in sending its players to Ireland was to produce the Irish classics on Irish soil – amid the very surroundings about which they were written. Therefore, when we view the rugged hills and the wildly romantic river of the picture, we are looking upon the self-same scenes in the south of Ireland of which Lover wrote. This charm of realism will have strong appeal.[125]

Similarly, the title card of *'You Remember Ellen'* noted it was 'Adapted from Thomas Moore's Poem', and its intertitles quoted lines from the poem.[126] *Moving Picture World* also suggested that the 'thoroughness of local and native detail gives educational value to the picture, and it may well be said that besides picturing the poem of *You Remember Ellen* the film is descriptive of Irish scenery, life and customs'.[127] Once again, publicity promised that viewers would see the 'Gap of Dunloe' and other 'charming scenery'.[128]

As for the other films shot on their second trip to Ireland, it is likely that either Gene Gauntier or Emmett Campbell developed the scenarios. One of them, *The O'Neill* (1912), bore some similarities to *Rory O'More*, though it was not based on a direct historical or literary antecedent; the film told the story of an Irish patriot who makes a successful escape to Paris with his lover.[129] Three others involved immigration stories: *The Fishermaid of Ballydavid* (1911), *His Mother* (1912) and *Far From Erin's Isle* (1912). *His Mother* tells the story of an Irish musician who achieves great success in America, forgetting Ireland and his mother until she arrives in New York for an emotional reunion.[130] By contrast, *The Fishermaid of Ballydavid* has a young Irish girl seeking love in America from a man who flirted with her in Ireland; he spurns her, and so she returns to her family in Ireland.[131] Similarly, *Far From Erin's Isle* told the story of a young Irish woman who moves to America seeking success, but finds only hardship; thanks to a 'kind landlady', she borrows money for return passage to Ireland.[132] Its narrative was an inversion of the 'American Dream' story depicted in previous Irish-to-America immigration films; the *New York Dramatic Mirror* praised its 'compelling' story.[133]

However, a review in *Moving Picture World* saw *Far from Erin's Isle* in very similar terms to the other O'Kalem films: 'Many bits of Irish land and sea scapes beautify this picture ... the cottage interiors attract attention for the careful arrangement of the details of those scenes'.[134] Likewise, in

**5.11** Publicity for *Arrah-na-Pogue*, as published on 18 November 1911 in the *Moving Picture World*.

Alaska, the *Fairbanks Daily Times* claimed *His Mother* was notable for being 'redolent of the "ould sod", with the beautiful hills, dales, rivers, and lakes for backgrounds'.[135] Films like *Far from Erin's Isle* and *His Mother* also featured the added publicity advantage of having been filmed 'in both Ireland and America', the combination suggesting a heavy expenditure of budget and an epic quality.[136]

Such expenditures apparently proved to be worthwhile investments. During November 1911, Frank J. Marion proposed a third overseas trip for Gauntier and Olcott (who were at the time working on films in Jacksonville, Florida), this time to 'Egypt and the Holy Land'.[137] *The Billboard* also claimed that the company would 'tour' through Italy and Spain.[138] The Gauntier-Olcott company left New York in December. *Motion Picture Story Magazine* wrote: 'When a section of the Kalem Company went to Ireland to make pictures, they were playfully designated as the O'Kalems and so, when the Egyptian tour was contemplated, their name was changed to El Kalem.'[139] During their trip, the El Kalems produced films in 'Egypt, Arabia, the Holy Land, Turkey, and so to Northern Europe'.[140] After a brief stay in England, they ended their trip in Ireland, where they became 'the O'Kalems again' for what became their third visit to the country.[141] Based upon surviving letters from Frank J. Marion to Sidney Olcott, it seems clear that the O'Kalems had arrived at Beaufort by July 1912, where they remained until returning to America.[142] They docked in New York on 12 October 1912, some ten months after they had begun their filming expedition.[143]

Numerous films emerged from the lengthy voyage, ranging from the fictional *The Fighting Dervishes of the Desert* (1912) to the non-fiction *The Kalemites Visit Gibraltar* (1912). However, the most successful film to emerge from the trip was *From the Manger to the Cross* (1912), which told the life story of Jesus Christ. Kalem heavily promoted the fact that the film was shot in 'authentic locations in Palestine and Egypt', as well as the fact that the film had been 'endorsed by clergy both in America and Europe'.[144] *From the Manger to the Cross* became Kalem's most successful film, and the film for which they were best remembered in the industry.[145] It also fulfilled Marion's goal from 1910, which had not been to shoot specifically in Ireland, but rather to shoot films on location in various countries other than the United States.

A newspaper article of 1912 extolled the virtues of companies like Kalem who were shooting films abroad, weaving 'a thread of story through a travel film, showing to thousands of people scenes in far away lands. Thus, at present, a branch of one of the leading film companies is operating in Egypt, combining the classic scenes with dramatic and Biblical

**5.12** A scene from *Rory O'More* (Kalem, 1912).

stories. A few months ago, this same company did practically the same thing in Ireland.'[146] Describing these moving pictures as 'travel film[s]', the newspaper article continued the argument made by *Moving Picture World* two years earlier when it had claimed that *The Lad from Old Ireland*'s chief interest was its 'scenery'. These comments suggest the extent to which these fictional films were compared to non-fiction films.

Writing to Olcott about *From the Manger to the Cross* in July 1912, Frank J. Marion noted that 'it is complete, dignified, reverent, and convincing'.[147] In terms of being 'convincing', the film exemplified Kalem's ongoing emphasis on authenticity. That same year, for example, *Moving Picture World* reported that two people were injured when an auto-sleigh went through the ice during the filming of a chase sequence for Kalem's film *The Banker's Daughter*, which was shot in New Jersey; the article's headline was 'Realism for Kalem Films'.[148] At the same time, Marion realized that on-screen realism had to be tempered with censorship. In October 1912, he wrote to Sidney Olcott, instructing him to avoid scenes in upcoming films that depicted 'shooting, stealing, ill-using children, insanity, poisoning, or any criminal act or intent', as cutting such sequences after the initial edit 'destroys the film altogether'.[149]

By the time Marion wrote that letter, Olcott was back in America, having just completed six fictional films in Ireland on the El Kalem/O'Kalem trip. The two most successful seem to have been *The Shaughraun* (1912) and *The Kerry Gow* (1912). As a newspaper article in Eau Claire, Wisconsin, told readers when the former was released, 'Dion Boucicault's famous play [*The Shaughraun*] has been a favorite for a half century and will never lack an appreciative audience.'[150] *Moving Picture World* said much the same, suggesting 'there are few theatres in this country where *The Shaughraun* has not at some time or other had its inning'.[151] The decision to produce those two films had stemmed once again from a desire to combine the use of on-location shooting with stage plays already famous and respected by the broader American public.

The decision also came as a result of successful negotiations for the rights. On 29 March 1912, Frank J. Marion wrote to Sidney Olcott, who was at that time in Egypt:

> We have offered Mrs Boucicault $500 for the exclusive rights, both European and American, to 'Con the Shaugran [*sic*].' The copyrights are still effective both here and in Europe and we have got to pay for both. Mrs Boucicault has accepted our proposition as to America and she has cabled to the other side to get the necessary consent there. I believe that inside of a week, we will have this, the most celebrated Boucicault play, corked up tight for your use in Ireland.
>
> We have finally located Joe Murphy. He is spending the winter in St Petersburg. His brother, who is a jeweller on Maiden Lane, has the necessary power of attorney from him and we expect to buy the exclusive rights to *Kerry Gow* and *Shaun Rue* within a week. When these matters are finally arranged we will of course cable you, and you can then use your best judgment as to when you will do them.

In a subsequent letter, Marion told Olcott that screenwriter 'Emmett Campbell Hall writes that he thinks he has succeeded in making [i.e. writing] a two-reel production out of *Shaun Rue* although very little of the original plot is left. I think we will give it a different name with a sub-title based on Joe Murphy's famous Irish play *Shaun Rue*.'[152] Though it was subsequently announced in *Moving Picture World*, Kalem did not produce a film version of *Shaun Rhue*.[153]

As for those films produced on the O'Kalem's third trip to Ireland, which occurred during the summer of 1912, publicity materials again underscored their authenticity.[154] One advertisement in Reno, Nevada, called *The Shaughraun* 'a genuine Irish drama played amid genuine Irish surroundings amid picturesque Ireland'.[155] The *New York Dramatic Mirror* praised 'the scenes along the rugged Irish sea coast', which made 'a splendid background'.[156] *Moving Picture World* agreed, suggesting that 'plates were made for the ensuring of real interiors of Irish huts and cottages and from these plates the artist and director arranged the interior settings'. They applauded the film for using 'subtitles' that relied on the 'text of the play whenever possible', and they remarked that 'happily, Sidney Olcott is an Irishman', even though he was actually born in Canada.[157]

The press said much the same of *The Kerry Gow*.[158] A newspaper in Utah claimed that the 'popular play has been presented thousands of times throughout the United States and Canada ... every theatre patron is familiar with the story, making it unnecessary to give a synopsis'.[159] A review of the film in a Minnesota newspaper praised its 'unmistakable air of realism' and suggested that 'every real characteristic of the Irish soil and Irish heart' would result in a 'tremendous revival of *The Kerry Gow* all over the country'.[160] In addition, some advertisements promoted the settings which had so often been explored in non-fiction moving pictures and lantern slides; for example, one promised: 'You will see the Lakes of Killarney, the Gap of Dunloe, the picturesque highways of old Ireland, and many typical, humorous types.'[161]

The other four films resulting from the final trip made by the O'Kalems to Ireland were not based on famous stage plays or poems; instead, they were probably written by either Emmett Hall or Gene Gauntier. They included *The Mayor From Ireland* (1912), which echoed *The Lad from Old Ireland* (and, to a lesser extent, *Caught by Wireless*) in its story of a 'typical Irish man' who immigrates to America with his wife Bridget and, after an initial period of struggle, beats a rival and becomes a mayor.[162] The *New York Dramatic Mirror* praised its 'realism'.[163] *The Wives of Jamestown* (1913) also offered a story of immigration to America, but added the novelty of a sixteenth-century setting. An Irish peasant named Bryan O'Sullivan falls in love with Lady Geraldine, but flees to America and becomes a colonist in Jamestown after a fight with a nobleman. After her castle is later besieged, Lady Geraldine is sent to Jamestown with other women who are to become wives to the colonists. She and O'Sullivan reunite for a happy ending.[164]

*Lady Peggy's Escape* (1913) – which would become the last of the O'Kalem films to be released – also offered a sixteenth-century setting, thus allowing the company to reuse some costumes and props from *The Wives of Jamestown*.[165] In it, the title character escapes from British troops after they seize her castle. She kills a soldier in a duel and saves a desperate Irish family from the clutches of the military.[166] The film revealed the increasing

**5.13** A scene from *Far from Erin's Isle* (Kalem, 1912).

anti-British sentiment expressed in the O'Kalem films, which was also expressed in *Ireland the Oppressed* (1912), one of only two O'Kalem films that did not star Gene Gauntier (the other being *The Kerry Gow*). In it, an old man at a 'modern Irish harvest party' recounts the story of the British red-coats who arrest a priest who has been saving tenants from eviction.[167] A secret society of Irish peasants rescues the priest, who escapes to America, which is once again pictured as the land of hope. However, the military sentences a young woman who helped the priest to seven years in prison. For this film, Kalem's publicity attempted to mimic the Irish dialect, an effect that consti-tuted yet another attempt to seem 'genuine', even though some might have read it as an offensive caricature.[168]

The O'Kalem and El Kalem films had an impact on other film compa-nies. For example, when a theatre in Lowell, Massachussetts screened *The Mayor from Ireland*, which they heralded for being 'photographed partly in Ireland', they screened Edison's *The New Squire* (1912) on the same bill; they promoted the fact it had been 'photographed in England by the Edison company'.[169] More specifically, the commercial success of O'Kalem films probably encouraged other companies to shoot Irish-themed films, such as Rex, which released *Where the Shamrocks Grow* – 'A Great Irish Drama' – in 1911.[170] That same year, the Yankee Film Company produced four Irish-themed films. In addition to their aforementioned *Kathleen Mavourneen* (1911), *The Colleen Bawn* (1911) and *For the Wearing of the Green* (1911), Yankee also shot and released *Inshavogue* (1911), an adapt-ation of a nineteenth-century Irish-themed stage play. The title character 'struck terror to the hearts of the enemies of Ireland and was worshipped by Ireland's peasants'.[171] Though imprisoned by the British, he is eventually paroled through the influence of friends.

**5.14** A scene from *His Mother* (Kalem, 1912).

Various other compa-
nies released Irish-themed
films during this period as
well. Imp's *The Brothers*
(1911) offered a tale of two
lovers fighting over the
same woman in Ireland;
their battle causes one to
fall over a cliff, though the
story is revealed to be a
priest's dream.[172] That same
year, Rex released the
aforementioned *Where the
Shamrock Grows*, in which
a woman is kidnapped by a
villain, though the hero
'Danny' rescues her.[173]
*Buttercups* (Vitagraph,
1913) presented a story of
Irish children who meet
fairies that can make gold.[174] Both Lubin's *An Irish Girl's Love* (1912) and
Edison's *A Willful Colleen's Way* (1913) told tragic stories of lovers who
drown at sea.[175] Of the former, *Moving Picture World* complained that 'the
Irishness of it, in playing and costumes, is artificial'.[176] Lubin's *His Niece
from Ireland* (1913) and American's *The Crucible* (1914) offered more
stories of Irish characters immigrating to America, while Powers' *My
Mother's Irish Shawls* (1914) features two characters travelling to
Ireland.[177] The Downtown Amusement Company of New York promoted
their 'talkaphone' version of the *Trial of Robert Emmett* in 1913.[178] And
Kay-Bee's *The Rightful Heir* (1914) and Reliance's *The Smugglers of Sligo*
(1914) offered stories of smuggling in Ireland.[179]

Publicity for some of these films tried to draw attention to their authenticity. Victor's *Rory o'the Bogs* (1913) starred the Irish-American actor J.
Warren Kerrigan in an 'Irish romance of the 18th century', and Solax's
*Brennan of the Moor* (1913) starred Irish-American actor Barney Gilmore
in an adaptation of a 'classical Irish legend'.[180] Similarly, Kay-Bee claimed
its film *The Squire's Son* (1914) was a 'story of old Ireland'; *Moving Picture
World* believed otherwise, arguing that it had 'little real Irish spirit'.[181]

The O'Kalem films – as well as previous Irish-themed illustrated lectures
and lantern slides – also provided inspiration for J. Theobald Walsh's four-
reel film *The Life of St Patrick: From the Cradle to the Grave* (1912), which

was produced by the Photo Historic Film Company of New York. Ads heralded the fact that the film was shot in Ireland at 'the exact spots made memorable by Ireland's apostle'.[182] Other publicity claimed that 'more than eleven months were spent in making the production and more than 400 people were utilized in the groupings and all were Irish peasants'.[183] Reacting as much to the locations as to the story, *Moving Picture World* noted:

> The views of The Giant's Causeway, The Seven Churches, and the Lakes of Killarney shown in the course of these four reels deserve unstinted praise. The producers chose a number of Irish peasants without any artistic training, but full of the natural talents for pantomime, which is the heritage of every son and daughter of Erin. While we may miss the fine finish of other productions, there is a decided and charming novelty in the use of this unlettered, but not ungifted peasantry... In the main the essential facts of the life of Ireland's great patron saint have been filmed with a due regard for history. There is at least a good historical background, if not absolute historical accuracy.[184]

These aspects of the film – as well as the fact that it was written and directed by an 'Irishman' – caused the Photo Historic Company to publicize *The Life of St Patrick* as 'a genuine Irish picture'.[185] *Moving Picture World* did not disagree with that assessment, but they did warn exhibitors that the film was of a 'distinctly Roman Catholic nature'.[186] *Motion Picture News* countered that argument, saying, 'While it should and probably will please Catholics, it cannot offend or displease non-Catholics; on the contrary, it will interest all.'[187]

It is clear that the O'Kalem influence did not always extend to other Kalem Company films. In 1913, for example, Kalem produced two Irish-American comedies, the first of which was *Frayed Fagin's Adventures* (1913), starring Irish-American actor John E. Brennan as an Irish hobo who finds himself in antics none too different from *Dope Head Clancy* (1909); Brennan's whiskers, beard and receding hairline resembled the make-up worn by actors playing the stage Irish caricatures.[188] Shortly thereafter, Kalem produced *The Laundress and the Lady* (1913), in which Bridget the cook mistakes Mary Hall, her boss's sweetheart, for an Irish laundress named Mary Flannagan.[189] The 'tyrannical' Bridget has the sweetheart 'cowering' under her command when her boss arrives to find the mistake. Kalem cast John E. Brennan to play Bridget, thus recalling *How Bridget Made the Fire* (1900), in which a male actor in drag played the title character.

In an apparent effort to add credibility to these 'stage Irish' comedies, Kalem released them on split reels with non-fiction films. For example, *Frayed Fagin's Adventures* was paired with *Ulster Day in Belfast*, which was in fact shot in Ireland, presumably during the O'Kalem's third visit to the country. Similarly, Kalem paired *The Laundress and the Lady* with *The Dublin Horse Show*, which was also shot in Ireland, presumably during the same trip as *Ulster Day in Belfast*. However, in both cases Kalem gave top billing to the fictional comedies. Kalem then dispensed with such non-fiction pairings altogether by the time they released their comedy short *McBride's Bride* (1914), in which an Irish policeman ends up marrying his bride in a jail cell because of opposition from the bride's 'suffragette mother'.[190]

In 1913, the *Kalem Kalendar* claimed that 'never in the history of photoplays has a particular series attracted such worldwide attention and offered such universal entertainment as the Kalem Irish dramas'.[191] However, rather than purchase the rights to other Irish-themed stage plays or develop new Irish stories of their own, Kalem proceeded with a different strategy, perhaps because Gene Gauntier and Sidney Olcott resigned in late 1912. In addition to the stage Irish comedies, in May 1913 the *Kalem Kalendar* announced that the company had procured the rights to *The Octoroon*, another of Boucicault's plays.[192] By the following month, a syndicated newspaper column echoed the same news, claiming that 'The success of the Kalem company in producing Dion Boucicault's famous plays, *The Colleen Bawn*, *Arrah-na-Pogue*, and *The Shaughraun* led to the purchase of the exclusive motion picture rights to *The Octoroon*, thought by many to be the best work of this celebrated playwright.'[193] A subsequent Kalem advertisement for *The Octoroon* attempted to build enthusiasm amongst exhibitors in much the same way as they had with their other Boucicault adaptations. 'Millions of people have seen the stage version', Kalem claimed, so its 'tremendous popularity' assured the film version of 'Big Business'.[194] It was as if they attributed at least some of the success of the O'Kalem films to Dion Boucicault, rather than specifically to the Irish themes and locations of particular Boucicault plays.

## The O'Gees and the Sidfilms

Having departed from the Kalem Company, Gene Gauntier formed her own company in late 1912, the Gene Gauntier Feature Players; she would write and star in her own films, Sidney Olcott would manage the company and direct Gauntier's scenarios, and Warner's Features would distribute them.[195] The company also included Allen Farnham, the 'clever scenic artist

**5.15** A scene from *The O'Neill* (Kalem, 1912).

and stage manager who was responsible for all the Irish and Egyptian, Scotch and English stage settings which were always a feature of the Kalem's international productions'.[196] As Kalem moved away from Irish topics, Gauntier and Olcott immediately planned a return to them.[197] In December 1912, *Moving Picture World* announced that an 'arrangement has already been made to produce more pictures along the line of such as the extremely popular *The Lad from Old Ireland* and other Irish successes'.[198] On 14 August 1913, they sailed on the *Adriatic* to Ireland to produce a series of new films, though they 'feared that the season suitable for picture making will be short'.[199] Hearkening back to the 'O'Kalem' moniker, *Moving Picture World* announced that the 'Gee Gees' (as the Gene Gauntier Feature Players were called in the industry trade publications) had become the 'O'Gees'.[200]

Two three-reel moving pictures resulted from their trip. The first to be released was *For Ireland's Sake* (1914), which told the story of 'a young Irish patriot and his sweetheart Eileen (Gene Gauntier) who run afoul of the British soldiers and are imprisoned on a charge of high treason'.[201] In this case, Olcott wrote the story, which recalled *Rory O'More*. An 'explanatory title' at the beginning of the film announces: 'This entire production was produced in County Kerry, Ireland, amid the beautiful

**5.16** A scene from *'You Remember Ellen'* (Kalem, 1912).

Killarney district. The Gap of Dunloe, the Black Valley, Muckross Abbey, Sweet Innisfallen and the lakes are shown among many other pretty spots famed in song and story.' Echoing the intertitles in such films as *The Colleen Bawn*, the explanatory title drew attention to the authenticity of the locations seen in the film. *Motion Picture News* responded favourably to such scenery, noting the film's 'naturally perfect' use of 'atmosphere'. The publication also praised the use of such 'natural settings' as the 'ruins of the famous Muckross Abbey', a site that had earlier been pictured in non-fiction lantern slides of the nineteenth century.[202]

Gene Gauntier then wrote the second O'Gees release, *Come Back to Erin* (1914), which offered the 'adventures of Peggy in America'. *Moving Picture World* noted:

> Half of the scenes are staged in New York where the runaway 'Peggy' has come to seek work. Jerry's arrival in the great metropolis is the signal for some sensational action; true Irish hero that he is, he gets into the thick of the action himself, and, after subduing a New York crook, vindicates his 'Peggy' and takes her back to his humble Irish cot as his wife.[203]

In yet another echo of the O'Kalem films, Gauntier's story includes some narrative elements that had been explored in *Far From Erin's Isle*.

The O'Gees used Beaufort in County Kerry as a base of operations, just as the O'Kalems had. However, the emphasis on authentic locations did not extend to casting. Gene Gauntier and her husband Jack J. Clark assumed the lead roles in both films, with Olcott playing a priest in *For Ireland's Sake*. *Moving Picture World* noted that, upon arrival in Queenstown, Olcott, Gauntier and Clark intended to leave the crew and travel immediately to England in order to secure 'additional players' rather than hire them in Ireland.[204]

Though it is difficult to determine his reason, in January 1914 Sidney Olcott resigned from the Gene Gauntier Feature Players, forming his own production company, Sid Olcott International Features, often referred to as 'Sidfilms' in the film industry trade publications.[205] Within six months, Olcott engaged a new leading lady, Valentine Grant, and planned an elaborate series of films to be shot in England, Ireland, France, Germany and Italy.[206] F.C. Gunning resigned his position as assistant general manager of Warner's Features to become Olcott's assistant director.[207] During their ocean voyage in June 1914, Olcott shot footage of Grant in the role of an Irish woman immigrating to America.[208]

After their arrival in England on 19 June 1914, the Sidfilms cast and crew soon travelled to Beaufort, Olcott using it once again as a familiar base of operations.[209] The industry press claimed that Olcott filmed footage at the Lakes of Killarney and the Gap of Dunloe, and also said that he would shoot scenes in County Wicklow and in the city of Dublin.[210] In addition to Valentine Grant and various American actors, the films included 'a number of Irish players'.[211] Such work resulted in what *Moving Picture World* called 'real Irish features with genuine backgrounds'.[212] Interviewed by a film fan magazine, Valentine Grant later promoted other authentic aspects of the Irish-themed Sidfilms:

> Those are genuine Irish brogans in the Irish pictures, big and clumsy, and heavy as lead; but I wouldn't have had them a particle smaller or lighter, because they are the actual boots that these fisher-girls wear. The little shawl I bought in 'Paddy's Market' in Cork. The holes in the petticoat were worn by the knees of a scrub-woman who had worked in it for years.[213]

Such efforts at 'genuine' films could not occur in Germany, Italy or France. Due to the war, Olcott's plans to shoot elsewhere were scrapped; he told *Moving Picture World* that in England 'everything was in a turmoil', and that it was with the 'greatest difficulty' that the cast and crew secured passage

**5.17** A scene from *The Kerry Gow* (Kalem, 1912).

back to the United States, where they returned at the end of August 1914.[214] Olcott expressed a desire to return to Europe to shoot other films, though he believed that would only be possible if the 'war is ended quickly'.[215]

It would be nearly a year before any of the three Irish 'Sidfilms' would be released. In 1914, before the trip to Ireland, the industry press announced that Warner's Features would distribute Olcott's films; by July 1915, Lubin ran advertisements for their 'Made in Ireland' films starring Valentine Grant.[216] The delay in release was possibly tied to the overall change in distributors. At any rate, the *New York Dramatic Mirror* noted that the films were 'filmed along the rugged cliffs and broken shores of South Kerry, and amid the picturesque scenery of the Gap of Dunloe and the Lakes of Killarney'.[217] The industry press also underscored the fact that three of the players – Eddie O'Sullivan, Norah Hines and an actor known only as 'Sonny' – were Irish players engaged overseas.[218] While some extras and supporting players had appeared in various Olcott-directed Irish films, this marked the first time that any of the indigenous Irish actors were named.

The first of the trio to be released (in July 1915) was the three-reel 'comedy-drama' *All for Old Ireland*.[219] The film told a 'story of the days of '98, when all Ireland was preparing to resist the grasp that was about to close around it'.[220] In it, Eileen (Grant) and Myles (Olcott) are in love, but their happiness is disrupted when an informer who is in love with Eileen lies to the British army that Myles is plotting against the Crown. Thanks to help from Eileen, who secretly gives Myles a metal bar and rope, Myles

**5.18** A scene from
*The Mayor from Ireland*
(Kalem, 1912).

**5.19** A scene from
*Ireland the Oppressed*
(Kalem, 1912).

escapes from prison and flees to France, where Eileen and her mother will eventually join him.[221] *Motography* noted: 'In the production the scenic beauties and fine photography far outweigh the acting and the story.'[222]

One month later, in August 1915, Lubin released *Bold Emmett, Ireland's Martyr*.[223] Its title seems to have been changed shortly before its release, as one month earlier it had been advertised as *Robert Emmett, Ireland's Martyr*.[224] The change may well have been an attempt to distinguish it from previous films, such as Thanhouser's 1911 *Robert Emmet*. *Moving Picture World* referred to *Bold Emmett, Ireland's Martyr* as a 'comedy drama' that told the story of the 'stormy days when Robert Emmett tried vainly to free Ireland'. Reviewing the film, the trade noted the 'scenic environment' was 'beautiful beyond description'.[225] *Motography* added that 'the beautiful scenery, one of Ireland's many assets, is artistically shown'.[226] Lubin's opening titles underscored the location shoot, claiming the film was 'Written and produced for the Lubin Manufacturing Company by Sidney Olcott amid the beautiful hills and dales and rugged shores of Ireland.' The information was only partially correct; Olcott had certainly not written and produced any of the three films for Lubin, as the company was involved only in their release, not their production.

*The Irish in America*, the third Sidfilms Irish-themed release through Lubin, came in September 1915; similar to the others, publicity materials claimed the film was a 'comedy drama'.[227] Its storyline, which was written by Olcott, echoed the narratives of many illustrated Irish songs of the nickelodeon period. Dan Murphy (Olcott) comes to America from Ireland, as he is too poor to marry his Irish sweetheart, Peggy O'Sullivan (Grant).

5.20  An advertisement published in the 11 March 1911 issue of the
*Moving Picture News*.

After he goes 'West' and 'strikes it rich', Peggy first travels 'the rocky road to Dublin' and then journeys across the Atlantic to marry her beloved Dan.[228] *Motion Picture News* declared it was the best of the Sidfilms releases.[229] *Motography* not only praised the scenic qualities of the film, but also its perceived ethnographic qualities, claiming that 'the every day existence of the Irish country folks, their homes, and their religion are carefully depicted in this picture'.[230] *Moving Picture World* also noted that Olcott had 'wisely' travelled to Ireland to obtain scenes of 'quiet beauty' and 'grandeur'. While the publication believed Grant's character was a 'real Irish type', they complained that Olcott's performance 'smacks a little of what has been called "the stage Irishman" '.[231] That became the first major occasion that the authenticity of an Olcott-directed Irish-themed moving picture had been challenged.

Olcott was not the only former O'Kalem member who continued to pursue Irish-themed storylines, however. Gene Gaunter also returned to the subject. Initially, her husband Jack J. Clark assumed Olcott's place as the manager of the Gene Gauntier Feature Players; however, by March 1915, Gauntier and Clark dissolved the company and signed contracts with Universal Studios.[232] The *Universal Weekly* declared that her first films for the company were 'being kept' as a 'profound secret', but that they would constitute 'something very big and important'.[233]

Those 'profound' secrets included five films that would be released in the summer of 1915: *The Woman Hater's Baby*, *The Mad Maid of the Forest*, *Gene of the Northland* and two Irish-themed stories. The first, *A Smuggler's Lass*, appeared in June 1915. It was a two-reel 'Irish sea coast drama' filmed not in Ireland, but in California. In it, Sheila (Gauntier) and Bryan (Clark) are sweethearts in Ireland, but their life is disrupted when Bryan is imprisoned for smuggling. Sheila then gives Brian a loaf of bread, within which is secreted a rope ladder that he uses to escape his jail. Brian then flees to France. The film bears some similarities to *All for Old Ireland*, though the similarities are probably coincidental; *The Smuggler's Lass* was shot after *All for Old Ireland*, but was released shortly before it.

Universal's publicity attempted to offset the fact that *The Smuggler's Lass* was not shot in Ireland by promoting the fact that the studio had carefully built the castle seen in the film to be an 'exact reproduction of a centuries old fortress fronting on the Irish sea not a hundred miles from Belfast'. The crew used a photograph that Gauntier had taken during one of the O'Kalem trips as a template.[234] The studio also publicized the jump from a forty-foot cliff into the sea that the character Sheila makes; Gauntier performed the stunt herself, something that Universal claimed added to the film's realism.[235]

In July 1915, Universal released what seems to have been Gauntier's final Irish-themed film, a two-reel moving picture entitled *The Ulster Lass*. Its storyline, which drew upon various earlier Irish-themed films, features two sweethearts, Teddy O'Neill (Clark) and Eileen Sullivan (Gauntier), whose romance is interrupted when Teddy is falsely accused of treason. After being arrested, escaping from prison and then being arrested again, Teddy is finally cleared of murder and reunites with Eileen. As with *A Smuggler's Lass*, *The Ulster Lass* was apparently set in the north of Ireland, which may have been a conscious attempt to differentiate these films from those Olcott had shot in County Kerry in 1914 or that Olcott and Gauntier had filmed together.[236]

*The Ulster Lass* bore another similarity to *The Smuggler's Lass* in that it was shot in California, rather than Ireland. However, *Moving Picture World* noted the fact that 'An entire village of thatched roof cottages was constructed, Irish jaunting cars were specially built, and domestic animals galore figure in the ensemble scenes.'[237] Noting the accurate appearance of the setting, the trade added: 'Irish colleens and husky lads of Ould Erin jig away the dull moments while the town fiddler discourses lively music.' These 'colleens' and 'lads' would have been extras and supporting players in southern California. However, Gauntier was hardly the first to appear in a film that was set in Ireland, but that was shot in America.

# Raymond B. West and the Domino Film Company

Outside of the post-Kalem Irish-themed films made by Sidney Olcott and/or Gene Gauntier, the O'Kalems major influence was on the Domino Film Company, which formed in 1913 due in large part to financial capital supplied by the New York Motion Picture Corporation.[238] From 1913 until some point in 1915, the Mutual Film Corporation distributed Domino's films, including their series of Irish-themed moving pictures directed by Raymond B. West.

Aside from Sidney Olcott, West was the most prolific and important director of Irish-themed fictional films in the early cinema period. Born in Chicago, West spent the early part of his career as a corporate attorney in Detroit. However, he soon left for Los Angeles, where he was hired as an assistant director at the 101 Bison Company.[239] His career successes came in part due to his affiliation with Thomas Ince. By 1914, *Moving Picture World* referred to West as 'one of the best directors in the business'.[240]

Before going to work for Domino, West directed the two-reel film *The Banshee* (1913) at Kay-Bee, another company in which the New York Motion Picture Corporation owned a controlling interest. Set in Ireland and starring J. Barney Sherry and Anna Little, the film told the story of Dan O'Farrell, a drunk who murders his landlord and his wife, only to hear the sound of the banshee. Dan then wakes up to learn he has experienced a nightmare; as a result, he declares he will never drink again.[241] Kay-Bee promoted the alleged accuracy of the film's costumes, perhaps because they could not truthfully say the film had been shot in Ireland.[242] Nonetheless, *Moving Picture World* claimed it had 'an Irish setting so realistic as to make the observer think he is in the Emerald Isle'.[243]

Only two weeks after Kay-Bee issued *The Banshee*, they released West's two-reel film *Flotsam* (1915). The *Hamilton Evening Journal* of Hamilton, Ohio, noted that the 'strangely titled' film chronicled 'life among the Irish fisher folk'.[244] According to *Moving Picture World*, the film's plot features a sea captain who rescues a teenager whose ship sinks in a terrible storm. The captain cares for her, and after five years the two marry. However, the young lady is actually in love with an artist. As a result, she struggles between 'love and duty'.[245] In a subsequent issue, the same trade publication reviewed the film, noting that the 'scenes are laid in Ireland, probably, and the release is one of about average merit'.[246]

At some point during the summer of 1913, West became a director at Domino, which rapidly put several Irish-themed stories into production. The first to be released (on 16 October 1913) was *A Romance of Erin*. In it, two lovers in Ireland marry, though a jealous suitor whom the wife had

**5.21** The *Universal Weekly*, Universal's house organ, publicizes *Rory O' the Bogs* (Victor, 1913, aka *Rory of the Bogs*).

earlier spurned frames the husband; following a trial, the suitor admits his guilt and the young couple are reunited.[247] While the *New York Dramatic Mirror* complained that the story was 'old and time-worn', *Moving Picture World* praised the handling of a dream sequence and the 'scenic' aspects of the story.[248] Directed by Reginald Barker and written by William H.

**5.22** The Gene Gauntier Players (the 'O'Gees') travelling to Ireland aboard the *S. S. Adriatic* in 1913.

**5.23** A scene from *For Ireland's Sake* (Gene Gauntier Feature Players, 1914).

Clifford, *A Romance of Erin* would be Domino's only Irish-themed film release that was not directed by West.

One week later, on 23 October 1913, Domino (through Mutual) released West's *The Heart of Kathleen*. Its plot, written by Richard V. Spencer, offered a tragedy of Kathleen, who – following the death of her father – forsakes her lover Denis for a 'stranger' from England; the stranger eventually leaves her a 'ruined' woman, whom Denis finds dead on the beach.[249] *Motography* claimed that West's first Irish-themed film for the company was 'a wonderful story of old Ireland, replete with stirring effects, sweet love scenes, and real atmosphere. A storm at sea is one of the sensational, scenic and photographic marvels of the film, and the impressive effect is said to be awe-inspiring in its grandeur and majesty.'[250] Publicity for the film claimed it had 'beautiful Irish settings' and 'vivid Irish types', though the film was shot entirely in America.[251] *Motography* added that the 'three reel feature was cut down from seven reels', a suggestion that its content was culled from an extensive shoot.[252] That hardly impressed *Moving Picture World*, which – while praising the acting of Dorothy Davenport, as well as the costumes and scenic shots – believed the story featured 'hackneyed' dialogue and 'moth-eaten' dramatic situations.[253]

*Widow Maloney's Faith*, the third Irish-themed Domino film, appeared in theatres at the end of the same month; its story, in which a young sailor exacts revenge on an enemy and reunites with his mother and sweetheart, bore some similarities to *Caught by Wireless* and *The Lad from Old Ireland*.[254] Raymond B. West directed, as he would do for every subsequent Irish-themed film that Domino produced. *Motion Picture News* noted that 'the picture seems true to life'.[255] It is difficult to know how financially successful this film or its Domino predecessors were, but they probably did quite well; Domino quickly placed six more Irish-themed fictional films into production, all of which were released during December 1913 and January 1914. One newspaper advertisement referred to them as a 'series of Irish pictures'.[256] As before, West shot his tales of Ireland using American locations and sets, though some advertisements explicitly claimed they were filmed in Ireland.[257] Other publicity would hint at 'striking scenes' that – in tandem with mention of their Irish setting – implied that they were filmed in Ireland.[258]

*The Filly* (1913), which was the first to be released, offered a tale written by William H. Clifford in which two sweethearts unite despite resistance from the young heroine's father.[259] *Motion Picture News* praised actor Richard Stanton's 'Irish impersonations', and the *New York Dramatic Mirror* announced actress Anna Little was 'indeed a beautiful specimen of the rollicking Irish girl'.[260] While referring to it as a 'dashing Irish story',

*Moving Picture World* – which lauded *The Filly* for being 'a lively picture throughout' – underscored the fact that it was 'a racing story of the old-time sort'.[261]

Approaching the Irish theme in a different way, William H. Clifford also wrote *The Ghost* (1913). Eschewing action and romance, the film offered the story of Tim O'Grath, who spends all of his money on alcohol rather than pay his landlord. Going to sleep, he 'enters the land where things are not what they seem and phantoms lurk within whiskey dreams'.[262] His dreams become nightmares, however. St Patrick appears to him, claiming he must disavow drinking or forever 'roam the earth in spirit'. Then Tim witnesses his friends discussing his death and even sees his body prepared for burial. Upon wakening, Tim takes the pledge to drink no more. As a result, the film was essentially a retelling of *The Banshee* (1913).

By contrast, the other Domino films – *Eileen of Erin* (1913, written by Richard V. Spencer), *True Irish Hearts* (1914), *The Harp of Tara* (1914, written by William H. Clifford) and *The Informer* (1914, written by Richard V. Spencer) – combined stories of romance with tales of the Irish struggle against England.[263] At the same time, each featured distinctive narrative devices. For example, *The Informer* featured an unhappy ending in which the hero was hanged, and *The Harp of Tara* included the legend of a harp which, if found by the right man, would bring freedom to Ireland. The publicity for these films attempted to highlight their unique qualities. For example, one newspaper description of *True Irish Hearts* promised: 'The story is different from all other Irish stories.'[264]

However, reviews of the films suggested otherwise. Speaking of *Eileen of Erin*, *Moving Picture World* praised the film, but noted that 'the situations resemble those of previous offerings along this line'.[265] They wrote that *The Informer* was 'another tale of the Irish rebellion, with several of the familiar devices for catching the interest'.[266] Their comment on *True Irish Hearts* was much the same, claiming that the 'drama drops readily into the category of Irish plays and pictures from time immemorial...First class Irish drama of the conventional type.'[267] One newspaper advertisement for *The Harp of Tara* was even more succinct, simply announcing 'Another Irish drama'.[268]

Some trade publications did draw distinctions between these films in terms of perceived quality. Both *Motion Picture News* and the *New York Dramatic Mirror* complained of the anachronistic use of a match to start a fire in *The Harp of Tara*; *Moving Picture World* also believed the 'situations' near the conclusion of the film were 'weak'.[269] *Motion Picture News* noted that *The Informer* was 'not so clever' as other Domino Irish-themed films, a view shared by *Moving Picture World*, which claimed it was 'not

**5.24** A scene from Raymond B. West's film *The Banshee* (Kay-Bee, 1913).

quite up to former standards'.[270] Similarly, *Moving Picture World* suggested that the storyline of *The Ghost* was 'not very new'.[271]

At the same time, trade publications heralded aspects of these films that they viewed as authentic. *Moving Picture World* and *Motion Picture News* praised the 'fight scenes' in *The Harp of Tara* and *Eileen of Erin*.[272] Of *True Irish Hearts*, *Motion Picture News* was even more favourable, claiming:

> Anna Little, Richard Stanton, and Thomas Chatterton have obtained a most enviable reputation for their work in Irish parts [in Domino films]. In a number of pictures which this company has issued featuring these persons, there has not been one failure. The keynote of their success seems to be an ability to get atmosphere. Clever acting and good costuming contain the secret of this desirable result.[273]

Similarly, the *New York Dramatic Mirror* praised *Eileen of Erin* for its 'delightfully realistic Irish atmosphere'.[274]

# DOMINOES are TRUMPS

A Beautifully Told Story of Ireland's Fight for Liberty in Which a Lad's Love for a Colleen Is Interwoven.

War Scenes in Which the Shellalah and Blackthorn Stick Overcome the Musket and Sword.

# The Heart of Kathleen

**THREE REELS**

**Released Thursday, Oct. 23d**

Thos. Ince, managing director of the Domino Films, says that outside of the Battle of Gettysburg this is the best picture he has ever directed.

# New York Motion Picture Corporation

*MUTUAL PROGRAM EXCLUSIVELY*

**42d Street and Broadway** **(Longacre Building)** **NEW YORK CITY**

**5.25** Advertisement published in the 25 October 1913 issue of the *Moving Picture World*. Despite the ad's claim, Raymond B. West directed *The Heart of Kathleen*.
*(Courtesy of the Free Library of Philadelphia)*

The final Irish-themed story that West directed for Domino was the two-reel film *For the Wearing of the Green*, which was released in early March 1914, presumably timed for St Patrick's Day screenings. Once again, West constructed a film out of the Irish struggle against England, though in this case – according to the plot synopses prepared by Domino – the love story component was less pronounced than that of an Irish rebel betraying his friends.[275]

Domino's choice to shoot these films in America probably resulted from financial considerations. Rather than put together a company of cast and crew members to become the 'O'Dominos', they had Raymond B. West direct these films on American soil. West's films proved that – in a post-O'Kalem period – it was possible to make moving pictures about Ireland without shooting on location. No charges against the verisimilitude of their setting appeared in the film industry trade press, which – in addition to their apparent financial success – suggests West had done with the moving picture what others had done with the illustrated song slide: (re)create Ireland in America.

## Walter MacNamara and *Ireland a Nation*

Aside from the work of Olcott and Gauntier, the key American fictional film of the early cinema period to be shot on location in Ireland was Walter MacNamara's *Ireland a Nation* (1914).[276] Born in Ireland, MacNamara immigrated to America in 1911; by the following year, he was writing scripts for film companies. *Motography* claimed that twenty-nine of his stories had been produced within a two-year period.[277] The most famous was *Traffic in Souls* (1913), in which he also appeared in a small role.[278] In November 1913, *Moving Picture World* noted that Universal had signed MacNamara and mentioned that he had 'practically created' the successful 'Binks' comedy series, and that he had also written 'King Baggott successes and most of the later successes of Miss Jane Gail'.[279] At Universal, MacNamara forged a career as the director of such films as *Who Killed Olga Carew?* (1913) and *His Hour of Triumph* (1913).[280]

By February 1914, MacNamara formed the MacNamara Feature Film Company, which was incorporated with $100,000. His intention was to produce 'six and seven reel' films, the first of which would be shot in Ireland over a three-week period.[281] He and his crew arrived in London on 22 February 1914, and then travelled to Ireland approximately two weeks later.[282] Their intention was to film *Ireland a Nation*, a feature that MacNamara had written and would also produce and direct.

Rather than a three-week shoot, MacNamara later claimed to have spent five months in Ireland; the latter part of his trip overlapping with the 'Sidfilms' shoot in County Kerry.[283] Given that he did not travel from America with actors, MacNamara cast Irish talent in all of the lead and supporting roles, something that later factored into the film's publicity.[284] That necessitated shooting at least some of the interior scenes in Ireland as well, for which MacNamara used a greenhouse as a studio; he would later claim that interior sets 'faithfully followed old prints [of Irish homes]'.[285] However, MacNamara's greatest problems came while shooting exteriors. He recalled that soldiers 'would come from everywhere and demand to see a permit', thus interrupting numerous scenes. MacNamara later even claimed to have been arrested during the trip for 'importing arms' that were in fact century-old props.[286]

The review in *Motion Picture News* repeated comments that had been made about previous Irish-themed films, claiming: 'Although the value of the picture lies in its historical teachings, it is a worthy scenic besides. It is photographed well throughout; some pretty views have been caught. It was made in Ireland of course and the principals and extras are all Irish.'[287] The *New York Times* noted these same qualities, suggesting 'there is no end of Irish flavor to the whole performance'.[288] By contrast, *Variety* claimed the film was 'not too well produced, and the acting cast, numbering sixteen, discloses but one capable actor in the person of Barney Magee. Barry O'Brien, while looking the part, fails to make the big scenes convincing.'[289] Such a comment separated the nationality of the actor and any authenticity it might possess from his acting talent, which allegedly detracted from the film's ability to be 'convincing'.

At any rate, *Ireland a Nation* became the first Irish-themed feature film produced by an American company, at least by definitions that suggest a feature film was five or more reels in length. The *New York Times* claimed:

> The story begins with the passing of Ireland's House of Parliament and the news is carried over hills and dales and to the dancers on the cross roads and to Father Tom Murphy, who has a price on his head. All swear to break the yoke which binds them to England.
>
> The next three reels are devoted pretty much to the life story of Robert Emmet and his death on the scaffold, but the last reel brings the patriots up to the passing of the Home Rule bill, and then Erin prints Robert Emmet's epitaph because Ireland has once again taken her place among the nations of the earth.[290]

**5.26** Advertisement published in the 30 January 1915 issue of the *Moving Picture World*.

*Moving Picture World* gave their own account of the film's narrative content, which suggested the final reel 'takes up Daniel O'Connell and the fatal duel he fought with D'Esterre. Next the famine and the Emigration period, and finally the passage of the Home Rule bill this year.'[291]

However, it is difficult to determine if the sprawling story of *Ireland a Nation* actually spanned five projected reels when it was first released in 1914. Various reviews speak of non-fiction actualities being screened at the beginning of each performance. *Motion Picture News* referred to an 'introductory reel' that was shown before the 'picture proper' started; *Variety* even praised the 'reel of Irish views preceding the picture' more than *Ireland a Nation*.[292] The *Chicago Tribune* said much the same, noting: 'A whole reel of Irish scenery introduces the story proper. It is beautifully photographed and the objects and pictorial display are excellently chosen for illustrative purposes to get one into the midst of things visually. And then the picture follows on, set about the same places, the same quaint cottages, the same wonderful cathedrals.'[293] Repeated mention of these images suggests the possibility that all or part of the first of the five reels may have been a non-fiction pictorial prologue to *Ireland a Nation*. In any event, newspapers echoed trade publications in emphasizing the scenic qualities of *Ireland a Nation*. One newspaper article spoke about the 'most excellent photography in the scenes in County Wicklow, in Ballingglass [sic], and the Killarney lake region'.[294]

At the conclusion of *Ireland a Nation*, the scene depicting the passage of the Home Rule bill incorporated some non-fiction footage, which meant that – given the non-fiction prologue – the film opened and concluded with non-fiction images in an apparent attempt to heighten the authenticity of the dramatized narrative sequences that came between them. However, footage of the Home Rule bill – as well as much of the film's re-enactments – also served a propaganda purpose. The film supported Irish nationalism and decried British involvement in the country. Earlier films had made similar arguments, but *Ireland a Nation*'s narrative and running time drew greater attention to them.

Following the release of *Ireland a Nation*, MacNamara returned to Universal, then moved onto Mirror Films, and then to Keystone; all of these career shifts happened between 1915 and 1917.[295] The MacNamara Feature Film Company folded, and at some point during either 1915 or 1916 MacNarama sold the rights to *Ireland a Nation*. The film changed significantly. It is difficult to know how much re-editing occurred, although later reviews claimed that it was seven reels, rather than the five it had been three years earlier.[296] The first major Irish-themed feature film had grown in length, though it was still narratively, thematically and cinematographically tied to the early cinema period.

# Conclusion

Writing about Biograph's 1914 film *The Fleur-De-Lis Ring*, *Moving Picture World* told readers that it 'reminded one of the old fashioned Irish or English dramas'.[297] By that time, after some eight years in the cinema and many decades of pre-cinema forerunners, the Irish-themed melodrama had become an understood type of film that operated with recognizable codes and conventions. It was also a category that remained vibrant until the end of the early cinema period. For example, Edison's *A Sprig of Shamrock* (1915) offered a story of Irish immigration to America in which a shamrock reunites a wife with her husband.[298] Gold Seal produced *The Duchess* (1915), which starred Cleo Madison in a 'rollicking devil-may-care drama of modern Irish life'. The *Universal Weekly* heralded the fact that a 'village consisting of eight field-stone cottages with thatched roofs' had been built specifically for the film, which appeared authentic even to the 'minutest particulars'.[299] The same company also produced *A Wild Irish Rose* (1915, also starring Cleo Madison), which presented yet another Irish love story, though *Moving Picture World* promised it was 'somewhat different from the usual Irish type'.[300] The *New York Dramatic Mirror* praised the film's sets, some of which were probably reused from *The Duchess*.[301] Those films were in addition to a 1915 American release of the British-made *It's A Long, Long Way to Tipperary* (1914), which was promoted for its use of Irish actors and Irish scenery. The *New York Dramatic Mirror* noted that 'the cast is wholly Celtic' and the 'surroundings ring true'.[302]

While it bore some distinctive characteristics, the Irish-themed moving picture melodrama functioned as a component of the broader category of American melodrama, and as a result borrowed its narrative and cinematic traditions. Indeed, the majority of the people writing, directing, producing and starring in Irish-themed melodramas worked on non-Irish themed melodramas during their careers, including Edwin S. Porter, D.W. Griffith, Sidney Olcott, Gene Gauntier, Raymond B. West, Walter MacNamara and many others. Their Irish-themed films made repeated efforts to be viewed as 'genuine'. That meant filming on location in Ireland or filming at American locations, as well as casting actors who were either Irish or were associated with Irish roles. Film-makers also relied upon various other methods to instil a sense of authenticity, including the use of pre-existing narrative source material, such as non-fiction historical tales. This relentless drive towards the 'genuine' was not unique to Irish-themed films, but was a goal that pervaded much of early American cinema.

# Notes

1. C. Musser, 'The Nickelodeon Era Begins: Establishing the Framework for Hollywood's Mode of Representation', *Framework*, 22/23 (Fall 1983), pp.4–11.
2. T. Gunning, 'The Cinema of Attractions: Early Film, Its Spectator, and the Avant-Garde', in T. Elsaesser and A. Barker (eds), *Early Cinema: Space, Frame, Narrative* (London: British Film Institute, 1990), pp.56–62, at p.60.
3. C. Keil, *Early American Cinema in Transition: Story, Style, and Film-making, 1907–1913* (Madison, WI: University of Wisconsin, 2001), p.35.
4. C.H. Claudy, 'It "Went Over" ', *Moving Picture World*, 4 February 1911, pp.231–2. The same publication printed various articles on the subject of 'realism' in the cinema. See, for example, W.S. Bush, 'Dealers and Brokers in Moving Picture Realism', *Moving Picture World*, 23 September 1911, p.868; 'Pictures and Stage Realism', *Moving Picture World*, 1 February 1913, p.477.
5. Keil, *Early American Cinema*, p.53.
6. *No. 79, The Irish Blacksmith* (Chicago, IL: Selig Polyscope Company, January 1908) [n.p.]. Available in *A Guide to Motion Picture Catalogs by American Producers and Distributors, 1894–1908: A Microfilm Edition* (New Brunswick, NJ: Rutgers University Press, 1985), Reel 2. See also 'The Irish Blacksmith', *Views and Film Index*, 25 January 1908, p.11, which offers a synopsis of the film. The very same synopsis appears in 'The Irish Blacksmith', *Moving Picture World*, 25 January 1908, pp.63–4.
7. '*Come Back to Erin*', *Moving Picture World*, 11 March 1911, p.549.
8. 'Youthful Singer Scores Big Hit', *Waterloo Reporter* (Waterloo, IA), 17 March 1913, p.5.
9. '*Irish Hearts*', *Moving Picture World*, 21 January 1911, p.153. (The following year, Bainbridge appeared as Mrs O'Brien in *Shamus O'Brien*.)
10. '*Wilful Peggy*', *Moving Picture World*, 27 August 1910, p.475. A copy of *Wilful Peggy* appears on *D.W. Griffith – Director*, Volume 6, DVD (Phoenix, AZ: Grapevine Video, 2009).
11. R. Abel, *The Red Rooster Scare: Making Cinema American, 1900–1910* (Berkeley, CA: University of California Press, 1999).
12. C. Musser, *Before the Nickelodeon: Edwin S. Porter and the Edison Manufacturing Company* (Berkeley, CA: University of California Press, 1991), p.364.
13. For example, revivals of the stage play *Kathleen Mavourneen* occurred in 1905 in Chicago, Illinois ('Amusements', *Suburbanite Economist* (Chicago, IL), 10 March 1905, p.8), Logansport, Indiana ('Local Talent to Try Out', 30 June 1905, *Logansport Pharos*, p.8) and Anaconda, Montana ('At the Empire Theatre', *Anaconda Standard*, 30 December 1905, p.4).
14. A copy of *Kathleen Mavourneen* appears on *Edison: The Invention of the Movies*, DVD (New York: Kino International, 2005).
15. Musser, *Before the Nickelodeon*, p.364.
16. T. Elsaesser, 'Introduction: Once More: Narrative', in Elsaesser and Barker (eds), *Early Cinema*, pp.150–60, at p.153.
17. Advertisement, *New York Clipper*, 2 March 1907, p.65.
18. 'The Bell', *Oakland Tribune*, 9 October 1906, p.4.
19. Advertisement, *Billboard*, 25 August 1906, p.38.
20. '*Kathleen Mavourneen*', *Views and Film Index*, 8 September 1906, p.9.
21. 'Moving Pictures', *Billboard*, 13 October 1906, p.25.
22. This is, in fact, Musser's interpretation. See C. Musser, *The Emergence of Cinema: The American Screen to 1907* (Berkeley, CA: University of California Press), p.460.
23. Advertisement, *New York Clipper*, 25 August 1906, p.712.
24. 'Edison Manufacturing Co.', *Optical Lantern and Kinematograph Journal* (January 1907), p.68.
25. 'Good Bill at Crystal This Week', *Logansport Journal* (Logansport, IN), 28 October 1906, p.3.
26. 'Amusements', *Salt Lake Tribune* (Salt Lake City, UT), 13 November 1906, p.10.
27. '*Kathleen Mavourneen*', *Moving Picture News*, 29 July 1911, p.18; '*Kathleen Mavourneen*', *Moving Picture World*, 5 August 1911, p.312.
28. '*Sogarth Aroon*', *Moving Picture World*, 16 March 1912, p.1004.
29. '*Sogarth Aroon*', *New York Dramatic Mirror*, 20 March 1912, p.33.
30. '*Sogarth Aroon*', *Moving Picture News*, 2 March 1912, p.45.
31. '*Sogarth Aroon*', *New York Dramatic Mirror*, p.33.

32. 'Princess Theatre', *San Antonio Light* (San Antonio, TX), 23 March 1913, p.34.

33. G. Blaisdell, '*Kathleen Mavourneen* (Imp)', *Moving Picture World*, 8 March 1913, p.978.

34. The cover of the 1 April 1913 issue of *The Edison Kinetogram* features a photograph of *Kathleen Mavourneen* (1913), as well as a caption that mentions its pending 19 April 1913 release date. See also '*Kathleen Mavourneen*', *Moving Picture World*, 29 March 1913, p.1240, 1336.

35. Advertisement, *Hamilton Evening Journal* (Hamilton, OH), 18 March 1913, p.8.

36. 'Oakland Photo', *Oakland Tribune* (Oakland, CA), 27 March 1913, p.7.

37. '*Kathleen, the Irish Rose*', *Moving Picture World*, 14 March 1914, p.1132; '*Kathleen, the Irish Rose*', *Motion Picture News*, 14 March 1914, p.48. (The *Moving Picture World* synopsis clearly indicates that the title character is 'Kathleen Mavourneen'.)

38. '*Kathleen, the Irish Rose*', *Moving Picture World*, 21 March, 1914, p.1526.

39. Musser, *Emergence of Cinema*, p.460.

40. '*The Shaughraun*', *Views and Film Index*, 11 January 1908, p.9; '*The Shaughraun*', *Moving Picture World*, 18 January 1908, p.50.

41. '*An Irish Hero*', *Moving Picture World*, 13 February 1909, p.181; '*An Irish Hero*', *New York Dramatic Mirror*, 20 February 1909, p.16.

42. Advertisement, *Daily Advocate* (Victoria, TX), 1 June 1909, p.3.

43. A copy of *An Irish Hero* exists at the Library of Congress in Washington, DC.

44. *Supplement No. 122, A Daughter of Erin* (Chicago, IL: Selig Polyscope Company, Inc., 1 October 1908) [n.p.]. Available in *Guide to Motion Picture Catalogs ... 1894–1908: Microfilm Edition*, Reel 2.

45. 'The Latest Films', *Views and Film Index*, 10 October 1908, p.10; '*A Daughter of Erin*', *Moving Picture World*, 3 October 1908, pp.265–6.

46. '*Colleen Bawn*', *Moving Picture News*, 5 August 1911, p.289.

47. Ibid., p.15.

48. V. Randolph (ed.), *Ozark Folksongs: Volume 4, Religious Songs and Other Items* (Columbia, MO: University of Missouri Press, 1980), p.259.

49. '*Shamus O'Brien* Good', *New York Times*, 6 January 1897, p.5.

50. '*Shamus O'Brien*', *Moving Picture World*, 21 March 1908, p.246.

51. See, for example, advertisement, *Anaconda Standard* (Anaconda, MT), 17 March 1908, p.6.

52. A copy of *Shamus O'Brien* exists at the Library of Congress in Washington, DC.

53. Advertisement, *Moving Picture World*, 16 March 1912, p.924.

54. '*Shamus O'Brien*', *Moving Picture World*, 9 March 1912, pp.878–9. See also '*Shamus O'Brien*' *Moving Picture News*, 2 March 1912, p.42; '*Shamus O'Brien*', *Moving Picture World*, 9 March 1912, p.896; '*Shamus O'Brien*', *Billboard*, 9 March 1912, p.30; '*Shamus O'Brien*', *Billboard*, 16 March 1912, p.15.

55. '*Shamus O'Brien*', *New York Dramatic Mirror*, 20 March 1912, p.33.

56. '*A Brave Irish Lass*', *New York Dramatic Mirror*, 27 March 1909, p.13; '*A Brave Irish Lass: The Story of an Eviction*', *Moving Picture World*, 10 April 1909, p.455.

57. '*Peg Woffington*', *New York Dramatic Mirror*, 6 August 1910, p.26.

58. 'Manufacturers Synopses of Films', *Moving Picture News*, 4 March 1911, p.16.

59. '*Robert Emmet*', *Moving Picture World*, 18 March 1911, p.608; '*Robert Emmet*', *Moving Picture World*, 1 April 1911, p.720.

60. Walton, 'Seen on the Curtain', *Moving Picture News*, 25 March 1911, p.13.

61. '*Irish Hearts*', p.152.

62. '*For the Wearing of the Green*', *Moving Picture World*, 13 April 1912, p.133. (See also '*For the Wearing of the Green*', *Moving Picture World*, 23 September 1911, p.914.)

63. '*For the Wearing of the Green*', *Moving Picture World*, 13 April 1912, p.133.

64. '*For the Wearing of the Green*', *Moving Picture News*, 16 September 1911, p.29.

65. '*The Gambler and the Devil*', *Moving Picture World*, 3 October 1908, p.267.

66. '*The Leprechawn*', *Moving Picture World*, 26 September 1908, p.241.

67. '*The Leprechawn*', *Moving Picture World*, 10 October 1908, p.279.

68. '*The Leprechawn*', *New York Dramatic Mirror*, 3 October 1908, p.8.

69. E. Bowser (ed.), *Biograph Bulletins, 1908–1912* (New York: Octagon Books, 1973), p.224.

70. Advertisement, *Moving Picture World*, 27 August 1910, p.474.

71. '*Wilful Peggy*', *Moving Picture World*, 27 August 1910, p.475.

72. A copy of *Caught by Wireless* appears on *D.W. Griffith as an Actor*, DVD (Phoenix, AZ: Grapevine Video, 2008).
73. 'Caught by Wireless', *Moving Picture World*, 21 March 1908, p.241.
74. Ibid.
75. Advertisement, *Moving Picture World*, 19 March 1910, p.440.
76. 'The Irish Boy', *Moving Picture World*, 2 April 1910, p.508.
77. Advertisement, *Moving Picture World*, 19 March 1910, p.440.
78. 'Wild Pat', *Vitagraph Bulletin*, 1–30 November 1912, p.43.
79. 'Wild Pat', *Moving Picture World*, 16 November 1912, p.692; 'Wild Pat', *Moving Picture World*, 7 December 1912, p.975.
80. 'The Molly Maguires, or, Labor Wars in the Coal Mines', *Moving Picture World*, 19 December 1908, p.485; 'Kalem Co.', *The Film Index*, 19 December 1908, p.9.
81. 'The Molly Maguires', *Moving Picture World*, 12 December 1908, p.485.
82. 'Kalem Company (Inc.)', *Moving Picture World*, 8 June 1907, p.223.
83. 'Kalem's Achievements as Pioneer', *Moving Picture World*, 10 March 1917, pp.1504–5.
84. 'The Cliff Dwellers', *Moving Picture World*, 21 May 1910, p.830.
85. 'Real Irish-American Pictures', *The Film Index*, 5 November 1910, p.11.
86. 'The Lad from Old Ireland', *Kalem Kalendar*, 1 August 1914, p.2; 'The Lad from Old Ireland', *Moving Picture World*, 26 November 1910, p.1246. A copy of *The Lad from Old Ireland* exists at the Irish Film Archive in Dublin.
87. R. Altman, 'The Early History of Travel Films', in J. Ruoff (ed.), *Virtual Voyages: Cinema and Travel* (Durham, NC: Duke University Press, 2006), p.70.
88. 'Kalem's Achievements as Pioneer', p.1505.
89. 'American Photoplayers in Ireland', *The Film Index*, 29 October 1910, pp.1, 31.
90. 'The Irish Honeymoon', *Moving Picture World*, 25 March 1911, p.656.
91. G. Gauntier, 'Blazing the Trail', *Woman's Home Companion*, 55, 12 (December 1928), pp.15, 16, 132, 134.
92. 'Real Irish-American Pictures', p.11.
93. 'Excursion to the Spreewald', *The Film Index*, 17 December 1910, p.4.
94. Ibid., p.4.
95. Ibid., p.11.
96. 'The Lad from Old Ireland', *Moving Picture World*, 3 December 1910, p.1296.
97. 'The Lad from Old Ireland', *Kalem Kalendar*, 1 August 1914, p.2. See also 'Photoplay', *The Pointer* (Riverdale, IL), 30 December 1910, p.1; advertisement, *Daily Independent* (Monessen, PA), 30 November 1910, p.1.
98. Advertisement, *The Film Index*, 4 March 1911, p.21.
99. Certainly the film industry press suggested that it was the most successful. See, for example, 'Kalem Sends Stock Company to Ireland', *Moving Picture World*, 3 June 1911, p.1242.
100. 'Kalem's Achievements as Pioneer', p.1504.
101. Ibid.
102. 'More Irish Pictures', *The Film Index*, 18 March 1911, p.3.
103. Ibid.
104. *Kalem Co., Appt., v. Harper Brothers, Marc Klaw, Abraham Erlanger, and Henry L. Wallace*. 222 US 55. Argued 31 October and 1 November 1911. Decided 13 November, 1911. See also 'Blow to Moving Pictures', *New York Times*, 14 November 1911, p.13.
105. 'Forming the O'Kalem Company', *The Film Index*, 15 April 1911, p.31.
106. 'O'Kalem Players Organized', *The Film Index*, 13 May 1911, p.25.
107. 'Kalem Sends Stock Company to Ireland', p.1242.
108. 'Kalem Active', *The Film Index*, 3 June 1911, p.6.
109. 'The O'Kalems Combine Business with Pleasure', *Moving Picture World*, 1 July 1911, p.1506.
110. 'Answers to Inquiries', *Motion Picture Story Magazine* (September 1911), p.143.
111. 'O'Kalem's Return', *Moving Picture World*, 14 October 1911, p.136.
112. 'Answers to Inquiries', *Motion Picture Story Magazine* (January 1912), p.134. In *The Irish Filmography: Fiction Films 1896–1996* (Dublin: Red Mountain Media, 1996), Kevin Rockett includes Kalem's *The Magic Flower* (1910), which he claims 'is described as an Irish fairytale, though its Irish elements are unclear from contemporary written descriptions' (p.248). Based upon a

survey of all trade descriptions, and screening the film at the George Eastman House in Rochester, New York, I concur, to the extent that I would say the film is not at all Irish-themed. Indeed, the *New York Dramatic Mirror*, 29 January 1910, indicated that the film was 'the second of the new children's series of trick and fairy pictures to be issued by the Kalem Company' (p.16). Rockett's *Irish Filmography* also lists *Losing to Win* (1911). However, no primary source has yet surfaced to suggest that *Losing to Win* was shot in part or in whole in Ireland. Certainly no synopses or advertisements for the film promoted an Irish connection.

Also, Rockett, in *Irish Filmography* (p.260), lists the film *The Vagabonds*, which starred Gene Gauntier, Sidney Olcott, Jack J. Clark and Alice Hollister. The film told the story of a man who forsakes his sweetheart, Jane, for a woman travelling with a group of vagabonds, only to lose his money and then reconcile with Jane. Rockett suggests the film was 'almost certainly filmed in Ireland' and that it may be the same film pictured in *Moving Picture World* as '*The Beggar's Maid*' (6 July 1912, p.260). However, neither the *Kalem Kalendar* (12 January 1912, p.9) nor other trade publications nor newspaper advertisements for the film suggest that its story is set in Ireland or that the film was shot in Ireland. Furthermore, the photograph in *Moving Picture World* (p.9) – which is simply captioned '*Beggar Maid*' – offers no information other than the fact that it is, as the caption also states, a 'Kalem Irish subject'. Given the release date of *The Vagabonds* and its apparent lack of an Irish story or setting, it is also possible that the Gauntier–Olcott company made this film in Florida after returning from their second trip to Ireland.

113. '*The Colleen Bawn*', *Moving Picture World*, 30 September 1911, pp.954, 946.
114. Advertisement, *Piqua Leader-Dispatch* (Piqua, OH), 20 November 1911, p.2.
115. 'Amusements', *Mansfield News* (Mansfield, OH), 31 October 1911, p.3.
116. '*Colleen Bawn* at the Grand', *Nevada State Journal* (Reno, NV), 5 November 1911, p.3.
117. H.K. Webster, 'An Irish Classic in Three Reels', *Motography*, October 1911, p.186.
118. 'Kalem's *Colleen Bawn*', *Billboard*, 30 September 1911, pp.14, 51.
119. Ibid., p.51.
120. A copy of *The Colleen Bawn* exists at the George Eastman House in Rochester, New York.
121. '*Arrah-na-Pogue*', *Moving Picture World*, 18 November 1911, p.536.
122. See, for example, 'Amusements', *Mansfield News* (Mansfield, OH), 31 October 1911, p.3; 'Irish Patriot Drama at Imperial Theatre', *Anaconda Standard*, 28 December 1911, p.7; '*Arrah-na-Pogue*', *Moving Picture World*, 2 December 1911, p.748. With regard to the film's musical score, see H. Reynolds, 'Aural Gratification with Kalem Films: A Case History of Music, Lectures, and Sound Effects, 1907–1917', *Film History*, 12, 4 (2000), pp.417–42, as well as 'Special Music for *Arrah-na-Pogue*', *Moving Picture World*, 18 November 1911, p.536.
123. 'Among the Theatres', *Charleroi Mail* (Charleroi, PA), 18 November 1911, p.7.
124. 'Theatre Voyons', *Lowell Sun* (Lowell, MA), 12 September 1911, p.17.
125. '*Rory O'More* (Kalem)', *Moving Picture World*, 19 August 1911, pp.445–6.
126. A copy of '*You Remember Ellen*' exists at the George Eastman House in Rochester, New York.
127. ' "*You Remember Ellen*" ', *Moving Picture World*, 30 March 1912, p.1145. See also ' "*You Remember Ellen*" ', *Moving Picture World*, 16 March 1912, p.962.
128. Advertisement, *Thousandsticks* (Middlesboro, KY), 18 April 1912, p.5.
129. '*The O'Neill*', *Kalem Kalendar*, 22 December 1911, p.9; '*The O'Neill*', *Moving Picture World*, 6 January 1912, p.56.
130. '*His Mother*', *Kalem Kalendar*, 5 January 1912, p.5; '*His Mother*', *Moving Picture World*, 20 January 1912, p.236; '*His Mother*', *Moving Picture World*, 10 February 1912, p.481.
131. '*The Fishermaid of Ballydavid*', *Moving Picture World*, 11 November 1911, p.494; '*The Fishermaid of Ballydavid*', *Moving Picture World*, 2 December 1911, p.724.
132. '*Far from Erin's Isle*', *Moving Picture World*, 10 February 1912, p.510.
133. '*Far from Erin's Isle*', *New York Dramatic Mirror*, 28 February 1912, p.31.
134. '*Far from Erin's Isle* (Kalem)', *Moving Picture World*, 3 February 1912, p.401. See also '*Far from Erin's Isle*', *Kalem Kalendar*, 19 January 1912, p.5.
135. '*His Mother*, Big Irish Drama at Orpheum Tonight', *Fairbanks Daily Times* (Fairbanks, AK), 28 December 1913, p.3.
136. 'An Irish Feature at the Jewel Saturday', *Hamilton Evening Journal*, 26 January 1912, p.2; advertisement, *Coshocton Daily Age* (Coshocton, OH), 21 March 1912, p.5
137. F.J. Marion, letter to Sidney Olcott, 25 November 1911. Photocopy courtesy of Kevin Brownlow.

138. 'Kalem in Italy and Spain', *Billboard*, 9 December 1911, p.47.
139. 'Answers to Inquiries', *Motion Picture Story Magazine* (June 1912), p.160.
140. 'Answers to Inquiries', *Motion Picture Story Magazine* (February 1912), p.152.
141. 'Answers to Inquiries' (June 1912), p.160.
142. F.J. Marion, letter to Sidney Olcott, 2 July 1912. Photocopy courtesy of Kevin Brownlow. When Marion wrote to Olcott on 11 June 1912, he mailed it care of a London address, which implies that Olcott had not yet arrived in Ireland. It would thus seem likely that the Gauntier–Olcott group left for Ireland in late June 1912.
143. 'Kalem Players Return', *Moving Picture World*, 26 October 1912, p.329.
144. Advertisement, *Moving Picture World*, 21 December 1912, p.1208. Similar language appeared in advertisements for the film in *Motography*, 1 March 1913, p.3; *Moving Picture World*, 28 December 1912, pp.1318–19; *Moving Picture World*, 29 March 1913, p.1349.
145. 'Kalem's Achievements as Pioneer', p.1505.
146. 'Olympic Games Coming Here', *Evening Independent* (Massillon, OH), 19 July 1912, p.1.
147. F.J. Marion, letter to Sidney Olcott, 15 July 1912.
148. 'Realism for Kalem Films', *Moving Picture World*, 3 February 1912, p.402.
149. F.J. Marion, letter to Sidney Olcott, 30 October 1912.
150. '*The Shaughraun*', *Eau Claire Leader* (Eau Claire, WI), 25 December 1912, p.8.
151. W.S. Bush, 'The Shaughraun', *Moving Picture World*, 14 December 1912, p.1065.
152. F.J. Marion, letter to Sidney Olcott, 2 July 1912.
153. '*Kerry Gow* and *Shaun Rhue* in Pictures', *Moving Picture World*, 25 May 1912, p.716. Though no primary sources indicate that *Shaun Rhue* was produced and released, Kalem did believe the rights to the story had monetary value. When Vitagraph purchased Kalem in 1919, the *Exhibitors Herald and Motography* named *Shaun Rhue* as one of Kalem's valuable story properties. Perhaps its value was tied to the fact that it had not yet been filmed. See 'Vitagraph Absorbs Kalem Company and Acquires Valuable Properties', *Exhibitors Herald and Motography*, 1 March 1919, p.26.
154. 'News Items of the Kalem Company', published in the 15 September 1912 issue of the *Kalem Kalendar*, claimed that Olcott's crew had been in County Kerry 'for the past three months'. The article added that they would return to America 'about September 27th' (p.4).
155. Advertisement, *Reno Evening Gazette* (Reno, NV), 19 February 1913, p.1.
156. '*The Shaughraun*', *New York Dramatic Mirror*, 1 January 1913, p.28.
157. W.S. Bush, 'The Shaughraun', *Moving Picture World*, 14 December 1912, p.1065.
158. W.S. Bush, 'The Kerry Gow (Kalem) Three Reels', *Moving Picture World*, 9 November 1912, p.530; '*The Kerry Gow*', *New York Dramatic Mirror*, 27 November 1913, p.28.
159. '*The Kerry Gow*', *Evening Standard* (Ogden, UT), 25 November 1912, p.10.
160. '*The Kerry Gow*', *Evening Tribune* (Albert Lea, MN), 4 January 1913, p.4.
161. Advertisement, *Mansfield News* (Mansfield, OH), 27 November 1912, p.12. The same language appears in '*The Kerry Gow*', *Lima News* (Lima, OH), 17 December 1912, p.6. The origin of such language appears in an advertisement for the film in the *Kalem Kalendar*, 15 October 1912, p.10.
162. Advertisement, *Moving Picture World*, 16 November 1912, p.634. See also '*The Mayor from Ireland*', *Kalem Kalendar*, 1 November 1912, p.15; '*The Mayor from Ireland*', *Moving Picture World*, 23 November 1912, p.804.
163. '*The Mayor from Ireland*', *New York Dramatic Mirror*, 11 December 1912, p.33.
164. Advertisement, *Moving Picture World*, 4 January 1913, pp.1316–17; '*The Wives of Jamestown*', *Moving Picture Story Magazine* (February 1913), pp.42–53.
165. *Lady's Peggy's Escape* was released on 8 February 1913. See 'News Items of the Kalem Company', *Kalem Kalendar*, 1 January 1913, p.4.
166. '*Lady Peggy's Escape*', *Kalem Kalendar*, 1 January 1913, p.15; '*Lady Peggy's Escape*', *Kalem Kalendar*, 15 January 1913, p.15; '*Lady Peggy's Escape*', *Moving Picture World*, 1 February 1913, p.494; '*Lady Peggy's Escape*', *Moving Picture World*, 22 February 1913, p.779.
167. '*Ireland the Oppressed*', *Moving Picture World*, 28 December 1912, p.1291.
168. '*Ireland the Oppressed*', *Kalem Kalendar*, 15 November 1912, p.15; '*Ireland the Oppressed*', *Moving Picture World*, 2 December 1912, p.1002.
169. 'Theatre Voyons', *Lowell Sun*, 5 December 1912, p.4.
170. '*Where the Shamrocks Grow*', *Moving Picture News*, 11 March 1911, p.19; '*Where the Shamrocks*

*Grow*', *Moving Picture World*, 18 March 1911, p.610; '*Where the Shamrocks Grow*', *Moving Picture World*, 1 April 1911, p.721.

171. '*Inshavogue*', *Moving Picture World*, 2 September 1911, p.648; '*Inshavogue*', *Moving Picture World*, 23 September 1911, p.892.

172. '*The Brothers*', *Moving Picture World*, 9 September 1911, p.710.

173. '*Where the Shamrock Grows*', *Moving Picture World*, 18 March 1911, p.610; '*Where the Shamrock Grows*', *Moving Picture World*, 1 April 1911, pp.720–1.

174. '*Buttercups*', *Moving Picture World*, 1 March 1913, p.887.

175. '*An Irish Girl's Love*', *Moving Picture World*, 26 October 1912, p.376; '*A Willful Colleen's Way*', *New York Dramatic Mirror*, 22 October 1913, p.38.

176. '*An Irish Girl's Love*', *Moving Picture World*, 9 November 1912, p.553.

177. '*His Niece from Ireland*', *Moving Picture World*, 19 July 1913, p.319; '*His Niece from Ireland*', *Moving Picture World*, 28 July 1913, p.1392; '*The Crucible*', *Moving Picture World*, 7 March 1914, p.1238; '*My Mother's Irish Shawls*', *Universal Weekly*, 14 February 1914, p.24; '*My Mother's Irish Shawls*', *Moving Picture World*, 14 February 1914, p.872.

178. Advertisement, *Moving Picture World*, 19 July 1913, p.333.

179. '*The Smugglers of Sligo*', *Moving Picture World*, 21 March 1914, p.1586; '*The Smugglers of Sligo*', *Moving Picture World*, 11 April 1914, p.214; '*The Rightful Heir*', *Moving Picture World*, 25 April 1914, pp.578, 580.

180. '*Rory o'the Bogs*', *Moving Picture World*, 20 December 1913, p.1414; '*Rory o'the Bogs*', *Moving Picture World*, 27 December 1913, p.1558; advertisement, *Evening Gazette* (Cedar Rapids, IA), 8 November 1913, p.8; '*Brennan of the Moor*', *Moving Picture World*, 6 September 1913, p.1070.

181. '*The Squire's Son*', *Moving Picture World*, 11 April 1914, p.214.

182. Advertisement, *Lowell Sun*, 12 April 1913, p.17.

183. '*Lecture on St Patrick at City Hall Tonight*', *Fitchburg Daily Sentinel* (Fitchburg, MA), 28 April 1913, p.2.

184. '*The Life of St Patrick* (Historic Photoplay Co.)', *Moving Picture World*, 30 November 1912, p.885.

185. Advertisement, *Moving Picture World*, 23 November 1912, p.732.

186. '*Life of Saint Patrick*', *Moving Picture World*, 25 October 1913, p.390.

187. '*The Life of St Patrick*', *Motion Picture News*, 22 November 1913, p.33.

188. '*Frayed Fagin's Adventures*', *Kalem Kalendar*, 1 December 1913, p.15.

189. The *Kalem Kalendar* ('*The Laundress and the Lady*', 15 November 1913, p.3) spells the character name as 'Flannagan' in its list of cast credits, but then changes the spelling to 'Flannigan' in its plot summary.

190. '*McBride's Bride*', *Moving Picture World*, 23 May 1914, p.1116.

191. '*Lady Peggy's Escape*', *Kalem Kalendar*, 15 January 1913, p.15.

192. '*News Items of the Kalem Companies*', *Kalem Kalendar*, 15 May 1913, p.4.

193. '*Photoplays and Photoplayers*', *San Antonio Light* (San Antonio, TX), 15 June 1913, p.42.

194. Advertisement, *Kalem Kalendar*, 15 November 1913, p.2.

195. '*Gene Gauntier Heads Company*', *New York Dramatic Mirror*, 18 December 1912, p.27.

196. '*Gene Gauntier Goes Abroad*', *Motography*, 6 September 1913, p.158.

197. Gauntier was not only thinking about shooting in Ireland, but in America as well. For example, *Moving Picture World* ('*Gene Gauntier Notes*', 7 March 1914, p.1250) claimed that her new studio in America was a former Catholic church.

198. '*Gauntier Feature Players*', *Moving Picture World*, 21 December 1912, p.1169.

199. '*Gauntier Players Go to Ireland*', *Moving Picture World*, 23 August 1913, p.848.

200. Ibid.

201. '*A New Gauntier Picture*', *Motography*, 24 January 1914, p.46; '*For Ireland's Sake*', *Moving Picture World*, 17 January 1914, p.346. It is possible that this film was also screened under another title. The article '*Photoplays and Photo Players*' in the *Anaconda Standard* (Anaconda, MT) 24 May 1914, p.9, spoke about a three-reel feature called *A Daughter of Old Ireland* starring Gene Gauntier. The synopsis seems quite similar to the story of *For Ireland's Sake*.

202. '*For Ireland's Sake*', *Motion Picture News*, 24 January 1914, p.42.

203. '*Come Back to Erin*', *Moving Picture World*, 4 April 1914, p.77. See also '*Come Back to Erin*', *Moving Picture World*, 28 March 1914, p.1744.

204. 'Gauntier Players Go to Ireland', p.848; G. Gauntier, 'Gauntier Players in Ireland', *Moving Picture World*, 4 October 1913, p.39.
205. 'New Picture Making Company', *Moving Picture World*, 10 January 1914, p.181.
206. 'Sid Olcott Going Abroad', *Moving Picture World*, 13 June 1914, p.1519.
207. 'Gunning Joins Olcott', *Moving Picture World*, 6 June 1914, p.1410.
208. 'Olcott Going Abroad', *New York Dramatic Mirror*, 10 June 1914, p.24; 'Olcott Leads Company to Ireland', *Motography*, 11 July 1914, p.49.
209. 'Olcott's Company Reaches London', *Moving Picture World*, 11 July 1914, p.231; 'Sid Olcott and Players in Ireland', *Moving Picture World*, 25 July 1914, p.576.
210. 'Old Glory in Ireland', *Motography*, 1 August 1914, p.172; 'Olcott Players Attract Tourists', *Moving Picture World*, 15 August 1914, p.950; 'Olcott Gets Unique Irish Background', *Motography*, 22 August 1914, p.262; 'Sid Olcott Going Abroad', p.1519.
211. 'Olcott's Irish Pictures', *Moving Picture World*, 17 July 1915, p.502. (According to this article, other actors who travelled with Olcott to Ireland included Laurene Santley, Pat O'Malley, Robert Rivers, Charles McConnel and Arthur Leigh.)
212. 'Olcott in the Gap of Dunloe', *Moving Picture World*, 22 August 1914, p.1078.
213. E.M. Nelson, 'A Girl Whose Feelings Changed Her Face', *Motion Picture Classic* (July 1917), p.47.
214. 'Sidney Olcott Back, Too', *Moving Picture World*, 12 September 1914, p.1518.
215. 'War Affects Olcott Players', *Motography*, 5 September 1914, p.330.
216. Advertisement, *Moving Picture World*, 17 July 1915, p.454. The term 'Made-in-Ireland' also appears in the article 'All for Old Ireland', *Moving Picture World*, 17 July 1915, p.310, as well as in 'Valentine Grant', *Motography*, 24 July 1915, p.150.
217. 'Lubin Irish Series', *New York Dramatic Mirror*, 30 June 1915, p.20.
218. Ibid; 'Olcott's Irish Pictures', p.502.
219. 'All for Old Ireland', *Exhibitors Film Exchange*, 15 July 1915, p.14.
220. Ibid., p.20.
221. 'All for Old Ireland', *Moving Picture World*, 10 July 1915, p.370; 'All for Old Ireland', *Motography*, 17 July 1915, p.132; 'All for Old Ireland', *Moving Picture World*, 24 July 1915, p.667.
222. H. Hoffman, 'All for Old Ireland', *Motography*, 24 July 1915, pp.160–1.
223. A copy of *Bold Emmett, Ireland's Martyr* exists at the Library of Congress in Washington, DC.
224. Advertisement, *Moving Picture World*, 17 July 1915, p.454.
225. 'Bold Emmett, Ireland's Martyr', *Moving Picture World*, 7 August 1915, p.1018; J.C. Garrett, 'Bold Emmett, Ireland's Martyr', *Motography*, 14 August 1915, p.311.
226. Garrett, 'Bold Emmett, Ireland's Martyr', p.311.
227. 'The Irish in America', *Moving Picture World*, 4 September 1915, p.1716; advertisement, *Denton Record-Chronicle* (Denton, TX), 26 October 1915, p.4.
228. 'The Irish in America', *Moving Picture World*, 4 September 1915, p.1669; 'The Irish in America', *Motography*, 11 September 1915, p.542.
229. I.P. Solomon, 'The Irish in America', *Motion Picture News*, 11 September 1915, p.83.
230. J.C. Garrett, 'The Irish in America', *Motography*, 11 September 1915, pp.532–3.
231. 'The Irish in America', *Moving Picture World*, 18 September 1915, pp.2007–8.
232. 'Gene Gauntier with Universal', *Moving Picture World*, 27 March 1915, p.1942.
233. 'Gene Gauntier and Jack Join the Universal', *Universal Weekly*, 20 March 1915, p.13.
234. 'Gene Gauntier in *The Smuggler's Lass*', *Universal Weekly*, 29 May 1915, p.26.
235. Ibid.
236. 'The Ulster Lass', *Moving Picture World*, 3 July 1915, p.86; 'The Ulster Lass', *Moving Picture World*, 3 July 1915, p.128; 'The Ulster Lass', *Motography*, 10 July 1915, p.92.
237. 'The Ulster Lass', *Moving Picture World*, 3 July 1915, p.86.
238. P.H. Davis, 'Investing in the Movies', *Photoplay* (February 1916), pp.71–3, 164.
239. 'Raymond B. West, Dean of Ince Directors', *Moving Picture World*, 19 May 1917, p.1129.
240. 'Raymond B. West', *Moving Picture World*, 28 November 1914, p.1240.
241. 'The Banshee', *Moving Picture World*, 26 July 1913, p.408.
242. Advertisement, *Moving Picture World*, July 1913, p.5
243. 'The Banshee', *Moving Picture World*, 12 July 1913, p.205.
244. 'Amusements', *Hamilton Evening Journal*, 2 August 1913, p.6.

245. '*Flotsam*', *Moving Picture World*, 19 July 1913, pp.358–9.
246. '*Flotsam*', *Moving Picture World*, 26 July 1913, p.430.
247. '*A Romance of Erin*', *New York Dramatic Mirror*, 22 October 1913, p.33.
248. Ibid; '*A Romance of Erin*', *Moving Picture World*, 25 October 1913, p.266.
249. '*Heart of Kathleen*', *Moving Picture World*, 25 October 1913, p.306. See also '*The Heart of Kathleen*', *Moving Picture World*, 25 October 1913, p.382.
250. 'Irish Feature Coming', *Motography*, 20 September 1913, p.220.
251. Domino apparently prepared this promotional text, as it appears identically in 'Amusements', *Hamilton Evening Journal*, 28 October 1913, p.4, as well as in an advertisement, *Alton Evening Telegraph* (Alton, IL), 3 December 1913, p.7.
252. 'Irish Feature Coming', p.220.
253. L.R. Harrison, '*The Heart of Kathleen*', *Moving Picture World*, 25 October 1913, p.248.
254. '*Widow Maloney's Faith*', *Moving Picture World*, 25 October 1913, p.424; '*Widow Maloney's Faith*', *Moving Picture World*, 1 November 1913, p.498. (Though the three films were different in many ways, in each one the young hero leaves Ireland only to return later, just in time to offer financial assistance to a loved one.)
255. '*Widow Maloney's Faith*', *Motion Picture News*, 1 November 1913, p.44.
256. Advertisement, *Syracuse Herald* (Syracuse, NY), 8 February 1914, p.13.
257. For example, one advertisement for *The Harp of Tara* claimed it was 'Taken in Ireland': see advertisement, *Hamilton Daily Republican-News* (Hamilton, OH), 16 January 1914, p.8. An advertisement for *Eileen of Erin* later made the same claim. See advertisement, *Daily Gazette* (Xenia, OH), 29 May 1914, p.13.
258. See, for example, the wording of the advertisement for *The Harp of Tara* in *Titusville Herald* (Titusville, PA), 6 March 1914, p.5, which features text prepared by Domino. Similarly, a newspaper description of *Eileen of Erin* extolled its 'beautiful scenic effects'. See 'Amusements,' *Daily Kennebec Journal* (Kennebec, ME), 7 February 1914, p.11.
259. '*The Filly*', *Moving Picture World*, 6 December 1913, p.1212.
260. '*The Filly*', *Motion Picture News*, 6 December 1913, p.43; '*The Filly*', *New York Dramatic Mirror*, 24 December 1913, p.41.
261. '*The Filly*', *Moving Picture World*, 13 December 1913, p.1280.
262. '*The Ghost*', *Moving Picture World*, 8 November 1913, p.660.
263. '*Eileen of Erin*', *Moving Picture World*, 27 December 1913, p.1594; '*True Irish Hearts*', *Moving Picture World*, 10 January 1914, p.220; '*The Harp of Tara*', *Moving Picture World*, 10 January 1914, p.220; '*The Informer*', *Moving Picture World*, 24 January 1914, p.414.
264. '*True Irish Hearts*, at Elite', *Woodland Daily Democrat* (Woodland, CA), 17 March 1914, p.3.
265. '*Eileen of Erin*', *Moving Picture World*, 27 December 1913, p.1545; '*Eileen of Erin*', *Moving Picture World*, 27 December 1913, p.1594.
266. '*The Informer*', *Moving Picture World*, 24 January 1914, p.414.
267. '*True Irish Hearts*', *Moving Picture World*, 27 December 1913, p.1545.
268. Advertisement, *Hamilton Daily Republican-News*,12 January 1914, p.4.
269. '*The Harp of Tara*', *Motion Picture News*, 27 December 1913, p.47; '*The Harp of Tara*', *New York Dramatic Mirror*, 7 January 1914, p.33; '*The Harp of Tara*', *Moving Picture World*, 10 January 1914, p.174.
270. '*The Informer*', *Motion Picture News*, 17 January 1914, p.41; '*The Informer*', *Moving Picture World*, 24 January 1914, p.414.
271. '*The Ghost*', *Moving Picture World*, 8 November 1913, p.738.
272. '*The Harp of Tara*', *Moving Picture World*, 10 January 1914, p.174; '*Eileen of Erin*', *Motion Picture News*, 20 December 1913, p.41.
273. '*True Irish Hearts*', *Motion Picture News*, 10 January 1914, p.39.
274. '*Eileen of Erin*', *New York Dramatic Mirror*, 31 December 1913, p.32.
275. '*For the Wearing of the Green*', *Moving Picture World*, 7 March 1914, p.1302.
276. A copy of *Ireland a Nation* exists at the Library of Congress in Washington, DC.
277. 'Brevities of the Business', *Motography*, 21 February 1914, p.143.
278. In *Irish Filmography*, Kevin Rockett notes scepticism over MacNamara's 'role' in the 1913 film *Traffic in Souls* (p.268). However, trade publications of the time repeatedly credited MacNamara with having written or co-written the film. At the time of its release, George Blaisdell (in '*Traffic in*

Souls', *Moving Picture World*, 22 November 1913, p.849), wrote: 'Walter MacNamara is the author of the script.' The article '*Traffic in Souls*, a Moral Play', in *Motography* (29 November 1913, p.397) noted: 'It was written by George L. Tucker and Walter MacNamara.' Moreover, a review in the *New York Dramatic Mirror* ('*Traffic in Souls*', 19 November 1913, p.33) announced that the film was 'Written by W. Macnamara [*sic*] and G.L. Tucker'. For more examples of MacNamara being credited as the writer of *Traffic in Souls*, see 'Brevities of the Business', *Moving Picture World*, 21 February 1914, p.143; 'Walter MacNamara Rejoins Universal', *Moving Picture World*, 1 January 1916, p.56; 'MacNamara with Mirror Films', *Moving Picture World*, 26 February 1916, p.1275; 'Walter MacNamara off for Keystoneville', *Moving Picture World*, 24 March 1917, p.1938.

279. 'Walter MacNamara to Direct for Imp', *Moving Picture World*, 1 November 1913, p.500; 'Walter MacNamara, Director', *Moving Picture World*, 8 November 1913, p.613.

280. 'MacNamara Produces Crime Picture Based on Latest Discovery of Science', *Universal Weekly*, 15 November 1913, p.12; 'Brevities of the Business,' p.143.

281. 'Brevities of the Business,' p.143.

282. [Untitled], *Motography*, 21 March 1914, p.214.

283. G. Blaisdell, 'Irish History on the Screen', *Moving Picture World*, 29 August 1914, p.1245.

284. [Untitled], *Motography*, 24 October 1914, p.570.

285. Blaisdell, 'Irish History on the Screen', p.1245. In *The Irish Filmography*, Rockett claims that the interiors were shot at 'Kew Bridge Studios, Twickenham, London' (p.272). This is at odds with Blaisdell. However, it is possible that some or all interiors were shot in London, and that MacNamara did not acknowledge this fact in America, as he may have wanted publicity to suggest the film was shot entirely in Ireland.

286. Blaisdell, 'Irish History on the Screen', p.1245.

287. '*Ireland a Nation*', *Motion Picture News*, 10 October 1914, p.79.

288. '*Ireland*, Good Film Play', *New York Times*, 24 September 1914, p.11.

289. '*Ireland a Nation*', *Variety*, 10 October 1914, p.716.

290. '*Ireland*, Good Film Play', p.11.

291. R.C. McElravy, '*Ireland a Nation*', *Moving Picture World*, 26 September 1914, p.67.

292. '*Ireland a Nation*', *Motion Picture News*, p.79; '*Ireland a Nation*', *Variety*, p.25. Discussion of this reel of non-fiction footage also appears in McElravy, '*Ireland a Nation*', who claimed: 'Prior to the beginning of the main production, a reel of scenic film was shown, giving intimate views of the famous county Glendalough, the Lakes of Killarney, and other beautiful scenes' (p.67).

293. K. Kelly, 'Flickerings from Film Land', *Chicago Tribune*, 10 February 1915, p.10.

294. 'The Bijou Theatre Gets Another Big Feature', *North Adams Evening Transcript* (North Adams, MA), 31 October 1914, p.9.

295. 'Walter MacNamara Rejoins Universal', p.56; 'MacNamara with Mirror Films', p.1275; 'Walter MacNamara Off for Keystoneville', p.1938.

296. 'Irish Picture at Hartford Theatre', *Hartford Courant* (Hartford, CT), 25 February 1917, p.X11.

297. 'The Fleur-De-Ling Ring', *Moving Picture World*, 28 November 1914, p.1231.

298. 'A Sprig of Shamrock', *Motography*, 14 August 1915, p.327; 'A Sprig of Shamrock', *Moving Picture World*, 14 August 1915, p.1203.

299. 'Cleo Madison Featured in Irish Romance', *Universal Weekly*, 27 March 1915, p.11.

300. 'Wild Irish Rose', *Moving Picture World*, 10 April 1915, p.292. See also 'Cleo Madison Stars in Wild Irish Rose', *Universal Weekly*, 10 April 1915, p.25.

301. 'A Wild Irish Rose', *New York Dramatic Mirror*, 21 April 1915.

302. 'It's a Long, Long Way to Tipperary', *Moving Picture World*, 30 January 1915, p.740; 'It's a Long, Long Way to Tipperary', *New York Dramatic Mirror*, 10 February 1915, p.31; 'It's a Long, Long Way to Tipperary', *Motography*, 13 February 1915, p.266; 'It's a Long, Long Way to Tipperary', *Moving Picture World*, 13 February 1915, p.985.

# Chapter Six

# *Film Characters*

In Kalem's 1913 film *A Plot for a Million*, character Dick Logan is the 'son of a wealthy broker' who spends the winter in the American south.[1] There he falls in love with Elsie, the daughter of a tugboat captain. Mr Logan journeys to visit Dick, causing Logan's secretary to launch a plan to 'attack Logan's holdings'. Logan does not approve of Elsie, but quickly has his hands full with mounting financial problems. In an effort to keep Logan from contacting his office, the secretary 'takes drastic measures and imprisons Logan' aboard his yacht. According to the *Kalem Kalendar*, 'Dick, who has been visiting Elsie on the tugboat, witnesses his father's struggles from a distance and immediately pursues the yacht...Jumping [aboard], Dick is soon master of the situation and, apprehending the secretary, he liberates his father. The latter comes to the conclusion that his son has made a wise choice [of sweetheart] after all.'[2]

The melodramatic tale reaches a happy conclusion, which, like the rest of the film, is not dependent on the ethnicity of the characters involved. Dick Logan is one example of the large number of different kinds of Irish/Irish-American characters who appeared in early moving pictures that were set in America. Many of these characters were lead roles, while others were secondary or even background characters.

At times the Irish heritage of these lead characters was important to the films in which they appeared. Indeed, some of them appeared in serious tales that drew on narratives previously explored in Irish-themed comedies. For example, in Edison's 1913 film *The Younger Generation*, labourer Michael Riley unexpectedly falls heir to $2,000.[3] The following year, the title character of *O'Brien Finds a Way* (Warner's, 1914) inherits a farm that is little more than a 'sandy tract'. His 'daughter's beau' helps him grow fruit successfully; as a result, O'Brien sells the land so that the young couple can get married.[4] *When Wealth Torments* (Essanay, 1915) features an inheritance story in which Mrs Mahoney sadly turns her back on Jim O'Brien, her daughter's suitor, after receiving news that she has come into a fortune.

After pretending to be a wealthy French count, Jim finally wins the family's attentions.[5]

Irish characters also appeared in a number of dramatic 'Meeting of Nationalities' melodramas that were set in America. In *Cohen and Murphy* (Powers, 1910), the title characters are business partners; when Murphy is murdered, Cohen sets out to find the culprit.[6] Two non-Irish characters vie for the love of Mary O'Toole in *The Trap* (Kay-Bee, 1914). In Vitagraph's *The Fire Escape* (1915), Minnie Schwartz loves Jack, though Minnie's father disapproves, believing she should instead marry Doyle, the ward boss. However, Jack saves Harris, a wealthy politician, from Doyle's machinations, causing Doyle to be sent to prison. As a result, Jack becomes Harris' secretary and Minnie's father reconsiders his position.[7]

Lead characters with Irish names also appeared in films with narratives that, like *A Plot for a Million*, were not dependent on their ethnicity. Such films echoed illustrated song slides like *Take Me Out to the Ballgame* (DeWitt C. Wheeler, 1908), *Take Me Out to the End of the Pier* (DeWitt C. Wheeler, 1908) and *Roll on the Rollaway* (Chicago Transparency, 1908), in which the characters' Irish heritage – as suggested by their names – did not factor into the stories in which they appeared. For example, Mary Pickford portrayed Kittie Ryan in D.W. Griffith's *The Renunciation* (Biograph, 1909).[8] Josephine Miller portrayed Mary Donnelly in Tom Mix's *Cactus Jake, the Heartbreaker* (Selig, 1914).[9] In *The Chorus Lady* (Lasky, 1915), character Patricia O'Brien is a 'keen-witted, clean lived' chorus girl who holds 'her own amid the temptations incident to her profession'.[10] Other examples include *Jack Logan's Dog* (Powers, 1910), *Tim Mahoney, the Scab* (Vitagraph, 1911), *A Tenacious Solicitor* (Edison, 1912), *Wynona's Revenge* (Bison, 1913), *Old Gorman's Gal* (Essanay, 1913), *While Mrs McFadden Looked Out* (Thanhouser, 1913), *Witness 'A 3-Center'* (Essanay, 1913), *The Decision of Jim O'Farrel* (Selig, 1914), *The Danger Signal* (Kleine, 1915) and *Larry O'Neill, Gentleman* (Imp, 1915).[11]

Some of these characters defied Irish stereotypes. James Neill portrayed Judge Moore in *The Political Boss* (Kalem, 1914). Nellie Nolan and Tom Clancy work at the same department store in *Young Romance* (Lasky, 1915).[12] In *Think Mothers* (Lubin, 1915) Nora Murray marries a man who later becomes a horrible drunk; the bride is Irish, but the groom and alcoholic-to-be ('Lansing') is not.[13] But nowhere is the non-stereotypical Irish character more pronounced than in the film *Her Mother's Voice* (Mutual, 1915):

> [a] well-to-do Irishman spends his money trying to make an
> opera singer of his wife. But her voice is so bad that she draws

a rain of vegetables with every outburst...Eighteen years
later, the Irishman's daughter returns from a vocal culture
school. She sings for him. The customers in a nearby barber-
shop think there is a fire. Construction hands on a new
building imagine it to be the whistle to quit work. A horse
runs away. A portrait on the wall slides out of its frame and
escapes.[14]

In this case, the humour had nothing to do with ethnicity; the film successfully avoided the use of stage Irish caricatures.

In addition to lead roles, the American cinema also featured many
supporting characters who were coded as Irish. Perhaps the earliest example came in *Alphonse and Gaston* (American Mutoscope & Biograph,
1902, aka *Alphonse and Gaston Helping an Irishman*), the first of many
films adapting Frederick Burr Opper's French cartoon characters to the
screen. A catalogue describes the film: 'The two polite Frenchmen attempt
to assist an Irish laborer, who has dropped his lunch while carrying a heavy
plank along a country road. Their antics are very amusing.'[15] In this case,
the Irish character was a stereotype.[16]

Further examples of stereotypical Irish supporting characters appeared
in such comedies as *The Lost Child* (American Mutoscope & Biograph,
1904), in which a mother wrongly believes her baby has been kidnapped;
her misperception triggers a chase narrative. An 'Irish washerwoman' is
among the many different characters seen during the chaos.[17] Similarly,
Edwin S. Porter's film *Cohen's Fire Sale* (Edison, 1907) features an array of
characters, including Cohen, who is Jewish, a group of 'Italian laborers',
and – in one scene – a 'bunch of Irish women [who] secure some of the
prizes' at a cakewalk.[18]

Supporting characters in dramatic narratives varied from those who
were influenced by stereotypes to those who eschewed them. For example,
O'Houlihan in *Poor Jimmy* (Pathé, 1912) was a tough drinker.[19] Pat
Maloney was an Irish labourer in *The Story of a Wallet* (Nestor, 1912).[20] In
*The Iconoclast* (Broncho, 1913), Mike Flannagan was 'in charge of the
construction gang of a railroad'.[21] In *Betty's Bondage* (Rex, 1915), Steve
Moran is a 'brutal drunkard'.[22] And in *Sunshine Molly* (Bosworth, 1915),
the Irish Pat O'Brien and his wife run a boarding home.[23] By contrast, *An
Unpaid Ransom* (Edison, 1915), features a 'frank, unsuspecting Irishman'
named Connelly who inadvertently acts as chauffeur for a kidnapper;
Connelly apparently bore no relation to stereotypical Irish characters.[24]

During the early cinema period, five particular Irish film characters
surfaced repeatedly: the Irish boxer, the Irish policeman, the Irish gangster,

the Irish priest and the Irish hero. Influenced by pre-cinema entertainment, they became enduring characters in the American cinema. However, none of them were particularly well-defined characters. For example, depending on the film, the Irish policeman could be smart and brave, or he could be stupid and scared. Such nebulous attributes helped allow these five characters to appear in a range of different genres, ranging from non-fiction to comedies, melodramas, westerns, action films, and so forth.

All five characters existed within the larger framework of the American cinema. To be sure, not all boxers, priests, policemen, gangsters and heroes of the period were coded as Irish. In fact, quite the opposite was true, including such famous cases as the Italian gangsters in *The Black Hand* (American Mutoscope & Biograph, 1906). Thus, these Irish characters and the moving pictures in which they appeared functioned as part of the broader American film industry. As a result, many of them became part of the ongoing debates over authenticity and 'realism'.

# The Boxer

In many respects, the story of the Irish-American in the cinema begins with James J. Corbett, the famed boxer who was dubbed by the media as 'Gentleman Jim'. As Chapter 1 noted, Corbett – a world heavyweight champion – regularly appeared onstage during the 1890s. Thanks to a large number of biographical articles in the press, Corbett's Irish heritage was well known throughout America. In an 1892 syndicated newspaper article, Corbett himself wrote about his father, Patrick J. Corbett, who moved to 'San Francisco from New Orleans, to which place he had come from his Irish home at Tuame [*sic*]'.[25]

In his first moving picture, Corbett fought Peter Courtney at Edison's Black Maria studio.[26] The result was *Corbett and Courtney before the Kinetograph* (1894), six rounds depicted in six one-minute films. According to Dan Streible, it 'became the most widely seen kinetoscope attraction, its popularity continuing into 1896 and 1897'.[27] Corbett then fought Bob Fitzsimmons, a much better known opponent, in Carson City, Nevada, on St Patrick's Day, 1897. Their fourteen rounds became Veriscope's 100-minute feature film *The Corbett–Fitzsimmons Fight* (1897). Projected as late as 1901, it became the most famous of the early fight films, as well as a crucial project in the formation of American cinema.[28]

*The Corbett–Fitzsimmons Fight* also spawned such film fakes as Lubin's *Corbett and Fitzsimmons, Films in Counterpart of the Great Fight* (1897). Lubin would later offer other faked versions of Corbett fights, such as the *Corbett and Sharkey Fight* (aka *Fac-Simile of the Corbett and Sharkey Fight*,

**CORBETT-FITZSIMMONS**

FIGHT REPRODUCED LIFE SIZE.

An exact reproduction of the encounter, with all movements, projected upon a screen by the

# NEW MAGNISCOPE

Is Certain to be an Immense Attraction and Big Financial Success.

Purchase outfit now, and become familiar with the machine and ready to take hold at once. Be one of the first in the field and reap the benefit. Parties purchasing an outfit from us will be informed as soon as the films are ready for the market.

## WESTERN PHONOGRAPH CO.,
### 153 La Salle St., Chicago, Ill.

**6.1** Advertisement published in the 3 April 1897 issue of the *New York Clipper*.

1898), *Reproduction of the Corbett and Jeffries Fight* (aka *Reproduction of the Jeffries and Corbett Fight*, 1899), *Reproduction of the Corbett and McCoy Fight* (1900) and *Reproduction of the Corbett–McGovern Fight (San Francisco, Cal, March 31, 1903)*. Though Lubin dominated the faked Corbett film market, he was not alone.[29] In 1903, the American Mutoscope & Biograph Company released its own fake, *Reproduction of the Jeffries–Corbett Contest*. Nowhere was the question of authenticity more pronounced in early cinema than in the Corbett fight films.

To suggest that a moving picture like *The Corbett–Fitzsimmons Fight* is an Irish-themed film is as problematic as calling it – based upon Fitzsimmons' heritage – a British-themed film. At the same time, such moving pictures meant that the already famous Corbett became a film star, arguably the first film star. Moreover, even though such films were not Irish-themed, they did transfer the character of the Irish boxer – earlier embodied by such nineteenth-century boxers as Paddy Ryan and John L. Sullivan – to the screen. Here again the boxing film was important in issues of authenticity, as Corbett (like Ryan and Sullivan) was indeed a boxer in

315

real life, but (also like Ryan and Sullivan) his fame led to work as an actor. Corbett's persona, built out of fact and fiction, continued to be a presence in films throughout the early cinema period. In 1910, for example, he starred in Vitagraph's *Corbett in How Championships Are Won and Lost* (aka *How Championships Are Won–And Lost*).[30]

Following from the success of the Corbett films, other boxers of Irish descent appeared on screen during the early cinema period, including Terry McGovern (as in Selig's 1900 *Gans-McGovern Fight Pictures*) and 'Philadelphia' Jack O'Brien (as in the Miles Brothers' 1906 film *O'Brien-Burns Contest, Los Angeles, Cal. Nov. 26th, 1906*). As with Corbett, controversies over fact and fiction continued to rage. Irish-born boxer Peter Maher appeared in a re-enactment of one of his fights (Zinematographe's 1897 film, *Maher-Choynski Glove Contest*). Lubin continued to produce faked versions of famous fights, including *Reproduction of the Jeffries and Sharkey Fight* (1899), which purported to depict the famous Irish boxer Tom Sharkey.[31] In some cases, audiences responded quite negatively to these moving pictures. In 1906, *Variety* noted that viewers 'hissed' at a faked version of the 'Fitzsimmons–O'Brien fight pictures'.[32] This was all in addition to the fact that some boxers of the period who were not Irish, such as Kid McCoy, adopted names for the ring that made them sound Irish.

As the nickelodeon era progressed, the number of Irish boxers in filmed matches (or faked versions of them) decreased while the number of Irish boxers in fictional films grew. These fictional characters were influenced by Corbett, Sullivan and others. In filmed melodramas, these on-screen boxers echoed both the successes and the tragedies associated with their real-life predecessors. Furthermore, in comedies such as *The Amateur Champion* (Lubin, 1907), the Irish boxer easily meshed with the knockabout physical humour that had long been associated with the stage Irish.[33]

*Moving Picture World* claimed the fictional film *Spike Shannon's Last Fight* (Essanay, 1911) featured a four-round boxing match 'which seems not posed, but the real thing'.[34] The title character enters the ring to raise money for his sick wife's surgery. *The Reformation of Kid Hogan* (Lubin, 1912) has its title character continuing to fight despite the pleas of his sweetheart.[35] Actor Herbert Rawlinson appeared in the lead role of *Kid Reagan's Hands* (Rex, 1914); 'The Kid' knocks out a rival in a two-round bout, and then proceeds to 'take vengeance on his enemies, bare-handed'.[36] In 1915, Gotham's *The Man Who Beat Dan Dolan* featured a young character named Willie who attempts to win $300 by 'lasting three rounds with the champion, Dan Dolan'.[37]

Of these films, *Ireland and Israel* (Champion, 1912) made the greatest effort to be viewed as authentic. Its storyline drew on the many illustrated

6.2  *Ireland and Israel* (Champion, 1912).

song slides, comedic films and vaudeville acts that paired an Irish character
with a Jewish character. In the film, Abie Wedertzsky, a recent immigrant,
is bullied by a 'gang of toughs' until Pat Riley, a 'champion pugilist', comes
to his aid and teaches him how to fight. The two become friends, and eventually Abie helps Pat after he becomes poverty stricken.[38] 'Race and
nationality be d——', one of the film's intertitles declared.[39] *Moving Picture
World* praised *Ireland and Israel*, which combined melodrama and
comedy.[40] Champion's advertisements drew particular attention to the fact
that the film included 'actual New York scenes' and – more importantly –
famed boxer Tom Sharkey in the role of a referee.[41]

In the final years of the early cinema period, a number of comedy films
featuring Irish boxers were produced, such as *The Rise and Fall of McDoo*
(Biograph, 1913), *Red Hicks Defies the World* (Biograph, 1913, featuring
a fighter named 'O'Shea') and *Knockout Dugan's Find* (Selig, 1915).[42] The
most popular films of this type were the 'One-Round O'Brien' comedies
produced by Majestic. The first film, *One Round O'Brien* (1912), featured
Fred Mace in the title role.[43] He and his friend Duffy are out of money, and
so O'Brien – after seeing a poster for a fight film – convinces a theatre

**6.3** *One-Round O'Brien* (Majestic, 1912).

manager that he can 'knock out "all comers" in one round'.[44] His plan is that Duffy, hidden behind a curtain, will hit opponents with a mallet. The scheme works fine until Duffy accidentally hits O'Brien, laying him out flat.

*One-Round O'Brien* was successful, so much so that it was 'featured in several first-class vaudeville theatres, including Hammerstein's, New York City'.[45] The film's popularity meant that Majestic produced the sequel *One-Round O'Brien Comes Back* (1913), again starring Fred Mace. Its storyline was similar to the first film, though now a sponge filled with chloroform was the means to knock out opponents.[46] According to *Moving Picture World*, it was only after the second film that Majestic approached Fred Mace about appearing in an ongoing series of One-Round O'Brien films. *One-Round O'Brien's Flirtation* (1913) was the 'first of the lot'.[47] In it, O'Brien's opponent agrees to 'lay down, but his anger rose because O'Brien flirted with his girl and he knocked the latter out'.[48] Despite receiving a positive notice in *Moving Picture World*, only one more film in the series followed, *One-Round O'Brien in the Ring Again* (Apollo, 1914).[49]

# The Policeman

Numerous films during the early cinema period featured policemen who were not intended to be Irish, as in Robert W. Paul's *Misguided Bobby at a Fancy Garden Party*, released in America by Edison in 1906. Many other films featured policemen without clear ethnic identities.[50] For example, the police officers in films like *The Cop and the Nurse Girl* (Edison, 1898), *Off His Beat* (American Mutoscope & Biograph, 1903) and *Policeman's Pal* (Lubin, 1905) do not necessarily seem to have been Irish.[51] The officers in Edwin S. Porter's *Life of an American Policeman* (Edison, 1905) are not specifically coded as Irish. Furthermore, Mack Sennett's Keystone Cops – the most famous and popular comedic depictions of the police in early American cinema – were not coded as Irish either.[52] However, within the broader spectrum of police characters in early cinema, the 'Irish cop' did appear in films of more than one genre.

Given the large number of Irish-Americans working in the New York City police force, some of them probably appear in such non-fiction films as American Mutoscope & Biograph's *Chief Devery at Head of N. Y. Police Parade* (1898), *New York Police Parade* (1898), *New York Police* (1899), and *N. Y. Police Parade, 1905* (1905), and/or in Edison's *New York Police Parade, June 1, 1899* (1899) and *New York City Police Parade* (1903).[53] The same is also presumably true of *New York Police Force* (Atlas, 1910), which consisted of a 'series of views of New York policemen drilling'.[54] Edison's *The Police Force of New York City*, which was also released in 1910, depicted 'some of the phases of police life in New York'.[55] These 'phases' included directing traffic, rescuing a drowning man and catching 'river thieves'. A surviving print of the film indicates that some of the footage is non-fiction, while other segments were staged.[56]

In terms of film comedy, the first appearance of an Irish policeman came in *Chinese Laundry Scene* (Edison, 1894), which is discussed in Chapter 4. Another early example was Edison's *Congress of Nations* (1900), which featured a 'decidedly Hibernian policeman from the flag of Erin's Isle'.[57] The following year, Edison's *How the Dutch Beat the Irish* (1901) had an Irish policeman admonishing a Dutch cook for leaving a barrel on a side-walk.[58] The cook secretly replaces the barrel, hiding a bulldog inside it. When the cop lifts it, the dog 'wrecks his brand new uniform'.[59]

Police officers in other pre-nickelodeon era comedy films like *Trouble in Hogan's Alley* (American Mutoscope & Biograph, 1900) might well have been intended to be Irish, though in some cases without surviving prints it is difficult to reach definite conclusions. In the 'Bridget' moving pictures *Mysterious Disappearance of a Policeman* (American Mutoscope &

**6.4** Barney Gilmore as the title character in
*Dublin Dan, the Irish Detective* (Solax, 1912).

Biograph, 1899) and *Spirits in the Kitchen* (American Mutoscope &
Biograph, 1899), the cops were apparently intended to be Irish. Indeed, a
Lubin catalogue summary refers to the amorous policeman in *Policeman's
Love Affair* (Lubin, 1905) as 'Michael McGinnis'.[60]

As noted in Chapter 4, numerous romantic comedies involving Irish
policemen were produced during the nickelodeon era, such as *Fickle
Bridget* (Solax, 1911), *Bridget's Sudden Wealth* (Edison, 1912), *For the
Love of Mike* (Kalem, 1914) and *The Cook's Mistake* (Edison, 1915).
Other examples include *Maggie Hoolihan Gets a Job* (Pathé Frères, 1910),
in which Officer Clancey marries the title character, a 'freshly landed Irish
girl', so that she can care for his ten children.[61] *Dooley's Scheme* (Biograph,
1911) has Officer Dooley competing with Mike Doyle for the attentions of
a 'pretty little housemaid'.[62] Particularly unique was *The Pie Eaters* (Lubin,
1915), in which the 'entire police force of Hotelsville revel in pie'. Regan
and Finn, the two champion pie eaters, 'enjoy a rough and tumble scrap'
over not one but two women.[63]

Other film comedies featured characters who join the police in order to
impress the women they love. The title character of *Mike, the Timid Cop*

(Kalem, 1913) quits his job as an iceman and becomes a cop in order to win the affection of Nora, the cook.[64] Similarly, *Off Agin – On Agin – Finnegan* (Joker, 1914) gets a job as a police officer in order to 'win the girl, whose father insists he must work'.[65] Sergeant Kelly demands that Finnegan keep hoboes off his beat, though Finnegan falls asleep and has an exciting dream.[66] When he awakes, a 'roundsman' gives him a 'dressing-down'.[67]

Not unexpectedly, given long-standing Irish stereotypes, numerous Irish-themed comedies featured stupid police officers. *Officer Muldoon's Double* (Lubin, 1910) has a hungry actor taking a coat and cap from a sleeping policeman.[68] He eats for free at numerous lunch stands, and then returns the coat to its owner, who receives blame for the impostor's activities.[69] Essanay's *A Flirty Affliction* (1910) finds Officer O'Rourke mistaking Molly's nervous affliction, which causes her to nod, for a come-hither flirtation.[70] The same company also released *Where Is Mulcahy?* (1910), in which the title character suffers at the hands of 'young vagabonds' in a series of 'adventures' that cause him to lose his trousers.[71] Then, in 1914, Thanhouser released *A Cooked Goose*, in which the 'tyrant' policeman Dan McCarty ends up in jail for fighting with a 'roundsman'.[72]

Some police comedies drew upon the 'Meeting of Nationalities' story-lines that had been explored in previous moving pictures, illustrated song slides and stage productions. For example, *Building a Trust* (Lubin, 1913) features a Chinese laundryman who lobbies an Irish police officer to keep his competition from splashing mud on his clothes.[73] *Murphy's I.O.U.* (Keystone, 1913) details the debt that policeman Murphy owes to Cohen; for repayment, Murphy gives Cohen his wife's jewellery.[74] One of the cops in *Scenting a Terrible Crime* (Biograph, 1913) is Irish, while the others are not.[75] *A Brewerytown Romance* (Lubin, 1914) features Cassidy the Cop; trouble occurs when Emil Schweitzer and Tango Heinz court Cassidy's old sweetheart.[76] Then, in *Two of the Bravest* (World Film, 1915), Meyer pretends to be a judge and his friend Mike pretends to be a constable.[77]

Another repeated storyline featured the Irish cop who makes good in the face of adversity, a kind of comedic version of the 'American Dream'. In *Brannigan's Promotion* (Nestor, 1912), Brannigan is a 'big, fat, and good-natured' policeman. His fellow officers make fun of him until he captures a group of 'marauders'.[78] Selig's *The Fire Cop* (1913) features Andy Brannigan, a cop who deceives others with his false tales of heroism; he later becomes a 'true hero' after saving lives during a tenement fire.[79] The title character of *The Rise of Officer Casey* (Lubin, 1914) is the 'boob' of the police force, but he eventually 'tumbles into his good luck by accident'.[80]

Not all comedies about Irish police officers featured male characters.[81] *Kate, the Cop* (Lubin, 1913) is a cook and is policeman Casey's 'mistress';

**6.5** *The Chief of Police* (Kalem, 1914) featured a burglar
named Jack Keenan (left).

when Casey gets scared of a crook and Kate makes the arrest, the Chief of
Police instructs them to change jobs.[82] *Officer Kate* (Vitagraph, 1914)
features actress Kate Price as a policewoman who obtains her job thanks to
'suffragettes'.[83] In *The Female Cop* (Lubin, 1914), character Myra
McGinnis is an old maid who – after hearing about women joining the
force – obtains a police coat and 'arrests everyone she meets'.[84] Then, in
Edison's 1915 film *Not Much Force*, the town makes Officer O'Toole's wife
the new police chief after tiring of O'Toole's failures.[85]

Irish police officers also appeared in a number of film melodramas.
Many of these police officers were serious characters who exuded intelligence and bravery. At times some of these moving pictures did include
humour, though the policemen were not the butt of the jokes. For example,
the film *Officer McCue* (Lubin, 1909) incorporated elements of comedy
into a melodrama that was described as being of a 'dime novel manner'.[86]
Similarly, George Kleine's 1915 five-reel production of the hit play *Officer
666* cast Dan Moyles as the title character, whose real name is Phelan.[87]
*Motography* noted that the film was a combination of 'quick, snappy
action and continual flashes of wit and humor'.[88]

By 1909, serious depictions of the Irish police officer began to proliferate. For example, Biograph's *One Touch of Nature* (1909) features the
brave Officer John Murray.[89] Vitagraph's *Clancy* (1910, aka *Clancy,
Romance of a Policeman*) told the story of a successful police officer who
is nearly killed by a vicious gang.[90] That same year, Biograph's *A Child of
the Ghetto* (1910) has Officer Quinn, a 'kindhearted and reasoning policeman', help clear the name of a young, falsely accused Jewish girl.[91] *Moving*

*Picture World* repeatedly praised its images of the ghetto, calling them the 'most realistic ever attempted'.[92] By contrast, the same publication said that *Playing for a Fortune* (Kalem, 1914), which featured a policeman named O'Sullivan, was 'not made realistic'.[93]

Some of these police officers achieve major successes against criminals. The title character of *Mounted Officer Flynn* (Selig, 1913) captures a spy and recovers secret documents. After winning a Congressional Medal, he says he 'merely worked along the line of duty'.[94] The exploitation film *Traffic in Souls* (Imp, 1913) featured Matt Moore as Officer Burke, who helps capture a gang of white slavers.[95] In 1914, Selig's *The Fates and Ryan* offered the story of the mounted policeman Michael Ryan, whose sweetheart has a counterfeiting uncle who has to be captured.[96] In Edison's 1915 film *Only the Maid*, Officer Carney, a 'blue-coated Romeo, subdues a murderer'.[97] That same year, Edison released *McQuade of the Traffic Squad*, starring Pat O'Malley as the lead character, who is 'one of the finest' men on the force.[98] Despite the best efforts of a rival officer, McQuade succeeds at his job and catches a jewel thief.[99]

Other Irish police characters fought crime while caring for others. Patrolman Mulvihill, 'large of frame and mighty of heart', looks after an infant in *The Policeman and the Baby* (Selig, 1913).[100] In *The Cop on the Beat* (Selig, 1914), Officer Casey looks after a friend's children and later catches a burglar attempting to rob his friend's family.[101] Van Dyke Brooke portrayed the title role in Vitagraph's *Officer John Donovan* (1914).[102] In it, the title character disguises himself as a criminal in order to capture a gang; he also adopts an orphan and cares for her until she 'grows into womanhood'.[103] *Moving Picture World* called the film a 'realistic crook drama'.[104]

Of the serious Irish police films, few if any were as well promoted or received as *How Callahan Cleaned Up Little Hell* (Selig, 1915).[105] Adapted from a magazine short story, the three-reel film featured its title character 'insisting upon doing his duty and breaking up crime in his precinct, even though the temptations to leave the straight and narrow path were many and hard to resist, and even though his life was threatened if he did not desist'.[106] As a result of his honest ways, Captain Callahan does battle with corrupt politicians led by Boss Jim O'Neill.[107] *Moving Picture World* praised the film's action ('not a dull moment'), while *Motography* suggested it was 'one of the best stories of corrupt municipal politics which has ever appeared on the screen'.[108] Addressing the issue of authenticity, the *New York Dramatic Mirror* wrote: 'Stage Policemen are usually a ludicrous farce to real policemen but [Thomas] Santachi [the film's director and lead actor] not only looks and acts real himself, but has succeeded in making the other members of the cast also act as if they had been "pounding pavement" all their lives.'[109]

Early American cinema also produced numerous examples of Irish detectives who were clever and brave, including Detective Murray in *The Woman and the Law* (Crystal, 1913) and Detective Kelly in *The Twin's Double* (Gold Seal, 1914), *The Mystery of the White Car* (Gold Seal, 1914) and *The Mysterious Rose* (Gold Seal, 1914).[110] In *McCarn Plays Fate* (Reliance, 1914), the title character – a 'veteran police detective' – cleverly outwits the 'noted crook', Bull Klein.[111] According to *Moving Picture World*, *Detective Kelly* (Pathé Frères, 1914) was a 'thrilling picture even if it does contain absurdities'.[112] Its title character uses clever disguises and a fast automobile to catch a jewel thief. *Jimmy Kelley and the Kidnapper* (Joker, 1914) features a despondent detective who nearly commits suicide; however, 'at the critical moment' he reads about a gang of kidnappers that he proceeds to apprehend.[113] Then, in *The Tip-Off* (Balboa, 1915), detective chief Charles Donnelly successfully rounds up the Spike Murray gang.[114]

The key example of the Irish detective on film was *Dublin Dan, The Irish Detective* (Solax, 1912), a three-reel film starring Barney Gilmore. Gilmore wrote the story, which he performed onstage in a touring production at least as early as 1908. The title character works for the 'secret service' and uses his intelligence and disguises to liberate abducted women from a vicious ring of counterfeiters. In addition to scenes of high adventure, the stage production afforded Gilmore the chance to sing 'Irish songs' and to offer an array of 'Irish witticisms'.[115] At some performances, Gilmore also presented a non-fiction stereopticon show entitled *A Trip to Ireland*.[116]

Newspaper articles promoting the film version of *Dublin Dan, The Irish Detective* often drew attention to Gilmore's lengthy and successful stage career.[117] Moreover, *Moving Picture World* compared *Dublin Dan's* use of melodrama to that of Dion Boucicault.[118] Solax advertised the film as a 'thrilling and sensational melodrama', and a 'tense story of crime, conspiracy, and punishment'.[119] Surviving plot synopses suggest that the film eliminated the stage play's use of music and comedy, though it is possible that the film featured a minimal amount of humour.[120]

Presumably due to the success of *Dublin Dan*, Gilmore starred in at least two more detective films. For example, he was Detective Delaney in *The Fight for Millions* (Blaché Features, 1913), a four-reel feature film.[121] The plot hinges on a gang leader kidnapping a banker and attempting to blame a man named Russell. Responding favourably to the film, *Moving Picture World* noted: 'There [are] plots and counter-plots, all interestingly and more or less excitingly worked out. The result of course is the triumph of the detective – the restoration of the banker to his daughter, the

**6.6** *The Gangsters* (Reliance, 1914, aka *The Gangsters of New York*).

rehabilitation of Russell, and the breaking up and capture of the gang.'[122] Two years later, Gilmore appeared in *The Game of Three* (Sterling Camera and Film, 1915), a five-reel feature film. In it, he portrayed Detective O'Bryan of the New York City police department, who is hot on the trail of a stolen diamond necklace.[123] Similar to *Dublin Dan*, the film attempted to offer scenes of high adventure and action.[124] *Moving Picture World* claimed that it was 'not always bound by the laws of probability, but [was] always thrilling, always exciting, and never standing still'.[125] While drawing attention to the 'director's carelessness' in some scenes, *Motion Picture News* lauded the film for shooting on location in the streets of New York, the result providing a sense of authenticity.[126]

## The Gangster

Though the Irish gangster did not emerge in American cinema until the nickelodeon period, the character became a clear antithesis to the Irish police officer. As different as the two were, both the policeman and the gangster were characters who could appear in films of various genres. For example, Dan Kelly in *Love and Duty* (Kay-Bee, 1914) is the leader of a gang of wagon thieves; the Irish gangster was not solely an urban or 'modern' or, for that matter, a serious character.[127]

Indeed, various kinds of Irish criminals appeared in film comedies. 'Spider' Burke robs Mr Shaughnessy in *The Hold-Up Held Up* (Edison, 1909), but his partner 'Buck' Malley unexpectedly turns the gun on him. As they squabble, Shaughnessy hits Buck over the head, seizes a revolver, and then sees that both men go to jail.[128] *Red Sweeney's Mistake* (Kalem, 1913) finds Sweeney attempting to pawn jewellery that is both fake and stolen, resulting in a 'protracted visit' to prison.[129] The title character of *Mickey Flynn's Escapade* (Kalem, 1914) robs a counterfeiter and unknowingly 'puts the spurious money into general circulation'.[130] In 1914, Universal released *The Yegg and the Eggs*; in it, 'Spike' Murphy breaks into a safe in order to steal some 'priceless eggs'.[131] The following year, *A Boob for Luck* (Kalem, 1915) featured confidence men Hoyle and Casey.[132]

As for dramatic gangster stories, some offered tales of characters who recant their lives of crime. The narrative of *The Disreputable Mr Reagan* (Edison, 1911) featured what *Moving Picture World* called 'the Sunday school idea of reform'.[133] In *Micky's Pal* (Solax, 1912), Micky is not reformed by three years in a penitentiary, but he subsequently becomes 'full of remorse' after fighting with his friend Tom.[134] *Conscience* (Broncho, 1913) offered the story of Haggerty, who flees West disguised as a minister to evade capture; he meets a young woman and quickly changes his ways.[135] Both Red McGee and his girlfriend Sal reform in *Salvation Sal* (Vitagraph, 1913), though Red dies at the film's conclusion; much the same occurs to 'bad man' Regan in *Regan's Daughter* (Vitagraph, 1914).[136] Then, in Kay-Bee's 1914 film *In the Clutches of Gangsters*, Red Corrigan is 'moved to lead an honourable life' after meeting a 'pretty girl'.[137]

As the early cinema period drew to a close, the numbers of Irish gangsters and crooks increased. They appeared in such films as *The Chief of Police* (Kalem, 1914), *The Bully's Doom* (Lubin, 1914), *Wolves of the Underworld* (Broncho, 1914), *Conscience* (Broncho, 1914), *Stop Thief* (Kleine, 1915), *Out of Bondage* (Majestic, 1915) and *The Web of Crime* (Selig, 1915).[138] Those examples were all in addition to character Mike Donegal, who appeared in Kalem's 'Girl Detective' series. Episode 13, entitled *Mike Donegal's Escape* (1915), covered his escape from prison and subsequent recapture.[139] *Moving Picture World* noted that Paul C. Hurst played the character with 'grim realism'.[140]

Of these various Irish gangster films, two became the most important: *The Gangsters* (Reliance, 1914, aka *The Gangsters of New York*) and *Regeneration* (Fox, 1915, aka *The Regeneration*). Directed by James Kirkwood and 'supervised' by D.W. Griffith, *The Gangsters* was a four-reel film starring Henry B. Walthall. Its story features Biff Dugan, leader of a tough Irish gang that fights a war with a group of rivals. Biff is wrongly convicted of murder and is sentenced to the electric chair.[141] *Moving Picture World* claimed: 'the gangster is shown to be primitive in all his methods, a savage injected into the midst of progressive civilizations... He knows of only one act deserving punishment, that of squealing, to which there is only one penalty attached – that of death.'[142]

Speaking of *The Gangsters*, the *Washington Post* claimed that James Kirkwood was a 'strict exponent of realism in pictures'.[143] A newspaper in Wisconsin agreed, noting the film showed 'the life of the New York gangster, and, while the film is filled with battle, murder, and sudden death in such an extent that it seems almost impossible that such conditions can exist in a modern city, the chronicles in the newspapers almost daily leave little room for doubt that such things do exist'.[144] The same newspaper drew particular attention to an electrocution scene, claiming it was both gruesome and believable, so much so that it could act as a deterrent to viewers. The *New York Dramatic Mirror* believed much the same, claiming that the film – which they viewed as extremely well produced – was an 'absolutely true picture of crime as it exists in the underworld of today', so much so that it could act as a 'sermon in morality and a plea for better conditions as well'.[145]

Raoul Walsh's *Regeneration* deserves an even more prominent position in the history of the gangster film genre.[146] Adapted from a novel by Owen Kildare that had already been presented on the stage, the film's epic story follows the character Owen Conway from childhood to manhood. His 'regeneration' – in which he disavows the gangster life – occurs thanks to the intervention of a 'pretty settlement worker'.[147] Conway's enemy eventually fires a shot that kills her, but 'her work in reforming Owen is complete'.[148] In some respects, *Regeneration* echoed earlier films in which gangsters recant their lives of crime.

To heighten the film's 'realism', Walsh shot numerous scenes on location in Chinatown, along the Bowery, and in the 'Three Deuces' tenement.[149] *Moving Picture World* praised the director's 'accurate' representation of the 'squalor of tenement life on the East Side of New York', which included a 'selection of types that are in no way an exaggeration of those to be found on the streets'.[150] *Motion Picture News* concurred, claiming that 'there are dozens of realistic touches in every reel comprising the feature'.[151]

# The Priest

Catholic priests made numerous appearances during the early cinema period, though in some cases they were not coded as Irish.[152] In other cases,

**6.7** Van Dyke Brooke (seated left) in *O'Hara as Guardian Angel* (Vitagraph, 1913).

given the lack of surviving film prints, it is difficult to determine what ethnicity various moving pictures ascribed to their priest characters. For example, a priest appeared in *The Washerwoman's Mistake* (Lubin, 1903). According to a catalogue synopsis, the washerwoman was Irish, but no mention is made of the priest's heritage.[153]

It does seem that Irish priests appeared more frequently on screen after 1910, including in some of the O'Kalem films described in Chapter 5. Other examples include *Sunshine* (Essanay, 1912), in which Father O'Brien visits a condemned man in prison.[154] Irish priests also appeared in at least four early feature films, one being the aforementioned *Regeneration* (1915). *The Boss* (World Film, 1915) featured two key Irish characters; one becomes a priest, while another becomes a powerful businessman.[155] In *The Greater Will* (Premo, 1915), Father Malone hears a millionaire's story of how his daughter died at the hands of a 'master of hypnotism'. Such narratives depended on priest characters, but not necessarily on their ethnicity.

By contrast, the seven-reel feature film *The Rosary* (Selig, 1915) founded its story on the Irish heritage of the key character, Brian Kelly, who becomes Father Kelly; as a result, its depiction of an Irish priest was probably the most developed and important of the early cinema period.[156] Early scenes depict Kelly as a youth in Ireland; he later immigrates to America and works in a tenement district of New York. Kelly cares for a young man named Bruce whose mother was Kelly's 'old sweetheart of long ago in Ireland'. Later, when Bruce tries to shoot a man, Kelly successfully intervenes and the film reaches a happy conclusion.[157]

The *New York Dramatic Mirror* praised *The Rosary* for including 'some of the finest touches it has been our pleasure to witness' and drew particular attention to the 'scenes supposedly laid in Ireland, in which there are some of the most realistic settings showing Irish peasant life'.[158] *Moving Picture World* had a similar reaction, claiming the film's dramatic situations were 'realistic', as were the settings in both Ireland and New York.[159]

In some cases, the traditional roles and traits associated with priests were transferred to non-priest characters. The key example would be Vitagraph's 'O'Hara' film series, which was created by W.A. Tremayne. Van Dyke Brooke starred in the title role, with Kate Price, William Shea and Hughie Mack appearing in supporting parts. 'Sure, he's a fine man', Vitagraph publicity claimed. 'He and his philosophy help others. He's a peace-maker and promoter of happiness...O'Hara is the embodiment of geniality and good sense.'[160] Tremayne's O'Hara stories included some humorous elements, but they were not comedies.

Vitagraph released *O'Hara, Squatter and Philosopher*, the first of the five films, in November 1912. In it, O'Hara brings peace to a man fighting with the father of the woman he loves.[161] The *New York Dramatic Mirror* praised its 'appealing spirit' and 'pleasant effect'.[162] *Moving Picture World* echoed that sentiment, claiming that 'the author of this picture of life in the shanty borders of Brooklyn deserves credit for a fresh and human glimpse of a few good Irish characters'.[163]

Subsequent films in the series featured similar narratives. *O'Hara Helps Cupid* (Vitagraph, 1913) has O'Hara helping a policeman win the heart of a widow who has another suitor.[164] *O'Hara's Godchild* (Vitagraph, 1913) returned to the young couple seen in *Squatter and Philosopher*; O'Hara helps them and their new son.[165] Less than two months later, Vitagraph released *O'Hara and the Youthful Prodigal* (Vitagraph, 1913), which featured the same young couple and their son, who is now 8 years old. The boy runs away from home after being punished for misbehaviour, but O'Hara 'brings him back to the fold'.[166] Then, in *O'Hara as a Guardian Angel* (Vitagraph, 1913), the title character 'protects his daughter from her husband's false friend and points out the way to real happiness'.[167]

*Guardian Angel* was the final moving picture in the series. It is difficult to say why Vitagraph did not produce further O'Hara films, though two reviews in *Moving Picture World* suggest a possible reason. The trade publication responded favourably to the first three films in the series, refer-ring to the first two as 'delightful' and noting that the third was 'very acceptable'.[168] However, their critique of *Youthful Prodigal* claimed it was an 'overwork[ed]' idea and that it 'lack[ed] spontaneity'.[169] They were even more harsh in discussing *Guardian Angel*, claiming that the 'plot is weak and rather illogical'. The trade also bemoaned the fact that 'no series can hold up for long'.[170]

While that comment may well have been true, the O'Hara films proba-bly inspired at least one other similar film. Selig's *Jimmy* (1915) was a one-reel moving picture that featured 'Jimmy Hennessy ... a keen witted lad of the slums' who works as a messenger boy.[171] Though far younger than O'Hara, Jimmy shared much in common with him. Describing the film's story, *Motography* wrote that he 'responds to the summons of Rose Hargreaves when she wishes to return her ring to Jack Peabody, with whom she has had a quarrel. In his boyish, frank manner, the boy proceeds to reunite the alienated couple.'[172]

# The Hero

Of the five key character types described in this chapter, the Irish hero was the least codified. Usually these heroes were lead roles, and usually their acts of bravery and ingenuity were not directly dependent on their ethnic-ity. That they were Irish was generally incidental, and sometimes not referred to outside of their character names. In other respects, these heroes could be quite different from one another, due in part to the fact that they appeared in various film genres.

Some of these Irish heroes were men in uniform. Edison's *On Donovan's Division* (1912) has a fireman who prevents a train from crashing.[173] Kalem's *The Fire-Fighting Zouaves* (1913) featured the 'Irish laddies' of the 'famous Zouave regiment, recruited from the fire laddies of the Bowery in New York City'.[174] The film's story depicts the group in war scenes that culminate in the rescue of a 'fair heroine from her home, set on fire by shells of the enemy'.[175] The following year, the title character of *Private Dennis Hogan* (Vitagraph, 1914) was a 'rollicking, devil-may-care Irishman' whose expertise at telegraphy serves him well in the army when he and his fellow soldiers fight the Sioux Indians.[176]

Other heroes were out of uniform, fighting against evil in more informal capacities. The title character of *Gallegher* (Edison, 1910) loses his job at a newspaper office, later regaining it after overcoming 'several obstacles' and making a 'scoop' by shadowing a wanted murderer.[177] In *The Wolf of the City* (Selig, 1913), police reporter Haggarty refuses a bribe to keep a story

**6.8** Darwin Karr as the title character in *Private Dennis Hogan* (Vitagraph, 1914).

out of his newspaper.[178] Similarly, the title character in *Steve O'Grady's Chance* (Vitagraph, 1914) moves to the 'south' after being discharged by his newspaper.[179] In a small town, he tracks and defeats a group of bank robbers in a 'spirited fight'.[180] The resulting story causes his former editor to rehire him.

Western films of the early cinema were populated with a number of Irish characters, as in *The Foiling of Red Dugan* (Essanay, 1911), *The Sheriff's Prisoner* (Lubin, 1912), *Broncho Billy's Pal* (Essanay, 1912), *Broncho Billy's Strategy* (Essanay, 1913), *Conscience* (Broncho, 1913) and *Red Sweeney's Defeat* (American, 1913).[181] A number of these characters were heroes, such as the title character in *Texas Kelly at Bay* (Kay-Bee, 1911), who 'holds back the bandits attacking a stagecoach in true border-hero style, until help comes'.[182] Two years later, according to one advertisement, the falsely accused Jim Dolan, of *The Escape of Jim Dolan* (Selig, 1913), was the 'ideal type of Westerner'.[183] Similar examples include Buck McGee in *The Fatherhood of Buck McGee* (Vitagraph, 1912), Sheriff McCarthy in *The Sheriff's Honeymoon* (Essanay, 1913), Tommy Maguire in *His First Performance* (Edison, 1913), and the title character of *O'Hara of the Mounted* (Federal, 1915).[184]

A number of other Irish heroes combated the problems that plagued poor urban neighbourhoods. In *The Samaritan of Coogan's Tenement* (Lubin, 1912), 'Red' Maguire gives money to a young man who has helped him.[185] In *Tim Grogan's Foundling* (Vitagraph, 1913), the title character (portrayed by Van Dyke Brooke) is an Irish bricklayer in Chicago. He defends a young child against kidnappers and blackmailers, and is thus able

**6.9** *Steve O'Grady's Chance* (Vitagraph, 1914).

to marry the Widow McGee (Kate Price).[186] Then, in *A Broth of a Boy* (Edison, 1915), the wealthy and retired Joseph Sullivan assists the poor but honest Tim Connelly.[187]

Not all of these heroes were men. In *The Tragedy of Ambition* (Selig, 1914), Madge O'Mara works in a 'chop-house' to support her mother; her father was a saloonkeeper who died in Sing Sing.[188] At one point, Madge saves a captured man from a group of 'conspirators'.[189] The title character of *The Heart of Maggie Malone* (Selig, 1914) rescues a young girl in the tenements from 'persecution and shame' at the hands of the evil 'Oily Jake'.[190] Similarly, Sandy McCarthy ('of Celtic blood') saves the title character in *The Salvation of Nance O'Shaughnessy* (Selig, 1914) from a man at a dance hall 'with a catapult to [his] jaw that leaves him on the floor'.[191]

Another type of Irish hero on screen was the Irish adventurer. One of the more notable examples was *Kelly from the Emerald Isle* (Solax, 1913), which starred Barney Gilmore. Solax promoted the film as a 'genuine feature' with 'quaint and characteristic Irish humour'.[192] Whatever comedic elements it contained, however, the film's emphasis was on Kelly's heroism in the face of the villainous Doolin. *Moving Picture World* praised its 'convincing touches of realism', which included such stunts as the 'escape of Kelly and Sheilah [the film's heroine] over the cliff, a feat that will make the audiences wonder how the players dared so risk their lives'.[193] Among many other perils, Kelly is even 'tied to the rails and all but run over by a fast train'.[194]

A different kind of Irish adventurer was Chimmie Fadden, a character created by E.W. Townsend of the *New York Sun*. Cecil B. DeMille directed the five-reel feature film *Chimmie Fadden* for Paramount in 1915.[195] Irish-American actor Victor Moore starred as the title character, a 'Bowery Boy' who lives in a New York slum with his mother and his brother Larry, who is a crook. Chimmie obtains a job as a butler and vies for the attentions of a French maid until he stumbles onto a burglary committed by Larry and another man.[196] Chimmie tries to protect Larry, but finds himself charged with the crime until Larry confesses. Chimmie convinces the burgled man not to press charges, thus freeing his brother and allowing Chimmie the chance to reunite with the French maid.[197] Both *Moving Picture World* and the *New York Dramatic Mirror* praised the film, which proved highly successful with audiences.[198]

DeMille quickly co-wrote and directed a five-reel sequel entitled *Chimmie Fadden Out West* (Paramount, 1915).[199] In it, Chimmie heads to Death Valley and claims to have discovered a non-existent gold mine in order to promote a railroad that runs through the territory.[200] His plan works well until his employers issue stock on the gold mine.[201] The *New York Dramatic Mirror* and *Motion Picture News* published positive reviews, as did *Moving Picture World*, which drew particular attention to Victor Moore and Mrs Lewis McCord, who portrayed 'Mother Fadden'.[202] As with the first film, DeMille combined humour and adventure to construct the storyline.

In terms of his number of screen appearances, adventurer Terence O'Rourke was the most prominent Irish hero of the early cinema period.[203] In August 1914, *Motography* announced that Universal had obtained the film rights to Louis Joseph Vance's character, which had been popularized in his short stories and books. Universal's choice for the lead role was J. Warren 'Jack' Kerrigan, one of the most popular of the early film stars. The publication referred to O'Rourke as 'the most pleasing, clean cut, gentleman adventurer who ever entertained an audience bent upon being thrilled, enchanted, and bodily carried away into the world of romance and heart-throb'.[204]

The first O'Rourke films – which Universal collectively referred to as *Terence O'Rourke, Soldier of Fortune* and which were released 'every other week' under the 'Victor' company name – were comprised of five two-reel stories (as opposed to the 'twenty odd' originally announced), thus creating a series akin to a film serial.[205] The inaugural release was *His Heart, His Hand and His Sword* (1914), followed by *The Empire of Illusion* (1914), *The Inn of the Winged God* (aka, *The Inn of the Winged Gods*, 1914), *The King and the Man* (1914) and *A Captain of Villainy* (1915).[206] The tales

**6.10** *The Salvation of Nance O'Shaughnessy* (Selig, 1914).

began with O'Rourke in Paris and then covered his exploits in the Sahara and the Balkans. Romance, murder and intrigue marked the series.

Approximately one year after the *Soldier of Fortune* films first played theatres, Universal revived the character for a second series entitled *The New Adventures of Terence O'Rourke*. Once again, Jack Kerrigan portrayed the lead role.[207] Three two-reelers, each of which was released only one week after the previous entry, comprised the series: *The Palace of Dust* (1915), *When a Queen Loved O'Rourke* (1915) and *The Road to Paradise* (1915).[208] Using his wits, his bravery and his 'eloquent Irish tongue', O'Rourke successfully pursued adventures in such locations as Egypt and India.[209]

# Conclusion

With a script from Burns Mantle, director Lawrence B. McGill shot his feature film *How Molly Made Good* (Kulee, aka *How Molly Malone Made Good*) in 1915; it appeared in theatres in the autumn of that year, just as the early cinema period came to a close. Marguerite Gale starred in the title role of Molly, a character who emigrates from Ireland to the United States to reunite with her brother, a journalist for the *New York Tribune*. Upon arrival, she learns that her brother has left to fight in the war effort, presumably for John Redmond's National Volunteer Force, though that is never stated. His absence leaves poor Molly forlorn and without any means of financial support.

Molly immediately looks to the *Tribune* for employment, promising to interview a famous opera star that she met aboard ship during her passage to the US. The *Tribune* editor is quickly impressed by her abilities, and assigns her another ten interviews with famous actors. For the next several reels, Molly conducts the interviews with actual celebrities who are playing themselves. To add a sense of conflict and an element of comedy, a rival female reporter attempts to thwart Molly's new career at every turn.

Importantly, Molly's Irish background is never mentioned or addressed in any way after she begins interviewing celebrities. She has come to America from Ireland, but she is already aboard ship when the film begins; Ireland, even in the form of a studio set, is never shown. Molly finds success in the entertainment business as a journalist, an interviewer. She becomes a part of the larger American entertainment industry, and her Irish roots are not a factor in her work. As a result, they are not a factor during the bulk of the film's running time, and so it operates quite differently from other immigration film narratives.

Some trade publication reviews, which were overwhelmingly favourable, briefly mentioned that Molly was an Irish character.[210] However, other articles and reviews did not draw attention to her ethnicity. In a newspaper article, Burns Mantle – the film's screenwriter – referred to her simply as a 'newspaper novice'.[211] Moreover, a survey of newspaper advertisements across the United States and of surviving publicity materials makes clear that the film was distributed as *How Molly Made Good*, rather than *How Molly Malone Made Good*, thus eliminating her Irish surname from the title.

What did the reviews discuss? The *Washington Post* spoke about the 'novelty of twelve stars in one feature picture'.[212] Other reviews in both trade publications and city newspapers emphasized that as well.[213] *Motography* believed that the film's popularity hinged on its star power, claiming: 'It is quite unlike any other feature picture ever made and it is

**6.11** A six-sheet movie poster for *How Molly Made Good* (Kulee, 1915).

quite unlikely that ever again twelve stars of equal importance will be seen in one feature.'[214] That the film was unique represented an overstatement, as it was essentially a remake of *How Cissy Made Good* (Vitagraph, 1915), in which the title character – who was not coded as Irish – interviews a number of film stars, including John Bunny and Kate Price.[215]

In an effort to summarize the history of the Irish film character, it would be tempting to suggest that Molly and *How Molly Made Good* are either representative of the early cinema period or are the culmination of some kind of evolution. But in fact, neither would be true. Too many Irish characters populated American film genres for any one of them to act as a stand-in for all of the others. Certainly the number and array of different

Irish film characters grew as the era progressed, but – as a study of the Irish-themed comedy genre makes clear – while there were many changes between 1894 and 1915, there was no clear, simple, linear evolution. Some film characters cast off the shackles of the stage Irish; others did not. Put another way, the arrival of the serious Irish policeman and detective in the nickelodeon era did not bring an end to the comedic Irish cop. The appearance of sympathetic characters like O'Hara or heroes like Terence O'Rourke did not alter either the proliferation or the depiction of Irish gangsters or Irish boxers on the screen.

All that said, *How Molly Made Good* can act as an important coda to the Irish film characters described in this chapter. The very fact that the Irish Molly – whose heritage hardly plays a role in her story – was a reincarnation of the non-Irish Cissy indicates just how malleable and how less than codified the Irish film character in early American cinema could be. Indeed, the connection between Molly and Cissy underscores once again how tethered both the Irish-themed film and the Irish-coded film character were to the broader American film industry, and, by extension, to its pre-cinema influences.

# Notes

1. 'A Plot for a Million', *Kalem Kalendar*, 1 April 1913, p.11.
2. Ibid.
3. 'The Younger Generation', *Moving Picture World*, 30 August 1913, p.980.
4. 'O'Brien Finds a Way', *Moving Picture World*, 26 December 1914, p.1842.
5. 'When Wealth Torments', *Moving Picture World*, 2 November 1912, p.478.
6. 'Cohen and Murphy', *Moving Picture World*, 23 July 1910, p.215; 'Cohen and Murphy', *Moving Picture World*, 30 July 1910, p.12.
7. 'The Fire Escape', *Motography*, 4 September 1915, p.492.
8. *Renunciation* is available on the DVD entitled *D.W. Griffith – Director, Volume Three* (Phoenix, AZ: Grapevine Video, 2006). See also 'Renunciation', *Moving Picture World*, 17 July 1909, p.97.
9. 'The Trap', *Moving Picture World*, 28 March 1914, p.1742,
10. 'The Chorus Lady', *Moving Picture World*, 30 October 1915, p.1034.
11. 'Jack Logan's Dog', *Moving Picture World*, 24 December 1910, p.1490; 'Tim Mahoney, the Scab', *Moving Picture World*, 10 June 1911, p.1313; 'Tim Mahoney, the Scab', *The Billboard*, 10 June 1911, p.14; 'Wynona's Revenge', *Moving Picture World*, 15 November 1913, p.778; 'Old Gorman's Gal', *Moving Picture World*, 8 March 1913, p.1012; 'While Mrs. McFadden Looked Out', *Moving Picture World*, 8 February 1913, p.614; 'Witness "A 3-Center" ', *Moving Picture World*, 21 June 1913, p.1278; 'The Decision of Jim O'Farrel', *New York Dramatic Mirror*, 2 September 1914, p.34; 'The Danger Signal', *Moving Picture World*, 20 November 1915, p.1510; 'Imp Stars in *Larry O'Neill, Gentleman*', *Universal Weekly*, 19 June 1915, p.29.
12. 'Young Romance', *Moving Picture World*, 13 February 1915, p.1050.
13. 'Think Mothers', *Moving Picture World*, 2 October 1915, p.126.
14. 'Her Mother's Voice', *Moving Picture World*, 2 January 1915, p.134.
15. *Picture Catalogue* (New York: American Mutoscope & Biograph Company, November 1902), p.49. Available in *A Guide to Motion Picture Catalogs by American Producers and Distributors, 1894–1908: A Microfilm Edition*, Reel 1.
16. A copy of *Alphonse and Gaston* exists at the Library of Congress in Washington, DC.

17. *Moving Picture World*, 12 October 1907, p.502.
18. Advertisement, *Moving Picture World*, 27 July 1907, p.325.
19. 'Poor Finney', *Moving Picture World*, 10 February 1912, p.64.
20. 'The Story of a Wallet', *Moving Picture World*, 13 August 1912, p.914.
21. 'The Iconoclast', *Moving Picture World*, 22 March 1913, p.1258.
22. 'Betty's Bondage', *Motography*, 7 August 1915, p.278.
23. 'Sunshine Molly', *Moving Picture World*, 20 March 1915, p.1840.
24. 'An Unpaid Ransom', *Moving Picture World*, 3 April 1915, pp.112–13.
25. James J. Corbett, 'Corbett's Own Story', *Dallas Morning News*, 4 September 1892, p.5.
26. 'Prize Fight Reproduced', *Newark Sunday Advocate* (Newark, OH), 9 September 1894, p.1.
27. Dan Streible, *Fight Pictures: A History of Boxing and Early Cinema* (Berkeley, CA: University of California Press, 2008), p.35.
28. Ibid., p.83.
29. For a thorough account of these films, see ibid., pp.126–63.
30. 'Corbett in How Championships Are Won and Lost', *New York Dramatic Mirror*, p.19.
31. Streible, *Fight Pictures*, p.107.
32. 'By Sime', *Variety*, 20 January 1906, p.9.
33. Advertisement, *New York Clipper*, 28 September 1907, p.888.
34. 'Spike Shannon's Last Fight', *Moving Picture World*, 19 August 1911, p.475; 'Spike Shannon's Last Fight', *Moving Picture World*, 9 September 1911, pp.714–16.
35. 'The Reformation of Kid Hogan', *Moving Picture World*, 13 April 1912, p.15; 'The Reformation of Kid Hogan', *Moving Picture World*, 20 April 1912, p.230.
36. 'Kid Reagan's Hands', *Moving Picture World*, 26 September 1914, p.1778.
37. 'The Man Who Beat Dan Dolan', *New York Dramatic Mirror*, 2 June 1915, p.32.
38. 'Ireland and Israel', *Moving Picture News*, 2 March 1912, p.30; 'Ireland and Israel', *Moving Picture News*, 9 March 1912, p.43; 'Ireland and Israel', *Moving Picture World*, 9 March 1912, p.874; 'Ireland and Israel', *Moving Picture World*, 16 March 1912, p.1000; 'Ireland and Israel', *Photoplay*, April 1912, pp.53–9.
39. 'Ireland and Israel', *New York Dramatic Mirror*, 27 March 1912, p.32.
40. 'Ireland and Israel', *Moving Picture World*, 6 April 1912, p.42.
41. Advertisement, *Moving Picture News*, 9 March 1912, p.37; advertisement, *Moving Picture World*, 16 March 1912, p.926.
42. 'The Rise and Fall of McDoo', *Moving Picture World*, 14 June 1913, p.1172; 'The Rise and Fall of McDoo', *Moving Picture World*, 5 July 1913, p.48; 'Red Hicks Defies the World', *Moving Picture World*, 21 June 1913, p.1252; 'Knockout Dugan's Find', *Motography*, 4 September 1915, p.493.
43. A copy of *One-Round O'Brien* exists at the Library of Congress in Washington, DC.
44. 'One-Round O'Brien', *Moving Picture World*, 29 June 1912, p.1264; 'One-Round O'Brien', *Moving Picture World*, 27 July 1912, p.343.
45. 'One-Round O'Brien Is a Series', *Moving Picture World*, 30 August 1913, p.965.
46. 'One-Round O'Brien Comes Back', *Moving Picture World*, 5 July 1913, p.49; 'One-Round O'Brien Comes Back', *Moving Picture World*, 5 July 1913, p.86.
47. 'One-Round O'Brien Is a Series', p.965.
48. 'One-Round O'Brien's Flirtation', *Moving Picture World*, 6 September 1913, p.1069.
49. 'One-Round O'Brien in the Ring Again', *Moving Picture World*, 21 February 1914, p.947.
50. Such films include: *The New Cop* (Essanay, 1909), *The Policeman's Romance* (1909), *The Masquerade Cop* (Essanay, 1910) and *The Stolen Policeman* (Great Northern, 1910).
51. Copies of *The Cop and the Nurse Girl* and *Off His Beat* exist at the Library of Congress in Washington, DC.
52. Other examples of non-Irish policemen in early American cinema include *Clarence the Cop* (American Mutoscope & Biograph, 1903), *Clarence the Cop on the Feed Store Beat* (American Mutoscope & Biograph, 1904), *In the Hands of the Black Hands* (Biograph, 1913) and *Snitz Joins the Force* (Sterling, 1914). With regard to the Keystone Cops, at least one film featuring an Irish character tried to emulate their police comedies, Royal's 1914 film *O'Flanagan's Luck*. See 'O'Flanagan's Luck', *Moving Picture World*, 19 September 1914, p.1645.
53. A copy of *New York City Police Parade* exists at the Library of Congress in Washington, DC.
54. 'New York Police Force', *New York Dramatic Mirror*, 16 July 1910, p.22.

55. '*The Police Force of New York*', *Moving Picture World*, 31 December 1910, p.1536.

56. A copy of *The Police Force of New York* appears on *Perils of the New Land: Films of the Immigrant Experience (1910–1915)*, DVD (Los Angeles, CA: Flicker Alley, LLC, 2008).

57. Quoted in Savada, p.213.

58. A copy of *How the Dutch Beat the Irish* exists at the Library of Congress in Washington, DC.

59. *No. 288, Edison Films*, p.17.

60. *Lubin's Films* (Philadelphia: S. Lubin, circa 1905–1906) unpaginated. Available in *A Guide to Motion Picture Catalogs by American Producers and Distributors, 1894–1905: A Microfilm Edition*, Reel 3.

61. '*Maggie Hoolihan Gets a Job*', *Moving Picture World*, 3 September 1910, p.537; '*Maggie Hoolihan Gets a Job*', *Moving Picture World*, 17 September 1910, p.631.

62. '*Dooley's Scheme*', *Moving Picture World*, 11 November 1911, p.494.

63. '*The Pie Eaters*', *Moving Picture World*, 6 June 1914, p.1442.

64. '*Mike, the Timid Cop*', *Kalem Kalendar*, 15 August 1913, p.15; '*Mike, the Timid Cop*', *Moving Picture World*, 13 September 1913, p.1175.

65. '*Off Agin – On Agin – Finnegan*', *Moving Picture World*, 17 October 1914, p.337.

66. 'Her Father Throttled in Mistake for Rival', *Universal Weekly*, 10 October 1914, pp.21, 24; '*On Again [sic] – Off Again [sic] Finnegan*', *Motography*, 17 October 1914, p.544.

67. '*On Again [sic] – Off Again [sic] Finnegan*', *Moving Picture World*, 10 October 1914, p.240.

68. '*Officer Muldoon's Double*', *New York Dramatic Mirror*, 18 June 1910, p 17.

69. '*Officer Muldoon's Double*', *Moving Picture World*, 4 June 1910, p.954.

70. '*A Flirty Affliction*', *The Essanay Guide*, 15 September 1910, pp.7–8.

71. '*Where Is Mulcahy?*', *Moving Picture World*, 28 May 1910, p.899.

72. '*A Cooked Goose*', *Moving Picture World*, 11 July 1914, p.344.

73. '*Building a Trust*', *Moving Picture World*, 26 July 1913, p.427.

74. '*Murphy's I.O.U.*', *Moving Picture World*, 21 April 1913, p.206.

75. '*Scenting a Terrible Crime*', *Moving Picture World*, 4 October 1913, p.66. A copy of *Scenting a Terrible Crime* exists at the Museum of Modern Art in New York City.

76. '*A Brewerytown Romance*', *Moving Picture World*, 29 May 1914, p.1298.

77. '*Two of the Bravest*', *Moving Picture World*, 5 June 1915, p.1694.

78. '*Brannigan's Promotion*', *Moving Picture News*, 10 February 1912, p.42.

79. '*The Fire Cop*', *Moving Picture World*, 30 November 1912, p.902.

80. '*The Rise of Officer Casey*', *Moving Picture World*, 14 March 1914, p.1384.

81. The Pathé Fréres' film *Female Police Force* (1908) also featured female police officers, though a surviving plot synopsis does not suggest that these characters were Irish. See '*Female Police Force*', *Views and Film Index*, 9 May 1908, p.11.

82. '*Kate, the Cop*', *Moving Picture World*, 13 May 1913, p.942.

83. A copy of *Officer Kate* exists at the UCLA Film Archive (University of California, Los Angeles).

84. '*The Female Cop*', *Moving Picture World*, 29 May 1914, p.1298.

85. '*Not Much Force*', *Motography*, 7 August 1915, p.272.

86. '*Officer McCue*', *New York Dramatic Mirror*, 5 June 1909, p.15.

87. '*Officer 666*', *Moving Picture World*, 26 December 1914, p.1904.

88. 'Klein's *Officer 666*', *Motography*, 2 January 1915, p.22.

89. '*One Touch of Nature*', *Moving Picture World*, 9 January 1909, p.9.

90. '*Clancy*', *Moving Picture World*, 7 January 1911, p.32; '*Clancy*', *Variety*, 7 January 1911, p.13.

91. Advertisement, *Moving Picture World*, 11 June 1910, p.1006. *A Child of the Ghetto* is available on the DVD entitled *D.W. Griffith, Director – Volume Five* (Phoenix, AZ: Grapevine Video, 2007). See also '*Renunciation*', *Moving Picture World*, 17 July 1909, p.97.

92. '*A Child of the Ghetto*', *Moving Picture World*, 11 June 1910, p.1005. The same publication offered similar praise in '*A Child of the Ghetto*', 18 June 1910, p.1048, claiming: 'The Ghetto pictures are as good as any ever put on the screen.'

93. '*Playing for a Fortune*', *Moving Picture World*, 14 February 1914, p.808.

94. '*Mounted Officer Flynn*', *Moving Picture World*, 29 November 1913, p.1034.

95. A copy of *Traffic in Souls* appears on the DVD *Perils of the New Land: Films of the Immigrant Experience (1910–1915)*.

96. '*The Fates and Ryan*', *Moving Picture World*, 21 November 1914, p.1122.

97. 'Only the Maid', Moving Picture World, 20 March 1915, p.1816.
98. 'McQuade of the Traffic Squad', Moving Picture World, 5 June 1915, p.1659; 'McQuade of the Traffic Squad', New York Dramatic Mirror, 9 June 1915, p.37; 'McQuade of the Traffic Squad', Moving Picture World, 26 June 1915, p.2095.
 99. A copy of McQuade of the Traffic Squad appears on the DVD Perils of the New Land: Films of the Immigrant Experience (1910–1915).
100. 'The Policeman and the Baby', Moving Picture World, 20 September 1913, p.1312.
101. 'The Cop on the Beat', Moving Picture World, 14 March 1914, p.1426.
102. 'Officer John Donovan', Motion Picture News, 31 January 1914, p.35.
103. 'Officer John Donovan', Vitagraph Life Portrayals, 1–31 January 1914, p.21.
104. 'Officer John Donovan', Moving Picture World, 24 January 1914, p.413.
105. 'How Callahan Cleaned Up Little Hell', Moving Picture World, 5 June 1915, p.1668.
106. 'How Callahan Cleaned Up Little Hell', New York Dramatic Mirror, 9 June 1915, p.34.
107. 'How Callahan Cleaned Up Little Hell Is a Story of Corrupt Municipal Politics', Paste-Pot and Shears, 24 May 1915.
108. 'How Callahan Cleaned Up Little Hell', Moving Picture World, 29 May 1915, p.1446; N.G. Caward, 'How Callahan Cleaned Up Little Hell', Motography, 5 June 1915, pp.879–80.
109. 'How Callahan Cleaned Up Little Hell', New York Dramatic Mirror, p.34.
110. 'The Woman and the Law', Moving Picture World, 4 October 1913, p.74; 'The Twin's Double', Moving Picture World, 7 March 1914, p.1298; 'The Mystery of the White Car', Moving Picture World, 4 April 1914, p.114; 'The Mysterious Rose', Moving Picture World, 21 November 1914, p.1124.
111. 'McCarn Plays Fate', Moving Picture World, 22 August 1914, p.1146; 'McCarn Plays Fate', Moving Picture World, 29 August 1914, pp.1242–3.
112. 'Detective Kelly', Moving Picture World, 25 April 1914, p.517.
113. 'Jimmy Kelley and the Kidnapper', Moving Picture World, 18 July 1914, p.476.
114. 'The Tip-Off', Moving Picture World, 23 January 1915, p.584.
115. 'In the Spotlight', Des Moines Daily News, 18 March 1908, p.5.
116. 'In the Theatres', The Post-Standard (Syracuse, NY), 21 January 1910, p.4.
117. 'Barney Gilmore at the Camera', Oakland Tribune, 22 October 1912, p.22.
118. Harrison, 'Dublin Dan', p.857.
119. Advertisement, Moving Picture World, 5 October 1912, p.11.
120. See, for example, L.R. Harrison, 'Dublin Dan', Moving Picture World, 7 September 1912, pp.956–7.
121. 'The Fight for Millions', New York Dramatic Mirror, 17 September 1913, p.28.
122. G. Blaisdell, 'The Fight for Millions', Moving Picture World, 20 September 1913, p.1287.
123. 'A Game of Three', Sterling Camera, Is Good Vehicle for Talents of Gilmore and Niederaur', Motion Picture News, 21 August 1915, p.64.
124. 'The Game of Three', Moving Picture World, 25 September 1915, p.2254.
125. W.S. Bush, 'The Game of Three', Moving Picture World, 21 August 1915, p.1324.
126. H.F. Thew, 'The Game of Three', Motion Picture News, 21 August 1915, pp.87-88.
127. 'Love and Duty', Moving Picture World, 18 April 1914, p.420.
128. 'The Hold-Up Held Up', Moving Picture World, 12 June 1909, p.794.
129. 'Red Sweeney's Mistake', Kalem Kalendar, 1 January 1913, p.5; 'Red Sweeney's Mistake', Moving Picture World, 11 January 1913, p.186; 'Red Sweeney's Mistake', Moving Picture World, 1 February 1913, p.465.
130. 'Mickey Flynn's Escapade', Moving Picture World, 7 November 1914, p.787.
131. 'The Yegg and the Eggs', Moving Picture World, 14 March 1914, p.1428.
132. 'A Boob for Luck', Kalem Kalendar, January 1915, p.17.
133. 'The Disreputable Mr Reagan', Moving Picture World, 8 April 1911, p.780.
134. 'Micky's Pal', Moving Picture World, 8 June 1912, p.960.
135. 'Conscience', Motion Picture News, 6 December 1913, p.43.
136. 'Salvation Sal', Vitagraph Life Portrayals, 1–30 September 1913, p.5; 'Salvation Sal', Moving Picture World, 27 September 1913, p.1416; 'Salvation Sal', Moving Picture World, 18 October 1913, p.263; 'Regan's Daughter', Vitagraph Life Portrayals, 1–30 September 1914, p.53.
137. 'In the Clutches of Gangsters', New York Dramatic Mirror, 28 October 1914, p.33.

138. 'The Chief of Police', *Kalem Kalendar*, 1 August 1914, p.5; 'The Bully's Doom', *Moving Picture World*, 4 April 1914, p.104; 'Wolves of the Underworld', *Moving Picture World*, 21 March 1914, p.1586; 'Conscience', *Moving Picture World*, 10 January 1914, p.222; 'Stop Thief', *Moving Picture World*, 10 April 1915, p.308; 'Out of Bondage', *Moving Picture World*, 22 May 1915, p.1332; 'The Web of Crime', *Moving Picture World*, 12 June 1915, p.1836.

139. 'Mike Donegal's Escape', *Moving Picture World*, 17 April 1915, p.439; 'Mike Donegal's Escape', *Moving Picture World*, 8 May 1915, p.900.

140. 'Mike Donegal's Escape', *Moving Picture World*, 8 May 1915, p.900.

141. 'The Gangsters', *Moving Picture World*, 17 April 1914, p.424.

142. L.R. Harrison, 'The Gangsters of New York', 21 February 1914, p.932.

143. 'Photoplays and Players', *Washington Post*, 18 January 1914.

144. 'Palace Theatre', *Sheboygan Press* (Sheboygan, WI), 14 May 1914, p.2.

145. 'The Gangsters', *New York Dramatic Mirror*, 4 March 1914, p.42.

146. *Regeneration*, DVD (Chatsworth, California: Image Entertainment, 1995).

147. 'The Regeneration', *Motography*, 9 October 1915, p.767.

148. P. Milne, 'The Regeneration', *Motion Picture News*, 2 October 1915, p.83.

149. 'Walsh Producing *Regeneration* for Fox', *Motion Picture News*, 10 July 1915, p.54.

150. L. Denig, 'The Regeneration', *Moving Picture World*, 2 October 1915, p.94.

151. Milne, 'The Regeneration', p.83.

152. In the 'Facts and Comments' column, *Moving Picture World*, 28 February 1914, noted complaints from one correspondent that 'too many Catholic priests appear in motion pictures, and that there are not enough ministers' (p.1063). The column made no mention of the ethnicity of the priest characters, though certainly some of them were not Irish. For example, Father Martin in *A Shattered Dream* (Méliès, 1911) was not Irish.

153. *Complete Catalogue of Lubin Films* (Philadelphia, PA: S. Lubin, January 1903), p.48. Available in *Guide to Motion Picture Catalogs ... 1894–1908: Microfilm Edition*, Reel 3.

154. 'Sunshine', *Moving Picture World*, 19 October 1912, p.270; J.S. McQuade, 'Sunshine', *Moving Picture World*, 26 October 1912, pp.322–3.

155. 'The Boss', *Variety*, 14 May 1915, p.19; 'The Boss', *Moving Picture World*, 15 May 1915, p.1168.

156. A copy of *The Rosary* exists at the British Film Institute in London.

157. N.G. Caward, 'Selig's *The Rosary*', *Motography*, 3 July 1915, pp.26–7.

158. 'The Rosary', *New York Dramatic Mirror*, 30 June 1915, p.28.

159. 'The Rosary', *Moving Picture World*, 26 June 1915, p.2105.

160. Advertisement, *Moving Picture World*, 30 November 1912, p.853.

161. 'O'Hara, Squatter and Philosopher', *Moving Picture World*, 23 November 1912, p.808.

162. 'O'Hara, Squatter and Philosopher', *New York Dramatic Mirror*, 11 December 1912, p.28.

163. 'O'Hara, Squatter and Philosopher', *Moving Picture World*, 14 December 1912, p.1081.

164. 'O'Hara Helps Cupid', *Moving Picture World*, 4 January 1913, p.80; 'O'Hara Helps Cupid', *Vitagraph Life Portrayals*, 1–31 January 1913, p.23.

165. 'O'Hara's Godchild', *Moving Picture World*, 1 March 1913, p.918; 'O'Hara's Godchild', *Vitagraph Life Portrayals*, 1–31 March 1913, p.7.

166. 'O'Hara and the Youthful Prodigal', *Moving Picture World*, 26 April 1913, p.410; 'O'Hara and the Youthful Prodigal', *Vitagraph Life Portrayals*, 1–30 April 1913, p.51.

167. 'O'Hara as a Guardian Angel', *Moving Picture World*, 12 July 1913, p.226; 'O'Hara as a Guardian Angel', *Vitagraph Life Portrayals*, 1–31 July 1913, p.26.

168. 'O'Hara's Godchild', *Moving Picture World*, 15 March 1913, p.1104.

169. 'O'Hara and the Youthful Prodigal', *Moving Picture World*, 10 May 1913, p.596.

170. 'O'Hara as a Guardian Angel', *Moving Picture World*, 26 July 1913, p.428.

171. 'Jimmy', *Paste-Pot and Shears*, 19 July 1915, p.2.

172. 'Jimmy', *Motography*, 31 July 1915, p.226; 'Jimmy', *Moving Picture World*, 25 January 1913, p.364.

173. 'On Donovan's Division', *New York Dramatic Mirror*, 11 December 1912, p.28; 'On Donovan's Division', *Moving Picture World*, 23 November 1912, p.806.

174. A copy of *The Fire-fighting Zouaves* exists at the George Eastman House in Rochester, New York.

175. 'The Fire-Fighting Zouaves', *Moving Picture World*, 3 May 1913, p.487.

176. 'Private Dennis Hogan', *Vitagraph Life Portrayals*, 1–31 August 1914, p.31; 'Private Dennis Hogan', *Moving Picture World*, 15 August 1914, p.992.

177. 'Gallegher', *Moving Picture World*, 7 May 1910, p.736; 'Galligher' [sic], *New York Dramatic Mirror*, 7 May 1910, pp.18-19.

178. 'The Wolf of the City', *Moving Picture World*, 27 December 1913, pp.1544, 1576, 1578.

179. 'Steve O'Grady's Chance', *Moving Picture World*, 26 September 1914, p.64.

180. 'Steve O'Grady's Chance', *Vitagraph Life Portrayals*, 1–30 September 1914, p.29.

181. 'The Foiling of Red Dugan', *Moving Picture World*, 16 December 1911, p.918; 'The Sheriff's Prisoner', *Moving Picture World*, 24 August 1912, p.794; 'Broncho Billy's Pal', *Moving Picture World*, 3 August 1912, p.453; 'Broncho Billy's Strategy', *Moving Picture World*, 21 June 1913, p.1278; 'Conscience', *Motion Picture News*, 6 December 1913, p.43; 'Red Sweeney's Defeat', *Moving Picture World*, 13 September 1913, p.1177.

182. 'Texas Kelly at Bay', *Moving Picture World*, 29 March 1911, p.1338.

183. Advertisement, *Moving Picture World*, 15 November 1913, p.819.

184. 'The Fatherhood of Buck McGee', *Moving Picture World*, 27 July 1912, p.372; 'The Sheriff's Honeymoon', *Moving Picture World*, 22 March 1913, p.1238; 'His First Performance', *Moving Picture World*, 25 October 1913, p.406; 'O'Hara of the Mounted', *Moving Picture World*, 30 October 1915, p.970.

185. 'The Samaritan of Coogan's Tenement', *Moving Picture World*, 23 November 1912, p.804; 'The Samaritan of Coogan's Tenement', *Moving Picture World*, 14 December 1912, p.1081.

186. 'Tim Grogan's Foundling', *Vitagraph Life Portrayals*, 1–28 February 1913, p.49; 'Tim Grogan's Foundling', *Moving Picture World*, 15 March 1913, p.1103.

187. 'A Broth of a Boy', *Moving Picture World*, 30 October 1915, p.1015.

188. A copy of *The Tragedy of Ambition* exists at the George Eastman House in Rochester, New York.

189. 'The Tragedy of Ambition', *Moving Picture World*, 7 March 1914, p.1294.

190. 'The Heart of Maggie Malone', *Moving Picture World*, 31 January 1914, p.588.

191. J.S. McQuade, 'The Salvation of Nance O'Shaughnessy', *Moving Picture World*, 14 March 1914, p.1507.

192. Advertisement, *Moving Picture World*, 24 May 1913, p.773.

193. H.C. Judson, 'Kelly from the Emerald Isle', *Moving Picture World*, 31 May 1913, p.925.

194. Ibid.

195. There is some debate regarding the length of *Chimmie Fadden*, specifically whether it was four or five reels in length. As most contemporary accounts suggest it was five reels, I have opted for that number in the main text.

196. 'Chimmie Fadden', *Motion Picture News*, 10 July 1915, p.70; 'Chimmie Fadden', *Motography*, 17 July 1915, p.139.

197. 'Chimmie Fadden', *Moving Picture World*, 10 July 1915, pp.398, 400.

198. W.S. Bush, 'Chimmie Fadden', *Moving Picture World*, 10 July 1915, p.322; 'Chimmie Fadden', *New York Dramatic Mirror*, 7 July 1915, p.28.

199. 'Victor Moore in *Chimmie Fadden Out West*', *Moving Picture World*, 20 November 1915, p.1514; 'Victor Moore in *Chimmie Fadden Out West* Makes Third Appearance on Paramount-Lasky', *Motion Picture News*, 27 November 1915, p.87.

200. 'Chimmie Fadden Out West', *Wid's*, 2 December 1915 [n.p.].

201. 'Chimmie Fadden Out West', *Exhibitors Herald*, 20 November 1915, p.25.

202. 'Chimmie Fadden Out West', *New York Dramatic Mirror*, 4 December 1915, p.28; W.R. Andrews, 'Chimmie Fadden Out West', *Motion Picture News*, 4 December 1915, p.87; W.S. Bush, 'Chimmie Fadden Out West', *Moving Picture World*, 27 November 1915, p.1680.

203. Occasionally the film industry press spelled the character name 'Terence' as 'Terrence', such as in: 'O'Rourke Stories Crowded with Excitement', *Universal Weekly*, 17 October 1914, p.17; 'Doings in Los Angeles', *Moving Picture World*, 23 January 1915, p.503.

204. 'Terence O'Rourke Stories Coming', *Motography*, 22 August 1914, p.264.

205. 'O'Rourke Stories Crowded with Excitement', p.17; advertisement, *Moving Picture World*, 7 November 1914, p.729.

206. 'His Heart, His Hand and His Sword', *Moving Picture World*, 7 November 1914, p.828; 'The Empire of Illusion', *Moving Picture World*, 21 November 1914, p.1128; 'The Inn of the Winged God', *Moving Picture World*, 5 December 1914, p.1426; 'The Inn of the Winged Gods', *Moving Picture World*, 12 December 1914, p.1525; 'The King and the Man', *Moving Picture World*, 26 December 1914, p.1888; 'A Captain of Villainy', *Moving Picture World*, 2 January 1915, p.134.

207. 'The New O'Rourke Adventures', *Moving Picture World*, 27 November 1915, p.1685.
208. '*The New Adventures of Terrance O'Rourke*', *Moving Picture World*, 4 December 1915, p.1901.
209. Ibid.
210. Such reviews included: '*How Molly Made Good*', *Wid's*, 14 October 1915; H.F. Thew, '*How Molly Made Good*', *Variety*, 15 October 1915, p.21; '*How Molly Made Good*', *Motion Picture News*, 23 October 1915, p.83; L. Denig, '*How Molly Malone Made Good*', *Moving Picture World*, 23 October 1915, p.626; '*How Molly Made Good*', *Exhibitors Herald*, 15 November 1915, p.6.
211. B. Mantle, 'The Nakedest of the New York Shows', *Chicago Tribune*, 24 October 1915, p.E1.
212. 'At the Theatres', *Washington Post*, 30 November 1915, p.11.
213. See, for example, T.C. Kennedy, '*How Molly Malone Made Good*', *Motography*, 23 October 1915, p.863; 'At the Theatres', *Logansport Pharos-Reporter* (Logansport, IN), 17 March 1916, p.7.
214. 'Why *Molly* Should Be Popular', *Motography*, 13 November 1915, p.1000.
215. '*How Cissy Made Good*', *Vitagraph Life Portrayals*, 1–30 January 1915, p.34.

Marguerite Gale, pictured here in a publicity still for
*How Molly Made Good* (Kulee, 1915).

# Chapter Seven
# *Audiences*

In 1912, as the nickelodeon period was coming to an end, L.M. Thornton published a poem entitled *The Power of a Nickel*:

> I'm only a nickel, so hasten to spend me –
> The doors are just open, file in with the rest;
> For no better use could my makers intend me,
> Since good Motion Pictures are life at its best;
> A Wild Western drama, a romance exciting,
> A hunt with the red men that boys call immense;
> A 'Fat Man's Mistakes,' everyone delighting;
> A naval manuever [*sic*], and all for five cents![1]

Within those few lines of verse, Thornton described the various kinds of films that were screened at nickelodeons. However, he did not address the issue of who hastened to spend those nickels, or who constituted the 'rest' of the audience?

Early histories of the motion picture, such as those written by Terry Ramsaye (1926), Benjamin Hampton (1931) and Lewis Jacobs (1939), argued that the working class constituted the vast majority of nickelodeon viewers.[2] Such arguments remained largely unchallenged until the 1970s, when Russell Merritt published an essay on Boston nickelodeons that claimed some exhibitors did not approve of working-class audiences and actively courted the middle class.[3] Then, in 1979, Robert C. Allen published an essay that used primary sources to argue that the majority of nickelodeons in New York City operated in areas associated with the middle class. Conversely, he found that working-class neighbourhoods that included immigrant groups had relatively few nickelodeons.[4]

The work of Merritt and Allen was not met with universal acceptance. Robert Sklar challenged their findings in a 1988 essay, but it was Ben Singer's 1995 article, 'Manhattan Nickelodeons: New Data on Audiences and Exhibitors', that caused the greatest controversy.[5] By using primary sources that suggested New York City possessed more nickelodeons than Allen had found, Singer challenged the notion that middle-class patrons represented the dominant audience. This in turn led him to conclude that the traditional view emphasizing 'the immigrant and working-class foundation of early exhibition may not have been as far off the mark as the revisionist historians maintain'.[6]

Singer's own conclusions were not readily embraced. Allen provided a response that challenged Singer's methodology, claiming that, 'our "picture" of early exhibition in Manhattan during this important decade is not at all that affected by [Singer's] impressive empirical research'.[7] Sumiko Higashi responded to the controversy with the suggestion that the middle-class people who did attend nickelodeons were probably lower middle class.[8] Judith Thissen raised questions about the *Trow Business Directory*, a key primary source used by Allen and Singer, specifically in terms of how representative it was in cataloguing the numbers and locations of New York City nickelodeons.[9] William Uricchio and Robert E. Pearson suggested that the archival record was flawed insofar as being able to supply accurate data on the numbers of nickelodeons in New York City.[10] Singer responded to his critics in two separate essays, conceding some points, but still arguing for the legitimacy of his key arguments.[11]

The Singer–Allen debate – which Uricchio and Pearson described as 'lively and at times feisty'[12] – became the most notable discussion on early cinema audiences in the history of film historiography. Melvyn Stokes declared the 'controversy has added a good deal to our knowledge of cinema exhibition in New York during the nickelodeon era', a statement that is without doubt accurate. However, the debate leaves film studies with as many questions as answers about the people who attended nickelodeons in New York City.[13] Stokes also wrote: 'it is still unclear what, if anything, can be generalized from the New York experience'.[14] Certainly both Allen and Singer understood that New York City's nickelodeon audiences were not necessarily representative of those that existed in other American cities and towns.

More important than the details of the Singer–Allen debate are the larger conclusions that can be drawn from it. Nickelodeons in New York City evolved during the period. They went in and out of business, for example. The films they screened changed during the period, as did their audiences. Such complexities emphasize the need for caution in posing arguments, particularly against constructing a singular and monolithic 'audience' in which each patron interacted with moving pictures in exactly the same ways.

7.1 A balanced programme, as advertised in the
*Daily Oklahoman* of 18 July 1915.

After all, the very same person who might have viewed films in 1896 on
a Kinetoscope was probably a different kind of viewer when he or she saw
films projected at a nickelodeon in 1906, and then again when he or she
saw films projected at a movie theatre in 1916. If even the same viewer and
his/her responses evolved over time (or even during the course of a single
screening, at which he/she could have experienced a range of reactions),
then it becomes particularly important to be wary of bold, overarching
claims made about large groups, such as ethnic groups, who would have

shared some attributes, but who also would have possessed some demographic and psychographic differences. Indeed, a moving picture audience is by its very definition a fragmentary coalition of people bounded by the running time of the film programme: the lights go up, and a new, equally fragmentary group replaces them.

That said, it is possible to find certain kinds of trends and repetitions in primary sources. For example, many film patrons held an interest in viewing films that were authentic, rather than faked. But how they chose to understand authenticity could vary. A 1905 screening in Grand Rapids, Wisconsin, featured a programme of fiction and non-fiction films, including 'many interesting views of England, Ireland, Scotland, Paris, India, Russia, and Japan'. The newspaper noted that some of the fictional films were 'so real as to make people feel nervous who sit in the front seats'.[15] According to the journalist, at least some of the audience members believed the fictional films to be at least as 'real' as the non-fiction films.

In terms of the Irish-themed film, the question remains as to who constituted their audience or, more accurately, audiences. It would be tempting to speculate that a monolithic Irish-American immigrant, working-class audience viewed these films in urban areas, responding favourably to, say, non-fiction films of Ireland and to those fictional films that eschewed ethnic stereotypes. By contrast, the same monolithic group opposed the 'stage Irish' films they saw. These Irish-Americans viewed Irish-themed films in Irish-American venues, such as nickelodeons in Irish-American neighbourhoods.

However, primary sources – as well as lessons learned from the Singer–Allen debate and other studies in this area – rightly suggest a far more complicated story, one in which many Irish-Americans did view Irish-themed films, but one in which they did not form a singular, monolithic 'audience'. Their individual responses to even the same film or group of films could vary greatly, and the bulk of the films that they saw did not feature 'Irish' content. Additionally, they often viewed films in audiences that were comprised of mixed ethnicities, rather than in all-Irish/Irish-American settings.

More important is the fact that the Irish-themed film was ubiquitous at moving picture exhibitions throughout America. Rather than being produced specifically for working-class Irish immigrants in urban areas like New York (or, for that matter, Irish-Americans in any region and of any income bracket), it is clear that moving picture companies targeted Irish-themed films at the general American audience who attended screenings in small towns and big cities across the country.

# The Pre-Nickelodeon Era

The problems of reconstructing audiences become apparent in examining the history of Edison's Kinetoscope, as well as subsequent peepshow devices like the Mutoscope. Most Kinetoscope viewers might well have been male, but some publicity claimed that the device was for 'both ladies and gentlemen'.[16] The topics of individual films may have also played a role in causing interest among women. Charles Musser argues: 'The first films had been made by men, primarily for men, and of men, but these conditions were to change soon after [the bodybuilder] Sandow's appearance [in a Kinetoscope moving picture].'[17] Ticket prices might also act as an indicator of who viewed Kinetoscope films. In 1894, for example, the Holland brother's Kinetoscope parlour charged twenty-five cents per ticket to view films on any one of their five machines.[18] Such prices hardly suggest that a working-class Irish immigrant audience watched films like *Chinese Laundry Scene* (1894).

Other details regarding early film audiences are limited. As Musser notes, 'ascertaining who watched the early motion-picture shows is a difficult task'.[19] For example, little is actually known about the people who attended the first public film screening at Koster and Bial's in New York City when the Vitascope made its debut on 23 April 1896. Ticket prices suggest that they were likely to be from the middle or upper classes. However, no specific breakdown of their ages or gender is available. Period publications speak to their collective reaction, though individual reactions remain unknown. The *New York Times* claimed that the crowd was 'enthusiastic', responding to moving pictures with 'vociferous cheering'.[20] During the weeks that followed, subsequent audiences at Koster and Bial's – which at times could have included some repeat customers – continued to 'applaud' the films, but specific audience members might well have preferred some moving pictures over others.[21] For example, on 4 May 1896, a 'surf scene' was 'shown twice in response to an encore'.[22] At the same time, it is possible that some audience members present that same day enjoyed other moving pictures more than the 'surf scene'.[23]

What is clear is that – even before most Americans viewed any moving pictures at all – a small number of viewers in New York City developed preferences for particular films. Reviewing the programme at Keith's Union Square Theatre in New York in August 1896, the *New York Clipper* mentioned new films that would be projected by the Lumière Cinematographe, as well as 'several old favorites'.[24] By November 1896, the *Clipper* made a similar claim, noting that 'audiences seem to take renewed delight in the reflection of many of the old favorite views', implying that

7.2 During the nickelodeon era, audiences saw far more Irish-themed
illustrated song slides than they did Irish-themed films.

Above: Slide 18 of *Arrah Wanna* (A. L. Simpson, 1906).

Below: Slide 9 of *Kelly's Gone to Kingdom Come!* (A. L. Simpson, 1910).

(Courtesy of the Marnan Collection, LLC, Minneapolis, Minnesota) some viewers not only desired to see films, but desired to see specific films, and to see them again and again.[25]

However, such repeat viewings were not always possible for audience members in other cities and towns. People who attended 1896 Vitascope screenings in such cities as Baltimore, Boston, Cleveland, Providence and Trenton might well have been different in some respects from those who attended screenings in New York City.[26] For example, who constituted the 'small audience' for a film screening on 12 October 1896 at the Opera House in San Antonio?[27] What specific films did they see, in what order did they see them, and how did they react? And did advertisements promoting 'Edison's Vitascope and Refined Concert Co.' in Steubenville, Ohio, that same year draw a particular kind of audience member by the use of Edison's name, by the use of the word 'Refined', and by tickets that cost as much as fifty cents?[28]

Similar questions are operative for much of the itinerant period of exhibition that continued during the late nineteenth and early twentieth centuries. In 1898, for example, film screenings occurred at the German Lutheran Church in Bueyrus, Ohio; the School Hall in Dalton, Ohio; the Town Hall in Poughkeepsie, New York; and a tent meeting in Bartlett, Illinois.[29] By 1900, the American Vitagraph had made appearances at the West End Park in New Orleans and at Kernan's River View Park in Baltimore.[30] Once again, ticket prices might well indicate that few members of the lower classes attended such performances, but financial cost was not always a prohibitive factor. For one week in 1898, for example, the Vitascope Concert Company gave free afternoon and evening concerts at Wisconsin's Lake Hallie.[31] Such variances in venue and price suggest that people of various backgrounds, economic and otherwise, viewed films throughout the United States. As Musser notes, 'from the outset ... the cinema drew its audiences from across the working, middle, and elite classes'.[32]

Until audiences began to identify faked films for what they were, images at early film screenings could possess much verisimilitude. An 1897 article in *Munsey's Magazine* claimed: 'These [moving] pictures are always full of life and activity, and form absolutely truthful records of the progress of events.'[33] Indeed, Musser suggests that the sheer fact that moving pictures were projected had an impact on their believability: 'Projected images were conceived as a novelty in which lifelike movement in conjunction with a life-size photographic image provided a sense of heightened realism and intensified interest in the quotidian. This new level of realism dramatically expanded the screen's importance as a source of commercial amusement.'[34]

It is difficult to know whether some audiences perceived the first Irish-themed films – which were comedies – to be authentic or realistic. However, it is clear that they were screened to what might be termed general audiences. In what is likely to be the earliest documented example of an Irish-themed film being projected to a specific audience, the Edison film *Irish Politics* (1896, aka *Irish Way of Discussing Politics* and *Irish Political Discussion*) was screened in Newark, Ohio, in October 1896. The *Newark Advocate* printed the film programme as follows:

> Leigh sisters, umbrella dance, with calcium effects; Herald Square, New York City; Irish politics; bucking bronco; fire scene, showing the brave firemen saving the lives of women and children; bicycle parade through Prospect Park, Brooklyn, NY; whirlpool rapids; Niagara Falls; elevated train pulling into 23d street station, New York City; opening scene of the second act Hoyt's 'A White Flag'; serpentine dance, by Miss Loui Fuller; sea waves, Manhattan beach; Monroe Doctrine; watermelon contest.[35]

In the same way that vaudeville bills offered a balanced programme – an aggregation of music acts, comedy acts, dramatic sketches, and so forth – the early moving picture programmes did much the same. A comedy like *Irish Politics* was embedded in a larger film show that included everything from dances and a watermelon contest to an array of non-fiction actualities. For the sake of variety, some moving picture exhibitions would even avoid programming two films on the same general topic – moving pictures of Native Americans, for example – in a row at the same screening, instead breaking them up by projecting other films in between them.[36] In many cases, these balanced moving picture programmes were then incorporated as one act of a larger vaudeville bill that was itself balanced, the moving picture segment reflective of the variety of the entire show.

The integration of moving picture performances into vaudeville shows meant that Irish-themed content in live acts would appear on the same bill with non-Irish themed moving pictures. For example, in Fort Wayne, Indiana, in 1898, a live performance of a 'realistic Irish comedy drama' was booked along with 'illustrated songs, calcium light dances, [and] animated pictures'.[37] The following year, Schiller's Vaudeville Company appeared in Davenport, Iowa, its acts including Major James Doyle (the 'Liliputian' Irish comedian) and a 'cinematographic' show.[38] Then, in April 1905, the Lyceum in Ogden, Utah, offered a vaudeville bill featuring the 'Irish Comedy' of the Mahers, along with six other acts, including a 'cartoonist', a comedy duo, a 'Scotch Nightingale', a 'Dutch Comedy' an 'Operatic' and the 'Moving Pictures'.[39] Such vaudeville programming was in addition to Gus Hill's touring version of the stage play *McFadden's Row of Flats* in

1899, which included a 'cineograph and stereopticon combines, and [a] set of films' as an added attraction.[40]

Despite the drive towards balanced programming, individual films could and did maintain their self-identity. On occasion, specific films were promoted more than others screened on the same bill, such as particular fight films and religious moving pictures. In January 1897, for example, a Lincoln, Nebraska, newspaper announcement heralded the Irish-themed comedy *Pat and the Populist* (1896, aka *Pat Vs Populist*) as the 'special picture tonight'.[41] Why that particular film became the featured film attraction at one show in Nebraska is difficult to discern. Perhaps the exhibitor believed it would have particular resonance with some or all of their patrons, or perhaps it was simply the first time it was being screened in the city, as opposed to other films on the same bill.

Purchased by travelling exhibitors, films like *Pat and Populist* were screened throughout America and not solely at vaudeville theatres. For example, the Reverend T.H. McLaughlin of the St Thomas Church in North Adams, Massachusetts, held a moving picture show in October 1903 that included 'scenes from Ireland', as well as the 'coronation of Deir Bar at Delhi, India, the launching of Shamrock III, the destruction of St Pierre and eruption of Mt Pelee, and many historic views'. McLaughlin's event also included a 'noted baritone' singing religious songs, an illustrated lecture on Robinson Crusoe, pictures of Pope Leo XIII, and various other stereopticon views.[42] The following year, St Joseph's Church in New Castle, Pennsylvania, offered a screening of a *Passion Play* film, as well as moving pictures of such topics as Joan of Arc, Rome, and 'scenes from Ireland, including the River Shannon, the noted tunnel on the Kenmere [sic] Road, showing coaches of tourists passing through the picturesque passageway which connects County Cork and County Kerry. Then there are views in Killarney and panoramic presentations of other picturesque scenes in the Emerald Isle.' The event also featured a baritone singing religious songs.[43]

Programmes dominated by moving pictures – rather than vaudeville or live music, for example – also employed the balanced programme strategy. For his spring 1905 programme, travelling exhibitor Archie L. Shepard featured the films *Uncle Tom's Cabin* (1903) and *Logging in Canada* (1903). At an appearance at the Academy in Washington, DC, Shepard completed his two-hour programme with '*The Prodigal Son* [1904], told in ten moving scenes, *A German Hunting Scene*, *The Girl and the Wolf*, *Scenes from Killarney*, and *Out in the Streets*, with the addition of a large line of splendid comedy subjects'.[44] Shepard's show focussed on moving pictures, but still relied on the use of a variety of fiction (ranging from comedy to drama) and non-fiction moving pictures.

Such approaches to programming continued even as the running times of individual films grew in length. For example, Edison's *Kathleen Mavourneen* (1906) appeared on vaudeville bills in numerous cities. In October 1906, it appeared at the Empress in Des Moines, Iowa, on a bill with a 'the Way Down East Couple', a 'Mexican Study', an 'Operatic Soprano', two 'Black Face Singing and Talking Comedians', a 'Most Wonderful Ventriloquist' and a 'Jolly Wag' comedian.[45] The following month, *Kathleen Mavourneen* appeared at the Orpheum in Salt Lake City on a vaudeville bill with a gymnastic team, a 'shadowgrapher', a 'pair of comedians', a 'wonderful child pianist' and a 'clever pair' offering a 'versatile' act that included dancing.[46]

Balanced programmes also occurred at exhibitions that were likely attended, at least in part, by Irish-Americans. One of the earliest documented cases of an Irish organization sponsoring moving pictures came in Brooklyn in 1898 when the Ancient Order of Hibernians sponsored an 'Irish Fair'. According to the *Brooklyn Daily Eagle*, the exhibits included 'many articles of interest' including 'side shows, such as vaudeville, electric, moving pictures, etc.'[47] No non-fiction films of Ireland had yet been released in America. As a result, the films viewed by attendees probably represented a balanced programme of the type already described, thus being an early example of how Irish-Americans would experience the cinema in the pre-nickelodeon era and beyond: the bulk of the films that they viewed would not be Irish-themed.

As non-fiction films of Ireland became available in the early years of the twentieth century, they were often included on balanced programmes at events that were probably attended by Irish-Americans. For example, a 1904 moving picture exhibition at the Academy of Music in Lowell, Massachusetts (a city with a sizeable Irish-American population), screened, '*Cowboys and Indians*, showing an attack on the stage coach, the abduction of a mother and daughter and the rescue, *Shooting the Rapids at Killarney, Jack and the Beanstalk*, and many others'; in addition, the 'well-known local tenor' Daniel McCaffrey presented illustrated songs.[48] The following year, a moving picture exhibition in the same city occurred 'under the auspices of the Rosary society of St Michael's Church'. At an afternoon screening, 'children crowded the hall and enjoyed the views'; adults constituted the bulk of the evening crowd. The bill included 'scenes in the Life of Christ, views of the late Pope Leo, and scenes in Ireland and Japan'. St Michael's, which does not seem to have charged admission fees, arranged live music for the 'religious pictures' and the 'views of Ireland', the latter being accompanied by such music as *The Harp That Once Through Tara's Hall* and *Ireland, I Love You*.[49]

These instances suggest what might already have been a safe assumption: some Irish-Americans viewed films during the pre-nickelodeon era. Indeed, given the sheer number of people living across the United States who considered themselves Irish or Irish-American, there is little doubt that a number of them viewed films in a vast array of towns and cities. In most cases during this period, they would have done so in larger audiences comprised of patrons from various backgrounds, all viewing what were in most cases non-Irish themed moving pictures. However, the infrequency of film screenings in most cities and towns during this period, as well as the variety of venues used when they were screened, makes it very difficult to argue that codified film audiences existed in the same manner as they would in the nickelodeon period and beyond. Instead, groups of people attended a film screening, but then could have gone weeks or months before seeing more films.

For those Irish-Americans who did view moving pictures, many issues other than/in addition to their ethnicity could have shaped their reactions to given films, including their religion (which would have included Protestants as well as Catholics), education, geography, age and gender. For example, it would be tempting to suggest that Irish-American film viewers would have been supportive of James J. Corbett, the Irish-American boxer who appeared in the moving pictures *Corbett and Courtney Before the Kinetograph* (1894) and the *Corbett–Fitzsimmons Fight* (1897). While that may well have been true in some instances, such films received a range of public responses, including outrage. Many people protested against the *Corbett–Fitzsimmons Fight*, and screenings of it were prohibited in some areas.[50] For example, on the one hand, exhibitions of the *Corbett–Fitzsimmons Fight* seem to have occurred in Lowell, Massachusetts, a town with a sizeable Irish-American population, without incident; on the other hand, it was a US Representative from Massachusetts who introduced a bill prohibiting the screening of fight films in the District of Columbia and the shipment of the same through the mail or through other interstate means.[51] The range of reactions from those Irish-Americans who viewed the film (or refused to view it, for that matter) could have been even more complex, given the release of Lubin's fake Corbett films, such as *Corbett and Sharkey Fight* (1898).[52] Others might have hoped to see the film, but did not live in an area where it was screened or could not have afforded the ticket price. In short, it seems likely that Irish-Americans gave various responses to the Corbett films and others of the period.

All that said, some film companies believed that Irish-Americans would respond positively to films featuring Irish characters. A Lubin catalogue suggested that *Irish Couple Dancing Breakdown* (1903) would 'appeal to our Celtic brothers and sisters'.[53] Of *Patrick Street at Cork, Ireland* (aka

*Patrick Street, Cork*, 1904), the same company said: 'This picture is most interesting to our Irish inhabitants, as it brings back memories of their childhood.'[54] It is not difficult to suspect that many of them would have appreciated the non-fiction *Patrick Street at Cork, Ireland*, but may have had varying reactions to *Irish Couple Dancing Breakdown*, which featured 'Moriarty and his "ould" woman', performers who may not have even been Irish.

In addition to moving picture company catalogues, newspapers are a key resource for understanding early film audiences, as they occasionally recorded reactions that audiences gave to moving picture exhibitions. Newspapers catering to specific ethnicities or nationalities at times offered similar information. Such reportage tends to describe generalized group reactions to films, rather than detail the differences, subtle or otherwise, that may have existed between patrons at the same performance. Nonetheless, this data offers important insight into responses that were otherwise unrecorded.

To the extent that Irish-American newspapers discussed the cinema in this period, it was in general terms, none too different from news that was published in other newspapers. For example, in the summer and autumn of 1896, the *Irish-American* reported on the 'wonders of the Lumière Cinematographe at Keith's Union Square Theatre' in New York.[55] However, *The Irish-American* and other Irish-American newspapers during the pre-nickelodeon era did not mention *Irish Politics*, *Pat and the Populist*, or any other Irish-themed moving pictures. Perhaps some of these newspapers and/or some of their readers might well have disapproved of such comedies, but they certainly did not bother writing about them.

By contrast, *The Irish-American* and other Irish-American newspapers regularly editorialized against 'stage Irish' characters in live acts and in music. In June 1902, the *National Hibernian* spoke out against such stereotypes, citing as an example the ongoing performances of the 1888 song *Drill Ye Tarriers, Drill*, which in turn inspired a film of the same name produced by American Mutoscope & Biograph in 1900.[56] However, the *National Hibernian* did not mention the film version, either directly or by implication. Such editorials instead focussed on offensive stage plays and vaudeville acts, both of which were well-publicized events that were often produced repeatedly at the same venue. Offensive sheet music and postcards were also a concern, as they might be sold in stores for months at a time. However, the fact that individual moving pictures in this period were not usually advertised by title, the fact that they were embedded into larger film programmes (which were themselves often featured on even larger vaudeville bills), and the fact that they were sometimes screened for only a day or a few days are likely reasons that they proved too small a target for editorial foes of the 'stage Irishman'.

Similarly, the Irish-American press also wrote favourable responses to entertainment they believed to be 'genuine', but generally ignored non-fiction Irish-themed moving pictures. The key exception was the *Irish-American Advocate* in late 1904 and early 1905. After describing some moving pictures of Irish 'scenery' as presented by the United Irish League in late 1904, the newspaper decided to sponsor its own film screening.[57] They reported that their *Take a Trip to Ireland!* event in New York City in January 1905 was a 'great success' and that – due to the 'many hundreds of ... subscribers who could not be present, together with many of those who were present' – it would be repeated.[58] They later reported that their second screening – which was retitled *A Trip Through Ireland* – was presented in a hall that was 'poorly adapted' for the purpose, causing a 'crush and bustle' in which many viewers had to stand.[59] Nonetheless, they offered four more screenings that spring and also one in December 1905.[60] The *Yonkers Herald* reviewed the event, claiming: 'It was delightful beyond measure ... The exhibition occupied nearly three hours, but so fascinating were the moving pictures that the time passed quickly by, and the people would have kept their seats for more.'[61]

The coverage of *A Trip Through Ireland* in the *Irish-American Advocate* occurred at least in part due to their sponsorship of the event. The newspaper otherwise followed the approach of the other Irish-American newspapers of the period, which was to ignore the moving picture and focus on other kinds of entertainment. Such publications printed a large number of articles on Irish-themed books, stage plays and musical events. They also regularly covered illustrated Irish travel lectures in the pre-nickelodeon era as well, which suggests an interest not only in the topic of Ireland, but also in authentic, non-fiction images of the same.[62] However, these newspapers did not generally discuss or publicize non-fiction films of Ireland, whether the Warwick releases that began to appear in America in 1903 or otherwise. Once again, this suggests that those newspapers and their readers – or at least the editors' perceptions of their readers – believed that other entertainment forms were more important. It also underscores once again that a monolithic Irish-American film audience did not exist in the pre-nickelodeon period.

# The Nickelodeon Era

If the film audience of the period between 1896 and 1905 seems shadowy and difficult to reconstruct, the audience of the nickelodeon period has been offered at times as a rather simplistic stereotype based on class and gender: most of them were working-class men. Tickets for nickelodeons, usually priced at five cents, appealed to members of the lower classes, including immigrants in urban areas like New York City.[63] Writing about film audiences and class in *Moving Picture World* in 1908, W. Stephen Bush examined the stereotype that had already emerged:

> It has been the fashion in certain quarters to look upon the electric theatre as chiefly the poor man's amusement. The undoubted friendship between the moving picture and the poor is a fact on which I love to dwell. Who can tell how much sunshine the pictures have brought into humble homes, where sunshine was unknown before? I have seen the eager faces of the young, chafing perhaps unconsciously under the restraints of poverty, come to the electric theatre as keen in their quest for knowledge as any student of the university. I have seen rough, coarse men, blunted in body and mind by the burden of incessant toil, come out of the theatre with changed expressions and with a plain touch of the spiritual on their faces.

While praising the effect of the moving picture on the poor, however, Bush underscored another key point: the 'growing patronage of the moving picture is, let it be plainly understood, by no means confined to what we are pleased to call the "lower classes"'.[64]

On the issue of age and gender, *Views and Film Index* reported in 1907 that 'whole families' were attending nickelodeons; in 1908, the same publication mentioned that children were the 'best patrons'.[65] By contrast, *Moving Picture World* claimed that same year that men made up the majority of audience members.[66] However, analyses published during the nickelodeon era all too often concentrated on urban areas like New York City, and even then they were more anecdotal than formal studies. That is all in addition to the fact that industry trade publications wanted to defend the industry, which may have skewed their reporting. At the same time, it should be said that their readership consisted largely of exhibitors who dealt with audiences on a daily basis, which may have limited the degree to which they could exaggerate or spread misinformation.

Regardless, it seems likely that nickelodeons in different cities and towns across the America attracted different kinds of audiences.[67] For example, in 1907, *Moving Picture World* reported that women and children originally comprised the largest number of patrons in Dallas, Texas; the publication

It's Irish through and through!
Adapted from a Classic Irish Poem by an Irishman!
Leading Performers are Irish. Producer Also an Irishman!

### THIS 2,000-FOOT IMP

is released THURSDAY, MARCH 14th, just before the Big Day that is Celebrated by Irishmen the world over, the glorious "sivinteenth." Remember the Imp's previous 2,000-foot picture, "From the Bottom of the Sea," and what a sensational money-maker it was for every exhibitor who used it. See that you get an early booking on "SHAMUS O'BRIEN." Go after it with all your heart and soul and might and main—AT ONCE!

| "Better than Gold" | Countess De Swirsky Dances for the Imp! | "The Man from the West" |
|---|---|---|
| *(Copyright 1912, Imp Films Co.)* | One of the many specialties which the Imp has secured at heavy expense is released on the Saturday Split Reel Imp of March 23rd. The Russian Countess whose dances have created a furore all over the world has posed in special dances for the Imp. It's a great big relief from the common-place. See that you get it. On the same reel we will release "The Tankville Constable," a rattling good comedy. | *(Copyright 1912, Imp Films Co.)* |
| Another splendid drama of the mining country. Released on THURSDAY, March 21st. Are you getting these great Thursday Imps? | | Released Monday, March 18th. Another film in which King Baggot takes the leading role. Enough said. See that you get it! |

### IMP FILMS COMPANY
#### 102 West 101st Street        New York
##### CARL LAEMMLE, Pres.
### Coming---"THE LOAN SHARK"

7.3   Advertisement published in the 16 March 1912 issue of the
*Moving Picture World.*

added that it was only later that men began 'to drop in'.[68] That same year, *Moving Picture World* spoke more broadly about the attendance of women and children at nickelodeons, claiming that 'mothers do not have to "dress" to attend them, and they take the children'.[69] By 1913, the *Chicago*

*Tribune* noted long lines of women and baby carriages in front of nick-elodeons in lower-class neighbourhoods.[70] In some communities, women attended in large enough numbers that the 'hat nuisance' arose as an issue; in 1908, the Germantown Citizens' Association went on record decrying women who refused to remove their hats in nickelodeons.[71] By 1910, other cities like Atlanta, Georgia, passed laws against women wearing hats in theatres.[72]

In addition to geographical differences, the passage of time also played a role, as early nickelodeon audiences were probably different from those of a later date. In 1911, *Moving Picture News* announced that the five million Americans who attended film screenings each day represented 'every occupation, class, and condition... The physician may frequently find himself next to a laborer, the refined and educated woman next to her own wash lady, the college student in close proximity to what would elsewhere be termed a "gallery god".'[73] As a result, they were 'delightfully democratic'.[74] Diversity at work, it seemed, except when it came to some Americans. Hispanics, African-Americans and some other ethnic groups were at times segregated or denied admission. In 1909, for example, two Italians sued a Chicago nickelodeon for refusing them admittance.[75] But those problems also varied from theatre to theatre, region to region and year to year.[76]

Such issues are in addition to the topic of film literacy, including the enduring stereotype of the audience member who was so captivated by moving pictures as to believe them to be real. It is certainly possible to document specific examples of this kind of viewer. In 1908, police arrested a man in Pittsburgh for having fired four shots at the screen, aiming at an on-screen villain who was mistreating a female character in a Western film; a similar incident occurred at a screening in Leavenworth, Kansas, in 1913.[77] In 1911, *Moving Picture Story Magazine* printed the story of a boy asking his father if he was enjoying a moving picture show. The father responded, 'It's a good show, I reckon. But we're sitting so far back I can't hear the actors speak.'[78] However, examples of such gullible viewers are exceptions, which is why they merited attention in the press at the time. Moreover, given their potential for humour, journalists might well have exaggerated some of these accounts.

By contrast, *Views and Film Index* wrote in 1906 about the increasing 'demand' for realism in moving picture shows.[79] Some audience members seemed acutely aware of minor inconsistencies and errors in the films they watched. In 1910, *Moving Picture World* noted that 'the number of critical and sharpeyed [sic] fans is increasing every day'.[80] The following year, the manager of a theatre in Aberdeen, South Dakota, wrote about his patrons, claiming that they bristled at the actions of on-screen cowboys in Western films that seemed at odds with their personal knowledge of real-life cowboys. He added:

> When they see a film representing a trip across the plains in '57 or '49, and showing a prairie schooner, rigged up on iron wheels, they shout in derision; just as they resent the incongruity of a woman, who has been found famishing for food, dressing up in a satin lined cloak and a big fashionable hat, when asked to a Thanksgiving dinner by the man who has discovered her need.[81]

Such patrons had become astute viewers, informal critics who were a far cry from, say, an audience member who was afraid to sit too close to moving pictures of waterfalls for fear of getting wet.

The wide range of viewers also had wide-ranging cinematic tastes. In 1906, *Views and Film Index* wrote:

> The exhibitor must use a great deal of foresight. Almost any audience will enjoy the ordinary comedy and chase films, but those who will appreciate the *Passion Play* will usually object to seeing a prize fight film, and those who would become enthusiastic about the latter would, as a rule, ask for something livelier than the *Passion Play*.
>
> At an exhibition of the *Passion Play* recently, the scenes which usually command intense silence were uproariously cheered – the audience actually applauded the crucifixion. Had the exhibitor in this case exercised the proper judgment, he would have quickly realized that this was the wrong audience for his church picture.[82]

Three years later, *Moving Picture World* claimed that the audience members of 1909 fell into various categories, preferring different genres and/or the film outputs of particular companies.[83] That may well have been true, but many other issues may also have prompted individual viewers to attend specific nickelodeons. After all, that same year, *Munsey's Magazine* claimed that 'over 10,000 theatres of various kinds screened moving pictures and between 500,000 to one million persons went to see them each day.'[84]

In 1912, *Moving Picture World* examined the complexities of where patrons lived and whether or not geographical region factored into what constituted the 'average patron'.[85] The average patron: a contradiction in terms. To identify the 'average patron', *Moving Picture World* pursued an elusive concept. With all that is unknown about the nickelodeon-era audience, it is clear that an array of demographic and psychographic differences marked the people who attended film screenings in this period. That was in addition to the fact that such patrons evolved; a film viewer in 1906 was probably different by 1909, and different again by 1912, changed in many ways, perhaps, but certainly due to his or her own ever-increasing history of viewing films. As Eileen Bowser has noted, the 'nickelodeon audience was neither monolithic nor immutable'.[86] In short, *Moving Picture World* might well have been unable to find the 'average patron', because such a person did not exist.

## Presentations of Irish-Themed Entertainment

The dominant form that Irish-themed entertainment assumed at nickelodeon theatres was the illustrated song slide. Hundreds of Irish-themed song slides were released from 1906 to 1913, as opposed to less than 300 Irish-themed fiction and non-fiction films released during those same years. Moreover, exhibitors generally rented their films and changed their programmes with great regularity. In some cases, they changed their films daily; in other cases, they changed their films every two or three days.[87] By contrast, while exhibitors could rent song slides from exchanges, they could also purchase them; in fact, on some occasions, they could be obtained for free from sheet music publishers. Nickelodeon audiences thus had much more opportunity to view Irish-themed song slides than Irish-themed films, given both the sheer numbers and – to a lesser extent – the greater potential they held for repeat performances.

The use of Irish-themed song slides was ubiquitous across the United States during the nickelodeon period. For example, Phil Conner sang the illustrated song *Colleen Bawn* at the Crystal Theatre in Logansport, Indiana, in 1906; that same year, Ruby Long sang *In Dear Old Ireland, Meet Me There* at the Bijou in Piqua, Ohio.[88] In 1907, Lee Borough sang *Arrah Wanna* at the Vaudette in Marshall, Michigan, and an unknown singer presented *My Irish Rosie* at the Nickelodeon in Emporia, Kansas.[89] The following year, performers sang *My Irish Rose* at the Bijou in Santa Fe, New Mexico; *Since Arrah Wanna Married Barney Carney* at the Acme in Woodland, California; and *Miss Killarney* at the Lyric in San Antonio, Texas.[90] Then, in 1909, the Electric Park Theatre in Eau Claire, Wisconsin, offered *My Irish Maid*; in 1910, the Portsmouth Theatre in Portsmouth, New Jersey, presented *My Irish Caruso*; and in 1912, the Reel Theatre in Anaconda, Montana, offered *The Roses of Erin*.[91] In some cases, the use of the Irish-themed illustrated song slide became the most publicized feature of the bill, as happened in Des Moines, Iowa, in 1907, when the Radium

Theatre promoted *My Irish Rose* above its two featured films, *The Soldier* (Edison, 1905) and *Scratch My Back* (Gaumont, 1907).[92]

Such illustrated songs were incorporated into nickelodeon bills that operated much the same as had moving picture exhibitions in the pre-nickelodeon period; the balanced programme remained the prevailing approach.[93] This practice also continued at vaudeville theatres that screened films on their bills. For example, New York's Eden Musée projected the Urban film *Irish Scenes and Types* in 1907 alongside an array of live acts.[94] The following year, the Chase Polite Vaudeville Theatre in Washington, DC, presented the American Vitagraph Company and their featured film *Ireland's Giants' Causeway* on a bill that included such live acts as May Irwin, 'Europe's Spectacular and Sensational *Mephisto Moderne*'; *Pantomime Mirth*, 'Holland's Greatest Balancers'; the 'Ludicrous Laird from Scotland'; and a comedy sketch entitled *The Lady Across the Hall*.[95]

On occasion, individual films on a nickelodeon's bill would be promoted above the others. This was true, for example, when Edison's *Kathleen Mavourneen* (1906) headlined at an airdome nickelodeon in San Antonio, Texas, in 1906, and when Selig's *Shamus O'Brien* (1908) was the sole advertised film at the American Theatre in Anaconda, Montana, in 1908.[96] However, in general the overall nickelodeon bill seems to have been the key consideration. For example, a screening of *Shamus O'Brien* at the Gem in Austin, Minnesota, in 1908 occurred in tandem with the following non-Irish-themed films: Vitagraph's *A Good Boy* ('Just what the name implies'), Pathé Frères' *Each in His Turn* ('A rattling comedy full of vim and ginger'), *A Chinese City* ('A beautiful Scenic picture'), Pathé Frères' *The Burglar's New Trick* ('100 laughs in ten minutes') and Pathé Frères' *A Lucky Accident* ('A combined comic and scenic subject well worth seeing').[97]

Another factor was that a number of Irish-themed films were released on split reels that paired two moving pictures; as a result, both had to be screened in a certain order within a larger nickelodeon programme.[98] Wherever the Vitagraph drama *An Irish Hero* (1909) was screened, it had to be followed with Vitagraph's non-Irish-themed comedy *Lost in a Folding Bed* (1909). In 1909, those two films headlined the Theatorium in Titusville, Pennsylvania, and appeared as the second and third billed films (after Selig's 1909 film *The King of the Ring*) at the Electric Theatre in Dothan, Alabama.[99] In Victoria, Texas, the Princess Theatre sandwiched the Vitagraph split reel between their two headliners – *Now I'm Here, I'll Stay* (Pathé Frères, 1909) and *An Exacting Father-in-Law* (Pathé Frères, 1909) – and the illustrated song *In the Light of the Same Old Moon*.[100] The Grand in Madison, Wisconsin, situated the same split reel in an even lower place on its bill, listing them below five other advertised films.[101]

What all of these examples prove is that the screening of Irish-themed films in the nickelodeon period was not bound by any particular geography. Such moving pictures appeared on screens across the United States. *The Irish Blacksmith* (1908) appeared in Texas, *A Daughter of Erin* (Selig, 1908) appeared in Utah, *Caught by Wireless* (Biograph, 1908) appeared in Wisconsin, *Robert Emmet* (Thanhouser, 1911) appeared in Ohio, and *Kathleen Mavourneen* (Yankee, 1911) appeared in Indiana.[102] Hundreds and hundreds of documented examples exist of Irish-themed films playing at nickelodeons throughout America, which indicates that they were intended for widespread release, something that is hardly surprising given the sheer profit motive of the cinema. In other words, film companies did not produce these Irish-themed moving pictures specifically for Irish-Americans, but rather for distribution to film exchanges and thus exhibitors across the United States in order to achieve the greatest possible financial return.

The extent to which Irish-themed films reached a broad spectrum of different kinds of patrons is further expressed by experiments undertaken in 1910 with mentally ill patients and moving pictures. Reporting on such work, the *Nickelodeon* noted: 'Like a crowd of sane [persons] when their attention is diverted, if you watch [the insane] closely you will easily see their expressions changing as they view *Unlucky Trousers* [Urban-Eclipse, 1907], *Ancient Egypt* [Nordisk, 1909, aka *In Ancient Egypt*], *The Lakes of Killarney* [Paul, 1909, aka *Killarney's Lakes*].'[103] Though this example represents a particularly unique kind of viewing experience, it does highlight the fact that Irish-themed films were screened in a wide range of venues and for a wide variety of audiences.

Examining the situation from England, the *Optical Lantern and Kinematograph Journal* pronounced their belief that the Urban Trading Company's Irish non-fiction series of 1906 would sell well in the United States because:

> apart from the large Irish-American section of Yankee society, whose interest in the country should bring money into the showman's pocket, the same large which class which went to see [Urban's] Scotch series [which had sold better in the United States than anywhere else] – those thinking of taking a holiday abroad – will also be interested in the Irish views.[104]

The implication here is that at least two kinds of audience members existed: those who were Irish-American, and those who were not, but who were interested in viewing images of Ireland or Irish topics.

*The Film Index* later commented on much the same topic, extolling the virtues of 'scenic' and 'educational' films that 'impart a general knowledge for a few nickels that would cost many dollars and many days of study to acquire' from other means.[105] They added:

> the famous show places of the world, that the very small minority alone have been privileged to admire, are brought to our eyes for a nickel or a dime, expanding our knowledge of the world and its strange inhabitants, both human and animal, as nothing else would enable us to grasp the reality of its vast and incomparably interesting diversities.

Then the publication discussed another component of the audience:

> But [what] the moving picture means to millions of foreign-born citizens, who see scenes of their homeland on the screen, can only be understood by those who speak many tongues; who hear parents tell their American-born children of the countries and the peoples from which they came; who see the deep emotion of the expatriated at sight of a familiar scene, of groups of men and women, among whom they will never see again.[106]

Despite considerations of 'foreign-born citizens', the film industry understood that non-fiction moving pictures needed to have vast appeal to be successful. For example, *Moving Picture World* promised exhibitors that Vitagraph's *Scenes of Irish Life* (1912) 'will please everybody'.[107]

In preparing their synopses of Irish-themed moving pictures, film companies, industry trades and exhibitors often promoted the fact that these films were meant for all audiences, not just Irish-Americans. For example, the Opera House in Kennebec, Maine, declared that *Caught By Wireless* (Biograph, 1908) 'should be seen by everyone'.[108] In 1910, *Moving Picture World*'s description of *The Irish Boy* (Lubin, 1910) claimed that the title character grappled with 'possibilities which open before any young man who chooses to take advantage of them'; on another occasion, the trade wrote that the film's 'appeal is not to be denied'.[109] The following year, Thanhouser's synopsis of *Robert Emmet* noted: 'whether or not a man be an Irishman, this picture will arouse the best impulses of his nature'.[110] Similarly, the *Billings Gazette* claimed that the general audience at a local screening of *Robert Emmet* in 1911 were 'most enthusiastic of their praise of the film'.[111] Two years later, *Moving Picture World* claimed that Imp's

**7.4** Advertisement published in the 30 June 1915 issue of the
*New York Dramatic Mirror*.

production of *Kathleen Mavourneen* would have 'universal appeal, for Irish plays, like Irish songs, reach every heart'.[112]

The music that accompanied such films was in at least some cases Irish-themed, but generally it, too, appealed to the expectations of general audiences. For example, rather than play traditional Irish music, musicians at nickelodeons often seem to have relied on popular selections associated with Ireland, including *Has Anybody Here Seen Kelly?* and *It's A Long Way to Tipperary*.[113] Writing in *Moving Picture World* in 1911, Clarence Sinn printed a list of countries around the world and made suggestions as to the 'most commonly used songs' for each. For Ireland, he offered the following list: '*The Harp that Once, Kathleen Mavourneen, Come Back to Erin, The Minstrel Boy, Rory O'Moore, Patrick's Day*'.[114] Such tunes, like those he offered for other countries, were efforts to evoke Ireland through music already recognizable to the broader American public.

In at least some cases, the reactions of general audiences were quite favourable to Irish-themed films. Reviewing *All for Old Ireland* (Lubin, 1915), Hugh Hoffman of *Motography* noted: 'as the picture went on the scenes [shot in Ireland] became more charming, so that by the time the second reel was reached there was a good deal of murmuring among spectators in approbation of the natural beauty in the picture'.[115] In that instance, it was the non-fiction footage of Irish landscapes within a fictional film that caused approval. In other cases, it might well have been the story material and/or the on-screen talent.

Rather than a singular effort to appeal to Irish-Americans, an emphasis on St Patrick's Day film screenings in the nickelodeon period also suggests an effort to reach general audiences. As early as 1906, a 17 March 'moving picture display' at St Mary's Hall in Elyria, Ohio, had:

> no especial bearing on the birthday of the Irish saint, but [was] calculated nevertheless for the enjoyment of all who attend. The chief subject of the pictures is to be the passion play of Ober-Ammergau, but among the other things presented are colored scenes from the principle places in Ireland, the revolutionary and riot scenes from Odessa and St Petersburg, a trip through Italy, and incidents from the life of Moses.[116]

In this instance, St Patrick's Day might have inspired the projection of Irish images, but they were included on a balanced programme comprised largely of non-Irish-themed films.

In 1907, *Views and Film Index* reported that Pathé Frères would release 'some very attractive new films of *Scenes of Ireland* for the holiday'.[117] That same year, advertisements appeared in *The Billboard* for inexpensive 'Shamrocks' and 'St Patrick's Day novelties', which exemplify both the increasingly widespread celebration of the holiday, as well as the kinds of cheap, stereotypical products that at times met with disdain from the Irish-American press.[118] By 1910, the Western Bargain House of Chicago, Illinois, advertised the very cheap 'Souvenir, No. 200', which was a 'Shamrock hod and pipe' that moving picture theatres across America could give away on St Patrick's Day.[119]

It is very clear that St Patrick's Day screenings occurred at nickelodeons throughout the United States. For example, the Bijou Theatre of Houston, Texas, screened *Shamus O'Brien* (Selig, 1908) on 17 March 1909.[120] Lubin specifically promoted *The Irish Boy* (1910) as a St Patrick's Day release in 1910, with *Moving Picture World* noting the success of the scheme, writing that 'one exchange wrote for three extra prints and later telegraphed for four more, and most of the exchanges came in from at least one extra print'.[121] For St Patrick's Day in 1911, Thanhouser issued *Robert Emmet*, and Rex released *Where the Shamrock Grows*. Powers did the same with *Sogarth Aroon* (1912) the following year, as did Imp with their version of *Shamus O'Brien* (1912).[122]

These releases timed for St Patrick's Day were in addition to nickelodeons planning their own special programmes. For example, in 1911, the Lyric in Fort Wayne, Indiana, screened Rex's *Where the Shamrock Grows* (1911) on a bill that also included a performance of the *Come Back to Erin* illustrated song.[123] That same year, a pianist in Oklahoma wrote about his own salute to the holiday in the pages of *Moving Picture World*: 'On St Patrick's night, I played *Echoes of Ireland* as an overture and got a good hand on it.'[124] However, the general approach towards St Patrick's holiday bills remained balanced programmes. For example, that was true of a screening of Imp's *Kathleen Mavourneen* (1913) in 1913 at the Crystal Theatre in Cedar Rapids, Iowa; advertisements also drew attention to the fact that the film would 'appeal to everybody, which means that it will have universal appeal'.[125]

The drive towards 'universal appeal' had always existed in the American cinema, but may have even increased over time. Writing about *The Heart of Kathleen* (Domino, 1913) for *Moving Picture World* in 1913, Louis Reeves Harrison declared:

> The idea of bringing in an English Lord as the heavy to put an honest Irish country boy in the limelight might have been all right in the days of uncombed Bowery audiences, when a

smooth-faced Harp with glassy eyes fixed on the gallery sung out of the corner of his mouth that Ireland was Ireland when England was a pup, but such stuff disappeared long ago in the melting pot.[126]

Harrison's comment underscores the film industry's desire to please all audience members, not just those of a particular demographic group, and that such desires may well have increased as the nickelodeon era progressed.

## Irish-American Audience Members

Little is known about Irish-American patrons of moving pictures in the nickelodeon era. Unlike the pre-nickelodeon era, Irish-Americans in most towns and cities across America could have viewed moving pictures frequently if they had so desired, given both the regularity of screenings and the inexpensive ticket prices at nickelodeon theatres. As for what Irish-Americans would have seen, it would be tempting to suggest that they viewed mainly American films. However, at least in some measure, that would be incorrect, given the sheer number of films distributed in America that were shot in other countries. Russell Merritt has discussed this matter in terms of Pathé Frères, whom he claims 'single-handedly released more films in the United States than the major American companies combined'.[127] It does seem evident that Irish-Americans would have seen the same kinds of films that other American viewers watched: various genres produced by various American and non-American companies.

O.E. Miller's 1912 poem *Motion Picture Lizzie* told the story of 'Lizzie Kelly', whose life was 'dull and slow' until the opening of a local 'moving picture show'.[128] Kelly becomes so enraptured by the cinema that she becomes known as 'Motion Picture Liz'. According to the poem:

> She would sit through bloody battles, gaze at reptiles and at bugs,
> Interwove with melo-drama, and its kisses, love, and hugs.
>
> She could tell the plots of novels, works, alas, she'd never read;
> And the history of heroes, who in days of knighthood bled;
> Many themes of modern science, and of ships that sail the skies,
> Till Mag Dun exclaimed in anger: 'Gee! But Liz is gettin' wise.'[129]

By the end of the poem, the 'erstwhile' Liz teaches grammar school, having been educated through viewing films and then being inspired to read books. Through fictionalized propaganda supporting the cinema, the poem does speak to the kind of films that Irish-Americans would have seen: fiction and non-fiction of all kinds, rather than a steady flow of Irish-themed films.

Perhaps it is more tempting, in an effort to construct a story of diasporic cinema-going, to suggest that Irish-Americans regularly viewed Irish-themed films. Certainly some Jewish nickelodeon audiences saw Jewish films, just as some Italian audiences saw Italian films. However, the Irish-American experience was different, at least in some respects. For example, Giorgio Bertellini notes that 'Between 1908 and 1916, roughly 1,600 Italian films circulated among American exchanges.'[130] During those same years, few Irish films circulated at American exchanges. It is true that Irish-themed films circulated at exchanges during those same years, but these were generally produced in America, save for a small number of fictional films shot in Ireland by American companies, and an array of non-fiction films shot in Ireland by American, British and French companies. Even if one were to tabulate all of these films, they would not at all constitute the kinds of numbers necessary to have fostered a situation in which Irish-American audiences regularly viewed Irish-themed films.

To what extent were Irish-Americans interested in any moving pictures? In a 1907 article in the *Saturday Evening Post*, Joseph Medill Patterson suggested that:

> In cosmopolitan city districts the foreigners attend in larger proportion than English speakers. This is doubtless because the foreigners, shut out as they are by their alien tongues from much of the life about them, can yet perfectly understand the pantomime of the moving pictures. As might be expected, the Latin races patronize the shows more consistently than Jews, Irish, or Americans.[131]

Patterson's comment is interesting, though his conclusions were based purely on personal experience and anecdotal information.

Certainly Irish-Americans attended moving pictures in the nickelodeon era. Using New York City as an extended example, it is also possible to suggest that some nickelodeons existed in Irish neighbourhoods, as was the case of Yorkville. Whether or not Yorkville was middle class (Allen and Singer have disagreed on this point), it was an area whose dominant ethnic groups were German and Irish.[132] Both groups probably attended some of the same nickelodeons. A similar situation probably occurred in Harlem, an area in which native-born Americans, Germans, German Jews and the Irish lived.[133] Irish-Americans might also have attended other nickelodeons in commercial areas like Union Square and Herald Square, as well as in the

Bowery, all of which would also have catered to many ethnicities.[134] Writing about the latter in 1911, a journalist for *The Outlook* claimed that Bowery audiences had 'none of your neighborhood spirit' and instead seemed 'chance-met'.[135]

Examining the East Side's ethnic composition, Singer notes that it was a 'less homogenous' area than the 'nickelodeon-rich' Jewish and Italian neighbourhoods, comprised as it was of 'Germans (20 percent), Irish (18 percent), Austrians (probably from Bohemia, now part of the Czech Republic) (13 percent), and Americans ("Native Whites of Native Parents") (12 percent). Italians, Hungarians, and Russians (probably Russian Jews) each constituted about 6 or 7 percent.' He then suggests that the East Side had fewer nickelodeons than other parts of New York City, but hesitates to attribute that fact to ethnicity, given the possible role of economic class.[136] When he examines the Middle West Side, which contained the famous Hell's Kitchen, Singer also finds an ethnic mix, with the Irish at 26 per cent, Americans at 18 per cent and Germans at 13 per cent. However, he finds 'many more nickelodeons per capita' in the Middle West Side than in the East Side, despite similarities of ethnic composition. 'The comparison', he says, 'points to class [meaning that the Middle West Side was a "much poorer neighborhood than the East Side"], rather than ethnicity as the key factor.'[137]

However, discussing nickelodeons in a given district proves difficult, not only because the tabulations of how many New York City nickelodeons existed are quite contradictory, but also due to the fact that – as Singer points out – 'scores of exhibitors went out of business every year, while at the same time dozens of others ventured into the game. The nickelodeon business was in a state of constant upheaval during these years.'[138] And, as Uricchio and Pearson have argued, 'even if Singer somehow managed to discover the location of all Manhattan nickelodeons in 1908 and 1909, such a list would not enable him to construct a demographic profile of their audiences'.[139] Moreover, as Allen suggested in his response to Singer, 'it was not at all uncommon for some movie theatres to draw patronage from well beyond the immediate neighborhood'.[140]

Taken as a whole, these observations lead to several possible conclusions. Many Irish-Americans in New York City may have attended nickelodeons, but many others may not have done so. Their interest in moving pictures and their ability to view them may have been the result of their class affiliation as much or more than the fact that they were Irish. If they chose to attend nickelodeons, these may or may not have been located in their own neighbourhoods. If the nickelodeons were located in their neighbourhoods, they would have been likely to draw patrons of mixed ethnicity, due both to the ethnic make-up of those neighbourhoods, as well as – depending on the area – transient viewers. Given such possibilities, the question then arises of the extent to which New York City possessed, for lack of a better term, 'Irish-American nickelodeons', or whether most Irish-Americans would have attended mixed nickelodeons.

In his own work on New York City nickelodeons, Patrick Mullins confidently notes that 'There were three Irish nickelodeons in Harlem at this time';[141] however, that is not necessarily true. What Mullins offers as evidence are three nickelodeons whose owners had what appear to be Irish names. As Singer has noted, 'Using standard genealogical reference tools, one is able to determine the ethnic descent [of owner's names] with reasonable accuracy', but there is no evidence that Mullins undertook such genealogical work.[142] Instead, it seems he has made his judgments solely 'from the listings in the *Trow Business Directory*, trying to determine ethnicity by surname alone, even to the extent of pronouncing the owners as "Irish", whereas their families could have lived in America for one or more generations and might be better classed as "Irish-American"'.[143]

Even if Mullins's results could be seen as a reasonably accurate estimate, other problems with his findings emerge. Singer and Allen both agree that the number of nickelodeons in New York City was higher than the number listed in *Trow*'s, so using that publication to calculate how many nickelodeon owners of given ethnicities existed is problematic. Most important, however, is the fact that even if the trio of exhibitors in Harlem were Irish, and even if that is a fairly accurate number of how many Irish-owned nickelodeons existed in Harlem, that does not all mean that these were 'Irish nickelodeons', but rather that they were Irish-owned. The ethnic make-up of their clientele was another matter, especially in an area like Harlem that was home to various ethnic groups.

Similar questions could be raised about Mullins's 'Table 1', which calculates the numbers of Jewish, Italian, Irish and German nickelodeon owners in New York City. He finds that there were two Irish owners in 1908, six in 1909, six in 1910 and three in 1911; however, he does not suggest whether or not any of these exhibitors survived more than one year of operation. Though he admits that 'simple identification by ethnic name cannot in itself definitely establish immigrant status or ethnic identification', his table proceeds to do just that, fixing the term 'Irish' on the sole basis of what he calls 'distinctly identifiable' names.[144] Even if there are no genealogical errors, 'Table 1' can suggest only one key fact: it seems that a very small number of nickelodeons in New York City were owned by someone Irish or of Irish descent, though the duration for which these were in operation is in question. Such evidence says nothing about whether or not these nickelodeons were patronized predominantly by Irish-Americans, or by other ethnic groups, or – more likely, given their locations – a mix of ethnic groups.[145]

As a result, it is difficult to establish the extent to which any nickelodeons catering solely to Irish-Americans existed in New York City. However, to conclude that there were such nickelodeons, even if small in number, would still provide little insight into the viewers who attended them. Individual patrons, even if they were entirely or predominantly Irish, may not have personally known the majority of their fellow audience members. After all, at different times of the day or week, the audience composition could well have varied in terms of age, gender, and so forth. Moreover, simply knowing other audience members would not necessarily have affected one's individual reactions to given films while they were being screened in the dark.

Whatever can be said about the Irish-Americans who attended nickelodeons in New York City, and it seems little can be, their experience cannot necessarily speak to that of Irish-Americans in other cities and towns across America. As Bowser notes, 'it seems no city can be taken as typical'.[146] During the nickelodeon period, there may well have been thousands of Irish-Americans attending moving picture shows throughout the United States. Probably some of them attended with regularity; others did not. Some were Catholic; others were Protestant. Some lived in urban areas; others lived in rural areas. Perhaps some nickelodeons catered predominantly to Irish-Americans in cities like Brooklyn, the Bronx, Syracuse, Boston or elsewhere, but it is probable that most Irish-Americans in cities and towns across the United States saw films in nickelodeons with mixed patronage.

As a result, it is quite clear that no monolithic 'Irish' or 'Irish-American' audience existed in the nickelodeon era, but it is possible to find some recorded responses of individual Irish-Americans. Perhaps the most notable, given its widespread publication, was the case of a Mrs McAfee in Macon, Georgia. A syndicated newspaper article of 1912 claimed:

> Two weeks ago, Mrs McAfee, a well-to-do widow, visited a moving picture show which, by curious coincidence, represented a plot corresponding in a measure to the hidden story of her own life. From that evening, her relatives say, she brooded and wept, until finally she confessed she had killed her husband in Ireland and pleaded to be taken back so she could pay the penalty.[147]

Though a dramatic story, it underscores two aspects of film viewing that are necessary to remember when considering Irish-American audience members. Firstly, non-Irish-themed films may have resonated with them as much as, or more than, Irish-themed films. Secondly, audience members are individuals and can respond in unique ways to given films, even if they might also fall into some broad demographic or psychographic categories. As a result, many recorded reactions to films of the period, including to Irish-themed films, have limited application.

For example, in May 1907, *Moving Picture World* reported that the mayor of Providence, Rhode Island, attended the film *Murphy's Wake* (Walturdaw, 1907) after receiving a message that its depiction of an Irish wake was offensive. Viewing the film, the mayor spoke to the theatre's manager:

> My friend, allow me to say that you are perpetrating a gross and criminal libel upon a time-honored custom among decent people...Let me tell you that but for my interference, you would have had a much different performance in your house this evening. I was called up on the telephone by an indignant citizen of Pawtucket who complained of the insult you are offering the Irish people, and who informed me that it was the intention of a number of his friends to come here to-night and rough-house your place, and they would have done so, too, had I not prevailed upon him and them not to resort to anything of a rash nature, but to allow me to act.[148]

The mayor ordered that local screenings of *Murphy's Wake* cease, and thus no rioting occurred. However, it is dangerous to generalize too much from this case, as no other reports of similar reactions were published in film trades or Irish-American newspapers. Moreover, the mayor's actions came as the result of one person's phone call, which may or may not have overstated the potential for rioting. Perhaps many other people across America were offended by the film, but not to the extent of making such threats. Perhaps others found the film humorous, or were swayed by the fact that it was allegedly an adaptation of Boucicault's *The Shaughraun*. At any rate, no surviving evidence suggests that these kinds of events were common, whether as a result of *Murphy's Wake* or any other Irish-themed comedies.

Another important but less dramatic incident occurred in 1907 when Lyman H. Howe screened an evening of *Scenes of Ireland* in 1907. The *Boston Globe* reported that a 'good-sized audience...gave every evidence

**Moving Picture Theatres**

Increase your box office receipts on

**ST. PATRICK'S DAY**

by giving away this
Souvenir, No. 200

**Shamrock**

Hod and Pipe

**Gross $2.75**

**WESTERN BARGAIN HOUSE**
242 E. Madison Street . Chicago. Ills.

7.5 Advertisement published in the *Moving Picture World* of 12 March 1910.

of thoroughly enjoying the entertainment'.[149] As Howe's event represented an unbalanced programme concentrating on Irish non-fiction films held in Boston, it seems likely that many members of that 'good-sized audience' were Irish-Americans. At any rate, the newspaper added, 'the amusements of the Irish folk [on screen] evoked much laughter'.[150] Various interpretations of that sentence could be made. Would such laughter have occurred because the 'Irish folk' were seen to be comedic? If so, what specifically provoked the laughter? Or is it possible that at least some of the laughter was not generated by comedy, but instead by nostalgia and fond memories? Whatever the case, it is also important to consider the possibility that not all audience members may have laughed, or even have laughed for the same reason(s).

With regard to studies examining the film experiences of particular ethnic groups, ethnic newspapers have at times provided valuable inform-ation. However, the key Irish-American newspapers of the nickelodeon period – specifically the *Gaelic American*, *The Irish-American*, the *Irish-American Advocate*, the *Irish World and American Industrial Liberator*, the *National Hibernian* and the Boston *Pilot* – published relatively little coverage of moving pictures, particularly on Irish-themed fictional films, and, by extension, audience reactions to moving pictures.[151] It is possible to suggest various reasons why that might have been the case, but – among other considerations – there is the fact that these newspapers did not co-ordinate their reportage or editorials. The *Gaelic American*, for example, regularly decried other editorial stances taken by newspapers like the *Irish World and American Industrial Liberator*.

However, could this lack of reportage on moving pictures have suggested some effort, even if not coordinated, on the part of these newspapers to appear more upstanding and middle class? That would not seem possible, as these newspapers did publish infrequent articles on moving pictures, many of which were positive in tone. In 1909, for example, the *Irish-American Advocate* ran a brief story about an exhibition of 'the first [moving picture] views of the Italian earthquake'.[152] Two years later, *The Irish-American* reprinted part of a *Chicago Tribune* article on 'Moving Pictures and the Eyes', which dealt with then-current fears over the dangers of film viewing to eyesight.[153] The same publication also published two brief articles on Kinemacolor, as well as an article written about 'movies' by a theatrical manager.[154] In 1912, the Boston *Pilot* announced that Pope Pius X witnessed a moving picture show featuring images of the 'inauguration of St Mark's Campanile at Venice'.[155] Such articles are little different from moving picture news that would have been published in general audience newspapers, and they hardly suggest a boycott on the subject. Moreover, on a few occasions, these same newspapers offered show listings for non-Irish-themed film screenings.[156]

In keeping with film coverage that appeared in general audience news-papers, the Irish-American press also addressed concerns about 'immoral films' and whether or not censorship was necessary, much as they did from time to time about 'evil' and 'immoral' dime novels, comics and – most of all – stage plays.[157] While *The Irish-American* printed one article about 'insidious' moving pictures, the *Pilot* took the lead role, which is hardly surprising, given that – of all the Irish-American newspapers – it was the most consistent and outspoken on religious issues.[158] The *Pilot* printed three articles against the 'moving picture nuisance' during 1910–1911.[159]

These editorials were not responding in any way to offensive ethnic caricatures and in no way whatsoever referred to 'stage Irish' depictions on
film. Instead, they were published during a campaign against 'immoral'
stage plays, meaning those that featured 'indecent' content. Spurred by the
New York Society for the Prevention of Cruelty to Children, the American
Federation of Catholic Societies (which was not a strictly Irish-American
organization) passed resolutions against 'indecent' books, plays, postcards
and moving pictures in 1908 and 1909.[160] The *Pilot* employed similar
language to those groups, writing about 'disgust[ing]' moving picture
content (which specifically included 'burglary' and 'elopement').[161] Their
editorials also warned of the 'vile men who often frequent these places in
order to lure the innocent to unmentionable deeds'.[162]

Such articles – although numbering less than five across the whole of the
Irish-American press for the nickelodeon era – proves once again that Irish-
American newspapers were not unwilling to discuss the cinema or its
potential negatives, just as on rare occasions they had praised the cinema.
Moreover, such reportage suggests once again the fact that Irish-American
film viewers watched and were more interested in non-Irish-themed films,
even if from a negative standpoint.

What these instances also prove is that the six major Irish-American
newspapers in America at the time were not unwilling to discuss the
cinema. However, the question remains as to why these newspapers did
not offer more coverage on the subject, and why they did not usually
discuss Irish-themed moving pictures. The answers might be many. For
one, such newspapers were not published daily, which could as a result
have limited their coverage. Secondly, none of these six publications regularly received advertising revenue from nickelodeons or others in the film
industry, which would probably have prompted more coverage on the
same. In her study of Jewish immigrant audiences in New York during the
nickelodeon era, Judith Thissen has noted the same was true of the Yiddish
press.[163]

However, even in consideration of such possibilities, the fact remains
that these six different newspapers chose to ignore in large measure the
Irish-themed moving picture. Had their readership – which consistently
made its voice heard through letters to the editors – desired coverage of
Irish-themed moving pictures at any point during the nickelodeon era, one
or more of these newspapers, including those based in New York that
competed with one another, would likely have acquiesced. In short, these
six newspapers may have avoided coverage of moving pictures, Irish-
themed or otherwise, because they did not perceive a large interest in them
amongst their readership. It is not necessarily a given, after all, that all

Irish-American nickelodeon patrons preferred Irish-themed films. Rather, it is quite possible that many, including children, preferred other kinds of moving pictures. It is also quite possible that many Irish-Americans saw moving pictures as little more than a tangential feature of their daily lives.

At any rate, outside of two advertisements in the *Irish-American Advocate* promoting screenings of Edison's *Kathleen Mavourneen* in 1906 and 1907, the Irish-American newspapers ignored the Irish-themed fictional film during the entire nickelodeon era.[164] None of the six afore-mentioned Irish-American newspapers mentioned the O'Kalem fictional films, either to describe the novelty of their being shot on location in Ireland or to announce their release, or even to publish advertisements for screenings of them. Nor did they publish any publicity or descriptions of Irish-themed fictional films produced by companies other than Kalem. That was as opposed to the consistent coverage that each of these publications gave of the subjects of Irish dance, Irish literature, Irish stage plays and other forms of Irish entertainment.

The same newspapers also generally ignored discussions of offensive, 'stage Irish' moving pictures. The key exception appeared in the *Irish-American Advocate* in 1910. The article described a specific negative reaction to Irish-themed fictional films at a specific theatre:

> On St Patrick's day last, the three daughters, Madge, May, and Mildred of Matt Brassell, the well known Kerry man, patron-ized the moving picture show in their neighborhood at the corner of Tompkins and DeKalb avenues, Brooklyn, where Irish and St Patrick's Day pictures were announced as a special attraction. The usual make-up of the stage Irishman was intro-duced on the canvas with mingled expressions of feelings; some clapped and others hissed; the latter Miss Madge Brassell led, and straightaway went to the box office and pleaded with the manager in a spirited manner so that the stage Irishman pictures were withdrawn from further exhibition.[165]

The 'moving picture show' in question was located near an Irish-American neighbourhood in Brooklyn. In this case, the exhibitor probably did not realize the potential for negative reaction, perhaps because he or she rented the films without thorough knowledge of their content. Though the exhibitor withdrew the films after the complaints were lodged, it is import-ant to remember that some audience members at this nickelodeon clapped when seeing the 'stage Irishman'. It is possible these patrons were not Irish-American, but it also is possible that they were, and that they reacted favourably to Irish caricatures, something that is not out of the question. Indeed, Musser has suggested the possibility that some Irish audiences might have found Irish-themed comedies funny rather than offensive.[166] It is this example more than any other that suggests the complexities of Irish-American film audiences and the kinds of varied responses they may have given to moving pictures.

The fact that the Brooklyn example was not one of many begs another question, namely, why was there not more backlash against offensive Irish-themed fictional films from the Irish-American community during the nickelodeon period? As James M. Curran has suggested, 'immigrant and ethnic stereotypes [of the Irish] abounded' in the period 'despite motion picture dependence on immigrant patrons'.[167] Certainly the Irish-American press decried the 'stage Irish' in its other manifestations with great regularity during the nickelodeon era, preferring instead what they deemed to be 'genuine' Irish entertainment and 'real' Irish drama.[168] Rather than arguing in the abstract, newspaper editorials, articles and letters to the editors were motivated by particular stage plays, vaudeville sketches, picture postcards, and cartoons in newspapers and magazines.[169] The key targets of the period were stage productions of *McFadden's Row of Flats* and *The Playboy of the Western World*, the latter causing by far the greatest outcry.[170] Many other plays and vaudeville sketches also caused intense negative reactions.[171]

In 1907, for example, a group of Irish-Americans received much attention from the police and the press for egging the Russell Brothers at the Orpheum Theatre in Brooklyn; twenty-two of approximately one hundred egg-throwers were arrested.[172] Disdain for the Russell Brothers came as a result of their sketch *The Irish Servant Girl*, though by the time they played Brooklyn, they had changed the title to *The Stage-struck Maid*. Publications like the *Gaelic American* railed against the Russell Brothers, just as they did against stage productions of *The Belle of Avenue A*, which depicted a drunken Irish woman, and *The Hod Carrier's Meeting*, which included such characters as 'Casey' and 'O'Brien'.[173] In other cases, they targeted fictional Irish characters named 'Pat' and 'Brigid' who had appeared in a magazine.[174]

Why not target the same kind of content in moving pictures that depicted comic Irish servant girls, drunks and hod carriers? There can be little doubt that those Irish-Americans offended by stage Irish humour – which would not necessarily have been all Irish-Americans – would likely have decried many of the films released during the nickelodeon era if they had seen them. In some cases, as the 1910 article in the *Irish-American Advocate* proves, at least some Irish-Americans did see Irish-themed comedy films. However, some of those who did see such films and found

**7.6** Advertisement published in the 29 August 1914 issue of the Boston *Pilot*.

380

them offensive might not have complained to exhibitors. Even if they had, they might not have informed the Irish-American press. In short, it seems quite likely that some patrons may have disliked such films, but they took little or no action to express their feelings.

It also must be said that no Irish-American newspaper or organization actively campaigned against moving pictures containing stage Irish stereotypes during the nickelodeon era. The fact that the Irish-American press concentrated their fight on offensive stage plays, vaudeville acts, postcards, and cartoons published in newspapers and magazines, rather than on moving pictures, is not difficult to understand. A stage play might be performed over and over again at a theatre that heavily publicized it; the same was true of famous vaudeville acts. Picture postcards might be sold at a store for weeks or months at a time. Many newspapers and magazines had large circulations that reached thousands and thousands of readers; offensive material in them was easy to see, as anyone could cheaply purchase the same.

By contrast, as has already been suggested of moving pictures in the pre-nickelodeon era, individual films screened at nickelodeons were not always advertised. Even when they were, individual moving pictures generally did not possess the reputation of famous stage plays or vaudeville acts. The fact that most nickelodeons changed their programmes two or three times a week, if not daily, meant that potentially offensive images could disappear from the screen before those Irish-Americans who might have taken umbrage ever saw them. If they did see such a film, by the time major protests could be mounted or editorials could be published, the film might have already disappeared from the screen. This is all in addition to the fact that some exhibitors located in or near Irish-American neighbourhoods might have chosen not to rent and screen potentially offensive moving pictures, as they would have been able to read film company synopses of the same in catalogues at film exchanges or in film industry trade publications.

As a result, issues of potentially offensive films were dealt with in film trade publications, presumably because they had acute and ongoing concerns for the overall welfare of the industry.[175] In 1912, for example, *Moving Picture World* editorialized about the 'ridiculing of national peculiarities', which they viewed to be 'always in bad taste'. They also noted that caricaturing the 'foibles and oddities' of ethnic groups had become 'intolerable'. Speaking of an unnamed 1912 film, presumably *An Accidental Millionaire* (Lubin, 1912), *Moving Picture World* told readers:

> A picture recently made shows the ridiculous antics of an Irishman who has become rich suddenly. There can be no objection to showing the foolish things that are often done by

the newly rich. The chances are that a newly rich Irishman would act very much like a newly rich Frenchman or American. If the producer had contented himself with characterizing instead of caricaturing the Irishman, there would have been no objection. Indeed, one of the classics of the more boisterous sort of comedies *Mr O'Brien in Society* is still remembered with pleasure by all who saw it.

This other and newer picture aims not so much as ridiculing the follies of the newly rich as at ridiculing the Irish race. Such at least is the opinion of an exhibitor of considerable intelligence and experience. This exhibitor has complained that the exhibition of the picture in his theatre caused great dissatisfaction. 'There was not a laugh in the house,' he said, speaking of the reel in question, 'and after the show many patrons stopped to speak to me and denounced the picture as an unwarranted libel on the Irish people.'[176]

The *Moving Picture World* editorial proceeded to repeat their belief that 'there is no need for this kind of pictures [*sic*]'. However, the publication added that it was 'quite possible that the producer meant no harm', and that 'it is quite possible too that the complaining patrons were too sensitive'.[177]

Presumably these 'sensitive' viewers were Irish-Americans, though *Moving Picture World* did not say; even if they were, the 'many patrons' who complained might still have constituted only a small contingent of the larger audience in that same venue. What is clear is that the trade publications generally tried to discourage films that would evoke controversial responses of any kind, fearing that the industry would be harmed. As a result, on at least one occasion in the late nickelodeon period, *Moving Picture World* attempted to gauge the authenticity of Irish-themed films. Of Lubin's *An Irish Girl's Love* (1912), the trade wrote that 'the story, though slight, has an interesting climax and was liked'. However, they added that 'the Irishness of it, in playing and costumes, is artificial'.[178] Here again, a film trade publication spoke about issues ignored by the Irish-American press.

Little information survives regarding those occasions on which Irish-Americans responded favourably to specific film screenings, but primary sources do suggest that some of them appreciated non-fiction films. In 1911, Lizzie Pinson's poem *The Irish Heart* appeared in *Motion Picture Story Magazine*. In it, a fictional Irish-American boy pleads with his mother to give him a nickel so that he can to a 'picture show terday [*sic*]'. He describes *Uncle Tom's Cabin*, which is 'gonta be dere' at the nickelodeon.

His mother, who apparently has never visited a nickelodeon, is puzzled by what her son says. Though he wants to see *Uncle Tom's Cabin*, he convinces his mother to go by mentioning an Irish-themed non-fiction film and an illustrated song:

> Oh, I near forgot ter tell yer
> dat I saw another card
> Wot said *Views of Ireland* an' some
> singin' by an Irish bard.
>
> Mike, avourneen, do yer mane that
> annybody could conthrive
> For to show us dear ould Ireland wid
> the people like alive?
> Troth, I'd go look at that no matter
> what I'd have to pay,
> For to feast me eyes on Erin's Isle,
> I'd beg or shteal me away!
> Arrah! grammachree 'acushla! just to
> get another glance
> At the glen down where the bouchals
> and their colleens used to dance,
> And adown the road the schoolhouse
> where I learned the rule o' three
> While your father, pace be wid him,
> would be makin' eyes at me.
>
> It's not cryin' I am, Mike, sure thim
> are only tears of joy!
> Get me bonnet an' me shawl – I'll go
> along wid yez, me bhoy,
> And for every spot they show me where
> the dear ould shamrock grows,
> Faith, I'll beathe me fondest blessin'
> on the Movin' Pitchur shows.[179]

Pinson's poem, due in part to its attempt to mimic the accents of its characters, was intended for a general readership, published as it was in the key moving picture fan magazine of its day. The mother's excited reaction to viewing non-fiction images of Ireland could just as easily have been represented by a non-Irish immigrant viewing films of his/her homeland. The

poem also attempts to depict an adult who had never attended a nickelodeon convinced to do so by her child, thus creating a story of family film
attendance that the film industry could encourage and endorse. All that
said, whether by accident or design, Pinson's poem implies that some Irish-
Americans did embrace the Irish-themed non-fiction moving picture.

Though the Irish-American press did not report on Irish-themed non-
fiction films with any regularity, they did print more about them than any
other kind of film. However, references to these films did not come in the
form of general reportage on 'new releases' or the like; instead, without
exception they refer to specific screenings of such films as sponsored by
various Irish-American organizations or newspapers. What this suggests is
that the Irish-themed non-fiction film held interest for at least some Irish-
Americans in such urban areas as Boston and New York City. Indeed, these
films must have held far more interest for them than the Irish-themed
fictional films, given that the latter were so ignored.

Aforementioned advertisements for *Kathleen Mavourneen* (Edison, 1906)
in the *Irish-American Advocate* promoted screenings of it in 1906 and 1907
on a dual bill with the non-fiction *A Trip Thro' Ireland* [aka *A Trip Through
Ireland*]; in all publicity for those screenings, *A Trip Thro' Ireland* was
promoted far more prominently than *Kathleen Mavourneen*.[180] For example,
a lengthy article published about the event in the *Irish-American Advocate*
concentrated on *A Trip Thro' Ireland* and another '100 pictures of historic
interest' that would also be screened; only one sentence was devoted to
*Kathleen Mavourneen*.[181] Rather than being a single film – such as the 1906
Lubin release *A Trip Through Ireland* or Hale's Tours' 1906 film *Trip
Through Ireland*, it seems likely that *A Trip Thro' Ireland* was an umbrella
title for various short films akin to screenings of *A Trip Through Ireland*
promoted by the same newspaper in 1905. In any event, it caused enough
interest to be screened at least more than three times, though no future
mention was ever made of Edison's *Kathleen Mavourneen* (1906).[182]

Then, for at least three events (two in 1909 and one in 1910), the *Irish-
American Advocate* sponsored a film, or films, entitled *A Holiday Trip
Through Ireland*. The evening consisted of 'two hours of the latest and
most fascinating tour of Ireland by life motion pictures'; in March 1909,
their advertisement promised that the films had not previously been seen in
New York, which if true meant that the film(s) screened were different than
in any incarnation of *A Trip Thro' Ireland/A Trip Through Ireland*.[183]
However, their advertisement for the second 1909 screening and the 1910
screening of *A Holiday Trip Through Ireland* also promised that the films
in question had never been screened.[184] Ads for these subsequent screenings
described the same content as earlier publicity, suggesting that the *Irish-*

*American Advocate* may well have projected the same film(s) as they had at the first 1909 screening. Then, in 1913, the *Irish-American Advocate* sponsored a New York screening of *A Trip Through Ireland* consisting of non-fiction films shot by Kalem in Ireland in 1912.[185] None of these events featured fictional Irish-themed films.

The same was true of events sponsored by other Irish-American organizations. In 1908, two chapters of the Ancient Order of Hibernians screened a programme of 'moving picture scenes from old Ireland' in New York in conjunction with a dance.[186] Three years later, the Los Angeles chapter of the Ancient Order of Hibernians sponsored a 'gala day for sons of Erin' which featured a variety of activities; according to the *Los Angeles Times*, the 'last and one of the most important events of the day [was] a moving picture show, at which 100 views of beautiful old Ireland [were] shown'.[187] In all of these cases, the organizations could have rented Irish-themed fictional films from exchanges, but they chose not to do so, opting instead for unbalanced programmes consisting solely of non-fiction films.

The key exception was Walter MacNamara's feature film *Ireland a Nation* (1914). The reasons are perhaps many, including the fact that the film was shot in Ireland, the fact it had perceived propaganda value, and the fact it included some non-fiction footage. The previous year, *The Irish-American* had written a brief article on 'Moving Pictures and Nationalism' in which they expressed regret that the cinema so 'seldom' depicted 'Irish scenes or incidents of Irish history', which suggests they either were unaware of or were unimpressed by the numerous films that had done just that, such as the O'Kalem films.[188]

In September 1914, *Ireland a Nation* premiered at a 'new picture house', the Forty-Fourth Street Theatre in New York City.[189] Its premiere screening included 'a host of moving picture people and friends of the producers', as well as a 'happy sprinkling of folks from the "ould sod"', who applauded the film story and the rollicking Irish music of the evening'.[190] *Motography* reported that its subsequent 'twice daily' screenings at the venue were 'successful', and *Variety* noted the audiences attending it were 'almost wholly Irish'.[191] They added that one audience for the film was 'intensely enthusiastic' and 'applauded even the titles'.[192] *Motion Picture News* said much the same, claiming that the audience their journalist witnessed 'applauded each time the heroes make their appearance and roundly hiss the opposition'.[193]

*Variety* predicted that a road show of the film could be successful, claiming, 'there are enough Gaelic societies throughout the country which can be relied upon for support', though *Motion Picture News* warned exhibitors to tell 'all Englishmen, Orangemen, and the opposition to the Home Rule bill to stay out, or else there will be quite a riot'.[194] Irish-American newspapers promoted many of these screenings, perhaps because some of them were sponsored by Irish-American organizations. In Boston, 'large audiences, in which were included many prominent Irish-Americans of the city, enthusiastically greeted the pictures', which – according to the Boston *Pilot* – left them 'well pleased'.[195] In Brooklyn, members of the Brooklyn Gaelic Society were present 'in a body' at the opening screening.[196] The Ancient Order of Hibernians held 'theatre parties' in Baltimore to 'witness' the film; they also turned out in large numbers for its lengthy stay in St Louis.[197] In Chicago, audiences saw a slightly different cut, as censors cut images of 'soldiers whipping woman; shooting in duel'.[198] The film then appeared in many cities and towns across America, including Cumberland, Maryland, Trenton, New Jersey, and North Adams, Massachusetts, where it was heralded as a 'valuable bit of propaganda'.[199]

## The Kalem Irish-Themed Films

Similar to other Irish-themed films of the nickelodeon era, the O'Kalem films were screened to general audiences across the United States. In March 1911, for example, *The Film Index* reported: 'Whatever the Kalem may undertake in the way of Irish pictures there is a reasonable certainty that the result will be well-received. Not in a long time has a picture been given as enthusiastic a reception as that given *The Lad from Old Ireland* in every part of the country.'[200]

Surviving evidence suggests that the O'Kalem films received a wide range of different responses. Kalem commonly publicized the fact that *The Lad from Old Ireland* was shot on location, but not every viewer was convinced by its attempt at authenticity. In January 1911, *The Film Index* published a letter from Thomas F. Giblin of the Bijou Theatre in Providence, Rhode Island. He complained of the inaccuracy of 'religious subjects' in moving pictures:

> *The Lad from Old Ireland*, by the Kalem Co., is a beautiful picture, a grand subject, and a most interesting story, but I lost my interest at the deathbed of the girl's mother. Why, oh, why did the man who was playing the priest cross the eyes and nose, mouth and ears of the woman? It was a very poor imitation of the last sacrament. The sacrament of the Extreme Unction, as the last sacrament is called, is administered by a priest wearing a stole.
>
> On a table nearby is a lighted candle, preferably two, a small vessel of water, a linen cloth, and holy oils the priest

brings with him, and at the conclusion he does not bless every one in the room, he is attending the dying person.

After going across the ocean to get a picture, who would believe a big mistake of that kind was made. Also, there was no need for the burlesque on Irish emotion or sorrow given by the two women. Why choose the low things to follow? Is not the cry of the hour progress; upward, elevate the business.[201]

Giblin also complained that there was no need for Kalem to offer a 'burlesque on Irish emotion or sorrow' as 'given by the two women'. Rather than 'choose the low things to follow', he argued that films should 'progress'.[202] That the film had been shot in Ireland was of little importance to him in comparison to the problems he identified.

Giblin's response may well have been a minority view, however, as Kalem continued to rely on location shooting to publicize subsequent Irish-themed films. In late 1911, the fan publication *Motion Picture Story Magazine* described the release of *The Colleen Bawn*:

Perhaps no photoplay ever had the advance publicity of the Kalem production of *The Colleen Bawn*. Great things were expected of Gene Gauntier, Director Olcott, and others of the 'O'Kalems' who went to Ireland to make this play, and when the pictures were shown last month, there was a country-wide interest to see if the much-heralded production was equal to its advance reputation. A photoplay is something like a cigar. If it is good, everybody who smokes will want a box; if it is bad, no amount of puffing will make it draw. Not only did *The Colleen Bawn* fully meet all expectations, but it has proved one of the best drawing cards of the year, and it will probably be in demand for many months to come.[203]

Audience inquiries about *The Colleen Bawn* and other O'Kalem films arrived at the office of *Motion Picture Story Magazine* from across the United States, ranging from San Diego to Brooklyn.[204] In addition to publishing an article entitled 'The "El Kalems" in Egypt', the same publication also featured lengthy, synopses-based articles on *The Colleen Bawn* and *Arrah-Na-Pogue*, replete with photographs for the benefit of their national readership.[205]

In March 1912, *Moving Picture World* interviewed Kalem president Frank Marion after he made a six-week trip speaking with exhibitors across the United States. He told the trade publication that the 'Kalem Irish pictures had interested exhibitors everywhere he went and that he was now deluged with inquiries regarding the pictures now being made by the El Kalems in Egypt.'[206] Writing to film director Sidney Olcott in March 1912, Marion noted:

> I made frequent stops across the [United States] interviewing exhibitors, and you certainly would be gratified to find how strong they all are for your work. The Irish pictures really stand in a class by themselves, and exhibitors always refer to them not only as triumphs of dramatic art, but as great money makers as well. This of course is the real test of a moving picture.

In July 1912, Marion wrote another letter to Olcott, claiming, 'there is very great interest in your coming Irish productions'.[207]

On occasion, trade publications did suggest the appeal the O'Kalem possessed for specific audience members. For example, *Moving Picture World* believed *The Kerry Gow* would provide 'high class entertainment' for everyone, but noted that it might resonate most with 'older picture followers' who would have been familiar with the stage version.[208] Certainly too there was the belief that Irish-Americans would be interested in the O'Kalem films. Speaking of *The Lad from Old Ireland* in 1910, *The Film Index* wrote that 'the view of scenes of the peat bog, of the farmers harvesting grain, and of the old thatched cottage will appeal to the thousands of Irish men and women who have found prosperity and happiness in America'. The trade continued by suggesting, 'There is no mistaking the scenes shot in Ireland, and every son and daughter of the "old sod" will recognize them.'[209]

Not everyone understood why these films were popular. In July 1912, an editorial in *Moving Picture World* noted:

> Of course the Irish are interested in Irish plays, and the Scotch in Scotch plays, and the Poles in the dramatic career of their unfortunate land, but the great mass of people in this country are getting very weary of what has been done to death in this respect. The outcry made by the vanquished races – those who are licked always make the most noise – should not be mistaken for popularity.[210]

However, the O'Kalem films excited many audience members, as did the El Kalem films. For example, one newspaper advertisement for Kalem's *A*

IRELAND
A
NATION

## 44th ST. THEATRE West of Broadway

Afternoons 2.30    Evenings, 8.30    Admission, 25-50c.

A soul-inspiring film showing the struggles of Ireland's undying patriots
ROBERT EMMET, MICHAEL DWYER, DANIEL O'CONNELL and
Brave FATHER TOM MURPHY, to win Nationalism for their beloved
Erin.

Written by Walter Macnamara and produced under his personal direction in County Wicklow, Ireland.

SEE the Historic, Beautiful and Sacred Places: GLENDALOUGH, BALTINGLASS, RATHFARNHAM, &c., &c.

Faithfully Portrayed by Masterful Motion Photography.

All the Old Songs—"Mother Machree, "Killarney," "The Days of the Kerry Dances," "Come Back to Erin," "A Low Back Car," &c.
Rendered by THE EMERALD QUARTET.
COMPLETE ORCHESTRA AND SPECIAL MUSIC.

7.7  Advertisement published in the 17 October 1914 issue of the
*Gaelic American*.

*Tragedy in the Desert* (1912) drew attention to the exotic scenery, particularly the 'garden of Luxor at night under an Egyptian moon', and in so doing reminded potential filmgoers that it was the 'same company that portrayed *Colleen Bawn* and *Arrah-Na-Pogue*'.[211] For some audience members, the O'Kalem films might have been interesting for the same reason as the El Kalems: foreign scenery as the background to stories featuring popular actors like Gene Gauntier.

At any rate, film industry trades continued to pronounce the fact that the O'Kalem moving pictures held interest for general viewers. Of *The O'Neill* (1912), *Moving Picture World* told exhibitors the film would 'touch the hearts of most audiences at once'; the same publication claimed that *Ireland, the Oppressed* (1912) would 'strike a ready chord' and would 'likely...be acceptable everywhere'.[212] Exhibitors likely believed such comments, perhaps due to the successes that they had experienced with *The Lad from Old Ireland*. For example, Kalem's *Far From Erin's Isle* (1912) appeared in such cities as Oakland, California, Racine, Wisconsin, and Coschocton, Ohio.[213] *'You Remember Ellen'* (1912) was screened in Tipton, Indiana, Abilene, Texas, and Middlesboro, Kentucky.[214] Theatres in such cities as Waterloo, Iowa, and Reno, Nevada, booked *The Shaughraun* (1912).[215] Local publicity for these films sometimes underscored their universal appeal; for example, a newspaper advertisement for *Ireland the Oppressed* (1912) in Titusville, Pennsylvania claimed, 'An Irishman is a good lover and a good fighter, and the world loves him on both counts. This picture, taken in Ireland, strikes a ready chord and will be liked by all.'[216]

Then, in December 1913, Kalem announced that it was contemplating the reissue of 'several of their pictures that were pronounced successes two and three years ago, notably *The Colleen Bawn, Arrah Na-Pogue* [sic], *Rory O'Moore*, etc'. In a newspaper article published in Waterloo, Iowa (and which was apparently printed in many newspapers across America), the company announced it was seeking 'an expression of opinion from exhibitors', encouraging them to write and say 'whether or not you would like' to screen the films again.[217] Apparently encouraged by the response, Kalem initiated an extensive reissue programme that began with *The Colleen Bawn* (1911) in March 1914 ('just in time for St Patrick's Day') and continued with *The Lad From Old Ireland* (1910) in August 1914 and *Rory O'Moore* (1911) in September 1914.[218]

Certainly the most elaborate publicity campaign for any Irish-themed film during the early cinema period was mounted for the 1914 reissue of *The Colleen Bawn*. *Moving Picture World* wrote that Kalem had imported soil 'dug from the base of the Colleen Bawn Rock, in one of the Lakes of Killarney' to be 'distributed, free of charge, among the enterprising exhibitors' who booked the reissue.[219] 'Come and Tread on Irish Soil!' Kalem's advertisements suggested to theatre managers, who could also obtain complimentary 'copies of affidavits from Father Fitzgerald, the parish priest, and municipality of Killarney, vouching for the authenticity of the soil'.[220] One newspaper advertisement later boasted that Kalem had 'imported 10,000 sacks of Irish soil'.[221]

Whether or not that number was an accurate estimate, it is clear that Kalem shipped the soil to exhibitors across the United States. Individual theatres received 'enough of the soil to fill a box about 4 feet square by 1 inch deep'.[222] For example, exhibitors in Syracuse, New York, in Cedar Rapids, Iowa, and in Lincoln, Nebraska, promoted the soil in their newspaper advertisements for the film.[223] When the soil appeared in Alton, Illinois, a local newspaper described how it would be used:

> The soil will be placed in front of the ticket office of the Princess [Theatre] this evening, and everybody who buys a ticket there tonight will have to stand on Irish soil to do so. Anybody who goes to that theatre tonight can always say afterwards he or she has stood on Irish soil and they need make no further explanation either. They will be telling the truth.[224]

A newspaper in Corning, Iowa, said much the same, inviting 'everybody in this vicinity' to take the 'opportunity soon', promising an experience 'long to be remembered for the sons of Erin especially... This will be like visiting Ireland again to breathe the atmosphere of the heather in this beautiful picture and have the pleasure to tread on the good "auld" soil.'[225]

How many 'sons of Erin' trudged across that imported soil is difficult to know. Certainly Syracuse had a sizeable Irish-American population; whether many Irish-Americans attended the film in a town such as Corning, Iowa, is difficult to determine. Regardless, by the time the reissue of *The Colleen Bawn* appeared in a city like Lowell, Massachusetts, in April 1914, the '10,000 sacks of Irish soil' may have been depleted, or perhaps the theatre there did not see it as a worthwhile form of publicity, as its advertisements made no mention of the soil.[226]

At any rate, Kalem's reissue programme soon expanded, with the company re-releasing an array of non-Irish-themed films in 1915, specifically some one-reel moving pictures starring Carlyle Blackwell and Alice Joyce.[227] Then, in 1916, Kalem reissued *The O'Neill* with a new title, *The Irish Rebel*. In this case, rather than build on the film's previous notoriety, as had happened with *The Colleen Bawn* and *The Lad from Old Ireland*, their purpose was to obscure its previous release in an effort to make it appear recent and thus relevant in terms of then-current events in Ireland. According to *Moving Picture World*, the film was shot 'on the spots that have figured so prominently in the news columns'; *Exhibitors Herald* echoed that claim, suggesting its scenes were 'laid in locations drenched with blood during recent days'.[228]

# Case Study: Lexington, Kentucky

The six Irish-American newspapers used for this study featured scant coverage of the cinema. However, a seventh publication – the *Kentucky Irish-American*, published in Louisville, Kentucky – reported on the topic far more than the others, particularly during the nickelodeon era. Information contained in the newspaper allows for a clearer picture to emerge of Irish-Americans in that city interacting with the cinema than it is possible to obtain for those Irish-Americans living in New York City, Boston, or elsewhere in America. Together, the articles and advertisements published in the *Kentucky Irish-American* form a useful case study that underscores the complexities of early film audiences, but that also provides some insight into Irish-American film viewing in a particular city.

The *Kentucky Irish-American* reported very little on the moving picture between 1898 (the year it began publication) and 1902. The earliest article to appear was an announcement for a 'cinematograph exhibition' of *Passion Play Pictures* at St Louis Bertrand's church in Louisville in 1899.[229] Brief mention was then made of the arrival of the Polyscope at the city's Temple Theatre; the newspaper drew particular attention to footage screened of the local fire department.[230] Then, between December 1902 and March 1905, the newspaper chronicled at least fifteen appearances of the 'Biograph' at the city's Hopkins Theatre, which drew on more than just Irish-Americans for patronage.[231] In 1904 and 1905, advertisements and reports on these events occasionally mentioned specific moving pictures, such as footage of the Russo-Japanese War, footage of the 'Washington Inaugural', *Kit Carson* (American Mutoscope & Biograph, 1903), *An Impossible Voyage* (Méliès, 1904) and *The Chicken Thief* (American Mutoscope & Biograph, 1904).[232] If any Irish-themed films were screened, no mention was made of them.

Similarly, during the final months of 1905, the newspaper's 'Amusements' column began to announce the occasional appearance of 'Kinodrome' moving pictures at the Hopkins Theatre. As had been the case with the Biograph screenings, the management screened 'Kinodrome' films on balanced programmes featuring various vaudeville acts.[233] Moving pictures continued to appear at the Hopkins in 1906, covered in brief in the 'Amusements' column, as well as in the theatre's advertisements.[234] The fact that the manager of the Hopkins purchased regular ads probably encouraged the newspaper to publish brief, one-paragraph articles about the theatre, which in September 1906 included news of the theatre's redecoration.[235]

In late 1906, the Hopkins' advertisements began to name featured 'Kinodrome' films alongside the names of the vaudeville acts. For example, in the 13 October 1906 issue of the newspaper, the advertised bill was headlined by 'Paul Spadoni, the Juggler of Two Extremes', and also included: 'Camille Comedy Trio, Performers on the Horizontal Bar, Carlin and Otto, Celebrated German Comedians; Morrisey & Rich, in a new Comedy Sketch; Magaz & Mazette, *The Tramp and the Brakeman*; Bill Van, the Minstrel – *That's All*; Hickman Bros – 3 Comedians, Singers, and Dancers; the Kinodrome, *The Silver Wedding* [American Mutoscope & Biograph, 1906] and other new pictures'.[236] Other films named in subsequent ads included Edison's *How the Office Boy Saw the Ball Game* (1906) and Pathé Frères' *The Holiday* (1906) and *The Magic Flute* (1906).[237] In October 1906, the Buckingham Theatre, one of the Hopkins' competitors, advertised a bill that headlined 'The Genuine Gans-Nelson Fight Pictures'.[238] However, outside of brief mention in the 'Amusements' column and theatre advertisements, the *Kentucky Irish-American* largely ignored moving pictures in 1906, writing instead about other kinds of entertainment, such as Irish music. The newspaper also decried specific examples of the 'stage Irishman' in live theatre, but made absolutely no mention of such stereotypes in the cinema.[239]

The same was true in 1907, though instead of promoting individual films, the Hopkins' advertisements – and, as an apparent result, the newspaper's 'Amusements' column – referred obliquely to 'new animated views' and the 'new and latest motion pictures'.[240] Only once that year did the *Kentucky Irish-American* draw attention to a particular moving picture, which was the 'already famous view of Richard Croker's [horse] Orby winning the recent English derby'.[241] Perhaps they drew attention to the film because of Croker's Irish heritage. At any rate, the newspaper wrote at length in 1907 about Irish music and Irish dance, as well as specific examples of the 'stage Irishman' in live theatre, but not in the moving picture.[242]

By February 1908, the Hopkins Theatre enacted a change in its programming. A new advertisement in the 15 February 1908 issue of the *Kentucky Irish-American* announced that the theatre was 'Now Open with High-Class Picture Entertainment'. The Hopkins promoted a 'marvellous exhibition of animated photography', which was accompanied with 'Illustrated Songs by Harry Browne'. The shows were 'continuous from noon until 11 PM', with a 'stay as long as you like' policy in exchange for a ten-cent ticket. The Hopkins management also announced that the theatre, which had abandoned vaudeville to focus on moving pictures, catered to 'women and children especially'.[243]

Noting the Hopkins' change in programming in early March 1908, the *Kentucky Irish-American*'s 'Amusements' column claimed:

> The motion pictures at Hopkins Theatre continue to draw
> large crowds every afternoon and night and every day this

7.8 Soil from Ireland used to promote Kalem's 1914 reissue of
*The Colleen Bawn* at the Dome Theatre in Youngstown, Ohio.

week the handsome playhouse has been filled from six to eight
times...Where there is tragedy, the scenes are strong and
performed by competent actors, but it is the comedy pictures
that delight the women and children. Lovers of good music,
too, enjoy the illustrated songs. Taking it all in all, there is no
better or cheaper amusement in Louisville.[244]

One week later, the same column noted the fact that all of the Hopkins'
moving picture shows were 'clean and pure'.[245]

For St Patrick's Day 1908, Edward Dustin, manager of the Hopkins,
programmed three films that the *Kentucky Irish-American* believed would
'appeal with much interest to the Irish folk of Louisville, particularly those
who were born upon the Little Isle of Green'.[246] From 15 March to 18
March, Dustin screened an unbalanced programme consisting of Urban's
*Glimpses of Erin* (1906), *From Galway to Dublin* (a mysterious film that
may have been a retitled version of some other non-fiction moving picture)
and Selig's *The Irish Blacksmith* (1908). This was the first instance in ten

years of publication that the *Kentucky Irish-American* mentioned Irish-themed films.

The following week, the 'Amusements' column noted that the St Patrick's Day bill had been of an 'admirable character and the Irish features were appreciated by the many who witnessed them'. The column proceeded to claim that the new programme would be 'even better but of a more varied nature'.[247] That comment implies that at least some patrons preferred a return to non-Irish-themed films, or at least a return to balanced programmes. Indeed, the following month, the 'Amusements' column reported increased business at the theatre, claiming that 'while the attendance was fair during the Lenten season, the increase during the present week was very noticeable and at times the house was crowded'.[248]

That the Hopkins saw improved ticket sales was fortunate, given the increased local competition that they faced. In March 1908, Macauley's Theatre and the Marvel Theatre published advertisements in the *Kentucky Irish-American* to promote their own film screenings; the former showed Kalem's *Ben Hur* (1907) and the latter showed a version of the *Passion Play*.[249] In April 1908, the newspaper also reported on the appearance of Howe's Moving Pictures in Louisville; that was all in addition to the general competition moving pictures had from the Kentucky Derby in May 1908.[250]

Despite such challenges, Edward Dustin pronounced that the Hopkins would remain open during the hot summer months.[251] The 'Amusements' column reported his growing success, noting in June that 'on two or three occasions every seat was taken and some of the spectators had to stand'; by August, the newspaper claimed that the Hopkins 'continues to be the mecca for lovers of moving pictures'.[252] The *Kentucky Irish-American* did not generally announce the specific moving pictures that Dustin screened during the rest of 1908, except for mentioning footage of Teddy Roosevelt in July and a film of a baseball game between Chicago and Detroit in October.[253] They also gave a strong review of a singer who temporarily replaced Harry Browne; he performed 'an Italian character song' in November that was 'highly appreciated'.[254]

The *Kentucky Irish-American* also continued to report on the growing number of local theatres that screened moving pictures. While they castigated the Avenue Theatre for screening a 'fake' version of the 'recent Nelson–Gans prize fight' in July 1908, they applauded the Princess, Bijou, Dreamland and Casino Theatres – all owned by the Princess Amusement Company – for projecting moving pictures.[255] Each theatre offered a change of programme 'several times a week', and drew crowds of 'women and children'.[256] In addition to the new venues offering moving pictures, the Hopkins Theatre also faced competition from the city's Coliseum; the *Kentucky Irish-American* reported on the popularity of its skating rink in late 1908.[257]

In February 1909, the *Kentucky Irish-American* published its longest story about moving pictures at the Hopkins, though it was still only two paragraphs long, rather than the usual one. It praised the theatre and its manager Edward Dustin, as well as its recent screening of Vitagraph's *Francesca da Rimini, or, the Two Brothers* (1908); however, the publicity may have been of little help against competition that was growing in strength.[258] During 1909, the Princess Amusement Company regularly advertised three moving picture theatres in the *Kentucky Irish-American*: the Casino, the Princess and the Columbia (formerly the Bijou). In addition to reports of their increasing business, the newspaper excitedly announced the appearance of the Cameraphone – a 1908 invention that combined moving pictures with synchronized sound recordings – at each of those venues. That was in addition to a screening of 'the fight between Burns and Johnson' at the Masonic Theatre in March.[259] Perhaps due to these pressures, Dustin changed the Hopkins back to a vaudeville theatre in April 1909, relegating moving pictures to a minor spot on the bill.[260]

The cinematic landscape in Louisville, at least as covered in the *Kentucky Irish-American*, changed a great deal in 1910. For reasons unknown, the Hopkins dropped their vaudeville acts, focussing once again on moving pictures and illustrated songs; by March of that year, they heavily promoted Emile Weber, their new singer.[261] That, in turn, seems to have caused the Princess Theatre to promote their illustrated songs, as well as their singer Cary Taylor.[262] During the summer, the situation continued to change. The Princess Amusement Company changed the name of the Princess Theatre to the Orpheum, and promoted it and the Casino as their two premiere moving picture theatres, with 'first run films' as their new 'motto'. By contrast, they advertised the Columbia as a five-cent theatre, which was apparently playing older films.[263]

Then, in August 1910, the *Kentucky Irish-American* reported that the Princess Amusement Company had taken over the Hopkins Theatre, something that apparently occurred during the summer when it was closed for redecoration. Under new management, it once again became a theatre featuring vaudeville and moving pictures. Dustin had apparently lost the battle to his competitors. Despite these many changes, one aspect of the *Kentucky Irish-American*'s coverage remained the same as before. Each week the newspaper mentioned the local theatres, but only rarely did they announce a specific moving picture by name.[264]

During these years, with the exception of the aforementioned St Patrick's Day programme at the Hopkins in 1908, the *Kentucky Irish-American* did not discuss any Irish-themed moving pictures, either by name or by description. Then, for only the second time in its history, the *Kentucky Irish-American* mentioned Irish-themed moving pictures in its 29 April 1911 edition.[265] The newspaper announced that Division 3 of the Ancient Order of Hibernians had arranged with the local Globe Theatre to screen a 'special moving picture show' on 3 May and 17 May 1911. The show's contents were not described until 13 May 1911, when the newspaper wrote that 'some very fine Irish views will be presented' on 17 May.[266] No other details were printed either before or after the screening, though it would seem that the show consisted of non-fiction films of Ireland.

In 1911, the Princess Amusement Company continued to advertise vaudeville shows at the Hopkins, as well as film screenings at the Casino and Orpheum. However, the only mention of a specific moving picture at either venue came in March after the Orpheum screened a film of 'Archbishop Ryan's funeral'.[267] Later in the same year, the *Kentucky Irish-American* promoted the fact that the Casino and the Orpheum had reduced their ticket prices to five cents each; both theatres also claimed that they would screen 'three new films each day'.[268] Increased competition may have caused these changes. Lyman H. Howe's *Travel Festival* appeared at Macauley's Theatre in April just as the local Avenue Theatre began its own regular film screenings.[269] The *Kentucky Irish-American* reported that 'The pictures [at the Avenue Theatre] alternate with the vaudeville turns.'[270] The Casino and Orpheum's other new competitor was the Crown Theatre, a newly erected vaudeville and moving picture theatre that was first mentioned in the *Kentucky Irish-American* in September 1911.[271]

Mention of the Crown disappeared from the pages of the *Kentucky Irish-American* in 1912, though advertisements and brief articles on the Casino, Orpheum and Columbia continued.[272] The articles, running only one paragraph in length, never mentioned specific films during 1912, instead offering such generalizations as 'meritorious motion picture dramas, pictorial history scenes, and some very hilarious comedy'.[273] The newspaper also noted 'usual every other day changes' of programme at the Casino and Orpheum (rather than the previous year's promise of three new films per day), and the fact that the Hopkins Theatre presented a combination of vaudeville and moving pictures.[274] Except for a brief article about the installation of a projector at the Cardome Academy School, the *Kentucky Irish-American* focussed on only one other film-related story in 1912. The local Walnut Street Theatre hosted Paul J. Rainey's *Motion Picture Exhibition* in September.[275] The topic was a 'great African hunt', featuring moving pictures of 'nearly every animal which Noah took into the ark, in its native haunts'.[276]

During 1913, the number of advertisements published in the *Kentucky Irish-American* promoting film screenings decreased sharply, which in turn probably caused a noticeable decrease in the number of stories that the newspaper published on local theatres. Aside from brief mention of the Walnut Street Theatre, which had begun to screen moving pictures along with their vaudeville bills, the newspaper generally ignored the cinema that year.[277] That said, they did promote a February 1913 screening of motion pictures showing 'His Holiness Pius X and the Vatican', as well as a screening of Kalem's *The Colleen Bawn* (1911) at a St Patrick's Day celebration organized by the Ancient Order of Hibernians.[278]

*The Colleen Bawn* reappeared in the pages of the *Kentucky Irish-American* one year later, when the National Theatre advertised it in mid-March 1914. Presumably they booked the film for St Patrick's Day, though the rest of their bill consisted of non-Irish themed vaudeville acts, including 'Hunting Morn, Black and White Posing Act' and 'Kumry, Boesch, Robinson, *Fun in a Music Store*', both of which were billed above *The Colleen Bawn* in the *Kentucky Irish-American* advertisement. However, the ad did invite readers to 'come and tread on Irish soil brought over from Killarney'. While brief, the ad also represents the most attention ever given by an Irish-American newspaper of the period to one of the O'Kalem films.[279]

In April 1914, the newspaper noted that the Hibernian Social Club would present a moving picture and vaudeville show in April, though no details were given of the films to be projected.[280] The newspaper ignored the cinema for the rest of that year, outside of briefly mentioning local screenings of *The Merchant of Venice* (Universal, 1914), *The Gangsters of New York* (Reliance, 1914) and a film described as 'Seeing South American with Col. Roosevelt'.[281]

In 1915, no theatres screening films purchased advertisements in the *Kentucky Irish-American*, which probably accounts for the fact that coverage of the cinema disappeared completely that year. However, the fact that theatres did purchase ads over and over again during many of the years under review does suggest that such exhibitors believed they were reaching potential and regular ticket buyers. Such readers-turned-audience members do not seem to have requested screenings of Irish-themed moving pictures at these venues or coverage of the same in the *Kentucky Irish-American*.

What this case study does suggest is that some – perhaps many – Irish-Americans in Louisville, Kentucky, were interested attending moving pictures, particularly during the nickelodeon period. It would seem that they normally viewed non-Irish-themed films, and it would further seem that they viewed them at venues frequented by other ethnicities. Such

7.9 Advertisement published in the 14 March 1914 issue of the
*Kentucky Irish-American.*

venues changed during the nickelodeon era, in terms of their programming
(all moving pictures versus a combination with vaudeville, as well as the
frequency with which they changed moving picture programmes), their
ownership, their ticket prices and their sheer numbers (as competition
increased).

## Conclusion

Based upon surviving evidence, including the sheer number of film screenings reported in newspapers across America, it is evident that Irish-themed
illustrated song slides and Irish-themed moving pictures in the early cinema
period were intended for widespread distribution to general audiences,
rather than being produced and distributed specifically to Irish-Americans.
Indeed, the majority of viewers for such entertainment were not Irish-
Americans, but rather Americans of various backgrounds attending
itinerant film exhibitions and, later, nickelodeons throughout the United

States. Such audiences usually viewed Irish-themed song slides and moving pictures as part of balanced programmes comprised largely of non-Irish themed films, song slides, and/or live vaudeville acts.

To the extent that they experienced Irish-themed entertainment at nickelodeons, Irish-Americans would have had many more opportunities to see Irish-themed illustrated song slides – based upon the sheer number of them produced and distributed – than Irish-themed moving pictures. Their reactions to either could have varied greatly due to a large array of demographic and psychographic factors. Though fictional, Lizzie Pinson's 1911 poem *The Irish Heart* underscores the lack of a monolithic 'Irish' or 'Irish-American' film audience in the United States, illustrating as it does the different film preferences of two family members based on age and personal film viewing histories. Indeed, reported reaction to the St Patrick's Day screening in Brooklyn in 1910 suggests that Irish-American audience members could apparently give diametrically opposed responses even to 'stage Irish' moving pictures.

Moreover, based upon the relatively small number of Irish-themed films produced in the early cinema period, as well as the consistent use of balanced film programmes, it is also evident that Irish-Americans who did attend film screenings would generally have viewed non-Irish-themed moving pictures produced in America, France and elsewhere. As a result, they participated in the larger project of American filmgoing, both in terms of the film content that they viewed and the fact that most of them attended screenings also frequented by non-Irish-Americans. Despite its limited coverage in the Irish-American press, the cinema may well have been important to some Irish-Americans, but unimportant to others.

# Notes

1. L.M. Thornton, 'The Power of a Nickel', *Motion Picture Story Magazine* (March 1912), p.131.
2. T. Ramsaye, *A Million and One Nights: A History of the Motion Picture through 1925* (New York: Simon & Schuster, 1926); B. Hampton, *A History of the Movies* (New York: Corvici, Friede Publishers, 1931); L. Jacobs, *The Rise of the American Film* (New York: Harcourt, Brace, 1939).
3. R. Merritt, 'Nickelodeon Theatres, 1905–1914: Building an Audience for the Movies', in T. Balio (ed.), *The American Film Industry* (Madison, WI: University of Wisconsin Press, 1976), pp.59–79.
4. R.C. Allen, 'Motion Picture Exhibition in Manhattan, 1906–1912', *Cinema Journal*, 18, 2 (Spring 1979), pp.2–15.
5. R. Sklar, 'Oh Althusser! Historiography and the Rise of Cinema Studies', *Radical History Review*, 41 (Spring 1988), pp.10–35; B. Singer, 'Manhattan Nickelodeons: New Data on Audiences and Exhibitors', *Cinema Journal*, 34, 3 (Spring 1995), pp.5–35.
6. Singer, 'Manhattan Nickelodeons', p.28.
7. R.C. Allen, 'Manhattan Myopia; Or, Oh! Iowa!' *Cinema Journal*, 34, 3 (Spring 1996), pp.75–103.
8. S. Higashi, 'Dialogue: Manhattan's Nickelodeons', *Cinema Journal* (Spring 1995), pp.72–4.
9. J. Thissen, 'Oy, Myopia! A Reaction from Judith Thissen on the Singer–Allen Controversy', *Cinema Journal*, 36, 4 (Summer 1997), pp.102–7.

10. W. Uricchio and R.E. Pearson, 'Dialogue: Manhattan's Nickelodeons. New York? New York!', *Cinema Journal*, 36, 4 (Summer 1997), pp.98–102.
11. B. Singer, 'New York, Just Like I Pictured It ...', *Cinema Journal*, 35, 3 (Spring 1996), pp.104–28; B. Singer, 'Manhattan Melodrama: A Response from Ben Singer', *Cinema Journal*, 36, 5 (Summer 1997), pp.107–12.
12. Uricchio and Pearson, 'Dialogue: Manhattan's Nickelodeons', p.98.
13. M. Stokes, 'Introduction: Reconstructing American Cinema's Audiences', in M. Stokes and R. Maltby (eds), *American Movie Audiences: From the Turn of the Century to the Early Sound Era* (London: British Film Institute, 1999), pp.1–11.
14. Stokes, 'Introduction: Reconstructing American Cinema's Audiences', p.5.
15. 'Twin City Entertainers', *Wisconsin Valley Leader* (Grand Rapids, WI), 18 May 1905, p.1.
16. 'A Great Attraction on Our Streets', *Times-Democrat* (Lima, OH), 3 August 1896 [n.p.].
17. C. Musser, *The Emergence of Cinema: The American Screen to 1907* (Berkeley, CA: University of California Press, 1990), p.78.
18. Ibid., p.81.
19. Ibid., pp.118, 183.
20. 'Edison's Vitascope Cheered', *New York Times*, 24 April 1896, p.5.
21. For example, on 16 May 1896, the *New York Clipper* noted that the Vitascope films at Koster and Bial's 'all received the approval of the audience', and on 23 May 1896 the same publication claimed that the Vitascope films were met with 'loud applause'. With regard to the changing programme, on 16 May 1896 the *New York Clipper* claimed that 'several new pictures were shown'.
22. 'Koster and Bial's', *New York Clipper*, 9 May 1896, p.152.
23. It is also possible that a projectionist offered the surf scene in response to a more general call for an encore, rather than a request to see that particular film again.
24. 'Keith's Union Square Theatre', *New York Clipper*, 22 August 1896, p.392.
25. 'Keith's Union Square Theatre', *New York Clipper*, 7 November 1896, p.570. (These comments were made in relation to a performance of the Lumière Cinematographe.)
26. 'Maryland', *New York Clipper*, 11 July 1896, p.292; 'Massachusetts', *New York Clipper*, 10 October 1896, p.507; 'Rhode Island', *New York Clipper*, 27 June 1896, p.279; 'Amusements', *Evening Times* (Trenton, NJ), 10 September 1896, p.2.
27. 'The Vitascope', *Daily Light* (San Antonio, TX), 13 October 1896, p.3.
28. Advertisement, *Steubenville Herald* (Steubenville, OH), 30 November 1896, p.8.
29. 'Where They Were Exhibited Last Month', *Phonoscope*, October 1898, p.16.
30. Advertisement, *New York Clipper*, 31 March 1900.
31. [Untitled], *Eau Claire Leader* (Eau Claire, WI), 13 July 1898, p.5.
32. Musser, *Emergence of Cinema*, p.183.
33. 'The Stage: Footlight Chat', *Munsey's Magazine*, 16 (January 1897), p.499.
34. Musser, *Emergence of Cinema*, p.118.
35. 'Edison's Vitascope', *Newark Daily Advocate* (Newark, OH), 23 October 1896, p.5.
36. For example, two films of Native Americans were screened at a moving picture show in Colorado Springs, Colorado, in 1902, but they were separated on the programme by three other films and an intermission. See 'Moving Pictures Will Start Tonight', *Colorado Springs Gazette* (Colorado Springs, CO), 5 August 1902, p.11.
37. 'Comedy To-Night', *Fort Wayne Morning Journal* (Fort Wayne, IN), 24 May 1898, p.2; advertisement, *Fort Wayne Morning Journal*, 24 May 1898, p.2.
38. 'Last Night's Show', *Davenport Daily Leader* (Davenport, IA), 18 December 1896, p.6.
39. Advertisement, *The Standard* (Ogden, UT), 15 April 1905, p.7.
40. Advertisement, *New York Clipper*, 1 April 1899, p.100.
41. 'Announcements', *Lincoln Evening News* (Lincoln, NE), 21 January 1897, p.4.
42. 'Moving Picture', *North Adams Evening Transcript* (North Adams, MA), 3 October 1903, p.7.
43. 'The *Passion Play* Is Presented', *New Castle News* (New Castle, PA), 17 February 1904, p.1.
44. 'Shepard's Motion Pictures at the Academy To-Night', *Washington Post*, 9 April 1905, p.A2.
45. Advertisement, *Des Moines Daily News* (Des Moines, IA), 28 October 1906, p.7.
46. Advertisement, *Salt Lake Tribune* (Salt Lake City, UT), 13 November 1906, p.10.
47. 'The Irish Fair To-Night', *Brooklyn Daily Eagle*, 1 October 1898, p.14.
48. 'Academy of Music', *Lowell Sun* (Lowell, MA) 13 December 1904, p.8.

49. 'Fine Views', *Lowell Sun*, 15 May 1905, p.2.

50. See, for example, 'Mrs Cougar on the Warpath', *Logansport Pharos* (Logansport, IN), 21 September 1897, p.2; 'Pueblo Against the Kinetoscope', *Dallas Morning News*, 5 May 1897, p.3; 'Anti-Kinetoscope Bill Passed', *Renwick Times* (Renwick, IA), 7 May 1897 [n.p.].

51. 'Prize Fight to a Finish', *Lowell Sun*, 7 September 1895, p.1; 'National Solons', *Semi-Weekly Cedar Falls Gazette* (Cedar Falls, IA), 2 April 1897, p.3.

52. For an extensive history and analysis of early fight (and fake fight) films, see Dan Streible, *Fight Pictures: A History of Boxing and Early Cinema* (Berkeley, CA: University of California Press, 2008).

53. *Lubin's Films, 1907*, (Philadelphia: S. Lubin). Available in *A Guide to Motion Picture Catalogs by American Producers and Distributors, 1894–1908: A Microfilm Edition*, Reel 3.

54. *Lubin's Films* (Philadelphia, PA: S. Lubin, May 1905), p.30. Available in *Guide to Motion Picture Catalogs ... 1894–1908: Microfilm Edition*, Reel 3.

55. 'Amusements', *The Irish-American*, 3 August 1896, p.1; 'Amusements', *The Irish-American*, 17 August 1896, p.5; 'Amusements', *The Irish-American*, 31 August 1896, p.4; 'Amusements', *The Irish-American*, 14 November 1896, p.8.

56. 'The Stage Irishman', *National Hibernian*, 15 June 1902, p.4.

57. 'Seeing Ireland in Moving Pictures', *Irish-American Advocate*, 3 December 1904, p.1.

58. 'A Trip to Ireland', *Irish-American Advocate*, 21 January 1905, p.1.

59. 'A Trip Through Ireland', *Irish-American Advocate*, 4 February 1905, p.4.

60. Advertisement, *Irish-American Advocate*, 4 February 1905, p.4; advertisement, *Irish-American Advocate*, 25 February 1905, p.4; advertisement, *Irish-American Advocate*, 18 March 1905, p.8; advertisement, *Irish-American Advocate*, 1 April 1905, p.4; advertisement, *Irish-American Advocate*, 2 December 1905, p.4.

61. 'A Trip Through Ireland', *Irish-American Advocate*, 20 May 1905, p.1.

62. See, for example, 'Lecture on Ireland', *The Irish-American*, 15 February 1902, p.4.

63. 'The "Nickel Craze" in New York', *Views and Film Index*, 5 October 1907, p.3.

64. W.S. Bush, 'Who Goes to the Moving Pictures?', *Moving Picture World*, 31 October 1908, p.336.

65. 'The Moving Picture Theatre', *Views and Film Index*, 24 August 1907, p.2. See also F.J. Haskin, 'Nickelodeon History', *Views and Film Index*, 1 February 1908, pp.5, 14.

66. 'The Cult of the Motion Picture Show', *Moving Picture World*, 8 August 1908, p.106.

67. For more information on children in the nickelodeon audience, see R. Pearson and W. Uricchio's ' "The Formation and Impressionable Stage": Discursive Constructions of the Nickelodeon's Child Audience', in Stokes and Maltby (eds), *American Film Audiences*, pp.64–78. For more information on women as viewers of early cinema, see L. Rabinovitz, *For the Love of Pleasure: Women, Movies, and Culture in Turn-of-the-Century Chicago* (New Brunswick, NJ: Rutgers University Press, 1998). See also S. Stamp, *Movie-Struck Girls: Women and Motion Picture Culture After the Nickelodeon* (Princeton, NJ: Princeton University Press, 2000).

68. 'Moving Pictures at Dallas', *Moving Picture World*, 23 March 1907.

69. 'The Nickelodeon', *Moving Picture World*, 4 May 1907, p.140.

70. 'Taking Baby to a Show', *Chicago Tribune*, 1 April 1913, p.8.

71. 'Hat Nuisance', *Views and Film Index*, 10 October 1908, p.8.

72. 'Hats Off, Ladies!', *Nickelodeon*, 15 May 1910, p.262. See also 'Those Hats Again', *Nickelodeon*, 15 March 1910, p.148; 'Arrested for Allowing Women to Wear Hats', *The Film Index*, 3 December 1910, p.8; 'Women Don't Want to Remove Hats', *The Film Index*, 10 December 1910, p.9.

73. A.L. Barrett, 'Moving Pictures and Their Audiences', *Moving Picture News*, 16 September 1911, pp.8–9.

74. L.R. Harrison, 'Why We Go to the Picture Show', *Moving Picture World*, 17 August 1912, p.640.

75. 'Theatre Shuts Out Odor and Is Sued', *Nickelodeon*, July 1909.

76. For more information on the attendance of different ethnic groups at nickelodeons, see, for example, J. Thissen's 'Jewish Immigrant Audiences in New York, 1905–1914', pp.15–28; G. Bertellini's 'Italian Imageries, Historical Feature Films, and the Fabrication of Italy's Spectators in Early 1900s New York', pp.29–45; and A. Griffiths and J. Latham's 'Film and Ethnic Identity in Harlem, 1896–1915', all of which appear in Stokes and Maltby (eds), *American Film Audiences*. See also Gregory Waller's 'Another Audience: Black Moviegoing from 1907 to 1916', in I.R. Hark (ed.), pp.2–24, *Exhibition, the Film Reader* (New York: Routledge, 2002). In addition, K.H. Fuller's *At the Picture Show: Small Town Audiences and the Creation of Movie Fan Culture* (Washington, DC:

# Audiences

Smithsonian Institution Press, 1996) offers an examination of the 'Regional Diversity of Moviegoing Practices' that offers details on the film attendance of African-Americans, Mexican-Americans, Japanese-Americans and Chinese-Americans, from the nickelodeon era to the 1930s.

77. 'Who Says Moving Pictures Are Not As Good as the Real Thing?', *Moving Picture World*, 23 May 1908; 'Shot a "Movie" Villain', *Evening News* (Ada, OK), 9 May 1913, p.1.
78. 'Almost a Good Show', *Moving Picture Story Magazine* (October 1911), p.47.
79. 'The Demand for Realistic Exhibitions', *Views and Film Index*, 13 October 1906, p.1.
80. 'The Random Shots of a Picture Fan', *Moving Picture World*, 21 October 1910, p.198.
81. J.S. McQuade, 'Chicago Letter', *The Film Index*, 21 January 1911, p.8.
82. 'Demand for Realistic Exhibitions', p.1.
83. 'The Variety of Moving Picture Audiences', *Moving Picture World*, 25 September 1909, p.406. The word 'genre' was used during this period, even if infrequently. See, for example, 'Films and Realism', *Views and Film Index*, 24 October 1908, p.11.
84. W.A. Johnston, 'The Moving-Picture Show, the New Form of Drama for the Million', *Munsey's Magazine*, 41 (August 1909), pp.633–5.
85. W.H. Kitchell, 'The Average Patron', *Moving Picture World*, 10 February 1912, p.466.
86. E. Bowser, *The Transformation of Cinema: 1907–1915* (Berkeley, CA: University of California Press, 1990), p.2.
87. For example, the nickelodeon in Portsmouth, Ohio, changed its films 'every day', as did the Star Theatre in Marshall, Michigan, whereas a nickelodeon in Centralia, Washington, changed its films every Monday and Thursday. See 'New Attractions', *Portsmouth Daily Times* (Portsmouth, OH), 1 October 1910, p.13; advertisement, *Daily News* (Marshall, MI) 8 April 1908: 3; advertisement, *Centralia Daily Chronicle* (Centralia, WA), 11 December 1908, p.6.
88. Advertisement, *Logansport Chronicle* (Logansport, IN), 25 August 1906, p.4; 'The Stage', *Piqua Leader-Dispatch* (Piqua, OH), 21 July 1906.
89. 'Local', *Daily Chronicle* (Marshall, MI), 26 June 1907, p.2; [untitled], *Emporia Daily Gazette*, 10 July 1907, p.2.
90. Advertisement, *Santa Fe New Mexican* (Santa Fe, NM), 1 December 1908, p.2; 'At the Acme', *Woodland Daily Democrat* (Woodland, CA), 31 July 1908, p.1; 'Lyric', *San Antonio Gazette* (San Antonio, TX), 17 June 1908, p.8.
91. Advertisement, *Eau Claire Leader*, 15 July 1909, p.2; advertisement, *Portsmouth Daily Herald* (Portsmouth, NJ), 6 January 1910, p.2; advertisement, *Anaconda Standard* (Anaconda, MT), 30 January 1912, p.4.
92. Advertisement, *Des Moines Daily News*, 12 July 1907, p.8.
93. See, for example, 'Balancing the Program', *Moving Picture World*, 10 June 1911, p.1303.
94. 'Vaudeville', *New York Times*, 3 November 1907, p.X1.
95. Advertisement, *Washington Post*, 12 January 1908, p.3.
96. Advertisement, *San Antonio Light* (San Antonio, TX), 29 June 1906; advertisement, *Anaconda Standard*, 17 March 1908, p.6.
97. Advertisement, *Austin Daily Herald* (Austin, MN), 1 August 1908, p.3.
98. At least two split reels contained two-Irish-themed films, such as Vitagraph's fictional film *Too Many Caseys* (1912) and non-fiction travelogue *Cork and Vicinity* (1912), as well as Keystone's comedy films *Murphy's I.O.U.* (1913) and *A Dollar Did It* (1913). Though they were unbalanced reels, they were screened on larger, balanced programmes at nickelodeons. For example, the New Photoplay Theatre in Gettysburg, Pennsylvania, screened *Too Many Caseys* and *Cork and Vicinity* on a bill that also included Kalem's 'comedy', *A California Snipe Hunt* (1912), Edison's 'actual' film entitled *A Forest Fire* (1912) and Kalem's 'comedy', *Something Wrong with Bessie* (1912). See advertisement, *Gettysburg Times* (Gettysburg, PA), 6 March 1913, p.1.
99. Advertisement, *Titusville Herald* (Titusville, PA), 26 February 1909, p.6; advertisement, *Dothan Eagle* (Dothan, AL), 20 April 1909, p.3.
100. Advertisement, *Daily Advocate* (Victoria, TX), 1 June 1909, p.3.
101. Advertisement, *Wisconsin State Journal* (Madison, WI), 17 April 1909, p.2.
102. Advertisement, *San Antonio Light*, 24 September 1908, p.10; 'Random References', *The Standard* (Ogden, UT), 7 October 1908, p.6; advertisement, *Janesville Daily Gazette* (Janesville, WI), 16 April 1908, p.8; advertisement, *Sandusky Star Journal* (Sandusky, OH), 18 March 1911, p.5; 'Good Bill at Crystal This Week', *Logansport Journal* (Logansport, IN), 28 October 1906, p.3.

103. *The Nickelodeon*, 1 November 1910, p.254.
104. 'The Month's New Films', *Optical Lantern and Kinematograph Journal*, March 1907, p.121.
105. 'Something to Print', *The Film Index*, 13 August 1910, p.25.
106. Ibid.
107. '*Scenes of Irish Life*', *Moving Picture World*, 9 November 1912, p.553.
108. 'Amusements', *Kennebec Journal* (Kennebec, ME), 2 July 1908, p.10.
109. '*The Irish Boy*', *Moving Picture World*, 2 April 1910, p.508; 'Lubin', *Moving Picture World*, 7 May 1910.
110. '*Robert Emmet*', *Moving Picture World*, 1 April 1911, p.720.
111. 'New Star Film of Interest to Irishmen', *Billings Gazette* (Billings, MT), 2 April 1911, p.6.
112. G. Blaisdell, '*Kathleen Mavourneen* (Imp)', *Moving Picture World*, 8 March 1913, p.978.
113. For example, in a cartoon published in *Moving Picture World* (21 January 1911, p.125), a piano player happily relies on *Has Anybody Here Seen Kelly?* even during the death scene of a non-Irish-themed film. Then, in 1915, *Motion Picture News*, 6 November 1915, wrote about the popularity of *It's a Long Way to Tipperary* (p.159).
114. C. Sinn, 'Music for the Picture', *Moving Picture World*, 10 June 1911, p.1307.
115. H. Hoffman, '*All for Old Ireland*', *Motography*, 24 July 1915, pp.161–2.
116. 'Moving Picture Show', *Elyria Republican* (Elyria, OH), 15 March 1906, p.5.
117. [Untitled], *Views and Film Index*, 21 March 1908, p.10.
118. Advertisements, *Billboard*, 23 February 1907, p.47. Certainly St Patrick's Day celebrations occurred in various cities throughout America by the time of the nickelodeon era. For example, a 'St Patrick's Day Dramatic and Musical Entertainment' occurred in San Antonio, Texas, in 1908. See advertisement, *San Antonio Light*, 16 March 1908, p.8. In terms of a backlash in the Irish-American community to some St Patrick's Day novelty items, see 'St Patrick's Day Postal Cards', *Gaelic American*, 26 February 1910, p.4.
119. Advertisement, *Moving Picture World*, 12 March 1910.
120. 'Houston Irish Observed Day of Patron Saint', *Galveston Daily News* (Galveston, TX), 18 March 1909.
121. Advertisement, *Moving Picture World*, 12 March 1910, p.396; 'Lubin Notes', *Moving Picture World*, 10 March 1910; 'Lubin Notes', *Moving Picture World*, 2 April 1910, p.511.
122. '*Sogarth Aroon*', *New York Dramatic Mirror*, 20 March 1912, p.33; 'Powers Will Have St. Patrick Feature', *Moving Picture World*, 9 March 1912, p.881; '*Shamus O'Brien*', *New York Dramatic Mirror*, 20 March 1912, p.33.
123. 'The Lyric', *Fort Wayne Daily News* (Fort Wayne, IN), 16 March 1911, p.4.
124. C.E. Sinn, 'Music for the Pictures', *Moving Picture World*, 15 April 1911, p.821.
125. Advertisement, *Evening Gazette* (Cedar Rapids, IA), 22 March 1913, p.3.
126. L.R. Harrison, '*The Heart of Kathleen*', *Moving Picture World*, 25 October 1913, p.245.
127. Merritt, 'Nickelodeon Theatre, 1905–1914', p.23.
128. O.E. Miller, 'Motion Picture Lizzie', *Photoplay*, June 1912, p.48.
129. Ibid.
130. Bertellini, 'Italian Imageries', p.30.
131. J.M. Patterson, 'The Nickelodeons: The Poor Man's Elementary Course in the Drama', *Saturday Evening Post*, 23 November 1907, pp.10–11, 38.
132. Ibid., p.15.
133. Ibid., p.17.
134. Ibid., p.19; M.H. Vorse, 'Some Picture Show Audiences', *Outlook*, 24 June 1911, pp.441–7.
135. Vorse, 'Some Picture Show Audiences', p.446.
136. Singer, 'Manhattan Nickelodeons', p.22–3.
137. Ibid., p.23
138. Ibid., p.27.
139. Uricchio and Pearson, 'Dialogue: Manhattan's Nickelodeons', p.99.
140. Allen, 'Manhattan Myopia; or, Oh! Iowa!', p.79.
141. P. Mullins, 'Ethnic Cinema in the Nickelodeon Era in New York City: Commerce, Assimilation, and Cultural Identity', *Film History*, 12, 1 (2000), pp.115–24.
142. Singer, 'Manhattan Nickelodeons', p.26.
143. Mullins,' Ethnic Cinema', p.116.

144. Ibid., p.121.

145. Ibid., p.121. Mullins also notes that his Table leaves out 'additional combinations of ethnic names, such as Irish/Jewish and Irish/German partnerships' (p.121).

146. Bowser, *Transformation of Cinema*, p.6.

147. 'The 'Movies' Score', *Reno Evening Gazette* (Reno, NV), 10 December 1912, p.2.

148. 'Trade Notes', *Moving Picture World*, 18 May 1907, p.167.

149. 'Fine Moving Pictures', *Boston Globe*, 16 March 1907, p.11.

150. Ibid.

151. I base this claim on a page-by-page examination of each surviving issue of the six Irish-American newspapers named in the main text for the years 1896–1915.

152. 'Will Show Motion Pictures of Italian Quake at the Hippodrome', *Irish-American Advocate*, 30 January 1909, p.3.

153. 'Moving Pictures and the Eyes', *The Irish-American*, 3 June 1911.

154. 'Wonderful Pictures', *The Irish-American*, 18 January 1913, p.8; 'Kinemacolor at the Vatican', *The Irish-American*, 22 August 1913, p.8; 'A Theatrical Manager on the Movies', *The Irish-American*, 21 February 1913, p.2.

155. 'Moving Pictures for Pope', *Boston Pilot*, 13 July 1912, p.1.

156. See, for example: 'Notes of Boston', *The Pilot*, 2 November 1907, p.8 ; 'Notes of Boston', *The Pilot*, 16 November 1907: 8 ; 'Notes of Boston', *The Pilot*, 23 November 1907, p.8; advertisement, *The Irish-American*, 18 October 1913, p.6.

157. In terms of the Irish-American press editorializing against 'immoral' and 'evil' stage plays, see 'The Demand for Clean Theatres', *The Pilot*, 5 June 1909, p.4; 'The Decadence of the Stage', *The Pilot*, 8 January 1910, p.4; 'The Theatre Evil', *The Pilot*, 28 May 1910, p.4; 'Public and Theatre', *The Pilot*, 31 December 1910, p.4; 'Against Evil Plays', *The Pilot*, 1 April 1911, p.4; 'Reason of Evil Plays', *The Pilot*, 8 April 1911, p.4; 'An Insulting Poster', *The Pilot*, 27 May 1911: 4; 'Theatrical Outrage', *The Pilot*, 2 September 1911, p.4; 'The Play and the Public', *The Irish-American*, 4 January 1913, p.4. Similar articles were published in *The Pilot* on the subject of dime novels ('Dime Novels', 5 November 1910, p.4) and comics ('The Comic Supplement', 30 April 1910, p.4).

158. 'Insidious Motion Pictures', *The Irish-American*, 25 January 1913, p.6.

159. 'The Moving Picture Nuisance', *The Pilot*, 3 September 1910, p.4; 'The Moving Picture Nuisance', *The Pilot*, 8 October 1910, p.4; 'Moving-Pictures', *The Pilot*, 2 December 1911, p.4.

160. See, for example, 'Close of Catholic Federation Convention', *The Pilot*, 22 August 1908, pp.1, 4; 'Catholic Federation Executive Board Meeting', *The Pilot*, 4 December 1909, p.5.

161. 'The Moving Picture Nuisance', *The Pilot*, 3 September 1910, p.4.

162. 'Moving-Pictures', p.4.

163. Thissen, 'Jewish Immigrant Audiences', p.19.

164. Advertisement, *Irish-American Advocate*, 1 December 1906, p.4; advertisement, *Irish-American Advocate*, 20 April 1907, p.8.

165. 'A Chip Off the Old Block', *Irish-American Advocate*, 26 March 1910, p.1. Unfortunately this article – which is reprinted in full in the text of this chapter – does not mention the name of the theatre. The section on Brooklyn in the *Trow Business Directory of Greater New York (Five Boroughs Combined)* for 1911 (published by the Trow Directory Printing and Bookbinding Co. of New York City) does not list a theatre or nickelodeon at the address listed in the *Irish-American Advocate* article.

166. C. Musser, 'Ethnicity, Role-Playing, and American Film Comedy: From Chinese Laundry Scene to Whoopee', in L. Friedman (ed.), *Unspeakable Images: Ethnicity and the American Cinema* (Urbana, IL: University of Illinois Press, 1991), p.49.

167. J.M. Curran, *Hibernian Green on the Silver Screen: The Irish and American Movies* (Westport, CT: Greenwood Press, 1989), p.17.

168. See, for example, 'Real Irish Drama', *Gaelic American*, 7 May 1904, p.7; 'Genuine Irish Night', *Gaelic American*, 24 February 1912, p.8; 'Genuine Irish Night', *Gaelic American*, 16 March 1912, p.8; 'Irish-American Plays for Irish-American', *The Irish-American*, 14 December 1912, p.5; 'The Drone: A Real Irish Play', *The Irish-American*, 4 January 1913, p.1; and 'Genuine Irish Night', *Gaelic American*, 8 March 1913, p.8.

169. For discussions of offensive cards and postcards, see: 'Maryland', *National Hibernian*, 15 April 1907, p.5; 'Stamp Out Caricatures', *Gaelic American*, 19 March 1910, p.4; 'Picture Post Cards',

*Gaelic American*, 29 October 1910, p.7; 'Post-Card Caricatures', *The Irish-American*, 29 June 1912, p.1. For discussions of offensive artwork in newspapers and magazines, see: 'Insulting Pictures', *The Irish-American*, 29 March 1902, p.4; 'A Vile Caricature', *The Irish-American*, 15 April 1904, p.4; 'Irish Caricatures', *Gaelic American,* 8 September 1906, p.2; S. MacManus, 'Caricaturing the Irish', *Gaelic American*, 20 March 1907, p.3; 'Irish Caricature in Pictures', *National Hibernian*, 15 May 1907, p.4.

170. With regard to *McFadden's Row of Flats*, see, for example: 'The Stage Irishman Hunted from Butte', *Gaelic American*, 30 December 1905, pp.1, 8; 'McFadden's Flats Again', *Gaelic American*, 14 April 1906, p.6; 'Plotting *McFadden's Flats*', *Gaelic American*, 5 May 1906, p.5; 'The Stage Irishman', *Gaelic American*, 8 February 1908, p.5. With regard to *The Playboy of the Western World*, see, for example: 'Irish Players Well Received in Boston', *Gaelic American*, 30 September 1911, p.1; 'Ordure and Art in Drama', *Gaelic American*, 21 October 1911, p.4; 'New York's Protest Against a Vile Play', *Gaelic American*, 2 December 1911, pp.1, 8; '*Playboy* Dead as a Nail in a Door', *Gaelic American*, 9 December 1911, pp.1, 5; 'MacManus Raps the Play', *Gaelic American*, 9 December 1911, p.5; 'An Irish-American's View', *Gaelic American*, 16 December 1911, p.3; 'Lady Gregory Ignorant of Irish', *Gaelic American*, 16 December 1911, p.4; 'Denial from Irish Girls', *Gaelic American*, 30 December 1911, p.5; 'The *Evening Sun*'s Impudent Lie', *Gaelic American*, 6 January 1912, p.5; 'O'Leary Answers Quinn', *Gaelic American*, 13 January 1912, p.3; 'Philadelphia Spanks *The Playboy*', *Gaelic American*, 20 January 1912, pp.1, 7; 'Pennsylvania Air Bad for *Playboy*', *Gaelic American*, 27 January 1912, p.1; 'Chicago Doesn't Want *Playboy*', *Gaelic American*, 3 February 1912, p.1; 'Conway Scores in Debate', *Gaelic American*, 3 February 1912, p.8; 'Author of *The Playboy*', *Gaelic American*, 10 February 1912, p.2; 'Obdurate Lady Gregory', *Gaelic American*, 10 February 1912, p.3; 'Last of *The Playboy*', *Gaelic American*, 17 February 1912, p.2; 'A Crazy *Playboy* in Boston', *Gaelic American*, 30 March 1912, p.4; 'Irish Nationality and Art', *Gaelic American*, 6 April 1912, p.4; 'A *Playboy* Washed and Cleaned', *Gaelic American*, 4 January 1913, p.4; 'The *Sun* Turns Knownothing', *Gaelic American*, 3 February 1915, p.4; 'The Return of the *Playboy*', *The Irish-American*, 15 February 1913, p.2; '*The Playboy* Barred in Boston', *The Irish-American*, 15 March 1913, p.5.

171. See, for example: 'The Stage Irishman', *The Irish-American*, 15 November 1902, p.4; 'Race Insult', *National Hibernian*, 15 April 1903, p.4; 'The Lingering Stage Irishman', *National Hibernian*, 15 January 1904, p.4; 'Reviving the Stage Irishman in NY', *The Irish-American*, 23 January 1904, p.1; 'The Stage Irishman', *The Irish-American*, 10 March 1906, p.4; 'Depravity on the Stage', *Gaelic American*, 9 February 1907, p.5; 'The Stage Irishman', *Gaelic American*, 12 December 1906, p.5; 'Cheap and Offensive', *Gaelic American*, 16 February 1907, p.6; 'Exit the Stage Irishman', *Gaelic American*, 2 March 1907, p.3; 'The Stage Irishman', *Gaelic American*, 24 December 1910, p.8; 'The Stage Irishman', *Gaelic American*, 20 May 1911, p.4; 'Robinson's Play Condemned as Vile', *Gaelic American*, 30 December 1911, p.5.

172. 'Egg Russell Brothers in a Brooklyn Theatre', *New York Times*, 1 February 1907, p.1; 'Hooted Off the Stage', *Gaelic American*, 2 February 1907, p.5; 'Stunning Blow for the Stage Irishman', *Gaelic American*, 20 April 1907, pp.1, 5.

173. 'Stage Indecency Suppressed', *Gaelic American*, 30 March 1907, p.8; 'Stage Irishman Again', *Gaelic American*, 18 March 1911, p.5.

174. 'The Buffoon Irishman', *Gaelic American*, 21 January 1911, p.7.

175. Though he did not mention the Irish, W. Stephen Bush addressed the issue of ethnic stereotypes in his editorial, 'National Traits in Films', *Moving Picture World*, 25 April 1914, p.488.

176. 'Facts and Comments', *Moving Picture World*, 7 December 1912, p.956.

177. Ibid.

178. '*An Irish Girl's Love*', *Moving Picture World*, 9 November 1912, p.553.

179. L. Pinson, 'The Irish Heart', *Motion Picture Story Magazine* (March 1911), p.128.

180. Advertisement, *Irish-American Advocate*, 1 December 1906, p.4.

181. 'Two Exhibitions of *A Trip Through Ireland*', *Irish-American Advocate*, 25 May 1907: 8.

182. Advertisement, *Irish-American Advocate*, 25 January 1908, p.8; 'Entertainment for Longford Church', *Irish-American Advocate*, 8 February 1908, p.1; advertisement, *Irish-American Advocate*, 2 April 1910, p.8.

183. Advertisement, *Irish-American Advocate*, 27 February 1909, p.8; 'Seeing Ireland in a Holiday Trip', *Irish-American Advocate*, 6 March 1909, p.1.

184. Advertisement, *Irish-American Advocate*, 8 May 1909, p.4; advertisement, *Irish-American Advocate*, 19 February 1910, p.7.
185. 'A Trip Through Ireland on St Patrick's Eve', *Irish-American Advocate*, 8 March 1913, p.1.
186. 'Divisions 8 and 13 A. O. H. to Dance', *Irish-American Advocate*, 8 February 1908, p.1.
187. 'Gala Day for Sons of Erin', *Los Angeles Times*, 29 September 1911, p.16.
188. 'Moving Pictures and Nationalism', *The Irish-American*, 26 April 1913.
189. '*Ireland*, Good Film Play', *New York Times*, 24 September 1914, p.11.
190. R.C. McElravy, '*Ireland a Nation*', *Moving Picture World*, 3 October 1914, p.67.
191. [Untitled], *Motography*, 24 October 1914, p.570.
192. '*Ireland a Nation*', *Variety*, 10 October 1914, p.716.
193. '*Ireland a Nation*', *Motion Picture News*, 10 October 1914, p.79.
194. '*Ireland a Nation*', *Variety*, p.716; '*Ireland a Nation*', *Motion Picture News*, p.79.
195. '*Ireland a Nation*', *Boston Globe*, 20 October 1914, p.4; '*Ireland a Nation*', *The Pilot* 24 October 1914, p.6; advertisement, *The Pilot*, 31 October 1914, p.6.
196. 'To See *Ireland a Nation*', *Gaelic American*, 24 October 1914, p.5.
197. 'Hibernians Have Theatre Parties', *Baltimore Sun*, 23 June 1915, p.14.
198. 'Among the Missing', *Chicago Tribune*, 2 February 1915, p.10.
199. '*Ireland a Nation*', *Evening Times* (Cumberland, MD), 30 November 1914, p.6; 'Ireland in Pictures', *Trenton Evening Times* (Trenton, NJ), 9 December 1914, p.7; 'Amusements', *North Adams Evening Transcript*, 31 October 1914, p.9.
200. 'More Irish Pictures', *The Film Index*, 18 March 1911, p.3.
201. T.F. Giblin, 'Wants Correct Church Films', *The Film Index*, 7 January 1911, p.27.
202. Ibid., p.27.
203. 'Musings of The Photoplay Philosopher', *Motion Picture Story Magazine* (December 1911), p.139.
204. 'Answers to Inquiries', *Motion Picture Story Magazine* (October 1911), p.141; 'Answers to Inquiries', *Motion Picture Story Magazine* (January 1912), p.139; 'Answers to Inquiries', *Motion Picture Story Magazine* (March 1912), p.154.
205. E.M.L., 'The "El Kalems" in Egypt', *Motion Picture Story Magazine* (June 1912), pp.37–40; S. Machefert, '*The Colleen Bawn*', *Motion Picture Story Magazine* (October 1911), pp.13–25; S. Machefert, '*Arrah-na-Pogue*', *Motion Picture Story Magazine* (3 December 1911), pp.39–53.
206. 'Marion Optimistic', *Moving Picture World*, 23 March 1912, p.1052.
207. F. Marion, letter to Sidney Olcott, 2 July 1912. Courtesy of Kevin Brownlow.
208. '*The Kerry Gow*', *Moving Picture World*, 30 November 1912, p.877.
209. '*The Lad from Old Ireland*', *The Film Index*, 12 November 1910, p.5.
210. Editorial, *Moving Picture World*, 6 July 1912, p.26.
211. Advertisement, *Titusville Herald* (Titusville, PA), 25 July 1912, p.5.
212. '*The O'Neill*', *Moving Picture World*, 20 January 1912, p.308; '*Ireland, the Oppressed*', *Moving Picture World*, 28 December 1912, p.1291.
213. 'Does the Truth Pay?', *Oakland Tribune*, 14 February 1912, p.7; 'Y.W.C.A. Notes', *Racine Journal-News* (Racine, WI), 25 May 1912, p.19; advertisement, *Coshocton Daily Age* (Coshocton, OH), 21 March 1912, p.5.
214. Advertisement, *Tipton Tribune* (Tipton, IN), 13 March 1912, p.5; advertisement, *Abilene Reporter* (Abilene, TX), 26 August 1912, p.6; advertisement, *Thousandsticks* (Middlesboro, KY), 18 April 1912, p.5.
215. 'Youthful Singer Scores Big Hit', *Waterloo Reporter* (Waterloo, IA), 17 March 1913, p.5; advertisement, *Reno Evening Gazette*, 19 February 1913, p.1.
216. Advertisement, *Titusville Herald*, 17 January 1913, p.5.
217. 'Kalem Re-Issues', *Waterloo Reporter*, 6 December 1913, p.10.
218. 'News of Photoplays and Photoplayers', *Washington Post*, 8 February 1914, p.51; '*The Colleen Bawn*', *Kalem Kalendar*, 1 March 1914, p.3; A.D. Michell, '*The Colleen Bawn*', *Motion Picture News*, 14 March 1914, p.39; '*The Colleen Bawn*', *Moving Picture World*, 28 March 1914, p.1681; advertisement, *New York Dramatic Mirror*, 15 July 1914, p.23; '*The Lad from Old Ireland*', *New York Dramatic Mirror*, 29 July 1914, p.34; '*Rory O'More*', *Kalem Kalendar*, September 1914, p.5; '*Rory O'More*', *Moving Picture World*, 19 September 1914, pp.1676, 1678.
219. 'Kalem's Irish Soil Arrives', *Moving Picture World*, 27 February 1914, p.1106.
220. Advertisement, *Kalem Kalendar* 15 March 1914, p.2.

221. Advertisement, *Cedar Rapids Daily Republican* (Cedar Rapids, IA), 22 March 1914, p.11.
222. 'News of Photoplays and Players', p.51.
223. Ibid., p.11; advertisement, *Syracuse Herald* (Syracuse, NY), 22 March 1914, p.56; '*Dolly of the Dailies* at the Lyric', *Lincoln Daily News* (Lincoln, NE), 17 March 1914, p.3.
224. 'Imported Irish Soil', *Alton Evening Telegraph* (Alton, IL), 9 April 1914, p.1.
225. 'Come and Tread on Irish Soil', *Adams County Free Press* (Corning, IA), 1 April 1914, p.2.
226. Advertisement, *Lowell Sun*, 3 April 1914, p.19.
227. 'To Reissue Old Kalem Subjects', *Moving Picture World*, 3 April 1915, p.74; Advertisement, *Kalem Kalendar* May 1915: 24.
228. 'Irish Film Timely', *Moving Picture World*, 20 May 1916, p.1357; 'Show Irish Rebellion Scenes', *Moving Picture World*, 3 June 1916, p.26.
229. 'Passion Play Pictures', *Kentucky Irish-American*, 18 February 1899, p.2.
230. 'Theatricals', *Kentucky Irish-American*, 19 January 1901, p.3. The Polyscope appeared at the Temple Theatre again near the end of 1901. See 'Theatricals', *Kentucky Irish-American*, 19 October 1901, p.3.
231. These include: 'Hopkins Theatre', *Kentucky Irish-American*, 13 December 1902, p.3; 'Hopkins' Theatre', *Kentucky Irish-American*, 20 December 1902, p.4; 'Hopkins' Theatre', *Kentucky Irish-American*, 10 January 1903, p.3; advertisement, *Kentucky Irish-American*, 24 January 1903, p.2; advertisement, *Kentucky Irish-American*, 7 February 1903, p.3; 'Hopkins' Theatre', *Kentucky Irish-American*, 3 October 1903, p.3; advertisement, 31 October 1903, p.3; 'Hopkins' Temple', *Kentucky Irish-American*, 5 September 1903, p.3; advertisement, *Kentucky Irish-American*, 24 September 1904, p.3; 'Hopkins' Theatre', *Kentucky Irish-American*, 1 October 1904, p.3.
232. 'Hopkins Theatre', *Kentucky Irish-American*, 24 December 1904, p.3; advertisement, *Kentucky Irish-American*, 14 January 1905, p.3; advertisement, *Kentucky Irish-American*, 4 February 1905, p.3; advertisement, *Kentucky Irish-American*, 1 April 1905, p.2; advertisement, *Kentucky Irish-American*, 25 March 1905, p.2.
233. See, for example, 'Amusements', *Kentucky Irish-American*, 7 October 1905, p.4; 'Amusements', *Kentucky Irish-American*, 2 December 1905, p.2.
234. See, for example, 'Amusements', *Kentucky Irish-American*, 17 February 1906, p.2; 'Amusements', *Kentucky Irish-American*, 31 March 1906, p.2; 'Amusements', *Kentucky Irish-American*, 27 October 1906, p.2.
235. 'Amusements', *Kentucky Irish-American*, 8 September 1906, p.3.
236. Advertisement, *Kentucky Irish-American*, 24 November 1906, p.2.
237. Advertisement, *Kentucky Irish-American*, 6 October 1906, p.2; advertisement, *Kentucky Irish-American*, 13 October 1906, p.2; advertisement, *Kentucky Irish-American*, 17 November 1906, p.2.
238. Advertisement, *Kentucky Irish-American*, 20 October 1906, p.2.
239. 'Irish Music', *Kentucky Irish-American*, 22 September 1906, p.1; 'The Stage Irishman', *Kentucky Irish-American*, 14 April 1906, p.2.
240. See, for example, advertisements for the Hopkins Theatre in the *Kentucky Irish-American*, 16 February 1907, p.2, and 16 March 1907, p.2.
241. 'Theatrical', *Kentucky Irish-American*, 12 October 1907, p.4.
242. See, for example, 'Irish Music', *Kentucky Irish-American*, 6 July 1907, p.6; 'Famous Irish Singer', *Kentucky Irish-American*, 23 November 1907, p.2; 'Irish Dance Music', *Kentucky Irish-American*, 7 December 1907, p.2; 'Actors Hooted', *Kentucky Irish-American*, 2 February 1907, p.2.
243. Advertisement, *Kentucky Irish-American*, 15 February 1908, p.2.
244. 'Amusements', *Kentucky Irish-American*, 7 March 1908, p.4.
245. 'Amusements', *Kentucky Irish-American*, 14 March 1908, p.4.
246. 'Amusements', *Kentucky Irish-American*, 21 March 1908, p.6.
247. 'Amusements', *Kentucky Irish-American*, 28 March 1908, p.6.
248. 'Amusements', *Kentucky Irish-American*, 25 April 1908, p.2.
249. Advertisements, *Kentucky Irish-American*, 21 March 1908, p.6.
250. 'Amusements', *Kentucky Irish-American*, 25 April 1908, p.2; 'Amusements', *Kentucky Irish-American*, 9 May 1908, p.2.
251. 'Amusements', *Kentucky Irish-American*, 9 April 1908, p.4.
252. 'Hopkins Theatre', *Kentucky Irish-American*, 6 June 1908, p.2; 'Pictures at Hopkins', *Kentucky Irish-American*, 1 August 1908, p.3.

253. 'Hopkins Theatre', *Kentucky Irish-American*, 4 July 1908, p.4; 'Hopkins Theatre', *Kentucky Irish-American*, 24 October 1908, p.2.
254. 'Hopkins Theatre', *Kentucky Irish-American*, 14 November 1908, p.2.
255. 'Fake Moving Pictures', *Kentucky Irish-American*, 25 July 1908, p.3.
256. 'Motion Pictures', *Kentucky Irish-American*, 21 November 1908, p.4; 'Motion Pictures', *Kentucky Irish-American*, 28 November 1908, p.2.
257. 'Coliseum', *Kentucky Irish-American*, 19 December 1908, p.6; 'Coliseum', *Kentucky Irish-American*, 26 December 1908, p.3.
258. 'Motion Pictures', *Kentucky Irish-American*, 22 February 1909, p.4.
259. 'Masonic Theatre', *Kentucky Irish-American*, 27 March 1908, p.3.
260. 'Hopkins Theatre', *Kentucky Irish-American*, 17 April 1909, p.3.
261. 'Pictures at Hopkins', *Kentucky Irish-American*, 19 March 1910, p.4.
262. 'Moving Pictures', *Kentucky Irish-American*, 30 April 1910, p.3.
263. Advertisement, *Kentucky Irish-American*, 27 August 1910, p.2.
264. In October 1910, the newspaper told readers that the Orpheum would screen 'pictures of the world's championship ball game'. See 'Moving Pictures', *Kentucky Irish-American*, 29 October 1910, p.4.
265. 'Special Picture Shows', *Kentucky Irish-American*, 29 April 1911, p.4.
266. 'Hibernians', *Kentucky Irish-American*, 13 May 1911, p.4.
267. 'Motion Pictures', *Kentucky Irish-American*, 4 March 1911, p.4.
268. 'Motion Pictures', *Kentucky Irish-American*, 4 November 1911, p.3.
269. 'Macauley's Theatre', *Kentucky Irish-American*, 8 April 1911, p.3.
270. 'Avenue Theatre', *Kentucky Irish-American*, 13 May 1911, p.3.
271. 'Crown Theatre', *Kentucky Irish-American*, 2 September 1911, p.4.
272. See, for example, the advertisement for all three theatres in the *Kentucky Irish-American*, 9 March 1912, p.2.
273. 'Moving Pictures', *Kentucky Irish-American*, 6 April 1912, p.4.
274. Ibid; 'Vaudeville', *Kentucky Irish-American*, 20 April 1912, p.4.
275. 'Walnut Street Theatre', *Kentucky Irish-American*, 7 September 1912, p.4.
276. Advertisement, *Kentucky Irish-American*, 7 September 1912, p.2.
277. 'Walnut Theatre', *Kentucky Irish-American*, 15 November 1913, p.2.
278. 'Vatican Motion Pictures', *Kentucky Irish-American*, 1 February 1913, p.4; 'St Patrick's Day', *Kentucky Irish-American*, 15 March 1913, p.1.
279. Advertisement, *Kentucky Irish-American*, 14 March 1914, p.6.
280. 'Pictures and Vaudeville', *Kentucky Irish-American*, 18 April 1914, p.3.
281. 'National Theatre', *Kentucky Irish-American*, 28 February 1914, p.4; advertisement, *Kentucky Irish-American*, 28 March 1914, p.2; 'Gayety Theatre', *Kentucky Irish-American*, 21 March 1914, p.2.

# Bibliography

Abel, R., ' "Don't Know Much About History," or the (In)vested Interests of Doing Cinema History',
 *Film History*, 6, 1 (Spring 1994), pp.110–15.

Abel, R. (ed.), *Silent Film* (New Brunswick, NJ: Rutgers University Press, 1996).

Abel, R., *The Red Rooster Scare: Making Cinema American, 1900–1910* (Berkeley, CA: University of
 California Press, 1999).

Abel, R., '"History Can Work for You, You Know How to Use It"', *Cinema Journal*, 44, 1 (Autumn
 2004), pp.107–12.

Abel, R., *Americanizing the Movies and 'Movie-Mad' Audiences, 1910–1914* (Berkeley, CA: University of
 California Press, 2006).

Abel, R., 'Fan Discourse in the Heartland: The Early 1910s', *Film History*, 18, 2 (2006), pp.140–53.

Abel, R. and Altman, R. (eds), *The Sounds of Early Cinema* (Bloomington, IN: University of Indiana
 Press, 2001).

Abel, R., Bertellini, G. and King, R. (eds), *Early Cinema and the 'National'* (Bloomington, IN: Indiana
 University Press, 2008).

Akenson, D.H., 'An Agnostic View of the Historiography of Irish-Americans', *Labour/Le Travail*, 14 (Fall
 1984), pp.123–59.

Allen, R.C., 'Motion Picture Exhibition in Manhattan, 1906–1912', *Cinema Journal*, 18, 2 (Spring 1979),
 pp.2–15.

Allen, R.C., *Vaudeville and Film, 1895–1915: A Study in Media Interaction* (New York: Arno Press,
 1980).

Allen, R.C., 'Manhattan Myopia; Or, Oh! Iowa!', *Cinema Journal*, 35, 3 (Spring 1996), pp.75–103.

Allen, R.C. and Gomery, D., *Film History: Theory and Practice* (Boston, MA: McGraw-Hill, 1985).

Altman, C.F., 'Towards a Historiography of American Film', *Cinema Journal*, 16, 2 (Spring 1977),
 pp.1–25.

Altman, R., *Silent Film Sound* (New York: Columbia University Press, 2004).

Altman, R., 'The Early History of Travel Films', in J. Ruoff (ed.), *Virtual Voyages: Cinema and Travel*
 (Durham, NC: Duke University Press, 2006), pp.61–76.

Anderson, T., 'Reforming "Jackass Music": The Problematic Aesthetics of Early American Film Music
 Accompaniment', *Cinema Journal*, 37, 1 (Autumn 1997), pp.3–22.

Appel, J.J., 'From Shanties to Lace Curtains: The Irish Image in *Puck*, 1876–1910', *Comparative Studies
 in Society and History*, 13, 4 (October 1971), pp.365–75.

Auerbach, J., 'McKinley at Home: How Early American Cinema Made News', *American Quarterly*, 51, 4
 (December 1999), pp.797–832.

Auerbach, J., 'Chasing Film Narrative: Repetition, Recursion, and the Body in Early Cinema', *Critical
 Inquiry*, 26, 4 (Summer 2000), pp.798–820.

Azlant, E., 'Screenwriting for the Early Silent Film: Forgotten Pioneers, 1897–1911', *Film History*, 9, 3
 (1997), pp.228–56.

Balio, T. (ed.), *The American Film Industry* (Madison, WI: University of Wisconsin Press, 1985).

Barber, X.T., 'The Roots of Travel Cinema: John L. Stoddard, E. Burton Holmes, and the Nineteenth-
 Century Illustrated Travel Lecture', *Film History*, 5, 1 (March 1993), pp.68–84.

Barnouw, E., *The Magician and the Cinema* (Oxford: Oxford University Press, 1981).

# Bibliography

Barnouw, E., *Documentary: A History of the Non-Fiction Film* (Oxford: Oxford University Press, 1983).

Barton, R., *Irish National Cinema* (London: Routledge, 2004).

Barton, R., *Acting Irish in Hollywood* (Dublin: Irish Academic Press, 2006).

Barton, R. (ed.), *Screening Irish-America: Representing Irish-America in Film and Television* (Dublin: Irish Academic Press, 2009).

Basinger, J., *Silent Stars* (Hanover, NH: Wesleyan University Press, 1999).

Bean, J. and Negra, D. (eds), *A Feminist Reader in Early Cinema* (Durham: Duke University Press, 2002).

Bell, D., 'The Lads and Lasses from Ould Ireland: The Irish and the Silent Screen', *Film Ireland* (March/April 2007), p.31.

Bertellini, G., *Italy in Early American Cinema: Race, Landscape, and the Picturesque* (Bloomington, IN: University of Indiana, 2010).

Bitzer, G.W., *Billy Bitzer: His Story* (New York: Farrar, Strauss & Giroux, 1973).

Bogdanovich, P., *Allan Dwan: The Last Pioneer* (New York: Praeger Publishers, Inc., 1971).

Boltwood, S., '"The Ineffaceable Curse of Cain": Race, Miscegenation, and the Victorian Staging of Irishness', *Victorian Literature and Culture*, 29, 2 (2001), pp.383–96.

Bordwell, D., *Narration and the Fiction Film* (Madison, WI: University of Wisconsin Press, 1985).

Bordwell, D., *On the History of Film Style* (Cambridge, MA: Harvard University Press, 1997).

Bordwell, D., Staiger, J. and Thompson, K., *The Classical Hollywood Cinema: Film Style and Mode of Production to 1960* (New York: Columbia University Press, 1985).

Bottomore, S., 'Out of the World: Theory, Fact, and Film History', *Film History*, 6, 1 (Spring 1994), pp.7–25.

Bottomore, S., 'An International Survey of Sound Effects in Early Cinema', *Film History*, 11, 4 (1999), pp.485–98

Bottomore, S., 'Rediscovering Early Non-Fiction Film', *Film History*, 13, 2 (2001), pp.160–73.

Bowser, E. (ed.), *Biograph Bulletins, 1908–1912* (New York: Octagon Books, 1973).

Bowser, E., *The Transformation of Cinema, 1907–1915* (Berkeley, CA: University of California Press, 1990).

Bradley, P., *Making American Culture: A Social History, 1900–1920* (New York: Palgrave Macmillan, 2009).

Brewster, B. and Jacobs, L., *Theatre to Cinema: Stage Pictorialism and the Early Feature Film* (New York: Oxford University Press, 1997).

Brownlow, K., *The Parade's Gone By* (New York: Bonanza Books, 1968).

Brownlow, K., *Behind the Mask of Innocence, Sex, Violence, Prejudice, Crime: Films of Social Conscience in the Silent Era* (Berkeley, CA: University of California Press, 1990).

Brownlow, K., *Mary Pickford Rediscovered* (New York: Harry N. Abrams, 1999).

Byrne, T., *Power in the Eye: An Introduction to Contemporary Irish Film* (Lanham, MD: Scarecrow Press, 1997).

Caldwell, G. (ed.), *The Man Who Photographed the World: Burton Holmes Travelogues 1892–1928* (New York: Harry N. Abrams, 1977).

Caldwell, G. (ed.), *Burton Holmes Travelogues: The Greatest Traveler of His Time* (New York: Taschen, 2006).

Camlot, J., 'Early Talking Books: Spoken Recordings and Recitation Anthologies, 1880–1920', *Book History* 6 (2003), pp.147–73.

Charney, L. and Schwartz, V., *Cinema and the Invention of Modern Life* (Berkeley, CA: University of California Press, 1995).

Christie, I., *The Last Machine: Early Cinema and the Birth of the Modern World* (London: British Film Institute, 1994).

Clark, D. and Lynch, W.J., 'Hollywood and Hibernia: The Irish in the Movies', in R.M. Miller (ed.), *The Kaleidoscopic Lens: How Hollywood Views Ethnic Groups* (Englewood Cliffs, NJ: James S. Ozer, 1980).

Clee, P., *Before Hollywood: From Shadow Play to Silver Screen* (New York: Clarion, 2005).

Coe, B., *The History of Movie Photography* (Westfield, NJ: Eastview Editions, 1984).

Cohen, P.M., *Silent Film and the Triumph of the American Myth* (New York: Oxford University Press, 2001).

Condon, D., 'Touristic Work and Pleasure: The Kalem Company in Killarney', *Film and Film Culture*, 2 (2003), pp.7–16.

Condon, D., *Early Irish Cinema, 1895–1921* (Dublin: Irish Academic Press, 2008).

Condon, D., 'Irish Audiences Watch Their First US Feature: *The Corbett–Fitzsimmons Fight* (1897)', in R. Barton (ed.), *Screening Irish-America: Representing Irish-America in Film and Television* (Dublin: Irish Academic Press, 2009), pp.135–147.

Curran, J.M., *Hibernian Green on the Silver Screen: The Irish and American Movies* (Westport, CT: Greenwood Press, 1989).

Daly, N., 'The Many Lives of the Colleen Bawn: Pastoral Suspense', *Journal of Victorian Culture*, 12, 1 (Spring 2007), pp.1–25.

Darby, P., 'Gaelic Sport and the Irish Diaspora in Boston, 1879', *Irish Historical Studies*, 33, 132 (November 2003), pp.387–403.

deCordova, R., *Picture Personalities: The Emergence of the Star System in America* (Urbana, IL: University of Illinois Press, 1990).

Dennett, A.S. and Warnke, N., 'Disaster Spectacles at the Turn of the Century', *Film History*, 4, 2 (1990), pp.101–11.

Doyle, D.N., 'Cohesion and Diversity in the Irish Diaspora', *Irish Historical Studies*, 31, 123 (May 1999), pp.411–34.

Dumaux, S.A., *King Baggot: A Biography and Filmography of the First King of the Movies* (Jefferson, NC: McFarland & Co., 2002).

Edelstein, S., 'Charlotte Perkins Gilman and the Yellow Newspaper', *Legacy*, 24, 1 (2007), pp.72–92.

Elsaesser, T. (ed.), *Early Cinema: Space, Frame, Narrative* (London: British Film Institute, 1990).

Fawkes, R., *Dion Boucicault: A Biography* (London: Quartet, 1979).

Feaster, P. and Smith, J., 'Reconfiguring the History of Early Cinema through the Phonograph, 1877–1908', *Film History*, 21, 4 (2009), pp.311–25.

Fell, J.L., *Film Before Griffith* (Berkeley, CA: University of California Press, 1983).

Fell, J., 'Motive, Mischief and Melodrama: The State of Film Narrative in 1907', *Film Quarterly*, 33, 3 (Spring 1980), pp.30–7.

Fielding, R. (ed.), *A Technological History of Motion Pictures and Television* (Berkeley, CA: University of California Press, 1967).

Fielding, R., 'Hale's Tours: Ultrarealism in the Pre-1910 Motion Picture', *Cinema Journal*, 10, 1 (Autumn, 1970), pp.34–47.

Fielding, R., *The American Newsreel, 1911–1967* (Norman, OK: University of Oklahoma, 1972).

Fields, A., *Tony Pastor, Father of Vaudeville* (Jefferson, NC: McFarland & Co., 2007).

Fuller, K.H., *At the Picture Show: Small-Town Audiences and the Creation of Movie Fan Culture* (Washington, DC: Smithsonian Institution Press, 1996).

Garcia, D.J., 'Subversive Sounds: Ethnic Spectatorship and Boston's Nickelodeon Theatres, 1907–1914', *Film History*, 19, 3 (2007), pp.214–27.

Gifford, D., *The British Film Catalogue, Volume Two: Non-Fiction Film, 1888–1994* (London: Fitzroy Dearborn, 2000).

Gilbert, D., *American Vaudeville: Its Life and Times* (New York: McGraw-Hill, 1940).

Gillespie, M.P., *The Myth of an Irish Cinema: Approaching Irish-Themed Films* (Syracuse, NY: Syracuse University Press, 2008).

Gomery, D., 'Movie Audiences, Urban Geography, and the History of American Film', *Velvet Light Trap*, 19 (1982), pp.23–9.

Gomery, D., *Shared Pleasures: A History of Movie Presentation in the United States* (Madison, WI: University of Wisconsin Press, 1992).

Gomery, D., *The Coming of Sound* (New York: Routledge, 2005).

Gomery, D., *The Hollywood Studio System: A History* (London: British Film Institute, 2005).

Graham, C.C., Higgins, S., Mancini, E. and Vieira, J.L., *D.W. Griffith and the Biograph Company* (Metuchen, NJ: Scarecrow Press, 1985).

Grieveson, L., *Policing Cinema: Movies and Censorship in Early-Twentieth-Century America* (Berkeley, CA: University of California Press, 2004).

Griffith, Mrs D.W., *When the Movies Were Young* (New York: Arno Press, 1977).

Griffiths, A., ' "To the World the World We Show": Early Travelogues as Filmed Ethnography', *Film History*, 11, 3 (1999), pp.289–90.

Griffiths, A., *Wondrous Difference: Cinema, Anthropology, and Turn-of-the-Century Visual Culture* (New York: Columbia University Press, 2002).

412

# Bibliography

Gunning, T., 'Non-Continuity, Continuity, Discontinuity: A Theory of Genres in Early Films', *Iris*, 2, 1 (1984), pp.101–12.

Gunning, T., ' "Primitive" Cinema: A Frame-up? Or the Trick's on Us', *Cinema Journal*, 28, 2 (Winter 1989), pp.3–12.

Gunning, T., 'Now You See It, Now You Don't: The Temporality of the Cinema of Attractions', *Velvet Light Trap*, 32 (1993), pp.41–50.

Gunning, T., *D.W. Griffith and the Origins of American Narrative Film: The Early Years at Biograph* (Urbana, IL: University of Illinois Press, 1994).

Gunning, T., 'The World as Object Lesson: Cinema Audiences, Visual Culture, and the St. Louis World's Fair, 1904', *Film History* 6, 4 (Winter 1994), pp.422–44.

Gunning, T., 'Before Documentary: Early NonFiction Films and the "View" Aesthetic', in D. Hertogs and N. De Klerk (eds), *Uncharted Territory: Essays on Early Nonfiction Film* (Amsterdam: Stichting Nederlands Filmmuseum, 1997), pp.9–24.

Gunning, T., ' "The Whole World Within Reach": Travel Images Without Borders', in J. Ruoff (ed.), *Virtual Voyages: Cinema and Travel* (Durham: Duke University Press, 2006), pp.25–41.

Haenni, S., *The Immigrant Scene: Ethnic Amusements in New York, 1880–1920* (Minneapolis, MN: University of Minnesota Press, 2008).

Hampton, B., *A History of the Movies* (New York: Corvici, Friede Publishers, 1931).

Handel, L., *Hollywood Looks at Its Audience* (Urbana, IL: University of Illinois Press, 1950).

Hansen, M., *Babel and Babylon: Spectatorship in American Silent Film* (Cambridge, MA: Harvard University Press, 1991).

Hanson, P.K. (ed.), *The American Film Institute Catalog of Motion Pictures Produced in the United States: Feature Films, 1911–1920* (Berkeley, CA: University of California Press, 1988).

Hargaden, J., 'The Stage Irishman in Modern Irish Drama', *Studies: An Irish Quarterly Review*, 79, 313 (Spring 1990), pp.45–54.

Hark, I.R. (ed.), *Exhibition: The Film Reader* (London: Routledge, 2002).

Harner, G.W., 'The Kalem Company, Travel and On-Location Filming: The Forging of an Identity', *Film History*, 10, 2 (1998), pp.188–207.

Harrington, J.P., 'Synge's *Playboy*, The Irish Players, and the Anti-Irish Irish Players', in J. P. Harrington (ed.), *The Irish Play on the New York Stage, 1874–1966* (Lexington, KY: University of Kentucky, 1997), pp.55–74.

Heininge, K., *Buffoonery in Irish Drama: Staging Twentieth-Century Post-Colonial Stereotypes* (New York: Peter Lang Publishing, 2009).

Herbert, S., *A History of Early Film: Volume I* (New York: Routledge, 2000).

Herbert, S., 'Photographic Slides', in D. Robinson, S. Herbert and R. Crangle (eds), *Encyclopaedia of the Magic Lantern* (London: Magic Lantern Society, 2001), p.232.

Herbert, S. and McKernan, L. (eds), *Who's Who of Victorian Cinema* (London: British Film Institute, 1996).

Higashi, S., *Cecil B. DeMille and American Culture: The Silent Era* (Berkeley, CA: University of California, 1994).

Higashi, S., 'Dialogue: Manhattan Nickelodeons', *Cinema Journal*, 34, 3 (Spring 1995), pp.72–4.

Hirschman, C., 'Immigration and the American Century', *Demography*, 42, 4 (November 2005), pp.595–620.

Humphries, S., *Victorian Britain through the Magic Lantern, Illustrated by Lear's Magic Lantern Slides* (London: Sidgwick & Jackson, 1989).

Ignatiev, N., *How the Irish Became White* (New York: Routledge, 1995).

Izod, J., *Hollywood and the Box-Office, 1895–1986* (London: Macmillan Press, 1988).

Jacobs, L., *The Rise of the American Film* (New York: Harcourt, Brace, 1939).

Jenkins, H., *What Made Pistachio Nuts? Early Sound Comedy and the Vaudeville Aesthetic* (New York: Columbia University Press, 1992).

Jesionowski, J.E., *Thinking in Pictures: Dramatic Structure in D.W. Griffith's Biograph Films* (Berkeley, CA: University of California Press, 1987).

Keane, D., 'Cartoon Violence and Freedom of Expression', *Human Rights Quarterly*, 30, 4 (November 2008), pp.845–75.

Keil, C., *Early American Cinema in Transition: Story, Style, and Film-making, 1907–1913* (Madison, WI: University of Wisconsin Press, 2001).

Keil, C. and Stamp, S., *American Cinema's Transitional Era: Audiences, Institutions, Practices* (Berkeley, CA: University of California, 2004).

Kekatos, K.J., 'Edward H. Amet and the Spanish-American War Film', *Film History*, 14, 3/4 (2002), pp.405–17.

Keller, M., *The Art and Politics of Thomas Nast* (New York: Oxford University Press, 1968).

Kirby, L., *Parallel Tracks: The Railroad and Silent Cinema* (Durham: Duke University Press, 1997).

Klenotic, J.F., 'The Place of Rhetoric in "New" Film Historiography: The Discourse of Corrective Revisionism', *Film History*, 6, 1 (Spring 1994), pp.45–58.

Knobel, D.T., 'A Vocabulary of Ethnic Perception: Content Analysis of the American Stage Irishman, 1820–1860', *Journal of American Studies*, 15, 1 (April 1981), pp.45–71.

Koszarski, R., *An Evening's Entertainment: The Age of the Silent Feature Picture, 1915–1928* (Berkeley, CA: University of California Press, 1990).

Koszarski, R., *Fort Lee: The Film Town* (Rome: John Libbey Publishing, 2004).

Kusmer, K.L., *Down and Out, On the Road: The Homeless in American History* (New York: Oxford University Press, 2001).

Lagny, M., 'Film History; or Film History Expropriated', *Film History*, 6, 1 (Spring 1994), pp.26–44.

Lavitt, P.B., 'First of the Red Hot Mamas: "Coon Shouting" and the Jewish Ziegfield Girl', *American Jewish History*, 87, 4 (December 1999), pp.253–90.

Lewis, R.M. (ed.), *From Travelling Show to Vaudeville: Theatrical Spectacle in America, 1830–1910* (Baltimore, MD: Johns Hopkins University Press, 2007)

Lindenblatt, J., *Frederick Burr Opper's Happy Hooligan* (New York: Nantier, Beall, Minoustchine, 2008).

Louvish, S., *Keystone: The Life and Clowns of Mack Sennett* (New York: Faber & Faber, 2003).

MacGowan, K., *Behind the Screen: The History and Techniques of the Motion Picture* (New York, Delacorte, 1965).

MacKillop, J., *Contemporary Irish Cinema: From* The Quiet Man *to* Dancing at Lughnasa (Syracuse, NY: Syracuse University Press, 1999).

McFeely, D., 'Between Two Worlds: Boucicault's *The Shaughraun* and Its New York Audience', in J.P. Harrington (ed.), *Irish Theatre in America: Essays on Irish Theatrical Diaspora* (Syracuse, NY: Syracuse University Press, 2009), pp.54–65.

McIllroy, B., *Irish Cinema: An Illustrated History* (Dun Laoghaire: Anna Livia Press, 1989).

McIllroy, B. (ed.), *Genre and Cinema: Ireland and Transnationalism* (London: Routledge, 2007).

McKernan, L. (ed.), *A Yank in Britain: The Lost Memoirs of Charles Urban* (Hastings, East Sussex: Projection Box, 1999).

McLoone, M., *Irish Film: The Emergence of a Contemporary Cinema* (London: British Film Institute, 2000).

Marks, M.M., *Music and the Silent Film: Contexts and Case Studies, 1895–1924* (New York: Oxford University Press, 1997).

Maryoga, M.G., *A Short History of the American Drama* (New York: Dodd, Mead & Co., 1943).

Maschio, G., 'Ethnic Humor and the Demise of the Russell Brothers', *Journal of Popular Culture*, 26, 1 (Summer 1992), pp.81–92.

Meagher, T.J., 'Abie's Irish Enemy: Irish and Jews, Social and Political Realities and Media Representations', in R. Barton (ed.), *Screening Irish-America: Representing Irish-America in Film and Television* (Dublin: Irish Academic Press, 2009), pp.45–60.

Merritt, R., 'Nickelodeon Theatres, 1905–1914: Building an Audience for the Movies', in T. Balio (ed.), *The American Film Industry* (Madison, WI: University of Wisconsin Press, 1976), pp.59–79.

Miller, A., 'The Panorama, the Cinema, and the Emergence of the Spectacular', *Wide Angle*, 18, 2 (1996), pp.34–69.

Miller, K.A., *Emigrants and Exiles: Ireland and the Irish Exodus to North America* (New York: Oxford University Press, 1985).

Miller, K., *Ireland and Irish America: Culture, Class, and Transatlantic Migration* (Dublin: Field Day Publications, 2008).

Moore, C., *Silent Star* (Garden City, NY: Doubleday, 1968).

Morash, C., *A History of Irish Theatre, 1601–2000* (Cambridge: Cambridge University Press, 2002).

Moss, K., 'St Patrick's Day Celebrations and the Formation of Irish-American Identity, 1845–1875', *Journal of Social History*, 29, 1 (Autumn 1995), pp.125–48.

Mullins, P., 'Ethnic Cinema in the Nickelodeon Era in New York City: Commerce, Assimilation and Cultural Identity', *Film History*, 12, 1 (2000), pp.115–24.

Murphy, M., 'Irish-American Theatre', in M.S. Seller (ed.), *Ethnic Theatre in the United States* (Westport, CT: Greenwood Press, 1983), pp.221–237.

Musser, C., 'The Nickelodeon Era Begins: Establishing the Framework for Hollywood's Mode of Representation', *Framework*, 22/23 (Fall 1983), pp.4–11.

Musser, C., *The Emergence of Cinema: The American Screen to 1907* (Berkeley, CA: University of California Press, 1990).

Musser, C., 'The Travel Genre in 1903–1904: Moving Towards Fictional Narrative', in T. Elsaesser (ed.), *Early Cinema: Space, Frame, Narrative* (London: British Film Institute, 1990), pp.123–132.

Musser, C., *Before the Nickelodeon: Edwin S. Porter and the Edison Manufacturing Company* (Berkeley, CA: University of California Press, 1991).

Musser, C., 'Ethnicity, Role-Playing, and American Film Comedy: From Chinese Laundry Scene to Whoopee', in L. Friedman (ed.), *Unspeakable Images: Ethnicity and the American Cinema* (Urbana, IL: University of Illinois Press, 1991), pp.39–81.

Musser, C., 'Pre-Classical American Cinema: Its Changing Modes of Film Production', *Persistence of Vision*, 9 (1991), pp.46–65.

Musser, C., *Edison Motion Pictures, 1890–1900* (Washington, DC: Smithsonian Institute, 1997).

Musser, C., 'Historiographic Method and the Study of Early Cinema', *Cinema Journal*, 44, 1 (Autumn 2004), pp.101–07.

Musser, C. and Nelson, C.S., *High-Class Moving Pictures: Lyman H. Howe and the Forgotten Era of Traveling Exhibition, 1880–1920* (Princeton, NJ: Princeton University Press, 1991).

Nasaw, D., *The Chief: The Life of William Randolph Hearst* (New York: First Mariner, 2000).

Negra, D., *Off-White Hollywood: American Culture and Ethnic Female Stardom* (New York: Routledge, 2001).

Negra, D. (ed.), *The Irish in Us: Irishness, Peformativity, and Popular Culture* (Durham, NC: Duke University Press, 2006).

Ní Bhroiméil, Ú., 'The Creation of an Irish Culture in the United States: The Gaelic Movement, 1870–1915', *New Hibernia Review*, 5, 3 (Autumn 2001), pp.87–100.

Niehaus, E.F., 'Paddy on the Local Stage and in Humor: The Image of the Irish in New Orleans, 1830–1862', *Louisiana History: Journal of the Louisiana Historical Association*, 5, 2 (Spring 1964), pp.117–34.

Niver, K.R., *Motion Pictures from the Library of Congress Paper Print Collection, 1894–1912* (Berkeley, CA: University of California Press, 1967).

Niver, K.R., *The First Twenty Years: A Segment of Film History* (Los Angeles, CA: Locare Research Group, 1968).

Niver, K.R. and Bergsten, B. (eds), *Biograph Bulletins, 1896–1908* (Los Angeles, CA: Locare Research Group, 1971).

Nowatzki, R., 'Paddy Jumps Jim Crow: Irish-Americans and Blackface Minstrelsy', *Éire Ireland*, 41, 3 and 4 (Fall/Winter 2006), pp.162–84.

O'Leary, L., *Rex Ingram: Master of the Silent Cinema* (London: British Film Institute, 1993).

O'Sullivan, P., 'Developing Irish Diaspora Studies: A Personal View', *New Hibernia Review*, 7, 1 (Spring 2003), pp.130–48.

Orel, G., 'Reporting the Stage Irishman', in J.P. Harrington (ed.), *Irish Theatre in America: Essays on Irish Theatrical Diaspora* (Syracuse, NY: Syracuse Univ. Press, 2009), pp.66–7.

Pearson, R.E., *Eloquent Gestures: The Transformation of Performance Style in the Griffith Biograph Films* (Berkeley, CA: University of California Press, 1992).

Perry, T., 'Formal Strategies as an Index to the Evolution of Film History', *Cinema Journal*, 14, 2 (Winter 1974–75), pp.25–36.

Phelan, M., ' "Authentic Reproductions": Staging the "Wild West" in Modern Irish Drama', *Theatre Journal* 61, 2 (May 2009), pp 235–48.

Pickford, M., *Sunshine and Shadow* (Garden City, NY: Doubleday, 1955).

Pierce, D., 'The Legion of the Condemned: Why American Silent Films Perished', *Film History*, 9, 1 (1997), pp.5–22.

Pramaggiore, M., *Irish and African American Cinema: Identifying Others and Performing Identities, 1980–2000* (Albany, NY: State University of New York Press, 2007).

Quigley, M., *Magic Shadows: The Story of the Origin of Motion Pictures* (New York: Biblo & Tannen, 1969).

Rains, S., *The Irish-American in Popular Culture* (Dublin: Irish Academic Press, 2007).

Ramsaye, T., *A Million and One Nights: A History of the Motion Picture Through 1925* (New York: Simon & Schuster, 1926).

Reynolds, H., 'Aural Gratification with Kalem Films: A Case History of Music, Lectures and Sound Effects, 1907–1917', *Film History* 12, 4 (2000), pp.417–42.

Ripley, J.W., 'All Join in the Chorus', *American Heritage*, 10, 4 (June 1959), pp.50–9.

Robinson, D., *From Peepshow to Palace: The Birth of American Film* (New York: Columbia University Press, 1996).

Rockett, K., 'The Irish Migrant and Film', in P. O'Sullivan (ed.), *The Creative Migrant* (London: Leicester University Press, 1994).

Rockett, K., *The Irish Filmography: Fiction Films 1896–1996* (Dublin: Red Mountain Media, 1996).

Rockett, K, Gibbons, L. and Hill, J., *Cinema and Ireland* (London: Croom Helm, 1987).

Rosen, P., 'Securing the Historical: Historiography and Classical Cinema', in P. Mellencamp and P. Rosen (eds), *Cinema Histories, Cinema Practices* (Frederick, MD: University Publications of America, 1984), pp.17–34.

Rosen, P., *Change Mummified: Cinema, Historicity, Theory* (Minneapolis, MN: University of Minnesota Press, 2001).

Ross, S.J., *Working-Class Hollywood: Silent Film and the Shaping of Class in America* (Princeton, NJ: Princeton University Press, 1998).

Ruchatz, J., 'Travelling by Slide: How the Art of Projection Met the World of Travel', in R. Crangle, M. Heard and I. van Dooren (eds), *Realms of Light: Uses and Perceptions of the Magic Lantern from the 17th to the 21st Century* (London: Magic Lantern Society, 2005), pp.34–41.

Ryan, P.M., 'The Hibernian Experience: John Brougham's Irish-American Plays', *MELUS*, 10, 2 (Summer 1983), pp.33–47.

Savada, E. (ed.), *The American Film Institute Catalog of Motion Pictures Produced in the United States: Film Beginnings, 1893–1910* (Lanham, MD: Scarecrow Press, 1995).

Shannon, C., 'The Bowery Cinderella: Gender, Class, and Community in Irish-American Film Narrative', in R. Barton (ed.), *Screening Irish-America: Representing Irish-America in Film and Television* (Dublin: Irish Academic Press, 2009), pp.77–90.

Short, E., *Fifty Years of Vaudeville* (Westport, CT: Greenwood Press, 1979).

Singer, B., 'Manhattan Nickelodeons: New Data on Audiences and Exhibitors', *Cinema Journal*, 34, 3 (Spring 1995), pp.5–35.

Singer, B., 'New York, Just Like I Pictured It ... ', *Cinema Journal*, 35, 3 (Spring 1996), pp.104–28.

Singer, B., *Melodrama and Modernity: Early Sensational Cinema and Its Contexts* (New York: Columbia University Press, 2001).

Sklar, R., 'Oh! Althusser!: Historiography and the Rise of Cinema Studies', *Radical History Review*, 41 (Spring, 1988), pp.10–35.

Sklar, R., 'Does Film History Need a Crisis?' *Cinema Journal*, 44, 1 (Autumn 2004), pp.134–8.

Slide, A., *The Big V: A History of the Vitagraph Company* (Metuchen, NJ: Scarecrow Press, 1987).

Slide, A., *Nitrate Won't Wait: Film Preservation in the United States* (Jefferson, NC: McFarland & Company, 1992).

Slide, A., *Early American Cinema* (Metuchen, NJ: Scarecrow Press, 1994).

Sloan, K., *The Loud Silents: Origins of the Social Problem Film* (Chicago, IL: University of Illinois Press, 1988).

Smith, A., *Shooting Cowboys and Indians: Silent Western Films, American Culture, and the Birth of Hollywood* (Boulder, CO: University of Colorado Press, 2003).

Snyder, R.W., *The Voice of the City: Vaudeville and Popular Culture in New York* (Chicago, IL: Ivan R. Dee, 2000).

Spadoni, R., 'The Figure Seen from the Rear, Vitagraph, and the Development of the Shot/Reverse Shot', *Film History*, 11, 4 (1999), pp.319–41.

Staiger, J., 'Mass-Produced Photoplays: Economic and Signifying Practices in the First Years of Hollywood', *Wide Angle*, 4, 3 (1980), pp.12–27.

Staiger, J., *Interpreting Films: Studies in the Historical Reception of American Cinema* (Princeton, NJ: Princeton University Press, 1992).

Stamp, S., *Movie-Struck Girls: Women and Motion Picture Culture after the Nickelodeon* (Princeton, NJ: Princeton University Press, 2000).

Staples, S., *Male–Female Comedy Teams in American Vaudeville, 1865–1932* (Ann Arbor, MI: UMI Research Press, 1984).

Stokes, M. and Maltby, R. (eds), *American Movie Audiences: From the Turn of the Century to the Early Sound Era* (London: British Film Institute, 1999).

Streible, D., *Fight Pictures: A History of Boxing and Early Cinema* (Berkeley, CA: University of California Press, 2008).

Thissen, J., 'Oy, Myopia! A Reaction from Judith Thissen on the Singer–Allen Controversy', *Cinema Journal*, 36, 4 (Summer 1997), pp.102–7.

Thompson, K., *Exporting Entertainment: America in the World Film Market, 1907–34* (London: British Film Institute, 1985).

Thompson, K., 'Narration in Three Early Teens Vitagraph Films', *Film History*, 9, 4 (1997), pp.410–34.

Thompson, K. and Bordwell, D., 'Linearity, Materialism, and the Study of Early American Cinema', *Wide Angle*, 5, 3 (1983), pp.4–15.

Toulmin, V., 'Telling the Tale: The Story of the Fairground Bioscope Shows and the Showmen Who Operated Them', *Film History*, 6, 2 (Summer 1994), pp.219–37.

Uricchio, W. and Pearson, R.E., *Reframing Culture: The Case of the Vitagraph Quality Films* (Princeton, NJ: Princeton University Press, 1993).

Uricchio, W. and Pearson, R.E., 'Constructing the Audience: Competing Discourses of Morality and Rationalization during the Nickelodeon Period', *Iris*, 17 (1994), pp.43–54.

Uricchio, W. and Pearson, R.E., 'Dialogue: Manhattan's Nickelodeons. New York? New York!', *Cinema Journal* 36, 4 (Summer 1997), pp.98–102.

Usai, P.C., *Silent Cinema: An Introduction* (London: British Film Institute, 2000).

Vardac, A.N., *Stage to Screen, Theatrical Origins of Early Film: David Garrick to D.W. Griffith* (New York: Da Capo Press, 1987).

Waldsmith, J., *Stereo Views: An Illustrated History and Price Guide* (Iola, WI: Krause Publications, 2002).

Walker, B.E., *Mack Sennett's Fun Factory* (Jefferson, NC: McFarland & Company, 2010).

Waller, G., *Main Street Amusements: Movies and Commercial Entertainment in an Southern City* (Washington, DC: Smithsonian Institution Press, 1995).

Waller, G. (ed.), *Moviegoing in America* (Malden, MA: Blackwell, 2002).

Williams, W.H.A., *'Twas Only an Irishman's Dream: The Image of Ireland and the Irish in American Popular Song Lyrics, 1800–1920* (Urbana, IL: University of Illinois Press, 1996).

Williams, W.H.A., 'Green Again: Irish-American Lace-Curtain Satire', *New Hibernia Review*, 6, 2 (Summer 2002), pp.9–24.

Wittke, C., 'The Immigrant Theme on the American Stage', *Mississippi Valley Historical Review*, 39, 2 (September 1952), pp.212–232.

Woods, L., *Transatlantic Stage Stars in Vaudeville and Variety* (New York: Palgrave Macmillan, 2006).

Yaszek, L., ' "Them Damn Pictures": Americanization and the Comic Strip in the Progressive Era', *Journal of American Studies*, 28, 1 (April 1994), pp.23–38.

Young, G., 'Funny Girls: Early American Screen Comediennes and Ethnicity', in R. Barton (ed.), *Screening Irish-America: Representing Irish-America in Film and Television* (Dublin: Irish Academic Press, 2009), pp.61–76.

# Index

Jacobs, Lewis, 345
Jermon, Irene, 59
Jerome, Billy, 106, 226
*Jerry Cohan's Irish Comedy Company*, 39
Jessop, George, 48, 257
*Jimmy* (film, 1915), 330
*Jimmy Kelley and the Kidnapper* (film, 1914), 324
*A Joke on the Old Maid* (film, 1900), 194
Jones, Ada, 102
Jones, Charles, 51
Joyce, Alice, 104, 270, 391
Joyce, Edwin, 42
*Just Like Kids* (film, 1915), 220

Kaiser, John, 29
Kalem Company, 12, 14, 19, 165, 167–70, 173–4, 188, 251, 265–82, 283, 385, 386–91
   *Kalem Kalendar* ('house organ'), 14, 174, 269, 282, 311
   Rockett on, 9, 10
*The Kalemites Visit Gibraltar* (film, 1912), 275
*Kansas Saloon Smashers* (film, 1901), 189
Kanzee, George, 74
*Kate, the Cop* (film, 1913), 321–2
'Kate' film series (Vitagraph), 230–1, 322
*Kate Killarney, I'll Put A Kiss Away For You* (illustrated song), 110, 126
*Kathleen, the Irish Rose* (film, 1914), 255–6
*Kathleen Mavourneen* (Edison film, 1906), 252–4, 256, 258, 354, 363, 378, 384
*Kathleen Mavourneen* (Edison film, 1913), 255
*Kathleen Mavourneen* (Imp film, 1913), 255, 367, 368
*Kathleen Mavourneen* (William Travers play), 37, 252–6
*Kathleen Mavourneen* (Yankee Film Company film, 1911), 254–5, 279, 364
*Katie O'Sullivan* (illustrated song), 127
'Katzenjammer Kids' films, 205
Kelly, H.P., 31
Kelly, John T., 42, 51, 59
Kelly, Nora, 60–1
*Kelly, USA* (film, 1911), 206
*Kelly From the Emerald Isle* (film, 1913), 332
*Kelly Goes to War* (film, 1912), 219
*The Kelly's Are At It Again* (illustrated song), 116, 126
*Kelly's Gone to Kingdom Come!* (illustrated song), 115–16, 125
*The Kentucky Irish-American* (newspaper), 15, 392–9
Keough, Edwin, 55
Kernell, Harry, 38, 55
Kernell, John, 42
Kerrigan, J. Warren, 280, 333, 334

*The Kerry Gow* (Kalem film, 1912), 277, 278, 279, 388
*Kerryana* (illustrated song), 112–13, 122–3
Keystone Cops, 319
*Kid Reagan's Hands* (film, 1914), 316
Kiel, Charlie, 249–50
Kildare, Owen, 327
*Killarney* (Briggs Company slide series), 73
*Killarney* (illustrated song), 102, 126
*Killarney, My Home O'er the Sea* (illustrated song), 110, 112, 120
*Killarney's Lakes* (retitled *Lakes of Killarney*) (film, 1909), 167, 364
*King Edward's Visit to Ireland* (film, 1903), 153, 158, 173
Kirkwood, James, 326, 327
*Kissing the Blarney Stone* (aka *Blarney Castle and Stone*, film, 1904), 140, 156, 269
*Kit Carson* (film, 1903), 1, 392
*Kitty's Knight* (film, 1913), 219
*Knockout Dugan's Find* (film, 1915), 317
Knowles, R.G., 148–9

*The Lad from Old Ireland* (film, 1910), 265–7, 268, 269–70, 276, 283, 293, 386–7, 388, 390, 391
*Lady Bountiful Visits the Murphys on Wash Day* (film, 1903), 190
*Lady Peggy's Escape* (film, 1913), 278–9
*The Lakes of Killarney* (film, 1903), 155
*The Lakes of Killarney* (film, 1909), 167, 364
*The Lakes of Killarney* (lantern slide set), 81
*Lakes of Killarney* (retitled from *Killarney's Lakes*) (film, 1909), 167, 364
Lancaster, John, 229
Langenheim brothers, 71, 76
*The Laundress and the Lady* (film, 1913), 174, 224, 281, 282
*The Laundry Lady's Luck* (film, 1911), 216
Lawler, W.F., 39
Le Clair, Maggie, 50, 59
Le Fanu, J. Sheridan, 257, 258
*Leaving the Lake Hotel, Killarney* (film, 1905), 156
*The Leprechawn* (film, 1908), 261
Letters, Will, 115
*Levi and Cohen, the Irish Comedians* (film, 1903), 189–90
*Levi and McGuinness Running for Office* (film, 1913), 221
Lewis, Joseph ('Barney O'Toole'), 26
*Life of an American Policeman* (film, 1905), 319
*The Life of St Patrick: From the Cradle to the Grave* (film, 1912), 280–1
*The Line at Hogan's* (film, 1912), 209
Little, Anna, 290, 293
*The Little Spreewald Maiden* (film, 1910), 268, 269

*Little Willie in Mischief Again* (film, 1899), 200
Long, Ruby, 362
*The Lost Child* (film, 1904), 313
*Love and Duty* (film, 1914), 325–6
*Love and Laundry* (film, 1913), 223
*Love Me Little, Love Me Long* (film, 1903), 194–5
*Love Me to a Yiddisha Melody (Oh! You Kiddisha!)* (illustrated song), 113, 119, 128, 211
Lover, Samuel, 257
*The Lovers, Coal Box, and Fireplace* (film, 1901), 190
*A Lucky Accident* (film, 1908), 363
*Lunch Time* (film, 1910), 209–10

Mace, Fred, 220, 317–18
MacEvoy, Frank, 39, 73
Mack, Andrew, 48, 53
Mack, Ollie, 50
MacManus, Seamus, 89–90
MacNamara, Walter, 8, 9, 11, 297–300, 301, 385–6
Madison, Cleo, 301
Magee, Barney, 298
*Maggie Hoolihan Gets a Job* (film, 1910), 320
Maglone, Patrick, 38
Maher, Peter, 316
*Maher-Choynski Glove Contest* (film, 1897), 316
Mahoney Brothers, 60
*The Maid's Strategem* (film, 1912), 214
*Make a Noise Like a Hoop and Roll Away* (illustrated song), 109
*The Man Who Beat Dan Dolan* (film, 1915), 316
Mantle, Burns, 335
Marion, Frank, 9, 266, 267, 275, 276–7, 387–8
*Market Day in Killarney* (stereo view, 1901), 155
Markey and Moran (comedy duo), 58
*Married Men* (film, 1914), 219
Marsden, Fred, 62
   *The Kerry Gow*, 32, 36, 41, 47, 55, 258, 277, 278, 279, 388
   *The Minstrel of Clare*, 47–8
   *Shaun Rhue*, 41, 47, 277
Martin and Buckley, 58
*Mary Fiske's English Blondes* (variety show, 1879), 33
*Mary Jane's Mishap; or Don't Fool with the Paraffin* (film, 1903), 203
Maryoga, Margaret G., 26
Mathew, Kathleen, 89
Maxwell and Simpson, 102
*The Mayor From Ireland* (film, 1912), 278, 279
McAfee, Mrs, 373–4
McAllister, T.H., 77–9, 80, 86, 97–9, 103, 125, 258
*McAvoy's Double Hibernicon* (travelling company), 45
*McBride's Bride* (film, 1914), 223, 282
McCaffrey, Daniel, 354